Major Problems
in
American Religious History

MAJOR PROBLEMS IN AMERICAN HISTORY SERIES

GENERAL EDITOR
THOMAS G. PATERSON

Major Problems
in
American Religious History

DOCUMENTS AND ESSAYS

EDITED BY

PATRICK ALLITT

EMORY UNIVERSITY

HOUGHTON MIFFLIN COMPANY
Boston   New York

Editor in Chief: Jean L. Woy
Senior Associate Editor: Frances Gay
Senior Project Editor: Christina M. Horn
Production/Design Coordinator: Jodi O'Rourke
Senior Marketing Manager: Sandra McGuire
Assistant Manufacturing Coordinator: Andrea Wagner

Cover image: John Steuart Curry, *Baptism in Kansas,* 1928. Oil on canvas, 40 × 50 in.
  Collection of Whitney Museum of American Art. Gift of Gertrude Vanderbilt Whitney,
  31.159.
Photograph: Copyright © 1999 Whitney Museum of American Art.

Printed in the U.S.A.

Library of Congress Catalog Card Number: 99-72023

ISBN: 0-395-96419-9

123456789-CRS-03 02 01 00 99

For Randolph James

Contents

CHAPTER 5
Religion in the Early Republic: 1790–1850
Page 126

CHAPTER 6
Antebellum Immigration and Social Tensions: 1830–1860
Page 161

C H A P T E R   7
War, Defeat, and Apocalyptic Religion: 1860–1890
Page 196

CHAPTER 14
New Immigrants and Religious Multiculturalism: 1970–2000
Page 428

CHAPTER 15
Religion, Politics, and the Constitution: 1960–2000
Page 464

Preface

More than a hundred million Americans take part in organized religious activities every week and more than two hundred million say they believe in an all-powerful God. Church membership and attendance were as high in the 1990s as at any time in the nation's history. Americans, in fact, are more involved in religious life than are any other people in the Western industrialized world. Religion has long been, and remains, a principal source of community strength, personal consolation, and explanation about humanity and the world. The First Amendment to the U.S. Constitution assures that no religion will be given special advantages by the government and that none will be persecuted. Even so, religion in America has always been controversial. Ever since the first Europeans settled in North America more than five hundred years ago, it has caused misunderstanding and conflict within and among groups. This book explores many of the most important issues in American religious history over those five hundred years.

The researching and writing of religious history presents special challenges. It is difficult enough for historians to find out exactly what happened in the past. It is more difficult to discover what the participants in historical events thought about their world. And it is more difficult still to find out what they *believed* about the great religious questions: the ultimate purpose of their lives, the origins of the world, the relationship between the natural and the supernatural, their destiny after death, and the moral meaning of their actions. Religious historians usually have to make inferences, or informed guesses, about faith on the basis of people's actions. They know that religious motivation can be powerful, that it can lead to constructive and destructive decisions, and that people belonging to the same religious group can act in different and opposed ways while claiming a common motivation.

The people who lived in North America before the Europeans arrived had a wide variety of religious beliefs and practices, integrated into their hunting, farming, fighting, and family life. Spanish, French, and English missionaries tried to convert them to Christianity and in doing so learned, and recorded, how American Indians understood the cosmos and their place in it. The missionaries were often unsympathetic, but their accounts, when read with care, enable us to reconstruct the religious world of the Indians in those days of early contact. Chapter 2 examines the clash of native and European religious systems.

Europeans disagreed with one another about the form of Christianity the Indians should adopt. The French and Spanish belonged to the Catholic church, which until the early sixteenth century had dominated western Europe. The settlement of the Americas took place at the same time as the Reformation, however, which replaced northern Europe's traditional Catholicism with various forms of Protestantism. New

England's early settlers (the Puritans) were militant Protestants who considered their migration a religiously momentous event. In the seventeenth century they struggled to create a godly Protestant community as an example to the rest of the world. The government-supported Church of England dominated religious life in the middle and southern colonies, though these areas also saw an influx of more diverse Protestant groups from Holland, Sweden, and Germany. Maryland began its colonial life as a Catholic enclave, and Pennsylvania began as a haven for Quakers. Colonists who fought for the American Revolution and those who opposed it (or opposed war altogether) often explained their roles as the carrying out of a religious duty. Religion in colonial and revolutionary America are the themes of Chapters 3 and 4.

Chapters 5 through 9 explore the increased religious diversity of America in the nineteenth century. The new Constitution gave at least some protection to dozens of new churches, a few of which (Baptists, Methodists, Mormons) grew far more rapidly than the republic's older churches (Chapter 5). Large-scale Catholic and German-Jewish immigration increased the nation's religious pluralism and the potential for interreligious conflicts (Chapter 6). Meanwhile the problem of slavery, itself supercharged with religious significance for slaves themselves, for their owners, and for abolitionists, precipitated the secession crisis and the Civil War of the 1860s (Chapter 7). In the late nineteenth century the rapid growth of an industrial economy and large cities, along with accelerated immigration from southern and eastern Europe, created an immense gap between the rich and the poor, generated new social tensions, and forced religious leaders to reconsider the nature of their ministry (Chapter 8). At the same time a series of intellectual revolutions challenged biblically based theories about the world's origins and meaning. Some religious writers saw them as threatening to their faith, others as opportunities to enrich it (Chapter 9).

The last six chapters explore American religious history in the twentieth century, a century of assimilation for religiously diverse immigrant groups, in which most tried to steer a middle path between preserving their distinctiveness and adapting to American society (Chapter 10). During the twentieth century, religious communities also tried to work out an appropriate response to global wars and, after 1945, to the possibility of nuclear annihilation (Chapter 11). Chapters 12 and 13 show how new social movements in America, including civil rights, feminism, environmentalism, and the counterculture, gave rise to new forms of spirituality after the 1960s. Chapter 14 returns to the theme of immigration and shows that the religious diversity it entailed continued throughout the twentieth century. Immigrants from Latin America and Asia in the 1980s and 1990s passed through stages of adaptation and resistance similar to those that Russian Jews and Italian Catholics had experienced seventy or eighty years before. Chapter 15 considers religious-political connections in recent decades. It emphasizes the vitality of religious conservatives and their perception of an excessive separation between church and state.

In this book, as in others from the *Major Problems in American History* series, each thematic chapter contains several documents followed by two or three essays by scholars. The exception to this format is Chapter 1, which includes four statements on the general character of American religion. In the nineteenth century Philip Schaff and many of his Protestant contemporaries believed that the American religious scene provided clues about God's plans for the whole world. Most twentieth-century observers, including the three excerpted in Chapter 1, have taken a more down-to-earth approach, describing and explaining the interplay of ethnic and social forces in American religious history without reference to God's will or divine providence. Chapter introductions and document and essay headnotes set the topics in historical perspective and identify key questions and approaches. Bibiliographies at the end of each chapter suggest readings for further exploration.

I would like to thank Thomas G. Paterson, general editor, for his invitation to contribute to the *Major Problems* series; Jean Woy, Leah Strauss, Frances Gay, and Christina Horn at Houghton Mifflin for their efficient and good-natured help in guiding me through the editing process; Shirley Webster for her persistence in clearing the permissions; and my friends and colleagues here at Emory University and around the country for sending suggestions, bibliographies, course outlines, and criticisms of the various chapter drafts. Thanks also to the following reviewers who gave me many useful suggestions for revising the selection of documents and essays: Debra Campbell, Colby College; Tona Hangen, Brandeis University; Susan E. Myers-Shirk, Middle Tennessee State University; and Rachel Wheeler, Lewis and Clark College. An indulgence and a special dispensation to James Fisher of St. Louis University, John McGreevy of Notre Dame, and Kate Joyce of Duke University for their advice, friendship, and support, and to Peter Agree of Ithaca, New York, for his patience and understanding. Special thanks to my nearest and dearest: Toni and Frances Allitt.

The dedication is to Randolph James, organist of St. Bartholomew's Episcopal Church, Atlanta, and director of its choir, to which I belong. Randolph has all the gifts of a brilliant director: the ability to inspire loyalty, superb musicianship, a domineering personality, skill in teaching us, and an inexhaustible supply of wit. Under his direction our singing, especially of the Psalms, sometimes opens up lines of direct communication between Earth and Heaven. May they remain open as the second millennium ends and the third begins.

P. A.

Major Problems
in
American Religious History

CHAPTER
1

Approaches to American
Religious History

Visitors from abroad have always been fascinated by America's religious vitality and by its religious diversity. In Europe it was normal for one church, usually supported by the state, to dominate the nation's religious life. In America, by contrast, dozens of churches existed side by side and, after the early decades of the nineteenth century, none enjoyed government support. In Europe, the nineteenth and twentieth centuries witnessed a long religious decline. Falling church attendance, less reliance on religious ideas to explain the world, militant atheism, and a marginal place for ministers, priests, and rabbis, led observers to expect that religion would eventually die out altogether. But the American situation suggested just the opposite. Church membership was growing, clergy were numerous and respected, new churches were constantly being founded, and nearly no one would admit to being an agnostic, let alone an atheist.

Historians, like foreign visitors, have tried to explain these surprising contrasts between religion in Europe and America and to speculate about a connection. Did American religion benefit from church-state separation at the time of the Revolution? Is there something intrinsically religious about America and its people? Why did immigrants who showed little enthusiasm for religion in their home countries become more *religious after arriving in America? Was God particularly attentive to American religious life?*

Through much of the nineteenth century, many Americans—historians included—believed that God had chosen their nation for a special mission, first to settle and subdue a continent, then to civilize and Christianize the rest of the world. But they were vexed to discover that, far from preparing itself for this great task by uniting its many churches, American society continued to fragment into an ever-growing diversity of sects, cults, and denominations. The historians, most of whom were also ministers, regretted this diversity. Some argued that the diversity so apparent on the surface was underlaid by an essential Protestant unity. Their more pragmatic twentieth-century successors have accepted the diversity as real while continuing to disagree about its causes and about the source of America's unflagging religious vitality. This opening chapter reviews some of the answers given to these two large questions that lie at the center of American religious history.

1

✒ E S S A Y S

Philip Schaff emigrated from Germany to Pennsylvania in 1843 and published his book *America* twelve years later. A professor at the Mercersberg seminary of the German Reformed church, he did not regard American religious pluralism as good in theory ("the sect system is certainly a great evil"). Nevertheless, as a shrewd observer he had to admit that it worked well in practice, generated a lot of enthusiasm, and showed that church-state separation did not mean a descent into indifference and atheism. H. Richard Niebuhr, an American Protestant of German descent and a member of a famous theological family, writing eighty years later as a professor at Yale Divinity School, explained the diversity of denominations as the result of economic and geographical conditions. The rich, the middle class, and the poor, in his view, had very different religious needs and these were expressed in the different denominations they joined. Similarly, the contrast in life between the American North, South, East and West stimulated diverse types of religious expression and furthered the denominational tendency. Niebuhr, borrowing a key idea from the historian Frederick Jackson Turner, argued that the frontier was as important in patterning American religious life as it had been in shaping American character.

More recently, Roger Finke of Purdue University and Rodney Stark of the University of Washington, both sociologists of religion, have reached two significant conclusions based on their intensive study of American church membership figures: first, that church membership has grown almost uninterruptedly throughout American history; and second, that the more intense and demanding a church's message, the greater its share of new members will be. Finke and Stark borrow from the methods and rhetoric of economics for their study, while R. Laurence Moore of Cornell University adapts the insights of psychology. Noting that many American religious groups depict themselves as "outsiders," he shows that, paradoxically, there is no surer way of becoming a familiar part of the national religious scene than to position your group on the margins and claim that it is persecuted. Moore, like Finke and Stark but unlike Schaff and Niebuhr, does not object to the massive diversity of religious groups in America; he strives to explain why it exists, and illustrates how well attuned the many churches and synagogues are to meeting Americans' religious and psychological needs.

Religious Vitality and Church-State Separation

PHILIP SCHAFF

It is a vast advantage to that country itself, and one may say to the whole world, that the United States were first settled in great part from religious motives; that the first emigrants left the homes of their fathers for faith and conscience' sake, and thus at the outset stamped upon their new home the impress of positive Christianity, which now exerts a wholesome influence even on those later emigrants, who have no religion at all.

The ecclesiastical character of America, however, is certainly very different from that of the Old World. Two points in particular require notice.

Philip Schaff, "Religion and the Church," in *America: A Sketch of Its Political, Social, and Religious Character* (1854; reprint, Cambridge, Mass.: Belknap of Harvard University Press, 1961), 72–81. Edited by Perry Miller. Copyright © 1961 by the President and Fellows of Harvard University. Reprinted by permission of the publisher.

The first is this. While in Europe ecclesiastical institutions appear in historical connection with Catholicism, and even in evangelical countries, most of the city and village churches, the universities, and religious foundations, point to a mediaeval origin; in North America, on the contrary, every thing had a Protestant beginning, and the Catholic Church has come in afterwards as one sect among the others, and has always remained subordinate. In Europe, Protestantism has, so to speak, fallen heir to Catholicism; in America, Catholicism under the wing of Protestant toleration and freedom of conscience, has found an adopted home, and is everywhere surrounded by purely Protestant institutions. True, the colony of Maryland, planted by the Catholic Lord Baltimore, was one of the earliest settlements of North America. But, in the first place, even this was by no means specifically Roman. It was founded expressly on the thoroughly anti-Roman, and essentially Protestant, principles of religious toleration. And then, again, it never had any specific influence on the character of the country; for even the prominent position of the city of Baltimore, as the American metropolis of the Roman Church, is of much later date. Far more important and influential were the settlements of the Puritans in New England, the Episcopalians in Virginia, the Quakers in Pennsylvania, the Dutch in New York, in the course of the seventeenth century, the Presbyterians from Scotland and North Ireland, and the German Lutherans and Reformed from the Palatinate, in the first half of the eighteenth. These have given the country its spirit and character. Its past course and present condition are unquestionably due mainly to the influence of Protestant principles. The Roman Church has attained social and political importance in the eastern and western States only within the last twenty years, chiefly in consequence of the vast Irish emigration; but it will never be able to control the doctrines of the New World, though it should increase a hundred fold.

Another peculiarity in the ecclesiastical condition of North America, connected with the Protestant origin and character of the country, is the separation of church and state. The infidel reproach, that had it not been for the power of the state, Christianity would have long ago died out; and the argument of Roman controversialists, that Protestantism could not stand without the support of princes and civil governments, both are practically refuted and utterly annihilated in the United States. The president and governors, the congress at Washington, and the state legislatures, have, as such, nothing to do with the church, and are by the Constitution expressly forbidden to interfere in its affairs. State officers have no other rights in the church, than their personal rights as members of particular denominations. The church, indeed, everywhere enjoys the protection of the laws for its property, and the exercise of its functions; but it manages its own affairs independently, and has also to depend for its resources entirely on voluntary contributions. As the state commits itself to no particular form of Christianity, there is of course also no civil requisition of baptism, confirmation, and communion. Religion is left to the free will of each individual, and the church has none but moral means of influencing the world.

This separation was by no means a sudden, abrupt event, occasioned, say, by the Revolution. The first settlers, indeed, had certainly no idea of such a thing; they proceeded rather on Old Testament theocratic principles, like Calvin, John Knox, the Scottish Presbyterians, and the English Puritans of the seventeenth century; regarding state and church as the two arms of one and the same divine will. In the colony of Massachusetts, the Puritans, in fact, founded a rigid Calvinistic state-church system.

They made the civil franchise depend on membership in the church; and punished not only blasphemy and open infidelity, but even every departure from the publicly acknowledged code of Christian faith and practice as a political offense. In Boston, in the seventeenth century, even the Quakers, who certainly acted there in a very fanatical and grossly indecent way, were formally persecuted, publicly scourged, imprisoned, and banished; and, in Salem, of the same State, witches were burnt as accomplices of the devil. The last traces of this state-church system in New England were not obliterated till long after the American Revolution, and even to this day most of the States have laws for the observance of the Sabbath, monogamy, and other specifically Christian institutions. Thus the separation of the temporal and spiritual powers is by no means absolute. While New England had Congregationalism for its established religion, New York also had at first the Dutch Reformed, and afterwards the English Episcopal church, and Virginia, and some other Southern States, also the English Episcopal, for their establishments. With these the other forms of Christianity were tolerated either not at all, or under serious restrictions, as formerly the Dissenters were in England.

But on the other hand, there prevailed in other North American colonies from their foundation, therefore long before the Revolution of 1776, entire freedom of faith and conscience; as in Rhode Island, founded by the Baptist, Roger Williams, who was banished from Massachusetts for heresy, and thus set by bitter experience against religious intolerance; in Pennsylvania, which the quaker, William Penn, originally designed as an asylum for his brethren in faith, but to which he soon invited also German Reformed and Lutherans from the Palatinate, guaranteeing equal rights to all, and leaving each to the guidance of the "inward light;" and, finally, in Maryland, founded by Lord Baltimore on the same basis of universal religious toleration.

After the American Revolution this posture of the State gradually became general. First, the legislature of Virginia, after the colony had separated from the mother-country, annulled the rights and privileges of the Episcopal establishment, and placed all the dissenting bodies on a perfectly equal footing with it in the eye of the law. Her example was followed by the other colonies, which had established churches. When Congress was organized at the close of the war, an article was placed in the Constitution, forbidding the enactment of laws about religion; and similar prohibitions are found in the constitutions of the several States.

We would by no means vindicate this separation of church and state as the perfect and final relation between the two. The kingdom of Christ is to penetrate and transform like leaven, all the relations of individual and national life. We much prefer this separation, however, to the territorial system and a police guardianship of the church, the Bride of the God-man, the free-born daughter of heaven; and we regard it as adapted to the present wants of America, and favorable to her religious interests. For it is by no means to be thought, that the separation of church and state there is a renunciation of Christianity by the nation; like the separation of the state and the school from the church, and the civil equality of Atheism with Christianity, which some members of the abortive Frankfurt Parliament were for introducing in Germany. It is not an annihilation of one factor, but only an amicable separation of the two in their spheres of outward operation; and thus equally the church's declaration of independence towards the state, and an emancipation of the state from bondage to a particular confession. The nation, therefore, is still Christian, though it refuses to be governed in this deepest concern of the mind and heart by the temporal power. In fact, under such circumstances, Christianity, as the free expression of personal conviction and of the national character, has even greater power over the mind, than when enjoined by civil laws and upheld by police regulations.

This appears practically in the strict observance of the Sabbath, the countless churches and religious schools, the zealous support of Bible and Tract societies, of domestic and foreign missions, the numerous revivals, the general attendance on divine worship, and the custom of family devotion—all expressions of the general Christian character of the people, in which the Americans are already in advance of most of the old Christian nations of Europe.

In fact, even the state, as such, to some extent officially recognizes Christianity. Congress appoints chaplains (mostly from the Episcopal, sometimes from the Presbyterian and the Methodist clergy) for itself, the army, and the navy. It opens every day's session with prayer, and holds public worship on the Sabbath in the Senate Chamber at Washington. The laws of the several States also contain strict prohibitions of blasphemy, atheism, Sabbath-breaking, polygamy, and other gross violations of general Christian morality.

Thus the separation is not fully carried out in practice, on account of the influence of Christianity on the popular mind. It is even quite possible that the two powers may still come into collision. The tolerance of the Americans has its limits and counterpoise in that religious fanaticism, to which they are much inclined. This may be seen in the expulsion of the Mormons, who so grossly offended the religious and moral sense of the people. Great political difficulties may arise, especially from the growth of the Roman church, which has been latterly aiming everywhere at political influence, and thus rousing the jealousy and opposition of the great Protestant majority. The Puritanic Americans see in Catholicism an ecclesiastical despotism, from which they fear also political despotism, so that its sway in the United States must be the death of Republican freedom. Thus the Catholic question has already come to be regarded by many as at the same time a political question, involving the existence of the Republic; and a religious war between Catholics and Protestants, though in the highest degree improbable, is still by no means an absolute impossibility; as, in fact, slight skirmishes have already occurred in the street fight between the two parties in Philadelphia in 1844, and the violent demolition of a Roman convent at Charlestown, Mass. The secret political party of the "Know-Nothings," which is just sweeping over the States with the rapidity of the whirlwind, but which, for this very reason, cannot last long in this particular form, is mainly directed against the influence of Romanism.

If, however, the great question of the relation of church and state be not by any means fully solved even in the United States, still the two powers are there at all events much more distant than in any other country.

The natural result of this arrangement is a general prevalence of freedom of conscience and religious faith, and of the voluntary principle, as it is called: that is, the promotion of every religious work by the free-will offerings of the people. The state, except in the few cases mentioned above, does nothing towards building churches, supporting ministers, founding theological seminaries, or aiding indigent students in preparation for the ministry. No taxes are laid for these objects; no one is compelled to contribute a farthing to them. What is done for them is far, indeed, from being always done from the purest motives—love to God and to religion—often from a certain sense of honor, and for all sorts of selfish by-ends; yet always from free impulses, without any outward coercion.

This duly considered, it is truly wonderful, what a multitude of churches, ministers, colleges, theological seminaries, and benevolent institutions are there founded and maintained entirely by free-will offerings. In Berlin there are hardly forty churches for a population of four hundred and fifty thousand, of whom, in spite of all the union of church and state, only some thirty thousand attend public worship. In New York, to a population of six hundred thousand, there are over two hundred and fifty well-attended churches, some of them quite costly and splendid, especially in Broadway and Fifth Avenue. In the city of Brooklyn, across the East River, the number of churches is still larger in proportion to the population, and in the country towns and villages, especially in New England, the houses of worship average one to every thousand, or frequently even five hundred, souls. If these are not Gothic cathedrals, they are yet mostly decent, comfortable buildings, answering all the purposes of the congregation often even far better than the most imposing works of architecture. In every new city district, in every new settlement, one of the first things thought of is the building of a temple to the Lord, where the neighboring population may be regularly fed with the bread of life and encouraged to labor, order, obedience, and every good work. Suppose the state, in Germany, should suddenly withdraw its support from church and university, how many preachers and professors would be breadless, and how many auditories closed!

The voluntary system unquestionably has its great blemishes. It is connected with all sorts of petty drudgery, vexations, and troubles, unknown in well endowed Established Churches. Ministers and teachers, especially among the recent German emigrants in America, who have been accustomed to State provision for religion and education, have very much to suffer from the free system. They very often have to make begging tours for the erection of a church, and submit to innumerable other inconveniences for the good cause, till a congregation is brought into a proper course, and its members become practised in free giving.

But, on the other hand, the voluntary system calls forth a mass of individual activity and interest among the laity in ecclesiastical affairs, in the founding of new churches and congregations, colleges and seminaries, in home and foreign missions, and in the promotion of all forms of Christian philanthropy. We may here apply in a good sense our Lord's word: "Where the treasure is, there the heart will be also." The man, who, without coercion, brings his regular offering for the maintenance of the church and the minister, has commonly much more interest in both, and in their prosperity he sees with pleasure the fruit of his own labor. The same is true of seminaries. All the congregations and synods are interested in the theological teacher, whom they support, and who trains ministers of the Word for them; while in Europe the people give themselves little or no trouble about the theological faculties.

It is commonly thought that this state of things necessarily involves an unworthy dependence of the minister on his congregation. But this is not usually the case. The Americans expect a minister to do his duty, and they most esteem that one who fearlessly and impartially declares the whole counsel of God, and presents the depravity of man and the threatenings of the Divine Word as faithfully as he does the comforting promises. Cases of ministers employed for a certain time, as hired servants, occur indeed occasionally in independent German rationalistic congregations, and perhaps among the Universalists, but not in a regular synod. A pious congregation well knows that by such a degradation of the holy office, which preaches reconciliation, and binds and looses in the name of Christ, it would degrade itself; and a minister, in any respectable church connection, would not be allowed to accept a call on such terms, even were he willing.

Favored by the general freedom of faith, all Christian denominations and sects, except the Oriental, have settled in the United States, on equal footing in the eye of the law; here attracting each other, there repelling; rivalling in both the good and the bad sense; and mutually contending through innumerable religious publications. They thus present a motley sampler of all church history, and the results it has thus far attained. A detailed description of these at present is forbidden, both by want of time and by the proportion of the discourse. Suffice it to say, in general, that the whole present distracted condition of the church in America, pleasing and promising as it may be, in one view, must yet be regarded on the whole as unsatisfactory, and as only a state of transition to something higher and better.

America seems destined to be the Phenix grave not only of all European nationalities, as we have said above, but also of all European churches and sects, of Protestantism and Romanism. I cannot think, that any one of the present confessions and sects, the Roman, or the Episcopal, or the Congregational, or the Presbyterian, or the Lutheran, or the German or Dutch Reformed, or the Methodist, or the Baptist communion, will ever become exclusively dominant there; but rather, that out of the mutual conflict of all something wholly new will gradually arise.

At all events, whatever may become of the American denominations and sects of the present day, the kingdom of Jesus Christ must at last triumph in the New World, as elsewhere, over all foes, old and new. Of this we have the pledge in the mass of individual Christianity in America; but above all, in the promise of the Lord, who is with his people always to the end of the world, and who has founded his church upon a rock, against which the gates of hell shall never prevail. And his words are yea and amen.

America's Geographical Diversity Encourages Numerous Religious Denominations

H. RICHARD NIEBUHR

The primary social sources of American denominationalism are to be sought in the European history of the churches which have immigrated to the new world. Yet many of the two hundred varieties of Christianity which flourish in the United States were born within its confines and many others which derive their origin from Europe owe the development of their present separate individuality to the operation of social forces native to the new environment. Among the factors which have been responsible for the continued division of European proletarian, bourgeois,

---

H. Richard Niebuhr, "Sectionalism and Denominationalism in America," chap. 6 in *The Social Sources of Denominationalism* (1929; reprint, New York: Henry Holt and Co., 1957), 135–164. Reprinted by permission of Richard R. Niebuhr.

and nationalist Christianity in America, for the development of new types of conflict between them, and for the rise of wholly American schisms, sectionalism, the heterogeneity of an immigrant population, and the presence of two distinct races are of primary importance. America replaced the horizontal lines of European class structure with the vertical lines of a sectionalized society and continued or originated church schisms in accordance with that pattern of provincial organization of East and West and North and South which underlies its economic and political history. It brought the diverse races of Europe, with their various religious organizations, into a new relationship in which new kinds of accommodation and new kinds of conflict greatly modified the character of their church life. The third set of social factors which have been responsible for a great deal of denominationalism in America have arisen out of the forced migration to the New World of the African race and out of the subsequent relations of whites and Negroes.

I

The part which the sectional conflict between North and South has played in the history of church schism in America is well-known. Less obviously but not less effectively the constantly recurring strife between East and West has left its mark on religious life in the United States and has been responsible for the divergent development of a number of denominations. It is to be noted that just as North and South may represent cultural and economic forces more than geographical areas, so also the terms East and West, in this connection, designate complex social structures and movements rather than geographic sections. Throughout a large part of the eighteenth and the whole of the nineteenth century the advancing Western frontier brought forth a typical culture of its own, which not only profoundly affected the whole civilization of the United States but also came into frequent conflict with the established society of the mercantile East. It produced its own type of economic life and theory, its own kind of political practice and doctrine and created its own typical, religious experience and expression. The result was the formation of peculiarly Western denominations. These followed partly in the tradition of the European churches of the poor but were, nevertheless, truly indigenous outgrowths of the American environment. The East, upon the other hand, clung fast to the established forms of European religious life and found itself unable to maintain unity with the frontier. Hence there came to pass a division of the churches which speciously appears to be simply the continuation of earlier European schisms, but which has its true source in the sectional differences and conflicts of American civilization. . . .

. . . The expansive tendencies of American enterprise were fostered for centuries by the challenging opportunities offered by free land and virgin soil and by the ever-renewed possibilities for conquest and fortune. Equalitarianism in political doctrine was nurtured less in the land of Puritans and Pilgrims than in the Western settlements, where the common struggle for existence allowed no distinctions between high and low and where success attended effort rather than the fortune of inherited privilege. The love of liberty was also bred on the border. . . .

The religious conflicts of the established societies of the East with the free civilization of the frontier arose out of the same circumstances that brought forth political and economic strife. The social conditions, which in the one case fostered the

Federalist and later Republican temper and theory of government and in the other case the Jeffersonian and Jacksonian attitude and views of political organization, nurtured contrasting theories and practices of religious experience and expression as well as of ecclesiastical organization in the churches. The religion of the urban, commercial East tended to take on or to retain the typical features of all bourgeois or national religion—a polity corresponding to the order and character of class organized society, an intellectual conception of the content of faith, an ethics reflecting the needs and evaluations of a stable and commercial citizenry, a sober, ritualistic type of religious expression. The religion of the West, on the other hand, accepted or produced anew many of the characteristics of the faith of the disinherited, for the psychology of the frontier corresponds in many respects to the psychology of the revolutionary poor. This is especially true of the emotional character of religious experience, which seems to be required in the one case as in the other. The isolation of frontier life fostered craving for companionship, suppressed the gregarious tendency and so subjected the lonely settler to the temptations of crowd suggestion to an unusual degree. In the camp-meeting and in the political gathering formal, logical discourse was of no avail, while the "language of excitement" called forth enthusiastic response. In addition to the isolation of the frontiersman other influences inclined him to make an uncritical emotional response to religious stimulation. The reduction of life on the border to the bare fundamentals of physical and social existence, the dearth of intellectual stimulation and the lack of those effective inhibitions of emotional expression which formal education cultivates, the awesome manifestations of nature, the effects of which were not checked by the sense of safe permanent dwellings and the nearness of other men convey—all these made the settler subject to the feverish phenomena of revivalism.

The religion of the frontier was further akin to the faith of the poor in the love of democracy which was expressed in it. Among the poor the desire for individual experience and responsibility in religion and for the religious support of their efforts toward political enfranchisement were brought forth in reaction against the long denial of their human rights. On the frontier, conversely, the enjoyment of economic and political liberty fostered the desire for similar privileges in religion, while the great interest in the retention of individual rights in every sphere naturally sought in faith the justification of practice. Furthermore, the same individualism which resented all absentee control in political and economic life and which prompted the Westerner to seek a personal religion in the immediacy of experience caused him to look with suspicion upon all administration of religion by superior powers ordained of God or of men. Hence lay preaching and preaching by men who, though ordained, were not separated from their fellows by the marks of superior education and culture, were favored on the frontier as they were among the disinherited. This democratic attitude also came to expression in the sectarian organization of the religious community. The churches of the frontier tended to be voluntaristic organizations, in harmony with the other social structures of the individualistic society and in conformity with the conception of religion as immediate and individual experience. The frontier influenced dogma and ethics also. The relaxation and liberation which adventurers from the East enjoyed when they found themselves on the border, free not only from the compulsions of legal restraint but also from the watchful surveillance of their neighbors, tended to break down much of their customary morality. Complaints against drunkenness, gambling, and sexual license, as well as against the profanation of the Sabbath and the prevalence of profanity, abound in the accounts of Eastern visitors to the frontier. This relaxation largely determined the character of the conversion which took place when religion struck home. Revivals under these circumstances were true revivals of those inhibitions which had been only partly overcome in a generation or two of frontier life and which continued in their suppression to foster a sense of guilt beneath the brave front of carelessness. The ethics which was prized under these circumstances was the ethics of individual morality and the negative ethics of restraint from the typical sins of the border. In this respect there was a marked difference between the moral ideals of the frontier and those of the religious poor; where the latter were social, growing out of the urban and industrial solidarity of labor and prizing sympathy and justice, the former were individualistic, rising out of the isolation of the settler and exalting self-reliant attitudes as well as personal probity and purity. . . .

II

Almost all of the churches of America have, at some time or another, lived on the frontier, and almost all of them have retained some of the marks of the character which it sought to impress upon them. In a very general sense it is true that under the influence of frontier conditions the churches of Europe after migrating to America have tended to become sects, and that with the passing of the frontier and with the establishment of ordered society the sects of Europe and America have tended to become churches. Yet the influence of the frontier on the denominations has been very unequal. Some of them, by virtue of a rigid constitution acquired in earlier history, were able to resist the influence of border life or were unable to adapt themselves to it; others, again by virtue of their earlier character, were attracted to the frontier as a fitting field for their labors and readily adjusted themselves to its needs; some denominations, from the beginning of their American history, sought their membership only among those European classes or nationalities which found their home in the mercantile East or in the semi-aristocratic, plantation South; others, again, needed to follow their European adherents to the wilderness and to remain alien to the interests of the established society; still other denominations were native born, having originated in frontier religious revolts. . . .

Of the denominations which were confined to the settled area of the early East both as a result of their constitution and of the cultural character of their membership the Anglican or Protestant Episcopal Church is a typical example. The same factors which prevented it, in England, from fully accepting the Wesleyan revival operated in America to keep it aloof from the vivid, popular religion of the frontier. As the church of the Southern plantation aristocracy, of English bureaucracy and mercantile groups in the ports and capitals of the colonies, it represented those interests of which the frontier was most suspicious. In Virginia it lost the border population to Baptists, Methodists, and Presbyterians. In Maryland, where also it was the established church, "the Methodists . . . swept the country; . . . the enthusiasm of the New Lights and other itinerant preachers found a hearty, if ignorant, response; . . . Quakers and Presbyterians from Pennsylvania gathered large numbers into their respective folds." In the northern colonies the obvious connection of the church with the Loyalists of 1776 brought on its almost complete ruin. When it was re-established as an American Episcopal church after the Revolution it gained, indeed, in vitality but did not change its character as the church of English middle classes in the East. It retained its sober, ritualist forms despite all the temptations offered by the frontier spirit of the new nation and became the refuge of many who were offended by the emotional enthusiasm of the revivals which, originating in the West, spread also to the East.

The Congregationalism of New England, in contrast to Episcopalianism, appeared to be endowed by constitution and training for religious work on the frontier. From its origin as a church of the poor in the early seventeenth century it had maintained the sectarian principle of organization and an apparently democratic character. On the first frontier of the new world, Massachusetts Bay, the development of these characteristics had been encouraged by the social organization in isolated communities and the Puritan majority had conformed to the pattern of the Separatist minority. But in few other respects was this early Puritan Congregationalism sympathetic to the needs of the border communities which began to take on definitely frontier character a century after the founding of New England. Its characteristics were not those of the religiously naïve, but those of established and cultured social classes. Puritanism rather than Separatism gave it its chief endowment. The early Puritan colonies "contained men of humble position, it is true, but their leaders were from good station in England, many of them of the country gentry, men of wealth, character and education. Their ministers . . . were the peers in learning and ability of any in the Puritan wing of the Church of England. . . . Probably no colony in the history of European emigration was superior to that of Massachusetts in wealth, station or capacity." Emotionalism in religion was abhorrent to these learned clergymen and substantial citizens; lay preaching was associated in their minds with an equally detested radicalism in political and religious theory. The lack of truly democratic principles among the Puritans has been pointed out. . . .

The American denomination, which, above all others, became the frontier church in the nineteenth century and which profited most by the religious spirit of the West was the Methodist Episcopal Church. Beginning just before the Revolution in humble fashion among the poor of the Eastern cities, its promise of growth was not great in the early years of its activity in the colonies. It was an American branch of the English movement and without the frontier its significance as a church would scarcely have been greater eventually than that of Methodism in England. . . . Methodism soon found its proper sphere on the borders of the colonies. With its fervent piety, its lay preaching, its early sectarian polity, it accorded well with the spirit of the West, while the itineracy and the circuit system were admirable devices for the evangelization of the frontier. While it is true that the centralization of control in the Wesleyan church ran counter to the provincial and individualistic temper of isolated pioneer communities, yet this form of organization gave Methodism direction and concentration of energy which the loose polity of the Baptist movement lacked. This centralization of control was a corollary of the itineracy; in combination they constituted a missionary strategy which conquered the West.

Before Methodism could become a frontier church, however, it needed to relinquish part of its inheritance as the child of Anglicanism and the autocratic Wesley. . . . "For some time the preachers [of the Methodist Church] generally read prayers on the Lord's Day," said an early historian of American Methodism, "and in some cases the preachers read part of the morning service on Wednesdays and Fridays; but some who had been long accustomed to pray extempore were unwilling to adopt this new plan, being fully satisfied that they could pray better and with more devotion while their eyes were shut than they could with their eyes open." Dislike of liturgical forms on the part of a large majority of the membership combined with this predilection of the clergy for extempore prayers and "after a few years the Prayer-Book was laid aside." With the Prayer-Book went the vestments. . . . It was not the least of Methodism's advantages on the border that its missionaries were distinguished in no way from the people with whom they dealt, save in the fervor of their piety and in the purity of their lives.

Church Membership Has Increased Throughout American History, Especially in the Most Demanding Groups

ROGER FINKE AND RODNEY STARK

The most striking trend in the history of religion in America is growth—or what we call the churching of America. . . . [Here we] attempt to explore and explain how and why America shifted from a nation in which most people took no part in organized religion to a nation in which nearly two thirds of American adults do. Along the way we shall discover that the churching of America was not simply a rise in participation. Many observers have discounted the rise in church membership on the grounds that it was accompanied by a decline in acceptance of traditional religious doctrines. But this simply isn't so. Not all denominations shared in this immense rise in membership rates, and to the degree that denominations rejected traditional doctrines and ceased to make serious demands on their followers, they ceased to prosper. The churching of America was accomplished by aggressive churches committed to vivid otherworldliness. . . .

. . . How religious was colonial America? Have church membership rates risen constantly over the past two centuries or have there been cycles of ups and downs? . . . [A]s our work progressed we were drawn to some rather blunt questions about the characteristics of winners and losers in a free market religious environment that exposed religious organizations to relentless competition. To be more specific, we were led to ask questions such as: Why had the leading denominations of 1776 gone into such rapid eclipse by the turn of the century? Why were the Methodists and the Baptists able to win such huge and rapid victories, making them the dominant religious organizations during the first half of the nineteenth century? And then what happened to the Methodists? Why did their nearly miraculous rise soon turn into a long downward slide? . . .

. . . *What* is American religion? For most historians, religion means theology, and therefore the history of American religion is the history of religious ideas.

R. Finke and R. Stark, "A New Approach to American Religious History," chap. 1 in *The Churching of America, 1776–1990: Winners and Losers in our Religious Economy* (New Brunswick, N.J.: Rutgers University Press, 1992), 1–5, 15–21. Reprinted by permission of Rutgers University Press.

There is nothing wrong with writing histories of ideas, of course. But when historians trace the history of American religious ideas they nearly always adopt (at least implicitly) a model of intellectual progress. Their history is organized on the basis of showing how new religious ideas arose and were progressively refined. Moreover, the standards against which refinement is usually judged are entirely secular— parsimony, clarity, logical unity, graceful expression, and the like. One never encounters standards of theological progress or refinement based on how effectively a doctrine could stir the faithful or satisfy the heart. As a result, the history of American religious ideas always turns into an historical account of the march toward liberalism. That is, religious ideas always become more refined (i.e., better) when they are shorn of mystery, miracle, and mysticism—when an active supernatural realm is replaced by abstractions concerning virtue.

Even so, if historians were very careful to limit themselves to a history of religious ideas, we would find little in their work to criticize. But many historians of religion slip over the line and soon are linking individuals and organizations to these ideas. And it is here that the very strong preference for a more refined theology causes profound misreporting. An example may prove helpful. [Later] we shall encounter the Holiness Movement. As presented by historians, those involved in the Holiness Movement were unsophisticated souls, sadly out of joint with modern times. They were losers: not only were these misguided conservatives expelled from the mainline bodies, they were thereby consigned to historical insignificance as well.

Such an interpretation is possible only if one values theological refinement more than religious commitment and participation. For it is only in terms of a progressive history of theology that the Holiness Movement can be assigned to the losing side. Any fair history based on the subsequent fate of religious organizations would have to acknowledge that the Holiness Movement gave birth to denominations that have been growing rapidly, while the denominations that drove out the Holiness Movement have been rapidly losing out ever since.

In this book the history of American religion is the history of human actions and human organizations, not the history of ideas (refined or otherwise). But this is not to say that we regard theology as unimportant. To the contrary, we shall argue repeatedly that religious organizations can thrive only to the extent that they have a theology that can comfort souls and motivate sacrifice. In a sense, then, we are urging an underlying model of religious history that is the exact opposite of that based on progress through theological refinement. We shall present compelling evidence that theological refinement is the kind of progress that results in organizational bankruptcy. . . .

At this point it seems appropriate to present the primary fruits of our adventures with religious statistics. [The figure on page 14] plots the overall trend in the rate of religious adherence for two centuries. This pattern can truly be called the churching of America. On the eve of the Revolution only about 17 percent of Americans were churched. By the start of the Civil War this proportion had risen dramatically, to 37 percent. The immense dislocations of the war caused a serious decline in adherence in the South, which is reflected in the overall decline to 35 percent in the 1870 census. The rate then began to rise once more, and by 1906 slightly more than half of the U.S. population was churched. Adherence rates reached 56 percent by 1926. Since then the rate has been rather stable although inching upwards. By 1980 church adherence was about 62 percent.

Rates of Religious Adherence, 1776–1980

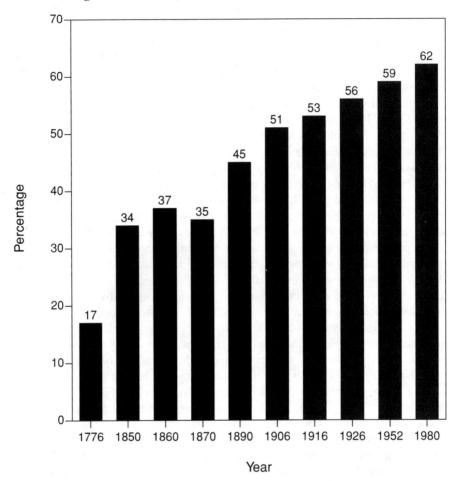

This is the phenomenon we shall try to explain. . . . Why did the rate rise so greatly? Which denominations contributed most to the great increase in religious adherence, and which failed to benefit? These issues lead directly to our key analytical device: religious economies.

On Religious Economies

Some readers may shudder at the use of "market" terminology in discussions of religion. But we see nothing inappropriate in acknowledging that where religious affiliation is a matter of choice, religious organizations must compete for members and that the "invisible hand" of the marketplace is as unforgiving of ineffective religious firms as it is of their commercial counterparts.

We are not the first to use an explicit market model to explore the interplay among religious organizations. Indeed, . . . Adam Smith did so very persuasively back in 1776. Moreover, it was typical for European visitors to use economic language to explain the religious situation in America to their friends back home. For example, Francis Grund, an Austrian who eventually became an American citizen, wrote in 1837: "In America, every clergyman may be said to do business on his own account, and under his own firm. He alone is responsible for any deficiency in the discharge of his office, as he alone is entitled to all the credit due to his exertions. He always acts as principal, and is therefore more anxious, and will make greater efforts to obtain popularity, than one who serves for wages. The actual stock in any of these firms is, of course, less than the immense capital of the Church of England; but the aggregate amount of business transacted by them jointly may nevertheless be greater in the United States."

We will use economic concepts such as markets, firms, market penetration, and segmented markets to analyze the success and failure of religious bodies. Religious economies are like commercial economies in that they consist of a market made up of a set of current and potential customers and a set of firms seeking to serve that market. The fate of these firms will depend upon (1) aspects of their organizational structures, (2) their sales representatives, (3) their product, and (4) their marketing techniques. Translated into more churchly language, the relative success of religious bodies (especially when confronted with an unregulated economy) will depend upon their polity, their clergy, their religious doctrines, and their evangelization techniques.

The use of economic tools in no way suggests that the content of religion is unimportant, that it is all a matter of clever marketing and energetic selling. To the contrary, we will argue that the primary market weakness that has caused the failure of many denominations, and the impending failure of many more, is precisely a matter of doctrinal content, or the lack of it. That is, we will repeatedly suggest that as denominations have modernized their doctrines and embraced temporal values, they have gone into decline.

The primary value of analyzing American religious history through a market-oriented lens is that in this way some well-established deductions from the principles of supply and demand can illuminate what might otherwise seem a very disorderly landscape (as it indeed often appears to be in standard histories of the subject). Consider the following examples.

First, as in the analysis of market economies, a major consideration in analyzing religious economies is their degree of regulation. Some are virtually unregulated; some are restricted to state-imposed monopolies. In keeping with supply and demand principles, to the degree that a religious economy is unregulated, pluralism will thrive. That is, the "natural" state of religious economies is one in which a variety of religious groups successfully caters to the special needs and interests of specific market segments. This variety arises because of the inherent inability of a single product to satisfy very divergent tastes. Or, to note the specific features of religious firms and products, pluralism arises because of the inability of a single religious organization to be at once worldly and otherworldly, strict and permissive, exclusive and inclusive, while the market will always contain distinct consumer segments with strong preferences on each of these aspects of faith. This occurs because of "normal" variations in the human condition such as social class, age, gender, health, life experiences, and socialization.

In fact, because of this underlying differentiation of consumer preferences, religious economies can never be successfully monopolized, even when a religious organization is backed by the state. At the height of its temporal power, the medieval church was surrounded by heresy and dissent. Of course, when repressive efforts are very great, religions in competition with the state-sponsored monopoly will be forced to operate underground. But whenever and wherever repression falters, lush pluralism will break through.

Sociologists have long been fascinated with religious pluralism and its consequences for the religious landscape. Unfortunately, their grasp of both economics and history has been imperfect. The received wisdom is that pluralism weakens faith—that where multiple religious groups compete, each discredits the other and this encourages the view that religion per se is open to question, dispute, and doubt. . . .

Historical evidence says otherwise. There is ample evidence that in societies with putative monopoly faiths, religious indifference, not piety, is rife. Our contrary perceptions are nostalgic error. As we shall see . . . in the Puritan Commonwealth of Massachusetts religious adherence probably never exceeded 22 percent. It is becoming increasingly well known that religious participation was very low in medieval Europe. . . . And today, close inspection of the religious situation in societies where "everyone" is a Roman Catholic reveals levels of religious participation that are astonishingly low compared with those in America—the exceptions being places such as Ireland and Quebec where the church has also served as the primary vehicle for political resistance to external domination.

In addition to being based on bad history, faith in the power of monopoly religions is rooted in bad economics. We have already noted that the inability of the monopoly church . . . to mobilize massive commitment is inherent in the segmentation of any religious economy. A single faith cannot shape its appeal to suit precisely the needs of one market segment without sacrificing its appeal to another. But a second, equally compelling, principle of economics also applies: Monopoly firms always tend to be lazy.

In contrasting the American and European religious situations, Francis Grund (1837) noted that establishment makes the clergy "indolent and lazy," because "a person provided for cannot, by the rules of common sense, be supposed to work as hard as one who has to exert himself for a living. . . . Not only have Americans a greater number of clergymen than, in proportion to the population, can be found either on the Continent or in England; but they have not one idler amongst them; all of them being obliged to exert themselves for the spiritual welfare of their respective congregations. The Americans, therefore, enjoy a threefold advantage: they have more preachers; they have more active preachers, and they have cheaper preachers than can be found in any part of Europe."

A similar argument was developed by the prominent and colorful English traveler William Cobbett (1818):

> Taxes and Priests; for these always lay on heavily together. . . . I will, on these subjects, address myself more immediately to my old neighbours of Botley, and endeavour to make them understand what America is as to taxes and priests. . . .
>
> I have talked to several farmers here about the tithes in England; and, they *laugh* . . . they seem, at last, not to believe what I say, when I tell them that the English farmer gives,

and is compelled [by law] to give, the Parson a tenth part of his whole crop. . . . They cannot believe this. They treat it as a sort of *romance*. . . .

But, my Botley neighbours, you will exclaim, "No *tithes!* Why, then, there can be no *Churches* and no *Parsons!* The people must know nothing of God or Devil; and must all go to hell!" By no means, my friends. Here are plenty of Churches. No less than three Episcopal (or English) Churches; three Presbyterian Churches; three Lutheran Churches; one or two Quaker Meeting-houses; and two Methodist places; all within *six miles* of the spot where I am sitting. And, these, mind, not poor shabby Churches; but each of them larger and better built and far handsomer than Botley Church, with the church-yards all kept in the neatest order, with a head-stone to almost every grave. As to the Quaker Meeting-house, it would take Botley Church into its belly, if you were first to knock off the steeple.

Oh no! Tithes are not necessary to promote *religion.* When our Parsons . . . talk about *religion,* or *the church,* being in danger; they mean that the *tithes* are in danger. They mean that they are in danger of being compelled to work for their bread.

But, the fact is, that it is the circumstances of the church being established by law that makes it of little use as to real religion. . . . Because . . . establishment forces upon the people, parsons whom they cannot respect. . . .

The most likely way to insure [a clergyman is both sincere and industrious] is to manage things so that he may be in the first place, selected by the people, and, in the second place, have no rewards in view other than those which are to be given in consequence of his perseverance in a line of good conduct.

And thus it is with clergy in America, who are duly and amply rewarded for their diligence, and very justly respected for the piety, talent, and zeal which they discover; but, who have no tenure of their places other than that of the will of the congregation.

Where many faiths function within a religious economy, a high degree of specialization as well as competition occurs. From this it follows that many independent religious bodies will, together, be able to attract a much larger proportion of a population than can be the case when only one or very few firms have free access.

This last point obviously helps to explain why American religious participation has been rising for two centuries.

Religious Outsiders and "Civil Religion"

R. LAURENCE MOORE

Throughout the nineteenth century most Protestant evangelicals who could be located within the Calvinist, Methodist, or Lutheran traditions warmly endorsed America's experiment in religious disestablishment. At the same time, they expected Americans to move toward a common faith which they thought would resemble their own sectarian outlooks. They were prepared to tolerate diversity, but they did not regard diversity as in itself a good thing. Too many sharply distinctive faiths in fact nullified not only their belief in the unity of the Reformed church but

R. Laurence Moore, *Religious Outsiders and the Making of Americans* (New York: Oxford University Press, 1986), 201–210. Used with permission of Oxford University Press, Inc.

their idea of a virtuous republic as well. To them, maintaining a sensible piety among the American people was a public concern.

Jefferson had spoken of a "wall of separation" between church and state, but Jefferson was not much of an evangelical. His metaphor badly characterized the attitude of ministers who took the lead in describing America's religious system. They viewed the United States as a Protestant Christian nation. Many of them wanted the Constitution to say so explicitly, and they lobbied for legislation that laid down broad guidelines for religious and moral behavior. The freedom to worship in odd ways did not, they believed, require governments to encourage people to exercise that freedom. Unfolding events in the nineteenth century did little to sustain the hopes of Protestants who were waiting for a fundamental religious unity to emerge. However, the situation was sufficiently complicated to lend plausibility to any number of interpretations. What one chose to describe remained very much under the influence of what one wished to prescribe.

By the middle of the twentieth century, the nineteenth-century Protestant desire clearly needed recasting. The permanence of diversity, diversity that included non-Protestant religious traditions, could no longer be doubted. Nonetheless, those who wanted to continue to emphasize some form of essential religious unity found ways to do so, none more persuasively than the American sociologist Robert Bellah. Bellah described the emergence of a civil religion in the United States which, while it did not replace or compete with individual churches, formed an arch of consensus over them. Civil religion, according to Bellah, had a life and institutional base of its own. Bellah argued that its major tenets were not even originally Protestant. But even if they were, the American mission which they sanctified had long ago expanded to include Catholics and Jews. Bellah found a good bit of the evidence for what he wanted to argue in the inaugural address of John Kennedy. America's first Catholic president molded his phrases to fit a tradition of public religious rhetoric that went all the way back to John Winthrop.

Without question, Bellah was onto something important, and he was not the only distinguished scholar who in the post–World War II era managed to locate an American faith that transcended the crazy quilt pattern of denominational divisions. Americans are nationalistic like other people, and their nationalism was and is frequently expressed in religious terms. The paradox has not been lost on European observers. A nation that supposedly is neutral about religion has made religion an obligatory part of public ceremonies. Americans cannot even begin a football game without calling on a clergyman, and it scarcely matters of what faith, to invoke the divine blessing that they assume is peculiarly theirs. Yet if the rites of civil religion suggest that Americans share religious myths, mere reference to them does not settle the issue of how much of themselves Americans invest in nonacrimonious religious observance and how much of themselves they invest in using religious lines to separate themselves from one another. Civil religion exists, but it too, like more ordinary religions, may have split Americans into separate camps as often as it has brought them together.

Common myths do not have to be read in the same way. That is one important caveat. Studies of popular culture have begun to take account of how people misread or creatively misinterpret texts that are assumed to have a clear and single meaning. Public ceremonies are no different from texts. Most Americans celebrate the commercially promoted holidays of Christmas and Thanksgiving, but what their private recreations on those days mean to them is anyone's guess. The same can be said about Inauguration Days, Fourth of July celebrations, and Memorial Days. Americans may or may not pay much attention to what presidents say when they take office; but since the ritual utterances are in the main bland (Jefferson, Lincoln, and Kennedy are exceptions), Americans are not forced into a single pattern of understanding meaning. Americans may remember on the Fourth of July that they are glad to be American, but whether that memory in most cases relates to feelings solemn or specific enough to qualify as religion is subject to doubt. Memorial Day celebrations in small towns give as much evidence of patterns of geographical tribalism as of a common faith. Insofar as the rites of a public religion evoke strong emotional response, they do most certainly reinforce American patriotism. However, as we have seen, patriotic flag waving permits a language that proclaims difference. A civil religion therefore turns into an arena of contested meanings where Americans make assertions about what makes them different from other Americans. The Civil War stands as an ample reminder of just how bad things can get. A functional unity of the majority may in normal times be the product of civic piety, but we ought not on that account forget the differences, or the ways in which what is called civil religion can reinforce the least attractive common denominators of the American people.

The last point, although acknowledged, is deemphasized in the prescriptive outlook that clearly underlies much of what has been written on the subject of civil religion. At its best, according to Bellah, American civil religion recognized that the nation stood under transcendent judgment. If regular denominational religions have had trouble keeping that point of view in mind, we should not be surprised that past American politicians have in their public piety fallen shorter of Bellah's idealism than Bellah wished to concede. When the "sixties" were over, some proponents of civil religion followed Bellah in writing sadly about the "empty and broken shell" of American civil religion. There was reason for sadness, but what they thought had failed was not failing for the first time in American life. Gratitude is due to anyone who tries to hold America to high expectations, but only historical forgetfulness can permit us to believe that the American past furnishes consistent encouragement to those expectations. What the original tribal inhabitants of North America learned about America's sense of national destiny was as relevant to understanding the uses of civil religion as Lincoln's Second Inaugural Address.

The success that the American people have had with their institutions was not necessarily in the design, for the system has often worked in ways that would have confounded the designers. Madison, in the celebrated tenth paper that he wrote to argue the Federalist position, came as close as anyone ever has to explaining the "genius" of American politics. Societies, according to Madison, are collections of groups or factions that seek to satisfy selfish, frequently economic, interests. In pure democracies or in small republics, factions posed grave dangers to individual liberty. Any one of them had a fair chance to become a majority and thus gain the unchecked power to impose its particular interests on everyone else. In a large republic, such as the United States was intended to be, the danger of factionalism was significantly reduced. Elected assemblies imposed a check on popular majorities. More important, large republics, spread over an extensive geographical area, multiplied the number of factions to the point that no one of them could become the majority. As a result, factions had to compromise and to be content with only part of what they wanted. They sometimes even had to concern themselves with the public good. Madison never imagined that the selfish desires responsible for the formation of factions would disappear or cease to be a primary motive in political behavior. He merely predicted, with reasonable accuracy, that the projected American system could control the dangerous consequences of factionalism.

The analysis that Madison applied to political behavior was just as prescient with respect to the American system of church voluntarism. American religious sects are a species of faction, and the religious history of the United States gives us little reason to think that tolerance would remain an entirely safe principle if any one of them gained an overwhelming majority. . . . However, the full extension of religious tolerance, if indeed full tolerance describes the present state of religious affairs in the United States, was more the product of conditions of pluralism which no one sect had the power to overcome as of an abstract belief in the value of pluralism. Contemporary studies that point to a strong correlation between religious affiliation and prejudice should remind us that religious tolerance was not the free gift of a dominant religious group, the Constitution notwithstanding, but the product of uneasy arrangements made between groups that did not much like one another. If Americans are now more religiously tolerant than they were in the nineteenth century, it is not because they are collectively more high-minded but because they care less about religion. A civil religion that guarantees an absolutely unqualified religious liberty to everyone has about the same standing in American life as Madison's realm of the public good. One has no trouble finding it proclaimed and respected, but it owes its existence to the frustration of sectarian interests rather than to the disappearance of selfish ambitions and dark suspicions about the value of someone else's religion.

In raising questions about the degree of religious consensus in the United States, we most certainly run the risk of exaggerating divergence. Any number of observers have remarked with respect to political behavior that the ideological differences among Americans have been relatively insignificant. Otherwise the American party system could not have operated as it has. An analogous observation about American religion suggests that although one can count hundreds of religious groups in the United States, the vast majority of religious Americans have gravitated toward a small number of "mainline" denominations. Edwin Gaustad, for example, argued on the basis of religious statistics gathered in 1965, that is, in a period marked by a seemingly large amount of religious splintering, that only ten major Christian denominational families existed in the United States. Despite journalistic attention given to new religions that attracted young students, the ten major denominational families together comprised 57.9 percent of the total national population and 90 percent of church membership.

Gaustad sensibly suggested, therefore, that America's system of religious pluralism has stopped well short of religious anarchy. . . . [Moreover, a]ny sophisticated theological perspective could instantly dissolve the importance of most beliefs that divide American Protestant groups. But religious modernists, who have yearned for a tolerance that flows from consensus, have tried to let an abstract possibility serve as reality. They have misread the facts that sectarian division is contrived, that religious groups exaggerate the differences that separate them, as evidence of incipient unity. What they have forgotten to ponder is why the divisions do not easily go away.

Andrew Greeley has persuasively noted that American churches have succeeded not merely because they have provided their adherents with a framework of religious meaning sufficient to explain the world they live in. If that were the only thing, secularism would long ago have worked more corrosively on American religious loyalties than it has. American churches have also provided a shelter for people who otherwise had no clear niche in a bewilderingly unstructured society. Americans needed an unusual differentiation of religious persuasions because they had an unusual need for a wide variety of social identities. The separation of church and state in America has not done as much for the virtue of either church or state as its proponents usually claim. It did not much help Americans to find God or public virtue. What it did do was enable them to find themselves.

This returns us to the problem of understanding the paradoxical relation between outsider religious groups and so-called "mainline" churches. What we have tried to suggest is that "mainline" has too often been misleadingly used to label what is "normal" in American religious life and "outsider" to characterize what is aberrational or not-yet-American. In fact the American religious system may be said to be "working" only when it is creating cracks within denominations, when it is producing novelty, even when it is fueling antagonisms. These things are not things which, properly understood, are going on at the edges or fringes of American life. They are what give energy to church life and substance to the claim that Americans are the most religious people on the face of the earth. This often unexamined cliche by the way only means that a lot of Americans go to church. It does not mean, at least not without more proof than is offered here, that Americans are an especially spiritually minded people.

All of the examples we have presented were meant to change the meaning of our common vocabularies by revealing their ambiguity. As the argument ends, we may concede that the Mormon church in 1840 is not usefully characterized as "mainline." Nonetheless, nothing was more central to American culture at the time than the Mormon "controversy." Americans discovered who they were by locating themselves with respect to it. Furthermore, nothing was more "normal" or "typical" of American life than the process of carving out a separate self-identification, a goal toward which all the early Mormon enterprise was directed. The same effort was being made by much larger groups, the Catholics for example, as well as by churches that already thought of themselves as being on the "inside." Unitarian belligerency in the face of Transcendentalism was the response of a group that was trying to balance feelings of cultural superiority with fears of social extinction. There is no way to deal with questions of inside and outside without sharply qualifying the objectivity which those labels seem to claim. What was in conventional terms outside the American religious mainstream turned American religious history into an interesting story. Pluralism may not have meant anarchy. But it did mean pluralism.

Many of the religious groups we have written about in these pages attracted people with strongly felt social insecurities. But what should we make of that? To call their activities marginal blinds us to the great number of Americans who have had to find ways to confront social insecurities. To call certain religious positions escapist or unrealistic because they failed to encourage political activity that promised relief to downtrodden groups conceals how little many people have gotten from politics even in what is theoretically as democratic a country as exists in the world. As the reader was warned in the beginning, the point of view of this analysis is not particularly optimistic.

On the other hand, if the time has long come when Americans must stop writing about their unique success, they may take certain satisfactions in reviewing the historical record. The United States absorbed a vast number of people who had no opportunities elsewhere. It did not do that without violence, oppression, and exploitation, but one can imagine a far worse scenario. On balance, the proliferation of religious identifications helped contain the worst tendencies in American life. That was not because the various religions taught brotherly love, although most of them did. Nor was it because religions sought to avoid antagonism. Quite the contrary. Nor was it because diversity did not really entail distinctiveness. What the proliferation did was to provide ways for many people to invest their life with a significance that eased their sense of frustration. For many, no doubt, that meant coming to terms with and accepting social and political powerlessness. For others, it led directly to gaining conventional forms of power in a world that was no longer primarily religious. America was potentially as great a religious battleground as had existed in the course of Western Civilization. That it did not become one of the worst is probably enough of a success so far as history goes. Consensus as a myth became believable, and the long-range effects of very real conflict were blunted. Whether that success, the result of a providential mistake, will continue in the future is another matter.

✎ *F U R T H E R   R E A D I N G*

Ahlstrom, Sidney. *A Religious History of the American People.* 2 volumes (1972).

Albanese, Catherine. *America: Religions and Religion.* 2nd edition (1992).

Bellah, Robert, and Frederick Greenspahn. *Uncivil Religion: Interreligious Hostility in America.* (1989).

Blau, Joseph. *Judaism in America.* (1976).

Butler, Jon, and Harry Stout, eds. *Religion in American History: A Reader* (1998).

Conkin, Paul, *American Origins: Homemade Varieties of Christianity* (1997).

Dillenberger, John, *The Visual Arts and Christianity in America* (1988).

Dolan, Jay P. *The American Catholic Experience: A History from Colonial Times to the Present* (1985).

Gaustad, Edwin. *Historical Atlas of Religion in America* (1962).

Hackett, David, ed., *Religion and American Culture* (1995).

Hall, David, ed., *Lived Religion in America: Toward a History of Practice* (1997).

Hatch, Nathan, and Mark Noll, eds. *The Bible in America: Essays in Cultural History* (1982).

Lippy, Charles, and Peter Williams, eds. *Encyclopedia of American Religious Experience* (1988).

McDannell, Colleen, *Material Christianity: Religion and Popular Culture in America* (1995).

Marsden, George. *Religion and American Culture* (1990).

Marty, Martin. *Pilgrims in Their Own Land: Five Hundred Years of Religion in America* (1984).

Mead, Sidney. *The Nation with the Soul of a Church* (1975).

Moore, R. Laurence. *Selling God: American Religion in the Marketplace of Culture* (1994).

Morris, Charles R. *American Catholic: The Saints and Sinners Who Built America's Most Powerful Church* (1997).

Noll, Mark, Nathan Hatch and George Marsden. *The Search for Christian America* (1989).

Roof, Wade, and William McKinney. *American Mainline Religion* (1993).

Schmidt, Lee. *Consumer Rites: The Buying and Selling of American Holidays* (1995).

Stout, Harry, and Darryl Hart, *New Directions in American Religious History* (1997).

Tweed, Thomas, ed. *Retelling U.S. Religious History* (1997).

Wentz, Richard. *Religion in the New World: The Shaping of Religious Traditions in the New World* (1990).

Williams, Peter. *America's Religions: Traditions and Cultures* (1990).

Wills, David. "The Central Themes of American Religious History: Pluralism, Puritanism, and the Encounter of Black and White," *Religion and Intellectual Life* 5. (Fall 1987), 30–41.

CHAPTER
2

European-Indian Encounters

The 1492 expedition of Christopher Columbus brought Europeans into contact with Native Americans (whom they called Indians) for the first time. Over the next four hundred years the Indians of the Americas suffered severely from Europeans' diseases, to which at first they had no immunity. They also endured defeat and dislocation as a result of the Europeans' technological superiority in war and their seizure of land for settlement and farming. Gradually, the Indians were compelled to adapt to the dominant white culture. Nevertheless elements of their religions and languages survive.

European settlers from Spain, France, Holland, and Britain hoped to convert the Indians to Christianity. They sometimes succeeded but more often failed because of the great cultural gulf between the two peoples and their mutual distrust. The most enterprising missionaries lived with the Indians, learned their languages and their explanations for the great mysteries of existence, then preached the Christian message in terms the Indians could grasp. Written descriptions by missionaries of the American Indians' way of life—their beliefs, rituals, and activities—help us to understand how these nonliterate peoples regarded themselves and their religion.

It is important to remember that "religion" is a concept of Western civilization and that Native Americans did not make a sharp distinction between the religious and secular aspects of their lives. Instead they inhabited a world in which sea, sky, rivers, trees, mountains, and animals all possessed spirits, all communicated with the Great Spirit, and all entered into arrangements with each other. It was also a world in which important messages and guidance could be presented in dreams. Missionaries were sometimes amused at the Indians' ideas of where the world and its people came from, what happened to people after death, and why people sometimes felt joy and sometimes pain. But as several of the documents and essays in this chapter show, the Indians could find the religious ideas of whites equally amusing and unconvincing. It is necessary to read missionaries' accounts with care because of their authors' bias, but they are immensely valuable to historians seeking to understand how these widely contrasting religious systems encountered each other.

Chronic frontier warfare between whites and American Indians sometimes led to the Indians taking English prisoners. They usually killed or ransomed adults but adopted children into their families and brought them up as full members of the tribes. If these children later rejoined the white society or found ways to bridge the gulf between the two peoples, they became excellent sources of sympathetic information. Such movement back and forth was not easy, however, and most *white colonists regarded with horror any white man or woman who "went native," which they regarded as becoming a savage. In the colonial era, then, certain whites befriended certain Indians, but most whites, lacking the concept of cultural relativism, had no interest in ensuring that the Indians' traditional way of life would persist. Indeed, with their fear of the Indians and their own regard for themselves as morally, socially, religiously, and technically superior, most whites were eager to see the native culture vanish as soon as possible. It is no coincidence that historians' sympathetic interest in the Native American culture rose in proportion to the decline in the threat they offered to the whites.*

 D O C U M E N T S

Spanish, French, and English views of the Indians are all represented in the following documents, along with a few glimpses of Indian views of the whites. Document 1 describes the dramatic encounter of Cortes's *conquistadores* with the Aztecs' ritual of human sacrifice in 1519. Document 2 (1542) shows a much more vulnerable Spanish explorer, Cabeza de Vaca, shipwrecked and far from help, adapting to Indian ways for the sake of his survival. In Document 3 (1610), Father Jouvency, a Jesuit priest in the St. Lawrence River Valley, now part of Canada, tells his French superiors about native funeral customs and about the strange turns his theological discussions with the Indians could take. Document 4 (1643), written by Roger Williams, the founder of Rhode Island, is an energetic Puritan's attempt to learn the language of the Narragansetts and to explain their religious ideas prior to attempting their conversion to Christianity. Document 5 is the account of Mary Jemison (c. 1750), a colonial farmer's daughter who was taken into captivity and raised by the Seneca Indians in what is now Upstate New York. She describes the rituals and ceremonies with which the Seneca greeted each New Year and the importance they attached to the sacrifice of white dogs. Documents 6 and 7 (c. 1750) are taken from English settlers who lived, hunted, and traded on the Indian frontier in the mid-eighteenth century. They describe the Indians' ideas about the Great Spirit; the importance of fortitude in the face of hunger, defeat, and death; and the Indians' view that they could communicate on equal terms with the animals, even criticizing them if they did not die with appropriate courage. Finally, Document 8 (1876) is an account by the environmentalist John Muir of how Alaskan natives, isolated until the mid-nineteenth century, abandoned their totem poles and turned to Christianity, a faith in which they found analogies to their own lives.

1. Bernal Diaz del Castillo Describes Cortes' Replacement of Human Sacrifice with the Cult of the Virgin Mary, c. 1519

[W]hen we had left those towns in peace and continued our march towards Cempoala, we met the fat cacique and other chiefs waiting for us in some huts with food, for although they were Indians, they saw and understood that justice is good and sacred, and that the words Cortés had spoken to them, that we had come to right wrongs and abolish tyranny, were in conformity with what had happened on that expedition, and they were better affected towards us than ever before.

Bernal Diaz del Castillo, *The Conquest of New Spain* (London: Hakluyt Society, 1908), 185–191.

We slept the night in those huts, and all the caciques bore us company all the way to our quarters in their town. They were really anxious that we should not leave their country, as they were fearful that Montezuma would send his warriors against them, and they said to Cortés that as we were already their friends, they would like to have us for brothers, and that it would be well that we should take from their daughters, so as to have children by them; and to cement our friendship, they brought eight damsels, all of them daughters of caciques, and gave one of these cacicas, who was the niece of the fat cacique, to Cortés; and one, who was the daughter of another great cacique, (called Cuesco in their language,) was given to Alonzo Hernández Puertocarrero. . . . Cortés received them with a cheerful countenance and thanked the caciques for the gift, but he said that before we could accept them and become brothers, they must get rid of those idols which they believed in and worshipped, and which kept them in darkness, and must no longer offer sacrifices to them, and that when he could see those cursed things thrown to the ground and an end put to sacrifices that then our bonds of brotherhood would be most firmly tied. He added that these damsels must become Christians before we could receive them, and the people must free themselves from sodomy, for there were boys dressed like women who went about for gain by that cursed practice, and every day we saw sacrificed before us three, four or five Indians whose hearts were offered to the idols and their blood plastered on the walls, and the feet, arms and legs of the victims were cut off and eaten, just as in our country we eat beef brought from the butchers. I even believe that they sell it by retail in the *tianguez* as they call their markets. Cortés told them that if they gave up these evil deeds and no longer practiced them, not only would we be their friends, but we would make them lords over other provinces. All the caciques, priests, and chiefs replied that it did not seem to them good to give up their idols and sacrifices and that these gods of theirs gave them health and good harvests and everything of which they had need; and that as for sodomy, measures would be taken to put a stop to it so that it should no longer be practiced.

When Cortés and all of us who had seen so many cruelties and infamies which I have mentioned heard that disrespectful answer, we could not stand it, and Cortés spoke to us about it and reminded us of certain good and holy doctrines and said: "How can we ever accomplish anything worth doing if for the honour of God we do not first abolish these sacrifices made to idols?" and he told us to be all ready to fight should the Indians try to prevent us; but even if it cost us our lives the idols must come to the ground that very day. We were all armed ready for a fight as it was ever our custom to be so, and Cortés told the caciques that the idols must be overthrown. When they saw that we were in earnest, the fat cacique and his captains told all the warriors to get ready to defend their idols, and when they saw that we intended to ascend a lofty *cue*—which was their temple—which stood high and was approached by many steps—I cannot remember how many (steps there were)—the fat cacique and the other chieftains were beside themselves with fury and called out to Cortés to know why he wanted to destroy their idols, for if we dishonoured them and overthrew them, that they would all perish and we along with them. Cortés answered them in an angry tone, that he had already told them that they should offer no more sacrifices to those evil images. . . .

When the Indians saw Cortés uttering these threats, and our interpreter Doña Marina knew well how to make them understood, and even threatened them with the power of Montezuma which might fall on them any day, out of fear of all this they replied that they were not worthy to approach their gods, and that if we wished to overthrow them it was not with their consent, but that we could overthrow them and do what we chose.

The words were hardly out of their mouths before more than fifty of us soldiers had clambered up [to the temple] and had thrown down their idols which came rolling down the steps shattered to pieces. The idols looked like fearsome dragons, as big as calves, and there were other figures half men and half great dogs of hideous appearance. When they saw their idols broken to pieces the caciques and priests who were with them wept and covered their eyes, and in the Totonac tongue they prayed their gods to pardon them, saying that the matter was no longer in their hands and they were not to blame, but these Teules who had overthrown them, and that they did not attack us on account of the fear of the Mexicans. . . .

. . . Cortés . . . made them a good speech through our interpreters, . . . and told them that . . . now they were not to have any more idols in their lofty temples he wished to leave with them a great lady who was the Mother of our Lord Jesus Christ whom we believe in and worship, and that they too should hold her for Lady and intercessor, and about this matter and others which were mentioned he made them an excellent discourse, so concisely reasoned, considering the time at his disposal, that there was nothing left to be said. He told them many things about our holy religion as well stated as only a priest could do it nowadays, so that it was listened to with good will. Then he ordered all the Indian masons in the town to bring plenty of lime so as to clean the place and he told them to clear away the blood which encrusted the cues and to clean them thoroughly. The next day when they were whitewashed, an altar was set up with very good altar cloths and he told the Indians to bring many of the roses which grew in the country and are very sweet-scented, and branches of flowers, and told the people to adorn the altar with garlands and always keep the place swept and clean. He then ordered four of the priests to have their hair shorn, for, as I have already said, they wore it long, and to change their garments and clothe themselves in white, and always keep themselves clean, and he placed them in charge of the altar and of that sacred image of our Lady, with orders to keep the place swept clean and decked with flowers. So that it should be well looked after, he left there as hermit one of our soldiers named Juan de Torres de Córdoba, who was old and lame. He ordered our carpenters, whose names I have already given, to make a cross and place it on a stone support which we had already built and plastered over.

The next morning, mass was celebrated at the altar by Padre Fray Bartolomé de Olmedo, and then an order was given to fumigate the holy image of Our Lady and the sacred cross with the incense of the country, and we showed them how to make candles of the native wax and ordered these candles always to be kept burning on the altar, for up to that time they did not know how to use the wax. The most important chieftains of that town and of others who had come together, were present at the Mass.

2. Alvar Nunez Cabeza de Vaca, a Spanish Castaway, Becomes an Indian Healer, 1542

These people love their children more and treat them better than any other people on earth. When someone's child happens to die, the parents and relatives and the whole village weep for him for a full year. The parents begin crying each morning before dawn, and then the whole village joins in. They do the same thing at midday and at sunrise. At the end of a year, they honor the dead child and wash themselves clean of the soot on their bodies. They mourn all their dead in this manner except old people, whom they ignore, saying that their time has passed and they are of little use, and that in fact they occupy space and consume food which could be given to the children. Their custom is to bury the dead, unless the dead man is a medicine man, in which case they burn the body, all dancing around the fire with much merriment. They grind the bones to a powder. A year later they honor the dead medicine man, scar themselves, and his relatives drink the powdered bones mixed with water.

Each one has a recognized wife. The medicine men have the greatest freedom, since they can have two or three wives, among whom there is great friendship and harmony. When someone gives his daughter in marriage, from the first day of the marriage onward, she takes all that her husband kills by hunting or fishing to her father's lodge, without daring to take or eat any of it. The husband's in-laws then take food to him. All this time the father-in-law and the mother-in-law do not enter his lodge and he does not enter their lodge nor the lodges of his brothers-in-law. If they encounter him somewhere, they move away the distance of a crossbow shot, and while they are moving away, they lower their heads and keep their eyes on the ground, because they think it is a bad thing for them to see each other. The women are free to communicate and converse with their in-laws and relatives. This custom is observed on the island and for a distance of more than fifty leagues inland.

Another custom of theirs is that, when an offspring or sibling dies, no one in the household looks for food for three months; they would sooner let themselves starve to death. Relatives and neighbors provide them with food. Since many of their people died while we were there and this custom and ritual was observed, there was great hunger in many households. . . .

On that island I have spoken of, they wanted to make us physicians, without testing us or asking for any degrees, because they cure illnesses by blowing on the sick person and cast out the illness with their breath and their hands. So they told us to be useful and do the same. We laughed at the idea, saying they were mocking us and that we did not know how to heal. They in turn deprived us of our food until we did as they ordered. Seeing our reluctance, an Indian told me that I did not know what I was talking about when I said that all that was useless. He knew that even

The Account: Alvar Nunez Cabeza de Vaca's Relación, trans. and ed. Martin A. Favata and Jose B. Fernandez (Houston, Tex.: Arte Publico Press, 1993).

rocks and other things found in the fields have beneficial properties, for he healed and took away pain by passing a hot rock across the stomach. And since, he said, we were powerful men, we were certain to have greater powers and properties. In brief, we were in such need that we had to do it, putting aside our fear that anyone would be punished for it.

Their manner of healing is as follows: when they are sick, they call a medicine man, and after they are cured they give him not only all their possessions, but also seek things from their relatives to give him. What the medicine man does is to make a cut where the pain is and suck around it. They cauterize with fire, a practice they consider very beneficial. I tried it and found that it gave good results. Afterwards they blow on the painful area, believing that their illness goes away in this manner.

We did our healing by making the sign of the cross on the sick persons, breathing on them, saying the Lord's Prayer and a Hail Mary over them, and asking God our Lord, as best we could, to heal them and inspire them to treat us well. God our Lord in his mercy deigned to heal all those for whom we prayed. Once we made the sign of the cross on them, they told the others that they were well and healthy. For this reason they treated us well, and refrained from eating to give us food. They also gave us hides and other small things. . . .

These Indians, and the ones we encountered before, told us a very strange thing which they reckoned had happened about fifteen or sixteen years earlier. They said that a man whom they called "Evil Thing" wandered that land. He had a small body and a beard, but they never were able to see his face. When he came to the house where they were, their hair stood on end and they trembled. Then there appeared at the entrance to the house a burning firebrand. Then he entered and took whomever he wanted and stabbed him three times in the side with a very sharp flint, as wide as a hand and two palms long. He would stick his hands in through the wounds and pull out their guts, and cut a piece of gut about a palm in length, which he would throw onto the embers. Then he would cut his victim three times in the arm, the second cut at the spot where people are bled. He would pull the arm out of its socket and shortly thereafter reset it. Finally he would place his hands on the wounds which they said suddenly healed. They told us that he often appeared among them when they were dancing, sometimes dressed as a woman and other times as a man. Whenever he wanted, he would take a *buhio* or a dwelling and lift it high. After a while he would let it drop with a great blow. They also told us that they offered him food many times but he never ate. They asked him where he came from and where he lived; he showed them an opening in the ground and said that his house was there below. We laughed a lot and made fun of these things that they told us. When they saw that we did not believe them, they brought many of the people who claimed he had taken them and showed us the marks of the stabbings in those places, just as they had said. We told them that he was evil, and, as best as we could, gave them to understand that, if they believed in God our Lord and became Christians as we were, they would no longer fear him, nor would he dare come to do those things to them. We assured them that as long as we were in their land he would not dare to appear. They were greatly relieved by this and lost much of their fear.

3. Joseph Jouvency, a Jesuit Priest, Discusses Death and Hell with Canadian Indians, 1610

They believe that there are two main sources of disease; one of these is in the mind of the patient himself, which desires something, and will vex the body of the sick man until it possesses the thing required. For they think that there are in every man certain inborn desires, often unknown to themselves, upon which the happiness of individuals depends. For the purpose of ascertaining desires and innate appetites of this character, they summon soothsayers, who, as they think, have a divinely-imparted power to look into the inmost recesses of the mind. These men declare that whatever first occurs to them, or something from which they suspect some gain can be derived, is desired by the sick person. Thereupon the parents, friends, and relatives of the patient do not hesitate to procure and lavish upon him whatever it may be, however expensive, a return of which is never thereafter to be sought. The patient enjoys the gift, divides a portion of it among the soothsayers, and often on the next day departs from life. Commonly, however, the sick recover, plainly because their illnesses are slight; for, in the case of more severe complaints, these soothsayers are more cautious, and deny the possibility of ascertaining what the patient desires; then they bewail him whom they have given up, and cause the relatives to put him out of the way. Thus they kill those afflicted with protracted illness, or exhausted by old age, and consider this the greatest kindness, because death puts an end to the sufferings of the sick. . . .

They never bear out the corpses of the dead through the door of the lodge, but through that part toward which the sick person turned when he expired. They think that the soul flies out through the smoke-hole; and, in order that it may not linger through longing for its old home, nor while departing breathe upon any of the children, who by such an act would be, as they think, doomed to death, they beat the walls of the wigwam with frequent blows of a club, in order that they may compel the soul to depart more quickly. They believe it to be immortal. That it may not thereafter perish with hunger, they bury with the body a large quantity of provisions; also, garments, pots, and various utensils of great expense, and acquired by many years' labor, in order, they say, that he may use them and pass his time more suitably in the kingdom of the dead. The tombs of the chiefs are raised a little from the ground; upon them they place poles joined in the form of a pyramid; they add a bow, arrows, shield and other insignia of war; but upon the tombs of the women they place necklaces and collars. They bury the bodies of infants beside paths, in order that their souls, which they think do not depart very far from the body, may slip into the bosoms of women passing by, and animate the yet undeveloped fetus. In mourning, they stain the face with soot. . . . When [a funeral] feast is completed the master of the funeral, who, in each distinguished family, permanently holds this office and is greatly honored, proclaims that the time for the burial has come. All give utterance to continuous lamentations and wailings. The corpse, wrapped in beaver skins and placed upon a bier made of bark and rushes, with his limbs bent and pressed tightly against his body in order that, as they say, he may be committed

Reuben G. Thwaites, ed., *The Jesuit Relations and Allied Documents*, vol. 1 (Cleveland: Burrows Brothers, 1896), 259–267 and 287–291.

to the earth in the same position in which he once lay in his mother's womb, is borne out on the shoulders of the relatives. The bier is set down at the appointed place, the gifts which each one offers to the dead are fastened to poles, and the donors are named by the master of the funeral. The mourning is renewed; finally, boys vie with each other in a mock contest.

Those who have been drowned are buried with greater ceremony and lamentation. For their bodies are cut open, and a portion of the flesh, together with the viscera, thrown into the fire. This is a sort of sacrifice, by means of which they seek to appease heaven. For they are sure that heaven is enraged against the race whenever any one loses his life by drowning. If any part of these funeral rites has not been duly and regularly performed, they believe that all the calamities from which they afterwards may suffer are a punishment for this neglect. They indulge their grief throughout an entire year. For the first ten days they lie upon the ground day and night, flat upon their bellies; it is impious then to utter any sound unless significant of grief, or to approach the fire, or to take part in feasts. . . . Every eight or ten years the Hurons, which nation is widely extended, convey all their corpses from all the villages to a designated place and cast them into an immense pit. They call it the day of the Dead. When this has been decreed by resolution of the elders, they drag out the corpses from their graves, some already decomposed, with flesh scarcely clinging to the bones, others thinly covered with putrid flesh, others teeming with vile worms and smelling fearfully. The loose bones they place in sacks, the bodies not yet disintegrated they place in coffins, and bear them, in the manner of suppliants, to the appointed place, proceeding amid deep silence and with regular step, uttering sighs and mournful cries. . . .

There is among them no system of religion, or care for it. They honor a Deity who has no definite character or regular code of worship. They perceive, however, through the twilight, as it were, that some deity does exist. What each boy sees in his dreams, when his reason begins to develop, is to him thereafter a deity, whether it be a dog, a bear, or a bird. They often derive their principles of life and action from dreams; as for example, if they dream that any person ought to be killed, they do not rest until they have caught the man by stealth and slain him. It is wearisome to recount the tales which they invent concerning the creation of the world. Soothsayers and worthless quacks fill with these the idle and greedy ears of the people in order that they may acquire an impious gain. They call some divinity, who is the author of evil, "Manitou," and fear him exceedingly. Beyond doubt it is the enemy of the human race, who extorts from some people divine honors and sacrifices. Concerning the nature of spirits, they go none the less astray. They make them corporeal images which require food and drink. They believe that the appointed place for souls, to which after death they are to retire, is in the direction of the setting sun, and there they are to enjoy feasting, hunting, and dancing; for these pleasures are held in the highest repute among them.

When they first heard of the eternal fire and the burning decreed as a punishment for sin, they were marvelously impressed; still, they obstinately withheld their belief because, as they said, there could be no fire where there was no wood; then, what forests could sustain so many fires through such a long space of time? This absurd reasoning had so much influence over the minds of the savages, that they could not be persuaded of the truth of the gospel. For, plainly, in the physical man, as some one from Sts. Peter and Paul says, the entire system of knowledge is based on vision. Nevertheless, a clever and ingenious priest overcame their obstinacy. He confidently declared that the lower world possessed no wood, and that it burned by itself. He was greeted by the laughter of the crowd of savages. "But," said he, "I will exhibit to you a piece of this land of Avernus, in order that, since you do not believe the words of God, you may trust the evidence of your own eyes." The novelty and boldness of the promise aroused their curiosity. Upon the appointed day they assembled from the whole neighborhood, and sat down together in an immense plain, surrounded by hills like an amphitheater. Twelve leading men of the tribe, persons of dignity and sagacity, were chosen to watch the priest, in order that neither fraud nor sorcery might be concealed. He produced a lump of sulphur and gave it to the judges and inspectors to be handled; after examining it with eyes, nose, and hand, they admitted that it was certainly earth. There stood near by a kettle containing live coals. Then the priest, under the eyes of the people at a distance, while the judges were gaping with their noses thrust down toward the coals, shook some grains from the lump of sulphur upon the coals, which suddenly took fire and filled the curious noses with a stifling odor. When this had been done a second and a third time, the crowd arose in astonishment, placing their hands flat over their mouths, by which gesture they signify great surprise; and believed in the word of God that there is a lower world.

4. Roger Williams Explains Rhode Island Indians' Language and Religion, 1643

Obs. He that questions whether God made the World, the *Indians* will teach him. I must acknowledge I have received in my converse with them many Confirmations of those two great points, *Heb.* II. *6. viz:*

1. That God is.
2. That hee is a rewarder of all them that diligently seek him.

They will generally confesse that God made all: but then in speciall, although they deny not that *English-mans* God made *English* Men, and the heavens and Earth there! yet their Gods made them and the Heaven, and Earth where they dwell.

Nummusquaunamúckqun manìt. | *God is angry with me?*

Obs. I have heard a poore *Indian* lamenting the losse of a child at break of day, call up his Wife and children, and all about him to Lamentation, and with abundance of teares cry out! O God thou hast taken away my child! thou art angry with me: O turne thine anger from me, and spare the rest of my children.

If they receive any good in hunting, fishing, Harvest &c. they acknowledge God in it.

Yea, if it be but an ordinary accident, a fall, &c. they will say God was angry and did it, *musquàntum manit* God is angry. But herein is their Misery.

First they branch their God-head into many Gods.

Roger Williams, *A Key into the Language of America* (1643; reprint, Providence, R.I.: Rhode Island and Providence Plantation Tercentenary Committee, Inc., 1963), 122–140.

Secondly, attribute it to Creatures.

First, many Gods: they have given me the Names of thirty seven which I have, all which in their solemne Worships they invocate: as

Kautántowwìt the great *South-West* God, to whose House all soules goe, and from whom came their Corne, Beanes, as they say.

Wompanand.	*The Easterne God.*
Chekesuwànd.	*The Westerne God.*
Wunnanaméanit.	*The Northerne God.*
Sowwanànd.	*The Southerne God.*
Wetuómanit.	*The house God.*

Even as the Papists have their He and Shee Saint Protectors as St. *George,* St. *Patrick,* St. *Denis,* Virgin *Mary,* &c.

Squáuanit.	*The Womans God.*
Muckquachuckquànd.	*The Childrens God,*

Obs. I was once with a *Native* dying of a wound, given him by some murtherous *English* (who rob'd him and run him through with a Rapier, from whom in the heat of his wound, he at present escaped from them, but dying of his wound, they suffered Death at new *Plymouth,* in *New-England,* this *Native* dying call'd much upon *Muckquachuckquànd,* which of other *Natives* I understood (as they believed) had appeared to the dying young man, many yeares before, and bid him when ever he was in distresse call upon him.

Secondly, as they have many of these fained Deities: so worship they the Creatures in whom they conceive doth rest some Deitie:

Keesuckquànd.	*The Sun God.*
Nanepaûshat.	*The Moone God.*
Paumpágussit.	*The Sea.*
Yotáanit.	*The Fire God,*

Supposing that Deities be in these, &c.

When I have argued with them about their Fire-God: can it say they be but this fire must be a God, or Divine power, that out of a stone will arise in a Sparke and when a poore naked *Indian* is ready to starve with cold in the House, and especially in the Woods, often saves his life, doth dresse all our Food for us, and if it be angry will burne the House about us, yea if a spark fall into the drie wood, burnes up the Country, (though this burning of the Wood to them they count a Benefit both for destroying of vermin, and keeping downe the Weeds and thickets?)

> *Presentem narrat quælibet herba Deum.*
> *Every little Grasse doth tell,*
>   *The sons of Men, there God doth dwell.*

Besides there is a generall Custome amongst them, at the apprehension of any Excellency in Men, Women, Birds, Beasts, Fish, &c. to cry out *Manittóo,* that is, it is a God, as thus if they see one man excell others in Wisdome, Valour, strength, Activìty &c. they cry out *Manittóo* A God: and therefore when they talke amongst themselves of the *English* ships, and great buildings, of the plowing of their Fields, and especially of Bookes and Letters, they will end thus: *Manittôwock* They are Gods: *Cummanittôo*, you are a God, &c. A strong Conviction naturall in the soule of man, that God is; filling all things, and places, and that all Excellencies dwell in God, and proceed from him, and that they only are blessed who have that Jehovah their portion.

| Nickómmo. | A Feast or Dance. |

Of this Feast they have publike, and private and that of two sorts.

First in sicknesse, or Drouth, or Warre or Famine.

Secondly, After Harvest, after hunting, when they enjoy a caulme of Peace, Health, Plenty, Prosperity, then *Nickómmo* a Feast, especially in Winter, for then (as the Turke faith of the Christian, rather the Antichristian,) they run mad once a yeare in their kind of Christmas feasting.

| Powwaw. | A Priest. |
| Powwaûog. | Priests. |

Obs. These doe begin and order their service, and Invocation of their Gods, and all the people follow, and joyne interchangeably in a laborious bodily service, unto sweatings, especially of the Priest, who spends himselfe in strange Antick Gestures, and Actions even unto fainting.

In sicknesse the Priest comes close to the sick person, and performes many strange Actions about him, and threaten and conjures out the sicknesse. They conceive that there are many Gods or divine Powers within the body of a man: In his pulse, his heart, his Lungs, &c.

I confesse to have most of these their customes by their owne Relation, for after once being in their Houses and beholding what their Worship was, I durst never bee an eye witnesse, Spectatour, or looker on, least I should have been partaker of Sathans Invention.

5. Mary Jemison Describes the Five Feasts by Which the Seneca Marked the Changing Seasons, c. 1750

In each year they have five feasts, or stated times for assembling in their tribes, and giving thanks to Nauwaneu, for the blessings which they have received from his kind and liberal and provident hand; and also to converse upon the best means of meriting a continuance of his favors. The first of these feasts is immediately after they have finished sugaring, at which time they give thanks for the favorable weather and great quantity of sap they have had, and for the sugar that they have been allowed to make for the benefit of their families. At this, as at all the succeeding feasts, the Chiefs arise singly, and address the audience in a kind of exhortation, in which they express their own thankfulness, urge the necessity and propriety of general gratitude, and point out the course which ought to be pursued by each individual, in order that Nauwaneu may continue to bless them, and that the evil spirit may be defeated.

James Everett Seaver, ed., *A Narrative of the Life of Mary Jemison* (1824; reprint, New York: American Scenic and Historic Preservation Society, 1925), 161–167.

On these occasions the Chiefs describe a perfectly straight line, half an inch wide, and perhaps ten miles long, which they direct their people to travel upon by placing one foot before the other, with the heel of one foot to the toe of the other, and so on till they arrive at the end. The meaning of which is, that they must not turn aside to the right hand or to the left into the paths of vice, but keep straight ahead in the way of well doing, that will lead them to the paradise of Nauwaneu.

The second feast is after planting; when they render thanks for the pleasantness of the season—for the good time they have had for preparing their ground and planting their corn; and are instructed by their Chiefs, by what means to merit a good harvest.

When the green corn becomes fit for use, they hold their third, or green corn feast. Their fourth is celebrated after corn harvest; and the fifth at the close of their year, and is always celebrated at the time of the old moon in the last of January or first of February. This last deserves a particular description.

The Indians having returned from hunting, and having brought in all the venison and skins that they have taken, a committee is appointed, says Mrs. Jemison, consisting of from ten to twenty active men, to superintend the festivities of the great sacrifice and thanksgiving that is to be immediately celebrated. This being done, preparations are made at the council-house, or place of meeting, for the reception and accommodation of the whole tribe; and then the ceremonies are commenced, and the whole is conducted with a great degree of order and harmony, under the direction of the committee.

Two white dogs, without spot or blemish, are selected (if such can be found, and if not, two that have the fewest spots) from those belonging to the tribe, and killed near the door of the council-house, by being strangled. A wound on the animal or an effusion of blood, would spoil the victim, and render the sacrifice useless. The dogs are then painted red on their faces, edges of their ears, and on various parts of their bodies, and are curiously decorated with ribbons of different colors, and fine feathers, which are tied and fastened on in such a manner as to make the most elegant appearance. They are then hung on a post near the door of the council-house, at the height of twenty feet from the ground.

This being done, the frolic is commenced by those who are present, while the committee run through the tribe or town, and hurry the people to assemble, by knocking on their houses. At this time the committee are naked, (wearing only a breech-clout,) and each carries a paddle, with which he takes up ashes and scatters them about the house in every direction. In the course of the ceremonies, all the fire is extinguished in every hut throughout the tribe, and new fire, struck from the flint on each hearth, is kindled, after having removed the whole of the ashes, old coals, &c. Having done this, and discharged one or two guns, they go on, and in this manner they proceed till they have visited every house in the tribe. This finishes the business of the first day.

On the second day the committee dance, go through the town with bear-skin on their legs, and at every time they start they fire a gun. They also beg through the tribe, each carrying a basket in which to receive whatever may be bestowed. The alms consist of Indian tobacco, and other articles that are used for incense at the sacrifice. Each manager at this time carries a dried tortoise or turtle shell, containing a few beans, which he frequently rubs on the walls of the houses, both inside and out.

This kind of manœuvering by the committee continues two or three days, during which time the people at the council-house recreate themselves by dancing.

On the fourth or fifth day the committee make false faces of husks, in which they run about, making a frightful but ludicrous appearance. In this dress, (still wearing the bear-skin,) they run to the council-house, smearing themselves with dirt and bedaub every one who refuses to contribute something towards filling the baskets of incense, which they continue to carry, soliciting alms. During all this time they collect the evil spirit, or drive it off entirely, for the present, and also concentrate within themselves all the sins of their tribe, however numerous or heinous.

On the eighth or ninth day, the committee having received all the sin, as before observed, into their own bodies, they take down the dogs, and after having transfused the whole of it into one of their own number, he, by a peculiar slight of hand, or kind of magic, works it all out of himself into the dogs. The dogs, thus loaded with all the sins of the people, are placed upon a pile of wood that is directly set on fire. Here they are burnt, together with the sins with which they were loaded, surrounded by the multitude, who throw incense of tobacco or the like into the fire, the scent of which they say, goes up to Nauwaneu, to whom it is pleasant and acceptable.

This feast continues nine days, and during that time the Chiefs review the national affairs of the year past; agree upon the best plan to be pursued through the next year, and attend to all internal regulations.

On the last day, the whole company partake of an elegant dinner, consisting of meat, corn, and beans, boiled together in large kettles, and stirred till the whole is completely mixed and soft. This mess is devoured without much ceremony—some eat with a spoon, by dipping out of the kettles; others serve themselves in small dippers; some in one way, and some in another, till the whole is consumed. After this they perform the war dance, the peace dance, and smoke the pipe of peace; and then, free from iniquity, each repairs to his place of abode, prepared to commence the business of a new year. In this feast, temperance is observed, and commonly, order prevails in a greater degree than would naturally be expected.

6. Tecaughretanego Explains Why the Great Spirit Sometimes Permits Men to Go Hungry Before Feeding Them, 1758

"*Brother,*—As you have lived with the white people, you have not had the same advantage of knowing that the great Being above feeds his people, and gives them their meat in due season, as we Indians have, who are frequently out of provisions, and yet are wonderfully supplied, and that so frequently, that it is evidently the hand of the great Owaneeyo that doth this. Whereas the white people have commonly large stocks of tame cattle, that they can kill when they please, and also their barns and cribs filled with grain, and therefore have not the same opportunity of seeing and knowing that they are supported by the Ruler of heaven and earth.

Samuel G. Drake, ed., *Tragedies of the Wilderness* (Boston: Antiquarian Bookstore and Institute, 1846), 226–231.

"*Brother,*—I know that you are now afraid that we will all perish with hunger, but you have no just reason to fear this.

"*Brother,*—I have been young, but am now old; I have been frequently under the like circumstances that we now are, and that some time or other in almost every year of my life; yet I have hitherto been supported, and my wants supplied in time of need.

"*Brother,*—Owaneeyo sometimes suffers us to be in want, in order to teach us our dependence upon him, and to let us know that we are to love and serve him; and likewise to know the worth of the favors that we receive, and to make us more thankful.

"*Brother,*—Be assured that you will be supplied with food, and that just in the right time; but you must continue diligent in the use of means. Go to sleep, and rise early in the morning and go a hunting; be strong, and exert yourself like a man, and the Great Spirit will direct your way." . . .

[The next night, w]hen we were all refreshed, Tecaughretanego delivered a speech upon the necessity and pleasure of receiving the necessary supports of life with thankfulness, knowing that Owaneeyo is the great giver. Such speeches from an Indian may be thought by those who are unacquainted with them altogether incredible; but when we reflect on the Indian war, we may readily conclude that they are not an ignorant or stupid sort of people, or they would not have been such fatal enemies. When they came into our country they outwitted us; and when we sent armies into their country, they outgeneralled and beat us with inferior force. Let us also take into consideration that Tecaughretanego was no common person, but was among the Indians as Socrates in the ancient heathen world; and it may be equal to him, if not in wisdom and in learning, yet perhaps in patience and fortitude. Notwithstanding Tecaughretanego's uncommon natural abilities, yet in the sequel of this history you will see the deficiency of the light of nature, unaided by revelation, in this truly great man. . . .

We remained here until some time in April, 1758. At this time Tecaughretanego had recovered so that he could walk about. We made a bark canoe, embarked, and went down Ollentangy some distance, but the water being low, we were in danger of splitting our canoe upon the rocks; therefore Tecaughretanego concluded we would encamp on shore, and pray for rain.

When we encamped Tecaughretanego made himself a sweat house, which he did by sticking a number of hoops in the ground, each hoop forming a semicircle; this he covered all round with blankets and skins. He then prepared hot stones, which he rolled into this hut, and then went into it himself with a little kettle of water in his hand, mixed with a variety of herbs, which he had formerly cured, and had now with him in his pack; they afforded an odoriferous perfume. When he was in, he told me to pull down the blankets behind him, and cover all up close, which I did, and then he began to pour water upon the hot stones, and to sing aloud. He continued in this vehement hot place about fifteen minutes. All this he did in order to purify himself before he would address the Supreme Being. When he came out of his sweat house, he began to burn tobacco and pray. He began each petition with *oh, ho, ho, ho,* which is a kind of aspiration, and signifies an ardent wish. I observed that all his petitions were only for immediate or present temporal blessings. He began his address by thanksgiving in the following manner:

"O Great Being! I thank thee that I have obtained the use of my legs again; that I am now able to walk about and kill turkeys, &c. without feeling exquisite pain and misery. I know that thou art a hearer and a helper, and therefore I will call upon thee.

"*Oh, ho, ho, ho,*

"Grant that my knees and ankles may be right well, and that I may be able, not only to walk, but to run and to jump logs, as I did last fall.

"*Oh, ho, ho, ho,*

"Grant that on this voyage we may frequently kill bears, as they may be crossing the Sciota and Sandusky.

"*Oh, ho, ho, ho,*

"Grant that we may kill plenty of turkeys along the banks, to stew with our fat bear meat.

"*Oh, ho, ho, ho,*

"Grant that rain may come to raise the Ollentangy about two or three feet, that we may cross in safety down to Sciota, without danger of our canoe being wrecked on the rocks. And now, O Great Being! thou knowest how matters stand; thou knowest that I am a great lover of tobacco, and though I know not when I may get any more, I now make a present of the last I have unto thee, as a free burnt offering; therefore I expect thou wilt hear and grant these requests, and I, thy servant, will return thee thanks, and love thee for thy gifts."

During the whole of this scene I sat by Tecaughretanego, and as he went through it with the greatest solemnity, I was seriously affected with his prayers. I remained duly composed until he came to the burning of the tobacco; and as I knew that he was a great lover of it, and saw him cast the last of it into the fire, it excited in me a kind of merriment, and I insensibly smiled. Tecaughretanego observed me laughing, which displeased him, and occasioned him to address me in the following manner.

"*Brother:* I have somewhat to say to you, and I hope you will not be offended when I tell you of your faults. You know that when you were reading your books in town I would not let the boys or any one disturb you; but now, when I was praying, I saw you laughing. I do not think that you look upon praying as a foolish thing; I believe you pray yourself. But perhaps you may think my mode or manner of praying foolish; if so, you ought in a friendly manner to instruct me, and not make sport of sacred things."

I acknowledged my error. . . .

7. John Heckwelder Describes the Delaware Indians' View of Bear Spirits, c. 1750

I have often reflected on the curious connexion which appears to subsist in the mind of an Indian between man and the brute creation, and found much matter in it for curious observation. Although they consider themselves superior to all other animals and are very proud of that superiority; although they believe that the beasts of the forest, the birds of the air, and the fishes of the waters, were created by the Almighty Being for the use of man; yet it seems as if they ascribe the difference between themselves and the brute kind, and the dominion which they have over them, more to their superior bodily strength and dexterity than to their immortal souls. All beings

---

John Heckwelder, *History, Manners, and Customs of the Indian Nations* (1876; reprint, New York: Arno, 1971), 255.

endowed by the Creator with the power of volition and self-motion, they view in a manner as a great society of which they are the head, whom they are appointed, indeed, to govern, but between whom and themselves intimate ties of connexion and relationship may exist, or at least did exist in the beginning of time. They are, in fact, according to their opinions, only the first among equals, the legitimate hereditary sovereigns of the whole animated race, of which they are themselves a constituent part. Hence, in their languages, these inflections of their nouns which we call *genders,* are not, as with us, descriptive of the *masculine* and *feminine* species, but of the *animate* and *inanimate* kinds. Indeed, they go so far as to include trees, and plants within the first of these descriptions. All animated nature, in whatever degree, is in their eyes a great whole, from which they have not yet ventured to separate themselves. They do not exclude other animals from their world of spirits, the place to which they expect to go after death.

I find it difficult to express myself clearly on this abstruse subject, which, perhaps, the Indians themselves do not very well understand, as they have no metaphysicians among them to analyse their vague notions, and perhaps confuse them still more. But I can illustrate what I have said by some characteristic anecdotes, with which I shall conclude this chapter.

I have already observed that the Indian includes all savage beasts within the number of his *enemies.* This is by no means a metaphorical or figurative expression, but is used in a literal sense, as will appear from what I am going to relate.

A Delaware hunter once shot a huge bear and broke its back-bone. The animal fell and set up a most plaintive cry, something like that of the panther when he is hungry. The hunter, instead of giving him another shot, stood up close to him, and addressed him in these words: "Hark ye! bear; you are a coward, and no warrior as you pretend to be. Were you a warrior, you would shew it by your firmness and not cry and whimper like an old woman. You know, bear, that our tribes are at war with each other, and that yours was the aggressor. You have found the Indians too powerful for you, and you have gone sneaking about in the woods, stealing their hogs; perhaps at this time you have hog's flesh in your belly. Had you conquered me, I would have borne it with courage and died like a brave warrior; but you, bear, sit here and cry, and disgrace your tribe by your cowardly conduct." I was present at the delivery of this curious invective; when the hunter had despatched the bear, I asked him how he thought that poor animal could understand what he said to it? "Oh!" said he in answer, "the bear understood me very well; did you not observe how *ashamed* he looked while I was upbraiding him?"

8. John Muir Witnesses the Conversion of Thlinkit Indians to Christianity, c. 1876

The Thlinkit tribes give a hearty welcome to Christian missionaries. In particular they are quick to accept the doctrine of the atonement, because they themselves practice it, although to many of the civilized whites it is a stumbling-block and rock of offense. As an example of their own doctrine of atonement they told Mr. Young and

---

John Muir, *Travels in Alaska* (1915; facsimile reprint, Boston: Houghton Mifflin, 1998), 198–201.

me one evening that twenty or thirty years ago there was a bitter war between their
own and the Sitka tribe, great fighters, and pretty evenly matched. After fighting all
summer in a desultory, squabbling way, fighting now under cover, now in the open,
watching for every chance for a shot, none of the women dared venture to the salmon-
streams or berry-fields to procure their winter stock of food. At this crisis one of the
Stickeen chiefs came out of his block-house fort into an open space midway between
their fortified camps, and shouted that he wished to speak to the leader of the Sitkas.

When the Sitka chief appeared he said:—

"My people are hungry. They dare not go to the salmon-streams or berry-fields
for winter supplies, and if this war goes on much longer most of my people will die
of hunger. We have fought long enough; let us make peace. You brave Sitka warriors go home, and we will go home, and we will all set out to dry salmon and
berries before it is too late."

The Sitka chief replied:—

"You may well say let us stop fighting, when you have had the best of it. You
have killed ten more of my tribe than we have killed of yours. Give us ten Stickeen
men to balance our blood-account; then, and not till then, will we make peace and
go home."

"Very well," replied the Stickeen chief, "you know my rank. You know that I
am worth ten common men and more. Take me and make peace."

This noble offer was promptly accepted; the Stickeen chief stepped forward
and was shot down in sight of the fighting bands. Peace was thus established, and
all made haste to their homes and ordinary work. That chief literally gave himself a
sacrifice for his people. He died that they might live. Therefore, when missionaries
preached the doctrine of atonement, explaining that when all mankind had gone
astray, had broken God's laws and deserved to die, God's son came forward, and,
like the Stickeen chief, offered himself as a sacrifice to heal the cause of God's
wrath and set all the people of the world free, the doctrine was readily accepted.

"Yes, your words are good," they said. "The Son of God, the Chief of chiefs,
the Maker of all the world, must be worth more than all mankind put together;
therefore, when His blood was shed, the salvation of the world was made sure."

A telling illustration of the ready acceptance of this doctrine was displayed by
Shakes, head chief of the Stickeens at Fort Wrangell. A few years before my first
visit to the Territory, when the first missionary arrived, he requested Shakes to call
his people together to hear the good word he had brought them. Shakes accordingly
sent out messengers throughout the village, telling his people to wash their faces,
put on their best clothing, and come to his block-house to hear what their visitor had
to say. When all were assembled, the missionary preached a Christian sermon on the
fall of man and the atonement whereby Christ, the Son of God, the Chief of chiefs,
had redeemed all mankind, provided that this redemption was voluntarily accepted
with repentance of their sins and the keeping of his commandments.

When the missionary had finished his sermon, Chief Shakes slowly arose, and,
after thanking the missionary for coming so far to bring them good tidings and taking
so much unselfish interest in the welfare of his tribe, he advised his people to accept
the new religion, for he felt satisfied that because the white man knew so much more
than the Indians, the white man's religion was likely to be better than theirs.

"The white man," said he, "makes great ships. We, like children, can only make
canoes. He makes his big ships go with the wind, and he also makes them go with

fire. We chop down trees with stone axes; the Boston man with iron axes, which are far better. In everything the ways of the white man seem to be better than ours. Compared with the white man we are only blind children, knowing not how best to live either here or in the country we go to after we die. So I wish you to learn this new religion and teach it to your children, that you may all go when you die into that good heaven country of the white man and be happy. But I am too old to learn a new religion, and besides, many of my people who have died were bad and foolish people, and if this word the missionary has brought us is true, and I think it is, many of my people must be in that bad country the missionary calls 'Hell,' and I must go there also, for a Stickeen chief never deserts his people in time of trouble. To that bad country, therefore, I will go, and try to cheer my people and help them as best I can to endure their misery."

 E S S A Y S

Catherine Albanese of the University of California, Santa Barbara, reconstructs aspects of the Native American nature religion partly from settlers' and missionaries' accounts and partly from the insights of later anthropologists and ethnographers, whose efforts to understand the Indians' frame of mind have been more searching and sympathetic. She reminds us that although there was an immense array of Indian tribes, languages, and traditions in North America, they shared enough characteristics to make some generalizations possible. Most important was that Native Americans did not make a sharp separation between animate and inanimate objects; to them rocks, rivers, rain, and mountains could speak. If Indian hunters killed an animal, the animal had consented and expected its remains to be treated in appropriate ritualized ways. James P. Ronda of the University of Tulsa, Oklahoma, argues that Native Americans, whatever their disadvantages in confronting the whites, were far from powerless. They took what they could use from the white settlers, both physically and psychologically, and rejected elements of the Christian outlook they could not understand. In some ways the two groups were similar—both believed in life after death, the reality of evil spirits, and the power of symbolic objects—but in other ways they were very different—the Indians scorned Christian ideas of sin and hell. Ronda cautions us to remember that traditions are fluid—constantly changing, adapting, and incorporating new elements without collapsing. Hence the ability of Native Americans to select certain elements of Christianity, blend them with traditional ideas, and create syncretistic movements of religious revitalization.

American Indians' Nature Religion

CATHERINE ALBANESE

Before Amerindians and Europeans encountered one another in the sixteenth and seventeenth centuries, anywhere from less than four to more than twelve million native North Americans dwelled in the area north of the Rio Grande River. Using perhaps 550 languages (as different from one another as, say, Chinese from English) and their dialects, Amerindians spoke in tongues that could be traced to nine linguistic stocks, each worlds apart from the other. Even when scholars attempt to

Catherine Albanese, *Nature Religion in America, from the Algonkian Indians to the New Age* (Chicago: University of Chicago Press, 1990), 16–33.

reduce this cultural diversity to manageable proportions, they confront a plethora of Indian nations, each with separate governance and self-understanding expressed in myth, custom, and ritual. Hence, in one way, to speak collectively of native North American tribal cultures is to do violence to the subjective sensibility of many different peoples. On the other hand, cast beside the European invaders, Amerindians and their religious ways shared much in common. Indeed, in southern New England, where Puritan and Amerindian met face-to-face, the underlying unity among a series of Indian cultures was reflected in their common Algonkian heritage of related language, social structure, and religious mentality.

However, before we examine the nature religion of the southern New England Algonkians, we need to pursue the more general understanding. We need to be clear about how Indians perceived what we, today, call nature, and we need to reflect on major characteristics of Amerindian religions.

Regarding the first, it is fair to say that the sense of nature as a collective physical whole—an ordered cosmos comprising the animal and vegetable kingdoms on earth as well as the stars and other heavenly bodies—is a product of the European heritage. Filtered through the lens of the eighteenth-century Enlightenment, . . . this understanding of nature grew more systemic and more mechanistic, providing an overarching frame within which humans could comprehend themselves and their cultural pursuits and activities. Amerindian peoples, on the other hand, recognized the nurturing (natural) matrix of their societies, but they sensed at once a more plural and more personal universe. Instead of the abstract and overarching "nature" of Europe, they saw a world peopled with other-than-human persons, often of mysterious powers and dispositions. Not all of what we name nature was identified by the Indians in personal terms, but the presence of persons animating "nature" radically grounded their nature religion. "Are *all* the stones we see about us here alive?" the anthropologist A. Irving Hallowell asked one old Ojibwa man in the 1950s. After reflecting a long time, the man replied, "No! But *some* are."

If native North Americans saw nature, as we know it, as inhabited by natural persons, that fact already opens the way to a survey of major themes in Amerindian religions. For Amerindians' view of their world was fundamentally relational. Bound to the sacred by ties of kinship, they could speak of preterhuman beings as Thunder Grandfathers or Spider Grandmothers or Corn Mothers. The Tewa remembered that in the beginning they had lived beneath Sandy Place Lake with the animals and the first mothers, "Blue Corn Woman, near to summer" and "White Corn Maiden, near to ice." But even beyond their relationship to individual nature beings, the Tewa—as other Amerindian peoples—understood that their relationship was with the earth itself. Sacred origin accounts of native North Americans told, in imaginative language, of their emergence from the womb of earth. Or they detailed how an earth-diving animal had plunged into the waters to come up with a speck of dirt that grew into the world. In the Tewa origin myth, the world above was still "green" and "unripe," but after an elaborate and ritualized migration the people emerged upon a ground that hardened. Expressing the strength of their relationship to the earth in the way they named themselves, ordinary Tewa were the Dry Food People, not unripe like the early earth but mature like the hardened grains of corn that nourished them.

For the Algonkians in the region of the Great Lakes, the animals embodied the power of the earth. A Great Hare had supervised the creation of the world, floating on a wooden raft with the other animals and taking the grain of sand, which the diving muskrat had found, to form from it the earth. When the first animals finally died, "the Great Hare caused the birth of men from their corpses, as also from those of the fishes which were found along the shores of the rivers which he had formed in creating the land." So the Algonkians derived "their origin from a bear, others from a moose, and others similarly from various kinds of animals." The Winnebago, in turn, could recall the antics and foibles of the Trickster/culture hero Coyote, from the remnants of whose mutilated penis came the crops. And numbers of Amerindian peoples acknowledged a "keeper" of the game, a spirit animal who long ago had made a pact pledging the members of his species to sacrifice themselves that the Indians might eat and survive.

For native North Americans the numinous world of nature beings was always very close, and the land itself expressed their presence. Indian peoples created religious geographies in which specific sites were inhabited by sacred powers and persons. Thus, the Eastern Cherokee knew that the spirit Little People had left their footprints within a cave behind a waterfall close to the head of the Oconaluftee River. And they located the game preserve of Kanati, the husband of the corn mother, in a cave on the northern side of Black Mountain, some twenty-five miles from Asheville, North Carolina. The Kiowa recalled the sinister Devil's Tower of the Black Hills, where a Kiowa boy playing with his seven sisters had unaccountably been turned into a bear, run after his terrified siblings, and scored the bark of a great tree they climbed as he chased them. The sisters had escaped, becoming the stars of the Big Dipper; the remnant of the tree was Devil's Tower.

The sense of continuity with the sacred—and natural—world that was revealed in this language had its counterpart in a mythic sense of time, in which what we call history was conflated, for Amerindians, with events that had occurred outside of ordinary time. In the Indian view, the present replicated the past, and one could discern the shape of contemporary events by reflecting on the message gleaned from the time of beginning. So the Kiowa, or "coming-out" people, are today a small tribe because once, at the origins of their earthly life, a pregnant woman became stuck while the people were emerging from a hollow log. Fertility had gotten "hung up," and only those who had come out before it was stopped could constitute the Kiowa nation.

Similarly, in one twentieth-century Hopi account that also includes the founding of the village of Hotevilla, the narrative begins as Hopi Birdmen perform their corn ceremony to help the quarreling people emerge to the earth. In the twentieth century, Hopis had quarreled again—this time about educating their children in United States government schools—and one group, evicted from the ancestral village of Oraibi, made their encampment at the site of Hotevilla. The twentieth-century tale of hostility evokes the time of origins, with conflict a recognized part of Hopi past and present. Ceremony, ordering the tribal life to the natural world, in each case fosters equilibrium.

As this relational view suggests, the well-being of Amerindian peoples depended in large measure on a correspondence between themselves and what they held sacred. The material world was a holy place; and so harmony with nature beings and natural forms was the controlling ethic, reciprocity the recognized mode of interaction. Ritual functioned to restore a lost harmony, like a great balancing act bringing the people back to right relation with the world.

What we, today, would call an ecological perspective came, for the most part, easily—if unselfconsciously—among traditional tribal peoples. Typically, one apologized to the guardian spirit of an animal or plant species for taking the life of the hunted animal or gathered vegetable crop. One paid attention, ceremonially, to the cardinal directions, orienting existence literally by placing oneself in space with reference to all of its beings and powers. A person lived by a ritual calendar in which the naming of months and times centered on growing and hunting seasons. And in disease or other illness, a person sought the cause in relational disharmony with a natural form or person—like a Navajo who encountered lightning in the sheepfold and then got sick or like a Cherokee who knew that overpopulation and overkilling of the animals had brought disease. Similarly, one found cure through the healer's—and patient's—identification with natural forms and through the healer's knowledge of herbal lore.

Meanwhile, healers, as shamans and seers, worked out of their sense of correspondence with natural forms. They were leaders in communication with other-than-human persons who dwelled in nature, sharers in the mysterious power that made things happen—the wakan of the Sioux, the orenda of the Iroquois, the manitou of the Algonkians. From this point of view, what we call magic and miracle were simply cases of like affecting like or of part affecting whole. United to natural forces and persons, Amerindians thought that all parts of the world—and their own societies—were made of the same material. Since everything was, in fact, part of everything else, it followed that one piece of the world could act powerfully on another, affecting change and transformation.

Such transformation often meant the shape-shifting of animals to human form and, likewise, the change of humans into animals. Amerindian myths are filled with accounts of encounters between humans and the other-than-human world. The Oglala Sioux received their sacred pipe and their full ceremonial panoply of seven rites when a strange wakan woman appeared among them with her gift, then moved around "in a sun-wise manner" and turned into a red and brown buffalo calf and subsequently into a white and a black buffalo. "This buffalo then walked farther away from the people, stopped, and after bowing to each of the four quarters of the universe, disappeared over the hill." Encouraged by her widowed mother, a Cherokee girl married her suitor, but when he failed to bring home a substantial hunt she followed him and found that, away from her, he changed into a hooting owl. Two Penobscots, in a contest with some Iroquois who had discovered them, changed themselves into a bear and a panther and got away.

In this world of animal/human transformations, Tricksters such as Coyote or Raven assumed human or animal form as they chose. Amerindians, who delighted in Trickster tales, also transformed themselves ritually by ceremonial clowning. These ritual clowns were deadly serious figures, like the *heyoka* among the Sioux, contorting the natural and accustomed order by doing things completely backward, saying yes when they intended no, and generally overturning canons of normalcy the more to underline them. In still other ritual transformations, Amerindians, like the Tewa healing Bears, portrayed the animal spirits by their clothing, accouterments, and even behavior.

In visions and dreams, too, natural persons appeared to guide Indian peoples. Expressed most explicitly in rituals of seeking for a guardian spirit, the naturalness of sacred things dominated the inner as well as the outer world. In his account of "crying for a vision" given to Joseph Epes Brown, Black Elk explained unequivocally how the powers came. The "lamenter" was required to "be alert to recognize any messenger which the Great Spirit may send to him, for these people often come in the form of an animal, even one as small and as seemingly insignificant as a little ant." "Perhaps," Black Elk continued, "a Spotted Eagle may come to him from the west, or a Black Eagle from the north, or the Bald Eagle from the east, or even the Red-headed Woodpecker may come to him from the south."

In short, Amerindian peoples lived symbolically with nature at center and boundaries. They understood the world as one that answered personally to their needs and words and, in turn, perceived themselves and their societies as part of a sacred landscape. With correspondence as controlling metaphor, they sought their own versions of mastery and control through harmony in a universe of persons who were part of the natural world. Nature religion, if it lived in America at all, lived among Amerindians.

Apparently, for all the changes history wrought, this picture drawn mostly from late nineteenth- and twentieth-century accounts applies as well to earlier times. There was a good deal of likeness between later and earlier expression; and, with only fragmentary—and often hostile—evidence from which to reconstruct seventeenth-century Amerindian lifeways, we can still trace the outlines, among the Algonkians of southern New England, of a fully developed nature religion.

The distinct groups whom the English Puritans first encountered were part of a related family of Indian nations. In the area framed by the Saco River, flowing southeast from present-day New Hampshire through southern Maine to the Atlantic, and the Quinnipiac River, flowing southward through central Connecticut to New Haven Harbor, Algonkian populations probably reached from seventy-two thousand to twice that number by the early seventeenth century. (By a century later the English population had only reached ninety-three thousand.) But from 1616 to 1618 and again from 1633 to 1634 epidemics swept through the tribes, decimating native populations by as much as ninety percent. No doubt caused by microbes from Europe brought first by trans-Atlantic traders, disease ravaged peoples who had no previous immunity and cultures that had no earlier preparation. Thus, the religions that Puritan observers would write about without comprehension were religions confounded by a double crisis—the jolt of foreign invasion and the catastrophe of a biological scourge worse in its relative effects than the Black Death of fourteenth-century Europe.

The four major Amerindian nations in the area—the Narragansett (of present-day Rhode Island), the Massachusett (of Massachusetts Bay), the Pokanoket, or Wampanoag (of Plymouth Colony), and the Pequot (of present-day Connecticut)—spoke related languages of the Eastern Algonkian family. They were united, too, by similar subsistence patterns and governance structures. In a mixed economy, they farmed the land, raising maize, beans, squash, and some tobacco, even as they gathered wild plants and also fished and hunted. With the coming of the English, they engaged in the fur trade. Dwelling in villages, with easy mobility to accommodate seasonal changes in the food supply (at least until the 1630s), these southern New Englanders were governed by sachems, political leaders whose power varied with each unit. On the whole, though, sachems ruled through prestige and moral authority, using generosity and persuasion more than outright coercion to gain their way.

Although the personal initiative of Algonkian Indian peoples has been cited, more striking still was their strong sense of community with one another and with nature. Their small-group life emphasized bonds of kinship. Their collective understanding of land tenure and their equation of ownership with use obviated European notions of private property that fostered individualism. Algonkian labor was often cooperative, as Roger Williams noticed among the Narragansetts: "When a field is to be broken up, they have a very loving sociable speedy way to dispatch it: All the neighbours men and Women forty, fifty, a hundred &c, joyne, and come in to help freely." Still more, the rich ceremonial life of these Amerindians reinforced their sense of mutuality and community.

Living closely as they did, Indian bands practiced an ethic of harmony within their communities. Roger Williams remarked on the lack of crime and violence among them, and William Wood—another seventeenth-century observer and probably not a Puritan—commented on their hospitality to strangers and their helpfulness. "Nothing is more hateful to them than a churlish disposition," he wrote, going on to discuss their equanimity, cheerfulness, and calm. Perhaps a sociologically conditioned survival tactic, the harmony ethic was also—if we can take later Amerindian experience as an indicator—an expression of their nature religion. A "connected" view of the environment would foster the connection of community.

Connection, however, did not mean amorphousness. The southern New England Algonkians, even read through fragmentary evidence, elaborated a systematic cosmology in which the world and human life were carefully named and ordered. Keeping themselves and their world in balance, which the harmony ethic enjoined, meant an intricate network of exchanges and interactions. And such a network had to be predicated on precise and detailed knowledge of parts of the larger whole. Hence, the unfamiliarity of a concept such as nature and the familiarity of nature persons made considerable sense in the Eastern Algonkian schema. Indeed, Neal Salisbury has rightly argued that the ethos of reciprocity was paramount, and he has noticed, too, the social, natural, and—as he termed it, somewhat problematically—"supernatural" worlds that needed to be maintained in equilibrium.

The equilibrium began, as in other Amerindian societies, with birth out of nature. Roger Williams told how the Narragansetts had heard from their fathers "that *Kautántowwit* made one man and woman of a stone, which disliking, he broke them in pieces, and made another man and woman of a Tree, which were the Fountaines of all mankind." "They say themselves, that they have *sprung* and *growne* up in that very place, like the very *trees* of the *Wildernesse*," he noted, just as tellingly, elsewhere. Further north, the missionary Daniel Gookin related the origin myth regarding two young squaws who swam or waded in the waters. "The froth or foam of the water touched their bodies, from whence they became with child; and one of them brought forth a male; and the other, a female child. . . . So their son and daughter were their [the people's] first progenitors."

If the people were themselves the gift of nature, so, too, were their foodstuffs, especially their corn. Stories of the sacred origins of corn run through numerous Amerindian cultures, many of them southwestern and southeastern. And in southern New England, even in an area near the northern boundary of corn cultivation, the mythology of corn throve with the growing crop. Williams explained the gingerly fashion in which the Narragansetts kept the birds away from the standing corn, citing the tradition "that the Crow brought them at first an *Indian* Graine of Corne in one Eare and an *Indian* or *French* Beane in another, from the Great God *Kautántouwits* field in the Southwest from whence they hold came all their Corne and Beanes." Corn ritual, too, figured prominently in the ceremonial life of the tribe.

Williams's references to Cautantowwit (the modern spelling) point to the pre-eminence of this figure (or Ketan, as he was known to the Narragansetts' neighbors) among the sacred beings who favored the Indians. Cautantowwit's home in the southwest was associated with the warm and nurturing wind that encouraged the growth of the corn. His home was also the place to which the people returned at death, and so he was linked to the life force itself, which originated from his house and again returned to it. "Ketan," wrote William Wood, "is their good god, to whom they sacrifice (as the ancient heathen did to Ceres) after their garners be full with a good crop; upon this god likewise they invoke for fair weather, for rain in time of drought, and for the recovery of their sick." Worship of Cautantowwit, in short, was invocation of a nature deity.

Less distinct but more pervasive than the worship of Cautantowwit was the southern New England orientation toward manitou. In a perception shared with other Algonkians, the word *manitou* carried meanings of wonder and extraordinary power, of a godliness inhering in numerous objects and persons. Williams remarked that at "any Excellency in Men, Women, Birds, Beasts, Fish, &c.," the Narragansetts would "cry out *Manittóo, that is, it is a God." Gookin, linking the manitou belief to Cautantowwit, spoke of acknowledgment of "one great supreme doer of good; . . . Woonand, or Mannitt." Other colonial New Englanders, such as Thomas Mayhew on Martha's Vineyard, noted the use of the term. What is clear from the references is that, if Cautantowwit possessed manitou or was manitou or a manitou, the manitou essence could also be found in other nature beings, in humans, and even in marvelous (for the Indians) technological objects such as English ships and great buildings. "The most common experience seems to be that of being overwhelmed by an all-encompassing presence," wrote William Jones in his classic essay on the subject. Referring to a property (adjectival) as well as referring to an object (substantive), manitou was closely linked to "the essential character of Algonkin religion . . . a pure, naive worship of nature."

Among the beings who possessed manitou were those whom Williams identified as deities of the sun, moon, fire, water, snow, earth, deer, and bear, some thirty-seven or thirty-eight in all. There were deities of the four directions, and a woman's god, a children's god, and a house god as well. On Martha's Vineyard, Thomas Mayhew likewise found knowledge of thirty-seven deities and noted their relation to "things in Heaven, Earth, and Sea: And there they had their Men-gods, Women-gods, and Children-gods, their Companies, and Fellowships of gods, or Divine Powers, guiding things amongst men, besides innumerable more feigned gods belonging to many Creatures, to their Corn, and every Colour of it." Daniel Gookin's testimony, if less extensive, was similar.

Moreover, it was clear, as Neal Salisbury has succinctly remarked, that the Indians were not "crypto-monotheists," conferring on Cautantowwit the role of creator of other gods. Indeed, the entire language of monotheism, god, and supernatural is forced and strained when made to fit Amerindian thinking. More to the mark, nature *manifested* sacred powers and revealed other-than-human persons of mysterious and numinous capacities. Instead of the opposition between divinity and creature or between supernatural and natural, there was—as already has been noted—a continuity between extraordinary and ordinary. While dualisms—such as body and spirit, for instance—existed, they were inserted into a different frame and bore a different, more intimate meaning than they did for Europeans.

If this observation be kept in mind, then the regard that southern New England Algonkians showed for animals assumes new and heightened significance. When the Narragansetts refused to kill crows or other birds that ate their crops, their behavior was consistent with other Indian practices. Thus, the English writer John Josselyn described the spiritual etiquette that attended the killing of a moose in the New England region: its heart, tongue, left rear foot, and sinews were ritually removed before the flesh was used, accomplishing the "gesture of reciprocity" that was the Amerindian response to beneficent power. Williams, in describing trapping practices for deer, cited the divine power the Indians saw in the animal to explain why the Narragansetts were "very tender of their Traps." Wood noticed that native peoples adorned themselves with earrings in the forms of birds, beasts, and fishes, and he also remarked on the depictions of animals and birds incised into their cheeks. And John Eliot, the New England missionary, placed first in his list of religious questions his would-be converts asked, *"Why have not beasts a soul as man hath, seeing they have love, anger, &c. as man hath?"*

The ceremonial forms of southern New England Algonkians expressed regard for animals and their power and, beyond that, regard and gratitude for vegetable life. Successful hunts and harvests were both marked by ritual (as were numerous other occasions in Indian life). Ceremonies accompanied spring fish runs and made supplication for rain in time of drought. The Narragansetts held a midwinter festival, according to Williams, and the feast may have been related to the time of solstice. Meanwhile, Williams also recorded the giveaways, in which people outdid one another in distributing their goods, imitating, perhaps, the bounty that animals and plants had shown to them. At various ceremonial times, dances were led by shamans or powwows, who garbed themselves in skins in order to imitate bears, wolves, and other animals, howling as they danced no doubt for the same purpose.

With all but one of their lunar months named for the planting cycle, Algonkian Indians expressed the significance of agriculture in their lives. But the ceremonial time of the community was supplemented by a round of other rituals, linked to hunting cultures, that focused more on individuals. Like the hunting cultures to the north and west, these Algonkians sought special guardian spirits in ritualized vision quests, and accounts tell of asceticisms and hardships incorporated into the practice. Thus, in one remarkable narrative, Williams wrote of a dying Narragansett's call to Muckquachuckquand, who had come to him many years before, bidding the Indian to seek him in time of distress. Likewise, southern New England Algonkians honored the menstrual hut used in hunting cultures. At the time of her menses, the fertility power of the woman was thought so strong that it could conflict with the other, male form of power needed in the hunt. Sequestered with her during her time in the hut, the woman's power did not endanger others.

The chief religious specialist among the New England tribes was the shaman or powwow, and much of the English commentary on native life was preoccupied, invariably negatively, with this figure. The shaman's tutelary deity and the power through whom he acted was Hobbamock (Abbomacho), who was also identified with Chepi, the shaman's helper. A terrestrial spirit believed to be involved in the onset of disease and suffering, Hobbamock roamed abroad at night, commanding fear. He signaled the negative powers of the sacred, the dangers it embodied, and the need for special knowledge and prowess to deal with it securely. In similar vein, Chepi's name was linked to terms for death, the departed, and the cold northeast wind. The English called Hobbamock the devil; and, in the language of their own dualistic understanding of good and evil, they were not completely wrong. Converted natives accepted the equation. It was true, too, that when Puritans first encountered the New England Indians the cult of Hobbamock seemed to be waxing and that of Cautantowwit declining—supporting the judgment that witchcraft beliefs are strategies for control that thrive in communal crises.

Shamans, as we noted, presided at the nature ceremonies of southern New England Algonkians. Such shamans entered their true estate when they became entranced, possessed and taken over by Hobbamock and the powers of manitou. On Martha's Vineyard, Thomas Mayhew related striking accounts of shamanic possession. He spoke of "Imps," whom the shamans called their "Preservers" and "treasured up in their bodies." One narrative suggested that inanimate substances, too, were alive, for the shaman Tequanonim claimed he had been "possessed from the crowne of the head to the soal of the foot with *Pawwawnomas,* not onely in the shape of living Creatures, as Fowls, Fishes, and creeping things, but Brasse, Iron, and Stone." Another shaman on the island told of his initiation through "Diabolical Dreams, wherein he saw the Devill in the likenesse of four living Creatures; one was like a man which he saw in the Ayre, . . . and this he said had its residence over his whole body. Another was like a Crow, . . . and had its residence in his head. The third was like a Pidgeon, and had its place [in] his breast. . . . The fourth was like a Serpent."

Healers of their people, the powwows employed herbal medicines and shamanic sucking cures in ritual fashion. Their identification, in the healing ceremony, with animals was suggested by William Wood's description of one such rite. Here the powwow proceeded "in his invocations, sometimes roaring like a bear, other times groaning like a dying horse, foaming at the mouth like a chased boar, smiting on his naked breast and thighs with such violence as if he were mad." Shamans also aided their people by their divinatory powers. In one anecdote remembered after King Philip's War, it was the shaman's vision of a bear—a ravenous animal and so a bad omen—that convinced the Indians they should retreat from Bridgewater, Massachusetts. Rainmaking was also the shaman's province. And, less benignly, the shaman could, on occasion and with preterhuman aid, inflict evil on another. Thomas Mayhew reported how, at the behest of the powwow, "the Devil doth abuse the real body of a Serpent, which comes directly towards the man in the house or in the field, . . . and do shoot a bone (as they say) into the Indians Body."

Significantly, even the southern New England Algonkian understanding of the afterlife expressed an Amerindian immersion in nature religion. We have already pointed to the connection between Cautantowwit's house for the dead and the warmth and life-bestowing properties of the southwest and its wind. Archeological evidence from New England burials supports the association, for not only were the dead aligned to the southwest but, in Narragansett burials, the dead were placed in fetal posture, suggesting the idea of rebirth. Similarly, red paint discovered in the graves suggests the blood and placenta that came with childbirth. And William Scranton Simmons has argued that the positioning of the skull to the southwest was related to the departure of the soul or souls in that direction.

Just as striking as evidence for a nature religion associated with death are the brief literary references of English contemporaries. Roger Williams likened Indian death hopes to the Turkish expectation of "carnall Joyes." William Wood, in words that bear full repetition, was more specific.

> They hold the immortality of the never-dying soul that it shall pass to the southwest Elysium, concerning which their Indian faith jumps much with the Turkish Alcoran [Quran], holding it to be a kind of paradise wherein they shall everlastingly abide, solacing themselves in odoriferous gardens, fruitful corn fields, green meadows, bathing their tawny hides in the cool streams of pleasant rivers, and shelter themselves from heat and cold in the sumptuous palaces framed by the skill of nature's curious contrivement; concluding that neither care nor pain shall molest them but that nature's bounty will administer all things with a voluntary contribution from the overflowing storehouse of their Elysian Hospital.

Nature religion, in sum, formed and framed native North American life from birth until death—and, in the Amerindian view, beyond. Nature religion shaped mentality; it lay behind behavior in symbolic and ordinary settings; it worked to achieve a harmony that was also an attempt to control the powers that impinged on life as native peoples knew it.

Indians' Views of Christian Missionaries

JAMES P. RONDA

Several scholars have recently . . . demonstrated that the Christian mission to native Americans was neither an attempt to save them from land-hungry settlers nor a guileless exercise in soul-winning. These historians view it as a revolutionary enterprise, designed to bring about a radical transformation of Indian culture. Native Americans were required to become like Europeans in all aspects of life—in matters of sex, marriage, economy, and government, as well as religion. The Indian who embraced Christianity was compelled, in effect, to commit cultural suicide. He was required to renounce not only his own personal past, but that of his forefathers as well, forsaking—and despising—all traditional beliefs and practices. Because missionaries demanded no less than "cultural revolution," their attacks on Indian religions "cannot be regarded simply as a matter of criticism of some abstract philosophical hypothesis." These attacks posed a threat to the very survival of native American society.

James P. Ronda, "We Are Well As We Are: An Indian Critique of 17thC. Christian Missions," *William and Mary Quarterly* 34 (January 1977): 66–82. Reprinted by permission of William and Mary Quarterly.

The new interpretations recognize the importance of that threat but still tend to emphasize only one side of the issue. They continue to concentrate upon the words and actions of missionaries to the neglect of Indian responses and initiatives. Native Americans reacted to missionary activity in a wide variety of ways, each of which deserves our attention if we are to understand the role of the mission in culture contact and change. Some Indians accepted the new religion and the new life-patterns it commanded. Others incorporated certain Christian elements into their lives while rejecting the essence of the white man's message. Most native Americans reaffirmed their traditional beliefs and strenuously resisted Christianity. But whatever their responses, Indian peoples did demonstrate that their traditions were dynamic intellectual systems, capable of change. The fact that most native Americans chose to retain their beliefs does not mean that Indian societies could not change; the evaluation and reaffirmation of accepted belief constitute in themselves a kind of transformation.

Failing to note this kind of change, historians have tended to view mission history as a one-sided struggle between ossified Indian traditions and a vital European Christianity. As a result, important Indian comments have been ignored or dismissed as the mere rantings of jealous Indian leaders. To restore the Indian critique of mission work to its proper place in the study of culture contact, historians must find and verify those crucial observations. This is often a complicated matter. Indian speeches were filtered through white interpreters, recorded by white secretaries, and ultimately arranged in the memoirs of white missionaries. Historians searching for Indian perspectives must read such accounts with caution. We must be sensitive to the circumstances surrounding each recorded speech or dialogue if we are to hear those Indian voices so long ignored.

Some of the most compelling voices were those of Huron and Montagnais Indians in New France. The Massachuset, Wampanoag, and Nipmuc tribes of southern New England also produced thoughtful critics who tried to construct sensible replies to the missionary assault on their cultures. These men and women reacted emphatically against the Christian theological ideas of sin, guilt, heaven, hell, and baptism. A reconstruction of the native American critique of the mission must begin with their responses to those ideas.

Sin and guilt were central themes in Christian dogma. From apostolic times missionaries knew that unless potential converts understood and accepted them, the mission would have little chance to win genuine believers. Many native American religions did not contain the idea of sin as either a primordial fault or a moral transgression against the will of God. These religions recognized personal wrongdoing but did not assign it any cosmic significance. Huron religion, for example, emphasized instead the presence of certain evil forces and the dangerous consequences that might result from failing to do proper service to a particular deity. Indians found the Christian view of sin and guilt both incomprehensible and useless. When a Jesuit urged a Huron to acknowledge her sins and be baptized, she and her friends protested that she had always lived in innocence and without sin. The woman clearly rejected the Christian insistence that a person who lived a moral life might also be a great sinner. *"May a good man sin sometimes?"* wondered one of John Eliot's New England converts. *"If a man be almost a good man and dyeth; whither goeth his soule?"* asked another. Eliot was closely questioned by an Indian who was interested in the origin of good and evil ideas. *"Do all evill thoughts come from the Devill,"* he asked, *"and all good ones from God?"* Most Indians simply dismissed the concept of personal sin and guilt. "It would be useless," insisted one Huron, "for me to repent of having sinned, seeing that I never have sinned." . . .

Indians tended to view the conceptions of heaven and hell with even less regard. The Huron, Montagnais, and New England native Americans all anticipated an after-life but assumed that it would be spent in morally neutral surroundings, not in a place of heavenly reward or hellish punishment. The Hurons spoke of a "village of souls" populated by the spirits of the dead. Life in those villages was believed to resemble life on earth with its daily round of eating, hunting, farming, and war-making. Missionary efforts to impress Indians with the delights of heaven met with disbelief and derision. Because the Jesuits described heaven in European material terms, the Hurons concluded that heaven was only for the French. When one Huron was asked why she refused to accept the offer of eternal life, she characteristically replied, "I have no acquaintances there, and the French who are there would not care to give me anything to eat." The father of a recently deceased convert child urged the missionaries to dress her in French garments for burial so that she would be recognized as a European and permitted entrance into heaven. Most native Americans rejected the European heaven, desiring to go where their ancestors were. The mission compounded this rejection by telling potential converts that heaven contained neither grain fields nor trading places, neither tobacco nor sexual activity—surely a dreary prospect. Some Indians resented the notion that one had to die in order to enjoy the blessings of conversion, while others observed that an everlasting life without marriage or labor was a highly undesirable fate.

Missionaries provoked an even stronger negative response when they preached about everlasting punishment in a fiery hell. The hell the Jesuits described must have profoundly affected their Indian listeners, for the Huron and Montagnais were no strangers to the horrors it was said to contain. The torture by fire of captured war-riors was a customary part of Iroquoian warfare, and Huron and Montagnais men knew that such would be their fate if they fell into enemy hands. They themselves practiced torture rituals on their own captives, applying burning brands and glowing coals to the bodies of the condemned before execution. Men and women who had participated in such events must have responded emphatically to the idea of hell. But the evidence suggests that most responded in disbelief. Though the torments of hell were all too imaginable, they were rejected because they seemed to serve no useful purpose. In fact, the most common objection to the Christian hell was that it only lessened the delights of earthly life. "If thou wishest to speak to me of Hell, go out of my Cabin at once," exclaimed one Huron. "Such thoughts disturb my rest, and cause me uneasiness amid my pleasures." Hurons resented what seemed to them a Christian obsession with death and punishment. This resentment may have sprung from Huron anxiety about death and about the uneasy relationship between the living and the spirits of the dead. Whether or not disturbed by this prospect, one Huron spoke for many when he said simply, "I am content to be damned."

Other native Americans went beyond rejecting hell as an unpleasant place to question the basic Christian assumptions about postmortem punishment. "We have no such apprehension as you have," said a Huron, "of a good and bad Mansion after this life, provided for the good and bad Souls; for we cannot tell whether every thing that appears faulty to Men, is so in the Eyes of God." . . .

To silence the skeptics the Jesuits in New France resorted to the use of highly colored pictures that depicted the torments of hell in gruesome detail. Indian critics soon turned the images against the missionaries. When the pictures were shown, Huron religious leaders proclaimed that those writhing in the flames were not the unbelievers but the converts. If hell existed at all, they seemed to be saying, it would surely be reserved for those traitors who have abandoned the way of their fathers. Most native Americans found the concept of hell a meaningless fiction. Even when presented with imagery bound to strike fear in their hearts, they concluded that the ideas of sin, heaven, and hell were just "so many Fabulous and romantick Stories."

Indians and missionaries might have debated endlessly the merits of those stories, but one Christian doctrine presented native Americans with a more immediate dilemma. The question of baptism and its consequences brought the confrontation to a matter of human survival. Jesuit policy was to withhold baptism from a potential convert until that person was at the moment of death or the missionaries were sure that he or she would not apostatize. Thus in the first years of the mission in New France most Indians who received the sacrament were soon dead. The critique of baptism developed by the Hurons grew slowly until by the late 1630s it consisted of several related arguments all devastating in their impact on the mission effort. At first, Hurons believed that baptism might restore health; they were inclined to view the sacrament as one more of the many healing ceremonies common to Huron life. Father Paul Le Jeune, superior of the Huron mission, was shocked to discover some who believed that the more water was used in baptism, the more healthful would be the consequences. This positive view quickly changed when smallpox swept the Huron villages. Since the Jesuits baptized only those on the verge of death, many Hurons concluded that the rite was the immediate cause of death. Charles Meiachkawat, a recent convert, was assailed by his wife who cried, "Dost thou not see that we are all dying since they told us to pray to God? Where are thy relatives, where are mine? the most of them are dead; it is no longer a time to believe."

Huron and Montagnais religious leaders employed the fear of baptism to diminish missionary influence. Huron shamans argued persuasively that missionaries "had a secret understanding with the disease" and used baptism to spread it. This belief became so widespread among the Hurons that by 1639 many political leaders, as well as ordinary people, were calling for the execution of the Jesuits as an act of self-preservation. By connecting baptism with the spread of smallpox, native Americans mounted a compelling indictment of the mission and its methods. The disease served as an ever-present warning that to abandon the traditional ways was to court death. Even the zealous mission worker Jerome Lalemant was forced to admit that "no doubt we carried the trouble with us, since, wherever we set foot, either death or disease followed us."

Indian critics found even greater fault with the missionary effort to discredit traditional healing ceremonies. Among the native Americans of southern New England the powwow was a rite that had both medical and religious significance. The Hurons held similar annual gatherings called *ononharoia.* In addition, Hurons when ill might employ the services of various curing societies. Missionaries who observed such healing rituals uniformly condemned them. Such condemnation was usually motivated by the desire to weaken the power of traditional religious leaders. Eliot bitterly attacked the healers as "great witches having fellowship with the old Serpent, to whom they pray." He described all Indian healing efforts as "sinfull and diabolicall." Jesuits also condemned the ceremonies. Healers were branded as "imps of satan" whose "art was founded upon falsehood."

Both Protestant and Catholic missionaries forbade their converts to take part in the ancient healing acts. This ban, coming as it did at the very moment when native Americans were suffering the effects of European diseases, provoked a torrent of angry criticism from both converts and traditionalists. The dilemma faced by converts was especially agonizing. They were required to abandon traditional sources of medicine and solace while watching members of their families die of strange and dread diseases. One powwow leader in Martha's Vineyard expressed astonishment that any Indian would turn away from the customary means of healing. He warned one convert of the recklessness of his stand. "I wonder that you that are a young Man," he chided, "and have a Wife and two Children, should love the *English* and their Ways, and forsake the *Pawwaws;* what would you do if any of you were sick? whither would you go for Help? If I were in your Case, there should be nothing to draw me from our *Gods* and *Pawwaws.*" As disease stalked the Hurons, similar pleas were made to those now derisively called "the Believers." "My nephew," entreated one Huron captain, "make a truce for one day with the Faith. Our Country is going to ruin; the sick are dying. Whither can we flee to avoid death? Why do you keep away from our dances? Why do you refuse to do this act of kindness to the People? It is the Christians who kill us, since they will not help us. Come and dance to-day, my nephew, and to-morrow thou shalt resume the practice of Faith." . . .

Angered at missionary attacks on customary healing rites and fearful of baptism as a carrier of disease, Indians in New France extended their criticism of the mission to an assault on the physical symbols of European Christianity. Before the smallpox epidemics began, Hurons and other Indians had found French material culture interesting and often amusing. Window glass, clocks, weather vanes, writing, and even doors were regarded with curiosity. But as disease and crop failures began to ravage Huronia, curiosity turned to suspicion. When a severe drought brought widespread crop damage in the summer of 1635, Huron religious leaders charged that the presence of Jesuit crosses had driven away the rain. Tehorenhaegnon, a prominent shaman, insisted that unless the crosses were removed and the missionaries expelled, no rain would fall. Even after rain did come, the fear of the Christian cross persisted. That fear was fueled in later years by the relentless smallpox. As the disease spread, Hurons became increasingly critical of other Christian symbols and images. Their criticism was based on the belief that all symbols possessed independent life and could be a source of grave personal danger. In the Huron mind the Christian cross was the living presence of an alien deity—a deity bent on destroying Hurons by unknown diseases. Similarly, instead of inspiring a fear of hell, the Jesuits' explicit pictures provoked a fear of all images. Even serene representations were considered hazardous. One missionary reported that many Hurons were convinced that "tainted influences issue . . . down into the chests of those who look" at images of Christ and the Holy Family. By 1640 all mission property, whether or not religious, had become suspect. The Jesuits' inkstands, books, and letters, as well as their sacred objects, were viewed with suspicion as potential hiding places for disease-bearing demons. The Indian assault on Christian symbols was motivated by neither simple iconoclasm nor fear alone. It was predicated on the premise that such symbols were deeply repugnant to true religion. This idea was prominent in the theologies of both the Indians and the missionaries. Both agreed that grave consequences would result if the offending emblems—the signs of the others' faith—were not removed.

Indians and missionaries shared another basic belief in their assessment of one another. Missionaries saw Indian religious leaders as devils, demons, sorcerers, and witches. Indian priests and shamans viewed their Christian counterparts in the same light. The Jesuits "are not men," contended one group of Huron leaders; "they are demons." . . .

In the eyes of Indian political leaders, the missionary-sorcerers were conniving imperialists as well—the advance guard of European political domination. Sachems, village elders, and band chiefs were intensely aware of the missions' attack on their sovereignty. Their resistance to Christianity was noted by nearly every missionary in early America. One New England sachem graphically explained what conversion would mean to his own political power. "If I be a praying Sachem, I shall be a poor and weak one, and easily be trod upon by others, who are like to be more potent and numerous; and by this means my Tribute will be small, and my people few, and I shall be a great loser by praying to God." The same sachem denounced Christianity and its political implications as "a bitter Pill, too hard for me to get down and swalow." . . .

. . . [M]any . . . thoughtful Indian critics . . . identified the "enemy" only after weighing the evidence. They carefully considered their positions before answering the missionaries. . . . [T]he exchanges between Indians and missionaries constituted genuine theological debates, in which both parties represented well-reasoned religious systems. To fully appreciate the scope and intensity of those debates we must move beyond the discussion of specific doctrinal ideas to glimpse some of the encounters in context. Both Le Jeune and Eliot participated in lively exchanges that may well typify native American responses to Christianity.

For Le Jeune the contest began shortly after his arrival in Quebec. During the winter of 1633–1634 he joined the roving hunt of a Montagnais band. Mixing language training with evangelism, he attached himself to the household of Carigonan, a noted holy man. The days were spent in grueling pursuit of moose and other game, but at night Le Jeune and Carigonan embarked on a quest of another kind. Inside dark, smoky bark cabins the French priest and the Montagnais shaman matched wits and challenged each other's theology. Their first major discussion contained all the elements of later ones. Predictably, Le Jeune began by asking Carigonan what he believed about life after death. All souls travel on foot to a great village beyond the western edge of the world, Carigonan replied. When the Jesuit ridiculed this interpretation, Carigonan snapped back, "Thou art mistaken . . . either the lands are united in some places, or there is some passage which is fordable over which our souls pass." Carigonan found it incomprehensible that Le Jeune would prefer to believe that souls float upward to a village in the sky. Le Jeune demanded to know what souls ate on their long trip, and was promptly told that they "eat bark . . . and old wood which they find in the forest." Le Jeune retorted that it was little wonder the Montagnais feared death, if that was what they would have to eat on such a tiresome journey. Undaunted, the Indian theologian described in more detail the activities of souls after death: they eat, hunt, and sleep as they had in life. Le Jeune scoffed, adding that Carigonan's idea of heaven was preposterous. Turning practical for the sake of argument, the Jesuit noted that Indians believed that all beings had souls and that no heaven could be large enough to contain them all. Carigonan was appalled by Le Jeune's apparent ignorance. "Thou art an ignoramus, thou has no sense," he declared. "Souls are not like us, they do not see at all during the day and see very clearly at night; their day is in the darkness of the night, and their night in the light of the day." When Le Jeune protested that Carigonan had hardly answered the question, the shaman cut him short. "Be silent," he commanded. "Thou askest things which thou dost not know thyself; if I had ever been in yonder country, I would answer thee."

Despite their many differences, Le Jeune and Carigonan shared more than they realized. Each embraced a religious system that emphasized the supernatural and its interaction with man. The Jesuit believed that human beings could be affected for good or ill by the actions of spirits and demons; Carigonan acknowledged the existence of equally influential beings called *khichikouai.* Both theologians accepted the dichotomy of soul and body as well. It was in the realm of religious practice—the manipulation of the sacred—that the differences between their theologies became most apparent. Le Jeune did not claim to have any personal supernatural powers, but Carigonan claimed direct communication with and control over supernatural forces. He believed himself capable of healing the sick, insuring good hunts, and killing distant enemies. He told Le Jeune that his soul could leave his body at will. Claims such as these reinforced Le Jeune's conviction that Carigonan was indeed a sorcerer and a formidable enemy of the faith. Le Jeune was further outraged by the rituals of the Montagnais. He witnessed dances, "eat-all" feasts, the ritual treatment of beaver and moose bones, and extended trances. His suspicions were heightened by the fact that shamans conducted some sacred ceremonies in secret.

Because neither Le Jeune nor Carigonan distinguished between belief and practice, their encounters continued to emphasize these differences. The severity of the early debates did not subside in subsequent meetings; the combatants argued, cajoled, and threatened well into the night each time. Each held his own. Le Jeune, a gifted professor of rhetoric, found Carigonan a worthy opponent. Carigonan demonstrated that Montagnais religion was as reasoned and systematic as Christianity. Several times in 1634 the shaman sought out Le Jeune to discuss troublesome points of doctrine in more detail. The evidence suggests that Carigonan's thought matured as a result of the debates. When Le Jeune's journey with the Montagnais was over, the Jesuit was grudgingly forced to admit that the Montagnais held to their faith as tenaciously as did any pious Christian. . . .

When confronted with Christian doctrines, symbols, and ceremonies, Indians asked searching questions. A few accepted the answers of the missionaries and were converted; others rejected what they saw as an alien ideology and reaffirmed their traditional beliefs. But native Americans did not respond to missionary activity solely by accepting or rejecting Christianity. So long as political autonomy was not totally compromised, Indians were able to produce positive religious movements to counter Christianity. Anthropologists have labeled these movements revitalization religions. Syncretistic in nature, revitalization religions often blended Indian and Christian theological elements around the central figure of an Indian prophet or savior. These movements were distinct from the kind of accommodation that seems to have occurred in many Indian convert congregations. The phenomenon was not limited to any one place or time. Revitalization prophets may be discerned throughout the Americas. From the Aztec Huichilobos to Handsome Lake and Wovoka, they represent a major and often neglected aspect of the native American response to Christianity.

As early as 1639, revitalization movements began to appear among the Hurons. A woman, deathly ill with smallpox, reported that she had seen a vision of an Indian savior while passing from life through death and back to life. This savior urged her to dress in red garments and studiously perform all the old rituals. Welcomed by Huron leaders as a sign of deliverance from the disease, the vision resulted in widespread feasting and public processions. The Jesuits angrily reported that the vision and the renewed zeal it inspired had cost the mission dearly. In the following year another exemplary episode of revitalization took place. A young Huron fisherman reported that a spirit had appeared to him and revealed his hopes for Huron regeneration. "I am Iouskeha," declared the spirit, "I am the one whom the French wrongly call Jesus, but they do not know me. I have pity on your country, which I have taken under my protection." Iouskeha, already known to the Hurons as the Master of the Earth, charged that the Jesuit mission was spreading death among the Huron people. "You can prevent this misfortune," insisted the spirit. "Drive out of your village the two black gowns who are there." Iouskeha instructed the young man to reinstitute traditional healing ceremonies and religious observances. Well into the 1640s visions of Huron prophets were regularly recounted by both laymen and religious leaders. Each visionary denounced Christianity as a dangerous, alien ideology, and stressed the value of Huron cultural unity. In New England the evidence for revitalization movements is lacking. The mission records of Eliot and others make no mention of Indian prophets or visionaries. It can be argued, however, that some Indians quietly embraced a kind of revitalization religion while accepting the outward forms of Christianity. Neal Salisbury has suggested that active Indian participation in congregational singing and church discipline invested "the imposed religion with traditional meaning." Demonstrating the continuing vigor of tradition, the revitalization movements offered both sharp criticism of the mission and an alternative for those unwilling to accept Christian conversion.

FURTHER READING

Albanese, Catherine. *Nature Religion in America: From the Algonkian Indians to the New Age* (1990).

Axtell, James. *The Invasion Within: The Contest of Cultures in Colonial North America* (1985).

Bender, Debra R. *Our Fires Have Nearly Gone Out: A History of Indian-White Relations on the Colonial Maryland Frontier* (1988).

Bowden, Henry Walker. *American Indians and Christian Missions: Studies in Cultural Conflict* (1981).

Calloway, Colin. *New Worlds for All: Indians, Europeans, and the Remaking of Early America* (1997).

Carmody, D. L., and J. T. Carmody. *Native American Religions: An Introduction* (1993).

Dennis, Matthew. *Cultivating a Landscape of Peace: Iroquois-European Encounters in Seventeenth Century America* (1993).

Dowd, Gregory. *A Spirited Resistance: The North American Indian Struggle for Unity, 1745–1815* (1992).

Dugan, Kathleen M. *The Vision Quest of the Plains Indians* (1985).

Gill, Sam. *Native American Religions: An Introduction* (1982).

———. *Native American Religious Action: A Performance Approach to Religion* (1987).

Grant, John Webster. *Moon of Wintertime: Missionaries and the Indians of Canada in Encounter Since 1534* (1984).

Gutierrez, Ramon. *When Jesus Came, the Corn Mothers Went Away: Marriage, Sexuality, and Power in New Mexico, 1500–1846* (1991).

Hultkrantz, Ake. *Essays on Native American Religions* (1976).

Krickeberg, Walter, et al. *Pre-Columbian American Religions* (1961).

Leger, Sister Mary Celeste. *The Catholic-Indian Missions in Maine: 1611–1820* (1929).

McLoughlin, William. *Cherokees and Missionaries, 1789–1839* (1984)

Martin, Calvin. *Keepers of the Game: Indian-Animal Relationships and the Fur Trade* (1978).

Martin, Joel. *Sacred Revolt: The Muskogees' Struggle for a New World* (1991).

Merrell, James H. *The Indians' New World: Catawbas and Their Neighbors from European Contact Through the Era of Removal* (1989).

Miller, Christopher. *Prophetic Worlds: Indians and Whites on the Columbia Plateau* (1985).

Paper, Jordan. *Offering Smoke: The Sacred Pipe and the Native American Religion* (1988).

Richter, Daniel K. *Beyond the Covenant Chain: The Iroquois and Their Neighbors in Indian North America, 1600–1800* (1987).

Terrell, John U. *The Arrow and the Cross: A History of the American Indians and the Missionaries* (1979).

Wood, P., G. Waselkov, and M. Hatley, eds., *Powhatan's Mantle: Indians in the Colonial Southeast* (1989).

Religious Life
in the British Colonies:
1620–1700

British settlers colonized a long section of the American Atlantic coast in the seven-teenth century, stretching from what is now Maine to South Carolina. Virginia, the earliest of these permanent settlements, began with a fortified town, Jamestown (founded 1607), but the opportunity to grow tobacco for the European market soon led the population to scatter onto widely dispersed plantations, which were worked first by indentured servants, later by slaves. The established Church of England (Anglican) was the nominal religion of most Virginia settlers, but it languished for lack of laymen's willingness to travel long distances for worship and their refusal to pay for churches and clergy.

Maryland, Virginia's neighbor to the north, was founded in the reign of King Charles I and had a comparable economy but was colonized largely by Roman Catholics. Pennsylvania, founded later in the century by William Penn under a license from King Charles II, took on the character of its founder, a convert to the Quaker faith. Quakers were an offshoot of the English Reformation who came to believe in absolute pacifism. This doctrine presented them with a dilemma during the colonial era's recurrent wars against the Indians, the French, and eventually the mother country itself. Around Pennsylvania, in what is now Delaware and parts of New York and New Jersey, Swedish, German, and Dutch Protestant colonists also settled, but all were eventually incorporated into the British Empire.

The New England colonies further north had a strongly Puritan character. English Puritans were not satisfied with the Anglican state church's attempts to incorporate a variety of religious views; this inclusiveness seemed to them more like contamination. The Plymouth Plantation of 1621 (the "Pilgrim Fathers") began as a sanctuary for religious separatists, militant Puritans who hoped to get away from Anglicanism altogether. The founders of the larger Massachusetts Bay Colony of 1630, by contrast, hoped that if they set up a "city on a hill" as a good example of purified Christianity to their brethren across the Atlantic, they would demonstrate that it could be done and so bring the English Reformation to a triumphant conclusion.

America confronted the colonists with unforeseen problems. Contact with the Indians, the demands of subsistence, the need to educate their own clergy, and catastrophic civil wars back in England all contributed to changing the settlers' view of their purposes and destiny. Economic opportunities enabled some settlers to get rich and to divert their thoughts slightly, away from heaven and toward the things of this world. Sermons by New England's highly educated and eloquent clergy show that they were dismayed at the "declension" (decline) of their godly experiment, and most saw it as a fall from an earlier state of grace. Historians today, however, recognize that changes were inevitable. The preachers' jeremiads, sermons full of gloom and threats of God's wrath, were not so much an accurate account of a deteriorating situation as ritualized reminders of the colonies' religious purpose.

English settlers in the seventeenth century interpreted all events as signs from God: miscarriages, storms, deaths, and harvest failures were God's tests to them as sinners, whereas good harvests or victories over the Indians were signs of His favor. They constantly compared their situation to that of biblical people (seeing New England, for example, as a wilderness comparable to that inhabited by the children of Israel after their escape from Egypt in the Book of Exodus, or as the wilderness in which Jesus prepared for his mission and resisted the devil's tempting). They felt surrounded by threats, natural and supernatural. The most notorious episode of the era was the Salem witch trials of the 1690s in which nineteen men and women, accused by their neighbors of consorting with the devil, were put to death with the active approval of the magistrates and clergy. Despite a widespread belief in the supernatural, however, not all British colonists, even in New England, belonged to a church. Secular distractions and religious indifference were as common then as in later generations, while church membership was, in most places, lower.

 D O C U M E N T S

John Winthrop and William Bradford were among the most influential Puritan writers, preachers, and politicians in the first generation of New England settlers. Document 1, Winthrop's "Model of Christian Charity" (1630)—preached onboard the *Arbella* during its Atlantic crossing—warns the Puritan colonists that they are to establish a model community, that the eyes of the world will be upon them, and that they must act toward one another as perfect Christians. Bradford, in his verses about the history of Massachusetts Bay Colony several decades later (Document 2), explains all its good and bad experiences as coded messages sent by God, and is distressed to find evidence of decline after an early era of divine favor. Harvard College, founded 1636, ensured that the tradition of a learned clergy, begun at Oxford and Cambridge Universities in England, would persist in the New World, and Document 3 (1643) outlines the students' way of life there. Document 4 is Maryland's 1649 Act of Religious Toleration, which acknowledges that the only way to keep the peace in the colony's religiously diverse population is to prohibit colonists from abusing each other's forms of Christianity, on pain of whipping, fines, or death. Document 5, Anne Bradstreet's poems on the death of two of her grandchildren in 1669, offers us a glimpse of the Puritan settlers' profound emotional life, their struggles to accept death as God's will, and their consolation in the knowledge that the children are with God in heaven, where families separated by death will ultimately be reunited. In Document 6 (1681), William Penn explains his view of human nature and the necessity for governments as a preface to Pennsylvania's first Frame of Government. "Government seems to me a part of religion itself," he declares, linking Adam's first sin to the need for rules, order, and discipline. Document 7 (1684) is an Anglican priest's gloomy assessment of the disarray of the church in Virginia at the end of the seventeenth century due, he says, to the inhabitants' worldliness, greed, and negligence and their refusal to preach to slaves and Indians. Document 8 (1692), written by Puritan minister Cotton Mather at the height of the Salem witch hunt, advises John Richards on methods to establish the guilt or innocence of witchcraft among the accused.

1. John Winthrop Outlines His Plan for a Godly Settlement, 1630

Thus stands the case between God and us. We are entered into a Covenant with Him for this work. We have taken out a commission. The Lord hath given us leave to draw our own articles. We have professed to enterprise these and those ends, upon these and those accounts. We have hereupon besought of Him favor and blessing. Now if the Lord shall please to hear us, and bring us in peace to the place we desire, then hath he ratified this Covenant and sealed our Commission, and will expect a strict performance of the articles contained in it; but if we shall neglect the observation of these articles which are the ends we have propounded, and, dissembling with our God, shall fall to embrace this present world and prosecute our carnal intentions, seeking great things for ourselves and our posterity, the Lord will surely break out in wrath against us; be revenged of such a (sinful) people, and make us know the price of the breach of such a Covenant.

Now the only way to avoid this shipwreck, and to provide for our posterity, is to follow the counsel of Micah, *to do justly, to love mercy, to walk humbly with our God.* For this end, we must be knit together, in this work, as one man. We must entertain each other in brotherly affection. We must be willing to abridge ourselves of our superfluities, for the supply of other's necessities. We must uphold a familiar commerce together in all meekness, gentleness, patience, and liberality. We must delight in each other; make other's condition our own; rejoice together, mourn together, labor and suffer together, always having before our eyes our commission and community in the work, as members of the same body. So shall we *keep the unity of the spirit in the bond of peace.* The Lord will be our God, and delight to dwell among us, as his own people, and will command a blessing upon us in all our ways. So that we shall see much more of his wisdom, power, goodness and truth, than formerly we have been acquainted with. We shall find that the God of Israel is among us, when ten of us shall be able to resist a thousand of our enemies; when he shall make us a praise and a glory, that men shall say of succeeding plantations, 'The Lord make it likely that of *New England.*' For we must consider that we shall be as a City upon a hill. The eyes of all people are upon us. Soe that if we shall deal falsely with our God in this work we have undertaken, and so cause him to withdraw his present help from us, we shall be made a story and a by-word throughout the world. We shall open the mouths of enemies to speak evil of the ways of God, and all professors for God's sake. We shall shame the faces of many of God's worthy servants, and cause their prayers to be turned into curses upon us till we be consumed out of the good land whither we are a-going.

Life and Letters of John Winthrop, vol. 2 (Boston: Little Brown, 1895), 18–20.

I shall shut up this discourse with that exhortation of Moses, that faithful servant of the Lord, in his last farewell to Israel (Deut. 30). *Beloved, there is now set before us life and good, Death and evil, in that we are commanded this day to love the Lord our God, and to love one another, to walk in his ways and to keep his Commandments and his Ordinance and his Lawes,* and the articles of our Covenant with him, that *we may live and be multiplied, and that the Lord our God may bless us in the land whither we go to possess it. But if our hearts shall turn away, so that we will not obey, but shall be seduced, and worship and serve other Gods,* our pleasure and profits, *and serve them;* it is propounded unto us this day, *we shall surely perish out of the good land whither we pass over this vast sea to possess it;* Therefore let us choose life that we, and our seed may live, by obeying His voice and cleaving to Him, for He is our life and our prosperity.

2. William Bradford Sees God's Mercy and Judgment in New England's Changing Fortunes, 1654

Famine once we had————
But other things God gave us in full store,
As fish and ground nuts, to supply our strait,
That we might learn on providence to wait;
And know, by bread man lives not in his need,
But by each word that doth from God proceed.
But a while after plenty did come in,
From his hand only who doth pardon sin.
And all did flourish like the pleasant green,
Which in the joyful spring is to be seen. . . .

But that which did 'bove all the rest excel,
God in his word, with us he here did dwell;
Well ordered churches, in each place there were,
And a learn'd ministry was planted here.
All marvell'd and said, "Lord this work is thine,
In the wilderness to make such lights to shine."
And truly it was a glorious thing,
Thus to hear men pray, and God's praises sing,
Where these natives were wont to cry and yell
To Satan, who 'mongst them doth rule and dwell.
Oh, how great comfort was it now to see,
The churches to enjoy free liberty!
And to have the gospel preach'd here with power,
And such wolves repell'd as would else devour;
And now with plenty their poor souls were fed,
With better food than wheat, or angels' bread,
In green pastures, they may themselves solace,
And drink freely of the sweet springs of grace;
A pleasant banquet, is prepar'd for these,

William Bradford, "A Description and Historical Account of New England," in *A Library of American Puritan Writings,* vol. 9, ed. Sacvan Bercovitch (New York: AMS Press, n.d.). Reprinted from *Collections of the Massachusetts Historical Society,* 1st Series, vol. 3, 1794.

Of fat things, and rich wine upon the lees;
"Eat O my friends, (saith Christ) and drink freely.
Here's wine and milk, and all sweet spicery;
The honey and its comb, is here to be had,
I myself for you, have this banquet made:
Be not dismayed, but let your heart rejoice
In this wilderness, O let me hear your voice;
My friends you are, whilst you my ways do keep,
Your sins I'll pardon and your good I'll seek."
And they, poor souls, again to Christ do say,
"O Lord thou art our hope, our strength and stay;
Who givest to us, all these thy good things,
Us shelter still, in the shadow of thy wings:
So we shall sing, and laud thy name with praise,
'Tis thine own work, to keep us in thy ways;
Uphold us still, O thou which art most high,
We then shall be kept, and thy name glorify,
Let us enjoy thyself, with these means of grace,
And in our hearts shine, with the light of thy face;
Take not away thy presence, nor thy word,
But we humbly pray, us the same afford."

    To the north or south, or which way you'll wind,
Churches now are spread, and you'll pasture find.
Many men of worth, for learning and great fame,
Grave and godly, into these parts here came:
As HOOKER, COTTON, DANFORTH, and the rest,
Whose names are precious and elsewhere express'd;
And many among these, you might soon find,
Who in some things, left not their like behind.
But some of these are dead, and others aged be,
Lord do thou supply, in thy great mercy;
How these their flocks did feed, with painful care,
Their labours, love and fruitful works declare;
They did not spare their time, and lives to spend,
In the Lord's work, unto their utmost end:
And such as still survive do strive the more,
To do like them that have gone before:
Take courage then, for ye shall have reward,
That in this work are faithful to the Lord.
Example take hereby, you that shall come,
In after time when these their race have run. . . .

    I am loth indeed to change my theme,
Thus of God's precious mercies unto them.
Yet I must do it, though it is most sad,
And if it prove otherwise I shall be glad.
Methinks I see some great change at hand,
That e're long will fall upon this poor land;
Not only because many are took away,
Of the best rank, but virtue doth decay,
And true godliness doth not now so shine,
As some while it did, in the former time;
But love and fervent zeal do seem to sleep,

Security and the world on men do creep;
Pride and oppression, they do grow so fast,
As that all goodness they will eat out at last.
Whoredom and drunkenness with other sin,
Will cause God's judgments soon to break in,
And whimsy errors have now got such a head,
And, under notion of conscience, do spread;
So as whole places with them now are stain'd,
Whereas goodness, sometime before hath reign'd.
Where godliness abates, evil will succeed,
And grow apace like to the noisome weed;
And if there be not care, their growth to stop,
All godliness, it soon will overtop.
Another cause of our declining here,
Is a *mixt multitude,* as doth appear;
Many for servants, hitherto were brought,
Others came for gain, or worse ends they sought:
And of these, many grew loose and profane,
Though some are brought to know God and his name.
But thus it is, and hath been so of old,
As by the scriptures we are plainly told;
For when, as from Egypt God's people came,
A mixed multitude got in among them.
Who with the rest murmur and lust did they,
In wants, and fell at *Kibroth Hatavah.*
And whereas the Lord doth sow his good seed,
The enemy, he brings in tares and weed;
What need therefore there is that men should watch,
That Satan them not at advantage catch;
For ill manners and example are such,
As others do infect and corrupt much.

3. Why Harvard College Was Founded, 1643

After God had carried us safe to *New-England,* and wee had builded our houses, provided necessaries for our liveli-hood, rear'd convenient places for Gods worship, and setled the Civill Government: One of the next things we longed for, and looked after was to advance *Learning,* and perpetuate it to Posterity; dreading to leave an illiterate Ministery to the Churches, when our present Ministers shall lie in the Dust. And as wee were thinking and consulting how to effect this great Work; it pleased God to stir up the heart of one Mr. *Harvard* (a godly Gentleman and a lover of Learning, there living amongst us) to give the one halfe of his Estate (it being in all about 1700. l.) towards the erecting of a Colledge, and all his Library: after him another gave 300. l. others after them cast in more, and the publique hand of the State added the rest: the Colledge was, by common consent, appointed to be at *Cambridge,* a place very pleasant and accommodate and is called (according to the name of the first founder) *Harvard Colledge.*

Nathanael Byfield, ed., *An Account of the Late Revolution in New England* (New York: Joseph Sabin, 1865).

The Edifice is very faire and comely within and without, having in it a spacious Hall; (where they daily meet at Commons, Lectures, Exercises) and a large Library with some Bookes to it, the gifts of diverse of our friends, their Chambers and studies also fitted for, and possessed by the Students, and all other roomes of Office necessary and convenient, with all needfull Offices thereto belonging. . . .

2. Rules, and Precepts that are observed in the Colledge.

1. When any Schollar is able to understand *Tully,* or such like classicall Latine Author *extempore,* and make and speake true Latine in Verse and Prose, *suo ut aiunt Marte;* And decline perfectly the Paradigim's of *Nounes* and *Verbes* in the *Greek* tongue: Let him then and not before be capable of admission into the Colledge.

2. Let every Student be plainly instructed, and earnestly pressed to consider well, the maine end of his life and studies is, *to know God and Jesus Christ which is eternall life,* Joh. 17. 3. and therefore to lay *Christ* in the bottome, as the only foundation of all sound knowledge and Learning.

And seeing the Lord only giveth wisedome, Let every one seriously set himselfe by prayer in secret to seeke it of him, *Prov.* 2, 3.

3. Every one shall so exercise himselfe in reading the Scriptures twice a day, that he shall be ready to give such an account of his proficiency therein, both in *Theoretticall* observations of the Language, and *Logick,* and in *Practicall* and spirituall truths, as his Tutor shall require, according to his ability; seeing *the entrance of the word giveth light, it giveth understanding to the simple,* Psalm. 119. 130.

4. That they eschewing all profanation of Gods Name, Attributes, Word, Ordinances, and times of Worship, doe studie with good conscience, carefully to retaine God, and the love of his truth in their mindes else let them know, that (notwithstanding their Learning) God may give them up *to strong delusions,* and in the end *to a reprobate minde,* 2 Thes. 2. 11, 12. Rom. 1. 28.

5. That they studiously redeeme the time; observe the generall houres appointed for all the Students, and the speciall houres for their owne Classis: and then dilligently attend the Lectures without any disturbance by word or gesture. And if in any thing they doubt, they shall enquire as of their fellowes, so, (in case of *Non Satisfaction*) modestly of their Tutors.

6. None shall under any pretence whatsoever, frequent the company and society of such men as lead an unfit, and dissolute life.

Nor shall any without his Tutors leave, or (in his absence) the call of Parents or Guardians, goe abroad to other Townes.

7. Every Schollar shall be present in his Tutors chamber at the 7th. houre in the morning, immediately after the sound of the Bell, at his opening the Scripture and prayer, so also at the 5th. houre at night, and then give account of his owne private reading, as aforesaid in Particular the third, and constantly attend Lectures in the Hall at the houres appointed? But if any (without necessary impediment) shall absent himself from prayer or Lectures, he shall bee lyable to Admonition, if he offend above once a weeke.

8. If any Schollar shall be found to transgresse any of the Lawes of God, or the Schoole, after twice Admonition, he shall be lyable, if not *adultus,* to correction, if *adultus,* his name shall be given up to the Overseers of the Colledge, that he may bee admonished at the publick monethly Act.

4. Maryland's Act of Religious Toleration, 1649

Acts and Orders of Assembly assented vnto

Enacted and made at a Genāll Sessions of the said Assembly held at St Maries on the one and twentieth day of Aprill Anno Dm̄ 1649 as followeth viz.:

An Act concerning Religion

fforasmuch as in a well governed and Xpian Com̄on Weath matters concerning Religion and the honor of God ought in the first place to bee taken, into serious consideracōn and endeavoured to bee settled. Be it therefore ordered and enacted by the Right Ho^{ble} Cecilius Lord Baron of Baltemore absolute Lord and Proprietary of this Province with the advise and consent of this Generall Assembly. That whatsoever pson or psons within this Province and the Islands thereunto belonging shall from henceforth blaspheme God, that is Curse him, or deny our Saviour Jesus Christ to bee the sonne of God, or shall deny the holy Trinity the ffather-sonne and holy Ghost, or the Godhead of any of the said Three psons of the Trinity or the Vnity of the Godhead, or shall use or utter any reproachfull Speeches, words or language concerning the said Holy Trinity, or any of the said three psons thereof, shalbe punished with death and confiscatōn or forfeiture of all his or her lands and goods to the Lord Proprietary and his heires, And bee it also Enacted by the Authority and with the advise and assent aforesaid. That whatsoever pson or psons shall from henceforth use or utter any reproachfull words or Speeches concerning the blessed Virgin Mary the Mother of our Saviour or the holy Apostles or Evangelists or any of them shall in such case for the first offence forfeit to the said Lord Proprietary and his heirs Lords and Proprietaries of this Province the sumē of ffive pound Sterling or the value thereof to be Levyed on the goods and chattells of every such pson soe offending, but in case such Offender or Offenders, shall not then have goods and chattells sufficient for the satisfyeing of such forfeiture, or that the same bee not otherwise speedily satisfyed that then such Offender or Offenders shalbe publiquely whipt and bee ymprisoned during the pleasure of the Lord Proprietary or the Leive^t of cheife Governor of this Province for the time being. . . .

. . . And be it also further Enacted by the same authority advise and assent that whatsoever pson or psons shall from henceforth vppon any occasion of Offence or otherwise in a reproachful manner or Way declare call or denominate any pson or psons whatsoever inhabiting residing traffiqueing trading or comerceing within this Province or within any the Ports, Harbors, Creeks or Havens to the same belonging an heritick, Scismatick, Idolator, puritan, Independant, Prespiterian popish prest, Jesuite, Jesuited papist, Lutheran, Calvenist, Anabaptist, Brownist, Antinomian, Barrowist, Roundhead, Sepatist, or any other name or terme in a reproachfull manner relating to matter of Religion shall for every such Offence forfeit and loose the somē or tenne shillings sterling or the value thereof to bee levyed on the goods and chattells of every such Offender and Offenders, the one half thereof to be forfeited and

Maryland Act of Religious Toleration, 1649, in *Archives of Maryland,* vol. 1, ed. William H. Browne (Baltimore: Maryland Historical Society, 1883), 244–247.

paid unto the person and persons of whom such reproachfull words are or shalbe spoken or vttered, and the other half thereof to the Lord Proprietary and his heires Lords and Proprietaries of this Province, But if such pson or psons who shall at any time vtter or speake any such reproachfull words of Language shall not have Goods or Chattells sufficient and overt within this Province to bee taken to satisfie the penalty aforesaid or that the same bee not otherwise speedily satisfyed, that then the pson or persons soe offending shalbe publickly whipt, and shall suffer imprisonm! without baile or maineprise vntill hee shee or they respectively shall satisfy the party soe offended or greived by such reproachfull Language by asking him or her respectively forgivenes publiquely for such his Offence before the Magistrate or cheife Officer or Officers of the Towne or place where such Offence shalbe given. And be it further likewise Enacted by the Authority and consent aforesaid That every person and persons within this Province that shall at any time hereafter p̄phane the Sabbath or Lords day called Sunday by frequent swearing, drunkennes or by any uncivill or disorderly recreacōn, or by working on that day when absolute necessity doth not require it shall for every such first offence forfeit 2^s 6^d sterling or the value thereof. . . . And whereas the inforceing of the conscience in matters of Religion hath frequently fallen out to be of dangerous Consequence in those commonwealthes where it hath been practised, And for the more quiett and peaceable governem! of this Province, and the better to p̄serve mutuall Love and amity amongst the Inhabitants thereof. Be it Therefore also by the Lo: Proprietary with the advise and consent of this Assembly Ordeyned & enacted (except as in this p̄sent Act is before Declared and sett forth) that noe person or psons whatsoever within this Province, or the Islands, Ports, Harbors, Creekes, or havens thereunto belonging professing to believe in Jesus Christ, shall from henceforth bee any waies troubled, Molested or discountenanced for or in respect of his or her religion nor in the free exercise thereof within this Province or the Islands thereunto belonging nor any way compelled to the beleife or exercise of any other Religion against his or her consent, soe as they be not unfaithfull to the Lord Proprietary, or molest or conspire against the civill Governem! established or to bee established in this Province vnder him or his heires.

5. Anne Bradstreet Commemorates Two Children's Deaths in Poems of 1669

In Memory of My Dear Grandchild Anne Bradstreet, Who Deceased June 20, 1669, Being Three Years and Seven Months Old.

> With troubled heart and trembling hand I write.
> The heavens have changed to sorrow my delight.
> How oft with disappointment have I met
> When I on fading things my hopes have set.
> Experience might 'fore this have made me wise
> To value things according to their price.

Charles Eliot Norton, ed., *Poems of Anne Bradstreet* (The Duodecimos, 1897), 251–252.

Was ever stable joy yet found below?
Or perfect bliss without mixture of woe?
I knew she was but as a withering flower,
That's here to-day, perhaps gone in an hour;
Like as a bubble, or the brittle glass,
Or like a shadow turning, as it was.
More fool, then, I to look on that was lent
As if mine own, when thus impermanent.
Farewell, dear child; thou ne'er shalt come to me,
But yet a while and I shall go to thee.
Meantime my throbbing heart's cheered up with this—
Thou with thy Saviour art in endless bliss.

On My Dear Grandchild Simon Bradstreet, Who Died on 16th November, 1669, Being But a Month and One Day Old.

No sooner come but gone, and fallen asleep;
Acquaintance short, yet parting caused us weep.
Three flowers—two scarcely blown, the last in bud—
Cropped by the Almighty's hand! Yet is he good.
With dreadful awe before him let's be mute.
Such was his will, but why let's not dispute.
With humble hearts and mouths put in the dust
Let's say he's merciful as well as just.
He will return, and make up all our losses,
And smile again, after our bitter crosses.
Go, pretty babe; go rest with sisters twain;
Among the blest in endless joys remain.

6. William Penn Gives Scriptural Justifications for His Pennsylvania Frame of Government, 1681

When the great and wise God had made the world, of all his creatures it pleased him to choose man his deputy to rule it; and to fit him for so great a charge and trust, he did not only qualify him with skill and power, but with integrity to use them justly. This native goodness was equally his honour and his happiness, and whilst he stood there, all went well; there was no need of coercive or compulsive means; the precept of divine love and truth in his bosom was the guide and keeper of his innocency. But lust prevailing against duty, made a lamentable breach upon it; and the law, that before had no power over him, took place upon him and his disobedient posterity, that such as would not live comfortable to the holy law within, should fall under the reproof and correction, of the just law without, in a judicial administration.

William Penn, "Preface to the First Frame of Government," 1681. Reprinted in Sylvester Stevens, ed., *Pennsylvania: The Keystone State* (New York: The American Historical Company, 1956), 23–26.

This the apostle teaches us in divers of his epistles. The law (says he) was added because of transgression: In another place, knowing that the law was not made for the righteous man; but for the disobedient and ungodly, for sinners, for unholy and prophane, for murderers, for whoremongers, for them that defile themselves with mankind, and for men-stealers, for liars, for perjured persons, &c. But this is not all, he opens and carries the matter of government a little further: Let every soul be subject to the higher powers, for there is no power but of God. The powers that be are ordained of God, whosoever therefore resisteth the power, resisteth the ordinance of God. For rulers are not a terror to good works, but to evil: wilt thou then not be afraid of the power? Do that which is good, and thou shalt have praise of the same.—He is the minister of God to thee for good.—Wherefore ye must needs be subject, not only for wrath but for conscience sake.

This settles the divine right of government beyond exception, and that for two ends; first, to terrify evil-doers; secondly, to cherish those that do well; which gives government a life beyond corruption, and makes it as durable in the world, as good men shall be. So that government seems to me a part of religion itself, a thing sacred in its institution and end. For if it does not directly remove the cause, it crushes the effects of evil, and is as such (tho' a lower yet) an emanation of the same Divine Power, that is both author and object of pure religion; the difference lying here, that the one is more free and mental, the other more corporal and compulsive in its operations: but that is only to evil-doers; government itself being otherwise as capable of kindness, goodness and charity, as a more private society. They weakly err, that think there is no other use of government than correction, which is the coarsest part of it: daily experience tells us that the care and regulation of many other affairs more soft and daily necessary, make up much the greatest part of government; and which must have followed the peopling of the world, had Adam never fell, and will continue among men on earth under the highest attainments they may arrive at, by the coming of the blessed second Adam, the Lord from Heaven. Thus much of government in general, as to its rise and end.

For particular frames and models, it will become me to say little; and comparatively I will say nothing. My reasons are: first, that the age is too nice and difficult for it; there being nothing the wits of men are more busy and divided upon. 'Tis true, they seem to agree in the end, to wit, happiness, but in the means they differ, as to divine, so to this human felicity; and the cause is much the same, not always want of light and knowledge, but want of using them rightly. Men side with their passions against their reason, and their sinister interests have so strong a bias upon their minds, that they lean to them against the good of the things they know. . . .

. . . [W]hen all is said, there is hardly one frame of government in the world so ill designed by its first founders, that in good hands would not do well enough; and story tells us, the best in ill ones can do nothing that is great or good; witness the Jewish and Roman states. Governments, like clocks, go from the motion men give them, and as governments are made and moved by men, so by them they are ruined too. Wherefore governments rather depend upon men, than men upon governments. Let men be good, and the government cannot be bad; if it be ill, they will cure it. But if men be bad, let the government be never so good, they will endeavor to warp and spoil it to their turn.

7. Morgan Godwin Describes the Troubles of the Anglican Church in Virginia, 1684

As it is a thing much to be lamented, so it is withal most certain, that in the Plantations, subject to his Majesties Government (among which New England in the Opinion of some is not to be reckoned) there is almost an Universal Declension of Christianity, and a Decay of all Religion, occasioned many ways, but chiefly by these following.

I. Their keeping their Parishes Vacant for many Years together, even where Ministers have offered themselves for their Supply, but have been rejected, their Law not compelling them to entertain any but at their own Leasure.

II. By their suffering other Parishes to Extend themselves to 60 or 70 miles, to save Charges; Or, else by permitting 4 or 5 Parishes (each of them 6, 8, or 10 Miles Square) to One Man's care, and he Perchance no Minister; Who for a pretty Salary from each, shall visit them Once a Month or Two: Notwithstanding, that the least might allow their full Maintenance (not answering to 40 *1. per Ann.* in *England,*) without Parting with more than the Hundredth Part of their Annual Increase.

III. By their scattering way of Living and Seating themselves; whereby, (together with their long Vacancies, and putting so many Parishes into One Man's Hand) diverse Persons and Families, are supposed hardly ever to have been Present at any Publick Exercise of Religion, tho' long residing there.

IV. By their Comissioning or Permitting Unordained Men (both Scandalous and Ignorant) to Preach, &c. And their Neglect of Catechizing.

V. By their Evil Entreating and Abusing of Ministers.

VI. By the want of Church Government; The Civil Governours there for the most Part Permitting the whole Care of the Church to their Parish Vestries, who have a kind of Arbitrary Power over the Ministers, and do even Dispose of them how they Please. From which Government of Vestries these Evils do proceed.

1. That Deacons, or (as before is said) meer Laymen are Permitted to Preach, and to Exercise all the Office of Priests; The Ministers being not allowed to view their Orders, nor to complain of the Abuse, tho' in itself most Evident and Notorious. The Vestries also having Divers times thrust out Presbyters or Priests to make way for those Pretenders, that they might enjoy Pluralities; Only for the Cheapness of the Bargain, which usually carries it for the next Comer.

Morgan Godwin, "A Brief Account of Religion in the Plantations" (Virginia), appended to Francis Brokesby, *Some Proposals Towards Propagating of the Gospel in Our American Plantations* (London: G. Sawbridges, 1708), 1–3.

2. Neither the King's Right of Patronage is preserved, nor any care taken to make due Certification of the Vacancies of Parishes, nor are the Legal Profits in the Interem secured for the ensuing incumbents, nor are they imployed to Purchase Glebes, Build Houses for the Ministers, nor Churches where they are wanting; but the whole Profits are Pocketed up by the people, which can be no small invitation to them to continue the Vacancy.

3. That Goods devoted to pious Uses, are kept in Private Hands, and Imbezelled to the great Discouragement of other Charitable and well Disposed People.

4. That the Ministers, being Hired for the most Part by the Year, or by the Sermon only, are so awed by their Parishioners, that they dare not with that Courage, which they ought to reprove Vice as Bold and Impudent in those Parts as it is: Much less acquaint their Charges with the Indespensable Necessity of Instructing and Baptizing, even those, *Negroes* or *Indians,* who understood *English,* no worse than our own people, of whom there are many Thousands, especially in *Barbadoes:* Nor dare they to extend this Charity to their own Slaves, whereby the Quakers have taken the Boldness in a kind of Sarcason, in one of their Printed Pamphlets Written by *Fox,* to demand of them, who made them Ministers of the Gospel, to the *White* People only, and not to the *Tawnies* and *Blacks* also? As in the said *Fox*'s Pamphlets is to be seen.

5. Hereby all manner of Licentiousness is Permitted: Particularly allowing Polygamy to their *Negroes,* as also openly to spend the Sundays in Idolatrous Dances and Drunkenness, or in Planting their own Provisions, no Time else being allowed them in the Week Days. Which Tolerations, and Impieties are no other than the Result of some Hellish Principles, *viz.* That *Negroes* are Creatures destitute of Souls, to be ranked among Brute Beasts, and Treated accordingly (as generally they are) and whom Religion (apt only to make Subjects Mutinous) doth no way Concern.

6. That in some Provinces Religion doth seem to be wholy Neglected and laid Aside there being no Ministry, Preaching, Service, nor Worship found amongst them, except only amongst some few *Papists* or *Quakers:* And this is Observed in *Mary-Land, Long* and *Rhode* Island, with divers other, both Islands and Places upon the Continent.

7. Hereby all Endeavours to Promote Christianity amongst the Heathen, is wholy Neglected and laid aside (except only in *New England*) to; but so much as Mention which in any of those Places, is Esteemed as most Ridiculous, and the effect of Madness. Which Neglect, how Sinful it is, and how Scandalous to the whole Reformation, I need not say; Since that thereby they, as much as in them lies do defeat and frustrate that very End, for which, as must be Piously supposed, God was Pleased to Discover and Possess us of those many Large and Fruitful Countries.

8. Cotton Mather Advises John Richards on Detecting Witches, 1692

I must humbly beg you that in the management of the affair in your most worthy hands, you do not lay more stress upon pure specter testimony than it will bear. When you are satisfied or have good, plain, legal evidence that the demons which molest our poor neighbors do indeed represent such and such people to the sufferers, tho' this be a presumption, yet I suppose you will not reckon it a conviction that the people so represented are witches to be immediately exterminated. It is very certain that the devils have sometimes represented the shapes of persons not only innocent, but also very virtuous, tho' I believe that the just God then ordinarily provides a way for the speedy vindication of the persons thus abused. Moreover, I do suspect that persons who have too much indulged themselves in malignant, envious, malicious ebullitions of their souls, may unhappily expose themselves to the judgment of being represented by devils, of whom they never had any vision, and with whom they have much less written any covenant. I would say this: if upon the bare supposal of a poor creature's being represented by a specter, too great a progress be made by the authority in ruining a poor neighbor so represented, it may be that a door may be thereby opened for the devils to obtain from the courts in the invisible world a license to proceed unto most hideous desolations upon the repute and repose of such as have yet been kept from the great transgression. If mankind have thus far once consented unto the credit of diabolical representations, the door is opened! Perhaps there are wise and good men that may be ready to style him that shall advance this caution, a witch advocate; but in the winding up, this caution will certainly be wished for.

III. Tho' 'tis probable that the devils may (tho' not often, yet sometimes) make most bloody invasions upon our exterior concerns, without any witchcrafts of our fellow creatures to empower them, and I do expect that as when our Lord was coming in His human nature among us, there was a more sensible annoyance of the destroyer upon our human nature than at other times, thus it will be just before our Lord's coming again in His human nature, when He will also dispossess the devils of their aerial region to make a New Heaven for His raised there. Nevertheless there is cause enough to think that it is a horrible witchcraft which hath given rise to the troubles wherewith Salem Village is at this day harassed; and the indefatigable pains that are used for the tracing [of] this witchcraft are to be thankfully accepted, and applauded among all this people of God.

IV. Albeit the business of this witchcraft be very much transacted upon the stage of imagination, yet we know that, as in treason there is an imagining which is a capital crime, and here also the business thus managed in imagination yet may not be called imaginary. The effects are dreadfully real. Our dear neighbors are most really tormented, really murdered, and really acquainted with hidden things, which are afterwards proved plainly to have been realities. I say, then, as that man is justly executed for an assassinate, who in the sight of men shall with a sword in his hand stab his neighbor into the heart, so suppose a long train laid unto a barrel

Cotton Mather to John Richards, 1692, *Selected Letters of Cotton Mather,* ed. Kenneth Silverman (Baton Rouge, La.: Louisiana State University Press, 1971), 36–40.

of gunpowder under the floor where a neighbor is, and suppose a man with a match perhaps in his mouth, out of sight, set fire unto the further end of the train, tho' never so far off. This man also is to be treated as equally a malefactor. Our neighbors at Salem Village are blown up, after a sort, with an infernal gunpowder; the train is laid in the laws of the kingdom of darkness limited by God himself. Now the question is, who gives fire to this train? and by what acts is the match applied? Find out the persons that have done this thing, and be their acts in doing it either mental, or oral, or manual, or what the devil will, I say *abeant quo digni sunt.*

V. To determine a matter so much in the dark as to know the guilty employers of the devils in this work of darkness, this is a work, this is a labor. Now first a credible confession of the guilty wretches is one of the most hopeful ways of coming at them, and I say a credible confession because even confession itself sometimes is not credible. But a person of a sagacity many times thirty furlongs less than yours, will easily perceive what confession may be credible, and what may be the result of only a delirious brain, or a discontented heart. All the difficulty is how to obtain this confession. For this I am far from urging the un-English method of torture, but instead thereof I propound these three things: first, who can tell but when the witches come upon their trials, they may be so forsaken, as to confess all. The Almighty God having heard the appeals of our cries to Heaven, may so thunder-strike their souls, as to make them show their deeds. Moreover, the devils themselves who aim at the entrapping of their own miserable clients, may treacherously depart from them in their examinations, which throws them into such toiling vexations that they'll discover all. Besides, when you come solemnly in God's name to exhibit yourselves as His viceregents, and when you come to form a most awful type of the Last Judgment, whereat the devils of all things tremble most, even they also may be smitten with such terrors as may contribute a little to their departure from the miscreants whom they have entangled. An unexpected confession, is that whereunto witches are very often driven. Secondly, I am ready to think that there is usually some expression or behavior whereto the devils do constantly oblige the witches, as a kind of sacrament, upon their least failure wherein the witches presently lose the thus forfeited assistances of the devils, and all comes out. Please then to observe, if you can find any one constant scheme of discourse or action, whereto the suspected seem religiously devoted, and (which may easily be done by the common policies of conversation) cause them to transgress that, a confession will probably then come on apace. Thirdly, whatever hath a tendency to put the witches into confusion is likely to bring them unto confession too. Here cross and swift questions have their use, but besides them, for my part, I should not be unwilling that an experiment be made whether accused parties can repeat the Lord's Prayer, or those other systems of Christianity which, it seems, the devils often make the witches unable to repeat without ridiculous depravations or amputations. The danger of this experiment will be taken away if you make no evidence of it, but only put it to the use I mention, which is that of confounding the lisping witches to give a reason why they cannot, even with prompting, repeat those heavenly composures. The like I would say of some other experiments, only we may venture too far before we are aware.

VI. But what if no confession can be obtained; I say yet the case is far from desperate. For if there have been those words uttered by the witches, either by way of threatening, or of asking, or of bragging, which rationally demonstrate such a knowledge of the woeful circumstances attending the afflicted people, as could not be had without some diabolical communion, the proof of such words is enough to fix the guilt. Moreover, I look upon wounds that have been given unto specters, and received by witches, as intimations broad enough, in concurrence with other things, to bring out the guilty. Tho' I am not fond of assaying to give such wounds, yet the proof such when given carries with it what is very palpable.

Once more, can there be no puppets found out? and here I would say thus much, I am thinking that some witches make their own bodies to be their puppets. If therefore you can find that when the witches do anything easy, that is not needful (and it is needful that I put in that clause "not needful" because it is possible that a prestigious demon may imitate what we do, tho' we are none of his) I say if you find the same thing, presently, and hurtfully, and more violently done by any unseen hand unto the bodies of the sufferers, hold them, for you have catched a witch. I add, why should not witch-marks be searched for? The properties, the qualities of those marks are described by diverse weighty writers. I never saw any of those marks, but it is doubtless not impossible for a chirurgeon, when he sees them, to say what are magical, and if these become once apparent, it is apparent that these witches have gone so far in their wickedness as to admit most cursed succages, whereby the devils have not only fetched out of them, it may be the spirits of which they make vehicles, wherein they visit the afflicted, but also they have infused a venom into them which exalts the malignity of their spirits as well as of their bodies; and it is likely that by means of this ferment they would be found buoyant (if the water-ordeal were made upon them).

VII. I begin to fear that the devils do more easily proselyte poor mortals into witchcraft than is commonly conceived. When a sinful child of man distempers himself with some exorbitant motions in his mind (and it is to be feared the murmuring phrensies of late prevailing in the country have this way exposed many to sore temptations) a devil then soon presents himself unto him, and he demands, Are you willing that I should go do this or that for you? If the man once comply, the devil hath him now in a most horrid snare, and by a permission from the just vengeance of God he visits the man with buffetings as well as allurements, till the forlorn man at first only for the sake of quietness, but at length out of improved wickedness, will commission the devil to do mischief as often as he requires it. And for this cause 'tis worth considering, whether there be a necessity always by extirpations by halter or fagot every wretched creature that shall be hooked into some degrees of witchcraft. What if some of the lesser criminals be only scourged with lesser punishments, and also put upon some solemn, open, public, and explicit renunciation of the devil? I am apt to think that the devils would then cease afflicting the neighborhood whom these wretches have stood them upon, and perhaps they themselves would now suffer some impressions from the devils, which if they do, they must be willing to bear till the God that hears prayer deliver them. Or what if the death of some of the offenders were either diverted or inflicted, according to the success of such their renunciation.

But I find my free thoughts thus freely laid before Your Honor, begin to have too much freedom in them. I shall now therefore add no more but my humble and most fervent prayers to the God who gives wisdom liberally, that you and your honorable brethren may be furnished from on high, with all that wisdom, as well as justice, which is requisite in the thorny affair before you. God will be with you. I am persuaded He will; and with that persuasion I subscribe myself,

Sir, Your very devoted servant

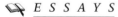 *E S S A Y S*

Perry Miller of Harvard University was among the greatest of all American historians. In the 1930s, when most American intellectuals looked back on the Puritans with disdain, treating them as no more than an embarrassing memory, something to be escaped, Miller's books explained the Puritans' mental outlook and their creative response to the world as they saw it. Miller, who was not religious, nevertheless forced skeptical historians to reckon with the vital importance of religious thought and feeling in American history. His influence persists even today, despite numerous attacks on his work. His essay "Errand into the Wilderness" explains the mission that the first and second generation of New England Puritan settlers undertook and describes how the ambiguities of the term "errand" mirror the ambiguity of their lives and actions.

Edward L. Bond of Alabama A and M University explains the quite different religious life of Virginia settlers in the late seventeenth and early eighteenth centuries. He shows that, despite a severe shortage of clergy, their colony was not as religiously destitute as Morgan Godwin (Document 7) had implied. It is true that Virginian Anglicanism—with its emphasis on order, repetition, and conventional morality—lacked the energy and fervor of New England Puritanism and that it was well suited to the pragmatic, profit-oriented tobacco farmers who had settled there. The Virginians' use of nautical metaphors in discussing religious life as a voyage underlines their awareness of the immense sea crossing that lay between them and their English homes. As Bond says, their inability to attend church regularly, and their dependence instead on personal devotions, gave an early premonition of Anglicanism's later decline.

The Puritans' Errand into the Wilderness

PERRY MILLER

Samuel Danforth's election sermon, delivered on May 11, 1670, [was titled] *A Brief Recognition of New England's Errand into the Wilderness*. . . . [A]ll the election sermons of this period—that is to say, the major expressions of the second generation, which, delivered on these forensic occasions, were in the fullest sense community expression—have interesting titles; a mere listing tells the story of what was happening to the minds and emotions of the New England people: John Higginson's *The Cause of God and His People In New-England* in 1663, William Stoughton's *New England's True Interest, Not to Lie* in 1668, Thomas Shepard's *Eye-Salve* in 1672, Urian Oakes's *New England Pleaded With* in 1673, and, climactically and most explicitly, Increase Mather's *A Discourse Concerning the Danger of Apostasy* in 1677.

All of these show by their title pages alone—and, as those who have looked into them know, infinitely more by their contents—a deep disquietude. They are troubled utterances, worried, fearful. Something has gone wrong. As in 1662 Wigglesworth already was saying in verse, God has a controversy with New England; He has cause to be angry and to punish it because of its innumerable defections. They say, unanimously, that New England was sent on an errand, and that it has failed.

To our ears these lamentations of the second generation sound strange indeed. We think of the founders as heroic men—of the towering stature of Bradford, Winthrop, and Thomas Hooker—who braved the ocean and the wilderness, who conquered both, and left to their children a goodly heritage. Why then this whimpering?

Some historians suggest that the second and third generations suffered a failure of nerve; they weren't the men their fathers had been, and they knew it. Where the founders could range over the vast body of theology and ecclesiastical polity and produce profound works like the treatises of John Cotton or the subtle psychological analyses of Hooker, or even such a gusty though wrongheaded book as Nathaniel Ward's *Simple Cobler,* let alone such lofty and rightheaded pleas as Roger Williams' *Bloudy Tenent,* all these children could do was tell each other that they were on probation and that their chances of making good did not seem very promising.

Since Puritan intellectuals were thoroughly grounded in grammar and rhetoric, we may be certain that Danforth was fully aware of the ambiguity concealed in his word "errand." It already had taken on the double meaning which is still carries with us. Originally, as the word first took form in English, it meant exclusively a short journey on which an inferior is sent to convey a message or to perform a service for his superior. In that sense we today speak of an "errand boy"; or the husband says that while in town on his lunch hour, he must run an errand for his wife. But by the end of the Middle Ages, errand developed another connotation: it came to mean the actual business on which the actor goes, the purpose itself, the conscious intention in his mind. In this signification, the runner of the errand is working for himself, is his own boss; the wife, while the husband is away at the office, runs her own errands. Now in the 1660's the problem was this: which had New England originally been—an errand boy or a doer or errands? In which sense had it failed? Had it been despatched for a further purpose, or was it an end in itself? Or had it fallen short not only in one or the other, but in both of the meanings? If so, it was indeed a tragedy, in the primitive sense of a fall from a mighty designation.

If the children were in grave doubt about which had been the original errand—if, in fact, those of the founders who lived into the later period and who might have set their progeny to rights found themselves wondering and confused—there is little chance of our answering clearly. . . .

. . . Massachusetts Bay was not just an organization of immigrants seeking advantage and opportunity. It had a positive sense of mission—either it was sent on an errand or it had its own intention, but in either case the deed was deliberate. It was an act of will, perhaps of willfulness. These Puritans were not driven out of England (thousands of their fellows stayed and fought the Cavaliers)—they went of their own accord.

So, concerning them, we ask the question, why? If we are not altogether clear about precisely how we should phrase the answer, this is not because they themselves were reticent. They spoke as fully as they knew how, and none more magnificently or cogently than John Winthrop in the midst of the passage itself, when he delivered a lay sermon aboard the flagship *Arbella* and called it "A Modell of Christian Charity." It distinguishes the motives of this great enterprise . . . from those of the masses who later have come in quest of advancement. Hence, for the student of New England and of America, it is a fact demanding incessant brooding that John Winthrop selected as the "doctrine" of his discourse, and so as the basic proposition to which, it then seemed to him, the errand was committed, the thesis that God had disposed mankind in a hierarchy of social classes, so that "in all times some must be rich, some poor, some highe and eminent in power and dignitie; others mean and in subjeccion." It is as though, preternaturally sensing what the promise of America might come to signify for the rank and file, Winthrop took the precaution to drive out of their heads any notion that in the wilderness the poor and the mean were ever so to improve themselves as to mount above the rich or the eminent in dignity. Were there any who had signed up under the mistaken impression that such was the purpose of their errand, Winthrop told them that, although other peoples, lesser breeds, might come for wealth or pelf, this migration was specifically dedicated to an avowed end that had nothing to do with incomes. We have entered into an explicit covenant with God, "we haue professed to enterprise these Accions vpon these and these ends"; we have drawn up indentures with the Almighty, wherefore if we succeed and do not let ourselves get diverted into making money, He will reward us. Whereas if we fail, if we "fall to embrace this present world and prosecute our carnall intencions, seeking greate things for our selves and our posterity, the Lord will surely breake out in wrathe against us be revenged of such a periured people and make us knowe the price of the breache of such a Covenant."

Well, what terms were agreed upon in this covenant? Winthrop could say precisely—"It is by a mutuall consent through a specially overruleing providence, and a more than ordinary approbation of the Churches of Christ to seeke out a place of Cohabitation and Consorteshipp under a due forme of Government both civill and ecclesiasticall." If it could be said thus concretely, why should there be any ambiguity? There was no doubt whatsoever about what Winthrop meant by a due form of ecclesiastical government: he meant the pure Biblical polity set forth in full detail by the New Testament, that method which later generations, in the days of increasing confusion, would settle down to calling Congregational, but which for Winthrop was no denominational peculiarity but the very essence of organized Christianity. What a due form of civil government meant, therefore, became crystal clear: a political regime, possessing power, which would consider its main function to be the erecting, protecting, and preserving of this form of polity. This due form would have, at the very beginning of its list of responsibilities, the duty of suppressing heresy, of subduing or somehow getting rid of dissenters—of being, in short, deliberately, vigorously, and consistently intolerant.

Regarded in this light, the Massachusetts Bay Company came on an errand in the second and later sense of the word: it was, so to speak, on its own business. What it set out to do was the sufficient reason for its setting out. About this Winthrop seems to be perfectly certain, as he declares specifically what the due forms will be attempting: the end is to improve our lives to do more service to the Lord, to increase the body of Christ, and to preserve our posterity from the corruptions of this evil world, so that they in turn shall work out their salvation under the purity and power of Biblical ordinances. Because the errand was so definable in advance, certain conclusions about the method of conducting it were equally evident: one, obviously, was that those sworn to the covenant should not be allowed to turn aside in a lust for mere physical rewards; but another was, in Winthrop's simple but splendid words, "we must be knit together in this worke as one man, wee must entertaine each other in brotherly affection." We must actually delight in each other, "always having before our eyes our Commission and community in the worke, our community as members of the same body." This was to say, were the great purpose kept steadily in mind, if all gazed only at it and strove only for it, then social solidarity (within a scheme of fixed and unalterable class distinctions) would be an automatic consequence. A society despatched upon an errand that is its own reward would want no other rewards: it could go forth to possess a land without ever becoming possessed by it; social gradations would remain eternally what God had originally appointed; there would be no internal contention among groups or interests, and though there would be hard work for everybody, prosperity would be bestowed not as a consequence of labor but as a sign of approval upon the mission itself. For once in the history of humanity (with all its sins), there would be a society so dedicated to a holy cause that success would prove innocent and triumph not raise up sinful pride or arrogant dissension.

Or, at least, this would come about if the people did not deal falsely with God, if they would live up to the articles of their bond. If we do not perform these terms, Winthrop warned, we may expect immediate manifestations of divine wrath; we shall perish out of the land we are crossing the sea to possess. And here in the 1660's and 1670's, all the jeremiads (of which Danforth's is one of the most poignant) are castigations of the people for having defaulted on precisely these articles. They recite the long list of afflictions an angry God had rained upon them, surely enough to prove how abysmally they had deserted the covenant: crop failures, epidemics, grasshoppers, caterpillars, torrid summers, arctic winters, Indian wars, hurricanes, shipwrecks, accidents, and (most grievous of all) unsatisfactory children. The solemn work of the election day, said Stoughton in 1668, is "Foundation-work"— not, that is, to lay a new one, "but to continue, and strengthen, and beautifie, and build upon that which has been laid." It had been laid in the covenant before even a foot was set ashore, and thereon New England should rest. Hence the terms of survival, let alone of prosperity, remained what had first been propounded:

> If we should so frustrate and deceive the Lords Expectations, that his Covenant-interest in us, and the Workings of his Salvation be made to cease, then All were lost indeed; Ruine upon Ruine, Destruction upon Destruction would come, until one stone were not left upon another.

Since so much of the literature after 1660—in fact, just about all of it—dwells on this theme of declension and apostasy, would not the story of New England seem to be simply that of the failure of a mission? Winthrop's dread was realized: posterity had not found their salvation amid pure ordinances but had, despite the ordinances, yielded to the seductions of the good land. Hence distresses were being piled upon them, the slaughter of King Philip's War and now the attack of a profligate king upon the sacred charter. By about 1680, it did in truth seem that shortly no stone would be left upon another, that history would record of New England that the founders had been great men, but that their children and grandchildren progressively deteriorated.

This would certainly seem to be the impression conveyed by the assembled clergy and lay elders who, in 1679, met at Boston in a formal synod, under the leadership of Increase Mather, and there prepared a report on why the land suffered. The result of their deliberation, published under the title *The Necessity of Reformation,* was the first in what has proved to be a distressingly long succession of investigations into the civic health of Americans, and it is probably the most pessimistic. . . .

First, there was a great and visible decay of godliness. Second, there were several manifestations of pride—contention in the churches, insubordination of inferiors toward superiors, particularly of those inferiors who had, unaccountably, acquired more wealth than their betters, and, astonishingly, a shocking extravagance in attire, especially on the part of these of the meaner sort, who persisted in dressing beyond their means. Third, there were heretics, especially Quakers and Anabaptists. Fourth, a notable increase in swearing and a spreading disposition to sleep at sermons (these two phenomena seemed basically connected). Fifth, the Sabbath was wantonly violated. Sixth, family government had decayed, and fathers no longer kept their sons and daughters from prowling at night. Seventh, instead of people being knit together as one man in mutual love, they were full of contention, so that lawsuits were on the increase and lawyers were thriving. Under the eighth head, the synod described the sins of sex and alcohol, thus producing some of the juiciest prose of the period: militia days had become orgies, taverns were crowded; women threw temptation in the way of befuddled men by wearing false locks and displaying naked necks and arms "or, which is more abominable, naked Breasts"; there were "mixed Dancings," along with light behavior and "Company-keeping" with vain persons, wherefore the bastardy rate was rising. In 1672, there was actually an attempt to supply Boston with a brothel (it was suppressed, but the synod was bearish about the future). Ninth, New Englanders were betraying a marked disposition to tell lies, especially when selling anything. In the tenth place, the business morality of even the most righteous left everything to be desired: the wealthy speculated in land and raised prices excessively; "Day-Labourers and Mechanicks are unreasonable in their demands." In the eleventh place, the people showed no disposition to reform, and in the twelfth, they seemed utterly destitute of civic spirit.

"The things here insisted on," said the synod, "have been oftentimes mentioned and inculcated by those whom the Lord hath set as Watchmen to the house of Israel." Indeed they had been, and thereafter they continued to be even more inculcated. At the end of the century, the synod's report was serving as a kind of handbook for preachers: they would take some verse of Isaiah or Jeremiah, set up the doctrine that God avenges the iniquities of a chosen people, and then run down the twelve heads, merely bringing the list up to date by inserting the new and still more depraved practices an ingenious people kept on devising. I suppose that in the whole literature of the world, including the satirists of imperial Rome, there is hardly such another uninhibited and unrelenting documentation of a people's descent into corruption.

I have elsewhere endeavored to argue that, while the social or economic historian may read this literature for its contents—and so construct from the expanding catalogue of denunciations a record of social progress—the cultural anthropologist will look slightly askance at these jeremiads; he will exercise a methodological caution about taking them at face value. If you read them all through, the total effect, curiously enough, is not at all depressing: you come to the paradoxical realization that they do not bespeak a despairing frame of mind. There is something of a ritual-istic incantation about them; whatever they may signify in the realm of theology, in that of psychology they are purgations of soul; they do not discourage but actually encourage the community to persist in its heinous conduct. The exhortation to a re-formation which never materializes serves as a token payment upon the obligation, and so liberates the debtors. Changes there had to be: adaptations to environment, expansion of the frontier, mansions constructed, commercial adventures under-taken. These activities were not specifically nominated in the bond Winthrop had framed. They were thrust upon the society by American experience; because they were not only works of necessity but of excitement, they proved irresistible—whether making money, haunting taverns, or committing fornication. Land specu-lation meant not only wealth but dispersion of the people, and what was to stop the march of settlement? The covenant doctrine preached on the *Arbella* had been for-mulated in England, where land was not to be had for the taking; its adherents had been utterly oblivious of what the fact of a frontier would do for an imported order, let alone for a European mentality. Hence I suggest that under the guise of this mounting wail of sinfulness, this incessant and never successful cry for repentance, the Puritans launched themselves upon the process of Americanization.

However, there are still more pertinent or more analytical things to be said of this body of expression. If you compare it with the great productions of the founders, you will be struck by the fact that the second and third generations had become ori-ented toward the social, and only the social, problem; herein they were deeply and profoundly different from their fathers. The finest creations of the founders—the disquisitions of Hooker, Shepard, and Cotton—were written in Europe, or else, if actually penned in the colonies, proceeded from a thoroughly European mentality, upon which the American scene made no impression whatsoever. The most striking example of this imperviousness is the poetry of Anne Bradstreet. . . .

The titles alone of productions in the next generation show how concentrated have become emotion and attention upon the interest of New England, and none is more revealing than Samuel Danforth's conception of an errand into the wilder-ness. . . . Their range is sadly constricted, but every effort, no matter how brief, is addressed to the persistent question: what is the meaning of this society in the wilderness? If it does not mean what Winthrop said it must mean, what under Heaven is it? Who, they are forever asking themselves, who are we?—and some-times they are on the verge of saying, who the Devil are we, anyway?

This brings us back to the fundamental ambiguity concealed in the word "errand," that *double entente* of which I am certain Danforth was aware when he published the words that give point to the exhibition. While it was true that in 1630, the covenant philosophy of a special and peculiar bond lifted the migration out of the ordinary realm of nature, provided it with a definite mission which might in the secondary sense be called its errand, there was always present in Puritan thinking the suspicion that God's saints are at best inferiors, despatched by their Superior upon particular assignments. Anyone who has run errands for other people, par-ticularly for people of great importance with many things on their minds, such as army commanders, knows how real is the peril that, by the time he returns with the report of a message delivered or a bridge blown up, the Superior may be interested in something else; the situation at headquarters may be entirely changed, and the gallant errand boy, or the husband who desperately remembered to buy the ribbon, may be told that he is too late. This tragic pattern appears again and again in modern warfare: an agent is dropped by parachute and, after immense hardships, comes back to find that, in the shifting tactical or strategic situations, his contribution is no longer of value. If he gets home in time and his service proves useful, he receives a medal; otherwise, no matter what prodigies he has performed, he may not even be thanked. He has been sent, as the devastating phrase has it, upon a fool's errand, than which there can be no more shattering blow to self-esteem.

The Great Migration of 1630 felt insured against such treatment from on high by the covenant; nevertheless, the God of the covenant always remained an unpredictable Jehovah, a *Deus Absconditus.* When God promises to abide by stated terms, His word, of course, is to be trusted; but then, what is man that he dare accuse Omnipotence of tergiversation? But if any such apprehension was in Winthrop's mind as he spoke on the *Arbella,* or in the minds of other apologists for the enterprise, they kept it far back and allowed it no utterance. They could stifle the thought, not only because Winthrop and his colleagues believed fully in the covenant, but because they could see in the pattern of history that their errand was not a mere scouting expedition: it was an essential maneuver in the drama of Christendom. The Bay Company was not a battered remnant of suffering Separatists thrown up on a rocky shore; it was an organized task force of Christians, executing a flank attack on the corruptions of Christendom. These Puritans did not flee to America; they went in order to work out that complete reformation which was not yet accomplished in England and Europe, but which would quickly be accomplished if only the saints back there had a working model to guide them. It is impossible to say that any who sailed from Southampton really expected to lay his bones in the new world; were it to come about—as all in their heart of hearts anticipated—that the forces of righteousness should prevail against Laud and Wentworth, that England after all should turn toward reformation, where else would the distracted country look for leadership except to those who in New England had perfected the ideal polity and who would know how to administer it? This was the large unspoken assumption in the errand of 1630: if the conscious intention were realized, not only would a federated Jehovah bless the new land, but He would bring back these temporary colonials to govern England.

In this respect, therefore, we may say that the migration was running an errand in the earlier and more primitive sense of the word—performing a job not so much for Jehovah as for history, which was the wisdom of Jehovah expressed through time. Winthrop was aware of this aspect of the mission—fully conscious of it. "For wee must Consider that wee shall be as a Citty upon a Hill, the eies of all people are uppon us." More was at stake than just one little colony. If we deal falsely with God, not only will He descend upon us in wrath, but even more terribly, He will make us "a story and a by-word through the world, wee shall open the mouthes of enemies to speake evill of the wayes of god and all professours for Gods sake." No less than John Milton was New England to justify God's ways to man, though not, like him, in the agony and confusion of defeat but in the confidence of approaching triumph. This errand was being run for the sake of Reformed Christianity; and while the first aim was indeed to realize in America the due form of government, both civil and ecclesiastical, the aim behind that aim was to vindicate the most rigorous ideal of the Reformation, so that ultimately all Europe would imitate New England. . . .

When we look upon the enterprise from this point of view, the psychology of the second and third generations becomes more comprehensible. We realize that the migration was not sent upon its errand in order to found the United States of America, nor even the New England conscience. Actually, it would not perform its errand even when the colonists did erect a due form of government in church and state: what was further required in order for this mission to be a success was that the eyes of the world be kept fixed upon it in rapt attention. If the rest of the world, or at least of Protestantism, looked elsewhere, or turned to another model, or simply got distracted and forgot about New England, if the new land was left with a polity nobody in the great world of Europe wanted—then every success in fulfilling the terms of the covenant would become a diabolical measure of failure. . . .

If an actor, playing the leading role in the greatest dramatic spectacle of the century, were to attire himself and put on his make-up, rehearse his lines, take a deep breath, and stride onto the stage, only to find the theater dark and empty, no spotlight working, and himself entirely alone, he would feel as did New England around 1650 or 1660. For in the 1640's, during the Civil Wars, the colonies, so to speak, lost their audience. . . .

In other words, New England did not lie, did not falter; it made good everything Winthrop demanded—wonderfully good—and then found that its lesson was rejected by those choice spirits for whom the exertion had been made. By casting out Williams, Anne Hutchinson, and the Antinomians, along with an assortment of Gortonists and Anabaptists, into that cesspool then becoming known as Rhode Island, Winthrop, Dudley, and the clerical leaders showed Oliver Cromwell how he should go about governing England. Instead, he developed the utterly absurd theory that so long as a man made a good soldier in the New Model Army, it did not matter whether he was a Calvinist, an Antinomian, an Arminian, an Anabaptist or even— horror of horrors—a Socinian! . . .

The most humiliating element in the experience was the way the English brethren turned upon the colonials for precisely their greatest achievement. It must have seemed, for those who came with Winthrop in 1630 and who remembered the clarity and brilliance with which he set forth the conditions of their errand, that the world was turned upside down and inside out when, in June 1645, thirteen leading Independent divines—such men as Goodwin, Owen, Nye, Burroughs, formerly friends and allies of Hooker and Davenport, men who might easily have come to New England and helped extirpate heretics—wrote the General Court that the colony's law banishing Anabaptists was an embarrassment to the Independent cause in England. . . . Out of the New Model Army came the fantastic notion that a party struggling for power should proclaim that, once it captured the state, it would recognize the right of dissenters to disagree and to have their own worship, to hold their own opinions. Oliver Cromwell was so far gone in this idiocy as to become a dictator, in order to impose toleration by force! Amid this shambles, the errand of New England collapsed. There was nobody left at headquarters to whom reports could be sent.

Many a man has done a brave deed, been hailed as a public hero, had honors and ticker tape heaped upon him—and then had to live, day after day, in the ordinary routine, eating breakfast and brushing his teeth, in what seems protracted anticlimax. . . . This sense of the meaning having gone out of life, that all adventures are over, that no great days and no heroism lie ahead, is particularly galling when it falls upon a son whose father once was the public hero or the great lover. He has to put up with the daily routine without ever having known at first hand the thrill of danger or the ecstasy of passion. True, he has his own hardships—clearing rocky pastures, hauling in the cod during a storm, fighting Indians in a swamp—but what are these compared with the magnificence of leading an exodus of saints to found a city on a hill, for the eyes of all the world to behold? He might wage a stout fight against the Indians, and one out of ten of his fellows might perish in the struggle, but the world was no longer interested. He would be reduced to writing accounts of himself and scheming to get a publisher in London, in a desperate effort to tell a heedless world, "Look, I exist!"

His greatest difficulty would be not the stones, storms, and Indians, but the problem of his identity. In something of this sort, I should like to suggest, consists the anxiety and torment that inform productions of the late seventeenth and early eighteenth centuries. . . .

The literature of self-condemnation must be read for meanings far below the surface, for meanings of which, we may be so rash as to surmise, the authors were not fully conscious, but by which they were troubled and goaded. They looked in vain to history for an explanation of themselves; more and more it appeared that the meaning was not to be found in theology, even with the help of the covenantal dialectic. Thereupon, these citizens found that they had no other place to search but within themselves—even though, at first sight, that repository appeared to be nothing but a sink of iniquity. Their errand having failed in the first sense of the term, they were left with the second, and required to fill it with meaning by themselves and out of themselves. Having failed to rivet the eyes of the world upon their city on the hill, they were left alone with America.

Anglicans in Virginia

EDWARD L. BOND

William Fitzhugh, an attorney and tobacco planter in Stafford County, reflected briefly in January 1686/7 on the difficulties of life in the Virginia colony. Education for children was hard to come by. Financial security rested upon too many contingencies and forced Fitzhugh to devote more time to worldly affairs than he thought proper. With the exception of that found in books, "good & ingenious" society was scarce. "[B]ut that which bears the greatest weight with me," he wrote, " . . . is the want of spirituall help & comforts, of which this fertile Country in every thing else, is barren and unfruitfull."

Edward L. Bond, "Anglican Theology and Devotion in James Blair's Virginia, 1685–1743: Private Piety in the Public Church," *The Virginia Magazine of History and Biography* 104 (Summer 1996): 313–340.

Complaints similar to Fitzhugh's were common throughout the seventeenth and eighteenth centuries. As early as 1611 the Reverend Alexander Whitaker had expressed concerns that would linger for more than a hundred years: "Our harvest is froward and great for want" of ministers. Conditions improved slowly. In 1662 a former colonial minister estimated that nearly 80 percent of the colony's parishes lay vacant. No more than ten or twelve ministers served a population approaching 26,000. Three decades later, in 1697, only twenty-two of Virginia's fifty parishes had ministers, and that for a population of approximately 62,800 souls. Not until the 1730s did an adequate supply of clergymen fill Virginia's churches.

Yet had ministers filled every vacant parish in the colony, the church's work still would have suffered, only to a lesser degree. The Church of England's mission in Virginia was hampered not only by a shortage of clergy but also by the colony's environment. Virginians learned early that their land's promise lay in tobacco. Consequently, they did not settle in towns as did inhabitants of England or its other colonies. Instead, they scattered across the countryside, often settling along one of the rivers that divided the Tidewater and Piedmont regions into a series of penin-sulas. This settlement pattern—essentially an accommodation to tobacco culture—hindered the public practice of religion. Parishes in Virginia were very large, and most contained more than one church. Colonial parsons served each on a rotating basis by officiating and preaching first at one church and then at the others in their turn on succeeding Sabbaths.

. . . Anglicanism in . . . Virginia was primarily a pastoral religion, concerned with the spiritual care and guidance of individuals rather than with theological polemic, intellectual debate, or a "prying into adorable Mysteries" beyond com-prehension by the human mind. Like Puritanism, Anglicanism addressed the devo-tional life, which for members of the Church of England meant a life that began in faith, proceeded through repentance and amendment of life, and culminated with the "sure and certain hope" of a glorious resurrection on the last day. The church's liturgy, ministers' sermons, the sacraments, devotional materials, and events in the natural world all helped create a general orientation pointing the faithful in the direc-tion of God, while leaving the essential work of salvation in the hands of individuals who would work out their own "with fear and trembling."

Virginians often spoke of this process as a pilgrimage or a voyage to Heaven. "Before I was ten years old," William Fitzhugh confessed to his mother, "I look'd upon this life here as but going to an Inn, no permanent being." By the late seven-teenth century, the pilgrimage motif was a well-known form of portraying the soul's journey to God. The Anglican notion of the journey, however, possessed its own dis-tinct qualities that emphasized neither the terrors of the wilderness typical of Puritan writers nor the mystical union with God common among Roman Catholic authors. Theirs was a low-key piety, deeply felt and involving the "whole individual" but given to order rather than to passion or ecstasy. Extremes harmed the spiritual life. John Page, for instance, warned his son against the emotional excesses of presump-tion and despair—those "two destructive rocks, upon either of which, if the ship of the soul dash, it is split in pieces"—as a missing of the religious life's golden mean. One deceived men and women into vain hopes of mercy; the other tormented them with "hellish fears of justice." Together they threatened both halves of the spiritual life. "Presumption," Page warned, "is an enemy to repentance, and despair to faith."

As Page's allusion suggests, Virginians often described their spiritual journeys through the metaphor of a ship at sea returning to its home port, a particularly evocative image for anyone who had survived an Atlantic crossing. James Blair [an Anglican minister] turned the metaphor into an analogy. He compared Christians to a well-disciplined ship's crew attending to its duties, "[s]uch as stopping the Leaks, mending the Sails, . . . preparing the Guns to make a Defence against an Enemy; and especially the keeping of a good Reckoning, and looking out sharp to avoid Shelves, and Rocks, and Quicksands, and all other Dangers both attending the Voyage at Sea, and the Piloting right into Harbour."

When Blair compared the spiritual journey to sailors going about their usual tasks of keeping the ship in order and bringing it to its intended destination, he captured the essence of the Anglican's movement to God. It was part of an individual's daily work, striking only in its ordinariness. People expected sailors to repair leaks, make preparations for enemy assaults, guide the vessel to port, and watch for shallow waters to prevent the ship from running aground. These were tasks common to the lives of seafaring men. For sailors to have neglected these chores would have been extraordinary. And this was perhaps the most distinctive quality of Anglican religion in colonial Virginia. It seemed unexceptional, a matter of performing the routine and habitual duties that naturally accompanied an individual's vocation. Religion was less something individuals believed than something they did, a practice rather than a set of propositions. . . . Virginians, then, thought mere belief in religious dogma denoted an insufficient faith. The mark of a good Christian was neither right doctrine nor a command of theological subtleties, but a life adorned with good morals. John Page's words to his son were typical: "A good life is inseparable from a good faith—yea, a good faith is a good life." Ministers occasionally maintained that the Sermon on the Mount with its teachings on behavior contained everything necessary for salvation.

Anglicans in Virginia conceived of religion as a form of duty, and this idea guided the way in which they ordered their relationships with God. Sometimes, as when James Blair preached that "Good Morality is Good Christianity," they simply equated religion with virtue, often in simplistic terms that could be misleading to people who did not share their understanding of religion. When Virginians referred to religion in this way, they meant more than performance of moral duties or some rationalist incarnation of virtue. Duty was a necessary facet of the Anglican believer's journey to Heaven, a response to God undertaken in faith. Had there been no God, there would have been no reason to attempt to control one's passions, to confess one's sins, or to marvel at God's "wise and mercifull Providence." But God did exist. He was merciful and good, and He had sent "Christ into the World to bring us to Heaven." The proper and natural response to God's loving action was obedience, for Virginians believed obedience was "perfective of our Natures." Duty, then, understood as a well-ordered life of prayer and obedience to God's laws, was the high mark of a person's earthly pilgrimage, the restoration of human nature as far as that was possible on earth. To live such a life, like the sailor who did his duty in Blair's analogy, was natural and what God expected.

Since Adam's fall, however, men and women had been incapable of the obedience God demanded. Virginians realized they were sinners and that more often than not their wicked ways fell short of a holy life. Yet they could comfort themselves with the knowledge that, despite their faults, God was merciful and did not want His creatures to suffer eternal damnation. For this reason He had sent His Son, Jesus Christ, into the world as a propitiation for the sins of mankind. Christ's death had pacified God's wrath toward humanity and granted "a title to eternal life" to all who accepted the Gospel's terms. God offered the promise of eternal life to the whole world, not just to a select few whom He had predestined for Heaven. John Page, a royalist who had emigrated to the colony during the English Civil War, offered one of the most powerful illustrations of this belief. Christ, the mediator between God and man, was born not in a "private house, but [at] an inn, which is open for all passengers," and in the "commonest place," a stable. Likewise, the Savior's crucifixion had not taken place within the city walls, "but without the gate, to intimate that it was not an Altar of the Temple, but the world." . . .

Virginians . . . focused their attention on the pastoral task of preventing the faithful from committing spiritual suicide by failing to repent and amend. Ministers preached of this duty, devotional literature recommended it, parents introduced their children to this truth by teaching them the church catechism, and condemned criminals urged the crowds gathered to witness their executions to "repent now, and continue repenting so long as you have an hour to live." In 1678 one young indentured servant who had been sentenced to death for murdering his master and mistress admonished onlookers in Charles City County to make their "Election sure" by forsaking their wicked paths. "Leave off sinning," he warned, "else God will leave you off." God also took part in the pastoral work of calling Virginians to repent by periodically sending epidemics and plagues of insects upon the colony to remind the settlers that they were sinners who needed to amend their lives. . . .

Repentance represented the essential reorientation of an individual's life. Despite the necessity of an amended life as evidence and the emphasis ministers placed on outward behavior, the process of repentance more accurately described an internal change within the believer's heart or mind . . . , which then resulted in a life that increasingly conformed to God's laws. "[T]he inner Man of the Heart, is the chief Thing that God aims to govern," preached Blair, for "like the main spring in a clock, the heart animates and directs all a person's thoughts and motions. As this main Spring of the Heart goes, the Man thinks, contrives, speaks and acts." Virginians often used the pilgrimage motif to express this shift in direction. Blair suggested that the disposition of the heart determined the port toward which a person sailed.

The heart's love also dictated the object that impressed itself upon the eyes. "*Heavenly Treasures* are fitted for our Heaven-born Souls," Blair told his Bruton Parish congregation, thereby noting man's natural end. "The more good we do with an Eye to Heaven, the more heavenly minded shall we prove, and the more directly shall we steer our Course to Heaven." What individuals saw or placed before their eyes was important to colonial Virginians, because they believed that sight conveyed knowledge more immediately than the elusive medium of sound. George Keith spoke for many in the colony when he observed that without frequent repetition, spoken words were "as soon forgot as heard, for most part." To set God before one's eyes was indicative both of a well-ordered heart and of one's embarkation on the path leading to Heaven. Felony indictments often illustrated this point in a negative way by citing the generally accepted explanation for the defendants' crimes: the malefactors were described as "not haveing the feare of God before thine eyes but being moved by the instigation of the devill." Lacking the proper orientation, men and women strayed from the precepts contained in the Gospels. They threatened their own salvation and disrupted the polity through acts such as theft, murder, and suicide. Robert Paxton urged his parishioners to follow a different course: "This therfor is an essential part of our relign, to set God always befor our eyes as the great pattern of our lives & actns." So oriented, obedience to God's laws provided evidence of a person's faith.

An active, sincere, and regular devotional life was the key to what Virginians called "evangelical obedience." Prayer and spiritual discipline could turn nominal Christians—those who were "Christian" by virtue of their Englishness—into professing Christians, or people who had made a conscious decision to make their lives a pilgrimage to God. George Keith employed nautical imagery to explain the importance of the devotional life. He compared the Bible to a compass and Christ's life to a map that could guide the faithful on their voyages. Prayer entreated God to send the winds of divine influence to fill the sails of human affections. The devotional life shaped the moral life and thus served as the link among faith and repentance and salvation.

In public as well as in private, the Book of Common Prayer was the single greatest influence shaping Virginians' devotional lives. Next to the Bible, it was the most common volume in the colonists' libraries. Its liturgy repeated weekly at public worship and read each day privately by many individuals provided a constant source of structure for the spiritual life. The Apostles' Creed and the Lord's Prayer were repeated at each office, and in the appointed lessons the Bible was read through every year. The liturgy in fact echoed the Bible; many of its prayers were crafted from the words of Holy Scripture. Day after day, week after week, it gave voice to the same themes in the same words that called the faithful to repentance at every service and offered them the means of grace. By repeating the same words at each service and by using the same forms, the set liturgies of the Book of Common Prayer were intended to work a gradual transformation in the lives of individuals. Thus, to describe Anglican worship (as some recent historians have) as "predictable and boring" misses the point because in effect it defines the Anglican approach to religion from an evangelical perspective. Unlike evangelicals and Nonconformists, Anglicans placed little emphasis on conversion, and their style of worship reflected this difference. Both as a devotional work and as a service book, the Book of Common Prayer aimed less at conversion than at helping the presumably converted maintain and deepen their faith. . . .

. . . By opening their minds to the words they heard, they allowed the liturgy to bring their affections into the right frame and temper. Repeatedly using the same set, brief forms encouraged this process and allowed the faithful to "recollect" their prayers, or, in [the Rev. William] Beveridge's words, to "look over our Prayers again, either in a Book, or in our Minds, where they are imprinted." Over time, spoken prayers thus gained the epistemological immediacy of sight. . . .

Devotional life played an important part in shaping a holy life, and Virginians did not restrict their spiritual regimen to the public liturgy and the sacred space of the parish church. They never viewed public worship as an end in itself and did not believe God could be approached only in the church building or through the set forms of the Book of Common Prayer. Nor did they believe public worship was necessarily the most important part of the spiritual journey. Unlike English divines, who treated private devotions as a form of preparation for the church's public worship, ministers in Virginia reversed this sequence. They placed greater emphasis on private devotions than on public and communal prayer. . . .

The emphasis Virginia's ministers placed on private prayer likely reflected the necessity imposed on Anglicans by the colony's [lack of ministers]. If the public worship of the church was to be the focal point for the piety of the faithful, the church had to provide regular opportunities for the devotion it encouraged. But relatively few ministers served Virginia's church, the Lord's Supper was usually celebrated just three or four times each year, and divine service was held only on Sundays, a practice ministers new to the colony sometimes complained about. Clergy tried to accommodate themselves to these circumstances as best they could and so often acted more like missionaries than settled ministers. Given their sporadic contact with the laity, necessitated by the colony's large parishes, ministers encouraged the faithful to make use of the means of grace in private. Most sermons preached in colonial Virginia, in fact, were how-to discourses on repentance urging the duty of private prayer and explaining its necessity. . . .

Not surprisingly, Anglicans in Virginia practiced much of their piety at home. Reading the Bible or other religious books, self-examination, and secret prayer all directed the faithful toward God. These exercises were designed to help Virginians forge spiritual resolutions and then to act upon them, to order their lives in keeping with the divine pattern. Bible reading was widely encouraged. John Page urged his son to read the Scriptures frequently and offered him the counsel of St. Ambrose: "Eat, and eat daily of this heavenly manna." The Scriptures provided "exact maps of the heavenly Canaan, drawn by the pen of the Holy Ghost." . . .

In addition to the Bible, Virginians turned to a variety of other religious works to guide their devotions. Philip Ludwell, Sr., kept a "poor little old [prayer] book" worn from use in his closet to help order his private spiritual exercises. Another colonist believed that for family or private devotions one "cannot make a better choice than of the church prayers." . . . These works advocated what came to be called "holy living," and like the Bible, they urged Virginians to imitate Christ. The colonists were likely as practical in their purchase of books as in their theology. Books were bought in order to be used. And apparently they were. In 1702 a group of Quakers in Chuckatuck complained that the Anglican practice of distributing devotional manuals hurt their own efforts to attract converts.

Family prayers, too, formed part of the Anglican spiritual regimen. Virginia's ministers recommended this exercise, as did the English clergy, especially for those people who were unable to attend public worship regularly. John Page urged his son to take up the practice of family devotions, not only as a means of grace but also as an example to his children. . . .

. . . By meditating on God's goodness, His providences, or His mercy in sending Jesus Christ to redeem mankind, men and women focused their eyes on the deity and thus oriented themselves for the journey to Heaven. These exercises brought the faithful *"Face to Face"* with God. So, too, did their daily observations of the natural world. Nature fascinated Virginians. It created within them a feeling of wonder that both frightened them and attracted them to the Creator. A great storm, the beauty of a flower, or the power of the sea that separated them from England all inspired this emotion, what one European philosopher called "a sudden surprise of the soul." Governor John Page remembered of the botanist John Clayton: "I have heard him say, whilst examining a flower, that he could not look into one, without seeing the display of infinite power and contrivance, and thus he thought it impossible for a BOTANIST to be an ATHEIST." The "most Dreadfull Hurry Cane" that struck Virginia in 1667 inspired a similar response. Councilor Thomas Ludwell believed "all the Elements were at Strife," contending to see "wch of them should doe most towards the reduction of the creation into a Second Chaos, it was wonderfull to consider the contrary effects of that Storme." Other colonists embraced illnesses, bad weather, and plagues of insects as calls to repentance. Understood properly, the entire world pointed toward God. . . .

Like other Christian theologies, Anglicanism in late seventeenth- and early eighteenth-century Virginia tried to assist the faithful along the path to Heaven. Although Anglican piety addressed the whole person by cultivating what James Blair called "the practice of the divine presence," Virginians demonstrated their piety most vividly through external behaviors. . . . Doing one's duty was a statement of faith and the product of a sincere devotional life. Unlike many Nonconformists, Anglicans did not seek in their earthly pilgrimages a mystical union with Christ, the "Bridegroom of the soul." Rather, they thought of Christ as a teacher of virtue, and with the assistance of God's grace they endeavored to imitate the divine pattern. William Byrd II could therefore define blasphemy as living a life of "Disorder." By so living, "instead of blessing his name, we are blaspheming it, & blotting out his Image in our Souls." . . .

The performance of devotional duties not only helped an individual grow in grace but also helped to establish a religious identity. This assumption of an identity had always been true of those who took on the disciplines of family and secret prayer, but by the end of the century it was becoming true of regular church attendance as well. In 1699 the House of Burgesses reduced the legal requirement for church attendance to once every two months. . . .

The colony's "occasions" had forced Virginians to adapt their devotional practices, not to abandon them. For those who wished to make use of them, the means of grace still existed. Virginia's ministers realized their church's problems, and pragmatic clergymen actively encouraged forms of prayer that potentially threatened the centrality of the institutional church. Despite the church's difficulties, the faithful were able to practice their piety and to continue their pilgrimage to Heaven. And although William Fitzhugh worried about the lack of "spirituall help & comfort" in Virginia, he also knew that a person could further her spiritual pilgrimage in the colony, even if the spiritual helps were not as readily available as some colonists may have wished. He wrote his mother in 1698 to thank her for the gift of her "choice Bible." Urging her to face a present illness with Christian patience and to see God's hand in it, he reported that his sister, who also lived in Virginia, had "died a true penitent of the Church of Engld."

Not only did the Anglicanism of James Blair's Virginia allow the faithful to continue their pilgrimages to Heaven, but it also created a mentality that helped to shape the colony's future. Although the private practice of piety that the colony's established church encouraged made it possible for Anglicans to adapt their devotional lives to a "novel environment," this emphasis carried with it a potential challenge to Virginia's institutional church. . . . That groups would eventually break away from the church . . . reflected less a disruption than an evolution of the colony's traditional approach to religion.

✎ *F U R T H E R   R E A D I N G*

Benes, Peter, and Philip D. Zimmerman. *New England Meeting House and Church, 1630–1850* (1979).

Boyer, Paul, and Stephen Nissenbaum. *Salem Possessed: The Social Origins of Witchcraft* (1974).

Breen, T. H. *Puritans and Adventurers: Change and Persistence in Early America* (1980).

Brown, Kathleen. *Good Wives, Nasty Wenches, and Anxious Patriarchs: Gender, Race, and Power in Colonial Virginia* (1996).

Davis, Vernon Perdue. *The Colonial Churches of Virginia* (1985).

Demos, John. *Entertaining Satan: Witchcraft and the Culture of Early New England* (1982).

Fogarty, Gerald. *Catholics in Colonial Virginia* (1993).

Gaustad, Edwin. *Liberty of Conscience: Roger Williams in America* (1991).

Hall, David. *The Faithful Shepherd: History of the New England Ministry in the Seventeenth Century* (1972).

———. *The Antinomian Controversy, 1636–1638* (1968).

Hambrick-Stowe, Charles. *The Practice of Piety: Puritan Devotional Discipline in Seventeenth Century New England* (1982).

———, ed. *Early New England Meditative Poetry: Anne Bradstreet and Edward Taylor* (1988).

Knight, Janice. *Orthodoxies in Massachusetts: Rereading American Puritanism* (1994).

Miller, Perry. *The New England Mind: The Seventeenth Century* (1939).

———. *Roger Williams* (1953).

Miller, Perry, and Thomas H. Johnson. *The Puritans: A Sourcebook of Their Writings* (1963).

Morgan, Edmund. *Visible Saints: The History of a Puritan Idea* (1963).

———. *The Puritan Dilemma: The Story of John Winthrop* (1958).

Morgan, John. *Godly Learning: Puritan Attitudes Towards Reason, Learning, and Education, 1560–1640* (1986).

Pilcher, George W. *Samuel Davies: Apostle of Dissent in Colonial Virginia* (1971).

Reis, Elizabeth. *Damned Women: Sinners and Witches in Puritan New England* (1997).

———, ed. *Spellbound: Women and Witchcraft in America* (1998).

Staloff, Darren. *The Making of an American Thinking Class* (1988).

Stout, Harry. *The New England Soul: Preaching and Religious Culture in Colonial New England* (1986).

Tolles, Frederick. *Meeting House and Counting House: The Quaker Merchants of Colonial Philadelphia, 1682–1763* (1948).

CHAPTER
4

Awakening and Revolution:

1730–1790

The Great Awakening was a series of religious revivals in the 1730s and 1740s, in which thousands of American colonists experienced dramatic emotional conversions to evangelical Christianity. Although scattered at first, it gained momentum with the arrival of George Whitefield from England in 1739. Colonists went miles to hear Whitefield, a charismatic twenty-six-year-old preacher who traveled throughout the Atlantic coast colonies and led open-air worship services. He galvanized religious energies and became probably the most widely known and popular man in America. His emotional style made him a religious hero to thousands, but not to all. Some influential ministers saw him as a potential threat to good order and to the colonies' established churches. Church divisions ensued. Among Presbyterians, for example, the "New Side" supported Whitefield, whereas the older, more conservative "Old Side" disliked his mobile and impassioned methods.

Another trend of eighteenth-century religion was the rational Enlightenment, embodied in the outlook of Benjamin Franklin and, later, of Thomas Jefferson. Tending to dismiss the fantastic tales and "special providences" of the previous century, Enlightenment figures saw God's work more in his maintenance of the regular laws of science than in his suspension of them and emphasized the virtues of charity and generosity. Opposed to the religious intolerance of their grandfathers, they played an influential role in the American Revolutionary War, which began in 1775.

The war itself presented troubling questions to American Christians. Unsettled political conditions, warfare, and social upheaval encouraged the creation of numerous new sects. Revolutionaries believed that in fighting against Britain they were doing God's will, and that the war's suffering constituted His punishment of their sins. Loyalists, by contrast, pointed out that Jesus was not a revolutionary and that he, like the apostles of the early church, had advised Christians to accept the rule of their governments, even if they were at times oppressive. A third position was taken by Quakers, who refused to fight for either side and, in consequence, were suspected of disloyalty by both. As the war continued, many Americans interpreted it in light of the prophetic books of Daniel and Revelation and saw it as evidence of the coming millennium.

*The war's end with the Treaty of Paris (1783) guaranteed American indepen-
dence. Thomas Jefferson, who had drafted the Declaration of Independence and
later became president, regarded his achievement of religious liberty in Virginia
(1786) as his greatest accomplishment (see Document 9).*

*Historians have long been interested in the links between the Great Awaken-
ing and the Revolution. Was the Great Awakening the event that turned Puritans
into Yankees and gave them the sense of independence to challenge not only their
religious traditions but their political leaders, too? Few would put it as baldly as
that, but it is reasonable to believe that the intensified religious life of the British
colonies in mid-century, and the schisms it provoked, obliged Americans to make
difficult choices and to begin thinking about the issues of law, authority, obedience,
and self-assertion.*

 D O C U M E N T S

In Document 1 (1738) Jonathan Edwards of Northampton, Massachusetts, the most
eloquent and learned of America's eighteenth-century Protestant ministers, describes the
moral reformation among the young people of his parish, as they turned from "frolics" to
religion. In Document 2 (1765) Connecticut farmer Nathan Cole recalls the feverish excitement with which he and his wife rode to hear one of George Whitefield's outdoor sermons
in 1741 and how the event led to his being "born again" after a period of spiritual tribulation. Document 3, an elegy at Whitefield's death (1770) was written by Phillis Wheatley,
the first black woman and slave to publish a book in America. Document 4 (1756) is a letter
from scientist, publisher, inventor, and polymath Benjamin Franklin to a friend, explaining
his worldly religious views and reproaching religious intolerance among others.

The second group of documents in this chapter is taken from the Revolutionary era.
In Document 5 (1776), Scottish immigrant and Presbyterian professor John Witherspoon
defends the Revolution as a godly cause, using close biblical and logical reasoning. The
Anglican priest Jonathan Boucher, by contrast (1775), makes the anti-Revolutionary or
Loyalist case with equal scriptural rigor in Document 6. Quakers Anthony Benezet (1776)
and Isaac Jackson (1777), who refused to fight on either side, explain why God supports
their attitude to the war and complain that they are being unjustly persecuted for their
principles in Documents 7 and 8. In Document 9 (1786), Thomas Jefferson explains that
God Himself is a defender of the principle of religious liberty, which will now be extended
to all the people of Virginia.

1. Jonathan Edwards Describes the Great Awakening
in Northampton, Massachusetts, 1738

Just after my Grandfather's Death, it seemed to be a time of extraordinary *Dulness*
in Religion: *Licentiousness* for some Years greatly prevailed among the *Youth* of
the Town; they were many of them very much addicted to *Nightwalking,* and fre-
quenting the *Tavern,* and *leud* Practices, wherein some, by their Example exceedingly corrupted others. It was their Manner very frequently to get together, in

A Faithful Narrative of the Surprising Work of God (Boston: S. Kneeland, 1738).

Conventions of both *Sexes,* for Mirth and Jollity, which they called *Frolicks;* and they would often spend the greater part of the *Night* in them, without regard to any *Order* in the Families they belonged to: and indeed *Family-Government* did too much fail in the Town. It was become very customary with many of our young People, to be *Indecent* in their Carriage at *Meeting,* which doubtless, would not have prevailed to such a degree, had it not been that my *Grandfather,* through his *great Age,* (tho' he retained his *Powers* surprizingly to the *last*) was not so able to *Observe* them. . . .

But in *two* or *three* Years after Mr. *Stoddard's* Death, there began to be a sensible Amendment of these Evils; the *young People* shew'd more of a Disposition to hearken to Counsel, and by degrees left off their *Frolicking,* and grew observably more *Decent* in their Attendance on the publick Worship, and there were more that manifested a *Religious Concern* than there used to be.

At the latter end of the Year 1733, there appeared a very unusual flexibleness, and yielding to Advice, in our young People. It had been too long their manner to make the *Evening after the Sabbath,* and after our publick *Lecture,* to be especially the Times of their *Mirth,* and Company keeping. But a *Sermon* was now preached on the Sabbath before the *Lecture,* to shew the *Evil Tendency* of the Practice, and to persuade them to reform it; and it was urged on *Heads* of *Families,* that it should be a thing *agreed* upon among them to govern their Families, and keep their Children at home, at these times; and withal it was more *privately* moved, that they should meet together, the next Day, in their several Neighbourhoods, to know each other's Minds: which was accordingly done, and the *Motion* complied with throughout the Town. But *Parents* found little, or no occasion for the exercise of Government in the Case: the *young People* declared themselves *convinced* by what they had heard from the *Pulpit,* and were willing of themselves to comply with the Counsel that had been given: and it was *immediately,* and, I suppose, almost *universally* complied with; and there was a thorough *Reformation* of these Disorders thenceforward, which has continued ever since.

Presently after this, there began to appear a *remarkable Religious Concern* at a little *Village,* belonging to the Congregation, call'd *Pascommuck,* where a few Families were settled, at about *three Miles* distance from the main Body of the Town. At this place, a number of Persons seemed to be savingly wrought upon. In the *April* following, *Anno* 1734, there happen'd a very *sudden and awful Death of a young Man,* in the Bloom of his Youth; who being violently seized with a *Pleurisy,* and taken immediately very *delirious,* died in about *two Days;* which (together with what was preached publickly on that Occasion) much *affected* many young People. This was followed with another Death of a young married *Woman,* who had been considerably *exercised* in Mind, about the Salvation of her *Soul,* before she was ill, and was in great *Distress,* in the beginning of her Illness; but seemed to have satisfying *Evidences* of God's saving *Mercy* to her, before her Death; so that she died very full of *Comfort,* in a most earnest and moving Manner *warning,* and counselling others. This seem'd much to *contribute* to the solemnizing of the Spirits of many young Persons: and there began evidently to appear more of a *Religious Concern* on People's Minds. . . .

. . . And *then* it was, in the latter part of *December, that the spirit of God* began extraordinarily to set in, and *wonderfully* to work amongst us; and there were, very *suddenly,* one after another, five or six Persons, who were to all appearance savingly converted, and some of them wrought upon in a very remarkable manner.

Particularly, I was surprized with the relation of a young *Woman,* who had been one of the greatest Company-Keepers in the whole Town: When she came to me, I had never heard that she was become in any wise serious, but by the Conversation I then had with her, it appeared to me, that what she gave an account of, was a glorious Work of God's infinite Power and sovereign Grace; and that God had given her a *new* Heart, truly broken and sanctified. I could not then doubt of it, and have seen much in my Acquaintance with her since to confirm it.

Tho' the Work was glorious, yet I was filled with concern about the *Effect* it might have upon others: I was ready to concinde [concede] (tho' too rashly) that some would be *harden'd* by it, in carelessness and looseness of Life; and would take occasion from it to open their Mouths, in *Reproaches* of Religion. But the Event was the *Reverse,* to a wonderful degree; God made it, I suppose, the *greatest occasion* of awakening to others of any thing that ever came to pass in the Town. I have had abundant Opportunity to know the Effect it had, by my private Conversation with many. The news of it seemed to be almost like a *flash of Lightning,* upon the Hearts of young People, all over the Town, and upon many others. Those Persons amongst us, who used to be *farthest* from seriousness, and that I most feared would make an ill Improvement of it, seemed greatly to be *awakened* with it; many went to talk with her, concerning what she had met with; and what appeared in her seemed to be to the Satisfaction of all that did so. . . .

But altho' People did not ordinarily neglect their worldly Business; yet there then was the Reverse of what commonly is: *Religion* was with all sorts the great Concern, and the *World* was a thing only by the Bye. The only Thing in their view was to get the Kingdom of Heaven, and every one appeared pressing into it: The Engagedness of their Hearts in this great Concern cou'd not *be hid,* it appear'd in their very *Countenances.* It then was a dreadful Thing amongst us to lie out of Christ, in danger every day of dropping into Hell; and what Persons minds were intent upon was to *escape for their Lives,* and to *fly from the Wrath to come.* All would eagerly lay hold of Opportunities for their Souls; and were wont very often to meet together in private Houses for religious Purposes: And such Meetings when appointed were wont greatly to be thronged.

There was scarcely a single Person in the Town, either old or young, that was left unconcerned about the great Things of the eternal World. Those that were wont to be the vainest, and loosest, and those that had been most disposed to think, and speak slightly of vital and experimental Religion, were now generally subject to great awakenings. And the Work of *Conversion* was carried on in a most *astonishing* manner, and increased more and more; Souls did as it were come by Flocks to Jesus Christ. From Day to Day, for many Months together, might be seen evident Instances of Sinners brought *out of Darkness into marvellous Light,* and delivered *out of an horrible Pit, and from the miry Clay, and set upon a Rock,* with a *new Song of Praise to God in their mouths.*

This Work of God, as it was carried on, and the Number of true Saints multiplied, soon made a glorious Alteration in the Town; so that in the Spring and Summer following, *Anno* 1735. the Town seemed to be full of the Presence of God: It never was so full of *Love,* nor so full of *Joy;* and yet so full of Distress as it was then. There were remarkable Tokens of God's Presence in almost every House. It was a time of Joy in *Families* on the account of Salvation's being brought unto them; *Parents* rejoicing over their Children as new born, and *Husbands* over their Wives, and *Wives* over their Husbands. *The goings of God* were then *seen in his Sanctuary,* God's *Day* was *a delight,* and his *Tabernacles* were *amiable.* Our publick *Assemblies* were then beautiful; the Congregation was *alive* in God's Service, every one earnestly intent on the Publick Worship, every *Hearer* eager to drink in the Words of the *Minister* as they came from his Mouth; the Assembly in general were from time to time *in Tears* while the Word was preached; *some* weeping with Sorrow and Distress, *others* with Joy and Love, *others* with Pity and Concern for the Souls of their Neighbours.

Our publick *praises* were then greatly enliven'd; God was then served in our *Psalmody,* in some measure, in the *Beauty of Holiness.*

2. Nathan Cole, Connecticut Farmer, Hears the Preaching of George Whitefield and Is Born Again (1741), 1765

I was born Feb 15th 1711 and born again octo 1741—

When I was young I had very early Convictions; but after I grew up I was an Arminian untill I was *near* 30 years of age; I intended to be saved by my own works such as prayers and good deeds.

[George Whitefield at Middletown]

Now it pleased God to send Mr Whitefield into this land; and my hearing of his preaching at Philadelphia, like one of the Old apostles, and many thousands flocking to hear him preach the Gospel; and great numbers were converted to Christ; I felt the Spirit of God drawing me by conviction; I longed to see and hear him, and wished he would come this way. I heard he was come to New York and the Jerseys and great multitudes flocking after him under great concern for their Souls which brought on my Concern more and more hoping soon to see him but next I heard he was at long Island; then at Boston and next at Northampton.

Then on a Sudden, in the morning about 8 or 9 of the Clock there came a messenger and said Mr Whitefield preached at Hartford and Weathersfield yesterday and is to preach at Middletown this morning at ten of the Clock, I was in my field at Work, I dropt my tool that I had in my hand and ran home to my wife telling her to make ready quickly to go and hear Mr Whitefield preach at Middletown, then run to my pasture for my horse with all my might; fearing that I should be too late; having my horse I with my wife soon mounted the horse and went forward as fast as I thought the horse could bear, and when my horse got *much* out of breath I would get down and put my wife on the Saddle and bid her ride as fast as she could and not Stop or Slack for me except I bad her and so I would run untill I was *much* out of breath; and then mount my horse again, and so I did several times to favour my horse; we improved every moment to get along as if we were fleeing for our lives; all the while

---

"The Spiritual Travels of Nathan Cole" (1740–1765), *William and Mary Quarterly* 33 (January 1976): 89–126.

fearing we should be too late to hear the Sermon, for we had twelve miles to ride double in little more than an hour and we went round by the upper housen parish.

And when we came within about half a mile or a mile of the Road that comes down from Hartford weathersfield and Stepney to Middletown; on high land I saw before me a Cloud or fogg rising; I first thought it came from the great River, but as I came nearer the Road, I heard a noise something like a low rumbling thunder and presently found it was the noise of Horses feet coming down the Road and this Cloud was a Cloud of dust made by the Horses feet; it arose some Rods into the air over the tops of Hills and trees and when I came within about 20 *rods* of the Road, I could see men and horses Sliping along in the Cloud like shadows and as I drew nearer it seemed like a steady Stream of horses and their riders, scarcely a horse more than his length behind another, all of a Lather and foam with sweat, their breath rolling out of their nostrils every Jump; every horse seemed to go with all his might to carry his rider to hear news from heaven for the saving of Souls, it made me tremble to see the Sight, how the world was in a Struggle; I found a Vacance between two horses to Slip in mine and my Wife said law our Cloaths will be all spoiled see how they look, for they were so Covered with dust, that they looked almost all of a Colour Coats, hats, Shirts, and horses.

We went down in the Stream but heard no man speak a word all the way for 3 miles but every one pressing forward in great haste and when we got to Middletown old meeting house there was a great Multitude *it was said to be 3 or 4000* of people Assembled together; we dismounted and shook of[f] our Dust; and the ministers were then Coming to the meeting house; I turned and looked towards the Great River and saw the ferry boats Running swift backward and forward bringing over loads of people and the Oars Rowed nimble and quick; every thing men horses and boats seemed to be Struggling for life; *The land and banks over the river looked black with people and horses* all along the 12 miles I saw no man at work in his field, but all seemed to be gone.

When I saw Mr Whitefield come upon the Scaffold he Lookt almost angelical; a young, Slim, slender, youth before some thousands of people with a bold undaunted Countenance, and my hearing how God was with him every where as he came along it Solemnized my mind; and put me into a trembling fear before he began to preach; for he looked as if he was Cloathed with authority from the Great God; *and a sweet sollome solemnity sat upon his brow* And my hearing him preach, gave me a heart wound; By Gods blessing; my old Foundation was broken up, and I saw that my righteousness would not save me; then I was convinced of the doctrine of Election: and went right to quarrelling with God about it; because that all I could do would not save me; and he had decreed from Eternity who should be saved and who not.

[Conversion Crisis]

I began to think I was not Elected, and that God made some for heaven and me for hell. And I thought God was not Just in so doing, I thought I did not stand on even Ground with others, if as I thought; I was made to be damned; My heart then rose against God exceedingly, for his making me for hell; Now this distress lasted Almost two years:—Poor—Me—Miserable me.—It pleased God to bring on my Convictions more and more, and I was loaded with the guilt of Sin, I saw I was undone for ever; I carried Such a weight of Sin in my breast or mind, that it seemed to me as if I should sink into the ground every step; and I kept all to my self as much as I could; I went month after month mourning and begging for mercy, I tryed every way I could think to help my self but all ways failed:—Poor me it took away *most* all my Comfort of eating, drinking, Sleeping, or working. Hell fire was most always in my mind; and I have hundreds of times put my fingers into my pipe when I have been smoaking to feel how fire felt: And to see how my Body could bear to lye in Hell fire for ever and ever. Now my countenance was sad so that others took notice of it.

Sometimes I had some secret hope in the mercy of God; that some time or other he would have mercy on me; And so I took some hopes, and thought I would do all that I could do, and remove all things out of the way that might possibly be an hindrance; and I thought I must go to my Honoured Father and Mother and ask their forgiveness for every thing I had done amiss toward them in all my life: if they had any thing against me; I went and when I came near the house one of my Brothers was there, and asked me what was the matter with me: I told him I did not feel well, and passed by; But he followed and asked again what was the matter. I gave him the same answer, but said he something is the matter more than Ordinary for I see it in your Countenance: I refused to tell at present—Poor me—I went to my Father and Mother and told them what I came for: and asked them to forgive me every think [*sic*] they had against me concerning my disobedience or whatso-ever else it might be; they said they had not any thing against me, and both fell aweeping like Children for Joy to see me so concerned for my Soul.

Now when I went away I made great Resolutions that I would forsake every thing that was Sinfull; And do to my uttermost every thing that was good; And at once I felt a calm in my mind, and I had no desire to any thing that was sin as I thought; But here the Devil thought to Catch me on a false hope, for I began to think that I was converted, for I thought I felt a real Change in me. But God in his mercy did not leave me here to perish; but in the space of ten days I was made to see that I was yet in the Gall of bitterness; my Convictions came on again more smart than ever—poor me—Oh then I long'd to be in the Condition of some good Man.

There was then a very Mortal disease in the land, the fever and bloody flux; and I was possest with a notion that if I had it I should die and goe right to hell, but I presently had it and very hard too: then my heart rose against God again for mak-ing me for hell, when he might as well have made me for heaven; or not made me at all:—Poor me—Oh that I could be a Dog or a toad or any Creature but Man: I thought that would be a happy Change for they had no Souls and I had. Oh what will become of me was the language of my mind; for now I was worse than ever, my heart was as hard as a Stone: my Eyes were dry, once I could weep for my Self but now cannot shed one tear; I was as it were in the very mouth of hell. The very flashes of hell fire were in my Mind; Eternity before me, and my time short here. Now when all ways failed me then I longed to be annihilated; or to have my Soul die with my body; but that way failed too. Hell fire hell fire ran Swift in my mind and my distemper grew harder and harder upon me, and my nature was just wore out—Poor me—poor Soul.

One night my brother Elisha came in to see me, and I spake to him and said I should certainly die within two or three days at the out Side for Nature cannot pos-sibly hold it any longer; and I shall certainly goe right to hell: And do you always remember that your poor brother is in hell; don't you never think that I am in heaven but take care of your self and always remember every day that your poor brother is in hell fire.—Misery—Miserable me; my brother got out of his Chair and went to speak to me, but he could not for weeping and went out of the house; and went away home and told my Father and Mother what I had said to him, and they were greatly distressed for me, and thought in the morning they would come and see me; but their distress grew so great for me that they could not stay but Came in the night.

And when they came into the house Mother seem'd to bring heaven into the house; but there was no heaven for me: She said Oh Nathan will you despair of the mercy of God, do not for a thousand of worlds, don't despair of the mercy of God, for he can have mercy at the very last gasp; I told her there was no mercy for me, I was going right down to hell, for I cannot feel grieved for my self, I can't relent, I can't weep for my self, I cannot shed one tear for my Sins; I am a gone Creature: Oh Nathan says she I have been so my self that I could not shed one tear if I might have had all the world for it; And the next moment I could cry as freely for Joy as ever I could for any thing in the world: Oh said she I know how you feel now, O if God should Shine into your Soul now it would almost take away your life, it would almost part soul and body; I beg of you not to despair of the mercy of God. I told her I could not bear to hear her talk so; for I cannot pray, my heart is as hard as a stone, do be gone, let me alone: do go home; you cannot do me any good, I am past all help of men or means, either for soul or Body, and after some time I perswaded them to go away; and there I lay all night in such a Condition until sometime the next day with pining thoughts in my mind that my Soul might die with my Body.

And there came some body in with a great Arm full of dry wood and laid it on the fire, *and went out* and it burnt up very briskly as I lay on my Bed with my face toward the fire looking on, with these thoughts in my mind, Oh that I might creep into that fire and lye there and burn to death and die for ever Soul and Body; Oh that God would suffer it—Oh that God would suffer it.—Poor Soul.

And while these thoughts were in my mind God appeared unto me and made me Skringe: before whose face the heavens and the earth fled away; and I was Shrinked into nothing; I knew not whether I was in the body or out, I seemed to hang in open Air before God, and he seemed to Speak to me in an angry and Sovereign way what won't you trust your Soul with God; My heart answered O yes, yes, yes; before I could stir my tongue or lips, And then He seemed to speak again, and say, may not God make one Vessel to honour and an other to dishonour and not let you know it; My heart answered again O yes yes before I cou'd stir my tongue or lips. Now while my Soul was viewing God, my fleshly part was working imaginations and saw many things which I will omitt to tell at this time.

When God appeared to me every thing vanished and was gone in the twinkling of an Eye, as quick as A flash of lightning; But when God disappeared or in some measure withdrew, every thing was in its place again and I was on my Bed. My heart was broken; my burden was fallen of[f] my mind; I was set free, my distress was gone, and I was filled with a pineing desire to see Christs own words in the bible; and I got up off my bed being alone; And by the help of Chairs I got along to the window where my bible was and I opened it and the first place I saw was the 15th Chap: John—on Christs own words and they spake to my very heart and every doubt and scruple that rose in my heart about the truth of Gods word was took right off; and I saw the whole train of Scriptures all in a Connection, and I believe I felt just as the Apostles felt the truth of the word when they writ it, every leaf line and letter smiled in my face; I got the bible up under my Chin and hugged it; it was sweet and lovely; the word was nigh me in my hand, then I began to pray and to praise God. . . .

Now I had for some years a bitter prejudice against three scornfull men that had wronged me, but now, all that was gone away Clear, and my Soul longed for them and loved them; there was nothing that was sinfull that could any wise abide the presence of God; And all the Air was love, now I saw that every thing that was sin fled from the presence of God: As far as darkness is gone from light or beams of the Sun for where ever the Sun can be seen clear there is no Darkness. I saw that Darkness could as well be in the Clear light of the Sun, as well as Sin in the presence of God; who is so holy and Sovereign.

Now I saw that I must Suffer as well as do for Christ, now I saw that I must forsake all and follow Christ; now I saw with new eyes; all things became new, A new God; new thoughts and new heart; Now I began to hope I should be converted some time or other, for I was sure that God had done some great thing for my soul; I knew that God had subdued my stubborn heart: I knew my heart would never rise so against God as it had done; here I saw in the aforesaid 15th Chap: of John where I opened the bible first that Christ says to his disciples if ye love me keep my Commandments and then says he this is my Commandment that ye love one another. Oh I thought I could die A thousand deaths for Christ, I thought I could have been trodden under foot of man, be mocked or any thing for Christ—Glory be to God.

3. Phillis Wheatley's Elegy at George Whitefield's Death, 1770

HAIL, happy saint, on thine immortal throne,
Possest of glory, life, and bliss unknown;
We hear no more the music of thy tongue;
Thy wonted auditories cease to throng.
Thy sermons in unequall'd accents flow'd,
And ev'ry bosom with devotion glow'd;
Thou didst, in strains of eloquence refin'd,
Inflame the heart, and captivate the mind.
Unhappy we the setting sun deplore,
So glorious once, but ah! it shines no more.

Behold the prophet in his tow'ring flight!
He leaves the earth for heav'n's unmeasur'd height,
And worlds unknown receive him from our sight.
There Whitefield wings with rapid course his way,
And sails to Zion through vast seas of day.
Thy pray'rs, great saint, and thine incessant cries
Have pierc'd the bosom of thy native skies.

"On the Death of the Rev. Mr. George Whitefield, 1790," in Phillis Wheatley, *Poems on Various Subjects, Religious and Moral* (reprinted from the London Edition by Barber and Southwick, for Thomas Spencer, 1793), 20–22.

Thou moon hast seen, and all the stars of light;
How he has wrestled with his GOD by night.
He pray'd that grace in ev'ry heart might dwell,
He long'd to see America excel;
He charg'd its youth that ev'ry grace divine
Should with full lustre in their conduct shine;
That SAVIOUR, which his soul did first receive,
The greatest gift that ev'n a GOD can give,
He freely offer'd to the num'rous throng,
That on his lips with list'ning pleasure hung.

    "Take him, ye wretched, for your only good,
"Take him ye starving sinners, for your food;
"Ye thirsty, come to this life-giving stream,
"Ye preachers, take him for your joyful theme;
"Take him, my dear Americans, he said,
"Be your complaints on his kind bosom laid:
"Take him, ye Africans, he longs for you,
"Impartial SAVIOUR is his title due:
"Wash'd in the fountain of redeeming blood,
"You shall be sons, and kings, and priests to GOD."

    Great Countess, we Americans revere
Thy name, and mingle in thy grief sincere;
New-England deeply feels, the orphans mourn,
Their more than father will no more return.

    But, though arrested by the hand of death,
Whitefield no more exerts his lab'ring breath,
Yet let us view him in th' eternal skies,
Let ev'ry heart to this bright vision rise;
While the tomb safe retains its sacred trust,
Till life divine re-animates his dust.

4. Benjamin Franklin Explains His Religious Views in a Letter, 1756

SIR:—I received your kind letter of the 2d inst., and am glad to hear that you increase in strength. I hope you will continue mending till you recover your former health and firmness. Let me know if you still use the cold bath, and what effect it has.

As to the kindness you mention, I wish it could have been of more service to you. But if it had, the only thanks I should desire is, that you would always be equally ready to serve any other person that may need your assistance, and so let good offices go round, for mankind are all of a family.

Benjamin Franklin to Joseph Huey, 1756, *The Works of Benjamin Franklin,* vol. 3 (New York: Putnam, 1904), 131–134.

For my own part, when I am employed in serving others, I do not look upon myself as conferring favours, but as paying debts. In my travels and since my settlement I have received much kindness from men, to whom I shall never have any opportunity of making the least direct return, and numberless mercies from God, who is infinitely above being benefited by our services. These kindnesses from men I can therefore only return on their fellow-men; and I can only show my gratitude for those mercies from God, by a readiness to help his other children and my brethren. For I do not think that thanks and compliments tho' repeated weekly, can discharge our real obligations to each other, and much less those to our Creator.

You will see in this my notion of good works, that I am far from expecting (as you suppose) that I shall ever merit heaven by them. By heaven we understand a state of happiness, infinite in degree and eternal in duration. I can do nothing to deserve such reward. He that for giving a draught of water to a thirsty person should expect to be paid with a good plantation, would be modest in his demands, compared with those who think they deserve heaven for the little good they do on earth. Even the mixed, imperfect pleasures we enjoy in this world are rather from God's goodness than our merit; how much more such happiness of heaven. For my own part, I have not the vanity to think I deserve it, the folly to expect it, nor the ambition to desire it; but content myself in submitting to the will and disposal of that God who made me, who hitherto preserv'd and bless'd me, and in whose fatherly goodness I may well confide, that he will never make me miserable, and that even the afflictions I may at any time suffer shall tend to my benefit.

The faith you mention has doubtless its use in the world; I do not desire it to be diminished, nor would I endeavour to lessen it in any man. But I wish it were more productive of good works than I have generally seen it. I mean real good works, works of kindness, charity, mercy, and publick spirit; not holiday-keeping, sermon reading or hearing, performing church ceremonies, or making long prayers, filled with flatteries and compliments,—despis'd even by wise men, and much less capable of pleasing the Deity. The worship of God is a duty, the hearing and reading of sermons may be useful; but if men rest in hearing and praying, as too many do, it is as if a tree should value itself in being water'd and putting forth leaves, tho' it never produc'd any fruit.

Your great Master tho't much less of these outward appearances and professions than many of the modern disciples. He preferr'd the doers of the word to the mere hearers; the Son that seemingly refus'd to obey his father and yet perform'd his command, to him that profess'd his readiness but neglected the work; the heretical but charitable Samaritan, to the uncharitable tho' orthodox priest and sanctified Levite; and those who gave food to the hungry, drink to the thirsty, raiment to the naked, entertainment to the stranger, and relief to the sick, &c., tho' they never heard of his name, he declares shall in the last day be accepted, when those who cry Lord, Lord, who value themselves on their faith, tho' great enough to perform miracles, but have neglected good works, shall be rejected, he professed that he came not to call the righteous but sinners to repentance; which imply'd his modest opinion that there were some in His time so good that they need not hear even him for improvement; but nowadays we have scarce a little parson, that does not think it the duty of every man within his reach to sit under his petty ministrations, and that whoever omits them [all the rest of this letter is torn out.]

5. John Witherspoon Preaches the Revolutionary War as God's Test to Sinners, 1776

The truth, then, asserted in this text, which I propose to illustrate and improve, is,— *That all the disorderly passions of men, whether exposing the innocent to private injury, or whether they are the arrows of divine judgment in public calamity, shall, in the end, be to the praise of God:* Or, to apply it more particularly to the present state of the American Colonies, and the plague of war,—*The ambition of mistaken princes, the cunning and cruelty of oppressive and corrupt ministers, and even the inhumanity of brutal soldiers, however dreadful, shall finally promote the glory of God, and in the meantime, while the storm continues, his mercy and kindness shall appear in prescribing bounds to their rage and fury.*

In discoursing of this subject, it is my intention, through the assistance of divine grace,

I. To point out to you in some particulars, how the wrath of man praises God.

II. To apply these principles to our present situation, by inferences of truth for your instruction and comfort, and by suitable exhortations to duty in the important crisis. . . .

In the *first* place, the wrath of man praises God, as it is an example and illustration of divine truth, and clearly points out the corruption of our nature, which is the foundation stone of the doctrine of redemption. Nothing can be more absolutely necessary to true religion, than a clear and full conviction of the sinfulness of our nature and state. . . .

. . . Both nations in general, and private persons are apt to grow remiss and lax in a time of prosperity and seeming security, but when their earthly comforts are endangered or withdrawn, it lays them under a kind of necessity to seek for something better in their place. Men must have comfort from one quarter or another. When earthly things are in a pleasing and promising condition, too many are apt to *find their rest,* and be satisfied with them as their only portion. But when the vanity and passing nature of all created comfort is discovered, they are compelled to look for something more durable as well as valuable. What therefore can be more to the praise of God, than that when a whole people have forgotten their resting place, when they have abused their privileges, and despised their mercies, they should by distress and suffering be made to *hearken to the rod,* and return to their duty.

There is an inexpressible depth and variety in the judgments of God, as in all his other works, but we may lay down this as a certain principle, that if there were no sin, there could be no suffering. Therefore they are certainly for the correction of sin, or for the trial, illustration, and perfecting of the grace and virtue of his own people. We are not to suppose, that those who suffer most, or who suffer soonest, are therefore more criminal than others. . . .

John Witherspoon, "The Dominion of Providence over the Passions of Men" (Philadelphia: R. Aitken, 1776).

. . . I would take the opportunity on this occasion and from this subject, to press every hearer to a sincere concern for his own soul's salvation. There are times when the mind may be expected to be more awake to divine truth, and the conscience more open to the arrows of conviction than at others. A season of public judgment is of this kind, as appears from what has been already said. That curiosity and attention at least are raised in some degree is plain from the unusual throng of this assembly. Can you have a clearer view of the sinfulness of your nature, than when the rod of the oppressor is lifted up, and when you see men putting on the habit of the warrior, and collecting on every hand the weapons of hostility and instruments of death? I do not blame your ardour in preparing for the resolute defence of your temporal rights. But consider I beseech you, the truly infinite importance of the salvation of your souls. Is it of much moment whether you and your children shall be rich or poor, at liberty or in bonds? Is it of much moment whether this beautiful country shall increase in fruitfulness from year to year being cultivated by active industry, and possessed by independent freemen, or the scanty produce of the neglected fields shall be eaten up by hungry publicans, while the timid owner trembles at the tax gatherers approach? And is it of less moment my brethren, whether you shall be the heirs of glory, or the heirs of hell? Is your state on earth for a few fleeting years of so much moment? And is it of less moment, what shall be your state through endless ages? Have you assembled together willingly to hear what shall be said on public affairs, and to join in imploring the blessing of God on the councils and arms of the united colonies, and can you be unconcerned, what shall become of you for ever, when all the monuments of human greatness shall be laid in ashes, for *the earth* itself *and all the works that are therein shall be burnt up.* . . .

From what has been said upon this subject, you may see what ground there is to give praise to God for his favours already bestowed on us, respecting the public cause. It would be a criminal inattention not to observe the singular interposition of providence hitherto, in behalf of the American colonies. It is however impossible for me in a single discourse, as well as improper at this time to go thro' every step of our past transactions, I must therefore content myself with a few remarks. How many discoveries have been made of the designs of enemies in Britain and among ourselves, in a manner as unexpected to us as to them, and in such season as to prevent their effect? What surprising success has attended our encounters in almost every instance? Has not the boasted discipline of regular and veteran soldiers been turned into confusion and dismay before the new and maiden courage of freemen in defence of their property and right? In what great mercy has blood been spared on the side of this injured country? . . .

While we give praise to God the supreme disposer of all events, for his interposition in our behalf, let us guard against the dangerous error of trusting in, or boasting of an *arm of flesh.* I could earnestly wish, that while our arms are crowned with success, we might content ourselves with a modest ascription of it to the power of the highest. It has given me great uneasiness to read some ostentatious, vaunting expressions in our news papers, though happily I think, much restrained of late. Let us not return to them again. If I am not mistaken, not only the holy scriptures in general, and the truths of the glorious gospel in particular, but the whole course of providence seems intended to abase the pride of man, and lay the vain-glorious in the dust. How many instances does history furnish us with of those who after exulting over, and despising their enemies, were signally and shamefully defeated. . . .

From what has been said you may learn what encouragement you have to put your trust in God, and hope for his assistance in the present important conflict. He is the Lord of hosts, great in might, and strong in battle. Whoever hath his countenance and approbation, shall have the best at last. I do not mean to speak prophetically, but agreeably to the analogy of faith, and the principles of God's moral government. Some have observed that true religion, and in her train dominion, riches, literature, and arts, have taken their course in a slow and gradual manner, from east to west since the earth was settled after the flood, and from thence forbode the future glory of America. I leave this as a matter rather of conjecture than certainty, but observe, that if your cause is just,—if your principles are pure,—and if your conduct is prudent, you need not fear the multitude of opposing hosts.

If your cause is just—you may look with confidence to the Lord and intreat him to plead it as his own. You are all my witnesses, that this is the first time of my introducing any political subject into the pulpit. At this season however, it is not only lawful but necessary, and I willingly embrace the opportunity of declaring my opinion without any hesitation, that the cause in which America is now in arms, is the cause of justice, of liberty, and of human nature. So far as we have hitherto proceeded, I am satisfied that the confederacy of the colonies, has not been the effect of pride, resentment, or sedition, but of a deep and general conviction, that our civil and religious liberties, and consequently in a great measure the temporal and eternal happiness of us and our posterity depended on the issue. The knowledge of God and his truths have from the beginning of the world been chiefly, if not entirely confined to these parts of the earth, where some degree of liberty and political justice were to be seen, and great were the difficulties with which they had to struggle from the imperfection of human society, and the unjust decisions of usurped authority. There is not a single instance in history in which civil liberty was lost, and religious liberty preserved entire. If therefore we yield up our temporal property, we at the same time deliver the conscience into bondage.

6. Jonathan Boucher's Loyalist Sermon Denounces the Revolution, 1775

In the infancy of Christianity, it would seem that some rumour had been spread (probably by Judas of Galilee, who is mentioned in the Acts) that the Gospel was designed to undermine kingdoms and commonwealths; as if the intention of our Saviour's first coming had been the same with that which is reserved for the second, viz. to *put down all rule, and all authority, and all power.* On this supposition the apparent solicitude of our Saviour and his Apostles, in their frequent and earnest recommendation of submission to *the higher powers,* is easily and naturally

---

Jonathan Boucher, *A View of the Causes and Consequences of the American Revolution* (1797; reprint, [New York]: Russell and Russell, 1967).

accounted for. Obedience to Government is every man's duty, because it is every man's interest: but it is particularly incumbent on Christians, because (in addition to it's moral fitness) it is enjoined by the positive commands of God: and therefore, when Christians are disobedient to human ordinances, they are also disobedient to God. If the form of government under which the good providence of God has been pleased to place us be mild and free, it is our duty to enjoy it with gratitude and with thankfulness; and, in particular, to be careful not to abuse it by licentiousness. If it be less indulgent and less liberal than in reason it ought to be, still it is our duty not to disturb and destroy the peace of the community, by becoming refractory and rebellious subjects, and *resisting the ordinances of God.* However humiliating such acquiescence may seem to men of warm and eager minds, the wisdom of God in having made it our duty is manifest. For, as it is the natural temper and bias of the human mind to be impatient under restraint, it was wise and merciful in the blessed Author of our religion not to add any new impulse to the natural force of this prevailing propensity, but, with the whole weight of his authority, altogether to discountenance every tendency to disobedience.

If it were necessary to vindicate the Scriptures for this their total unconcern about a principle which for many other writings seem to regard as the first of all human considerations, it might be observed, that, avoiding the vague and declamatory manner of such writings, and avoiding also the useless and impracticable subtleties of metaphysical definitions, these Scriptures have better consulted the great general interests of mankind, by summarily recommending and enjoining a conscientious reverence for law whether human or divine. To respect the laws, is to respect liberty in the only rational sense in which the term can be used; for liberty consists in a subserviency to law. "Where there is no law," says Mr. Locke, "there is no freedom." The mere man of nature (if such an one there ever was) has no freedom: *all his lifetime he is subject to bondage.* It is by being included within the pale of civil polity and government that he takes his rank in society as a free man.

Hence it follows, that we are free, or otherwise, as we are governed by law, or by the mere arbitrary will, or wills, of any individual, or any number of individuals. And liberty is not the setting at nought and despising established laws—much less the making our own wills the rule of our own actions, or the actions of others—and not bearing (whilst yet we dictate to others) the being dictated to, even by the laws of the land; but it is the being governed by law, and by law only. . . .

[The] popular notion, that government was originally formed by the consent or by a compact of the people, rests on, and is supported by, another similar notion, not less popular, nor better founded. This other notion is, that the whole human race is born equal; and that no man is naturally inferior, or, in any respect, subjected to another; and that he can be made subject to another only by his own consent. The position is equally ill-founded and false both in it's premises and conclusions. In hardly any sense that can be imagined is the position strictly true; but, as applied to the case under consideration, it is demonstrably not true. Man differs from man in every thing that can be supposed to lead to supremacy and subjection, *as one star differs from another star in glory.* It was the purpose of the Creator, that man should be social: but, without government, there can be no society; nor, without some relative inferiority and superiority, can there be any government. . . .

It was not to be expected from an all-wise and all-merciful Creator, that, having formed creatures capable of order and rule, he should turn them loose into the world under the guidance only of their own unruly wills; that, like so many wild beasts, they might tear and worry one another in their mad contests for pre-eminence. His purpose from the first, no doubt, was, that men should *live godly and sober lives.* But, such is the sad estate of our corrupted nature, that, ever since the Fall, we have been averse from good, and prone to evil. We are, indeed, so disorderly and unmanageable, that, were it not for the restraints and the terrors of human laws, it would not be possible for us to dwell together. But as men were clearly formed for society, and to dwell together, which yet they cannot do without the restraints of law, or, in other words, without government, it is fair to infer that government was also the original intention of God, who never decrees the end, without also decreeing the means. Accordingly, when man was made, his Maker did not turn him adrift into a shoreless ocean, without star or compass to steer by. As soon as there were some to be governed, there were also some to govern: and the first man, by virtue of that paternal claim, on which all subsequent governments have been founded, was first invested with the power of government. For, we are not to judge of the Scriptures of God, as we do of some other writings; and so, where no express precept appears, hastily to conclude that none was given. On the contrary, in commenting on the Scriptures, we are frequently called upon to find out the precept from the practice. Taking this rule, then, for our direction in the present instance, we find, that, copying after the fair model of heaven itself, wherein there was government even among the angels, the families of the earth were subjected to rulers, at first set over them by God: *for, there is no power, but of God; the powers that be are ordained of God.* The first father was the first king: and if (according to the rule just laid down) the law may be inferred from the practice, it was thus that all government originated; and monarchy is it's most ancient form. . . .

Even where the Scriptures are silent, they instruct: for, in general, whatever is not therein commanded is actually forbidden. Now, it is certain that mankind are no where in the Scriptures commanded to resist authority; and no less certain that, either by direct injunction, or clear implication, they are commanded to *be subject to the higher powers:* and this subjection is said to be enjoined, not for our sakes only, but also *for the Lord's sake.* The glory of God is much concerned, that there should be good government in the world: it is, therefore, the uniform doctrine of the Scriptures, that it is under the deputation and authority of God alone that *kings reign and princes decree justice.* Kings and princes which are only other words for supreme magistrates) were doubtless created and appointed, not so much for their own sakes, as for the sake of the people committed to their charge: yet are they not, therefore, the creatures of the people. So far from deriving their authority from any supposed consent or suffrage of men, they receive their commission from Heaven; they receive it from God, the source and original of all power. However obsolete, therefore, either the sentiment or the language may now be deemed, it is with the most perfect propriety that the supreme magistrate, whether consisting of one or of many, and whether denominated an emperor, a king, an archon, a dictator, a consul, or a senate, is to be regarded and venerated as the vicegerent of God.

7. Anthony Benezet, Quaker, Denounces War, 1776

But the true Christian spirit being much departed from the earth, true Christian knowledge, as its inseparable companion, is departed with it, and men seem to be gone back again to their old animal life: and tho' in speculation and idea they profess an assent to the truths of revelation, yet in heart and practice they are apt to consider the course of all things as connected only with temporal good and evil, and themselves as the center and circumference, the first cause, and the last end of all, ascribing *to human understanding, designs which only infinite Wisdom can form, and to human power, events which Omnipotence only can produce.* If the Christian, however, recollects himself, he will find war to be a sad consequence of the apostacy, and fall of man, when he was abandoned to the fury of his own lusts and passions, as the natural and penal effects of breaking loose from the divine government, the fundamental law of which is LOVE: *Thou shall love the Lord thy God with all thy heart, with all thy soul, with all thy mind, with all thy strength, and thy fellow creatures as thyself.*

The consequences of war, when impartially examined, will be found big, not only with outward and temporal distress, but also with an evil that extends itself (where in the darkness and tumult of human passions, it is, by many, neither expected nor conceived to reach) even into the regions of eternity. That property is confounded, scattered, and destroyed, that laws are trampled under foot, government despised, and the ties of all civil and domestic order broken into pieces; that fruitful countries are made deserts, and stately cities a heap of ruins, that matrons and virgins are violated; and neither the innocence of unoffending infancy, nor the impotence of decrepit age, afford protection from the rage and thirst for blood: this is but the mortal progeny of this teeming womb of mischief; the worst, even the dreadful effect it has upon the immortal soul, is still behind; and tho' remote from those senses and passions that are exercised only by present good and evil, must yet, upon the least recollection, impress with horror every mind that believes there is a righteous God, and a state of retribution, that is to last forever. Under these considerations, what must the real Christian feel; he who is fully convinced that the fall of man, is a fall from meekness, purity, and love, into sensuality, pride, and wrath; that the Son of God became incarnate, and suffered and died to restore that first life of meekness, purity, and love; and that for these in whom the restoration of that life is not begun, in the present state the Son of God incarnate, it is to be feared, suffered and died in vain. What must he feel for those immortal spirits, who in the earliest dawn of their day of purification, are by hundreds and thousands driven into eternity, in the bitterness of enmity and wrath—some inflamed with drunkenness, some fired with lust; and all stained with blood? In these direful conflicts, which are maintained with so much rage, that when the vanquished, at last, retreats with the loss of *twenty thousand human beings,* the victor finds he has purchased some little advantage, at the expence of more than half that number. Heaven and earth! what a possibility is here of a sacrifice made to the *prince of darkness,* the first and chief

---

Anthony Benezet, *Thoughts on the Nature of War* (Philadelphia, 1776).

apostate, who rejoices in beholding men, through the abuse of those benefits which undeserved mercy has conferred upon them, transformed into enmity and hatred of God and their brethren; forsaken by God, and destroying one another, and thus hastening once more into his horrid society; that having been accomplices in his rebellion, they may become partakers of his misery and torment.

Now if the man of valour, whom consenting nations have dignified with the title of *hero,* and *the man devoted to the world,* are asked, From whence this immortal mischief, that may thus extend its influence into the regions of eternity, can proceed, what must they answer? Indeed what can they answer, but that it is engendered by the love of human glory—as vain a phantom as ever played before *a mad man's eye:* by the lust of dominion; the avarice of wealth, or some other pursuit that centers in this present life. May all those who are called to be the followers of Christ be preserved from these *earthly,* these *sensual* and *malignant motives,* so repugnant to the generous, compassionate and forgiving temper, which, through the influence of redeeming mercy, is concomitant with the pure beams of heavenly light, that light which is intended to remove all the darkness of human corruption, and transform selfish, sensual, proud spirits, into angels of patience, humility, meekness, purity and love; *the children and heirs of God; the brethren and joint heirs of Christ.*

8. Isaac Jackson, Quaker, Protests Persecution, 1777

A Testimony given Forth from our Yearly Meeting held at Philadelphia, for Pennsylvania and New Jersey, by Adjournments from the 29th Day of the Ninth Month to the 4th of the Tenth Month inclusive, 1777.

A Number of our Friends having been imprisoned and banished, unheard, from their Families, under a Charge and Insinuation that "they have in their general Conduct and Conversation evidenced a Disposition inimical to the "Cause of America;" and from some Publications intimating that "there is strong Reason to apprehend that these Persons maintain a correspondence highly prejudicial "to the public safety;" may induce a Belief that we have in our Conduct departed from the peaceable Principles which we profess; and apprehending that the Minds of some may thereby be misled; for the clearing of Truth, we think it necessary publicly to declare, that we are led out of all Wars and Fightings by the Principle of Grace and Truth in our own Minds, by which we are restrained either as private Members of Society, or in any of our Meetings, from holding a Correspondence with either Army; but are concerned to spread the Testimony of Truth and the peaceable Doctrines of Christ, to seek the good of all—to keep a Conscience void of Offence toward God and Man—to promote the Kingdom of the Messiah, which we pray may come, and be experienced in Individuals, in Kingdoms and Nations; that they may beat their Swords into Plow-shares and the Spears into Pruning-hooks, and

---

Isaac Jackson, "A Testimony Given Forth . . ." (Philadelphia, 1777).

Nation not lift up Sword against Nation, neither learn War any more, Isai. ii. 4. And we deny in general Terms, all Charges and Insinuations which in any Degree clash with this our Profession.

As to a nameless Paper lately published, said to be dated at Spank-Town Yearly Meeting, and found among the Baggage on Staten-Island, every Person who is acquainted with our Stile, may be convinced it was never wrote at any of our Meetings, or by any of our Friends. Besides, there is no Meeting throughout our whole Society of that Name; nor was that Letter, or any one like it, ever wrote in any of our Meetings since we were a People. We therefore solemnly deny the said Letter and its Authors; and wish that those who have assumed a fictitious Character to write under, whether with a View to injure us or to cover themselves, might find it their Place to clear us of this Charge by stating the Truth.

And as from the Knowledge we have of our banished Friends, and the best Information we have been able to obtain, we are convinced that they have done nothing to forfeit their just Right to Liberty; we fervently desire that all those who have any hand in sending them into Banishment, might weightily consider the Tendency of their own Conduct, and how contrary it is to the Doctrines and Example of our Lord and Lawgiver Christ Jesus; and do them that Justice which their Case requires, by restoring them to their afflicted Families and Friends; And this we are well assured will conduce more to their Peace than keeping them in Exile.—We give forth this Admonition in the Fear of God, not only with a View to the Relief of our Friends, but also to the real Interest of those concerned in their Banishment.

Signed by Order and in Behalf of the Yearly Meeting, by
Isaac Jackson, Clerk.

9. Thomas Jefferson Establishes Religious Freedom in Virginia, 1786

An ACT for establishing Religious Freedom, *passed in the Assembly of Virginia in the beginning of the year* 1786.

Well aware that Almighty God hath created the mind free; that all attempts to influence it by temporal punishments or burdens, or by civil incapacitations, tend only to beget habits of hypocrisy and meanness, and are a departure from the plan of the Holy Author of our religion, who being Lord both of body and mind, yet chose not to propagate it by coercions on either, as was in his Almighty power to do; that the impious presumption of legislators and rulers, civil as well as ecclesiastical, who, being themselves but fallible and uninspired men have assumed dominion over the faith of others, setting up their own opinions and modes of thinking as the only true and infallible, and as such endeavouring to impose them on others, hath established

Thomas Jefferson, "An Act for Establishing Religious Freedom, passed in the Assembly of Virginia, 1786" in *Notes on the State of Virginia* (Philadelphia: R. T. Rawle, 1801), 432–436.

and maintained false religions over the greatest part of the world, and through all time; that to compel a man to furnish contributions of money for the propagation of opinions which he disbelieves, is sinful and tyrannical; that even the forceing him to support this or that teacher of his own religious persuasion, is depriving him of the comfortable liberty of giving his contributions to the particular pastor whose morals he would make his pattern, and whose powers he feels most persuasive to right-eousness, and is withdrawing from the ministry those temporal rewards, which proceeding from an approbation of their personal conduct, are an additional incite-ment to earnest and unremitting labours for the instruction of mankind; that our civil rights have no dependance on our religious opinions, more than our opinions in physics or geometry; that therefore the proscribing any citizen as unworthy the public confidence by laying upon him an incapacity of being called to the offices of trust and emolument, unless he profess or renounce this or that religious opin-ion, is depriving him injuriously of those privileges and advantages to which in common with his fellow citizens he has a natural right; that it tends also to corrupt the principles of that very religion it is meant to encourage, by bribing, with a mo-nopoly of worldly honours and emoluments, those who will externally profess and conform to it; that though indeed these are criminal who do not withstand such temptation, yet neither are those innocent who lay the bait in their way; that to suf-fer the civil magistrate to intrude his powers into the field of opinion and to restrain the profession or propagation of principles, on the supposition of their ill tendency, is a dangerous fallacy, which at once destroys all religious liberty, because he be-ing of course judge of that tendency, will make his opinions the rule of judgment, and approve or condemn the sentiments of others only as they shall square with or differ from his own; that it is time enough for the rightful purposes of civil govern-ment, for its officers to interfere when principles break out into overt acts against peace and good order; and finally, that truth is great and will prevail if left to her-self, that she is the proper and sufficient antagonist to error, and has nothing to fear from the conflict, unless by human interposition disarmed of her natural weapons, free argument and debate, errors ceasing to be dangerous when it is permitted freely to contradict them.

Be it therefore enacted by the General Assembly, That no man shall be compelled to frequent or support any religious worship, place or ministry whatsoever, nor shall be enforced, restrained, molested, or burthened in his body or goods, nor shall otherwise suffer on account of his religious opinions or belief; but that all men shall be free to profess, and by argument to maintain, their opinions in matters of religion and that the same shall in no wise diminish, enlarge, or affect their civil capacities.

And though we well know that this Assembly, elected by the people for the ordinary purposes of legislation only, have no power to restrain the acts of suc-ceeding Assemblies, constituted with the powers equal to our own, and that there-fore to declare this act irrevocable, would be of no effect in law, yet we are free to declare, and do declare, that the rights hereby asserted are of the natural rights of mankind, and that if any act shall be hereafter passed to repeal the present or to narrow its operation, such act will be an infringement of natural right.

✐ E S S A Y S

Patricia Bonomi of New York University explains how the Great Awakening of the 1730s and 1740s began to educate Americans to think in new ways, first about their religion and later about politics, too. She describes conflicts that began within denominations, such as the Presbyterians, as clergy feuded with each other and with their parishioners over appropriate styles of worship. The more emotional and evangelical New Side, led at first by Gilbert Tennent, wanted freedom to preach beyond the communities in which they were licensed, and enjoyed a great boost to their claim with the arrival of George Whitefield. But, as Bonomi shows, the Old Side Presbyterians' fear that itinerancy (traveling preachers) could lead to social disorder was not entirely unfounded: excitement over Whitefield claimed five people who were trampled to death in Boston when he first preached there. In Bonomi's view, the experience and rhetoric of the Great Awakening encouraged Americans to think more in terms of themselves as individuals, as well as to be more willing to factionalize and to challenge the established authorities in the decades before the Revolutionary War.

Stephen Marini of Wellesley College describes the hill-town revivals that accompanied the Revolution and the upsurge of charismatic sects it created. Many sects anticipated the imminent end of the world and their doctrines strove to make their followers perfect in preparation for Jesus's return, especially when odd natural phenomena such as the "Dark Day" (May 19, 1780) occurred. The figures Marini describes, such as Jemima Wilkinson, the "Public Universal Friend," had grown up in the years after the Great Awakening and were certainly willing to make bold and creative breaks from convention in the belief that they were fulfilling the will of a God who had spoken to them directly.

The Great Awakening

PATRICIA U. BONOMI

The Great Awakening—that intense period of revivalist tumult from about 1739 to 1745—is one of the most arresting subjects of American history. The eighteenth century, and the latter part of the seventeenth, were . . . punctuated with religious episodes that seemed to erupt without warning and draw entire communities into a vortex of religious conversions and agitations of soul. Yet those episodes tended not to spread beyond the individual churches or towns in which they originated. By the third decade of the eighteenth century, however, a number of currents were converging to prepare the way for an unprecedented burst of religious fervor and controversy.

The two major streams of thought shaping western religious belief in the eighteenth century—Enlightenment rationalism and Continental pietism—were by the 1720s reaching increasing numbers of Americans through the world of print, transatlantic learned societies, and such recently arrived spokesmen as the Anglican moderate George Berkeley, on the one side, and the Dutch Reformed pietist Theodore Frelinghuysen, on the other. By the 1730s, American clergymen influenced by the spiritual intensity and emotional warmth of Reformed pietism were vigorously asserting that religion was being corrupted by secular forces; in their

---

view a conversion experience that touched the heart was the only road to salvation. The rationalists demurred, preferring a faith tempered by "an enlightened Mind . . . not raised Affections." This contest between reason and innate grace was in one sense as old as Christianity itself. . . .

Adding to currents of religious unease in the early eighteenth century were a number of other developments: an accelerating pace of commercial growth; land shortages as well as land opportunities; the unprecedented diversity of eighteenth-century immigration; and a rapid climb in total population. Population growth now created dense settlements in some rural as well as urban areas, facilitating mass public gatherings. Moreover, the proliferation of churches and sects, intensifying denominational rivalries, and smallpox and earthquake alarms that filled meeting-houses to overflowing all contributed to a sense of quickening in church life.

Into this volatile and expectant environment came some of the most charismatic and combative personalities of the age. And as the electricity of a Tennent crackled, and the thunder of a Whitefield rolled, a storm broke that in the opinion of many would forever alter American society. The Great Awakening created conditions uniquely favorable to social and political, as well as religious, reform by piercing the facade of civility and deference that governed provincial life to usher in a new age of contentiousness. By promoting church separations and urging their followers to make choices that had political as well as religious implications, the Awakeners wrought permanent changes in public practices and attitudes. Before it subsided, the revival had unsettled the lives of more Americans and disrupted more institutions than any other single event in colonial experience to that time. . . .

The Great Awakening began not as a popular uprising but as a contest between clerical factions. Thus only those churches with a "professional" clergy and organized governing structure—the Presbyterian, Congregational, Dutch Reformed, and eventually the Anglican—were split apart by the revival. The newer German churches and the sects, having little structure to overturn, remained largely outside the conflict. These events have usually been viewed from the perspective of New England Congregationalism, though the first denomination to be involved in the Awakening was the Presbyterian Church in the Middle Colonies. All of the strains and adjustments experienced by other colonial denominations over a longer time span were compressed, in the Presbyterian case, into the fifty years from the beginning of Ulster immigration around 1725 to the Revolution. Thus the Presbyterian example serves as a kind of paradigm of the experience of all churches from their initial formation through the Great Awakening and its aftermath. It reveals too how a dispute between ministers rapidly widened into a controversy that tested the limits of order and introduced new forms of popular leadership that challenged deferential traditions.

Presbyterians looked to the future with reasonably high hopes by the third decade of the eighteenth century. To all appearances they possessed a more stable and orderly church structure than any of their middle-colony competitors. . . .

Yet the controls imposed by the Presbyterian hierarchy were hardly all that they appeared to be. Beneath orderly processes were tensions which had been expanding steadily before finally bursting forth in fratricidal strife and schism after 1739. Any reading of eighteenth-century Presbyterian records discloses at least three kinds of strains beneath the surface: between parishioners, between people and minister, and within the professional clergy itself.

The Presbyterian Church was the focal point and mediator of Scotch-Irish community life from the late 1720s on, when thousands of Ulster Scots began entering the colonies annually. As the westward-migrating settlers moved beyond the reach of government and law, the Presbyterian Church was the only institution that kept pace with settlement. By stretching resources to the limit, the synod, and especially the presbyteries, kept in touch with their scattered brethren through itinerant preachers and presbyterial visitations. Ministers, invariably the best educated persons on the early frontier, were looked to for leadership in both religious and community affairs, and they often took up multiple roles as doctors, teachers, and even lawyers. So closely did the Scotch-Irish identify with the Kirk that it was often said they "could not live without it." . . .

The Great Awakening split the Presbyterian Church apart, and through the cracks long-suppressed steam hissed forth in clouds of acrimony and vituperation that would change the face of authority in Pennsylvania and elsewhere. As the passions of the Awakening reached their height in the early 1740s, evangelical "New Side" Presbyterians turned on the more orthodox "Old Sides" with the ferocity peculiar to zealots, charging them with extravagant doctrinal and moral enormities. The internecine spectacle that ensued, the loss of proportion and professional decorum, contributed to the demystification of the clergy, forced parishioners to choose between competing factions, and overset traditional attitudes about deference and leadership in colonial America.

The division that surfaced in 1740–1741 had been developing for more than a decade. Presbyterian ministers had no sooner organized their central association, the Synod of Philadelphia, in 1715 than the first lines of stress appeared, though it was not until a cohesive evangelical faction emerged in the 1730s that an open split was threatened. Most members of the synod hoped to model American Presbyterianism along orderly lines, and in 1729 an act requiring all ministers and ministerial candidates to subscribe publicly to the Westminster Confession had been approved. In 1738 the synod had further ruled that no minister would be licensed unless he could display a degree from a British or European university, or from one of the New England colleges (Harvard or Yale). New candidates were to submit to an examination by a commission of the synod on the soundness of their theological training and spiritual condition. The emergent evangelical faction rightly saw these restrictions as an effort to control their own activities. They had reluctantly accepted subscription to the Westminster Confession, but synodical screening of new candidates struck them as an intolerable invasion of the local presbyteries' right of ordination.

The insurgents were led by the Scotsman William Tennent, Sr., and his sons, William, Jr., Charles, John, and Gilbert. . . .

. . . [Then] George Whitefield made his sensational appearance. Whitefield's visits to New Jersey and Pennsylvania in the winter of 1739–1740 provided tremendous support for the Presbyterian insurgents, as thousands of provincials flocked to hear him and realized, perhaps for the first time, something of what the American evangelists had been up to. The public support that now flowed to [Gilbert]

Tennent and his sympathizers exhilarated . . . [the revivalists], inciting them to ever bolder assaults on the synod.

The revivalists had to this point preached only in their own churches or in temporarily vacant pulpits, but that winter they began to invade the territory of the regular clergy. This action raised the issue of itinerant preaching, perhaps the thorniest of the entire conflict, for it brought the parties face to face on the question of who was better qualified to interpret the word of God. It was in this setting that Gilbert Tennent was moved on March 8, 1740 to deliver his celebrated sermon, *The Danger of an Unconverted Ministry,* to a Nottingham congregation engaged in choosing a new preacher. It was an audacious, not to say reckless, attack on the Old Side clergy, and Tennent would later qualify some of his strongest language. But the sermon starkly reveals the gulf that separated the two factions by 1740. It also demonstrates the revivalists' supreme disregard for the traditional limits on public discussion of what amounted to professional questions.

Tennent began by drawing an analogy between the opposers in the Philadelphia Synod who rejected experiential religion, and the legalistic Pharisees of old who had rejected the radical teachings of Jesus. The Pharisees, he declared, were bloated with intellectual conceit, letter-learned but blind to the truths of the Saviour. They "loved the uppermost Seats in the Synagogues, and to be called Rabbi, Rabbi." They were masterly and positive in their sayings, "as if forsooth Knowledge must die with them." Worst of all, they "had their Eyes, with Judas, fixed upon the Bag. Why, they came into the Priest's Office for a Piece of Bread; they took it up as a Trade . . . O Shame!" For all these worldly conceits Jesus had denounced them as hypocrites and a generation of vipers. Tennent went on to pronounce a similar judgment on the Pharisees of his own time—"unconverted [and] wicked Men" who as nearly resembled the old Pharisees "as one Crow's Egg does another." If men are not called to the ministry by a "New Birth. . . . their Discourses are cold and sapless, and as it were freeze between their lips."

Tennent's solution to the problem of unconverted ministers, in addition to prayer for their "dear fainting Souls," was "to encourage private Schools, or Seminaries of Learning, which are under the Care of skilful and experienced Christians." As for itinerant preachers, Tennent assured his Nottingham auditors that it was no sin but a right well within their Christian liberty to desert their parish minister for a converted preacher. "Birds of the Air fly to warmer Climates in order to shun the Winter-cold, and also doubtless to get better Food"; should humankind do less? . . .

. . . The typical New Side minister was about thirty-two at the time of the schism, or a decade younger than his Old Side counterpart.

. . . The Old Sides, more mature than their adversaries, were also more settled in their professional careers; further, their Scottish education and early professional experiences in Ulster may have instilled a respect for discipline and ecclesiastical order that could not easily be cast aside. . . .

The New Side party, on the other hand, cared less about professional niceties than about converting sinners. Its members were at the beginning of their careers, and most, being native-born or coming to the colonies in their youth, were not so likely to be imbued with an Old World sense of prerogative and order. They never doubted that an educated clergy was essential, but education had to be of the right sort. By the 1730s Harvard and Yale were being guided, in their view, by men of rationalist leanings who simply did not provide the type of training wanted by the revivalists. Thus the New Sides chafed against the controls favored by their more conservative elders, controls that restricted their freedom of action, slowed their careers, and were in their opinion out of touch with New World ways.

The anti-institutionalism of the revivalists caused some critics to portray them as social levellers, though there were no significant distinctions in social outlook or family background between Old and New Sides. But as with any insurgent group that relies in part on public support for its momentum, the New Sides tended to clothe their appeals in popular dress. At every opportunity they pictured the opposers as "the Noble & Mighty" elders of the church, and identified themselves with the poor and "common People"—images reinforced by the Old Sides' references to the evangelists' followers as an ignorant and "wild Rabble."

The revivalists may not have been deliberate social levellers, but their words and actions had the effect of emphasizing individual values over hierarchical ones. Everything they did, from disrupting orderly processes and encouraging greater lay participation in church government, to promoting mass assemblies and the physical closeness that went with them, raised popular emotions. Most important, they insisted that there were choices, and that the individual himself was free to make them. . . .

Whitefield's initial visit to Boston in September 1740 was greeted with tremendous interest, for the "Grand Itinerant" was the first figure of international renown to tour the colonies. During an eleven-day period he preached at least nineteen times at a number of different churches and outdoor sites, including New South Church where the huge crowd was thrown into such a panic that five were killed and many more injured. Fifteen thousand persons supposedly heard Whitefield preach on Boston Common. Even allowing for an inflated count, these were surely the largest crowds ever assembled in Boston or any other colonial city. As Samuel Johnson once said, Whitefield would have been adored if he wore a nightcap and preached from a tree. Whitefield's tours outside of Boston, and then into western Massachusetts and Connecticut, were attended by similar public outpourings. No one, it seems, wanted to miss the show. In December Gilbert Tennent arrived in Boston, having been urged by Whitefield to add more fuel to the divine fires he had kindled there. Tennent's preaching, which lacked Whitefield's sweetness but none of his power, aroused a popular fervor that matched or exceeded that inspired by the Englishman.

Most Congregational ministers, including those at Boston, had welcomed Whitefield's tour as an opportunity to stimulate religious piety. Tennent's torrid preaching may have discomfited some, but it was not until 1742 that three events led to a polarization of the clergy into "New Light" supporters and "Old Light" opposers of the Great Awakening. First came the publication in Boston of Tennent's sermon, *The Danger of an Unconverted Ministry,* which one Old Light would later blame for having "sown the Seeds of all that Discord, Intrusion, Confusion, Separation, Hatred, Variance, Emulations, Wrath, Strife, Seditions, Heresies, &c. that have been springing up in so many of the Towns and Churches thro' the Province. . . ." Another was the publication of Whitefield's 1740 *Journal,* in which he criticized "most" New England preachers for insufficient piety and observed of Harvard and Yale that "their

Light is become Darkness." The final provocation was the arrival in Boston on June 25, 1742 of the Reverend James Davenport, a newly fledged evangelist who already had Connecticut in an uproar and would soon have all Boston by the ears.

Davenport had been expelled from Connecticut on June 3 after being adjudged "disturbed in the rational Faculties of his Mind." Now the twenty-six-year-old evangelist was determined to share his special insights with the people of Boston. Forewarned about Davenport's odd behavior, the ministers of Boston and Charlestown (the majority of whom favored the Awakening) requested that the intruder restrain his "assuming Behavior . . . especially in judging the spiritual State of Pastors and People," and decided not to offer him their pulpits. Davenport was undeterred. He preached on the Common and in the rain on Copp's Hill; he proclaimed first three and then nine more of Boston's ministers "by name" to be unconverted; and he announced that he was "ready to drop down dead for the salvation of but one soul." Davenport was followed, according to one critic, by a "giddy Audience . . . chiefly made up of idle or ignorant Persons" of low rank. To some of Boston's soberer citizens the crowd appeared "menacing," and one newspaper essayist found Davenport's followers "so red hot, that I verily believe they would make nothing to kill Opposers." Such was the anarchy threatened by religious enthusiasm. . . .

In the months that followed, New Englanders, like middle-colony Presbyterians before them, would witness and then be drawn into a fierce struggle between the two factions, as their once-decorous ministers impugned the intelligence and integrity of their rivals in public sermons and essays. The Old Light writers were especially bellicose, losing no opportunity to rebuke the "enthusiastic, factious, censorious Spirit" of the revivalists. Schisms were threatened everywhere, and as early as 1742 some congregations had "divided into Parties, and openly and scandalously separated from one another." As the Connecticut Old Light, Isaac Stiles, warned, the subversion of all order was threatened when "Contempt is cast upon Authority both Civil and Ecclesiastical." Most distressing to those who believed that "Good Order is the Strength and Beauty of the World," was the Awakening's tendency to splinter New England society. "Formerly the People could bear with each other in Charity when they differ'd in Opinion," recalled one writer, "but they now break Fellowship and Communion with one another on that Account."

Indeed, awakened parishioners were repeatedly urged to withdraw from a "corrupt ministry." "O that the precious Seed might be preserved and *separated* from all gross Mixtures!" prayed the Connecticut New Light Jonathan Parsons. And spurred on by Parsons and other New Lights, withdraw they did. In Plymouth and Ipswich, from Maine to the Connecticut River Valley, the New England separatist movement gained momentum from 1743 onward.

Religion has always been considered a likely agent of radicalism. Nor is there reason to doubt that the tremendous stir of the Great Awakening altered the social and political equilibrium of colonial life. Just as the revival marked a significant divide in popular thought and practice, so too it would supply the most pertinent and usable model for radical activists in the years that lay ahead. Many features of the Awakening foreshadowed what was to come.

Since the Awakeners began as an insurgent minority in every church, they could advance their religious ideology only by overturning the orthodox majority, or, when that failed, by withdrawing from or bringing down the institutional structures that sheltered orthodoxy and fortified its authority. For such work they required allies, and owing to the importance of the laity in colonial church life, as well as shifting values in eighteenth-century provincial society at large, the revivalists found their allies among the people. Together they launched a mass movement that made bold assaults on established forms of church government and traditional assumptions about deference and social order. Evangelical preachers constantly exhorted their followers not to shrink from painful choices between alternative religious doctrines, and urged them to act on those decisions by separating from unregenerate churches. The separatists constructed parallel—in the eyes of some, "extra-legal"—organizations to compete with those from which they had seceded. Impelled to justify their opposition, the revivalists developed novel arguments defending the rights of minorities, and they increasingly characterized the authority against which they were rebelling as illegitimate, even tyrannical.

In all these actions the dissidents and their followers cut through the still powerful proscriptions against opposition to settled authority, and they did so not only in theory but in practice. The institutional disruptions and church separations of the Great Awakening thus provided a kind of "practice model" which enabled the provincials to "rehearse"—though unwittingly—a number of the situations, and the arguments appropriate to them, that would reappear with the political crisis of the 1760s and 1770s. . . .

As evangelical factions formed in congregations throughout the Middle Colonies and New England, leaders of the revival were pressed ever harder to justify their divisive behavior. In an age when factionalism was widely denounced as destructive of the larger common good, the revivalists were on slippery ground. Their primary experience—and everyone else's—was with political factions, but these always carried a taint of impropriety, if not of positive corruption, and strictures against them were so strong that no systematic theory of parties emerged during the eighteenth century. In the religious sphere, on the other hand, the situation was not so clear. Religious factions had a long and almost respectable history in the eighteenth-century mind, making it easier to justify divisions over questions of eternal truth. Thus, beginning in the 1740s and continuing into the next decade, Presbyterian and Congregational separatists constructed a defense that stressed the rights of minorities against majorities and of individuals against the whole, in matters of conscience. . . .

As the Great Awakening broke down social cohesion in America, it simultaneously elevated the individual. During the more communal seventeenth century, colonists had rarely conceived of themselves apart from a larger collectivity—the family, the congregation, or the town. But the eighteenth-century revival penetrated and shattered that unitary cosmos by directing its message to the individual. In exhorting their followers to make personal decisions for God, and then to act on those decisions regardless of their effect on the larger society, the revivalists gave sanction to a new dynamic in human relationships.

How the Revolution Stimulated New Religious Movements

STEPHEN MARINI

The most important religious event in rural New England during the Revolution was a revival that swept across the hill country and maritime Canada between 1776 and 1783. At the outbreak of hostilities all Evangelicals prescribed a new awakening, whether to purify Patriots and enlist God's aid in the struggle—as urged by New Light Congregationalists—or to proclaim as did Radicals "a spiritual assurance which rejected and transcended the tribulations of the secular world." Rhetoric of the former kind buttressed the established order against ideological and institutional depredations of war and formed a powerful religious appeal to soldiers and citizens alike to persevere in revolutionary activity.

The latter sort of evangelism sparked a renewal of charismatic religion and Radical Evangelical growth in the new settlements. The revival, called the New Light Stir in New England and the New Light Revival in Canada, established Baptists as a principal religious group on the frontier and also fostered the appearance of many local schismatic sects. Out of the Stir also came permanent indigenous religions of rural New England—Shakers, Universalists, and Freewill Baptists— each transmuting Radical Evangelicalism into new forms under the combined force of revival, revolution, and frontier. The Stir was a declaration of identity for the new settlements, a religious analogue to the cultural and political turmoil assaulting the northern frontier. Its eventual consequence was the creation of new New England religions. . . .

. . . [T]he rural revivalists seized on millennialism and perfectionism as vehicles of persuasion. Belief in the imminent Second Coming of Christ and the concomitant search for complete sanctification among the "saved remnant" in the Last Days were irresistible and effective themes for evangelists responding to revolutionary "wars and rumors of war."

Congregationalist divines also proclaimed "the promised day of the Lord," but there was a significant and revealing difference between the two visions of the future. The Congregationalist view, typified by Ezra Stiles's 1783 sermon *The United States Elevated to Glory and Honor,* focused on America as the chosen nation of God, blessed by the Lord with millennial holiness, virtue, prosperity, and empire. Proceeding from this endorsement and support of the Revolution, Congregationalists articulated a sanguine expectation for an earthly millennial kingdom in America. Radical Evangelicals, on the other hand, held to the notion that war confirmed human sinfulness and depravity and that the revival itself signaled the speedy end of history and the imminent establishment of the otherworldly kingdom of the New Jerusalem.

It was a conflict between premillennialism and postmillennialism—whether the thousand-year reign of the saints would precede or follow the cataclysmic Second Coming of Christ. The rural saints of the New Light Stir were certain that their reign would commence only after the imminent return of Christ, and instead of finding hope and solace in America's military triumph they sought "the signs of the times" in political events and natural omens to discern the moment of millennial dawn.

One such event—the Dark Day of 1780—occurred about midway through the Stir and served to drive it to new heights of chiliastic fervor. On 19 May 1780, from early morning in the Hudson Valley to mid-afternoon as far east as Casco Bay, Maine, all of New England was plunged into an eerie and profound darkness. At Worcester, "the Obscurity was so great that those who had good eyesight could scarcely see to read common print; the birds and fowls in many places retired to roost as tho' it had been actually night, and people were obliged to light candles to dine by." Accounts from Amenia, New York; Rupert, Vermont; Ipswich, Massachusetts; Portsmouth, Maine; and elsewhere all confirmed the story, amplifying it with reports of distant thunderings and other omens. At Newport, for example, "a Ball of fire was seen to pass swiftly and southerly over the water" in the afternoon darkness.

The impact of the Dark Day was electric: To the already indubitable millennial signs of war and revival, God had added yet another through dramatic natural omens. Even in sophisticated New Haven, Ezra Stiles reported that "the inhabitants were thrown into a Consternation, as if the appearance was preternatural." Observers in other urban centers registered similar popular dismay; on the frontier the message of the darkness was even more fearful and compelling. Even Stiles himself, though convinced that the condition was caused by smoke from slash-and-burn land clearing on the northern frontier, could not resist speculation about the meaning of the event. "It is not recollected from History," he mused, "that a darkness of equal Intenseness & Duration has ever happened in any parts of the world, except in Egypt, and at the miraculous Eclipse at the Crucifixion of our Blessed Savior." Stiles did not follow the implication that New England might soon see the climax of the divine drama begun with Exodus and the Crucifixion, but he did mirror the reaction of many that "the unusual appearances in the Natural World ought to lead our Tho'ts up to the Author of Nature, & the Energies of his irresistible power, that we may be filled with reverential awe of the divine majesty."

For rural revivalists, the Dark Day, the wartime atmosphere, and the revival itself all were indications of prophetic fulfillment portending the Last Days. Understanding themselves as experiencing the narrative of the Book of Revelation, revivalists urged their hearers to join the last witnesses to the gospel and claim the powers of spiritual and physical perfection granted to the apostolic remnant. The theme of millennial expectation suffused the New Light Stir. The larger and more intense the awakening became, the more self-validating evidence it provided that Divine Providence was preparing to introduce "the period so often spoken of in God's word, when the earth shall be full of knowledge of the Lord, as the waters cover the sea." Radical Evangelicals vigorously pursued their mission of proclaiming the Last Days of grace to rural New Englanders, urging them to join the hosts of saints "crying in union, come Lord Jesus, come quickly." . . .

The largest and best-known local sect was the Universal Friends, led by the prophetess Jemima Wilkinson, which flourished in Rhode Island and Connecticut from 1776 to 1789. Wilkinson was born in 1752 at Cumberland, Rhode Island, the eighth child of a prosperous Quaker family. She came under Radical Evangelical influence during the late 1760s quite possibly through the itinerancy of George

Whitefield. By 1776 she had rejected the plain style of Quakerism and embraced the charismatic faith of a Separate congregation at nearby Abbott Run. The year of revolution was a time of religious and moral turmoil in the Wilkinson family. Jemima's elder sister, Patience, was dismissed from Smithfield Lower Friends Meeting in 1776 for bearing an illegitimate child, and three elder brothers were expelled the same year because they frequented "Trainings for Military Service and endeavor[ed] to Justify the Same."

Amidst this disintegration of familial and religious bonds Jemima experienced renewed conviction and ascetic physical mortification. In October 1776 she contracted an "illness" during which "she appeared to meet the Shock of Death." In her delirium she saw two archangels who announced that the Last Days were come and that "the Spirit of Life from God, had descended to earth, to warn a lost and guilty, perishing and dying world, to flee from the wrath to come." The Spirit "was waiting to assume the body which God had prepared," the body of Jemima Wilkinson. She experienced the departure of her own soul to heaven and its replacement by "the Spirit of Life from God," which henceforth "took full possession" of her. Immediately Wilkinson began to exhort and itinerate, wearing a clerical costume of robes and cravat-bands, surmounted by a high-crowned white Quaker hat. She called herself "the Public Universal Friend," a minister whose mission was to witness to the Spirit within her and preach salvation to all who would listen in "the eleventh hour."

Wilkinson preached an Arminian theology that each soul enjoyed a "day of grace" in which it was free to choose salvation or damnation. Millennialism and perfectionism were also salient dimensions of Wilkinson's message. To war-ravaged Narragansett society she offered a life of holiness and moral discipline in preparation for the Last Judgment. "As in war an Error is death," she proclaimed, "so in death an Error is damnation. Therefore live as you intend to die and die as you intend to live." The decisive element in Wilkinson's ministry, however, was her personal charisma. "She exhorts in a pathetic manner," reported an early convert, "with great Confidence and Boldness . . . says that she has an immediate Revelation for all she delivers." Wilkinson's sermons, usually delivered at taverns or private homes, were often accompanied by prophecies, ecstatic prayer, and the gift of spiritual discernment. Her gender, costume, meticulous appearance, and social skills also contributed to her messianic impact on hearers. Although stopping short of asserting the power to judge and forgive sin, Wilkinson presented herself as an infallible, inspired guide in all matters of human life, possessing "the Voice that spake as never Man spake."

Wilkinson's first converts were members of her immediate family. Her father, four sisters ranging in age from twelve to twenty-nine, and a younger brother who had served in the military all professed faith in her by the end of 1777. But the most important early convert was Judge William Potter of South Kingston, Rhode Island, a wealthy and distinguished member of the Narragansett elite. Potter, whose household included thirteen children and twelve slaves in 1774, built a fourteen-room addition to the family mansion to house the Public Universal Friend. From this social base Wilkinson was able to gather other families into the sect: the Hathaways, a prominent Tory family of New Bedford; the Smith family of Stonington and Groton, Connecticut; the five sons of Benjamin Brown of New London and their families; and several clans at East Greenwich and New Milford, Connecticut.

These first converts gathered into typical Radical Evangelical congregations. In 1783 the Universal Friends built a meetinghouse at East Greenwich and issued a public declaration of faith stating "that it was by obeying the Divine Counsil Spoken to us by & through the Dear Universal Friend of friends that we are redeemed from wrath to come and are brought into Union with God & his holy one." Similar congregations appeared at South Kingston, Stonington, and New Milford in the mid-1780s. The center of community life was worship and moral discipline. Universal Friends worshiped daily in a variety of formats: silent meetings, sermonic meetings, and prayer meetings. These sessions embodied a synthesis of Quaker and Separate spirituality and emphasized the exercise of charismatic gifts. During one meeting Wilkinson was inspired to perform a healing; during another, Alice Potter Hazard cast devils out of her mentally ill brother.

At an early date, however, Universal Friends' congregations developed into more intimate biological communities. "Four of Jemima Wilkinson's sisters, her earliest converts, married members of the society. Thus the Wilkinsons of Cumberland were allied with the Potters of South Kingston and the Botsfords married Hathaways from New Bedford. Eventually all the leading families in the society of Universal Friends were linked together by ties by marriage."

The prophetess was resistant to familism, however, enjoining celibacy on her followers as the spiritually purest way of life. Yet she did not forbid marriage and took a more positive tack on the question by rewarding continent members, especially females, with special responsibilities for mission, worship, and moral oversight. Intermarriage paradoxically enforced another aspect of Wilkinson's communal leadership. With members living in such close physical and biological proximity, every aspect of their behavior was prescribed. The prophetess issued detailed rules for personal hygiene, dress, food preparation, indoor and outdoor labor, social contact, and all other matters of life-style. The sect thus became an unusual social composition, a kinship network of nuclear families governed by a charismatic celibate matriarchy. This tribal organization lent stability and discipline to the commitment of members and reflected the manner in which sectarian religion constructed new forms of primary community. . . .

Another Radical sect appeared around 1775 at Harvard, Massachusetts, "a typical subsistence community" thirty miles west of Boston. Harvard experienced a classic pattern of religious pluralization after the Great Awakening. Separates organized in 1753, calling Charlestown pipefitter Shadrach Ireland as their minister. By 1776, however, a sizable proportion of the Separates had become Baptists, and in that year they organized a congregation under their local leader Isaiah Parker. Ireland, meanwhile, became increasingly eccentric and extreme in his religious teaching. Around 1770 he abandoned his wife and family and professed the doctrine of "spiritual wifery." Ireland persuaded his followers to construct "the Square House," a large brick dwelling in which Ireland resided with his new spiritual wife and a retinue of other female disciples. About 1775 he proclaimed himself immortal and urged followers to obey his instructions so that they too would achieve physical and spiritual perfection. Included in his rules were a ban on marriage for single converts and a demand for married partners "not to lodge with each other." The Irelandites abandoned the biological family and occupied the Square House, where the prophet molded them into a celibate perfectionist sect.

Ireland's movement flourished for two more years, until his failing health made it impossible to sustain his claim to immortality. In preparing the community for his death, Ireland shifted to an apocalyptic focus, predicting the imminent arrival of Christ. According to Isaac Backus, Ireland pronounced on his deathbed, "I am going but don't bury me; for the time is short; God is coming to take the church." After his death in September 1778, Ireland's disciples obeyed, leaving his corpse reposing in a lime-filled box for more than six weeks before finally burying it. Utilizing their esoteric interpretations to the fullest, the disciples regarded Ireland's departure as a prophetic sign of the Second Coming, and the sect survived its founder. Irelandites remained at the Square House until 1781, when many of them were converted by the Shakers.

Other kinds of local sectarian activity took place elsewhere in the hill country during the New Light Stir. . . .

By 1779 the Come-Outers [of Gorham, Maine] were practicing ecstatic worship quite reminiscent of James Davenport's followers in the Great Awakening. The charismatic leaders were "generally females" who "wrought themselves up to complete frenzy, even to frothing at the mouth, dancing, stamping, and whirling around." This exercise eventuated in a trance state that they regarded as "holding communion with God." When conscious again these charismatics confronted individual sinners, "assailing them with a torrent of invectives . . . not forgetting to remind the poor culprit of each and every known fault, or deviation from the path of right, which he had been known to take from his infancy."

At its peak the Come-Outer movement embraced "strange notions" of physical and spiritual perfection as well as pacifism. The sectarians also embraced a radical life-style marked by shunning, separation from the world, and strict sumptuary codes. "Ribbons, ruffles, jewelry, and ornaments of all kinds were in their estimation especially articles of temptation used by the devil to work evil and ruin the soul of the wearer."

In 1780 the Come-Outers continued their campaign against the Old Lights, locking the parish church, rioting, and disrupting services. They in turn were beaten and stoned for their pacifism and radical deviance. The violence ended only with the assertion of civil and military order, along with "an epidemic of some sort" that forced cooperation between the competing religious groups. Active hostility subsided after 1781, but Gorham remained permanently divided on religious grounds. . . .

Similar movements occurred in Maine at New Gloucester, Alfred, and Sanford. In Sanford the Radicals were called "the Merry Dancers" for their unbridled ecstasy. Made up mainly of young war veterans, the Merry Dancers repeatedly disrupted the Congregationalist parish before gathering their own meeting in 1780. The perfectionism of this youthful group soon grew out of hand, bringing about "drinking to excess . . . and indecent and immoral practices." The Dancers also engaged in strange antics such as "hooting the Devil." Members dressed in strange garb while screaming, "Woe! Woe! Woe!" which was "audible in the stillness of the evening nearly the distance of one mile." The Merry Dancers explained such excesses as purification rites for perfection, "a sort of carnal slough through which they were doomed to pass, preparatory to spiritual regeneration."

The Come-Outers, Merry Dancers, and New Lebanon New Lights illustrated the process of sect development on the northern frontier. Renewed religious concern, a rapid influx of settlers, and returning veterans created unstable socioreligious conditions, characterized by mounting division between New Lights and Old Lights. When revival struck in such circumstances, institutional fluidity permitted swift growth of heterodox doctrine and charismatic experience. Young men and women emerged as sectarian leaders on the basis of their extraordinary gifts while millennial expectation, new communal identity, and Old Light opposition kept revival at fever pitch. Typically these sectarian movements rose to a paroxysm of ecstatic deviance—chiliasm, orgiastic purification, violence. These episodes often passed quickly, leaving the sects in an ambiguous position that they resolved by either returning to the larger community or remaining apart in a kind of spiritual limbo, awaiting "further light." . . .

A different pattern of local sectarianism appeared in the rise of the New Israelites of Middletown, Vermont. This community was inspired by Nathaniel Wood, a Separate from Norwich, Connecticut, who was one of Middletown's original settlers and sire of its leading family. . . .

[His] new family sect soon assumed a menacing tone, pronouncing "supernatural agencies and special judgments of God" on local citizens. This defensive posture was elaborated into theological terms with "Priest" Wood's assertion that his followers were "modern Israelites or Jews, who were under the special guardianship of the Almighty while the Gentiles—all who were opposed to them—would suffer from their hostility." For about ten years Priest Wood and his New Israelites adopted rigorous dietary and sumptuary codes based on their reading of the Mosaic Law and manifested prophetic and other spiritual gifts. During this period the sect grew to a modest size, including in its numbers Joseph Smith, Sr., father of the Mormon prophet, and Oliver Cowdery, Sr., father of one of the three Mormon Witnesses.

Around 1799 the New Israelites came under the influence of a diviner named Wingate who convinced the Woods that secret prophecies and miraculous root medicines could be discovered by use of divining rods. Priest Wood pronounced the rods to be instruments of God's judgment and used their powers to make increasingly bizarre demands on his followers. For example, the rods revealed to Wood that Satan was inhabiting the clothes of two adolescent females in the sect, who were then directed to strip and hike naked over a nearby mountain to purify themselves. A temple was built and then abandoned by command of the rods, and for several years New Israelites spent their summers digging for treasure under their guidance.

This sectarian jumble of divination, prophecy, and alienation crystallized in Wood's prediction that "the destroyer would pass through the land and slay a portion of unbelievers" on the night of 14 January 1801 and that a great earthquake would obliterate the remaining unfaithful. The New Israelites recognized the prophecy as a second Passover preparatory to the end of the world. They abandoned their homes, painting over the doorposts the slogan "Jesus our passover was sacrificed for us" as a sign for their possessions to be spared. They then gathered in a schoolhouse to observe the Passover by fasting, prayer, and exhortation. The local militia was mustered to meet any insurrectionary action by the New Israelites, but the night passed quietly. Wood announced a slight miscalculation, then eight weeks later instructed believers to contribute their specie to pave the streets of the New Jerusalem. At this point the diviner Wingate was exposed as a convicted counterfeiter, and the movement collapsed. The Wood, Smith, and Cowdery families left Middletown in disgrace for upstate New York, where their religious enthusiasm passed to a new generation. . . .

The evidence, though fragmentary, suggests that literally dozens of local sects were spawned in rural New England by the New Light Stir and its aftermath. Revivalism is an uncontrollable form of religious transformation, and when it struck an already fragmented culture in the hill country the result was an explosion of enthusiasm and heterodoxy. A region mired in the throes of war, political struggle for self-determination, precarious economic conditions, and frontier isolation did not possess the means to routinize religious renewal into stable institutional form. . . .

. . . [T]he sects articulated basic social and intellectual discontent with colonial religion in all its forms and pointed toward new religious identities appropriate to unprecedented circumstances. Three interlocking dimensions of this emerging identity seem particularly important. First, the sects expressed an overwhelming need for deep and transforming personal religious experience. Virtually all the local sects were charismatic. They displayed a range and variety of gifts limited only by the imagination and creativity of the sectarians themselves. Their spirituality was so intense that it extended into the realm of sensory and physical reality, transforming even sexuality into an instrument for divine use, whether through celibacy, continence, or spiritual wifery. For the sectarians, religion was above all an experiential mode that gave access to new spiritual understanding and physical powers of sinlessness.

The sects also undertook to redefine social and economic order through the model of the extended family. They practiced separation from the world and built new social practices upon the kinship networks that comprised most of their membership. Marginal economic conditions helped extend this social reorientation through collective farming and communal property arrangements. Local sects tended to be economically egalitarian and socially authoritarian, with the charismatic leadership functioning often as symbolic "spiritual parents" to believing children. Extensive rituals and detailed prescription of daily activity followed from such an arrangement, providing concrete social and economic behaviors through which spiritual authority could be mediated. These characteristics suggest that rural sectarians absorbed the most distinctive social and economic traits of their environment— clans and friendship circles, egalitarian class structure, and cooperative subsistence economics—into their visions of religious community, thereby sacralizing and legitimating the life patterns of the new New England.

Finally, the local sects unmistakably modified the Calvinist theological tradition. Each group based its beliefs on a rejection of some salient feature of post-Awakening Calvinist thought, and no matter how bizarre the protests seemed, they contained serious intellectual content. Jemima Wilkinson, Shadrach Ireland, and William Dorrell challenged the uneasy Calvinist anthropology of innate depravity and spiritual sensation, claiming an essentially Arminian perfectionism. Annihilationists and Nothingarians, Merry Dancers and Come-Outers applied the logic of determinism in alternative ways, the former arguing that the damned had no existence after death, the latter that the elect were doomed to sin as a precondition for grace. Nathaniel Wood stood Evangelical Calvinist exegesis on its head, claiming that the Old rather than the New Testament was the norm for Christian faith and practice. Joseph Meacham surveyed the signs of the times and asserted that the gradual earthly appearance of Christ's kingdom argued by Edwards was erroneous. Rather, a violent and sudden Second Advent was about to commence.

FURTHER READING

Bloch, Ruth. *Visionary Republic: Millennial Themes in American Thought, 1756–1800* (1985).

Bonomi, Patricia. *Under the Cope of Heaven: Religion, Society and Politics in Colonial America* (1986).

Bushman, Richard. *The Great Awakening: Documents on the Revival of Religion, 1740–1745* (1970).

Demos, John. *The Unredeemed Captive: A Family Story from Early America* (1994).

Essig, James. *The Bonds of Wickedness: American Evangelicals Against Slavery, 1770–1808* (1982).

Gaustad, Edwin. *The Great Awakening in New England* (1957).

Griffin, Kevin. *Revolution and Religion: The American Revolutionary War and the Reformed Clergy* (1994).

Hatch, Nathan. *The Sacred Cause of Liberty: Republican Thought and the Millennium in Revolutionary New England* (1977).

Hatch, Nathan, and Harry Stout, eds. *Jonathan Edwards and the American Experience* (1988).

Heimert, Alan. *Religion and the American Mind from the Great Awakening to the Revolution* (1966).

Heyrman, Christine. *Southern Cross: The Beginnings of the Bible Belt* (1997).

Hughes, Richard, and C. Leonard Allen. *Illusions of Innocence: Protestant Primitivism in America, 1630–1875* (1988).

Isaac, Rhys. *The Transformation of Virginia* (1982).

Juster, Susan. *Disorderly Women: Sexual Politics and Evangelicalism in Revolutionary New England* (1994).

May, Henry. *The Enlightenment in America* (1976).

Miller, Perry. *The New England Mind: From Colony to Province* (1953).

Miller, Perry, and Alan Heimert. *The Great Awakening: Documents Illustrating the Crisis and Its Consequences* (1967).

Noll, Mark. *Christians in the American Revolution* (1977).

———. *Princeton and the Republic, 1768–1822* (1989).

Scherer, Lester B. *Slavery and the Churches in Early America, 1619–1819* (1975).

Schmidt, Leigh Eric. *Holy Fairs: Scottish Communions and American Revivals in the Early Modern Period* (1989).

Stout, Harry. *The New England Soul: Preaching and Religious Culture in Colonial New England* (1986).

———. *The Divine Dramatist: George Whitefield and the Rise of Modern Evangelicalism* (1991).

Tracy, Patricia. *Jonathan Edwards, Pastor* (1980).

Woolverton, John. *Colonial Anglicanism in North America* (1984).

CHAPTER
5

Religion in the Early Republic:
1790–1850

The First Amendment to the Constitution prohibited Congress from establishing a church or preventing free exercise of religion. Even so, several states continued to have state-supported churches, including Connecticut until 1816 and Massachusetts until 1833. Since then all states have followed the principles embodied in the First Amendment and every church has been left free to recruit members and to raise funds for its ministers' pay. The overwhelming majority of the population throughout the nineteenth century was still Christian, however, and regarded certain kinds of conduct (such as Mormon polygamy) as intolerable. Their view was upheld by the judiciary, whose members also looked on America as a "Christian Republic."

The early national period was another era of vigorous revivalism, often referred to by historians as the Second Great Awakening. Baptists and Methodists, hitherto small denominations, proved extremely well adapted to recruiting the westward-moving population as it extended the republic beyond the Appalachians, along the Ohio River, and out to the Mississippi. Before 1850 they had become the nation's two largest denominations, leaving far behind the Congregationalists, Presbyterians, and Episcopalians who had dominated on the eve of the Revolution. The Methodists' circuit-riders, mobile preachers seeking out every new settlement, were tenacious in winning converts. The Baptists, who believed that preachers were chosen directly by God and that seminary training was unnecessary, had an ample supply of voluntary preachers.

The Shakers, the Disciples of Christ, and the Mormons were among the new, American-invented churches that began their history in this era. They all originated in an area of Upstate New York known as the "burned-over district" because of the frequency of religious upheavals and experiments there. Promoting revivals became almost a science in the hands of Charles Grandison Finney, a charismatic preacher in the tradition of Whitefield. The Protestant denominations now had to compete against each other for adherents; their arguments and rivalries were often acrimonious. For the first time certain individuals, including Joseph Smith and Orestes Brownson, tried to make up their own minds by sampling several churches in fairly quick succession, only to find them all wanting. The social and psychological experience of pluralism became, and remained thereafter, a characteristic element of American religious life.

Some southern slaveowners, prior to the Revolution, had tried to convert their slaves to Christianity, but others had feared that conversion might lead to revolts. Northern states began to abolish slavery soon after the Revolution; the trans-Atlantic slave trade was eliminated in 1808. The southern states reacted by mounting a more vigorous intellectual defense of slavery and by converting more of their slaves to Christianity, although masters were rarely able to control the forms their slaves' religion actually took. Slave Christianity incorporated elements of African religions and a variety of beliefs involving haunting and witchcraft. It also taught lessons about human dignity and freedom that would contribute to undermining the slave system and to creating an independent black community.

 D O C U M E N T S

Document 1 is the record of an anxious young woman who found her dreams literally coming true when she visited Mother Ann Lee, founder of the Shakers, in the later days of the Revolutionary War (c. 1780). The Shakers' strenuous way of life and absolute celibacy attracted recruits for more than a century. In Document 2 (1857), Orestes Brownson gives a humorous description of his failed attempt to live up to the Presbyterians' code of conduct in about 1820. He wrote the passage after his later conversion to Roman Catholicism to show that, contrary to popular prejudice, the Protestant churches were actually much *more* repressive than the Catholic. In Document 3 (1835), Charles Grandison Finney justifies the emotional manipulation involved in revival preaching. In his view it is just a way of giving the Holy Spirit a nudge in the right direction. Document 4 (1842) is testimony from Joseph Smith, the founder of the Mormon church, about his early religious life, his visits from the angel Moroni, his translation of the Book of Mormon from golden tablets, and the persecution of his church. Shortly after writing it he was murdered at Carthage, Illinois, leaving his successor, Brigham Young, to take the Mormons to Utah. Document 5, by Ralph Waldo Emerson (1841), is a classic statement of the New England Transcendentalists, former Unitarians who had abandoned conventional Christian doctrines but who had a vivid sense of participating in a connected and supernatural universe. Documents 6, 7, and 8 are accounts of slaves' religious rituals, of the benevolence of Quakers to escaping slaves, and of the difficulties faced by a black preacher who lived north of the Mason-Dixon Line.

1. Lucy Wight Meets Shaker Leader Mother Ann Lee (c. 1780), 1826

When I was young I used to be much affected with reading about the sufferings and persecutions which Christ and his disciples endured from the wicked; and I often thought if I had lived in that day, I would have been one of Christ's disciples. When I was about nineteen years old, I was taken very sick with a nervous fever so that my life was despaired of, both by myself and others. In the time of this sickness I

Testimonies Concerning the Character and Ministry of Mother Ann Lee (Albany: Packard and Van Benthuysen, 1827), 65–69.

fell into a kind of trance, and thought I died. Finding myself alone in the world of spirits, as I thought, and no one to help me, I was in great trouble, and prayed that some one would come to my assistance, and conduct me to a place of happiness. And there appeared to me a very pure, bright looking man, who conducted me to a house, as it seemed, where I saw a number of people who looked so pure and clean that I began to feel greatly ashamed of myself. Among the rest I saw a man who seemed to be walking the floor, under the operations of the power of God.

The sight of such heavenly purity as these people seemed to possess, and the sense I felt of my own impurity and unfitness for such a place, brought excessive tribulation upon me, and I felt as tho I wanted to get away and hide myself. I told the people that when I was in the body, I thought when I died I should go to Heaven but I could not find Heaven, because I had come there in my sins; and I asked them if there was not some place where I could go and repent of my sins and be saved, and not go to hell. They said there was; and I might go and repent.

About this time my father came to my bed-side and took hold of my hand, and I awoke from my trance. I asked him if he thought I was dying. He said he thought I was, and asked me if I did not think so. I answered No. He asked me if I was willing to die. I replied that I was not; for I was yet in my sins; and if I should die in my sins, I could not be saved. My vision in this sickness greatly awakened my feelings, and led me to search for some way out of sin. In this search I continued for several years without success—no way appeared; but I did not then know the cause.

In the year 1779, there was a great revival of religion in New-Lebanon, in which I received a witness that the time of Christ's second appearance was near at hand; but in what manner it would take place I could not tell: for I believed his second appearance, like the first, would take place in a manner contrary to all human calculation. And I was afraid I should be like the unbelieving Jews, and should oppose Christ in his coming.

In the spring of the following year, (1780,) there were various reports in circulation about a strange sort of people living up above Albany; and I felt a great anxiety to go and search them out, and see whether there was any thing good among them or not. Accordingly I set out with six or seven others to make them a visit. While on our journey, one of the company asked me if I was going to join them. I replied that I had searched a great deal after religion; but had never yet found any that had any solid foundation; and if their religion had no better foundation than any that I had ever found before, I should not join them: for, said I, "they cannot catch old birds with chaff."

We went to John Partington's and staid over night. The next morning, being Sabbath, we went on to the place where Mother and the Elders lived, and arrived there just before they began their morning worship, and attended their meeting, which was unspeakably powerful, solemn and striking. We also attended their afternoon meeting. The mighty power of God was evidently present in visible operations among the people. I was so affected with a sense of fear, guilt and shame, on account of my own wretched and lost state, and my unfitness to be with a people of such purity, that I drew back and kept out of sight as much as possible. Among other extraordinary manifestations of the power of God which I noticed, one of the Elders, while walking the floor under the visible operations of divine power suddenly extended his hand towards me, and came directly up to me, saying, "God knows what is there, and so do his servants." This struck me very forcibly; I fully believed what he said, and felt as tho all my sins were as plain and open to their view as they were to my own; and I felt as much tribulation as I was able to endure.

We again attended the evening meeting, when I again stepped in behind the people and sat down on a bench, in hopes of keeping out of sight. Elder James Whittaker soon came and sat down with me, and said, "Woman, what do you think of this great work of God?" I answered, "I know it is the work of God." "So you do; (said he,) but you are like the Jews of old, who waited long for a Messiah; but when he came, he was too mean for them; so is this work of God too mean for you." I replied, that I did not think there was any way of God for me. Then Mother and the Elders came and kneeled down before me; my head was bowed down into my lap and I was unable to raise it up, or to help myself. Mother wept and cried for a few minutes, and then began to sing, and sung very melodiously. They then told me that there was a way of God for me, if I would confess and forsake my sins. This I fully believed, and in obedience to the faith I then received, I went immediately out and confessed my sins honestly before Mother; and I found her to be a Mother indeed. I found that releasement from the burden of sin which I had never felt before, and which I had never been able to find in any other way tho I had long sought for it.

The vision which I had seen in my sickness, more than four years before, came fresh to my mind. Here was the house and the people. I remembered the guilt and confusion I had felt in my vision, and now I had realized it. The man who came to me with out-stretched hand, I found to be Elder John Hocknell; and I knew him to be the same man that I saw in my vision, walking the floor under the operations of divine power. All the scenes of that singular vision were this day realized to me in a very striking manner. I now felt as tho I had got upon a sure foundation, where I could safely stand. We continued there the following day; during this time Mother faithfully instructed us in the way of God. On Tuesday morning we took our leave of them and returned home greatly satisfied with our visit. When I got home, I told my father I had found the people I saw in my vision, and I knew Elder John Hocknell to be the same man I saw walking the floor under the power of God; and my father recollected the vision. . . .

Altho it is now nearly forty-two years since Mother Ann's decease; yet that same testimony which I first received from her, still remains like a living witness in my soul; and in obedience to its teaching, I have received many blessed gifts of God, and many precious seasons of heavenly joy and comfort. I have enjoyed many feeling sensations of Mother's spirit and presence since she left the body. In times of tribulation, I have often felt her present with me, to comfort me. These things are not fanciful dreams of the imagination; but as real as the light of the sun in a clear day. Could I believe the charges of the wicked against Mother, I must believe that a corrupt tree can bring forth good fruit: for I know I have received much good and heavenly fruit from her; and I never received any thing from her but what was good; nor did I ever see anything but goodness in her, from the first day I saw her to the day of her decease.

LUCY WIGHT.
New-Lebanon, June 10th, 1826.

2. Orestes Brownson Recalls His Quest for the Right Religion as a Young Man (c. 1820), 1857

The Monday following my reception into the Presbyterian communion we had a covenant meeting, or a meeting of all the members of the church. The Presbyterians, like most of the Protestant sects in this country, adopt the doctrine of the old Dona-tists, that the church is composed of the elect, the just, or the saints only, and they therefore distinguish between the church and the congregation, or between those who are held to be saints, and those held to be sinners; that is, between those who profess to have been regenerated, and those who make no such pretension, although they may have been baptized. The church members, to the number of about six hun-dred, came together on Monday, and after being addressed by the pastor, and stirred up to greater zeal for the promotion of Presbyterianism, renewed their covenant obligations, and bound themselves to greater efforts for the conversion of sinners, the common name given to all not of the sect, even though members of the congre-gation, and born of Presbyterian parents. In this meeting we all solemnly pledged ourselves, not only to pray for the conversion of sinners, but to mark them wherever we met them, to avoid them, to have no intercourse with them that could be helped, and never to speak to them except to admonish them of their sins, or so far as it should be necessary on business. There was to be no interchange of social or neigh-borly visits between us and them, and we were to have even business relations with them only when absolutely necessary. We were by our manner to show all, not members of the Presbyterian Church, that we regarded them as the enemies of God, and therefore as our enemies, as persons hated by God, and therefore hated by us; and we were, even in business relations, always to give the preference to church members, and, as far as possible, without sacrificing our own interests, to treat those not members as outcasts from society, as pariahs; and thus, by appeals to their busi-ness interests, their social feelings, and their desire to stand well in the community, to compel them to join the Presbyterian Church. The meeting was animated by a singular mixture of bigotry, uncharitableness, apparent zeal for God's glory, and a shrewd regard to the interests of this world.

About the time I speak of, and for several years after, meetings of the sort I have described, were common in the Presbyterian churches; and a movement was made, in 1827, to induce all the members throughout the Union to pledge them-selves to non-intercourse with the rest of the community, except for their conver-sion, and to refuse in the common business affairs of life to patronize any one not a member of the church. How far it succeeded, I am not informed; but as, taking the country at large, the Presbyterians were but a small minority, and by no means able to control its business operations, I suppose it was only partially successful, and its abettors had to soften their rules a little so as to bring within the privileged the members of the other Evangelical sects.

It may readily be believed that the exhibition I saw was not over and above pleasing to me, and that it was only with a wry face that I took the pledges with the

Orestes Brownson, *Works,* vol. 5 (1888; reprint, New York: AMS Press, 1966), 3–30.

rest. I was in for it, and I would do as the others did. I saw at once that I had made a mistake, that I had no sympathy with the Presbyterian spirit, and should need a long and severe training to sour and elongate my visage sufficiently to enjoy the full confidence of my new brethren. Every day's experience proved it. In our covenant we had bound ourselves to watch over one another with fraternal affection. I was not long in discovering that this meant that we were each to be a spy upon the others, and to rebuke, admonish, or report them to the Session. My whole life became constrained. I dared not trust myself, in the presence of a church member, to a single spontaneous emotion; I dared not speak in my natural tone of voice, and if I smiled, I expected to be reported. The system of espionage in some European countries is bad enough, and it is no pleasant reflection that the man you are talking with may be a *mouchard,* and report your words to the *Préfet de Police;* but that is nothing to what one must endure as a Presbyterian, unless he has enough of malignity to find an indemnification for being spied in spying others. We were allowed no liberty, and dared enjoy ourselves only by stealth. The most rigid Catholic ascetic never imagined a discipline a thousandth part as rigid as the discipline to which I was subjected. The slightest deviation was a mortal sin, the slightest forgetfulness was enough to send me to hell. I must not talk with sinners; I must take no pleasure in social intercourse with persons, however moral, amiable, well-bred, or worthy, if not members of the church; I was forbidden to read books written by others than Presbyterians, and commanded never to inquire into my belief as a Presbyterian, or to reason on it, or about it.

I tried for a year or two to stifle my discontent, to silence my reason, to repress my natural emotions, to extinguish my natural affections, and to submit patiently to the Calvinistic discipline. I spent much time in prayer and meditation, I read pious books, and finally plunged myself into my studies with a view of becoming a Presbyterian minister. But it would not do. I had joined the church because I had despaired of myself, and because, despairing of reason, I had wished to submit to authority. If the Presbyterian Church had satisfied me that she had authority, was authorized by Almighty God to teach and direct me, I could have continued to submit; but while she exercised the most rigid authority over me, she disclaimed all authority to teach me, and remitted me to the Scriptures and private judgment. "We do not ask you to take this as your creed," said my pastor, on giving me a copy of the Presbyterian Confession of Faith; "we do not give you this as a summary of the doctrines, you must hold, but as an excellent summary of the doctrines which we believe the Scriptures teach. What you are to believe is the Bible. You must take the Bible as your creed, and read it with a prayerful mind, begging the Holy Ghost to aid you to understand it aright." But while the church refused to take the responsibility of telling me what doctrines I must believe, while she sent me to the Bible and private judgment, she yet claimed authority to condemn and excommunicate me as a heretic, if I departed from the standard of doctrine contained in her Confession.

This I regarded as unfair treatment. It subjected me to all the disadvantages of authority without any of its advantages. The church demanded that I should treat her as a true mother, while she was free to treat me only as a stepson, or even as a stranger. Be one thing or another, said I; either assume the authority and the responsibility of teaching and directing me, or leave me with the responsibility my freedom. If you have authority from God, avow it, and exercise it. I am all submission.

I will hold what you say, and do what you bid. If you have not, then say so, and forbear to call me to an account for differing from you, or disregarding your teachings. Either bind me or loose me. Do not mock me with a freedom which is no freedom, or with an authority which is illusory. If you claim authority over my faith, tell me what I must believe, and do not throw upon me the labor and responsibility of forming a creed for myself; if you do not, if you send me to the Bible and private judgment, to find out the Christian faith the best way I can, do not hold me obliged to conform to your standards, or assume the right to anathematize me for departing from them. . . .

In becoming a Presbyterian on the ground I did, I committed a mistake, and placed myself in a false position, which it took me years to rectify. It was a capital blunder. Not that I was insincere, or governed by bad motives, but because, feeling the insufficiency of my own reason to guide me, I turned my back on reason, and took up with what I supposed to be authority without a rational motive for believing it divinely commissioned. As far as I could, I abnegated my own rational nature, denied reason to make way for revelation, rational conviction to make way for authority. Unhappily, the religious belief of my Protestant countrymen, as far as religious belief they have, is built on scepticism, and hence, if they think at all, they have a perpetual struggle in their minds between faith and reason. The two are presented, not each as the other's complement, but as antagonistic, the one to advance only over the dead body of the other. All those with whom I came into relation, either denied reason to make way for revelation, or revelation to make way for reason. At least such was their tendency. The one class declaimed against reason, used reason against reason, and sometimes assigned, apparently, a very good reason why reason ought not to be used. The other class either openly denied all supernatural revelation, or, admitting it in words, explained away all its supernaturalness, and brought it within the sphere of the natural order, and subjected it to the dominion of natural reason.

3. Charles Grandison Finney Stirs Up Religious Emotions at Revival Meetings, c. 1835

1. Revivals were formerly regarded as miracles. And it has been so by some even in our day. And others have ideas on the subject so loose and unsatisfactory, that if they would only *think,* they would see their absurdity. For a long time, it was supposed by the church, that a revival was a miracle, an interposition of Divine power which they had nothing to do with, and which they had no more agency in producing, than they had in producing thunder, or a storm of hail, or an earthquake. It is only within a few years that ministers generally have supposed revivals were to be *promoted,* by the use of means designed and adapted specially to that object. Even in New England, it has been supposed that revivals came just as showers do, sometimes in one town, and sometimes in another, and that ministers and churches

---

Charles Grandison Finney, *Lectures on Revivals of Religion* (New York: Fleming H. Revell, 1868), 18–20.

could do nothing more to produce them than they could to make showers of rain come on their own town, when they were falling on a neighboring town.

It used to be supposed that a revival would come about once in fifteen years, and all would be converted that God intended to save, and then they must wait until another crop came forward on the stage of life. Finally, the time got shortened down to five years, and they supposed there might be a revival about as often as that.

I have heard a fact in relation to one of these pastors, who supposed revivals might come about once in five years. There had been a revival in his congregation. The next year, there was a revival in a neighboring town, and he went there to preach, and staid several days, till he got his soul all engaged in the work. He returned home on Saturday, and went into his study to prepare for the Sabbath. And his soul was in an agony. He thought how many adult persons there were in his congregation at enmity with God—so many still unconverted—so many persons *die* yearly—such a portion of them unconverted—if a revival does not come under five years, so many adult heads of families will be in hell. He put down his calculations on paper, and embodied them in his sermon for the next day, with his heart bleeding at the dreadful picture. As I understood it, he did not do this with any expectation of a revival, but he felt deeply, and poured out his heart to his people. And that sermon awakened *forty heads of families,* and a powerful revival followed; and so his theory about a revival once in five years was all exploded.

Thus God has overthrown, generally, the theory that revivals are miracles.

2. Mistaken notions concerning the sovereignty of God have greatly hindered revivals.

Many people have supposed God's sovereignty to be some thing very different from what it is. They have supposed it to be such an arbitrary disposal of events, and particularly of the gift of his Spirit, as precluded a rational employment of means for promoting a revival of religion. But there is no evidence from the Bible that God exercises any such sovereignty as that. There are no facts to prove it. But every thing goes to show that God has connected means with the end through all the departments of his government—in nature and in grace. There is no *natural* event in which his own agency is not concerned. He has not built the creation like a vast machine that will go on alone without his further care. He has not retired from the universe, to let it work for itself. This is mere atheism. He exercises a universal superintendence and control. And yet every event in nature has been brought about by means. He neither administers providence nor grace with that sort of sovereignty that dispenses with the use of means. There is no more sovereignty in one than in the other.

And yet some people are terribly alarmed at all direct efforts to promote a revival, and they cry out, "You are trying to get up a revival in your own strength. Take care, you are interfering with the sovereignty of God. Better keep along in the usual course, and let God give a revival when he thinks it is best. God is a sovereign, and it is very wrong for you to attempt to get up a revival, just because *you think* a revival is needed." This is just such preaching as the devil wants. And men cannot do the devil's work more effectually than by preaching up the sovereignty of God, as a reason why we should not put forth efforts to produce a revival.

3. You see the error of those who are beginning to think that religion can be better promoted in the world without revivals, and who are disposed to give up all efforts to produce religious awakenings. Because there are evils arising in some

instances out of great excitements on the subject of religion, they are of opinion that it is best to dispense with them altogether. This cannot, and must not be. True, there is danger of abuses. In cases of great *religious* as well as all other excitements, more or less incidental evils may be expected of course. But this is no reason why they should be given up. The best things are always liable to abuses. Great and manifold evils have originated in the providential and moral governments of God. But these *foreseen* perversions and evils were not considered a sufficient reason for giving them up. For the establishment of these governments was on the whole the best that could be done for the production of the greatest amount of happiness. So in revivals of religion, it is found by experience, that in the present state of the world, religion cannot be promoted to any considerable extent without them. The evils which are sometimes complained of, when they are real, are incidental, and of small importance when compared with the amount of good produced by revivals. The sentiment should not be admitted by the church for a moment, that revivals may be given up. It is fraught with all that is dangerous to the interests of Zion, is death to the cause of missions, and brings in its train the damnation of the world.

4. Joseph Smith Explains How an Angel Guided Him to Found the Latter-Day Saints (Mormons), 1842

I was born in the town of Sharon Windsor co., Vermont, on the 23d of December, A. D. 1805. When ten years old my parents removed to Palmyra New York, where we resided about four years, and from thence we removed to the town of Manchester.

My father was a farmer and taught me the art of husbandry. When about fourteen years of age I began to reflect upon the importance of being prepared for a future state, and upon enquiring the plan of salvation I found that there was a great clash in religious sentiment; if I went to one society they referred me to one plan, and another to another; each one pointing to his own particular creed as the summum bonum of perfection: considering that all could not be right, and that God could not be the author of so much confusion I determined to investigate the subject more fully, believing that if God had a church it would not be split up into factions, and that if he taught one society to worship one way, and administer in one set of ordinances, he would not teach another principles which were diametrically opposed. Believing the word of God I had confidence in the declaration of James: "If any man lack wisdom let him ask of God who giveth to all men liberally and upbraideth not and it shall be given him." I retired to a secret place in a grove and began to call upon the Lord, while fervently engaged in supplication my mind was taken away from the objects with which I was surrounded, and I was enwrapped in a heavenly vision and saw two glorious personages who exactly resembled each other in features, and likeness, surrounded with a brilliant light which eclipsed the sun at noon-day. They told me that all religious denominations were believing in incorrect doctrines, and that none of them was acknowledged by God as his church

Dean C. Jesse, ed., *The Personal Writings of Joseph Smith* (Salt Lake City: Deseret Books, 1984).

and kingdom. And I was expressly commanded to "go not after them," at the same time receiving a promise that the fulness of the gospel should at some future time be made known unto me.

On the evening of the 21st of September, A. D. 1823, while I was praying unto God, and endeavoring to exercise faith in the precious promises of scripture on a sudden a light like that of day, only of a far purer and more glorious appearance, and brightness burst into the room, indeed the first sight was as though the house was filled with consuming fire; the appearance produced a shock that affected the whole body; in a moment a personage stood before me surrounded with a glory yet greater than that with which I was already surrounded. This messenger proclaimed himself to be an angel of God sent to bring the joyful tidings, that the covenant which God made with ancient Israel was at hand to be fulfilled, that the preparatory work for the second coming of the Messiah was speedily to commence; that the time was at hand for the gospel, in all its fulness to be preached in power, unto all nations that a people might be prepared for the millennial reign.

I was informed that I was chosen to be an instrument in the hands of God to bring about some of his purposes in this glorious dispensation.

I was also informed concerning the aboriginal inhabitants of this country, and shown who they were, and from whence they came; a brief sketch of their origin, progress, civilization, laws, governments, of their righteousness and iniquity, and the blessings of God being finally withdrawn from them as a people was made known unto me: I was also told where there was deposited some plates on which were engraven an abridgement of the records of the ancient prophets that had existed on this continent. The angel appeared to me three times the same night and unfolded the same things. After having received many visits from the angels of God unfolding the majesty, and glory of the events that should transpire in the last days, on the morning of the 22d of September A. D. 1827, the angel of the Lord delivered the records into my hands.

These records were engraven on plates which had the appearance of gold, each plate was six inches wide and eight inches long and not quite so thick as common tin. They were filled with engravings, in Egyptian characters and bound together in a volume, as the leaves of a book with three rings running through the whole. The volume was something near six inches in thickness, a part of which was sealed. The characters on the unsealed part were small, and beautifully engraved. The whole book exhibited many marks of antiquity in its construction and much skill in the art of engraving. With the records was found a curious instrument which the ancients called "Urim and Thummim," which consisted of two transparent stones set in the rim of a bow fastened to a breastplate.

Through the medium of the Urim and Thummim I translated the record by the gift, and power of God.

In this important and interesting book the history of ancient America is unfolded, from its first settlement by a colony that came from the tower of Babel, at the confusion of languages to the beginning of the fifth century of the Christian era. We are informed by these records that America in ancient times has been inhabited by two distinct races of people. The first were called Jaredites and came directly from the tower of Babel. The second race came directly from the city of Jerusalem, about six hundred years before Christ. They were principally Israelites, of the descendants of Joseph. The Jaredites were destroyed about the time that the Israelites came from Jerusalem, who succeeded them in the inheritance of the country. The principal nation of the second race fell in battle toward the close of the fourth century. The remnant are the Indians that now inhabit this country. This book also tells us that our Saviour made his appearance upon this continent after his resurrection, that he planted the gospel here in all its fulness, and richness, and power, and blessing; that they had apostles, prophets, pastors, teachers and evangelists; the same order, the same priesthood, the same ordinances, gifts, powers, and blessing, as was enjoyed on the eastern continent, that the people were cut off in consequence of their transgressions, that the last of their prophets who existed among them was commanded to write an abridgement of their prophesies, history &c., and to hide it up in the earth, and that it should come forth and be united with the bible for the accomplishment of the purposes of God in the last days. For a more particular account I would refer to the Book of Mormon, which can be purchased at Nauvoo, or from any of our travelling elders.

As soon as the news of this discovery was made known, false reports, misrepresentation and slander flew as on the wings of the wind in every direction, the house was frequently beset by mobs, and evil designing persons, several times I was shot at, and very narrowly escaped, and every device was made use of to get the plates away from me, but the power and blessing of God attended me, and several began to believe my testimony.

On the 6th of April, 1830, the "Church of Jesus Christ of Latter-Day Saints," was first organized in the town of Manchester, Ontario co., state of New York. Some few were called and ordained by the spirit of revelation, and prophesy, and began to preach as the spirit gave them utterance, and though weak, yet were they strengthened by the power of God, and many were brought to repentance, were immersed in the water, and were filled with the Holy Ghost by the laying on of hands. They saw visions and prophesied, devils were cast out and the sick healed by the laying on of hands. From that time the work rolled forth with astonishing rapidity, and churches were soon formed in the states of New York, Pennsylvania, Ohio, Indiana, Illinois and Missouri; in the last named state a considerable settlement was formed in Jackson co.; numbers joined the church and we were increasing rapidly; we made large purchases of land, our farms teemed with plenty, and peace and happiness was enjoyed in our domestic circle and throughout our neighborhood; but as we could not associate with our neighbors who were many of them of the basest of men and had fled from the face of civilized society, to the frontier country to escape the hand of justice, in their midnight revels, their sabbath breaking, horseracing, and gambling, they commenced at first ridicule, then to persecute, and finally an organized mob assembled and burned our houses, tarred, and feathered, and whipped many of our brethren and finally drove them from their habitations; who houseless, and homeless, contrary to law, justice and humanity, had to wander on the bleak prairies till the children left the tracks of their blood on the prairie, this took place in the month of November, and they had no other covering but the canopy of heaven, in this inclement season of the year; this proceeding was winked at by the government and although we had warrantee deeds for our land, and had violated no law we could obtain no redress.

There were many sick, who were thus inhumanly driven from their houses, and had to endure all this abuse and to seek homes where they could be found. The result was, that a great many of them being deprived of the comforts of life, and the necessary attendances, died; many children were left orphans; wives, widows; and husbands widowers.—Our farms were taken possession of by the mob, many thousands of cattle, sheep, horses, and hogs, were taken and our household goods, store goods, and printing press, and type were broken, taken, or otherwise destroyed.

5. Ralph Waldo Emerson Describes the "Over-Soul," 1841

There is a difference between one and another hour of life, in their authority and subsequent effect. Our faith comes in moments; our vice is habitual. Yet is there a depth in those brief moments, which constrains us to ascribe more reality to them than to all other experiences. For this reason, the argument, which is always forthcoming to silence those who conceive extraordinary hopes of man, namely, the appeal to experience, is forever invalid and vain. A mightier hope abolishes despair. We give up the past to the objector, and yet we hope. He must explain this hope. We grant that human life is mean; but how did we find out that it was mean? What is the ground of this uneasiness of ours; of this old discontent? What is the universal sense of want and ignorance, but the fine inuendo by which the great soul makes its enormous claim? . . . The philosophy of six thousand years has not searched the chambers and magazines of the soul. In its experiments there has always remained, in the last analysis, a residuum it could not resolve. Man is a stream whose source is hidden. Always our being is descending into us from we know not whence. The most exact calculator has no prescience that somewhat incalculable may not baulk the very next moment. I am constrained every moment to acknowledge a higher origin for events than the will I call mine.

As with events, so is it with thoughts. When I watch that flowing river, which, out of regions I see not, pours for a season its streams into me,—I see that I am a pensioner,—not a cause, but a surprised spectator of this ethereal water; that I desire and look up, and put myself in the attitude of reception, but from some alien energy the visions come.

The Supreme Critic on all the errors of the past and the present, and the only prophet of that which must be, is that great nature in which we rest, as the earth lies in the soft arms of the atmosphere; that Unity, that Over-Soul, within which every man's particular being is contained and made one with all other; that common heart, of which all sincere conversation is the worship, to which all right action is submission; that overpowering reality which confutes our tricks and talents, and constrains every one to pass for what he is, and to speak from his character and not from his tongue; and which evermore tends and aims to pass into our thought and hand, and become wisdom, and virtue, and power, and beauty. We live in succession,

Ralph Waldo Emerson, "The Over-Soul," in *Essays: First Series* (Philadelphia: David McKay, 1898), 287–323.

in division, in parts, in particles. Meantime within man is the soul of the whole; the wise silence; the universal beauty, to which every part and particle is equally related; the eternal ONE. And this deep power in which we exist, and whose beatitude is all accessible to us, is not only self-sufficing and perfect in every hour, but the act of seeing, and the thing seen, the seer and the spectacle, the subject and the object, are one. We see the world piece by piece, as the sun, the moon, the animal, the tree; but the whole, of which these are the shining parts, is the soul. It is only by the vision of that Wisdom, that the horoscope of the ages can be read, and it is only by falling back on our better thoughts, by yielding to the spirit of prophecy which is innate in every man, that we can know what it saith. . . .

If we consider what happens in conversation, in reveries, in remorse, in times of passion, in surprises, in the instructions of dreams wherein often we see ourselves in masquerade,—the droll disguises only magnifying and enhancing a real element, and forcing it on our distinct notice,—we shall catch many hints that will broaden and lighten into knowledge of the secret of nature. All goes to show that the soul of man is not an organ, but animates and exercises all the organs; is not a function, like the power of memory, of calculation, of comparison,—but uses these as hands and feet; is not a faculty, but a light; is not the intellect or the will, but the master of the intellect and the will;—is the vast back-ground of our being, in which they lie,—an immensity not possessed and that cannot be possessed. From within or from behind, a light shines through us upon things, and makes us aware that we are nothing, but the light is all. . . .

Of this pure nature every man is at some time sensible. Language cannot paint it with his colors. It is too subtle. It is undefinable, unmeasurable, but we know that it pervades and contains us. We know that all spiritual being is in man. A wise old proverb says, "God comes to see us without bell:" that is, as there is no screen or ceiling between our heads and the infinite heavens, so is there no bar or wall in the soul where man, the effect, ceases, and God, the cause, begins. The walls are taken away. We lie open on one side to the deeps of spiritual nature, to all the attributes of God. Justice we see and know, Love, Freedom, Power. These natures no man ever got above, but always they tower over us, and most in the moment when our interests tempt us to wound them.

6. Anonymous Ex-Slave Sees the Ghost of Her Dead Master, c. 1850

I used to see haunts when I was young. One day I was coming from the spring and had a bucket of water on my head and two buckets in my hands when I came up to the door it was in the evening and Mars' B. had been dead over a year. I looked up as I started up the steps and there I saw his ghost. It was exactly like him standing, leaning against the side of the door with his red handkerchief around his neck and his legs crossed. He was looking across the pasture towards the big hill. I said,

George P. Rawick, ed., *The American Slave,* vol. 19. (Nashville: Fisk University Social Science Institute, 1945), 205–210.

"Mars' Bill." He didn't move or speak but just stood looking up the hill as he did every day while he was living to call the hogs. I just stooped and went under his arm. When I went in Mistress said, "Who was that you were talking to? Hush, you black liar, I heard you calling Mars' Bill, you black kinky haired bitch. I will kill you." With that she struck me and almost beat me to death.

One other time I saw him. It was one night while I was carrying supper to the cabin-lot, to mamma. I heard something walking behind me and when I looked around I saw Mars' Bill, a great tall man nearly as tall as a tree. Usually I wasn't scared of him because I was his pet in his lifetime and he used to keep mistress from whipping me. But when I looked up at him and saw that he didn't have any head on, it nearly scared me to death. He was all dressed up in a black coat and pants and white shirt but he didn't have no head. His hat was on his neck. He was right on me when I looked up and saw him and I ran through it breaking off the latch and fell in the door where mamma was lying sick. I didn't spill her supper but the pan slipped out of my grip and slid under her bed. Some of them heard me hollering and came to see what the trouble was. They picked me up and layed me on the bed, but it was some time before I got over the scare enough to tell them what I had seen.

When my mistress heard about it the next day, she beat me again. "You black ugly snotty-nosed bitch, I will teach you to be going around here talking about seeing your Mars' Bill." But in spite of her beatings I still stuck to it that I did see him.

Not long after this she saw him and he like to have scared her to death. She was sitting in the room alone by the fire when he appeared before her and such hollering you never heard. When I went in to find out the trouble she tried to make believe that a big rat scared her. She said this because she didn't want me to know that she had seen him. But she got [so] nervous that she was afraid to stay in the house. I guessed what the trouble was even before it got to be hinted around that his spirit was coming back tormenting her. She beat me for saying that I had seen him and my God was just causing her to suffer for her meanness. She lived until after the war. I heard of her before she died. She went out of this world just like she lived— fussing and cursing.

I used to see haunts so much I prayed to God that I might not see any more. And I don't see them now like I did then since I became an elect in the House of God. He has taken fear out of me. He shows me things but they are spiritual and come from His matchless wisdom and the world can't see nor understand them. I profess to know nothing about the world nor its ways. I can't read a line either of the Scriptures or any other kind of writing, but I do know this: Whenever the truth from heaven is read before me I can talk to the Father. Others may read and talk but I go to the telephone that is always in operation and ask the Father who is never too busy to answer. So I may not speak the words just like they are in His printed book but I am right anyhow and know it. I often wish I did know how to read, but since I didn't have the chance to learn—being fearsome to be seen with a book when I was a slave—God has seen my need and made me satisfied. He has taken me—a fool— for sometimes my head was beat so I thought I was foolish—and hidden with me the secret of eternal life. He has made me to stand up on my feet and teach the world-wise out of His wisdom that comes from on high.

Sometimes I am caused to feel sad because I see people going around telling lies and talking about religion when I know they don't know what they are talking about.

When such people come around me, I usually go to God and say, "Lord, am I right?" And He never leaves me in ignorance. Neither does He leave any that trust Him in ignorance. The soul that trusts in God need never stumble nor fall, because God being all wise and seeing and knowing all things, having looked down through time before time, foresaw every creeping thing and poured out His spirit on the earth. . . .

I know nothing about what God said to the prophets of old but I do know what He has said to me. And I know that I have a counselor in Him that never fails. When danger comes, He works on my mind and conscience and causes me to walk around the snares set for me by my enemies. What earthly friend could do this? Why the latter would say, "I would have warned you, but I didn't know there was danger ahead." That is why I trust in God, because He sees and knows all things. And because I trust in God, He leads me into all wisdom and shows me the failings of hypocrits and liars.

7. Henry Bibb, a Slave, Uses Conjuring to Prevent Harm and Attract Women, 1849

There is much superstition among the slaves. Many of them believe in what they call "conjuration," tricking, and witchcraft; and some of them pretend to understand the art, and say that by it they can prevent their masters from exercising their will over their slaves. Such are often applied to by others, to give them power to prevent their masters from flogging them. The remedy is most generally some kind of bitter root; they are directed to chew it and spit towards their masters when they are angry with their slaves. At other times they prepare certain kinds of powders, to sprinkle about their masters' dwellings. This is all done for the purpose of defending themselves in some peaceable manner, although I am satisfied that there is no virtue at all in it. I have tried it to perfection when I was a slave at the South. I was then a young man, full of life and vigor, and was very fond of visiting our neighbors slaves, but had no time to visit only Sundays, when I could get a permit to go, or after night, when I could slip off without being seen. If it was found out, the next morning I was called up to give an account of myself for going off without permission; and would very often get a flogging for it.

I got myself into a scrape at a certain time, by going off in this way, and I expected to be severely punished for it. I had a strong notion of running off, to escape being flogged, but was advised by a friend to go to one of those conjurers, who could prevent me from being flogged. I went and informed him of the difficulty. He said if I would pay him a small sum, he would prevent my being flogged. After I had paid him, he mixed up some alum, salt and other stuff into a powder, and said I must sprinkle it about my master, if he should offer to strike me; this would prevent him. He also gave me some kind of bitter root to chew, and spit towards him, which would certainly prevent my being flogged. According to order I used his remedy, and for some cause I was let pass without being flogged that time.

Narrative of the Life and Adventures of Henry Bibb, a Slave, in Gilbert Osofsky, *Puttin' on Ole' Massa* (New York: Harper and Row, 1969), 70–73.

I had then great faith in conjuration and witchcraft. I was led to believe that I could do almost as I pleased, without being flogged. So on the next Sabbath my conjuration was fully tested by my going off, and staying away until Monday morning, without permission. When I returned home, my master declared that he would punish me for going off; but I did not believe that he could do it, while I had this root and dust; and as he approached me, I commenced talking saucy to him. But he soon convinced me that there was no virtue in them. He became so enraged at me for saucing him, that he grasped a handful of switches and punished me severely, in spite of all my roots and powders.

But there was another old slave in that neighborhood, who professed to understand all about conjuration, and I thought I would try his skill. He told me that the first one was only a quack, and if I would only pay him a certain amount in cash, that he would tell me how to prevent any person from striking me. After I had paid him his charge, he told me to go to the cow-pen after night, and get some fresh cow manure, and mix it with red pepper and white people's hair, all to be put into a pot over the fire, and scorched until it could be ground into snuff. I was then to sprinkle it about my master's bedroom, in his hat and boots, and it would prevent him from ever abusing me in any way. After I got it all ready prepared, the smallest pinch of it scattered over a room, was enough to make a horse sneeze from the strength of it; but it did no good. I tried it to my satisfaction. It was my business to make fires in my master's chamber, night and morning. Whenever I could get a chance, I sprinkled a little of this dust about the linen of the bed, where they would breathe it on retiring. This was to act upon them as what is called a kind of love powder, to change their sentiments of anger, to those of love, towards me, but this all proved to be vain imagination. The old man had my money, and I was treated no better for it. . . .

As all the instrumentalities which I as a slave, could bring to bear upon the system, had utterly failed to palliate my sufferings, all hope and consolation fled. I must be a slave for life, and suffer under the lash or die. The influence which this had only tended to make me more unhappy. I resolved that I would be free if running away could make me so. I had heard that Canada was a land of liberty, somewhere in the North; and every wave of trouble that rolled across my breast, caused me to think more and more about Canada, and liberty. But more especially after having been flogged, I have fled to the highest hills of the forest, pressing my way to the North for refuge; but the river Ohio was my limit. To me it was an impassable gulf. I had no rod wherewith to smite the stream, and thereby divide the waters. I had no Moses to go before me and lead the way from bondage to a promised land. Yet I was in a far worse state than Egyptian bondage; for they had houses and land; I had none; they had oxen and sheep; I had none; they had a wise counsel, to tell them what to do, and where to go, and even to go with them; I had none. I was surrounded by opposition on every hand. My friends were few and far between. I have often felt when running away as if I had scarcely a friend on earth. . . .

. . . I had been taught by the old superstitious slaves, to believe in conjuration, and it was hard for me to give up the notion, for all I had been deceived by them. One of these conjurers, for a small sum agreed to teach me to make any girl love me that I wished. After I had paid him, he told me to get a bull frog, and take a certain bone out of the frog, dry it, and when I got a chance I must step up to any girl whom I wished to make love me, and scratch her somewhere on her naked skin with this bone, and she would be certain to love me, and would follow me in spite of herself; no matter who she might be engaged to, nor who she might be walking with.

So I got me a bone for a certain girl, whom I knew to be under the influence of another young man. I happened to meet her in the company of her lover, one Sunday evening, walking out; so when I got a chance, I fetched her a tremendous rasp across her neck with this bone, which made her jump. But in place of making her love me, it only made her angry with me. She felt more like running after me to retaliate on me for thus abusing her, than she felt like loving me. After I found there was no virtue in the bone of a frog, I thought I would try some other way to carry out my object. I then sought another counsellor among the old superstitious influential slaves; one who professed to be a great friend of mine, told me to get a lock of hair from the head of any girl, and wear it in my shoes this would cause her to love me above all other persons. As there was another girl whose affections I was anxious to gain, but could not succeed, I thought, without trying the experiment of this hair, I slipped off one night to see the girl, and asked her for a lock of her hair; but she refused to give it. Believing that my success depended greatly upon this bunch of hair, I was bent on having a lock before I left that night let it cost what it might. As it was time for me to start home in order to get any sleep that night, I grasped hold of a lock of her hair, which caused her to screech, but I never let go until I had pulled it out. This of course made the girl mad with me, and I accomplished nothing but gained her displeasure.

Such are the superstitious notions of the great masses of southern slaves. It is given to them by tradition, and can never be erased, while the doors of education are bolted and barred against them.

8. Samuel Ringgold Ward Escapes from Slavery and Becomes a Minister (1820), 1855

[When Ward was a child in slavery he became gravely ill, but his mother nursed him back to health.]

But the more certain these poor slaves [his parents] became that their child would soon be well, the nearer approached the time of my mother's sale. Motherlike, she pondered all manner of schemes and plans to postpone that dreaded day. She could close her child's eyes in death, she could follow her husband to the grave, if God should so order; but to be sold from them to the far-off State of Georgia, the State to which Maryland members of Churches sold their nominal fellow Christians—sometimes their own children, and other poor relations—*that* was more than she could bear. Submission to the will of God was one thing, she was prepared for that, but submission to the machinations of Satan was quite another thing; neither her womanhood nor her theology could be reconciled to the latter. Sometimes pacing the floor half the night with her child in her arms—sometimes kneeling for hours in secret prayer to God for deliverance—sometimes in long earnest consultation with

Samuel Ringgold Ward, *Autobiography of a Fugitive Negro* (1855. Chicago: Johnson Publishing, 1970), 14–23.

my father as to what must be done in this dreaded emergency—my mother passed days, nights, and weeks of anguish which wellnigh drove her to desperation. But a thought flashed upon her mind: she indulged in it. It was full of danger; it demanded high resolution, great courage, unfailing energy, strong determination; it might fail. But it was only a thought, at most only an indulged thought, perhaps the fruit of her very excited state, and it was not yet a plan; but, for the life of her, she could not shake it off. She kept saying to herself, "supposing I should"—Should what? . . . "William," said she to my father, "we must take this child and run away." . . .

. . . [O]n a certain evening, without previous notice, my mother took her child in her arms, and stealthily, with palpitating heart, but unfaltering step and un-daunted courage, passed the door, the outer gate, the adjoining court, crossed the field, and soon after, followed by my father, left the place of their former abode, bidding it adieu for ever. I know not their route; but in those days the track of the fugitive was neither so accurately scented nor so hotly pursued by human sagacity, or the scent of kindred bloodhounds, as now, nor was slave-catching so complete and regular a system as it is now. . . .

At the time of my parents' escape it was not always necessary to go to Canada; they therefore did as the few who then escaped mostly did—aim for a Free State, and settle among Quakers. This honoured sect, unlike any other in the world, in this respect, was regarded as the slave's friend. This peculiarity of their religion they not only *held,* but so *practised* that it impressed itself on the ready mind of the poor victim of American tyranny. To reach a Free State, and to live among Quakers, were among the highest ideas of these fugitives; accordingly, obtaining the best di-rections they could, they set out for Cumberland County, in the State of New Jersey, where they had learned slavery did not exist—Quakers lived in numbers, who would afford the escaped any and every protection consistent with their peculiar tenets—and where a number of blacks lived, who in cases of emergency could and would make common cause with and for each other. Then these attractions of Cumberland were sufficient to determine their course.

I do not think the journey could have been a very long one: but it must be trav-elled on foot, in some peril, and with small, scanty means, next to nothing; and with the burden (though they felt it not) of a child, nearly three years old, both too young and too weakly to perform his own part of the journey. . . .

Struggling against many obstacles, and by God's help surmounting them, they made good progress until they had got a little more than midway their journey, when they were overtaken and ordered back by a young man on horseback, who, it seems, lived in the neighborhood of my father's master. The youth had a whip, and some other insignia of slaveholding authority; and knowing that these slaves had been accustomed from childhood to obey the commanding voice of the white man, young or old, he foolishly fancied that my parents would give up the pursuit of freedom for themselves and their child at *his bidding. They thought otherwise;* and when he dismounted, for the purpose of enforcing authority and compelling obe-dience by the use of the whip, he received so severe a flogging at the hands of my parents as sent him home nearly a cripple. . . .

After this nothing serious befell our party, and they safely arrived at Green-wich, Cumberland County, early in the year 1820. They found, as they had been told, that at Springtown, and Bridgetown, and other places, there were numerous coloured people; that the Quakers in that region were truly, practically friendly, "not loving in word and tongue," but in deed and truth; and that there were no slaveholders in that part of the State, and when slave-catchers came prowling about the Quakers threw all manner of *peaceful* obstacles in their way, while the Negroes made it a little too *hot* for their comfort. . . .

. . . [Growing up in New Jersey and New York, he still encountered race prejudice.] So, if I sought a trade, white apprentices would leave if I were admitted; and when I went to the house of God, as it was called, I found all the Negro-hating usages and sentiments of general society there encouraged and embodied in the Negro pew, and in the disallowing Negroes to commune until *all the whites,* however poor, low, and degraded, had done. I know of more than one coloured person driven to the total denial of all religion, by the religious barbarism of white New Yorkers and other Northern champions of the slaveholder.

However, at the age of sixteen I found a friend in George Atkinson Ward, Esq., from whom I received encouragement to persevere, in spite of Negro-hate. In 1833 I became a clerk of Thomas L. Jennings, Esq., one of the most worthy of the coloured race; subsequently my brother and I served David Ruggles, Esq., then of New York, late of Northampton, Massachusetts, now no more.

In 1833 it pleased God to answer the prayers of my parents, in my conversion. . . .

In May, 1839, I was licensed to preach the gospel by the New York Congregational Association, assembled at Poughkeepsie. In November of the same year, I became the travelling agent of first the American and afterwards the New York Anti-slavery Society; in April, 1841, I accepted the unanimous invitation of the Congregational Church of South Butler, Wayne Co., N. Y., to be their pastor; and in September of that year I was publicly ordained and inducted as minister of that Church. I look back to my settlement among that dear people with peculiar feelings. It was my first charge: I there first administered the ordinances of baptism and the Lord's supper, and there I first laid hands upon and set apart a deacon; there God honoured my ministry, in the conversion of many and in the trebling the number of the members of the Church, most of whom, I am delighted to know, are still walking in the light of God. The manly courage they showed, in calling and sustaining and honouring as their pastor a black man, in that day, in spite of the too general Negro-hate everywhere rife (and as professedly pious as rife) around them, exposing them as it did to the taunts, scoffs, jeers, and abuse of too many who wore the cloak of Christianity—entitled them to what they will ever receive, my warmest thanks and kindest love. But one circumstance do I regret, in connection with the two-and-a-half years I spent among them—that was, not the poverty against which I was struggling during the time, nor the demise of the darling child I buried among them: it was my exceeding great inefficiency, of which they seemed to be quite unconscious. Pouring my tears into their bosoms, I ask of them and of God forgiveness.

✒ *E S S A Y S*

Before 1800 most Christians thought of God as "Lord" or "King." But the American Revolution had overthrown monarchy and aristocracy. How would the Christian message change to fit a democracy? And how would Americans' daily religious experiences and activities influence their political attitudes? In the first essay Nathan Hatch of the University of Notre

Dame explores the close connection between Christianity and democracy in the new republic. He notes that religion played a larger part in many Americans' lives than any other social or group activity and that as they learned to make their own choices in religion, deciding between the claims of rival denominations, so they learned to make political choices. The many new or rapidly growing religions of the era, including the Methodists, Baptists, Mormons, and Disciples of Christ, were not organized democratically. Some, such as the Mormons, lived under the discipline of patriarchs. Nevertheless, they were democratic in the sense that they did not have a learned ministry set apart from their unlettered members, in their acceptance of the reality of emotional and supernatural experiences, and in their belief that God was using them to unify America and give it a new spiritual birth.

Slaves were among the many Americans gaining a new sense of their own identity through religion. Albert Raboteau of Princeton University relates how slaves adapted Christianity to their plight. Even when restricted by illiteracy and the inability to move freely, they found ways to celebrate Christianity rather than confine their religious lives to sitting at the back of their white masters' churches. At times, as Raboteau shows, slaves could even have a profound religious effect on their masters. But if a shared faith sometimes brought master and slave closer together, at other times it prepared the way for their eventual separation.

Christianity and Democratic Politics

NATHAN O. HATCH

[A]t the very inception of the American republic the most dynamic popular movements were expressly religious. However powerful working-class organizations became in cities such as New York and Baltimore, their presence cannot compare with the phenomenal growth, and collective elán, of Methodists, Baptists, Christians, Millerites, and Mormons. It was lay preachers in the early republic who became the most effective agents in constructing new frames of reference for people living through a profoundly transitional age. Religious leaders from the rank and file were phenomenally successful in reaching out to marginal people, in promoting self-education and sheltering participants from the indoctrination of elite orthodoxies, in binding people together in supportive community, and in identifying the aspirations of common people with the will of God.

The vitality of these religious ideologies and mass movements has had a considerable long-term effect upon the character and limits of American politics. Churches, after all, came to serve as competing universes of discourse and action. And the political implications of mass movements that were democratic and religious at the same time are far more profound than merely predisposing members to vote Federalist or Republican, Democrat or Whig. As mass popular movements, churches came to be places in which fundamental political assumptions were forged: ideas about the meaning of America, the priority of the individual conscience, the values of localism, direct democracy, and individualism, and the necessity of dynamic communication, predicated on the identification of speaker or author with an audience.

Nathan O. Hatch, "The Democratization of Christianity and the Character of American Politics," in Mark Noll, ed., *Religion and American Politics* (New York: Oxford University Press, 1990), 92–120.

. . . [T]o understand the democratization of American society, one must look at what happened to Protestant Christianity in the years 1780–1830. In an age when people expected almost everything from religion (and churches) and almost nothing from politics (and the state), the popular churches are essential to comprehending the enduring shape of American democracy. . . .

The American Revolution is the single most crucial event in American history. . . .

. . . [It] dramatically expanded the circle of people who considered themselves capable of thinking for themselves about issues of freedom, equality, sovereignty, and representation; and it eroded traditional appeals to the authority of tradition, station, and education. Ordinary people moved towards these new horizons as they gained access to a powerful new vocabulary, a rhetoric of liberty that would not have occurred to people were it not for the Revolution. . . .

The profoundly transitional age between 1776 and 1830 left the same kind of indelible imprint upon the structures of American Christianity as it did upon those of American political life. . . . The age of the democratic revolutions unfolded with awesome moment for people in every social rank. Amidst such acute uncertainty, many humble Christians in America began to redeem a dual legacy. They yoked together strenuous demands for revivals, in the name of Whitefield, and calls for the expansion of popular sovereignty, in the name of the Revolution. It is the linking of these equally potent traditions that sent American Christianity cascading in so many creative directions in the early republic. Church authorities had few resources to restrain these movements fed by the passions of ordinary people. American Methodism, for example, under the tutelage of Francis Asbury, veered sharply from the course of British Methodism. . . . After 1800, the leaders of British Methodism were able to bar the eccentric American revivalist Lorenzo Dow from contaminating their meetings. In America, however, Dow took the camp meeting circuit by storm despite periodic censure from bishops and presiding elders. Given his effectiveness and popular support, they were unable to mount a direct challenge to his authority.

A diverse array of evangelical firebrands went about the task of movement-building in the generation after the Revolution. While they were intent on bringing evangelical conversion to the mass of ordinary Americans, rarely could they divorce that message from contagious new vocabularies and impulses that swept through American popular cultures in an era of democratic revolution: an appeal to class as the fundamental problem of society, a refusal to recognize the cultural authority of elites, a disdain for the supposed lessons of history and tradition, a call for reform using the rhetoric of the Revolution, a commitment to turn the press into a sword of democracy, and an ardent faith in the future of the American republic.

At the same time, Americans who espoused evangelical and egalitarian convictions, in whatever combination, were left free to experiment . . . unopposed by civil or religious authority. . . .

The reality of a nonrestrictive environment permitted an unexpected and often explosive conjunction of evangelical fervor and popular sovereignty. It was this engine that greatly accelerated the process of Christianization with American popular culture, allowing indigenous expressions of faith to take hold among ordinary people, both white and black. This expansion of evangelical Christianity did not proceed primarily from the nimble response of religious elites meeting the challenge before them. Rather, Christianity was effectively reshaped by ordinary people who molded it in their own image and threw themselves into expanding its influence. Increasingly assertive common people wanted their leaders unpretentious, their doctrines self-evident and down-to-earth, their music lively and singable, their churches in local hands. It was this upsurge of democratic hope that characterized so many religious cultures in the early republic and brought Baptists, Methodists, Disciples, and a host of other insurgent groups to the fore. The rise of evangelical Christianity in the early republic is, in some measure, a story of the success of common people in shaping the culture after their own priorities rather than the priorities outlined by gentlemen, such as the Founding Fathers. A style of religious leadership that the public had deemed "untutored" and "irregular" as late as the First Great Awakening became overwhelmingly successful, even normative, in the first decades of the new nation.

It is easy to miss the profoundly democratic character of the early republic's insurgent religious movements. The Methodists, after all, retained power in a structured hierarchy under the control of bishops; the Mormons reverted to rule by a single religious prophet and revelator; and groups such as the Disciples of Christ, despite professed democratic structures, came to be controlled by powerful individuals such as Alexander Campbell, who had little patience with dissent. As ecclesiastical structures, these movements often turned out to be less democratic than the congregational structure of the New England Standing Order.

The democratization of Christianity, then, has less to do with the specifics of polity and governance and more with the very incarnation of the church into popular culture. In at least three respects the popular religious movements of the early republic articulated a profoundly democratic spirit. First, they denied the age-old distinction that set the clergy apart as a separate order of men and they refused to defer to learned theologians and received orthodoxies. All were democratic or populist in the way [they] instinctively associated virtue with ordinary people rather than with elites. . . .

Second, these movements empowered ordinary people by taking their deepest spiritual impulses at face value rather than subjecting them to the scrutiny of orthodox doctrine and the frowns of respectable clergymen. In the last two decades of the century, preachers from a wide range of new religious movements openly fanned the flames of religious ecstasy. Rejecting in 1775 the Yankee Calvinism of his youth, Henry Alline found that his soul was transported with divine love, "ravished with a divine ecstasy beyond any doubts or fears, or thoughts of being then deceived." What had been defined as "enthusiasm" increasingly became advocated from the pulpit as an essential part of Christianity. Such a shift in emphasis, accompanied by rousing gospel singing rather than formal church music, reflected the success of common people in defining for themselves the nature of faith. In addition, an unprecedented wave of religious leaders in the last quarter of the century expressed their own openness to a variety of signs and wonders—in short, an admission of increased supernatural involvement in everyday life. Scores of preachers' journals, from Methodists and Baptists, from North and South, from white and black, indicated a ready acceptance to interpret dreams and visions as inspired by God, normal manifestations of divine guidance and instruction. "I know the word of God is our infallible guide, and by it we are to try all our dreams and feelings," conceded the Methodist stalwart Freeborn Garrettson. "But," he added, "I also know, that both sleeping and waking, things of a divine nature have been revealed to me." . . .

The early republic was also a democratic moment in a third sense. Religious outsiders were flushed with confidence about their prospects and had little sense of their own limitations. They dreamed that a new age of religious and social harmony would spring up naturally out of their own efforts to overthrow coercive and authoritarian structures. This upsurge of democratic hope, this passion for equality, led to a welter of diverse and competing forms, many of them structured in highly undemocratic ways. The Methodists under Francis Asbury, for instance, used authoritarian means to build a church that would not be a respecter of persons. This church faced the curious paradox of gaining phenomenal influence among laypersons with whom it would not share ecclesiastical authority. Similarly, the Mormons used a virtual religious dictatorship as the means to return power to illiterate men. Yet, despite these authoritarian structures, the fundamental impetus of these movements was to make Christianity a liberating force, giving people the right to think and act for themselves rather than being forced to rely upon the meditations of an educated elite. The most fascinating religious story of the early republic is the signal achievements of these and other populist religious leaders, outsiders who brought to bear the full force of democratic persuasions upon American culture.

The wave of popular religious movements that broke upon the United States in the half-century after independence did more to Christianize American society than anything before or since. Nothing makes that point clearer than the growth of Methodists and Baptists as mass movements among white and black Americans. Starting from scratch just prior to the Revolution, the Methodists in America grew at a rate that terrified other denominations, reaching a quarter of a million members by 1820 and doubling again by 1830. Baptist membership multiplied tenfold in the three decades after the Revolution, the number of churches increasing from 500 to over 2500. The black church in America was born amidst the crusading vigor of these movements and quickly assumed its own distinct character and broad appeal among people of color. By the middle of the nineteenth century, Methodist and Baptist churches had splintered into more different denominational forms than one cares to remember. Yet together these movements came to constitute nearly 70 percent of Protestant church members in the United States and two-thirds of its ministers.

. . . [The] mass movements that came to the fore early in the nineteenth century . . . [were] led by young men of relentless energy who went about movement-building as self-conscious outsiders. They shared an ethic of unrelenting labor, a passion for expansion, a hostility to orthodox belief and style, a zeal for religious reconstruction, and a systematic plan to labor on behalf of their ideals. However diverse their theologies and church organizations, they were able to offer common people, especially the poor, compelling visions of individual self-respect and collective self-confidence. . . .

. . . [T]hese upstarts were radically innovative in reaching and organizing people. Passionate about ferreting out converts in every hamlet and crossroads, they sought to bind them together in local and regional communities. They continued to refashion the sermon as a profoundly popular medium, inviting even the most unlearned and inexperienced to respond to a call to preach. These initiates were charged to proclaim the gospel anywhere and every day of the week—even to the limit of their physical endurance. The resulting creation, the colloquial sermon, employed daring pulpit storytelling, no-holds-barred appeals, overt humor, strident attack, graphic application, and intimate personal experience. These young builders of religious movements also became the most effective purveyors of mass literature in the early republic, confronting people in every section of the new nation with the combined force of the written and spoken word. In addition, this generation launched bold experiments with new forms of religious music, new techniques of protracted meetings, and new Christian ideologies that denied the mediations of religious elites and promised to exalt those of low estate.

The result of these intensive efforts was nothing less than the creation of mass movements that were deeply religious and genuinely democratic at the same time. . . .

. . . As one new Methodist convert recalled, "I now found myself associated with those who loved each other with a pure heart fervently, instead of being surrounded by those with whom friendship was a cold commerce of interest." These new movements could also impart to ordinary people, particularly those battered by poverty or infirmity, what Martin Luther King called "a sense of somebodiness"—the kind of consolation that another Methodist found so appealing in worship held in the crude environment of a log cabin: "an abiding confidence that he was a subject of that powerful kingdom whose Prince cared for his subjects." These movements also allowed common people to trust their own powerful religious impulses. They were encouraged to express their faith with fervent emotion and bold testimony. In the most democratic gesture of all, some preachers even began to take their cues for evidence of divine power from expressions in the audience. During a camp meeting on an island in the Chesapeake Bay, Lorenzo Dow was interrupted by a woman who began clapping her hands with delight and shouting "Glory! Glory!" In a response that was the opposite of condescension, Dow proclaimed to the audience: "The Lord is here! *He is with that sister.*"

The dissident movements of the early republic championed nothing more than the separation of church and state. Yet they were given to embrace the American republic with as much enthusiasm as had any of the orthodox traditions that still yearned for a Christian nation. These dissidents endowed the republic with the same divine authority as did defenders of the Standing Order such as Timothy Dwight and Noah Webster, but for opposite reasons. The republic became a new city on a hill not because it kept faith with Puritan tradition, but because it sounded the death knell for corporate and hierarchic conceptions of the social order. In sum, a government so enlightened as to tell the churches to go their own way must have also had prophetic power to tell them which way to go.

This is certainly not to suggest that political idioms uniformly colored the thinking of popular preachers in the early republic or that their message was not profoundly religious in purpose and scope. The early Methodist preachers, for instance, were preeminently soul savers and revivalists and saw political involvement as a distraction at best. Their transatlantic connections furthermore kept before them the movement of Providence abroad as well as at home. Yet even Francis Asbury was given to affectionate reflections on the religious privileges offered in his adopted land. Repeatedly he made a sharp contrast between the state of Methodism in America and in Great Britain, noting the success of the daughter in outstripping the parent. A Methodist preacher without the slightest interest in politics or in the millennium still had to take note of the phenomenal growth on these shores of a movement that began as "the offscouring of all things."

Even the Mormons, who seemed to have rejected American values and who seemed to impose biblical models upon politics rather than vice versa, developed an eschatology that was explicitly American. Joseph Smith made the Garden of Eden a New World paradise, with America becoming the cradle of civilization. In due time, the *Book of Mormon* recounts, God prevailed upon Columbus "to venture across the sea to the Promised Land, to open it for a new race of free men." A variety of Mormon authors suggest that it was the free institutions of America that prepared the way for the new prophet, Joseph Smith. The early Mormon missionaries to Great Britain made a literal appeal that converts should leave the Old World, bound in tyranny and awaiting destruction, and travel to the New. . . .

Not political in any conventional sense, the early Latter-day Saints envisioned a theology of America that was less explicit but far more concrete than any of their rivals. Despite extreme dissent from mainstream America, the Mormons never claimed that the entire stream of American identity, like that of the church, had become polluted. There was a special character to this land and its people that would allow the kingdom of heaven to be restored even if the current generation remained mired in corruption and oppression. This ambivalence allowed Joseph Smith to establish an independent kingdom at Nauvoo while at the same time announcing his candidacy for the presidency of the United States, calling Americans to "rally to the standard of Liberty" and "trample down the tyrant's rod and the oppressor's crown." . . .

It is also important to emphasize that popular denominations were socially uniform and thus politically predictable. By the second decade of the century a struggle occurred within Baptists and Methodists between those who wanted respectability, centralization, and education and those who valued the tradition of democratic dissent—localism, antielitism, and religious experience fed by the passions of ordinary people. The fault line often ran between cosmopolitans and localists, between urban and rural interests. The example of Nathan Bangs superbly captures the tension in popular denominations between democratic dissent and professional respectability.

Although he declined election as bishop of the Methodist Church in 1832, Nathan Bangs left an indelible imprint upon the church in the generation after Francis Asbury. Bangs's early career was typical of those called to service in Asbury's missionary band. A largely self-educated young man who spent his youth in Connecticut and his teenage years in rural New York, Bangs moved to Canada at the age of twenty-one and taught school in a Dutch community near Niagara. Troubled by the perplexities of Calvinism, Bangs came under the influence of a Methodist itinerant, James Coleman, experienced a riveting conversion and sanctification, and, conforming to severest Methodist custom, removed the ruffles from his shirts and cut his long hair, which he had worn fashionably in a cue. In 1801, a year after he joined the church and three months after he was approved as an exhorter, he was licensed to preach and given a circuit. Riding circuits from Niagara to Quebec for the next decade, Bangs became the principal force in establishing Methodism in the lower St. Lawrence Valley.

In 1810, the New York Conference presented a charge to Nathan Bangs that would profoundly alter the emphasis of his ministry: he was named "preacher in charge" of the five preachers, five preaching places, and 2,000 members that comprised the single circuit of New York City. Bangs remained a dominant influence in Methodist affairs until the time of the Civil War—when Methodists could boast sixty churches and 17,000 members in the city. Yet despite the Methodist rule of biennial change of appointment, Bangs never managed to leave New York. His career and influence represent the tremendous allure of respectability that faced insurgent religious movements in Jacksonian America as their own constituencies grew in wealth and social standing and it became more difficult to define leaders' pastoral identity as defiant and alienated prophets. Bangs envisioned Methodism as a popular establishment, faithful to the movement's original fire but tempered with virtues of middle-class propriety and urbane congeniality. If Asbury's career represented the triumph of Methodism as a populist movement, with control weighted to the cultural periphery rather than to the center, then Bangs's pointed to the centripetal tug of respectable culture. In America, dissenting paths have often doubled back to lead in the direction of learning, decorum, professionalism, and social standing.

From the time Nathan Bangs arrived in New York City he set his face to dampen the popular spontaneity that had infused Methodist worship. "I witnessed," he said, "a spirit of pride, presumption, and bigotry, impatience of scriptural restraint and moderation, clapping of the hands, screaming, and even jumping, which marred and disgraced the work of God." Bangs called together the Methodists of New York in the John Street Church and exhorted them to be more orderly in their social meetings. Later Bangs also went on record as opposed to the spiritual songs of the camp meeting, "ditties" that in his words, "possessed little of the spirit of poetry and therefore added nothing to true intellectual taste." . . .

. . . After serving for two years as the presiding elder for the New York Conference, he was elected the agent of the Methodist Book Concern in 1820, a position which would keep him permanently in New York and provide a strategic base from which to promote Methodist publications, missions, Sunday schools, and educational institutions. Under his direction the Book Concern grew from a struggling agency embarrassed by debt and without premises of its own to a publishing house which was the largest in the world by 1860. . . .

. . . In his tenure as doorkeeper of Methodist thinking, Bangs used his considerable resources to accelerate a process by which many Methodists, particularly those in urban settings, shed their populist distinctives and stepped into ranks of "influential" Christians. By 1844 even the bishops of the church were forced to confess that the church was well on the way to selling its original birthright: "in some of the Conferences little or nothing remains of the itinerant system."

The Slaves' Own Religion

ALBERT J. RABOTEAU

One of the perennial questions in the historical study of American slavery is the question of the relationship between Christianity and the response of slaves to enslavement. Did the Christian religion serve as a tool in the hands of slaveholders to make slaves docile or did it serve in the hands of slaves as a weapon of resistance and even outright rebellion against the system of slavery? Let us acknowledge from the outset that the role of religion in human motivation and action is very complex; let us recognize also that Christianity played an ambiguous role in the stances which slaves took toward slavery, sometimes supporting resistance, sometimes accommodation. That much admitted, much more remains to be said. Specifically, we need to trace the convoluted ways in which the egalitarian impulse within Christianity overflowed the boundaries of the master-slave hierarchy, creating unexpected channels of slave autonomy on institutional as well as personal levels. To briefly sketch out some of the directions which religious autonomy took among slaves in the antebellum South is the purpose of this essay.

Institutional Autonomy

From the beginning of the Atlantic slave trade in the fifteenth century, European Christians claimed that the conversion of slaves to Christianity justified the enslavement of Africans. For more than four centuries Christian apologists for slavery would repeat this religious rationalization for one of history's greatest atrocities. Despite the justification of slavery as a method of spreading the gospel, the conversion of slaves was not a top priority for colonial planters. One of the principal reasons for the refusal of British colonists to allow their slaves religious instruction was the fear that baptism would require the manumission of their slaves, since it was illegal to hold a fellow Christian in bondage. This dilemma was solved quickly by colonial legislation stating that baptism did not alter slave status. However, the most serious obstacle to religious instruction of the slaves could not be legislated away. It was the slaveholder's deep-seated uneasiness at the prospect of a slave laying claim to Christian fellowship with his master. The concept of equality, though only spiritual, between master and slave threatened the stability of the system of slave control. Christianity, complained the masters, would ruin slaves by allowing them to think themselves equal to white Christians. Far worse was the fear, supported by the behavior of some Christian slaves, that religion would make them rebellious. In order to allay this fear, would-be missionaries to the slaves had to prove that Christianity would make better slaves. By arguing that Christian slaves would become obedient to their masters out of duty to God and by stressing the distinction between spiritual equality and worldly equality, the proponents of slave conversion in effect built a religious foundation to support slavery. Wary slaveholders were assured by missionaries that "Scripture, far from making an Alteration in Civil

Albert J. Raboteau, "Slave Autonomy and Religion," *Journal of Religious Thought* 38 (1981–2): 51–64. Reprinted in Paul Finkelman, ed., *Articles on American Slavery* (New York: Garland, 1989), 593–614.

Rights, expressly directs, *that every Man abide in the Condition wherein he is called, with great Indifference of Mind* concerning outward circumstances."

In spite of missionary efforts to convince them that Christianity was no threat to the slave system, slaveowners from the colonial period on down to the Civil War remained suspicious of slave religion as a two-edged sword. Clerical assurances aside, the masters' concern was valid. Religious instruction for slaves had more than spiritual implications. No event would reveal these implications as clearly as the series of religious revivals called the Great Awakenings which preceded and followed the Revolution. The impact of revival fervor would demonstrate how difficult it was to control the egalitarian impulse of Christianity within safe channels.

The first Great Awakening of the 1740s swept the colonies with the tumultuous preaching and emotional conversions of revivalistic, evangelical Protestantism. Accounts by Whitefield, Tennent, Edwards, and other revivalists made special mention of the fact that blacks were flocking to hear the message of salvation in hitherto unseen numbers. Not only were free blacks and slaves attending revivals in significant numbers, they were taking active part in the services as exhorters and preachers. The same pattern of black activism was repeated in the rural camp meetings of the second Great Awakening of the early nineteenth century.

The increase in slave conversions which accompanied the awakenings was due to several factors. The evangelical religion spread by the revivalists initiated a religious renaissance in the South where the majority of slaves lived. The revival became a means of church extension, especially for Methodists and Baptists. The mobility of the Methodist circuit rider and the local independence of the Baptist preacher were suited to the needs of the rural South. Among the Southerners swelling the ranks of these denominations were black as well as white converts.

Moreover, the ethos of the revival meeting, with its strong emphasis upon emotional preaching and congregational response, not only permitted ecstatic religious behavior but encouraged it. Religious exercises, as they were termed, including fainting, jerking, barking, and laughing a "holy laugh," were a common, if spectacular, feature of revivals. In this heated atmosphere slaves found sanction for an outward expression of religious emotion consonant with their tradition of danced religion from Africa. While converting to a belief in a "new" God, slaves were able to worship in ways hauntingly similar to those of old.

Extremely important for the development of black participation in revival religion was the intense concentration upon individual inward conversion which fostered an inclusiveness that could become egalitarianism. Evangelicals did not hesitate to preach to racially mixed congregations and had no doubt about the capacity of slaves to share the experience of conversion to Christ. Stressing plain doctrine and emotional preaching, emphasizing the conversion experience instead of religious instruction, made Christianity accessible to illiterate slave and slaveholder alike. The criterion for preachers was not seminary training but evidence of a converted heart and gifted tongue. Therefore, when an awakened slave showed talent for preaching, he preached, and not only to black congregations. The tendency of evangelical Protestantism to level the souls of all men before God reached its logical conclusion when blacks preached to and converted whites.

By the last quarter of the eighteenth century a cadre of black preachers had begun to emerge. Some of these pioneer black ministers were licensed, some not;

some were slaves, others free. During the 1780s a black man named Lewis preached to crowds as large as four hundred in Westmoreland County, Virginia. Harry Hosier traveled with Methodist leaders, Asbury, Coke, Garretson, and Whatcoat and was reportedly such an eloquent preacher that he served as a "drawing card" to attract larger crowds of potential converts, white and black. In 1792 the mixed congregation of the Portsmouth, Virginia Baptist Church selected a slave, Josiah Bishop, as pastor, after purchasing his freedom and also his family's. Another black preacher, William Lemon, pastored a white Baptist church in Gloucester County, Virginia, for a time at the turn of the century.

In 1798, Joseph Willis, a freeman, duly licensed as a Baptist preacher, began his ministry in southwest Mississippi and Louisiana. He formed Louisiana's first Baptist church at Bayou Chicot in 1812 and served as its pastor. After developing several other churches in the area, he became the first moderator of the Louisiana Baptist Association in 1818. Uncle Jack, an African-born slave, joined the Baptist church and in 1792 began to preach in Nottoway County, Virginia. White church members purchased his freedom and he continued to preach for over forty years. Henry Evans, a free black licensed as a local preacher by the Methodists, was the first to bring Methodist preaching to Fayetteville, North Carolina. Initially preaching to black people only, he attracted the attention of several prominent whites and eventually the white membership of his congregation increased until the blacks were crowded out of their seats. Evans was eventually replaced by a white minister, but continued to serve as an assistant in the church he had founded until his death.

That black preachers should exhort, convert, and even pastor white Christians in the slave South was certainly antithetical to the premise of slave control. Though such occasions were rare, they were the ineluctable result of the impulse unleashed by revivalistic religion. Of greater importance for the development of autonomy in the religious life of slaves was the fact that black preachers, despite threats of punishment, continued to preach to slaves and in some few cases even founded churches. An early historian of the Baptists applauded the anonymous but effective ministry of these black preachers:

> Among the African Baptists in the Southern states there are a multitude of preachers and exhorters whose names do not appear on the minutes of the associations. They preach principally on the plantations to those of their own color, and their preaching though broken and illiterate, is in many cases highly useful.

Several "African" Baptist churches sprang up before 1800. Some of these black congregations were independent to the extent that they called their own pastors and officers, joined local associations with white Baptist churches, and sent their own delegates to associational meetings. Though the separate black church was primarily an urban phenomenon, it drew upon surrounding rural areas for its membership, which consisted of both free blacks and slaves. Sometimes these black churches were founded amidst persecution. Such was the case with the African Baptist Church of Williamsburg, Virginia, whose history was chronicled in 1810:

> This church is composed almost, if not altogether of people of colour. Moses, a black man, first preached among them, and was often taken up and whipped, for holding meetings. Afterwards Gowan Pamphlet . . . became popular among the blacks, and began to baptize, as well as to preach. It seems, the association had advised that no person of colour should be allowed to preach, on the pain of excommunication; against this

regulation, many of the blacks were rebellious, and continued still to hold meetings. Some were excluded, and among this number was Gowan. . . . Continuing still to preach and many professing faith under his ministry, not being in connexion with any church himself, he formed a kind of church out of some who had been baptized, who, sitting with him, received such as offered themselves; Gowan baptized them, and was moreover appointed their pastor; some of them knowing how to write, a churchbook was kept; they increased to a large number; so that in the year 1791, the Dover association, stat[ed] their number to be about five hundred. The association received them, so far, as to appoint persons to visit them and set things in order. These making a favourable report, they were received, and have associated ever since. . . .

The labors of these early black preachers and their successors were crucial in the formation of slave religion. In order to adequately understand the development of Christianity among the slaves, we must realize that slaves learned Christianity not only from whites but from other slaves as well. Slave preachers, exhorters, and church-appointed watchmen instructed their fellow slaves, nurtured their religious development, and brought them to conversion in some cases without the active involvement of white missionaries or masters at all. The early independence of black preachers and churches was curtailed as the antebellum period wore on, particularly in periods of reaction to slave conspiracies, when all gatherings of blacks for whatever purpose were viewed with alarm. For slaves to participate in the organization, leadership, and governance of church structures was perceived as dangerous. Surely it was inconsistent, argued the guardians of the system, to allow blacks such authority. As the prominent South Carolinian planter, Charles Cotesworth Pinkney, declared before the Charleston Agricultural Society in 1829, the exercise of religious prerogatives left slaves too free from white control. "We look upon the habit of Negro preaching as a wide-spreading evil; not because a black man cannot be a good one, but . . . because they acquire an influence independent of the owner, and not subject to his control. . . . when they have possessed this power, they have been known to make an improper use of it." No doubt, Pinkney and his audience had in mind the African Methodist Church of Charleston which had served as a seedbed of rebellion for the Denmark Vesey conspiracy of 1822. (Following discovery of the plot, whites razed the church to the ground.)

Regardless of periodic harassment by civil and ecclesiastical authorities, black preachers continued to preach and separate black churches continued to be organized. . . . In various sections of the antebellum South, black churches kept gathering members, over the years swelling in size to hundreds and in a few instances thousands of members. Certainly, the vast majority of slaves attended churches under white control. However, even in racially mixed churches some black Christians found opportunities to exercise their spiritual gifts and a measure of control over their religious life. This was so especially in Baptist churches because Baptist polity required that each congregation govern itself. In some churches committees of black members were constituted to oversee their own conduct. . . .

Personal Autonomy

Like their colonial predecessors, antebellum missionaries to the slaves had to face objections from whites that religion for slaves was dangerous. Beginning in the 1820s, a movement led by prominent clerics and laymen attempted to mold southern opinion in support of missions to the slaves. Plantation missionaries created an ideal image of the Christian plantation, built upon the mutual observance of duties by masters and by slaves. One leader of the plantation mission stated the movement's basic premise when he predicted that "religious instruction of the Negroes will *promote our own morality and religion.*" For, when "one class rises, so will the other; the two are so associated they are apt to rise or fall together. Therefore, servants do well by your masters and masters do well by your servants." In this premise lay a serious fallacy; for while the interests of master and slave occasionally coincided, they could never cohere. No matter how devoted master was to the ideal of a Christian plantation, no matter how pious he might be, the slave knew that the master's religion did not countenance the slaves' freedom in this world.

Precisely because the interests of master and slave extended only so far and no further, there was a dimension of the slaves' religious life that was secret. The disparity between the master's ideal of religion on the plantation and that of the slaves led the slaves to gather secretly in the quarters or in brush arbors (aptly named hush harbors) where they could pray, preach, and sing, free from white control. Risking severe punishment, slaves disobeyed their masters and stole off under cover of secrecy to worship as they saw fit. Here it was that Christianity was fitted to their own peculiar experience.

It was the slaveholding gospel preached to them by master's preacher which drove many slaves to seek true Christian preaching at their own meetings. "Church was what they called it," recalled former slave Charlie Van Dyke, "but all that preacher talked about was for us slaves to obey our masters and not to lie and steal." To attend secret meetings was in itself an act of resistance against the will of the master and was punished as such. In the face of the absolute authority of the Divine Master, the authority of the human master shrank. Slaves persisted in their hush harbor meetings because there they found consolation and communal support, tangible relief from the exhaustion and brutality of work stretching from "day clean" to after dark, day in and day out. "Us niggers," remarked Richard Carruthers, describing a scene still vivid in his memory many years later, "used to have a prayin' ground down in the hollow and sometimes we came out of the field . . . scorchin' and burnin' up with nothin' to eat, and we wants to ask the good Lawd to have mercy. . . . We takes a pine torch . . . and goes down in the hollow to pray. Some gits so joyous they starts to holler loud and we has to stop up they mouth. I see niggers git so full of the Lawd and so happy they draps unconscious."

In the hush harbor slaves sought not only substantive preaching and spiritual consolation; they also talked about and prayed for an end to their physical bondage. "I've heard them pray for freedom," declared one former slave. "I thought it was foolishness then, but the old time folks always felt they was to be free. It must have been something 'vealed unto 'em." Though some might be skeptical, those slaves who were confident that freedom would come, since God had revealed it, were able to cast their lives in a different light. Hope for a brighter future irradiated the darkness of the present. Their desire for freedom in this world was reaffirmed in the songs, prayers, and sermons of the hush harbor. This was just what the master—those who didn't believe in prayer, as well as those who did—tried to prevent. The external hush harbor symbolized an internal resistance, a private place at the core of the slaves' religious life which they claimed as their own and which, in the midst of bondage, could not be controlled.

For evangelical Christians, black or white, full admission into membership in the church required that the candidate give credible testimony about the inner workings of the Spirit upon his or her heart. The conversion experience, as described by ex-slaves, was typically a visionary one, inaugurated by feelings of sadness and inner turmoil. Frequently the individual "convicted of sin" envisioned Hell and realized that he was destined for damnation. Suddenly, the sinner was rescued from this danger and led to a vision of Heaven by an emissary from God. Ushered into God's presence, the person learned that he was not damned but saved. Awakening, the convert realized that he was now one of the elect and overwhelmed with the joyful feeling of being "made new" shouted out his happiness. For years afterwards, this "peak" experience remained a fixed point of identity and value in the convert's life. He knew that he was saved, and he knew it not just theoretically but experientially. Confident of their election and their value in the eyes of God, slaves who underwent conversion, gained in this radical experience a deeply rooted identity which formed the basis for a sense of purpose and an affirmation of self-worth—valuable psychic barriers to the demeaning and dehumanizing attacks of slavery.

Conversion, as an experience common to white and black Christians, occasionally led to moments of genuine emotional contact, in which the etiquette of racial relationships was forgotten. A dramatic instance of one such occasion was recounted by a former slave named Morte:

> One day while in the field plowing I heard a voice . . . I looked but saw no one . . . Everything got dark, and I was unable to stand any longer . . . With this I began to cry. Mercy! Mercy! Mercy! As I prayed an angel came and touched me, and I looked new . . . and there came a soft voice saying, "My little one, I have loved you with an everlasting love. You are this day made alive and freed from hell. You are a chosen vessel unto the Lord." . . . I must have been in this trance more than an hour. I went on to the barn and found my master waiting for me. . . . I began to tell him of my experiences. . . . My master sat watching and listening to me, and then he began to cry. He turned from me and said in a broken voice, "Morte I believe you are a preacher. From now on you can preach to the people here on my place. . . . But tomorrow morning, Sunday, I want you to preach to my family and my neighbors." . . . The next morning at the time appointed I stood up on two planks in front of the porch of the big house and, without a Bible or anything, I began to preach to my master and the people. My thoughts came so fast that I could hardly speak fast enough. My soul caught on fire, and soon I had them all in tears . . . I told them that they must be born again and that their souls must be freed from the shackles of hell.

The spectacle of a slave reducing his master to tears by preaching to him of his enslavement to sin certainly suggests that religion could bend human relationships into interesting shapes despite the iron rule of slavery. Morte's power over his master was spiritual and (as far as we know) it was temporary. It was also effective.

While commonality of religious belief might lead to moments of religious reciprocity between blacks and whites, by far the more common relationship, from the slaves' side, was one of alienation from the hypocrisy of slaveholding Christians. As Frederick Douglass put it, "Slaves knew enough of the orthodox theology of the time to consign all bad slaveholders to hell." On the same point, Charles Ball commented that in his experience slaves thought that heaven would not be heaven unless slaves could be avenged on their enemies. "A fortunate and kind master or mistress, may now and then be admitted into heaven, but this rather as a matter of favour, to the intercession of some slave, than as a matter of strict justice to the whites, who will, by no means, be of an equal rank with those who shall be raised from the depths of misery in this world." Ball concluded that "The idea of a revolution in the conditions of the whites and blacks, is the cornerstone of the religion of the latter. . . ."

Slaves had no difficulty distinguishing the gospel of Christianity from the religion of their masters. Ex-slave Douglas Dorsey reported that after the minister on his plantation admonished the slaves to honor their masters whom they could see as they would God whom they could not see, the driver's wife who could read and write a little would say that the minister's sermon "was all lies." Charles Colcock Jones, plantation missionary, found that his slave congregation did not hesitate to reject the doctrine preached in a sermon he gave in 1833:

> I was preaching to a large congregation on the *Epistle of Philemon:* and when I insisted upon fidelity and obedience as Christian virtues in servants and upon the authority of Paul, condemned the practice of *running away,* one half of my audience deliberately rose up and walked off with themselves, and those that remained looked any thing but satisfied, either with the preacher or his doctrine. After dismission, there was no small stir among them; some solemnly declared "that there was no such an Epistle in the Bible;" others, "that I preached to please the masters;" others, "that it was not the Gospel;" others, "that they did not care if they ever heard me preach again!" . . . There were some too, who had strong objections against me as a Preacher, because I was a *master,* and said, "his people have to work as well as we." . . .

Not all slaves, however, were able to distinguish master's religion from authentic Christianity, and were led to reject this religion totally. In 1839, Daniel Alexander Payne explained how this could happen:

> The slaves are sensible of the oppression exercised by their masters; and they see these masters on the Lord's day worshipping in his holy Sanctuary. They hear their masters professing Christianity; they see their masters preaching the gospel; they hear these masters praying in their families, and they know that oppression and slavery are inconsistent with the Christian religion; therefore they scoff at religion itself—mock their masters, and distrust both the goodness and justice of God.

Frederick Douglass too remembered being shaken by "doubts arising . . . from the sham religion which everywhere prevailed" under slavery, doubts which "awakened in my mind a distrust of all religion and the conviction that prayers were unavailing and delusive." Unable to account for the evil of slavery in a world ruled by a just God, some slaves abandoned belief. "I pretended to profess religion one time," recalled one former slave, "I don't hardly know what to think about religion. They say God killed the just and unjust; I don't understand that part of it. It looks hard to think that if you ain't done nothing in the world you be punished just like the wicked. Plenty folks went crazy trying to get that straightened out." There is no way of estimating how many slaves felt these doubts, but they indicate how keenly aware slaves were of the disparity between the gospel of Christ and what they termed "white man's religion."

At the opposite extreme from the agnostic slave was the slave who developed a life of exemplary Christian virtue which placed him in a position of moral superiority over his master. William Grimes, for example, was possessed of a sense of righteousness which led him to take a surprising attitude toward his master when punished for something he had not done:

> It grieved me very much to be blamed when I was innocent. I knew I had been faithful to him, perfectly so. At this time I was quite serious, and used constantly to pray to my God. I would not lie nor steal. . . . When I considered him accusing me of stealing, when I was so innocent, and had endeavored to make him satisfied by every means in my power, that I was so, but he still persisted in disbelieving me, I then said to myself, if this thing is done in a green tree what must be done in a dry? I forgave my master in my own heart for all this, and prayed to God to forgive him and turn his heart.

Grimes is of course alluding to the sacrifice of Christ and identifying himself with the innocent suffering servant who spoke the words concerning green and dry wood on his way to death on Calvary. From this vantage point Grimes is able to forgive his master. Note however the element of threat implied in the question, "if this thing is done in a green tree (to the innocent) what must be done in a dry (to the guilty)?" Those who are guilty of persecuting the innocent, like Grimes's master, will be judged and punished. (The full context of the biblical allusion includes a terrifying prediction of the destruction of Jerusalem.) What did it mean to Grimes's self-image to be able to have moral leverage by which he might elevate his own dignity? . . .

The emotional ecstasy of slave religion has been criticized as compensatory and otherworldly, a distraction from the evils of this world. And so it was. But it was much more. Individually, slaves found not only solace in their religion but, particularly in the conversion experience, a source of personal identity and value. Collectively, slaves found in the archetypical symbol of biblical Israel their identity as a community, a new chosen people bound for Divine deliverance from bondage. From this communal identity mutual support, meaning, and hope derived. In the ecstasy of religious performance individual and communal identity and values were dramatically reaffirmed time and time again. In the hand-clapping, footstomping, headshaking fervor of the plantation praisehouse, the slaves, in prayer, sermon, and song, fit Christianity to their own peculiar experience and in the process resisted, even transcended the dehumanizing bonds of slavery.

 F U R T H E R   R E A D I N G

Bozeman, Theodore D. *Protestants in an Age of Science: The Baconian Ideal and Antebellum American Religious Thought* (1977).

Braude, Ann. *Radical Spirits: Spiritualism and Women's Rights in Nineteenth Century America* (1989).

Brereton, Virginia. *From Sin to Salvation: Stories of Women's Conversions, 1800 to the Present* (1991).

Bushman, Richard L. *Joseph Smith and the Beginnings of Mormonism* (1984).

Butler, Jon. *Awash in a Sea of Faith: Christianizing the American People* (1990).

Calhoon, Robert. *Evangelicals and Conservatives in the Early South: 1740–1861* (1988).

Cawardine, Richard. *Evangelicals and Politics in Antebellum America* (1993).

Conkin, Paul K. *Cane Ridge: America's Pentecost* (1990).

———. *The Uneasy Center: Reformed Christianity in Antebellum America* (1995).

Conser, Walter. *God and the Natural World: Religion and Science in Antebellum America* (1993).

Dieter, Melvin. *The Holiness Revival of the 19th Century* (1980).

Gaustad, Edwin. *Neither King nor Prelate: Religion and the New Nation, 1776–1826* (1993).

Genovese, Eugene. *Roll, Jordan, Roll: The World the Slaves Made* (1972).

Hambrick-Stowe, Charles. *Charles G. Finney and the Spirit of American Evangelicalism* (1996).

Hardman, Keith J. *Charles Grandison Finney, 1792–1875: Revivalist and Reformer* (1987).

Hatch, Nathan. *The Democratization of American Christianity* (1989).

Hughes, Richard. *The American Quest for the Primitive Church* (1988).

Johnson, Curtis. *Islands of Holiness: Rural Religion in Upstate New York, 1790–1860* (1989).

McLoughlin, William. *Modern Revivalism: Charles Grandison Finney to Billy Graham* (1959).

Mathews, Donald. *Religion in the Old South* (1977).

Powell, Milton. *The Voluntary Church: American Religious Life, 1740–1860, Seen Through the Eyes of European Visitors* (1967).

Schneider, Gregory. *The Way of the Cross Leads Home: The Domestication of American Methodism* (1993).

Shipps, Jan. *Mormonism: The Story of a New Religious Tradition* (1985).

Stein, Stephen. *The Shaker Experience in America* (1992).

Thomas, George. *Revivals and Cultural Change: Christian Nation Building and the Market in the 19th Century United States* (1989).

Wosh, Peter. *Spreading the Word: The Bible Business in Nineteenth Century America* (1994).

CHAPTER
6

Antebellum Immigration and Social Tensions: 1830–1860

The American religious scene, with its dozens of competing Protestant denominations, became even more complex when a large number of Catholic immigrants began to arrive. Ever since the foundation of Maryland in the 1630s, a handful of Catholics had co-existed uneasily with the colonies' Protestant majority. One Catholic, Charles Carroll, had signed the Declaration of Independence, and his brother had become the first American Catholic bishop. The arrival of thousands of poor Irish Catholics from the 1820s through the 1850s, however, transformed the situation, especially when, in the late 1840s, the migration became an escape from the catastrophes of harvest failure and famine. The Irish, who came from rural peasant backgrounds, usually settled in the seaboard cities and formed an impoverished working class. The men got unskilled laboring jobs as canal and railroad builders; the women often became domestic servants.

Most American Protestants feared and detested Catholicism, which they saw as a foreign despotic system, the antithesis of American freedom. The illiterate Irish, who had no experience of political independence, did nothing to soothe their fears. Some Protestants also saw Catholicism as the embodiment of the antichrist. As soon as they were able, the Catholics began to defend themselves against anti-Catholic propaganda, to argue that their religion was perfectly compatible with democracy, and that they did not have divided loyalties. Nevertheless pitched street battles between Protestant and Catholic gangs disturbed city life in Boston and Philadelphia in the 1830s and 1840s. Catholic churches and convents—which some Protestants thought of as brothels for hypocritical priests—were attacked and burned. The "Know Nothing" party of the 1850s was explicitly anti-Catholic; it tried to restrict Catholics' citizenship rights and to ensure that America's public schools taught a Protestant form of Christianity to immigrants' children. Meanwhile the immigration of Reform Jews, mainly from Germany, who also gathered in eastern cities, provided the further possibility, or challenge, that the nation might not always be Christian.

Protestant reformers in the antebellum era linked their faith not only to anti-Catholicism but also to various social reforms: the first women's rights movement, the early temperance movement (against alcohol), sabbatarianism (the keeping of Sunday free from all worldly activities), and above all the abolition of slavery. But while the abolitionist movement tried to mobilize northern Christians'

161

sentiments, southern defenders of slavery turned to their *Bibles to make the godly defense of their system more explicit than ever. The religious debate over slavery was one of many nineteenth-century occasions where both sides of a controversy could quote appropriate biblical passages to the satisfaction of their supporters, without converting their opponents. It is difficult to avoid the conclusion that, although each sought the moral high ground through an appeal to Scripture, each had actually decided beforehand what to find in the Bible and just singled out the most suitable texts.*

🔖 D O C U M E N T S

Alexis de Tocqueville made only one visit to America (nine months in 1831) but the two-volume study he wrote in the following years, *Democracy in America,* has had a lasting impact on Americans' ideas about themselves, and many of his observations remain eerily accurate even today. Tocqueville, a 26-year-old aristocrat from a Catholic family, believed that Catholics could be excellent citizens of the republic (Document 1, 1835). Most Protestants of the era disagreed and were willing to believe the worst of their new Catholic neighbors. Document 2 (1836) comes from Maria Monk's wildly inaccurate tale about being forced, as a young nun, to have sex on demand with priests and to participate in the murder of another nun who refused to strangle an illegitimate child. Monk's book remained a bestseller among Protestants even when its author had been discredited. Document 3 (1887) describes Irish famine victims arriving in the New World in the late 1840s and the Catholic church's efforts to alleviate their suffering. It also praises Catholic girls' dogged defense of their faith and their virtue while working among Protestants. Document 4 (1854) is an anxious Jewish father's letter to his son, a migrant from Germany, giving moral and religious advice about the dangers and temptations of American life.

Document 5 is a sentimental evocation of sabbatarianism at its best (1853) by Harriet Beecher Stowe, the wife of a Protestant minister. Stowe is better known for her novel *Uncle Tom's Cabin* (1852), which galvanized antislavery sentiment in the North and contributed to the onset of the Civil War. Antislavery literature drew heavily on the Bible, as Document 6 (1838) shows. Its author, Angelina Grimke, was particularly unusual in that she was a southerner and the daughter of a slaveholder. Her belief that the Bible and Christianity condemned slavery was shared by former slave and abolition activist Frederick Douglass as demonstrated in Document 7 (1845), taken from his autobiography. Defenders of slavery like Thornton Stringfellow, however (Document 8, 1860), were equally adept at producing biblical passages to show that neither the Old nor the New Testament condemned slavery.

1. Alexis de Tocqueville Sees Catholicism and Democracy as Compatible, 1835

RELIGION CONSIDERED AS A POLITICAL INSTITUTION WHICH POWERFULLY CONTRIBUTES TO THE MAINTENANCE OF A DEMOCRATIC REPUBLIC AMONG THE AMERICANS. *North America peopled by men who professed a democratic and republican Christianity—*

Alexis de Tocqueville, *Democracy in America,* vol. 1, ed. Daniel Boorstin (New York: Vintage, 1990), 300–303.

Arrival of the Catholics—Why the Catholics now form the most democratic and most republican class.

By the side of every religion is to be found a political opinion, which is connected with it by affinity. If the human mind be left to follow its own bent, it will regulate the temporal and spiritual institutions of society in a uniform manner, and man will endeavor, if I may so speak, to *harmonize* earth with heaven.

The greatest part of British America was peopled by men who, after having shaken off the authority of the Pope, acknowledged no other religious supremacy: they brought with them into the New World a form of Christianity which I cannot better describe than by styling it a democratic and republican religion. This contributed powerfully to the establishment of a republic and a democracy in public affairs; and from the beginning, politics and religion contracted an alliance which has never been dissolved.

About fifty years ago Ireland began to pour a Catholic population into the United States; and on their part, the Catholics of America made proselytes, so that, at the present moment more than a million Christians professing the truths of the Church of Rome are to be found in the Union. These Catholics are faithful to the observances of their religion; they are fervent and zealous in the belief of their doctrines. Yet they constitute the most republican and the most democratic class in the United States. This fact may surprise the observer at first, but the causes of it may easily be discovered upon reflection.

I think that the Catholic religion has erroneously been regarded as the natural enemy of democracy. Among the various sects of Christians, Catholicism seems to me, on the contrary, to be one of the most favorable to equality of condition among men. In the Catholic Church the religious community is composed of only two elements: the priest and the people. The priest alone rises above the rank of his flock, and all below him are equal.

On doctrinal points the Catholic faith places all human capacities upon the same level; it subjects the wise and ignorant, the man of genius and the vulgar crowd, to the details of the same creed; it imposes the same observances upon the rich and the needy, it inflicts the same austerities upon the strong and the weak; it listens to no compromise with mortal man, but, reducing all the human race to the same standard, it confounds all the distinctions of society at the foot of the same altar, even as they are confounded in the sight of God. If Catholicism predisposes the faithful to obedience, it certainly does not prepare them for inequality; but the contrary may be said of Protestantism, which generally tends to make men independent more than to render them equal. Catholicism is like an absolute monarchy; if the sovereign be removed, all other classes of society are more equal than in republics.

It has not infrequently occurred that the Catholic priest has left the service of the altar to mix with the governing powers of society and to take his place among the civil ranks of men. This religious influence has sometimes been used to secure the duration of that political state of things to which he belonged. Thus we have seen Catholics taking the side of aristocracy from a religious motive. But no sooner is the priesthood entirely separated from the government, as is the case in the United States, than it is found that no class of men is more naturally disposed than the Catholics to transfer the doctrine of the equality of condition into the political world.

If, then, the Catholic citizens of the United States are not forcibly led by the nature of their tenets to adopt democratic and republican principles, at least they are not necessarily opposed to them; and their social position, as well as their limited number, obliges them to adopt these opinions. Most of the Catholics are poor, and they have no chance of taking a part in the government unless it is open to all the citizens. They constitute a minority, and all rights must be respected in order to ensure to them the free exercise of their own privileges. These two causes induce them, even unconsciously, to adopt political doctrines which they would perhaps support with less zeal if they were rich and preponderant.

The Catholic clergy of the United States have never attempted to oppose this political tendency; but they seek rather to justify it. The Catholic priests in America have divided the intellectual world into two parts: in the one they place the doctrines of revealed religion, which they assent to without discussion; in the other they leave those political truths which they believe the Deity has left open to free inquiry. Thus the Catholics of the United States are at the same time the most submissive believers and the most independent citizens.

It may be asserted, then, that in the United States no religious doctrine displays the slightest hostility to democratic and republican institutions. The clergy of all the different sects there hold the same language; their opinions are in agreement with the laws, and the human mind flows onwards, so to speak, in one undivided current.

I happened to be staying in one of the largest cities in the Union when I was invited to attend a public meeting in favor of the Poles and of sending them supplies of arms and money. I found two or three thousand persons collected in a vast hall which had been prepared to receive them. In a short time a priest in his ecclesiastical robes advanced to the front of the platform. The spectators rose and stood uncovered in silence while he spoke in the following terms:

"Almighty God! The God of armies! Thou who didst strengthen the hearts and guide the arms of our fathers when they were fighting for the sacred rights of their national independence! Thou who didst make them triumph over a hateful oppression, and hast granted to our people the benefits of liberty and peace! turn, O Lord, a favorable eye upon the other hemisphere; pitifully look down upon an heroic nation which is even now struggling as we did in the former time, and for the same rights. Thou, who didst create man in the same image, let not tyranny mar thy work and establish inequality upon the earth. Almighty God! do thou watch over the destiny of the Poles, and make them worthy to be free. May thy wisdom direct their councils, may thy strength sustain their arms! Shed forth thy terror over their enemies; scatter the powers which take counsel against them; and permit not the injustice which the world has witnessed for fifty years to be consummated in our time. . . .

". . . Save the Poles, we beseech thee, in the name of thy well-beloved Son, our Lord Jesus Christ, who died upon the cross for the salvation of all men. Amen."

The whole meeting responded: "Amen!" with devotion.

2. Maria Monk Shocks Protestant Readers with Allegations of Sex and Violence in a Nunnery, 1836

After taking the vows, I proceeded to a small apartment behind the altar, accompanied by four nuns, where was a coffin prepared with my nun name engraven upon it:

"Saint Eustace."

My companions lifted it by four handles attached to it, while I threw off my dress, and put on that of a nun of Sœur Bourgeoise; and then we all returned to the chapel. I proceeded first, and was followed by the four nuns; the Bishop naming a number of worldly pleasures in rapid succession, in reply to which I rapidly repeated—"Je renonce, je renonce, je renonce"—[I renounce, I renounce, I renounce.]

The coffin was then placed in front of the altar, and I advanced to lay myself in it. This coffin was to be deposited, after the ceremony, in an outhouse, to be preserved until my death, when it was to receive my corpse. . . . A large, thick black cloth was then spread over me, and the chanting of Latin hymns immediately commenced. My thoughts were not the most pleasing during the time I lay in that situation. The pall, or Drap Mortel, as the cloth is called, had a strong smell of incense, which was always disagreeable to me, and then proved almost suffocating. . . .

When I was uncovered, I rose, stepped out of my coffin, and kneeled. The Bishop then addressed these words to the Superior, "Take care and keep pure and spotless this young virgin, whom Christ has consecrated to himself this day." After which the music commenced, and here the whole was finished. I then proceeded from the chapel, and returned to the Superior's room, followed by the other nuns, who walked two by two, in their customary manner, with their hands folded on their breasts, and their eyes cast down upon the floor. The nun who was to be my companion in future, then walked at the end of the procession. On reaching the Superior's door, they all left me, and I entered alone, and found her with the Bishop and two priests.

The Superior now informed me, that having taken the black veil, it only remained that I should swear the three oaths customary on becoming a nun; and that some explanations would be necessary from her. I was now, she told me, to have access to every part of the edifice, even to the cellar, where two of the sisters were imprisoned for causes which she did not mention. I must be informed, that one of my great duties was, to obey the priests in all things; and this I soon learnt, to my utter astonishment and horror, was to live in the practice of criminal intercourse with them. I expressed some of the feelings which this announcement excited in me, which came upon me like a flash of lightning, but the only effect was to set her arguing with me, in favor of the crime, representing it as a virtue acceptable to God, and honorable to me. The priests, she said, were not situated like other men, being forbidden to marry; while they lived secluded, laborious, and self-denying

---

Maria Monk, *Awful Disclosures of the Hotel Dieu Nunnery in Montreal* (1836).

lives for our salvation. They might, indeed, be considered our saviours, as without their services we could not obtain the pardon of sin, and must go to hell. Now, it was our solemn duty, on withdrawing from the world, to consecrate our lives to religion, to practice every species of self-denial. We could not become too humble, nor mortify our feelings too far; this was to be done by opposing them, and acting contrary to them; and what she proposed was, therefore, pleasing in the sight of God. I now felt how foolish I had been to place myself in the power of such persons as were around me.

From what she said I could draw no other conclusion, but that I was required to act like the most abandoned of beings, and that all my future associates were habitually guilty of the most heinous and detestable crimes. When I repeated my expressions of surprise and horror, she told me that such feelings were very common at first, and that many other nuns had expressed themselves as I did, who had long since changed their minds. She even said, that on her entrance into the nunnery, she had felt like me. . . .

She gave me another piece of information which excited other feelings in me, scarcely less dreadful. Infants were sometimes born in the convent; but they were always baptized and immediately strangled! This secured their everlasting happiness; for the baptism purified them from all sinfulness, and being sent out of the world before they had time to do anything wrong, they were at once admitted into heaven. How happy, she exclaimed, are those who secure immortal happiness to such little beings! Their little souls would thank those who kill their bodies, if they had it in their power!

Into what a place, and among what society, had I been admitted! How differently did a Convent now appear from what I had supposed it to be! The holy women I had always fancied the nuns to be, the venerable Lady Superior, what were they? And the priests of the seminary adjoining, some of whom indeed I had had reason to think were base and profligate men, what were they all? I now learnt they were often admitted into the nunnery, and allowed to indulge in the greatest crimes, which they and others called virtues. . . .

Nothing important occurred until late in the afternoon, when, as I was sitting in the community-room, Father Dufrèsne called me out, saying he wished to speak with me. I feared what was his intention; but I dared not disobey. In a private apartment, he treated me in a brutal manner; and from two other priests I afterward received similar usage that evening. Father Dufrèsne afterward appeared again; and I was compelled to remain in company with him until morning. . . .

[A few days later she was in a group.] The young nun was standing alone near the middle of the room; she was probably about twenty, with light hair, blue eyes, and a very fair complexion. I spoke to her in a compassionate voice, but at the same time with such a decided manner, that she comprehended my full meaning—

"Saint Francis, we are sent for you."

Several others spoke kindly to her, but two addressed her very harshly. The poor creature turned round with a look of meekness, and without expressing any unwillingness or fear, without even speaking a word, resigned herself to our hands. The tears came into my eyes. I had not a moment's doubt that she considered her fate as sealed, and was already beyond the fear of death. She was conducted, or rather hurried to the staircase, which was near by, and then seized by her limbs and clothes, and in fact almost dragged up-stairs, in the sense the Superior had intended. . . .

[She told the Mother Superior] that she did not repent of words she had uttered, though they had been reported by some of the nuns who had heard them; that she still wished to escape from the Convent; and that she had firmly resolved to resist every attempt to compel her to the commission of crimes which she detested. She added, that she would rather die than cause the murder of harmless babes.

"That is enough, finish her!" said the Bishop.

Two nuns instantly fell upon the young woman, and in obedience to directions, given by the Superior, prepared to execute her sentence.

She still maintained all the calmness and submission of a lamb. Some of those who took part in this transaction, I believe, were as unwilling as myself; but of others I can safely say, that I believe they delighted in it. Their conduct certainly exhibited a most blood-thirsty spirit. But, above all others present, and above all human fiends I ever saw, I think Sainte Hypolite was the most diabolical. She engaged in the horrid task with all alacrity, and assumed from choice the most revolting parts to be performed. She seized a gag, forced it into the mouth of the poor nun, and when it was fixed between her extended jaws, so as to keep them open at their greatest possible distance, took hold of the straps fastened at each end of the stick, crossed them behind the helpless head of the victim, and drew them tight through the loop prepared as a fastening.

The bed which had always stood in one part of the room, still remained there; though the screen, which had usually been placed before it, and was made of thick muslin, with only a crevice through which a person behind might look out, had been folded up on its hinges in the form of a W, and placed in a corner. On the bed the prisoner was laid with her face upward, and then bound with cords, so that she could not move. In an instant another bed was thrown upon her. One of the priests, named Bonin, sprung like a fury first upon it, and stamped upon it, with all his force. He was speedily followed by the nuns, until there were as many upon the bed as could find room, and all did what they could, not only to smother, but to bruise her. Some stood up and jumped upon the poor girl with their feet, some with their knees, and others in different ways seemed to seek how they might best beat the breath out of her body, and mangle it, without coming in direct contact with it, or seeing the effect of their violence. . . .

After the lapse of fifteen or twenty minutes, and when it was presumed that the sufferer had been smothered, and crushed to death, Father Bonin and the nuns ceased to trample upon her, and stepped from the bed. All was motionless and silent beneath it.

They then began to laugh at such inhuman thoughts as occurred to some of them, rallying each other in the most unfeeling manner, and ridiculing me for the feelings which I in vain endeavoured to conceal. . . . After spending some moments in such conversation, one of them asked if the corpse should be removed. The Superior said it had better remain a little while. After waiting a short time longer, the feather-bed was taken off, the cords unloosed, and the body taken by the nuns and dragged down stairs. I was informed that it was taken into the cellar, and thrown unceremoniously into the hole which I have already described, covered with a great quantity of lime, and afterwards sprinkled with a liquid of the properties and name of which I am ignorant. This liquid I have seen poured into the hole from large bottles, after the necks were broken off, and have heard that it is used in France to prevent the effluvia rising from cemeteries.

3. John Francis Maguire Recounts the Suffering of Irish Catholic Immigrants (1846), 1887

I have more than once referred to the unfavourable circumstances under which the vast majority of the Irish arrived in America, and the difficulties with which, in a special degree, they had to contend; but the picture would be most imperfect were not some reference made to the disastrous emigration of the years 1847 and 1848—to that blind and desperate rush across the Atlantic known and described, and to be recognised for time to come, as the Irish Exodus. . . . A glance even at a single quarantine—that of Grosse Isle, in the St. Lawrence, about thirty miles below Quebec—while affording a faint idea of the horrors crowded into a few months, may enable the reader to understand with what alarm the advent of the Irish was regarded . . . and how the natural terror they inspired, through the terrible disease brought with them across the ocean, deepened the prejudice against them, notwithstanding that their sufferings and misery appealed to the best sympathies of the human heart.

On the 8th of May, 1847, the "Urania," from Cork, with several hundred immigrants on board, a large proportion of them sick and dying of the ship-fever, was put into quarantine at Grosse Isle. This was the first of the plague-smitten ships from Ireland which that year sailed up the St. Lawrence. But before the first week of June as many as eighty-four ships of various tonnage were driven in by an easterly wind; and of that enormous number of vessels there was not one free from the taint of malignant typhus, the offspring of famine and of the foul ship-hold. This fleet of vessels literally reeked with pestilence. . . .

The authorities were taken by surprise, owing to the sudden arrival of this plague-smitten fleet, and, save the sheds that remained since 1832, there was no accommodation of any kind on the island. These sheds were rapidly filled with the miserable people, the sick and the dying, and round their walls lay groups of half-naked men, women, and children, in the same condition—sick or dying. Hundreds were literally flung on the beach, left amid the mud and stones, to crawl on the dry land how they could. "I have seen," says the priest who was then chaplain of the quarantine, and who had been but one year on the mission, "I have one day seen thirty-seven people lying on the beach, crawling on the mud, and dying like fish out of water." Many of these, and many more besides, gasped out their last breath on that fatal shore, not able to drag themselves from the slime in which they lay. Death was doing its work everywhere—in the sheds, around the sheds, where the victims lay in hundreds under the canopy of heaven, and in the poisonous holds of the plague-ships, all of which were declared to be, and treated as, hospitals.

John Francis Maguire, *The Irish in America* (New York: D. and J. Sadlier, 1887).

From ship to ship the young Irish priest carried the consolations of religion to the dying. Amidst shrieks, and groans, and wild ravings, and heart-rending lamentations,—over prostrate sufferers in every stage of the sickness—from loathsome berth to loathsome berth, he pursued his holy task. So noxious was the pent-up atmosphere of these floating pest-houses, that he had frequently to rush on deck, to breathe the pure air, or to relieve his over-taxed stomach; then he would again plunge into the foul den, and resume his interrupted labours.

There being, at first, no organisation, no staff, no available resources, it may be imagined why the mortality rose to a prodigious rate, and how at one time as many as 150 bodies, most of them in a half-naked state, would be piled up in the dead-house, awaiting such sepulture as a huge pit could afford. Poor creatures would crawl out of the sheds, and being too exhausted to return, would be found lying in the open air, not a few of them rigid in death. When the authorities were enabled to erect sheds sufficient for the reception of the sick, and provide a staff of physicians and nurses, and the Archbishop of Quebec had appointed a number of priests, who took the hospital duty in turn, there was of course more order and regularity; but the mortality was for a time scarcely diminished. The deaths were as many as 100, and 150, and even 200 a day, and this for a considerable period during the summer. . . .

About the middle of June the young chaplain was attacked by the pestilence. For ten days he had not taken off his clothes, and his boots, which he constantly wore for all that time, had to be cut from his feet. A couple of months elapsed before he resumed his duties; but when he returned to his post of danger the mortality was still of fearful magnitude. Several priests, a few Irish, the majority French Canadians, caught the infection; and of the twenty-five who were attacked, seven paid with their lives the penalty of their devotion. Not a few of these men were professors in colleges; but at the appeal of the Archbishop they left their classes and their studies for the horrors and perils of the fever sheds.

It was not until the 1st of November that the quarantine of Grosse Isle was closed. Upon that barren isle as many as 10,000 of the Irish race were consigned to the grave-pit. . . .

This deplorable havoc of human life left hundreds of orphans dependent on the compassion of the public; and nobly was the unconscious appeal of this multitude of destitute little ones responded to by the French Canadians. Half naked, squalid, covered with vermin generated by hunger, fever, and the foulness of the ship's hold, perhaps with the germs of the plague lurking in their vitiated blood, these helpless innocents of every age—from the infant taken from the bosom of its dead mother to the child that could barely tell the name of its parents—were gathered under the fostering protection of the Church. They were washed, and clad, and fed; and every effort was made by the clergy and nuns who took them into their charge to discover who they were, what their names, and which of them were related the one to the other, so that, if possible, children of the same family might not be separated for ever. A difficult thing it was to learn from mere infants whether, among more than 600 orphans, they had brothers or sisters. But by patiently observing the little creatures when they found strength and courage to play, their watchful protectors were enabled to find out relationships which, without such care, would have been otherwise unknown. If one infant ran to meet another, or caught its hand, or smiled at it, or kissed it, or showed pleasure in its society, here was a clue to be followed; and in many instances children of the same parents were thus preserved to each other. Many more, of course, were separated for ever, as these children were too young to tell their own names, or do anything save cry in piteous accents for "mammy, mammy!" until soothed to slumber in the arms of a compassionate Sister.

The greater portion of the orphans of the Grosse Isle tragedy were adopted by the French Canadians, who were appealed to by their *curés* at the earnest request of Father Cazeau, then Secretary to the Archbishop, and now one of the Vicars General of the Archdiocese of Quebec. . . .

. . . There lived, as a "help," in the house of a Protestant family, an intelligent and high-spirited Irish girl, remarkable for her exemplary conduct, and the zeal with which she discharged the duties of her position. Kate acted as a mother to a young brother and sister, whom she was bringing up with the greatest care; and a happy girl was Kate when she received good tidings of their progress in knowledge and piety. Kate, like many other people in the world, had her special torment, and that special torment was a playful-minded preacher who visited at the house, and who looked upon "Bridget"—he *would* call her Bridget—as a fair butt for the exercise of his pleasant wit, of which he was justly proud. It was Kate's duty to attend table; and no sooner did she make her appearance in the dining-room, than the playful preacher commenced his usual fun, which would be somewhat in this fashion: "Well, Bridget, my girl! when did you pray last to the Virgin Mary? Tell me, Bridget, when were you with Father Pat? What did you give him, Bridget? What did the old fellow ask for the absolution this time? Now, I guess it was ten cents for the small sins, and $1 for the thumpers! Come now, Bridget, tell me what penance did that priest of yours give you?" Thus would the agreeable jester pelt the poor Irish girl with his generous pleasantries, to the amusement of the thoughtless, but to the serious annoyance of the fair-minded, who did not like to see her feelings so wantonly wounded. . . . On one memorable day, however, his love of the humorous carried him just too far. A large company was assembled round the hospitable table of the mistress of the house. The preacher was present, and was brimming over with merriment. Kate entered the room, bearing a large tureen of steaming soup in her hands. "Ho, ho Bridget!—how are you, Bridget? Well, Bridget what did you pay Father Pat for absolution this time? Come to me, Bridget, and I will give you as many dollars as will set you all straight with the old fellow for the next six months, and settle your account with purgatory too. Now, Bridget, tell us how many cents for each sin?" The girl had just reached the preacher as he finished his little joke; and if he wished to see the Irish eye flash out its light, and the Irish blood burn in the cheek, he had an excellent opportunity for enjoying that treat. It was Bridget's turn to be playful. Stopping next to his chair, and looking him steadily in his face, while she grasped the tureen of rich green-pea soup more firmly in her hands, she said: "Now, sir, I often asked you to leave me alone, and not mind me, and not to insult me or my religion, what no real gentleman would do to a poor girl; and now, sir, as you want to know what I pay for absolution, here's my answer!" and, suiting the action to the word, she flung the hot steaming liquid over the face, neck, breast—entire person—of the playful preacher! . . . The condition of the preacher may best be described as abject: morally as well as physically, he was overwhelmed. Kate rushed to her room, locked herself in, and relieved her excitement in a cry—"as if her heart would break." In a short time her mistress tapped at the door, told her to come out, that all was right, and that Mr. Blank was sorry that he had annoyed her—as, no doubt, he was. The sentiment—the generous American sentiment—was in Kate's favour, as she might have perceived in the manner of the guests. For the poor preacher, it may be said that the soup "spoiled his dinner" for that day. He did not make his appearance again for some time; but when he did, it was as an altered and much-improved gentleman, who appeared to have lost all interest in the religious peculiarities of Kate, whom, strange to say, he never more called by the name of Bridget. The warm bath, so vigorously administered, had done him much service—Kate said, "a power of good."

When once her worth is recognised, the most unlimited trust is placed in the Irish girl. There are thousands of houses in the United States in which everything is left to her charge and under her control; and, unless in some rare instances, in which fanaticism is more than a match for common sense, the more devoted she is to the practices of her religion, the more she is respected and confided in by those with whom she lives. Occasional betrayals of trust there may be, for humanity is not perfect; but as a rule, broad and sweeping, confidence and kindness are rewarded with unswerving fidelity.

In the hotels of America the Irish girl is admittedly indispensable. Through the ordeal of these fiery furnaces of temptation she passes unscathed. There, where honesty and good conduct are most essential, she is found equal to the test, while in cheerful willing industry none can surpass her. Such is the testimony which is readily borne to the Irish girl in every State of the Union.

I remember asking one of the best-known hotel proprietors of America, why it was that all the young women in the establishment were Irish, and his replying— "The thing is very simple: the Irish girls are industrious, willing, cheerful, and honest—they work hard, and they are strictly moral. I should say that is quite reason enough." I agreed with him.

There are testimonies, also, borne to her in a very different spirit, but equally honouring—those extorted from the baffled tempter, who finds all his arts of seduction fail before the seven-fold shield of an austerity as unexpected as unwished-for. Nothing is more common than for one who has failed in his attempts against the honour of an Irish girl to warn his companions from a similar folly—"Oh, hang her!—don't lose your time with *her;* she is one of those d——d Irish girls—the priest has a hold of her—she goes to confession, and all that kind of nonsense— don't lose your time, for it's no use." Quite true: temptations assail her in vain; in her faith and piety she is invincible.

The Irish woman is naturally religious; the fervent character of her mind is adapted to devotional enthusiasm; and in the practices of her faith she finds occupation for her leisure time, as well as strength for her soul and consolation for her heart. If she happen to be in a new mission, where everything—church, school, asylum, hospital—is to be erected, she enters into the holy task with congenial ardour. To build up, finish, or decorate a church—to her, the House of God and Temple of her Ancient Faith—she contributes with generous hand. It is the same in a long-established parish, whose spiritual necessities keep pace with its growing population; there, also, the Irish girl is unfailing in her liberality.

4. Benjamin Roth Warns His Emigrant Son Solomon About Moral and Religious Dangers in America, 1854

My Dear Son:

It is doubtful whether we shall see each other again in life; and from afar I cannot warn you against such dangers as often threaten youth. Yet, even from the further-most distance I shall think of you only with fatherly love and tenderness, and will at all times do everything in my power to help you. No sacrifice is too great for a father's love to bring willingly. In whatever situation you may find yourself, turn to me; and I will always show you that I am yours with an unending love, now and forever. Always have confidence in me. Before you give your confidence to a stranger—trust your father.

At this moment of our parting, since I can no longer be near you, let me give you the following precepts for life to take with you. Obey them, follow them, and you will never be unhappy. Whatever situations you may enter into, you will be able to take hold of yourself, to comfort yourself; and God, to whom I pray daily for your welfare, will let it be well with you.

1. Always seek to keep your conscience clear; i.e., never commit an action which you will have to regret afterwards. . . .

2. Consider what you possess as a trust given you by God. Be thrifty with it, and seek to enlarge it in an honest manner. Consider it just as much the possession of your brothers and sisters, and therefore . . . let no sacrifice appear too great for you. Wealth should never come to diminish your honor and your clear conscience. Also, never say in the manner of the cold Englishman or American: "Help your own self!" Instead, aid rather to the full extent of your powers every poor man and anyone who needs your help. In short: be thrifty for yourself, that you may be able to aid a suffering humanity with your wealth.

3. Never leave the religion that is yours by birth, the faith of your parents and ancestors. Neither wealth, nor friendship, nor the possibility of a brilliant career in life, nor seduction, nor even the love of a girl should move you or have the power to make you change your religion. Should you be forced, partly through circumstances, partly because of the dictates of reason, to omit the ceremonial observances, you must nevertheless under no circumstances depart from the basis of religion: "The Eternal, your God, is one, unique, single being." Reason and conviction can never force you to desert Judaism, since the Jewish religion is really the only one whose basic teachings can be brought into harmony with philosophy. Therefore, desertion would be for worldly advantages, and these are never valuable enough to sacrifice the Eternal One or our conscience. I feel I must recommend this to you doubly, since you have a tendency towards frivolity which could lead you to an easier acceptance of this type of seduction.

Also, never have any contact with missionaries. You do not have enough knowledge of the Holy Scriptures. That way, you cannot engage in disputations with them; for they could easily lead you astray. Consider them therefore only as self-seeking

Benjamin Roth to his son Solomon, 1854, *American Jewish Archives* 6 (January 1954), 6–12.

cheats, or as ranting visionaries, as I have come to know them. And, indeed, in my conversations with them I frequently exhibited them as such in the presence of company, something I could do since I have studied Scripture from my childhood days. And yet, even then it was a difficult task.

4. Do not become acquainted—not to mention closer relationships—with women. Be polite and well-mannered towards them; for the rest, as far as it is possible, keep your distance. Consider them like a sharp, pointed toy, with which one can play only occasionally—and then with the greatest of care. Seek to keep your heart free; guard it; and be not seduced by the tempting, destructive speech and actions of your contemporaries. This last demands your closest attention.

Have no relations with a prostitute. Her breath is poison, her word the bite of a snake; and they are all alike. However, let me add here, in praise of Jewish womanhood, that with a few exceptions they have preserved much purer morals than the girls of other races; and they have contained themselves from selling their charms for money.

I recommend the above to you in particular as injunctions to be followed. With your fine appearance and cheerful temperament you will be exposed to many temptations and opportunities in regard to women. And I do not want to say much on this point, leaving it rather to your wisdom and unspoiled instincts. My deepest prayer is that you may guard the latter; and, if it is your firm intention to remain pure, the good Lord will aid you in this task. . . .

And thus I transmit to you, my beloved son, these rules for life. Seek to follow them. I particularly recommend to you that you seek to emulate your brother Moses and that you obey him; partly because he is your older brother, partly because he has an excellent, steadfast, and firm character. I do not censure you for the fact that big-city life and your growing up among strangers have in some ways been detrimental to you. This is the reason why you have almost discarded by now that steadfastness of spirit which you took with you from your parents' home. It remained longer in Moses, who stayed at home till he was seventeen, and whose character could therefore develop further. Really, you could not give me more pleasure than by living together peacefully and in brotherly harmony; as you could also give me no greater pain and sorrow than by not doing this. I do not doubt that both of you will follow my wishes, and in that way you will also fulfill the words of our sages [Hebrew]: "How good and how pleasant it is for brethren to live together in unity."

I assure you that my whole happiness exists in the happiness of my children. Believe me, no sacrifice would be too great for me to bring willingly if I could make you happy. It was a great inward struggle for me (and I had to conceal my feelings from you as from mother) to send you away from me while you were yet so young. But it was your firm desire—and I did not want to take it from you. For all eternity my feelings towards you will be those of the deepest love.

And with this I give you, now, my blessing; may it follow you on all your paths with the words [Hebrew]:

> The angel who hath redeemed me from all evil bless thee; and let my name be named in thee, and the name of my fathers, Abraham and Isaac; and mayest thou grow into a multitude in the midst of the earth.

The Lord bless thee, and keep thee.
The Lord make His face to shine upon thee, and be gracious unto thee.
The Lord lift up His countenance upon thee, and give thee peace.

God make thee as Ephraim and Manasseh, like Moses in his humility, like Solomon in his wisdom, like Samson in his strength, like Absalom in his beauty, like Hezekiah in his righteousness, and like David in his reverence.

Hechingen, June, 1854   B. M. ROTH

5. Harriet Beecher Stowe Advocates Enlightened Observance of the Sabbath, 1853

"All will come in good time," said Mrs. Fletcher. "But tell me, my dear children, are you sure that you are quite ready for the Sabbath? You say that you have put away the books and the playthings; have you put away, too, all wrong and unkind feelings? Do you feel kindly and pleasantly towards everybody?"

"Yes, mother," said Willie, who appeared to have taken a great part of this speech to himself; "I went over to Tom Walters this very morning to ask him about that chicken of mine, and he said that he did not mean to hit it, and did not know he had till I told him of it; and so we made all up again, and I am glad I went."

"I am inclined to think, Willie," said his father, "that if everybody would make it a rule to settle up all their differences *before Sunday,* that there would be very few long quarrels and lawsuits. In about half the cases a quarrel is founded on some misunderstanding, that would be got over in five minutes if one would go directly to the person for explanation."

"I suppose I need not ask you," said Mrs. Fletcher, "whether you have fully learned your Sunday-school-lessons?"

"Oh, to be sure," said William. "You know, mother, that Susan and I were busy about them through Monday and Tuesday, and then this afternoon we looked them over again, and wrote down some questions."

"And I heard Robert say his all through, and shewed him all the places on the Bible Atlas," said Susan.

"Well, then," said my friend, "if everything is done, let us begin Sunday with some music."

Thanks to the recent improvements in the musical instruction of the young, every family can now form a domestic concert, with words and tunes adapted to the capacity and the voices of children; and while these little ones, full of animation, pressed round their mother as she sat at the piano, and accompanied her music with the words of some beautiful hymns, I thought that, though I might have heard finer music, I had never listened to any that answered the purpose of music so well.

It was a custom at my friend's to retire at an early hour on Saturday evening, in order that there might be abundant time for rest, and no excuse for late rising on the

Harriet Beecher Stowe, *Four Ways of Observing the Sabbath* (Liverpool, England: Pearce and Brewer, 1853).

Sabbath; and, accordingly, when the children had done singing, after a short season of family devotion, we all betook ourselves to our chambers, and I, for one, fell asleep, with the impression of having finished the week most agreeably, and with anticipations of very great pleasure on the morrow.

Early in the morning I was aroused from my sleep by the sound of little voices singing with great animation, in the room next to mine, and, listening, I caught the following words:

> "Awake! awake! your bed forsake,
>   To God your praises pay;
> The morning sun is clear and bright,
> With joy we hail his cheerful light.
>   In songs of love
>   Praise God above—
>   It is the Sabbath day!" . . .

It was a beautiful summer morning, and the voices of the children within accorded well with the notes of birds and bleating flocks without—a cheerful, yet Sabbath-like and quieting sound.

"Blessed be children's music!" said I to myself; "how much better this is than the solitary tic-tic of old Uncle Fletcher's tall mahogany clock."

The family bell summoned us to the breakfast-room just as the children had finished their hymn. The little breakfast-parlour had been swept and garnished expressly for the day, and a vase of beautiful flowers, which the children had the day before collected from their gardens, adorned the centre-table. The door of one of the bookcases by the fireplace was thrown open, presenting to view a collection of prettily bound books, over the top of which appeared in gilt letters the inscription, "Sabbath library." The windows were thrown open to let in the invigorating breath of the early morning, and the birds that flitted among the rose-bushes without seemed scarcely lighter and more buoyant than did the children as they entered the room. It was legibly written on every face in the house, that the happiest day in the week had arrived, and each one seemed to enter into its duties with a whole soul. . . .

"It seems to me that this work must be very expensive," I remarked to my friend, as we were turning the leaves [of Calmet's illustrated dictionary].

"Indeed, it is so," he replied; "but here is one place where I am less withheld by considerations of expense than in any other. . . . Whatever will give my children a better knowledge of, or deeper interest in, the Bible, or enable them to spend a Sabbath profitably and without weariness, stands first on my list among things to be purchased. . . . Two large drawers below were filled with maps and scriptural engravings, some of them of a very superior character. . . .

"But," said I, "would not the Sunday-school library answer all the purpose of this?"

"The Sabbath-school library is an admirable thing," said my friend; "but this does more fully and perfectly what that was intended to do. It makes a sort of central attraction at home on the Sabbath, and makes the acquisition of religious knowledge and the proper observance of the Sabbath a sort of family enterprise. You know," he added, smiling, "that people always feel interested for an object in which they have invested money."

The sound of the first Sabbath-school bell put an end to this conversation. The children promptly made themselves ready, and, as their father was the superintendent of the school, and their mother one of the teachers, it was quite a family party.

One part of every Sabbath at my friend's was spent by one or both parents with the children, in a sort of review of the week. The attention of the little ones was directed to their own characters, the various defects or improvements of the past week were pointed out, and they were stimulated to be on their guard in the time to come, and the whole was closed by earnest prayer for such heavenly aid as the temptations and faults of each particular one might need.

6. Angelina Grimke Uses the Bible to Justify Abolishing Slavery, 1838

Now the Bible is my ultimate appeal in all matters of faith and practice, and it is to *this test* I am anxious to bring the subject at issue between us. Let us then begin with Adam and examine the charter of privileges which was given to him. "Have dominion over the fish of the sea, and over the fowl of the air, and over every living thing that moveth upon the earth." In the eighth Psalm we have a still fuller description of this charter which through Adam was given to all mankind. "Thou madest him to have dominion over the works of thy hands; thou hast put all things under his feet. All sheep and oxen, yea, and the beasts of the field, the fowl of the air, the fish of the sea, and whatsoever passeth through the paths of the seas." And after the flood when this charter of human rights was renewed, we find *no additional* power vested in man. "And the fear of you and the dread of you shall be upon every beast of the earth, and every fowl of the air, and upon all that moveth upon the earth, and upon all the fishes of the sea, into your hand are they delivered." In this charter, although the different kinds of *irrational* beings are so particularly enumerated, and supreme dominion over *all of them* is granted, yet *man* is *never* vested with this dominion *over his fellow man;* he was never told that any of the human species were put *under his feet;* it was only *all things,* and man, who was created in the image of his Maker, *never* can properly be termed a *thing,* though the laws of Slave States do call him "a chattel personal;" *Man* then, I assert *never* was put *under the feet of man,* by that first charter of human rights which was given by God, to the Fathers of the Antediluvian and Postdiluvian worlds, therefore this doctrine of equality is based on the Bible.

But it may be argued, that in the very chapter of Genesis from which I have last quoted, will be found the curse pronounced upon Canaan, by which his posterity was consigned to servitude under his brothers Shem and Japheth. I know this prophecy was uttered, and was most fearfully and wonderfully fulfilled, through the immediate descendants of Canaan, i. e. the Canaanites, and I do not know but it has been through all the children of Ham, but I do know that prophecy does *not* tell us what *ought to be,* but what actually does take place, ages after it has been delivered, and that if we justify America for enslaving the children of Africa, we must also justify Egypt for reducing the children of Israel to bondage, for the latter was foretold as

Angelina Grimke, *Appeal to the Christian Women of the South* (n.d. [circa 1840]; reprint, New York: Arno, 1969).

explicitly as the former. I am well aware that prophecy has often been urged as an excuse for Slavery, but be not deceived, the fulfilment of prophecy will *not cover one sin* in the awful day of account. Hear what our Saviour says on this subject; "it must needs be that offences come, but *woe unto that man through whom they come."* . . .

Shall I ask you now my friends, to draw the *parallel* between Jewish *servitude* and American *slavery?* No! For there is *no likeness* in the two systems; I ask you rather to mark the contrast. The laws of Moses *protected servants* in their *rights* as *men and women,* guarded them from oppression and defended them from wrong. The Code Noir of the South *robs the slave of all his rights* as a *man,* reduces him to a chattel personal, and defends the *master* in the exercise of the most unnatural and unwarantable power over his slave. They each bear the impress of the hand which formed them. The attributes of justice and mercy are shadowed out in the Hebrew code; those of injustice and cruelty, in the Code Noir of America. Truly it was wise in the slaveholders of the South to declare their slaves to be "chattels personal;" for before they could be robbed of wages, wives, children, and friends, it was absolutely necessary to deny they were human beings. It is wise in them, to keep them in abject ignorance, for the strong man armed must be bound before we can spoil his house—the powerful intellect of man must be bound down with the iron chains of nescience before we can rob him of his rights as a man; we must reduce him to a *thing* before we can claim the right to set our feet upon his neck, because it was only *all things* which were originally *put under the feet of man* by the Almighty and Beneficent Father of all, who has declared himself to be *no respecter* of persons, whether red, white or black.

But some have even said that Jesus Christ did not condemn slavery. To this I reply that our Holy Redeemer lived and preached among the Jews only. The laws which Moses had enacted fifteen hundred years previous to his appearance among them, had never been annulled, and these laws protected every servant in Palestine. If then He did not condemn Jewish servitude this does not prove that he would not have condemned such a monstrous system as that of American *slavery,* if that had existed among them. But did not Jesus condemn slavery? Let us examine some of his precepts. *"Whatsoever* ye would that men should do to you, do *ye even so to them,"* Let every slaveholder apply these queries to his own heart; Am *I* willing to be a slave—Am *I* willing to see *my* wife the slave of another—Am *I* willing to see my mother a slave, or my father, my sister or my brother? If *not,* then in holding others as slaves, I am doing what I would *not* wish to be done to me or any relative I have; and thus have I broken this golden rule which was given *me* to walk by.

But some slaveholders have said, "we were never in bondage to any man," and therefore the yoke of bondage would be insufferable to us, but slaves are accustomed to it, their backs are fitted to the burden. Well, I am willing to admit that you who have lived in freedom would find slavery even more oppressive than the poor slave does, but then you may try this question in another form—Am I willing to reduce *my little child* to slavery? You know that *if it is brought up a slave* it will never know any contrast, between freedom and bondage, its back will become fitted to the burden just as the negro child's does—*not by nature*—but by daily, violent pressure, in the same way that the head of the Indian child becomes flattened by the boards in which it is bound. It has been justly remarked that *"God never made a slave,"* he made man upright; his back was *not* made to carry burdens, nor his neck to wear a yoke, and the *man* must be crushed within him, before *his* back can be *fitted* to the burden of perpetual slavery; and that his back is *not* fitted to it, is manifest by the insurrections that so often disturb the peace and security of slaveholding countries. Who ever heard of a rebellion of the beasts of the field; and why not? simply because *they* were all placed *under the feet of man,* into whose hand they were delivered; it was originally designed that they should serve him, therefore their necks have been formed for the yoke, and their backs for the burden; but *not so with man,* intellectual, immortal man! I appeal to you, my friends, as mothers; Are you willing to enslave *your* children? You start back with horror and indignation at such a question. But why, if slavery is *no wrong* to those upon whom it is imposed? . . .

. . . Northern women may labor to produce a correct public opinion at the North, but if Southern women sit down in listless indifference and criminal idleness, public opinion cannot be rectified and purified at the South. It is manifest to every reflecting mind, that slavery must be abolished; the era in which we live, and the light which is overspreading the whole world on this subject, clearly show that the time cannot be distant when it will be done. Now there are only two ways in which it can be effected, by moral power or physical force, and it is for *you* to choose which of these you prefer. Slavery always has, and always will produce insurrections wherever it exists, because it is a violation of the natural order of things, and no human power can much longer perpetuate it. The opposers of abolitionists fully believe this; one of them remarked to me not long since, there is no doubt there will be a most terrible overturning at the South in a few years, such cruelty and wrong, must be visited with Divine vengeance soon. Abolitionists believe, too, that this must inevitably be the case if you do not repent, and they are not willing to leave you to perish without entreating you, to save yourselves from destruction; well may they say with the apostle, "am I then your enemy because I tell you the truth," and warn you to flee from impending judgments.

But why, my dear friends, have I thus been endeavoring to lead you through the history of more than three thousand years, and to point you to that great cloud of witnesses who have gone before, "from works to rewards?" Have I been seeking to magnify the sufferings, and exalt the character of woman, that she "might have praise of men?" No! no! my object has been to arouse *you,* as the wives and mothers, the daughters and sisters, of the South, to a sense of your duty as *women,* and as Christian women, on that great subject, which has already shaken our country, from the St. Lawrence and the lakes, to the Gulf of Mexico, and from the Mississippi to the shores of the Atlantic; *and will continue mightily to shake it,* until the polluted temple of slavery fall and crumble into ruin. I would say unto each one of you, "what meanest thou, O sleeper! arise and call upon thy God, if so be that God will think upon us that we perish not." Perceive you not that dark cloud of vengeance which hangs over our boasting Republic? Saw you not the lightnings of Heaven's wrath, in the flame which leaped from the Indian's torch to the roof of yonder dwelling, and lighted with its horrid glare the darkness of midnight? Heard you not the thunders of Divine anger, as the distant roar of the cannon came rolling onward, from the Texian country, where Protestant American Rebels are fighting with Mexican Republicans—for what? For the re-establishment of *slavery;* yes! of American slavery in the bosom of a Catholic Republic, where that system of robbery, violence, and wrong, had been legally abolished for twelve years. Yes! citizens of the United States, after plundering

Mexico of her land, are now engaged in deadly conflict, for the privilege of fastening chains, and collars, and manacles—upon whom? upon the subjects of some foreign prince? No! upon native born American Republican citizens, although the fathers of these very men declared to the whole world, while struggling to free themselves from the three penny taxes of an English king, that they believed it to be a *self-evident* truth that *all men* were created equal, and had an *unalienable right to liberty.*

7. Frederick Douglass Compares Southern Slaveowners' Religion with That of Jesus, 1845

Between the Christianity of this land, and the Christianity of Christ, I recognize the widest possible difference—so wide, that to receive the one as good, pure, and holy, is of necessity to reject the other as bad, corrupt, and wicked. To be the friend of the one, is of necessity to be the enemy of the other. I love the pure, peaceable, and impartial Christianity of Christ: I therefore hate the corrupt, slaveholding, women-whipping, cradle-plundering, partial and hypocritical Christianity of this land. Indeed, I can see no reason, but the most deceitful one, for calling the religion of this land Christianity. I look upon it as the climax of all misnomers, the boldest of all frauds, and the grossest of all libels. Never was there a clearer case of "stealing the livery of the court of heaven to serve the devil in." I am filled with unutterable loathing when I contemplate the religious pomp and show, together with the horrible inconsistencies, which every where surround me. We have men-stealers for ministers, women-whippers for missionaries, and cradle-plunderers for church members. The man who wields the blood-clotted cowskin during the week fills the pulpit on Sunday, and claims to be a minister of the meek and lowly Jesus. The man who robs me of my earnings at the end of each week meets me as a class-leader on Sunday morning, to show me the way of life, and the path of salvation. He who sells my sister, for purposes of prostitution, stands forth as the pious advocate of purity. He who proclaims it a religious duty to read the Bible denies me the right of learning to read the name of the God who made me. He who is the religious advocate of marriage robs whole millions of its sacred influence, and leaves them to the ravages of wholesale pollution. The warm defender of the sacredness of the family relation is the same that scatters whole families,—sundering husbands and wives, parents and children, sisters and brothers,—leaving the hut vacant, and the hearth desolate. We see the thief preaching against theft, and the adulterer against adultery. We have men sold to build churches, women sold to support the gospel, and babes sold to purchase Bibles for the *poor heathen! all for the glory of God and the good of souls!* The slave auctioneer's bell and the church-going bell chime in with each other, and the bitter cries of the heart-broken slave are drowned in the religious shouts of his pious master. Revivals of religion and revivals in the slave-trade go hand in hand together. The slave prison and the church stand near each other. The clanking of fetters and the rattling of chains in the prison, and the pious psalm and solemn

Frederick Douglass, *Narrative of the Life of Frederick Douglass, an American Slave,* ed. Benjamin Quarles (Cambridge: Belknap Press of Harvard University Press, 1968).

prayer in the church, may be heard at the same time. The dealers in the bodies and souls of men erect their stand in the presence of the pulpit, and they mutually help each other. The dealer gives his blood-stained gold to support the pulpit, and the pulpit, in return, covers his infernal business with the garb of Christianity. Here we have religion and robbery the allies of each other—devils dressed in angels' robes, and hell presenting the semblance of paradise. . . .

Dark and terrible as is this picture, I hold it to be strictly true of the overwhelming mass of professed Christians in America. They strain at a gnat, and swallow a camel. Could any thing be more true of our churches? They would be shocked at the proposition of fellowshipping a *sheep*-stealer; and at the same time they hug to their communion a *man*-stealer, and brand me with being an infidel, if I find fault with them for it. They attend with Pharisaical strictness to the outward forms of religion, and at the same time neglect the weightier matters of the law, judgment, mercy, and faith. They are always ready to sacrifice, but seldom to show mercy. They are they who are represented as professing to love God whom they have not seen, whilst they hate their brother whom they have seen. . . .

Such is, very briefly, my view of the religion of this land; and to avoid any misunderstanding, growing out of the use of general terms, I mean, by the religion of this land, that which is revealed in the words, deeds, and actions, of those bodies, north and south, calling themselves Christian churches, and yet in union with slaveholders. It is against religion, as presented by these bodies, that I have felt it my duty to testify.

8. Thornton Stringfellow Argues That the Bible Is Proslavery, 1860

[C]an we believe that God put them [the children of Israel] into these schools of affliction in Egypt and Babylon to teach them, (and all others through them,) the sinfulness of slavery, and yet, that he brought them out without giving them the first hint that involuntary slavery was a sin? And let it be further considered, that it was the business of the prophets which the Lord raised up, *to make known to them the sins for which his judgments were sent upon them.* The sins which he charged upon them in all his visitation are upon record. Let any man find involuntary slavery in any of God's indictments against them, and I will retract all I have ever written.

In my original essay, I said nothing of Paul's letter to Philemon, concerning Onesimus, a run-away slave, converted by Paul's preaching at Rome; and who was returned by the Apostle, with a most affectionate letter to his master, entreating the master to receive him again, and to forgive him. O, how immeasurably different Paul's conduct to this slave and his master, from the conduct of our abolition brethren! Which are we to think is guided by the Spirit of God? It is *impossible* that both can be guided by that Spirit, unless sweet water and bitter can come from the same fountain. This letter, itself, is sufficient to teach any man, capable of being

---

Thornton Stringfellow, "The Bible Argument, or, Slavery in the Light of Divine Revelation," in *Cotton Is King and Pro-Slavery Arguments,* ed. E. N. Ellitt (Augusta, Ga.: Pritchard, Abbott, and Loomis, 1860), 461ff.

taught in the ordinary way, that slavery is not, *in the sight of God, what it is in the sight of the abolitionists. . . .*

Now, my dear sir, if from the evidence contained in the Bible to prove slavery a lawful relation among God's people under every dispensation, the assertion is still made, in the very face of this evidence, that slavery has *ever been* the greatest sin—*everywhere, and under all circumstances*—can you, or can any sane man bring himself to believe, that the mind capable of such a decision, is not capable of trampling the word of God under foot upon any subject?

If it were not known to be the fact, we could not admit that a Bible-reading man could bring himself to believe, with Dr. Wayland, that a thing made lawful by the God of heaven, was, notwithstanding, the greatest sin—and that Moses under the law, and Jesus Christ under the gospel, had sanctioned and regulated in practice, the greatest known sin on earth—and that Jesus had left his church to find out as best they might, that the law of God which established slavery under the Old Testament, and the precepts of the Holy Ghost which regulate the mutual duty of master and slave under the New Testament, were laws and precepts, to sanction and regulate among the people of God the greatest sin which was ever perpetrated.

It is by no means strange that it should have taken seventeen centuries to make such discoveries as the above, and it is worthy of note, that these discoveries were made at last by men who did not appear to know, at the time they made them, what was in the Bible on the subject of slavery, and who now appear unwilling that the teachings of the Bible should be spread before the people—this last I take to be the case, because I have been unable to get the Northern press to give it publicity. . . .

You ask me for my opinion about the emancipation movement in the State of Kentucky. I hold that the emancipation of hereditary slaves by a State is not commanded, or in any way required by the Bible. The Old Testament and the New, sanction slavery, but under no circumstances enjoin its abolition, even among saints. Now, if religion, or the duty we owe our Creator, was inconsistent with slavery, then this could not be so. If pure religion, therefore, did not require its abolition under the law of Moses, nor in the church of Christ—we may safely infer, that our political, moral and social relations do not require it in a State; unless a State requires higher moral, social, and religious qualities in its subjects, than a gospel church.

Masters have been left by the Almighty, both under the patriarchal, legal, and gospel dispensations, to their individual discretion on the subject of emancipation.

The principle of justice inculcated by the Bible, refuses to sanction, it seems to me, such an outrage upon the rights of men, as would be perpetrated by any sovereign State, which, to-day, makes a thing to be property, and to-morrow, takes it from the lawful owners, *without political necessity or pecuniary compensation.* Now, if it be morally right for a majority of the people (and that majority possibly a meagre one, who may not own a slave) to take, without necessity or compensation, the property in slaves held by a minority, (and that minority a large one,) then it would be morally right for a majority, without property, to take any thing else that may be lawfully owned by the prudent and care-taking portion of the citizens.

As for intelligent philanthropy, it shudders at the infliction of certain ruin upon a whole race of helpless beings. If emancipation by law is philanthropic in Kentucky, it is, for the same reasons, philanthropic in every State in the Union. But nothing in the future is more certain, than that such emancipation would begin to work the degradation and final ruin of the slave race, from the day of its consummation.

Break the master's sympathy, which is inseparably connected with his property right in his slave, and that moment the slave race is placed upon a common level with all other competitors for the rewards of merit; but as the slaves are inferior in the qualities which give success among competitors in our country, extreme poverty would be their lot; and for the want of means to rear families, they would multiply slowly, and die out by inches, degraded by vice and crime, unpitied by honest and virtuous men, and heart-broken by sufferings without a parallel.

So long as States let masters alone on this subject, good men among them, both in the church and out of it, will struggle on, as experience may dictate and justify, for the benefit of the slave race. And should the time ever come, when emancipation in its consequences, will comport with the moral, social, and political obligations of Christianity, then Christian masters will invest their slaves with freedom, and then will the good-will of those follow the descendants of Ham, who, without any agency of their own, have been made in this land of liberty, their providential guardians.

Yours, with affection,

THORNTON STRINGFELLOW.

ESSAYS

The following two essays explore aspects of conservative religious thought. Until recently, historians of the antebellum era were most interested in reformers and the ways in which they used their religious faith to argue for changes in society. Now a generation of historians is studying *resistance* to change and finding that it, too, was based on strong religious traditions and theological arguments. Jay Dolan of the University of Notre Dame is a specialist in Catholic history. Here he explains that Irish and German Catholic immigrants in the years before the Civil War believed not in social or religious equality but in hierarchy. Their solution to American cities' social problems was to be charitable as individuals and to act in personally virtuous and Christ-like ways. The members of each social class had special duties attached to their special privileges, they said; by fulfilling them they would preserve social order as well as their immortal souls. Ironically, although the vast majority of these Catholic immigrants settled in cities, they, like their Protestant neighbors, believed that rural life was morally superior.

Eugene Genovese, now retired, and Elizabeth Fox-Genovese of Emory University are two of the most brilliant and influential living historians, whose work has transformed our understanding of the history of slavery. In their essay they take the reader into the minds of southern slaveholders and explain how they could reconcile their ownership of other humans with faith in Christ. As the Genoveses show, the slaveowners were on stronger ground than abolitionists when they argued from the Bible (which makes clear that the children of Israel *were* slaveowners, even though they had had to escape from their own enslavement in Egypt, and that Jesus did not condemn slavery). Slaveowners and proslavery intellectuals could also point to the suffering and insecurity of the industrial working classes in Europe and the American North to argue that their own system, which looked after slave children and the elderly, was morally superior. The Genoveses' rhetorical skill permits us to share for a moment the proslavery advocates' feelings of intellectual superiority while reminding us that they were devoting their brilliance to a wicked and doomed system.

Catholic Charity and Protestant Suspicions

JAY P. DOLAN

In the ante-bellum period the spirit of reform was in the air. Americans were challenging traditional institutions of society; and such issues as abolition, prison reform, the role of women, public education, and evangelical theology made up the galaxy of reforms that absorbed people's energies. At mid-century Catholics were alienated from these movements of reform and looked upon them with a great deal of suspicion. They appeared to be only American versions of Red republicanism, communism, or socialism, and the strong Protestant tone of many reform movements only made them more suspect. The nativist crusade reinforced these suspicions, and the church remained aloof from the arena of reform; in adopting this position it demonstrated how alienated it was from the rest of American society. This did not mean that Catholics ignored social problems, but it did indicate that the problems and their solutions would be defined in terms of the Catholic tradition, not in terms of the American reform movement.

Catholics defined social reform in a very traditional and conservative manner: it was basically carrying out the corporal works of mercy and was directed toward the poor, the hungry, and the homeless. It was a crusade of charity and not one of social change. The emphasis was on bettering the lot of the individual, with the guiding principle always being the salvation of one's soul. The goal was to make the situation of the oppressed more humane—a stepping stone to salvation, not a stumbling block.

This view of social reform was rooted in Catholic theology and was judged by Catholics to be antithetical to reform movements abroad in America. "Social evils which afflict mankind are the result of Adam's sin," one priest wrote, and "all reform, properly understood, begins with a return to religion and the Church." Orestes Brownson further developed the Catholic position:

> The Church teaches us to rely on moral power, the grace of God, and individual conscience. She demands the intervention of government only in the material order, for the maintenance or vindication of justice; what lies entirely in the moral or spiritual order, she regards as no proper object of governmental suppression. So of great moral and philanthropic objects. She does not call upon the government to enact them, and make it a legal offense to neglect them. Hence, she leaves the care of the poor, the provision for orphans, emancipation of slaves and similar good works, to the charity of the faithful, without calling upon the government to exact them as a matter of justice.

In his opinion the American reform movement led to either despotism or anarchy; charity on the individual level was the only true avenue of reform. Society was a static, stratified social system, and man could not alter it. The charity of Catholics thus was able to adapt itself to capitalism as readily as it had to feudalism. This conservative view of society and social reform was the tradition that immigrants brought with them to the United States.

Jay P. Dolan, "Social Catholicism," in *The Immigrant Church* (Notre Dame, Ind.: University of Notre Dame Press, 1983), 121–140. Copyright © 1983 by University of Notre Dame Press.

Irish immigrants came from a land where poverty, unemployment, and hunger were every day occurrences; the peasant was idealized and not disparaged. Confronted with such widespread suffering, the response of the church was, in the words of one priest to his hungry flock, "to have confidence in God." A priest could comfort a dying man with the assurance that "when one has had as little happiness as you have had in this world, and when one has known how to profit by its miseries, one has nothing to fear in the next." The Irish peasant was sustained by a religion that was little concerned with social reform, and by keeping his sights on the world beyond, he could find solace in the hardships of the earthly kingdom. Poverty, self-denial, and resignation to God's will were Christian ideals aptly suited for a peasant society, and Irish clergy were trained to reinforce this world view.

German immigrants brought with them a similar tradition. During the first half of the century Catholics in Germany evidenced little concern for social questions. As in Ireland, the principal task of the church was to renew Catholic life in a changing social order. Political questions were paramount. Social problems were accepted as part of the divine plan, and no one could change the law of God. Unlike in Ireland, Catholicism in Germany eventually acquired a social awareness through the reform movement spearheaded by the bishop of Mainz, Emmanuel von Ketteler. But as late as 1869 von Ketteler was able to describe the German clergy as having little interest in the fate of the working classes "because they are ignorant of the existence and the impact of the dangers which lurk in these threatening social conditions, because they have failed to size up the character and the breadth of the social question, finally because they have no conception of possible remedies." This was the prevailing tradition that clergy and laity brought with them to the United States, and it influenced the social thought of American Catholics until late in the nineteenth century.

The church's opposition to American reform movements underlined the foreignness of Catholics. Nativist attacks emphasized this aspect of Catholicism, and Catholics were forced to counterattack such charges by demonstrating their compatibility with the American system. This was the principal social issue confronting Catholics in the ante-bellum period, and the debate against Protestants and nativists left little time to examine the church's attitude toward the presence of human suffering in the New World. In fact, why should one question the hallowed tradition of Christian charity that had worked so well in the past? American Protestants were moving along the same traditional path, and Catholics had little time or little reason to question its validity. What worked in the old country was sure to work in America, since it was God's plan to have rich and poor live together so that one could practice almsgiving and the other patience and resignation.

Few people dared to question this divine order. Archbishop Hughes emphasized this perception of society to a Baltimore audience:

> To every class and condition [the church] assigned its own peculiar range of Christian obligations: To sovereigns and legislators, those of justice and mercy in the enactment and execution of laws. To the rich, moderation in enjoyment and liberality toward the poor. To the poor, patience under their trials and affection toward their wealthier brethren. Toward all, the common obligation of loving one another, not in word, but in deed.

God had permitted poverty, and the church was the protector of the poor; they were representatives of Christ, and Catholics were reminded that "to extend a generous and charitable hand to a fellow creature in distress is one of the most exalting and noble acts of man."

This interpretation of society was echoed in the pulpit, the lecture hall, and the press. The salvation of one's soul was the highest law, and "as for the rest, though you should be reduced to the lowest condition; though you should be stripped of all your worldly possessions, all this is nothing if you arrive at length at the happy term of salvation." . . . The press also reinforced this attitude. The *Catholic World* was a progressive publication, alert to the social problems of urban life, but its outlook was very traditional: Christianity was the foundation of society; without religion, society was doomed to failure. The journal urged Catholics to give more attention to the city's poor through "practical benevolence" (in this context "practical benevolence" meant almsgiving and establishing institutions for the sick and the poor). The practice of good works, long a Christian tradition, still remained the fundamental approach to human suffering for nineteenth-century Catholics. If they exercised such charity, poverty, in the words of John Hughes, "would never have existed at all."

Catholic fiction also idealized poverty and faithful resignation to God's will. . . . One of the more popular Catholic novels was *Willy Burke; or, The Irish Orphan in America,* written by Mary Sadlier in 1850. Like most Catholic fiction at that time, it was a moralistic exhortation written to support the Catholic religion in Protestant America. Willy Burke gained success by keeping his mind fixed on God and remaining faithful to his religion. As long as he had trials to bear, he could not forget God; and trusting in Him was the way to sustain the sufferings of this world.

Catholics could emerge from poverty through hard work and fidelity to God. Such attitudes merited their reward in heaven as well as on earth. Because he remained faithful to his religion, Willy Burke inherited five thousand dollars from his employer, who was converted to Catholicism through Willy's example. Other Catholic novelists, writing for both German and Irish readers, reiterated this theme of a moral life meriting material rewards. The main characters in these novels were often poor Catholics, but poverty was scarcely a hindrance to leading a good moral life. It was a way of life imitative of Jesus, who had "led a most holy life, in poverty and suffering"; his followers could expect no less, and they were continually reminded of how difficult it was for a rich man to enter heaven. For the poor the key to success was to persevere in one's state in life, trust in God, and possibly reap a tangible reward for living a good life.

Readers used in Catholic schools further reinforced the ideal of resigning oneself to God's will and to one's position in society. Tales depicted the heroic resignation of early Christian martyrs and other saints. . . .

A central figure in the social apostolate of the parish was the priest. Father Varela, pastor of Transfiguration, came to New York with the reputation of one "exclusively dedicated to the good of others." While in New York, he lived up to this reputation. He visited the sick and poor at all hours of the day. His labors took him to quarantined ships; and during the cholera epidemic of 1832 it was said that he "lived in the hospitals." Soon stories began to circulate about his unselfish work with the poor and sick. Tales recounted how he gave his clothes, his watch, and even his bedding to the poor who often gathered outside his window to receive such gifts. His friends gave him a watch to replace one that he had given away, but in a few days it was gone; later it was found in the hands of a poor parishioner ready to pawn it. While visiting the sick he often gave away the clothes on his back. When he ran out of clothes, he would call upon his friends to replenish his supply. People claimed that he gave away everything he owned.

Another priest in the parish gained a similar reputation. Father Alexander Mupiatti worked at Transfiguration for only five years, but when he died in 1846, large crowds followed his body to the cemetery, and in later years people remembered him as a saint. An historical epitaph noted that "his day was divided between the confessional and the bedside of the sick . . . and all flocked to him for advice and direction." . . .

The one significant difference between the Irish and German social apostolates was in their attitudes toward the temperance movement. Although German Catholics did not support the temperance movement in New York, they did not come out in favor of intemperance. Mission sermons portrayed its evil consequences, and good German Catholics were told to avoid the disruptive environment of rowdy taverns. At the same time, however, they were called on to support the good taverns and *Biergartens* of Little Germany. A recommended spot, owned by a German Catholic, was located directly opposite the church on Third Street. The newspaper commented on the good quality of the clientele and claimed that they "were always a sober group, mostly people from the community, orderly people"; it was a place "where one can have a good glass of beer or wine and also carry on a Christian discourse." Germans regarded beer "as healthy and nourishing," and unlike the Irish press, German newspapers always printed advertisements for beer and wine, as well as for German *Biergartens*. Among the Irish, however, temperance became a holy crusade.

For Irish Catholics a principal cause of poverty was intemperance. A standard sermon in the parish mission concerned drunkenness; preachers were advised to denounce it in every sermon, but its evil effects demanded that "a special and a most powerful sermon be given on this vice." The spiritual ruin caused by intemperance received special emphasis, since it led to eternal damnation. Equally significant were the social consequences of drunkenness. As a vice it inevitably was denounced as a source of misery and poverty for the family. The preacher claimed that poverty could not exist if temperance and industry prevailed; for the virtuous man material success was possible in this life, but intemperance closed off this possibility. Thus, as a virtue temperance became a means of improving one's position in life. . . .

Another aspect of Catholic benevolence was institutions for the care of a special group of individuals—young single women. Like the hospital, these institutions cared for females from all parishes; the dangers of urban life were a more motivating impulse than fears of Protestant proselytization. Priests did advise single girls to avoid romantic links with Protestant boys, since difference in religion was a source of great unhappiness and a drawback to love and would ultimately raise problems in their children's education. Survival handbooks for Catholic women portrayed the Protestant Bible as an evil book; and if the only employment they could find was with Protestant families, the young ladies were to insist that time be allowed for Sunday Mass. But in addition to this customary anti-Protestant counsel, the city was singled out as a particularly degenerate locale for young immigrant girls. In the opinion of John Hughes, New York needed a special home where "the virtue and innocence of destitute females of good character might be shielded from the snares and dangers to which their destitution exposes them in a wealthy and corrupt metropolis like New York." . . .

Some girls were not as successful as others in warding off the evils of city life. To respond to the needs of these delinquent females a group of Catholic women sought to establish a special institution. John Hughes approved their plan, though with some hesitation, and the House of the Good Shepherd opened in 1857. The program of reform of the Sisters of the Good Shepherd centered on religion, education, and work. Like the Sisters of Mercy, the Sisters of the Good Shepherd trained the girls in domestic trades needed in the city; spiritually they sought to strengthen the young women so that they could lead a virtuous life in a locale described by one priest as "the Sodom of Atlantic cities."

The negative attitude of Catholics toward the city was shared by most Americans. Underlying this mentality was the idealization of rural life. In the face of increasing urbanization, Americans sought to cling to the pastoral ideals of the recent past. The hallowed traditions of rural origins and a country environment received increased emphasis during this period of transformation. The country was portrayed as a garden of innocence and virtue, while the city remained a den of sin and corruption. Guidebooks for immigrant Catholics reinforced this mentality. They instructed Irish newcomers to settle on the rural frontier, where work was better; there a man could preside over his own homestead and watch his "family grow up prosperous and industrious removed from the pestilential examples and practices of city life." Irish authors idealized the image of the "simple innocent countryman" and extolled the frontier as a place where the immigrant could enjoy "not merely a home, but comfort and independence." In vilifying the city, preachers praised agricultural life as "incomparably more wholesome, more happy, and more favorable to virtue and piety than the feverish, comfortless, and unnatural existence to which the mass of the laboring class are condemned in large cities." . . .

In addition to the twofold impulse of charity and self-protection, the myth of the pastoral ideal exercised considerable influence on the child care enterprise. The moral superiority of the country was quite evident in the practice of "binding out" city children to the country, which was a general pattern among reformers and which quite naturally became part of the program of the Roman Catholic Orphan Asylum. The practice of moving children from the institution to a home was present from the very beginning, but such a practice did not always mean that the child was sent to live on a farm in the West. On the contrary, children were often placed in homes in the city to learn a trade useful in the urban economy. Gradually, however, the pattern shifted, and more emphasis was placed on binding out children to the country, preferably to a farm. It is difficult to pinpoint exactly when the shift occurred, but certainly by 1858 the Catholic Orphan Asylum was actively encouraging the removal of city boys and girls to the country. . . .

The emphasis on the moral superiority of rural life and the anti-urban bias of Catholics reinforced their social conservatism. Since the city was portrayed as basically evil with few if any redeeming qualities, reformers tended to ignore the possibility of changing it; rather, they sought to reform the individual even if this meant removing him from the city. They accepted the poverty and disorganization present in the city as a natural state of existence and did not dare to challenge what God had ordered. Resigned to His will, they endeavored to ameliorate the condition of the less fortunate through a parochial and citywide benevolent enterprise. It was only later in the century that Catholics, along with Protestants, began to question the social order and challenge the hallowed tradition of laissez-faire economics. Only then did they shift their focus from the individual to the environment and look upon poverty more from an economic point of view than from a moralistic perspective. . . .

The patterns of the past provided guidelines for the church in the United States. Transplanted from across the ocean, time-honored practices outweighed any attempts at improvisation in the New World. This was especially evident in handing on the faith to immigrant newcomers. A transatlantic voyage did not alter or rearrange the truths of Catholicism: they were packaged and shipped across the ocean to reappear intact in America.

Slaveholders and the Bible

EUGENE D. GENOVESE
ELIZABETH FOX-GENOVESE

For the southern slaveholders any social order worthy of the name, and therefore its appropriate social relations, had to be grounded in divine sanction. In this conviction they did not depart radically from their contemporaries in the North and in Europe, or indeed from their predecessors and successors in the Western tradition, but they did differ significantly from others in their views of the appropriate relation of the human to the divine and of the legitimate relations among people. For, during the portentous century in which the Western tradition as a whole was repudiating its own long-standing acceptance of unfree labor, especially slave labor, southern slaveholders not merely persisted in the defense of slavery, they purposefully raised it to an abstract model of necessary social order.

The slaveholders cohered as a ruling class on the basis of their ownership of human beings. From an opportunistic reliance upon slaves as the most convenient laborers available during the seventeenth century, they progressed to a commitment to slavery as a social system. Their intellectual hegira led from the acceptance of slavery as a necessary evil to the defense of slavery as a positive good, which ultimately led to a defense of slavery in the abstract—to a defense of slavery as the best possible bulwark against the corrosive and un-Christian impact of industrial capitalism and its cruel and morally irresponsible market in human labor-power.

The slaveholders' insistence upon the legitimacy and charity of their own society took shape in tandem with the revolution in thought that attended and articulated the triumph of capitalism. This revolution, which resulted in the consolidation of bourgeois individualism, haunted the slaveholders at every turn. The proslavery argument never reduced to a reactionary celebration of the "ways of our mothers and fathers," much less to the celebration of feudalism or medievalism. Rather, it strove to fashion an alternate view of social order for modern times. But the slaveholders

---

Eugene D. Genovese and Elizabeth Fox-Genovese, "The Divine Sanction of Social Order: Religious Foundations of the Southern Slaveholders' World View," *Journal of the American Academy of Religion* 55: 211–233.

differed from their bourgeois contemporaries in the values they chose to promote and in their assessment of the social relations that could sustain decent and humane values, which to them meant Christian values. . . .

At the heart of the conflict between antislavery and proslavery thought lay contrasting visions of the relation of the individual to society. For opponents of slavery, each individual must be free to dispose of his or her person, including his or her labor-power. Ultimately, the individual—understood as equal to and logically interchangeable with all other individuals—constituted the only legitimate rationale for social institutions that in some ways necessarily hampered the exercise of the individual's innate right to freedom. Order depended upon freedom, to which it was logically subordinated. Defenders of slavery reversed the priorities. Freedom could be understood only as a function of order, upon which it depended and to which it was logically subordinated. Against opponents of slavery, who saw individual right as universal, defenders of slavery preached individual right as particular. Individuals were good not in the abstract, but only as representatives of their kind and in their station. For southerners, slavery as a social system articulated and embodied this general principle.

In defending slavery as the foundation of social order, southerners drew heavily upon a religious discourse that they shared in large measure with their bourgeois opponents. Antebellum southern intellectuals have largely been forgotten or have been dismissed by historians as an inferior breed. This is nonsense. Their eclipse suggests nothing so much as the common fate of those who back losing causes, especially causes judged immoral. The southern intellectuals concerned themselves with modern developments in science and epistemology, in social, political, and economic theory, and in theology. And in the South as in the North theology and religious studies developed as inseparable from social thought. . . .

During 1830–1860 northern abolitionists took second place to none in their invocation of divine sanction for their hallowed cause, but they increasingly retreated to the swampy terrain of individual conscience. . . . The individual conscience emerged in their thinking as the ultimate custodian of God's purpose. In this progress they radically reduced the social relations to which the Bible applied directly. They rested their case on the spirit of the Bible, not on its specific prescriptions. In so doing, they abstracted further and further from the Bible's words. . . . Southerners, by contrast, took great comfort in the Bible's demonstrable justification of slavery, which led them to attend carefully to the Bible's pronouncements on other matters as well, for the Word of God referred directly, not abstractly, to their society. . . .

Consider, for example, the words of James Henley Thornwell, president of the immensely influential South Carolina College, editor of the *Southern Presbyterian Review,* unquestionably the greatest theologian in the South and, arguably, second to none in the United States. . . . Referring to the deepening struggle of the South against abolitionism and the concentration of national power, he wrote in 1841 that abolitionism was only one form of the "madness," "fanaticism," and "great disease" that were convulsing both church and state.

In 1850 he denounced the European revolutions of 1848–1849 and "the mad speculations of philosophers, the excesses of unchecked democracy," and the "despotism of the masses." He asserted that the "parties in this conflict are not merely Abolitionists and Slaveholders; they are Atheists, Socialists, Communists, Red

Republicans, Jacobins on the one side and the friends of order and regulated freedom on the other."

The South, then, stood as God's bastion against all the isms that were threatening Christian civilization. The South had a social order that hemmed in the evil inevitable in a world haunted by sin—a social order that imposed the discipline necessary to permit the flowering of the God-inspired good in man. For slavery provided the social, institutional, and political structures within which morally frail human beings could live together safely in a manner pleasing to God—with each given according as his work shall be, with each free to serve God in his or her proper station and thereby to prepare for salvation through Christ, if God through His grace willed it.

Thornwell had studied Rousseau and the great philosophers from Plato and Aristotle to Kant and Hegel. His social writings show overwhelming evidence of his learning in history and political economy, notably of his having studied Smith and Say, Ricardo and Malthus. And as a supporter of the Baconian inductive method in science, he accepted the laws of political economy as valid in their appropriate sphere. Hence, he viewed with foreboding the laws of diminishing returns in agriculture, of the falling rate of profit, and of the tendency of population geometrically to outstrip subsistence. For these laws, left to work themselves out in a society based upon freedom of labor, capital, and trade, must end by skewing society between rich and poor in a desperate class struggle.

In that struggle, the masses of mankind would inescapably be ground up if they did not rise with fearful violence to destroy the social classes that imposed such misery on them. Could anyone who called himself a Christian accept these alternatives? accept the immiseration of the masses by a cold-hearted bourgeoisie that refused responsibility for its laborers and left them to starve and, even worse, to plunge into a despair that would drive them from Christ and their own salvation? Conversely, could anyone who called himself a Christian support the revolutionary violence of those desperate souls? support the destruction of the very foundations of social hierarchy and order that God, in His mercy, had provided for a weak and sinful humanity after its Fall? To ask such questions was to answer them. Thornwell, ever the logician, did not hesitate. Social stratification under a ruling class that accepted the responsibility to be its brothers' keeper must prevail over siren calls to a false and oppressive freedom. Labor must be subordinated to capital and thereby disciplined, but it must also be protected and nourished. Slavery, in one form or another, must everywhere prevail over the cash nexus of the market—a slavery, to be sure, grounded in biblical principles and regulated by Christian doctrine, a slavery at once humane and stern, compassionate and firm, paternalistic and demanding. Thus he declared on the eve of secession and war that the capitalist countries must everywhere institute slavery or everywhere disintegrate.

. . . For Thornwell, . . . and for southern slaveholders as a class, the question of social order assumed three analytically discrete yet systemically related forms: first, as order in the family, understood as the basic experience of social dependence; second, in the household, understood as the basic unit of economy and community; and third, in the polity, understood as the community writ large as region and nation. The slaveholders took for granted that the families, households, and polity with which they were concerned were those of a Christian society that would stand or fall in accordance with its adherence to Christian principles. And those principles made God's will manifest in the legitimate authority that some, as members of specific groups, wielded over others.

The first of those Christian principles was the God-ordained power of men over women and the attendant duty of Christian women to submit to the authority of fathers and husbands. Almost all the scriptural defenses of slavery—and scriptural defenses probably accounted for a majority of all published defenses—and a great many of the secular defenses as well, rooted the subjection of slaves to masters and of blacks to whites in the prior subjection of women to men. Thus, superordination and subordination by gender constituted the foundation of God's ordination of hierarchy in social relations. Distinctions of class and race were similarly God-ordained as extensions of the principle of family order and male authority. In consequence, notwithstanding the slaveholders' commitment to individual liberty, to republicanism, and to the political equality of slaveholders and indeed of all white men, the individual was strictly defined as a social being. The state of nature was a mischievous myth. With Aristotle, they denied that the individual could exist outside society, and they made the family, considered as society in microcosm, the foundation not merely of civilization but of life itself.

In southern slave society the step from family to household was short; or rather, the one naturally articulated the other. The household provided the fundamental embodiment of God-ordained property, defined to include property in human beings. Property had arisen with human life itself. The slaveholders, in other words, viewed property as inherent in man's social nature and not as a creation of society, much less of the state. In this view, as in others, they betrayed their indebtedness to bourgeois thought and took their place with Locke and his followers against Filmer and Hobbes. Withal, they placed the emphasis differently than did Locke's northern successors. For they denied the theoretical right of all to that most basic form of property—property in one's own person and labor-power. For all the freedom attributed to the white male, the foundation of his freedom lay more in his social role as head of household than in his innate attributes as a laboring individual.

In the southern mind, family and household resisted disentangling. From our perspective it is tempting to view the two terms as different cognitive perspectives on a single system: For individual slaveholders, "family" designated a complex social, economic, affective, and political unit; for society as a whole, "household" designated the same unit. Society consisted in a network of households, the inhabitants of which were encouraged to view themselves as members of a family. The common expression "my family, white and black" was therefore no passing sentimentality or mere rationalization for the exercise of despotic power over labor. It laid bare the sense of a Christian community as an extended family within which the laborers were assimilated to an organic relation with their masters, whose duties included protection and succor as well as discipline and the imposition of order. . . .

. . . The male heads of households exercised their power legitimately only when they exercised it in accordance with the Mosaic Law, the Sermon on the Mount, and the entire body of laws and commandments laid down in the Old and New Testaments. . . .

. . . [M]en faced each other as Christian masters who represented the interests of the entire household—its wife, children, and slaves, each of whom constituted different kinds of dependents in a web of social dependencies. . . .

We need not belabor the obvious: The reality ranged far from this ideal, and the crime against an enslaved black people constituted the greatest enormity in an age well marked by enormities. Here, we purpose to understand how a deeply committed Christian people could have viewed their world and their claims to power as they did and, in time, lay down their lives in terrible numbers to preserve their way of life. We ought, however, to note that religious leaders, as well as eminent jurists and other secular leaders, did rail against the evils—the abuses—of the system, did call for the legalization of slave marriage and slave literacy, and did demand that cruel masters be severely punished. Before the War, but especially during it, as Confederate losses piled up, they warned that if a proud and sinful southern people did not repent and reform, it would face the judgment of a God of Wrath. But to the bitter end, they denied that slavery was inherently sinful and argued that all human institutions lay open to abuse and injustice. Slavery as a social relation was ordained of God, who thereby charged the masters with a heavy responsibility toward those in their custody. It would be the fault of a sinful people, not of the social system, if those chosen to rule abused their privileges, failed in their Christian responsibilities, and provoked an angry God to withdraw His sanction.

No more than southern society itself did southern thought follow some preordained path. Like the society the values of which it articulated, southern thought developed in response to its internal logic, to countervailing voices within southern society, and to the pressures of the bourgeois world in which it was embedded. Southern social thought developed dramatically between 1820 and 1860. It passed from an apologetic defense of slavery as a necessary evil to a militant defense of slavery as a positive good for masters, slaves, and society as a whole. . . .

First, in a society that was witnessing a dramatic increase in the number of professing Christians, the Bible provided the natural grounding for the moral defense of slavery. Abolitionist critics tried to dismiss the purported biblical sanction for slavery as self-serving and hardly worthy of serious refutation, but they sorely underestimated the scholarship and learning of the southern clergy. The gyrations of abolitionist critics notwithstanding, the slaveholding theologians had little trouble in demonstrating that the Bible did sanction slavery and that, specifically, God had sanctioned slaveholding among His chosen people of Israel. The abolitionists lost the battle . . . of scholarly inquiry into the nature of the Israelite social system. The slaveholders' version stood up during the antebellum debates and has been overwhelmingly confirmed by modern scholarship. . . .

Some southerners, including clergymen, tried to reconcile the biblical sanction of slavery with racism by arguing that the Canaanite and other non-Hebrew slaves of the Israelites had in fact been black Africans. . . . The leading southern theologians . . . saw clearly that the slavery sanctioned in the Bible had little to do with race. Hence, the scriptural defense of slavery decisively emerged as a question of social stratification and class power within which racially inferior Africans presented a special case of the general subjugation of labor. The scriptural defense of slavery thereby passed into a defense of what came to be called "slavery in the abstract."

Second, the southern defense of the slavery actually practiced in the South led to a wholesale assault on the free-labor system of the North and Western Europe—an assault on capitalism as a social sytem. The slaveholders never tired of saying that they treated their slaves better than capitalists treated free workers—that their slaves had better and immeasurably more secure living conditions than most of the world's proletarians and peasants. The slaveholders regularly received reports on the misery of the peasants of Eastern Europe and Asia and held up the cradle-to-grave security of their slaves in shining contrast. Now, if these comparisons were valid, as up to a point they were, did it not follow that a Christian ruling class had a duty to protect labor by assuming personal responsibility for the health and welfare of its laborers? . . .

In these ways and others, southern writers transformed the proslavery argument into an argument for slavery as the solution to the Social Question for all countries that were being locked into a self-propelling economic development. By the 1840s the defense of slavery in the abstract had infected the southern intellectuals as a group and was sinking deep roots among the slaveholders as a class. In particular, the enormously influential southern theologians and ministers, from the sophisticated to the down-home, embraced the argument *con amore* and endowed it with biblical foundations.

No one should be surprised, for in the intensely religious South no social theory, and certainly not one as radical as this, could have gotten a hearing unless grounded in scripture. Even the secular proslavery theorists almost invariably began their treatises and addresses by assuring their audience that everything that they were about to say conformed to Christian teaching. And they knew enough to quote the Bible correctly, for they were talking to people who read it, even if many of them read little else, and who routinely judged their preachers by their ability to make a sermon actually elaborate its text. . . .

Augustus Baldwin Longstreet, . . . one of the South's most widely read and appreciated literary figures, . . . owned a plantation from which he never did earn a living. He made his fortune by practicing law and won a considerable reputation as a judge. He also taught school and rose to become president of several southern colleges, including South Carolina College. And he was a Methodist preacher who played a modest but by no means trivial role in splitting the national communion in 1844 over the slavery question and in launching the Methodist Church, South. He and countless other ministers, from the most eminent to the humblest, accepted the slaveholding world they found around them and tried to make it correspond more closely to Mosaic law and to the Christian model of social relations.

Even by their own standards they failed, as their wartime jeremiads demonstrate. They had to fail, for however honest their purposes, slavery remained a massive injustice that poisoned the lives of all it affected. Yet up to a point they did remarkably well in their efforts to bring a Christian conscience to the slaveholding class. Whatever security and succor their slaves had, whatever decency and humanity they found in their masters, derived in no small part from the spread of Christian conscience among the slaveholders. To be sure, the high price of slaves occasioned by the closing of the African slave trade propelled the masters into more humane policies so as to guarantee reproduction of their labor force. But the correspondence of economic interest with deepening religious sensibility does not render the latter mere rationalization or pretense. The evidence for that deepening religious sensibility and its positive social consequences may be found everywhere, most notably in the private diaries, journals, and letters of slaveholding men and women.

If we can understand the extent and depth of the effort to place slavery on Christian ground and to erect upon that very ground a God-ordained, class-stratified social order, then we can at least begin to understand the readiness of the southern white people as a whole to defend a social system so offensive, then as now, to most of the Western world. And that readiness appears nowhere so poignantly as in the diaries, journals, and letters of ordinary slaveholders. Thus the diaries and even the plantation daybooks that recorded business matters are dotted with prayers and cries for God's grace. One after another—but in no sense by formula or rote—the authors prayed from the depths of their souls for the strength to be good husbands and fathers, dutiful wives and mothers. But they also prayed for the strength to be kind and humane slave masters and mistresses. And they did so in words that, in one variation or another, we find uttered time and time again: "This we ask in Christ's name, and for His sake."

FURTHER READING

Abzug, Robert H. *Cosmos Crumbling: American Reform and the Religious Imagination* (1994).

Billington, Ray A. *The Protestant Crusade 1800–1860* (1962).

Boydston, J., M. Kelley, and A. Margolis. *The Beecher Sisters on Women's Rights and Women's Sphere* (1988).

Carey, Patrick. *People, Priests, and Prelates: Ecclesiastical Democracy and the Tensions of Trusteeism* (1987).

Diner, Hasia. *Erin's Daughters: Irish Immigrant Women in the Nineteenth Century* (1983).

Franchot, Jenny. *Roads to Rome: The Antebellum Protestant Encounter with Catholicism* (1994).

Friedman, Lawrence. *Gregarious Saints: Self and Community in American Abolitionism, 1830–1870* (1982).

Fuller, Robert C. *Alternative Medicine and American Religious Life* (1989).

Griffin, Clifford. *Their Brothers' Keepers: Moral Stewardship in the United States, 1800–1865* (1960).

Hardesty, Nancy. *Your Daughters Shall Prophesy: Revivalism and Feminism in the Age of Finney* (1991).

Holifield, Brooks. *The Gentlemen Theologians: American Theology in Southern Culture, 1795–1860* (1978).

Lazerow, Jama. *Religion and the Working Class in Antebellum America* (1995).

Lesick, Lawrence. *The Lane Rebels: Evangelicalism and Abolitionism in Antebellum America* (1980).

Levine, Lawrence. *Black Culture and Black Consciousness: Afro-American Folk Thought from Slavery to Freedom* (1977).

Lincoln, Eric, and Lawrence H. Mnamiya. *The Black Church in the African-American Experience* (1990).

Johnson, Curtis. *Redeeming America: Evangelicals and the Road to Civil War* (1993).

McKivigan, John, and Mitchell Snay, eds. *Religion and the Antebellum Debate over Slavery* (1998).

Miller, Kerby. *Emigrants and Exiles: Ireland and the Irish Exiles to North America* (1985).

Numbers, Ronald, and Jonathan Butler. *The Disappointed: Millerism and Millenarianism in the Nineteenth Century* (1993).

Perry, Lewis. *Radical Abolitionism* (1973).

Raboteau, Albert. *Slave Religion: The "Invisible Institution" in the Antebellum South* (1978).

———. *A Fire in the Bones: Reflections on African-American Religious History* (1995).

Sernett, Milton. *Black Religion and American Evangelicalism: White Protestants, Plantation Missions, and the Flowering of Negro Christianity* (1975).

Shaw, Richard. *Dagger John: The Unquiet Life and Times of Archbishop John Hughes of New York* (1977).

Sklar, Katherine. *Catharine Beecher* (1973).

Smith, Timothy. *Revivalism and Social Reform: American Protestantism on the Eve of the Civil War* (1980).

Wilentz, Sean, and Paul Johnson. *The Kingdom of Matthias* (1994).

Wyatt-Brown, Bertram. *Lewis Tappan and the Evangelical War Against Slavery* (1969).

Yee, Shirley. *Black Women Abolitionists: A Study in Activism, 1828–1860* (1992).

War, Defeat, and Apocalyptic Religion: 1860–1890

Confederate and Union soldiers alike fought the Civil War in the belief that they were justified. Seceding southerners appealed to the tradition of the American Revolution and to the primacy of state sovereignty; the Union argued that secession was illegal and that the southerners were rebels. Both sought God's blessing for their cause and tried to explain their actions in Christian terms, seeing their losses and hardships as tests sent by God or as a punishment for their sins. Union clergy often argued that God was chastising them for permitting slavery to continue so long in their midst and that they, like the children of Israel in the biblical books of Joshua and Judges, had to redeem themselves by fighting against foes God had intentionally raised up against them.

The slaves whom President Abraham Lincoln freed by decree on January 1, 1863, saw him as the Great Liberator, a second Moses leading his children out of the "Egypt" of slavery. His assassination by John Wilkes Booth just as the war ended led northern clergy to compare Lincoln to Christ, dying a sacrificial death for the sins of the people he had loved and served. Meanwhile, the end of the war forced Confederates to come to terms with defeat. They too drew comfort from the comparison with Christ crucified. Earthly glory, after all, was not the Christian way, so while the victors saw themselves as men rewarded for righteousness, the vanquished consoled themselves with the thought that Christ, too, finished his earthly mission in the disaster and defeat of the cross.

The horrific suffering of the war, in which tens of thousands died in battle and even more in epidemics, drove Americans to consider not only the warlike parts of the Bible and the warrior God, but also the prophetic books of Daniel and Revelation. Were the events of the 1860s fulfilling prophecies of Christ's Second Coming and the chaos that precedes the millennium of peace? The books are cryptic, difficult to understand and interpret. One group of Protestants, the "premillennialists," believed that the world was degenerating in accordance with a divine plan and that people were powerless to stop it. Jesus would have to come down from heaven and seize those he had chosen before the last catastrophes of earth's history, featuring the antichrist and the Battle of Armageddon, could take place. Others, "postmillennialists," had a more optimistic view of human nature and believed that by their own striving they could build the millennial kingdom before Jesus returned.

The decades after the Civil War were a time of great social upheaval, urbaniza- tion, and industrialization, as well as southern Reconstruction. They were character- ized by a heightened enthusiasm for biblical prophecy interpretation and for claims that the end of the world was near. The Jehovah's Witnesses, for example, founded in the 1870s by a Pennsylvania businessman, Charles Taze Russell, believed that the "Millennial Dawn" had come in 1874 and that the world would end with Christ's return in 1914.

History was ending in a different sense for the Plains Indians. Their victory over George Custer's Seventh Cavalry at the Battle of the Little Big Horn in 1876 was the last success in their long struggle to preserve an independent way of life. By the end of 1877, the remains of the victorious tribes had been forced to sur- render and to accept life on reservations under government supervision. Whites had hunted the great buffalo herds almost to extinction. News that a Paiute Indian in Nevada, named Wovoka, had enjoyed visions of the whites' disappearance and the buffalo's return, however, helped spark the "Ghost Dance" religion in 1889 and 1890. It mixed traditional Indian and Christian themes and convinced some Indians that their "ghost shirts" protected them from bullets. The U.S. Army, fearing that a fervent new religious movement might revive the Indian wars, pre-emptively massacred a group of three hundred Sioux Indians at Wounded Knee, South Dakota, in 1890.

 ## D O C U M E N T S

Document 1, a letter written in 1861 by a prominent southern educator to his son in the Confederate army, reminds the youth that he is fighting in a godly cause and that his moral behavior in the army must be exemplary. Document 2 (1868), from the Union side of the lines, recounts the work of the Christian Commission, a medical and religious mission to the Army of the Potomac in 1863, whose members tended the wounded during and after battles but preached revival sermons as often as time permitted, trying to ensure the eternal as well as the temporal salvation of the souls in their care. Document 3 (1864) is an account by a white officer from Boston of the expressive religious customs of the southern black soldiers (many of them recently released slaves and Union volunteers) in his regiment. He finds widespread piety but is also surprised by a touch of skepticism from one orator. Document 4 (1863) recounts how Catholic nuns bravely tended the wounded at the Battle of Shiloh and tried to console the dying. Document 5 is composed of a pair of sermons by eminent ministers, preached in sorrow to commemorate Abraham Lincoln on the first Sunday after his assassination in 1865. The second sermon, by Phillips Brooks, quotes a long section of Lincoln's Gettysburg Address and confirms that this speech was already becoming a classic religious statement of the Union's case less than two years after its original delivery. When Lincoln's body was shipped by train to Illinois for burial, it was treated by most who saw it as a sacred relic. In Document 6 (c. 1870), a young southern black woman in the Reconstruction South, working like her forebears in the cotton fields, is struck down and converted by a visitation from God; she recalls it in language strongly reminiscent of the book of Revelation. Charles Russell, author of Document 7 (1889), explains the timetable of the "End Times" as 1914 approaches, while in Document 8 E. A. Dyer, a Nevada settler, remembers his friend Jack Wilson, or Wovoka, whose visions (1889) inaugurated the Ghost Dance religion among remnants of the Plains Indian tribes.

1. Robert Ryland Reminds His Son That the Confederate Cause Is Godly, 1861

A Letter to a Son in camp.

AT HOME, July 17, 1861.

My Dear Son: It may have seemed strange to you that a professing Christian father so freely gave you, a Christian son, to enlist in the volunteer service. My reason was that I regarded this as a *purely defensive war.* Not only did the Southern Confederacy propose to adjust the pending difficulties by peaceful and equitable negotiations, but Virginia used again and again the most earnest and noble efforts to prevent a resort to the sword. These overtures having been proudly spurned, and our beloved South having been threatened with invasion and subjugation, it seemed to me that nothing was left us but stern resistance or abject submission to unconstitutional power. A brave and generous people could not for a moment hesitate between such alternatives. A war in defence of our homes and firesides—of our wives and children—of all that makes life worth possessing is the result. While I most deeply deplore the necessity for the sacrifice, I could not but rejoice that I had a son to offer to the service of the country, and if I had a dozen *I would most freely give them all.* As you are now cheerfully enduring the hardships of the camp, I know you will listen to a father's suggestions touching the duties of your new mode of life. . . .

. . . An undisciplined army is a curse to its friends and a derision to its foes. Give your whole influence, therefore, to the maintenance of lawful authority and strict order. Let your superiors feel that whatever they intrust to *you* will be faithfully done. Composed of such soldiers, and led by skilful and brave commanders, our army, by the blessing of God, will never be defeated. It is, moreover, engaged in a holy cause, and must triumph.

Try to maintain your Christian profession among your comrades. I need not caution you against strong drink as useless and hurtful, nor against profanity, so common among soldiers. Both these practices you abhor. Aim to take at once a decided stand for God. If practicable, have prayers regularly in your tent, or unite with your fellow-disciples in prayer-meetings in the camp. Should preaching be accessible, always be a hearer. Let the world know that you are a Christian. Read a chapter in the New Testament which your mother gave you, every morning and evening when you can, and engage in secret prayer to God for his Holy Spirit to guide and sustain you. I would rather hear of your death than of the shipwreck of your faith and good conscience.

As you will come into habitual contact with men of every grade, make special associates of those whose influence on your character is felt to be good. . . . They can relax into occasional pleasantries, without violating modesty. They can be loyal to their government without indulging private hatred against her foes. They can be cool and brave in battle, and not be braggarts in the absence of danger. Above all,

---

Rev. J. William Jones, *Christ in the Camp* (Atlanta: Martin and Hoyt, 1887/1904), 28–31.

they can be humble, spiritual, and active Christians, and yet mingle in the stirring and perilous duties of soldier life. Let these be your companions and models. You will thus return from the dangers of camp without a blemish on your name.

Should it be your lot to enter into an engagement with the enemy, lift up your heart in secret ejaculations to the ever-present and good Being, that He will protect you from sudden death; or, if you fall, that He will receive your departing spirit, cleansed in the blood of Jesus, into His kingdom. It is better to trust in the Lord than to put confidence in princes. Commit your eternal interests, therefore, to the keeping of the Almighty Saviour. You should not, even in the hour of deadly conflict, cherish personal rage against the enemy, any more than an officer of the law hates the victim of the law. How often does a victorious army tenderly care for the dead and wounded of the vanquished. War is a tremendous scourge which Providence sometimes uses to chastise proud and wicked nations. Both parties must suffer, even though one may get the advantage. There is no occasion, then, for adding to the intrinsic evils of the system the odious feature of animosity to individuals. In the ranks of the foe are thousands of plain men who do not understand the principles for which we are struggling. They are deceived by artful demagogues into a posture of hostility to those whom, knowing, they would love. It is against such men that you may perhaps be arrayed, and the laws of war do not forbid you to pity them, even in the act of destroying them. It is more important that *we* should exhibit a proper temper in this unfortunate contest, because many professed Christians and ministers of the Gospel at the North are breathing out, in their very prayers and sermons, threatenings and slaughter against us! Oh! how painful that a gray-headed pastor should publicly exclaim, *"I would hang them as soon as I would shoot a mad dog."*

Providence has placed you in the midst of thoughtless and unpardoned men. What a beautiful thing it would be if you could win some of them to the Saviour! Will you not try? You will have many opportunities of speaking a word in season. The sick, you may comfort; the wavering, you may confirm; the backslidden, you may reclaim; the weary and heavy laden, you may point to Jesus for rest to the soul. It is not presumptuous for a young man, kindly and meekly, to commend the Gospel to his brother soldiers. The hardest of them will not repel a gentle approach, made in private. And many of them would doubtless be glad to have the subject introduced to them. They desire to hear of Jesus, but they lack courage to inquire of his people. An unusually large proportion of pious men have entered the army, and I trust they will give a new complexion to military life. Let them search out each other, and establish a fraternity among all the worshippers of God. To interchange religious views and administer brotherly counsel will be mutually edifying. "He that watereth shall be watered also himself."

And now, as a soldier has but little leisure, I will not occupy you longer. Be assured that every morning and evening we remember you, at the family altar, to our Father in Heaven. We pray for a "speedy, just, and honorable peace," and for the safe return of all the volunteers to their loved homes. All the children speak often of "brother," and hear your letters read with intense interest. That God Almighty may be your shield and your exceeding great reward is the constant prayer of your loving father.

"RO. RYLAND."

2. Lemuel Moss Describes the Christian Commission's Work with the Union Army in 1863 (1868)

The work of the Christian Commission in the army was one of constant change. The year, indeed, was made up of many distinct *campaigns,* the one differing so greatly from the other that, although the same men were actors in each, one would with difficulty identify them as the same. This week the Delegates may be distributing religious papers and books, preaching the Gospel to crowds of healthy, vigorous men; the next, preparing with their own hands some soothing draught or nourishing food for those who are languishing with disease in some remote hospital. This week preparing reading-rooms and chapels, feeding the mind with that which is wholesome and abiding, inciting to temperance, purity, and piety; the next, with coats off, before a fire of logs, cooking coffee and soup for the hungry, or bearing stimulants and nutriment to those who are perishing. To-day, living quietly in "winter quarters;" to-morrow, off for the battle-field, with a blanket alone for house and shelter.

During the month of January, at the stations before mentioned, the Delegates of the Commission performed a twofold work,—one party with a wagon visiting camps and field hospitals, taking both hospital stores and religious reading; the other remaining at the station, preparing food and drink for the hundreds of sick who, on their way to the hospital, were detained sometimes many hours at the railroad station. Before the close of the month, however, a new and more important field was opened. The army made one more attempt to gain the heights of Fredericksburg before resting in winter quarters. Again the effort failed. Scarcely had the long lines of infantry, cavalry, and artillery started upon their rapid night-march when a terrible storm of rain and sleet arose, breaking up the roads and making all advance impossible. Chilled and exhausted, floundering through the mud in the bitter cold wind of that winter night, the soldiers struggled back to their cheerless camps, but thousands who had escaped unharmed from a score of battles now fell the victims of this memorable "mud campaign." . . . To this scene of distress the Delegates came. A small tent served as their storehouse and quarters. A dispatch to Washington and Philadelphia soon furnished them with a thousand loaves of soft bread, and boxes of clothing, cordials, and fruits. These they distributed throughout the camp, wherever the need was most urgent. They passed from tent to tent, ministering to the physical wants of the suffering, and directing the hearts of all to Jesus, the great Physician of souls. Often they were called to the side of the dying, to give counsel in that last trying hour, and commit the departing soul to God. The dead were followed to the grave with the rites of Christian burial, and the record of the last moments and of the place of interment forwarded to the distant home friends. After the work of the day the Delegates would go from tent to tent, and read a few verses of Scripture and offer a prayer for God's blessing upon all. The effect of these ministrations was very manifest. Many who seemed near to death were recovered by the tender nursing and nutritious food. As the condition of the hospital improved, the Delegates found more time to devote to the spiritual wants of the men. An empty cookhouse was obtained for a chapel, where services were held on the

Lemuel Moss, *Annals of the U.S. Christian Commission* (Philadelphia: Lippincott, 1868), 374–9.

Sabbath, and meetings for prayer each evening of the week. All felt the presence of the Holy Spirit. At one meeting fifty persons announced their desire and determination to begin a Christian life. Many who had come to that dreary camp a few weeks before, as they thought to die, found life instead, even life eternal. . . .

This campaign over, vigorous measures were taken for the next. Acting upon the experience gained at Windmill Point, it was resolved to undertake to supply every regiment in the army with copies of the New Testament. . . . Each station was complete in itself, and contained from three to seven Delegates. Hospital stores, Testaments, and religious reading were at each, and were distributed under the direction of committees appointed for the purpose. At each, where practicable, a house or tent for religious worship was secured and meetings held every evening, while on the Sabbath appointments for preaching to regiments or brigades were filled by the clerical Delegates. . . .

Stoneman's Station was the scene of a remarkable revival. The tents used as a chapel formed a room nearly sixty feet long. Meetings were held nightly, and to them officers and men came in crowds. The tents stood upon an elevation, commanding an extended view, and, as the evening hour drew near, men, singly and in squads and companies, could be seen wending their way from the various camps towards the house of prayer. "Mount Zion," the soldiers called it; and, like Mount Zion of old, it was indeed "beautiful" when, crowded to its utmost capacity and throngs about the open doors, strains of some familiar home-loved hymn floated out upon the evening air. Here were heard, from veterans who had passed through all the temptations and trials of a soldier's life, testimonies of the strength and comfort they had experienced all the way along from the religion of Jesus; here soldiers would ask what they should do to be saved; and here many, with joy beaming on the countenance, would tell of the blessing they had found in the assurance of sins forgiven through the blood of Christ. The number of men who in these meetings gained a knowledge of Jesus no earthly record will ever show; but we know that there were scores who dated the commencement of their Christian life from those meetings at Stoneman's, and hundreds, many of whom have joined the company of saints in heaven, will thank God through eternity for His spirit there bestowed. . . .

[The Commission moved to the site of another battle.] Threading their way through woods and fields filled with wagons, ambulances, and guns, after a journey of many hours the ford was reached. . . . There was no lack of work,—on all sides, at every house and barn and shed, in gardens and door-yards, under trees and the shelter of walls, lay wounded and bleeding men. With soap and bandages and pails, strong arms and willing hearts, the services of these Delegates were offered to the surgeons in charge and gladly accepted, and from that time they were hard at work. Their supply of stimulants and food was soon exhausted, but was reinforced by another wagon-load sent from Falmouth.

The party left behind in the mean time were not idle. The Second and Sixth Corps, storming the heights of Fredericksburg, carried everything before them in victory. The "old flag" waved in triumph from height to height; but in the city the red signals hanging at every corner, at church-doors, and the market-place, told how fearful was the cost,—hospitals on every side, houses filled with the prostrate forms of dying men, who but an hour ago rushed forward to the charge. But why tarry here? No pen can describe such scenes or record such labors. The history of

Chancellorsville is known by all; its gallant achievements, its bitter disappointment, its herculean labors, and its fruitless end. It is enough to say that the Delegates of the Christian Commission worked amid those scenes as any other fathers
or brothers would have toiled, had they been permitted to be there.

Wearied and sad, the remnant of the great army came back to the old camps.
The old walls are again covered and echo to the sounds of life; but how many
whose voices one week before were heard in the cabins and the streets are now forever silent in the soldier's grave!

3. Thomas Wentworth Higginson Witnesses the Religious Life of Black Soldiers, 1864

All over the camp the lights glimmer in the tents, and as I sit at my desk in the open
doorway, there come mingled sounds of stir and glee. Boys laugh and shout,—a
feeble flute stirs somewhere in some tent, not an officer's,—a drum throbs far away
in another,—wild kildeer-plover flit and wail above us, like the haunting souls of
dead slave-masters,—and from a neighboring cook-fire comes the monotonous
sound of that strange festival, half pow-wow, half prayer-meeting, which they
know only as a "shout." These fires are usually enclosed in a little booth, made
neatly of palm-leaves and covered in at top, a regular native African hut, in short,
such as is pictured in books, and such as I once got up from dried palm-leaves for a
fair at home. This hut is now crammed with men, singing at the top of their voices,
in one of their quaint, monotonous, endless, negro-Methodist chants, with obscure
syllables recurring constantly, and slight variations interwoven, all accompanied
with a regular drumming of the feet and clapping of the hands, like castanets. Then
the excitement spreads: inside and outside the enclosure men begin to quiver and
dance, others join, a circle forms, winding monotonously round some one in the
centre; some "heel and toe" tumultuously, others merely tremble and stagger on,
others stoop and rise, others whirl, others caper sideways, all keep steadily circling
like dervishes; spectators applaud special strokes of skill; my approach only en-
livens the scene; the circle enlarges, louder grows the singing, rousing shouts of
encouragement come in, half bacchanalian, half devout, "Wake 'em, brudder!"
"Stan' up to 'em, brudder!"—and still the ceaseless drumming and clapping, in
perfect cadence, goes steadily on. Suddenly there comes a sort of *snap,* and the
spell breaks, amid general sighing and laughter. And this not rarely and occasionally, but night after night, while in other parts of the camp the soberest prayers and
exhortations are proceeding sedately. . . .

Beside some of these fires the men are cleaning their guns or rehearsing their
drill,—beside others, smoking in silence their very scanty supply of the beloved
tobacco,—beside others, telling stories and shouting with laughter over the broadest
mimicry, in which they excel, and in which the officers come in for a full share. The
everlasting "shout" is always within hearing, with its mixture of piety and polka, and

---

Thomas Wentworth Higginson, *Army Life in a Black Regiment* (1870; reprint, Boston: Beacon, 1962).

its castanet-like clapping of the hands. Then there are quieter prayer-meetings, with pious invocations and slow psalms, "deaconed out" from memory by the leader, two lines at a time, in a sort of wailing chant. . . . Elsewhere, it is some solitary old cook, some aged Uncle Tiff, with enormous spectacles, who is perusing a hymn-book by the light of a pine splinter, in his deserted cooking booth of palmetto leaves. By another fire there is an actual dance, red-legged soldiers doing right-and-left, and "now-lead-de-lady-ober," to the music of a violin which is rather artistically played, and which may have guided the steps, in other days, of Barnwells and Hugers. And yonder is a stump-orator perched on his barrel, pouring out his exhortations to fidelity in war and in religion. To-night for the first time I have heard an harangue in a different strain, quite saucy, sceptical, and defiant, appealing to them in a sort of French materialistic style, and claiming some personal experience of warfare. "You don't know notin' about it, boys. You tink you's brave enough; how you tink, if you stan' clar in de open field,—here you, and dar de Secesh? You's got to hab de right ting inside o' you. You must hab it 'served [preserved] in you, like dese yer sour plums dey 'serve in de barr'l; you's got to harden it down inside o' you, or it's notin'." Then he hit hard at the religionists: "When a man's got de sperit ob de Lord in him, it weakens him all out, can't hoe de corn." He had a great deal of broad sense in his speech; but presently some others began praying vociferously close by, as if to drown this free-thinker, when at last he exclaimed, "I mean to fight de war through, an' die a good sojer wid de last kick,—dat's *my* prayer!" and suddenly jumped off the barrel. I was quite interested at discovering this reverse side of the temperament, the devotional side preponderates so enormously, and the greatest scamps kneel and groan in their prayer-meetings with such entire zest. It shows that there is some individuality developed among them, and that they will not become too exclusively pietistic. . . .

. . . [T]heir religious spirit grows more beautiful to me in living longer with them; it is certainly far more so than at first, when it seemed rather a matter of phrase and habit. It influences them both on the negative and positive side. That is, it cultivates the feminine virtues first,—makes them patient, meek, resigned. This is very evident in the hospital; there is nothing of the restless, defiant habit of white invalids. Perhaps, if they had more of this, they would resist disease better. Imbued from childhood with the habit of submission, drinking in through every pore that other-world trust which is the one spirit of their songs, they can endure everything. This I expected; but I am relieved to find that their religion strengthens them on the positive side also,—gives zeal, energy, daring. They could easily be made fanatics, if I chose; but I do not choose. Their whole mood is essentially Mohammedan, perhaps, in its strength and its weakness; and I feel the same degree of sympathy that I should if I had a Turkish command,—that is, a sort of sympathetic admiration, not tending towards agreement, but towards co-operation. Their philosophizing is often the highest form of mysticism; and our dear surgeon declares that they are all natural transcendentalists. The white camps seem rough and secular, after this; and I hear our men talk about "a religious army," "a Gospel army," in their prayer-meetings. They are certainly evangelizing the chaplain, who was rather a heretic at the beginning; at least, this is his own admission. We have recruits on their way from St. Augustine, where the negroes are chiefly Roman Catholics; and it will be interesting to see how their type of character combines with that elder creed.

4. George Barton Remembers a Pious Irish-American Nun Nursing the Wounded at Shiloh, 1863

". . . A cold, drizzling rain commenced about nightfall and soon came harder and faster, then turned to pitiless, blinding hail. This storm raged with unrelenting violence for three hours. I passed long wagon trains filled with wounded and dying soldiers without even a blanket to shield them from the driving sleet and hail which fell in stones as large as partridge eggs until it lay on the ground two inches deep."

It was by the work that she did at and after this battle that Sister Anthony, a notable member of the Sisters of Charity, won enduring laurels. She left Cincinnati for Shiloh, accompanied by two other Sisters of Charity, Dr. Blackman, of Cincinnati; Mrs. Hatch and daughter, Miss McHugh, Mrs. O'Shaughnessy and some charitable ladies of the Queen City. This trip was made on Captain Ross' boat, under the care of Dr. Blackman. Sister Anthony, whose mind is unimpaired and whose memory is excellent, thus tells of her experience at Shiloh:

"At Shiloh we ministered to the men on board what were popularly known as the floating hospitals. We were often obliged to move farther up the river, being unable to bear the terrific stench from the bodies of the dead on the battlefield. This was bad enough, but what we endured on the field of battle while gathering up the wounded is simply beyond description. At one time there were 700 of the poor soldiers crowded in one boat. Many were sent to our hospital in Cincinnati. Others were so far restored to health as to return to the scene of war. Many died good, holy deaths. . . .

"There was one young man under the care of Sister De Sales. This Sister spoke to him of heaven, of God and of his soul. Of God he knew nothing, of heaven he never heard, and he was absolutely ignorant of a Supreme Being. He became much interested in what the Sister said and was anxious to know something more of this good God of whom the Sister spoke. This good Sister of Charity instructed him, and, no priest being near, she baptized him and soon his soul took its flight to that God whom he so late learned to know and love.

"Were I to enumerate all the good done, conversions made, souls saved, columns would not suffice. Often have I gazed at Sister De Sales, as she bent over the cots of those poor boys, ministering to their every want, in the stillness of the night. Ah! here is one to whom she gives a cool drink, here another whose amputated and aching limbs need attention, there an old man dying, into whose ears she whispers the request to repeat those beautiful words: 'Lord, have mercy on my soul!' I asked myself: 'Do angels marvel at this work?'

"Day often dawned on us only to renew the work of the preceding day, without a moment's rest. Often the decks of the vessels resembled a slaughter house, filled as they were with the dead and dying."

The following is what an eye-witness says of Sister Anthony: "Amid this sea of blood she performed the most revolting duties for those poor soldiers. Let us follow her as she gropes her way among the wounded, dead and dying. She seemed to me like a ministering angel, and many a young soldier owes his life to her care and charity. Let us gaze at her again as she stands attentive kindness and assists

---

George Barton, *Angels of the Battlefield* (Philadelphia: Catholic Art, 1897), 41–44.

Dr. Blackman while the surgeon is amputating limbs and consigning them to a watery grave, or as she picks her steps in the blood of these brave boys, administering cordial or dressing wounds."

A Sister relates a sad story of a young man who was shot in the neck. The wound was very deep. From the effect of this and the scorching rays of the sun he suffered a burning thirst. He was too weak to move, when suddenly the rain fell down in torrents. Holding out his weak hands, he caught a few drops, which sustained life until he was found among the dead and dying on the battlefield. Cordials were given which relieved him. His looks of gratitude were reward enough. Many other soldiers who were thought to be dying eventually recovered.

After the Sisters had finished their work at Shiloh they followed the army to Corinth, where the Confederates had retreated. The river was blocked by obstacles in the stream and progress by boat was necessarily slow. Finally the impediments became so thick that the boat was stopped altogether. The vessel was crowded and the situation was a critical one. The captain finally said that it was a matter of life and death and that the Sisters would have to flee for their lives. To do this it would have been necessary to abandon their patients, who were enduring the greatest misery on the boat. This the Sisters heroically refused to do. All expressed their willingness to remain with the "wounded boys" until the end and to share their fate, whatever it might be. Such heroism melted the hearts of hardened men. The Sisters fell on their knees and called on the "Star of the Sea" to intercede for them, that the bark might be guarded from all harm.

5. Union Sermons Mourn Abraham Lincoln, 1865

Gilbert Haven

The appalling deed of the last Good Friday begins to put on the fixed lineaments of the past. As that face and form, then so full of life, are frozen in death, so he who animated them is fast becoming solidified and shapen in the unchanging marble of history.

Still standing in the horrible shadow, how can we carve the features of the immortal dead? The chisel shakes in our trembling hand. The rain of sorrow blinds our eyes. In the ghastly darkness, we but faintly discern the spiritual form that has so suddenly and forever vanished from the eyes of man. He, who but yesterday was the center of all human observation; whose every word, as he himself declared but three nights before his death, was in no unimportant sense a national decree; from whom were the issues of life and death to the imperious leaders of the rebellion and their too willing subjects; upon whose course foreign potentates fastened watchful eyes, and foreign peoples were yet more intent; the foremost man in all the world—now lies he low in his shroud of blood. A nation weeps around his bier. The world bemoans his fate.

Never before did so wide and bitter a cry pierce the skies. Never before were the heads of so many millions waters, and their eyes fountains of tears, weeping day and

Gilbert Haven, "The Uniter and Liberator of America," in *Sermons Speeches, and Letters on Slavery and Its War* (Boston: Lee and Shepard, 1869).

night for the slain of the daughter of their people. The great day of the Church has become yet more solemn in the annals of America. Let not the 15th of April be considered the day of his death, but let Good Friday be its anniversary. For then the fatal blow was struck. He died to the conscious world ere the day had died. We should make it a movable fast, and ever keep it beside the cross and the grave of our blessed Lord, in whose service and for whose gospel he became a victim and a martyr. . . .

. . . He held every one in his heart of hearts; he felt a deep and individual regard for each and all; he wept over the nation's dead boys at Gettysburg as heartily as over his own dead boy at Washington. Their death, more than his own child's, was the means of bringing him into an experimental acquaintance with Christ. That sorrow wrought in him a godly sorrow, which has become a joy forever.

Here then may we properly conclude his portraiture. It arises, like that of Him in whose image he and all of us are made, into the hights of love. Without profanity we may say Abraham Lincoln is love. By that nature will the future hail him. A John among the disciples, he, of all our public men, the most truly possessed and expressed the nature of his Lord and Master. Without revenge, without malice, without hardness or bitterness of heart, he held loyal and disloyal, slave and master, black and white, rebel soldier and rebel leader, in his equal love. Had his dying lips been allowed to utter one sentence, we think it would have been the dying words of Christ.

Phillips Brooks

So let him lie here in our midst to-day, and let our people go and bend with solemn thoughtfulness and look upon his face and read the lessons of his burial. As he paused here on his journey from his western home and told us what by the help of God he meant to do, so let him pause upon his way back to his western grave and tell us with a silence more eloquent than words how bravely, how truly by the strength of God he did it. God brought him up as he brought David up from the sheepfolds to feed Jacob, his people and Israel his inheritance. He came up in earnestness and faith and he goes back in triumph. As he pauses here to-day, and from his cold lips bids us bear witness how he has met the duty that was laid on him, what can we say out of our full hearts but this—"He fed them with a faithful and true heart and ruled them prudently with all his power." The *Shepherd of the People!* that old name that the best rulers ever craved. What ruler ever won it like this dead President of ours? He fed us faithfully and truly. He fed us with counsel when we were in doubt, with inspiration when we sometimes faltered, with caution when we would be rash, with calm, clear, trustful cheerfulness through many an hour when our hearts were dark. He fed hungry souls all over the country with sympathy and consolation. He spread before the whole land feasts of great duty and devotion and patriotism on which the land grew strong. He fed us with solemn, solid truths. He taught us the sacredness of government, the wickedness of treason. He made our souls glad and vigorous with the love of Liberty that was in his. He showed us how to love truth and yet be charitable— how to hate wrong and all oppression, and yet not treasure one personal injury or

Phillips Brooks, *The Life and Death of Abraham Lincoln* (Philadelphia: H. B. Ashmead, 1865).

insult. He fed *all* his people from the highest to the lowest, from the most privileged down to the most enslaved. Best of all, he fed us with a reverent and genuine religion. He spread before us the love and fear of God just in that shape in which we need them most, and out of his faithful service of a higher Master who of us has not taken and eaten and grown strong. "He fed them with a faithful and true heart." Yes, till the last. For at the last, behold him standing with hand reached out to feed the South with Mercy and the North with Charity, and the whole land with Peace, when the Lord who had sent him called him and his work was done.

He stood once on the battle-field of our own State, and said of the brave men who had saved it words as noble as any countryman of ours ever spoke. Let us stand in the country he has saved, and which is to be his grave and monument, and say of Abraham Lincoln what he said of the soldiers who had died at Gettysburg. He stood there with their graves before him, and these are the words he said: "We cannot dedicate, we cannot consecrate, we cannot hallow this ground. The brave men who struggled here have consecrated it far beyond our power to add or detract. The world will little note nor long remember what we say here, but it can never forget what they did here. It is for us the living rather to be dedicated to the unfinished work which they who fought here have thus far so nobly advanced. It is rather for us to be here dedicated to the great task remaining before us, that from these honored dead we take increased devotion to that cause for which they gave the last full measure of devotion; that we here highly resolve that these dead shall not have died in vain; that this nation, under God shall have a new birth of freedom, and that Government of the people, by the people and for the people shall not perish from the earth."

May God make us worthy of the memory of ABRAHAM LINCOLN.

6. Daughter of a Freed Slave Describes Her Conversion Experience, c. 1870

My parents were good Christians and they took me to church every Sunday. I heard a great deal of shouting and preaching but I thought mostly of amusements like dancing. I had to work hard every day in the field and at home but I was always taught to thank God for His blessings—life and the daily food. I began to long for the peace of rest called heaven but I was told that God had a chosen people and called whomsoever he chose. I began to pray but I still continued to serve the devil of whom I was very much afraid. Finally I decided that I was no good and gave up praying entirely.

One day, a year later, I was out chopping in the field. The corn was high and the weather was hot. I was feeling joyous and glad for I wanted to eat and I was thinking of the coming dance and the good time I was going to have. Suddenly I heard a voice. It called "Mary! Mary!" It sounded so sweet and it seemed to ring all through me. I looked all around the field but I saw not a single person and I was alone. I suddenly became weak and faint and fell to the ground unconscious. While lying in this condition the voice spoke to me again and said, "My little one, I am God Almighty. I have loved you from the foundation of the world even with an

"Behold the Travail of Your Soul," in *The American Slave*, vol. 19, ed. George Rawick (Westport, Conn.: Greenwood, 1972), 49–52.

everlasting love. I have freed your soul from hell and you are free indeed. You are the light of the world. Go and tell the world what great things God had done for you and lo, I am with you always. Behold the travail of your soul."

I looked and lo, and behold, there were two Marys! There is a being in a being, a man in a man. Little Mary was standing looking down on old Mary, on this temple, my body, and it lay on the very brinks of hell. There was a deep chasm filled with ravenous beasts and old satan was there with a ball and chain on his leg. He had a great ball in his hand and threw this at me but it missed me and fell far on the other side of the narrow path. I became afraid and became faint again and there began a crying on the inside, saying, "Mercy! Mercy! Mercy! Lord!" Then I began to cry and as I wept I looked and there by my side stood a little man, very small and with waxen hair. His eyes were like fire, his feet as burnished brass. On his shoulder he carried a spear and on the end of it was a star that outshone the morning sun. I saw the real sun go down and there was great darkness and I began to tremble with fear, but the little man spoke and said, "Be not afraid and follow me for lo, I am a swift messenger and I will ever be thy guide. Keep thy feet in the straight and narrow path and follow Me and all the demons in hell shall not be able to cause thee to stumble or to fall."

I journeyed on and finally came face to face with God. He was seated on a high throne and a multitude of angels hovered round and about Him. As I came up my guide vanished and I saw God. He looked neither to the right nor to the left. As I entered all the angels heaved and in one cry moaned, "Welcome! Welcome! Welcome! Welcome to the House of God!" I looked to the right and left and beyond the throne and behold! I saw a beautiful green pasture and grazing there were thousands of sheep and they turned towards me and all in one bleat cried out, "Welcome! Welcome! to the House of God." I fell at the throne of God and a voice began to cry on the inside, "Unworthy! Unworthy!" I began to weep and lo! an angel came out and with a blood-stained garment wiped my tears away and said unto me, "Weep not for behold! thou hast found favor with God." I stood up on my feet and there was a great silence. Then one of the angels nearby said, "Behold the Lamb of God, even He who was slain from the foundation of the world." I looked and there coming up from the east I saw Jesus coming with great power, having on His breast-plate, His buckler and shield and His face outshone the sun. He spoke and out of His mouth came fire. A great smoke enveloped Him and He cried with a loud voice, "Behold I have overcome both hell and death and the grave and henceforth I am at the right hand of power. Peace on earth and good-will, for I have removed the sting of death and robbed the grave of her victory."

I do not remember how long I was in this state for immediately I regained consciousness I began to shout and cry. I rushed to the house, my body all drenched in perspiration and my clothes torn from my body. I shouted the rest of the day and thought no more of the coming dance. I went to church on the following Sunday, having been directed in the spirit to an old preacher named Rev. Mason who, after hearing my testimony, reached me among his flock.

At times, though, I became slack being tempted by old satan. Whenever the spirit moved me to do something I felt very heavy and if I did not go as I felt I ought to go, a great fear would come over me and a voice that seemed loud enough for everyone to hear would cry on the inside, "Remember, I have called you with a holy call and for your disobedience I will chastise you and you shall go."

7. Charles Taze Russell Argues That the "End Times" Are Imminent, 1889

The time is at hand for the establishment of the Redeemer's Kingdom. . . . Nothing intervenes. We are already living in the seventh millennium—since Oct. 1872. The lease of power to the Gentile kingdoms must terminate with the year 1914. The great antitypical Jubilee, the Times of Restitution of all things, had its beginning in the year 1874, when the presence of the great Restorer was also due. The manner of his return and the character of his work up to the present time are in exact correspondence with the details of prophecy thus far. The closing features of this dispensation, now observed, are in perfect accord with those of its Jewish type. The Elias has come, and is received as foretold; and the predicted curse—the great time of trouble—is already impending. The Man of Sin has been revealed in all his hateful deformity, and has almost run his predicted course. The establishment of the long promised Kingdom of Messiah is therefore the great event just before us. Not only so, but its establishment is now in progress. The necessary undermining and overturning of the kingdoms of this world under the prince of darkness—"the prince of this world"—are now visible to some extent even to the natural eye of the children of this world, but are much more clearly seen, as they should be, by those who look upon transpiring events through the field-glass of God's Word, which at proper focus brings distant matters and results close to view, and enables God's children to recognize the minutiae which the natural eye cannot discern, as well as the leading features which the world's statesmen and philosophers see in but dim outline. Even the worldly-wise can discern the social trouble fomenting, as the dominance of ignorance gives place to greater general knowledge and personal independence. And though they vainly hope for some unknown and unexpected favorable turn of affairs to occur, yet, as described in the Scriptures, their hearts are failing them for fear and for looking after the things coming upon the earth—because they see the shaking of the symbolic heavens now in progress, and perceive that with such a shaking and removal of the power of error, superstitions and religious restraints from the masses of the people, violence and anarchy must result.

But, from God's standpoint, from which the waking ones of the household of faith are privileged to look, not only the severity of the trouble is more distinct, but also the blessed results, which under God's providence it shall subserve by ushering in the Millennial Kingdom. And this is a comfort, and more than an offset for all the tribulation, even though we or our dearest ones may share it.

That we might now have the comfort of this knowledge, and not be in doubt and perplexity, was but part of the object in the giving of the time-prophecies. Another object was, that, as the representatives of that kingdom among men, we should be aware of the great dispensational changes now in progress, and able to bear testimony before the world, regarding God's plan, etc., which, though unheeded now, will greatly benefit them by and by, and help them the sooner to recognize the Lord's presence in the great day of wrath, drawing on. Another object is, that the faithful, thus armed and

---

Charles Taze Russell, *The Time Is at Hand* (1889; reprint, Brooklyn, N.Y.: Watch Tower Bible and Tract Society, 1912).

strengthened by God's Word, may be enabled to stand firm, when so many will be falling into infidelity and various other deceptive errors, which will soon sweep over "Christendom." Another object is, to give force and point to the entire Plan of the Ages: for it is a general experience that, while the first glimpse of God's gracious plan for blessing the whole world through the Church, during the Millennial age, fills the hearts and enlists the zeal of his faithful children to the utmost, yet as their efforts to enlighten others are coldly received, and they find that only a very few, comparatively, have "an ear to hear," the tendency is to settle down to the quiet enjoyment of the precious knowledge, in such a manner as will bring the least reproach and opposition.

Seeing this, our natural weakness, the Lord has provided time-prophecies as a spur, to quicken and awaken us fully, and keep us active in his service. Being already in the "harvest" time, harvest work should engage the time, service and thoughts of the Lord's servants, who now, like the disciples at the first advent, are to do the reaping work. (John 4: 35–38.) Let us each seek to do what our hands find to do, in obedience to the instructions of the great Chief Reaper. But, with reference more particularly to the time and order of events in this "harvest," we must refer the reader to the succeeding volume of this series, wherein the conclusions of the foregoing and other time prophecies are brought to a focus, and the various foretold signs and corroborative testimonies of the Master's presence and the progress of his work are marked, proving—that the "Time of the End" has come; that the Days of Waiting for the Kingdom are fulfilled; that the Cleansing of the Sanctuary is accomplished; that the great Harvest Work is in progress; that the Re-gathering of Israel is apparent; that the Battle of the Great Day of God Almighty is impending; and that the complete establishment of the glorious Kingdom of God at the time appointed, the end of the Times of the Gentiles, is an unquestionable certainty; and showing, further, the work of the saints during the harvest; marking the close of the "high calling," and the "change" of those saints who "are alive and remain;" and showing, also, that the Great Pyramid of Egypt is one of God's Witnesses (Isa. 19: 19, 20), whose wonderful message is a full and complete corroboration of God's plan of the ages, together with its times and seasons.

8. E. A. Dyer, Sr., Remembers Wovoka, a Paiute Indian Who Originated the Ghost Dance Religion, 1889

As a child and adult I mingled with the Pahute [Paiute] Indians and learned to speak their language fluently. At 18 years of age I joined the Nevada State Militia, formed to deal with Indian uprising and am the last surviving member of Company I of that organization. . . .

I first knew Jack Wilson as a grown man somewhat older than I, when in my teens I started a store in Yerington. . . . The Wilson family had a partial hand in the raising of the Indian lad and furnished him with his American name. . . . The early day members of the Wilson family, like many pioneers were of a devout turn of mind. The young Indian, accepted into the house, was thus exposed to some religious

E. A. Dyer, Sr., "Wizardry," in *Wovoka and the Ghost Dance* (Carson City, Nev.: Grace Dangberg Foundation, 1990).

teaching through family Bible readings, evening prayers, grace before meat and similar family devotions. Indeed, some particular effort was made by the lady of the house to read to the boy some of the better known Bible stories. What he heard he may not have thoroughly understood but he was vastly interested and impressed. More to the point he learned that the white men had certain leaders, wisemen and prophets whom they revered and by whose laws and precepts they endeavored to live. Just as today's boy might day dream of becoming a space pilot, yesterday's young Indian might envision himself as some sort of an Indian version of an Old Testament prophet. Later events lend a certain credibility to the supposition. . . .

. . . [H]e did claim to have some facility in the matter of prophesy; he could perform certain feats beyond the abilities of most mortals; he could describe the delights of the Happy Hunting Grounds from personal observation—he'd gone there on short trips. . . .

. . . Jack Wilson was a tall, well-proportioned man with piercing eyes, regular features, a deep voice and a calm and dignified mien. He stood straight as a ramrod, spoke slowly and by sheer projection of personality commanded the attention of any listener. He visibly stood out among his fellow Indians like a thoroughbred among a bunch of mustangs.

Like all who claim unusual abilities he had his skeptics and eventually he had to demonstrate or shut up. And demonstrate he did. He caused ice to come down from the sky. . . . He went into trances in which he remained for as long as two days and when he awakened, announced that he had been to the Indian Heaven and was able to give a thorough-going description. He painted such an enticing picture that a few of his most faithful believers decided to hurry things up by eating wild parsnip root (water hemlock). I personally witnessed the demise of one deluded victim and can attest that it was a long drawn out and agonizing death. Eating of wild parsnip to commit suicide was not an uncommon method among the Indians. In this case and several others, the victim not only was in a hurry to visit Heaven but also was assured that he could return again as Jack had done, to find earth a much improved place, for better days were coming for the red men. Jack Wilson's trances were, at least to Indians, very impressive productions. I can speak only as a layman in such matters but it is my belief that they were truly self induced hypnotic trances of a rather deep nature. He wasn't shamming. His body was as rigid as a board. His mouth could not be pried open and he showed no reaction to pain inducing experiments. . . .

. . . When out on a rabbit drive, they said Jack was in the habit of dropping a pinch of snow or sand into the muzzle of his gun and forthwith bringing down a jackrabbit. He didn't need orthodox power and shot. They knew this to be true as they had seen it with their own eyes. This business with substitute ammunition led naturally to another act of which I pieced together a complete picture from descriptions of many of those who had also seen "with their own eyes." . . . He announced well in advance that he couldn't be killed by a gun. He simply was able to render his body impervious to lead. Moreover he could create powder and shot out of dust and sand. . . .

Understandably the Indians were interested. If one of them could become bullet proof maybe the condition could be made to rub off on the rest of the tribe. The average Indian was becoming thoroughly fed up with the white man by this time and longed to shoot all of them out of hand but the white man was prone to shoot back with deadly accuracy and moreover he controlled the supply of powder and shot. It is difficult to wage a war when one is dependent on the enemy for supplies. . . .

Naturally news of such a phenomenon as a bullet proof Indian with its possible application by other and more disgruntled Indians soon spread by word of mouth beyond the immediate tribal area and in the course of time reached the Plains Indians and those of Oklahoma Territory. . . . [M]any dances were held: a sort of religious fervor was generated. Fuel was added to the fire by the Prophet's declaration that better and happier times for Indians were coming soon. . . .

Gradually the belief built up that the Indian peoples had something at long last. They came to regard Jack Wilson as a veritable Messiah come to punish the Indian's enemies. There is no concrete evidence to show that Jack deliberately cultivated such a belief. He was content merely to bask in the adulation and veneration of his fellow Indians. But his fellow Indians having ideas of his own, ran off with the ball. They asked for Wilson's garments, particularly shirts. They began, by extension to attribute miraculous powers to shirts he had worn, owned, touched, looked upon or simply just thought about. . . .

But his build up among the Indians everywhere went on unabated and they began to get restless. Hotheads among them clamored for some action. It remained for the Sioux, perhaps the most warlike of the plains Indians, to precipitate trouble. By this time government authorities had become aware of trouble brewing. To cool things off a bit it was decided to take into custody as a sort of hostage for good behavior, the nominal head of the Sioux, Sitting Bull. His followers objected strenuously, some sort of a hassle developed and in the melee Sitting Bull was killed. That dropped the fat practically into the fire but before a general war could be started a parlay was arranged with the Indians. It took place Dec. 29, 1890 near Pine Ridge in southern South Dakota. Neither side trusted the other. In consequence as arrangements shaped up, troops armed with the new Gatling gun (a forerunner of the modern machine gun) occupied the heights overlooking the conference area. Within the area were hundreds of blanketed Indians who were supposed to be unarmed as were the government spokesmen who were to confer with them.

Just what happened next has never been satisfactorily determined. Indians claimed overt acts and bad faith on the part of the whites. They in turn claimed the same of the Indians. It was said that Indians began to drop blankets, expose (sic) rifles and prepare to use them. Again, the first shot was attributed to a jittery soldier. It is futile to speculate at this late date but it is known that a shot rang out, several more followed and then the Gatling guns were turned loose. The result was little short of a massacre. Some 300 Indians lay dead with many more wounded. The surviving Indians were stunned and apparently the Army was somewhat astounded by this first bloody demonstration of the effectiveness of mechanized carnage. It took its place in history as the battle of Wounded Knee. To the victors of the Little Big Horn it was final and bitter defeat. No other tribe was prepared to face a similar debacle. Other isolated skirmishes among various tribes occurred well into the 20th century and several were accounted "the last Indian battle" but Wounded Knee for all practical purposes marked the end of the Indian wars. A bloody period had been placed at the end of the last chapter of the annals of an era.

Inquiries among the surviving insurgents turned up many references to "ghost shirts" and the belief that their wearers were safe from bullets. Further probing revealed the name of Jack Wilson. . . .

Mr. Mooney and I drove to the camp in my buggy and found Wilson "at home." After introductions and assurances that nothing disagreeable was in store he was persuaded to talk. Thus began the first of many all day sessions of questions and answers. The catechism was thorough and when the subject of the ghost shirts and the prophet's connection thereto was exhausted, Mr. Mooney went into tribal lore and religious beliefs. I translated legends, stories, songs and dance chants, all of which were duly recorded in Mr. Mooney's notebook. Wilson was cooperative, neither cringing, bellicose nor evasive. At the end he posed, upon the promise of a print, for a formal photograph which Mooney took with professional skill. I was thoroughly convinced that Jack Wilson had at no time attempted deliberately to stir up trouble. He never advocated violence. Violence was contrary to his very nature. Others seized upon his prophecies and "stunts" and made more out of them than he intended. On the other hand it should be said that there is no evidence to show that he tried to restrain over zealous followers. In a way, once started, he was riding a tiger. It was difficult to dismount. And at the end, he evinced a very real regard at what had happened. There were no more demonstrations of wizardry. . . .

And now, strangely enough, Jack Wilson acquired that which he sought all along, namely a quiet veneration by Indians everywhere. No Indian blamed him for the debacle at Wounded Knee.

☙ E S S A Y S

James Moorehead of North Carolina State University researched hundreds of sermons and pamphlets by northern clergy to determine how they explained the outbreak of the Civil War. As he shows in this extract from his book *American Apocalypse,* they were convinced that it came from God, as punishment for their sins but also, perhaps, as a way of removing obstacles to the coming millennium. Therefore, they concluded, it would be sinful not to fight to the end. They shied away from the idea that it might be just a matter of power politics and instead interpreted each event as encapsulating a clue as to God's will for the Union.

Charles Reagan Wilson of the University of Mississippi studied the long aftermath of the Civil War in the defeated Confederacy. As he explains, Confederate veterans and their families commemorated their exploits in a language and style that mixed political and religious imagery, statues, songs, poems, speeches, and tributes. They thought of themselves retrospectively as Christian warriors who, despite their defeat, had had God's favor and the priceless assurance that they had been doing his work. Wilson is very precise as to how these Confederate rituals developed, and he draws on a body of anthropological literature that explains the central role of ritual in creating religious traditions.

Civil War as Battle of Armageddon

JAMES MOOREHEAD

Several weeks after the surrender of Fort Sumter, the *Presbyterian* confessed its perplexity with the dark events that had befallen the Union. The United States had been "raised up and commissioned of God to serve as a light and a deliverer to those long down-trodden and degraded populations" of the earth. Yet at the very moment when democracy had taken root in Europe and ancient barriers to missions

---

James Moorehead, "The Armageddon of the Republic," chap. 2 in *American Apocalypse* (New Haven: Yale University Press, 1978), 42–59.

had begun to crumble, the nation destined to lead this world renovation had succumbed to internecine strife. That America should stumble when its golden hour
had come, concluded the paper, "is surely one of the most lamentable, and one of
the most inexplicable providences in the history of nations or of mankind."

War forced the churches to reconsider their previous understanding of the manner in which the Kingdom of God would come. In spite of the growing sense of crisis
in the 1850s, many had not given up hope that the United States might be spared
tribulation and that its mission would be one of peace. In a sermon to the Foreign
Missionary Society the week after Lincoln's election, the Reverend Walter Clarke
summarized the role that churchmen expected to play in the transformation of the
world. "The people of God have no need to assail the nations; they have no use for
arms, and no license for invasion. They have only to keep their Christian virtues, and
exercise them, and by this simple process they shall at length acquire a Kingdom. . . .
And they are to do all this as the leaven does its transforming and restless work; by
the secret infusion into all parts of the social organism, of the spirit of their master,
the spirit of equity, and truth, and love." Whatever wars might augur the Kingdom
would likely fall upon the earth's benighted peoples, its victims of despotic princes
and religious superstition; the American Republic, unperturbed in its peaceful mission, would be happily exempt from the travail. After 12 April 1861, however, these
hopes were awash in a sea of blood. The *Christian Review* expressed the anguish of
the religious community: "Coming into existence in an age and region remote from
the political corruptions, the diplomatic intrigues, the hereditary feuds, and the tra-
ditionary abuses of the Old World, we had flattered ourselves that we should escape
the desolating wars which have marked the fluctuating fortunes of the European
Empire, and that in a pathway of unbroken peace we should sweep forward into the
cloudless splendors of the Millenial [*sic*] era. . . . Our visions have been suddenly,
rudely dispelled."

Almost as soon as the first guns had fired, Protestants set about reevaluating
their conception of the historical process and of national destiny. Drawing upon the
Puritan tradition of pulpit jeremiads, the clergy suggested that the nation's hope had
gone awry because the people had sinned. Since their virtue and piety had declined
from the glorious example of their revolutionary ancestors, God demanded expia-
tion in blood. Simultaneously Protestants concluded that the woes of the Apocalypse
applied even to the United States. Here, too, the Kingdom could come only through
travail and the clash of arms. God was violently overturning the old, corrupt order
and was bringing the disparate forces of history to a climactic resolution in one
place and time. It had been granted to Americans to fight the definitive battle that
would ensure the future happiness of the nation and the world. The Armageddon of
the Republic had begun.

"No truth is more patent in American history," wrote Edward McNall Burns some
years ago, "than the fact that this nation is an Old Testament people." The chosen
vessel of the millennium, the United States was also believed to be the modern
successor to the ancient Jewish state. Herman Melville, far from the orthodox
community, indicated the pervasiveness of this sentiment when he observed, "We
Americans are the peculiar, chosen people—the Israel of our time; we bear the ark
of the liberties of the world." As he had done with Israel, God entered into a special

covenant with the American people and conferred great blessings upon them. A covenant, however, entails mutual obligations, and if either party defaults, the agreement can be annulled. From the beginning of the colonial enterprise, Americans sensed, albeit dimly at times, that election thus carried a threat as well as a promise. Governor John Winthrop of the Massachusetts Bay Colony gave classic expression to this awareness in 1630 in his sermon to the immigrants on the *Arbella:* "Thus stands the cause between God and us, we are entered into Covenant with him for this work . . . ; but if we shall neglect the observation of these Articles which are the ends we have propounded, and dissembling with our God, shall fall to embrace this present world and prosecute our carnal intentions seeking great things for our selves and our posterity, the Lord will surely break out in wrath against us, be revenged of such a perjured people, and make us know the price of the breach of such a Covenant." As Perry Miller has shown, later Puritan preaching virtually institutionalized this motif in a sermonic form, the jeremiad, which affirmed that whatever evils befell the people came as punishment for the transgression of the covenant. The jeremiad was considerably modified during the Revolutionary and early National periods, but it never fully disappeared as a theological rationale for the sufferings of a chosen people.

The tragedy of civil war reinvigorated the jeremiadic tradition, and these thunderings of judgment seemed peculiarly appropriate to the crisis. . . . At the national fast on 30 April 1863, Byron Sunderland framed the charge . . . sharply to his Washington, D.C., congregation: "We have sinned, while holding in trust the noblest heritage ever held by any people, while having charge in effect of the last and most precious hopes of human nature." Unless God stayed his wrath, the country would soon "sink into an abyss of shame and infamy such as no people ever contracted, not even the doomed and wandering house of Israel."

False to its covenant bonds, the nation was summoned to hear anew the word of the prophets that the Lord is an avenging God. "The Old Testament, in our current notions and sympathies," suggested A. L. Stone, "has been almost outlawed from human affairs. We have turned its leaves for its curious and quaint old histories, but felt as though we were living under a new dispensation. And now the days have come upon us, for which these strong-chorded elder Scriptures have been waiting. Their representations of God, as the rewarder of the evil doer; the Avenger of the wronged, the Asserter of his own trampled prerogatives, . . . suit the day and hour of the intense present." . . .

The sword had fallen upon the nation for sins that the entire people had committed, and the North was as much the object of divine wrath as was the South. "Let no one section of our common country," insisted Roswell Hitchcock of Union Seminary, "angrily upbraid another for its vices or crimes. We are offenders all of us, North and South, East and West." According to Methodist George Peck, the meaning of the crisis could be learned from the actions of God during the Assyrian invasion of Judah, when the Lord raised up a heathen king to smite his own people for their wickedness. Thus "as God often uses one wicked people for the punishment of another, he is permitting this slaveholders' rebellion to inflict upon us terrible chastisement." The North similarly was being used by God to inflict a "judicial punishment" upon the South for its iniquitous slave system. Unwittingly the two parties to the conflict had become the rods by which God was scourging both for their sins. . . .

Frequently these confessions enumerated alleged violations of virtually every prohibition in the Scriptures. George Duffield's widely circulated *God of Our Fathers,* for example, uncovered a catalog of transgressions among which were ingratitude, intemperance, violation of the Sabbath, infidelity, adultery, murder, unjust wars, and oppression. In spite of their inclusivity, the jeremiads were not merely time-honored rhetorical broadsides lacking specific relevance to the contemporary situation. Clergy recognized that the manifold sins of the Republic were traceable to two chief moral failures: the toleration of slavery and the want of an effective internal discipline within American democracy.

For those who seriously pondered the American heritage, it was a scandal of shocking proportions that a people affirming certain inalienable rights for all should have so long endured human bondage in their midst. The Reverend M. L. P. Thompson of Cincinnati suggested that the nation's hypocritical retreat from its first faith had prompted the present judgment: "Like the Israelites taking possession of their promised land, who disobediently spared some of the idolatrous nations whom God had commanded them to drive out, and were ever after vexed by them in all their generations—so, we, denying in practice the holy doctrine of our Exodus, with which God accompanied us as a friend, and established us in our inheritance, left in the heart of our land the very flail with which he is now threshing us." In this extremity, a cheap repentance could no longer suffice. Payment for slavery must be made, said Baptist minister George Ide, in "rivers of blood and oceans of treasure."

Another indictment explained the calamity: the people had succumbed to an overweening selfishness that threatened chaos. To many perceptive observers, it seemed that the young republic was a nation without internal cohesion. Relative social egalitarianism and economic mobility atomized the citizenry into competitive individuals, each striving for material gain and security. . . .

In an address to the Plymouth Congregational Church of Milford, Connecticut, the editor of the *American Presbyterian and Theological Review* suggested that all the particular vices of the nation might be traced to this primal sin. Preoccupied with "style and luxury and extravagance," Americans had deserted the "republican simplicity" of the fathers. . . . The end result of such disregard for order could be only that which the nation was now experiencing—a bloody insurrection. The vital center of American nationality had been dissipated by unbridled individualism, and until this defect was remedied, "God will keep his hand heavy down upon us."

God's judgment upon the United States was not part of an endless cycle of sin and chastisement, for the divine wrath systematically moved toward a final victory over evil. Although the nations had indeed sinned repeatedly and received condign punishment, each convulsion marked the defeat of a particular iniquity, which, once vanquished, would never flourish again. George Prentiss of Union Seminary in New York remarked that current upheavals only appeared to replicate past ones. "A new cycle of events begins," he explained. "A fresh chapter is opened in history. Humanity takes a step never taken before toward the fulfillment of its grand destiny. The hand on the dial-plate of time is moved forward, and no mortal power is strong enough ever to put it back again." According to the *Independent,* the deity of the Scriptures was the *deus eversor,* God the destroyer. Never content with the world as it was, he subverted, one by one, the barriers to the millennium. "This is the burthen [*sic*] of all prophecy—this the light that shines along the track of time, growing brighter as the world advances and God's plan unfolds itself in history. God 'overturns, overturns, overturns'; one power after another, one nation after another, one mighty iniquity after another, falls and is no more; while earth and heaven are waiting till he shall come whose right it is to reign." And if such were God's way of working, the American Christian could only conclude of the Civil War: "We are in the midst of such an overturning." . . .

Dr. George Ide repeated the assertion that violence was a necessary tool of the Kingdom of God. Although the "normal character of His dispensations" was found in the "persuasive ministry" of the Gospel, God inaugurated truly significant periods of history by political strife and wars. A provocative sermon title gave Ide's theme away: "Great Eras Marked by Great Judgments." He called attention to the nexus of events that surrounded previous advances, each of which had been accompanied by bloodshed. For example, the Hebrew nation could not enter upon its divinely commissioned vocation until the hosts of Pharaoh were slaughtered; and Jesus's advent, hardening the Jews, led to their political destruction by the legions of Vespasian. Ide concluded: "When individuals or communities have become so sunk in degeneracy, or so wedded and sold to enormous vices, as to be insensible to every motive derived from His goodness; and, especially, when from wicked laws, institutions or governments, obstacles stand in the way of His purposes which ordinary appliances fail to remove then it is that He makes bare His arm for judgment; then it is that 'by terrible things in righteousness,' He answers prayer, and annihilates the barriers that oppose the going forth of His salvation." Within Ide's remarks lay the outlines of a dialectical view of divine activity within history, for God wielded alternately the suasion of the Gospel and the hammer of violence. . . .

As one of the upheavals necessary to this consummation, the Civil War could be intelligible only within the framework of world history. Indeed the logic of millennialism prohibits that any event be merely parochial, for history is not the random eruption of economic struggles, dynastic rivalries, or chauvinistic vendettas; it is essentially one struggle between two opposing forces. God and Satan—Christ and Antichrist—are the only real contestants; all others are mere epiphenomena. . . .

If every event was part of one struggle, the most minute historical occurrence was never lost. A civilization in each success bequeathed a valuable legacy to its successors or in each failure a moral warning. All fit perfectly into the plan of the Kingdom. "With infinite wisdom and sovereign authority," explained the Reverend Daniel March of Philadelphia, "He [God] assigns to nations their periods of trial and of conflict, of prosperity and of repose, in such order as best to secure the ultimate triumph of righteousness and truth. The great world-wide contest is ever-going on, not always with the sword, but always with resources of vast extent and with weapons of mighty power." Although the United States had hoped to avoid writing "another page of the bloodstained annals of war," such innocence had been denied. "But the active conflict which the powers of darkness are ever waging for the possession of this world, has at last rolled toward that quarter of the field where the Divine Commander has assigned us our station. And we must take our turn in resisting the attack, considering what we do and suffer in this contest is not for ourselves alone, but for the ages and generations of the human family in all the future." The American war had global significance because it was the current theater of operations in a much larger struggle;

and in such universal strife whatever happens in one arena, even if removed by thousands of miles, affects every other sphere of hostilities. It was therefore axiomatic to Protestants that the Civil War was fraught with incalculable consequences, and the *Christian Advocate and Journal* echoed March: "There is not an island in the sea, nor a hamlet on the broad continents, that has not a stake in the issue." . . .

Their conception of history converted the Civil War into a crusade for Protestants. If the chosen light should fail, how great would be the darkness! The collapse of the model republic would sink the aspirations of freedom-loving people everywhere, and thus the contest had to be pressed with unceasing vigor. In the first Presbyterian Church of Pittsburgh W. W. Eells affirmed: "We hold up the banner of terror to tyrants, the banner of hope to oppressed millions. And justly do we contend to the utmost, lest in our failure, gloomy darkness spread its pall over all lands, and it be held as proven, that man is not worthy to be free." . . .

Victory for the Union would undeniably conclude another of those periodic upheavals by which the progress of the Kingdom was traced, but triumph might well mean even more. The unique position of America in history suggested that the current conflict might well be part of the final battle. The Reverend Joel Bingham asked a Buffalo audience to consider the future of the Republic after the guns fell silent. Could it be otherwise than that America would offer "such a home of liberty, such a scene of peaceful order and contented industry, . . . such a land of right and virtue and religion as would well answer to the figure of millennial glory and the reign of the Redeemer of men upon earth?"

By the time of the Civil War, Protestants had been introduced to schemes purporting to draw from the Scriptures, verse by verse, a time-specific scenario for the millennium. William Miller, whose prediction of the end of the world in 1844 created national attention, was merely the best known of the "watchers for the Second Coming." From the British Isles emanated a more literate variety of prophetic speculation. After 1840 the works of such English authors as John Nelson Darby, George S. Faber, and John Cumming were widely disseminated in America, and in 1859–60, Michael Baxter, a Church of England missionary, had toured the United States preaching a message encapsulated in the title of his later published work, *The Coming Battle and the Appalling National Convulsion Foreshadowed in Prophecy Immediately to Occur During the Period 1861–1867. Prophetic Times,* a Philadelphia-based interdenominational publication, was established in 1863 to promote careful study of the prophecies; and in the same year the *Christian Intelligencer,* the organ of the Dutch Reformed Church, attracted widespread attention with a spirited debate about the millennial timetable. Most Protestants scoffed at these theories. The Millerite fiasco had severely discredited efforts to predict the Second Coming, and, in any event, these prophetic schedules usually operated upon premises rejected by most clergy. Such schemes tended to be, almost without exception, premillennial, and they claimed a greater foreknowledge than Protestants generally thought attainable. Nevertheless, the war did induce a few people to seek scriptural evidence that the details of the current crisis had been predicted.

An obscure Methodist preacher, L. S. Weed of Brooklyn, provides a representative guide into these exotic realms. Weed surveyed the contemporary scene rife with "debates in Congress, and Parliament, and Chambers; insurrections in the

Ottoman Empire and Greece; the upheaval of society in Russia; the Italian difficulties; the discontent of Hungary and Poland; the dissensions of Germany; the unrest of France and Spain; the tramp of foreign mercenaries in Mexico, and the rage of civil conflict and the boom of cannon on our shores." Turmoil on such a global scale, he concluded, could be only the "ascending dust of the world's gathering squadrons for the decisive conflict."

Weed was confident that the specifics of this apocalyptic drama could be learned from the Scriptures. In particular he turned to the dream of Nebuchadnezzar in the second chapter of Daniel—a book that has frequently inspired millennial speculation—to find a clue to the present world situation. In this dream, the Chaldean king sees a human image whose body is divided into four sections composed of different substances. A stone cut without human hands smashes the image and becomes a great mountain filling the entire earth. Daniel interprets the human figure as a symbolic representation of the future succession of earthly empires, the head signifying Nebuchadnezzar's own kingdom and the remaining portions of the body three political powers to arise later. The great stone indicates a fifth empire that will destroy every trace of the preceding ones and will establish a permanent dominion throughout the earth. Following a standard interpretation, Weed suggested that the political units foreshadowed by the image had virtually passed away, although remnants of the fourth empire—the Roman—persisted in the modern nations of Europe. Since Europe's turmoil indicated it was in decline, the hour of the fifth and universal empire was at hand. "Our country," suggested Weed with no false modesty, "is the exact fulfillment" of this prophecy.

Weed found explicit prediction of the Civil War and its outcome in the twelfth chapter of the Apocalypse, which recounts a celestial conflict between the Archangel Michael and the dragon. After stubborn resistance, this satanic rebellion collapses, and the dragon's hosts are cast from heaven—a symbolic representation, according to Weed, of the certain defeat of the Confederacy. This expulsion proved to Weed's satisfaction that tyranny would henceforth be confined to Europe, whose tottering aristocracies would attempt a final abortive alliance against the Union. Near the end of the secession struggle, the United States and these corrupt powers would confront one another, probably on the field of battle; and as prophesied in the thirty-eighth and thirty-ninth chapters of Ezekiel, this coalition against the American Israel would be "entirely overthrown." Then revolutions would reverberate around the globe, and all nations would submit to the Gospel and to democracy as exemplified by the United States.

Confederates' Defeat as Chastisement from God

CHARLES REAGAN WILSON

RICHMOND REMEMBERED. It had been the capital of the Southern Confederacy, and when the drive for independence failed, Richmond became the eternal city of Southern dreams. It, in turn, preserved the memory of its past and catered to the activities

Charles Reagan Wilson, *Baptized in Blood: The Religion of the Lost Cause* (Athens, Ga.: University of Georgia Press, 1980).

of the Lost Cause. Appropriately, therefore, one of the first large postwar gatherings of defeated Confederate veterans occurred in the city in October, 1875, a decade after the war's end and one year before the nation's centennial celebration. The Confederates met for a celebration, but not of the American nation: they celebrated ritualistically the Confederate nation that still lived in their minds. "Memory-fraught Richmond, the soldier's Mecca," as one Southerner later described it, was the site on October 26, 1875, of the dedication of the first statue in the South to Stonewall Jackson.

As the South's monument-making obsession gathered momentum, days like this one became ever more frequent, reaching a peak between 1890 and 1910. Richmond augmented its position as the capital of the Lost Cause. By 1920 the city boasted a sixteen-acre Hollywood Cemetery, holding the graves of 16,000 Confederate soldiers, including 3,000 from the Gettysburg battlefield; the Hollywood Cemetery Monument, a massive, ninety-foot-high Egyptian-like pyramid of James River granite; the Soldiers' and Sailors' Monument in Libby Hill Park, a seventy-two-foot-high shaft, topped by an eighteen-foot-high bronze Confederate; the Confederate Memorial Institute, known as the South's Battle Abbey; the White House of the Confederacy, which had been made into the United Daughters of the Confederacy Museum; and a carefully maintained Monument Boulevard, with statues of J. E. B. Stuart, Stonewall Jackson, Robert E. Lee, and an elaborate Jefferson Davis monument, dedicated in 1907 before 200,000 people, the largest crowd ever to assemble to honor the Confederates. The 1875 gathering thus represented a beginning of the movement that lasted for generations. Its events and tone were representative of the hundreds of future dedications. It was a truly region-wide meeting to celebrate and to mourn the Confederacy. The Lost Cause was an intellectual attitude, with a marble embodiment in the monuments that proliferated throughout the South after 1875. . . .

The day of the dedication displayed a curious mixture of joy and sadness, perfectly capturing the essence of the Lost Cause itself. Balmy Indian summer weather contributed to a festive summer atmosphere among the people; but one could not escape noticing that the year was dying, and that the Indian summer was only postponing death. General Daniel Harvey Hill wrote that the autumn winds sang "a requiem to the 'Lost Cause,' and the dead leaves falling on the base of the pedestal seemed to be Nature's tribute to the lost hero." Richmond spared no expense in decorating for the occasion, but the decorations also contributed to the mixed mood. The American flags on the streets were all new, with deep, rich colors, while the Confederate flags, torn and faded, were authentic ones used in the Civil War. One observer noted, "The flag that floats over the Capitol-grounds is the flag of the conqueror. The conquered banner is wrapped around the dead hero's body in the dead hero's grave." The Confederate veterans dressed in their gray uniforms. Many of the city's decorations blended religious and military motifs; one of the most striking was the Grand Arch at a downtown corner. A Richmond reporter described it:

> It was thirty-two feet high and sixteen wide. It was constructed with two turreted towers covered with evergreen, with an arch connecting them. On the west side of the arch was inscribed in large letters "Warrior, Christian, Patriot." Just above this was a painting representing a stone-wall, upon which was resting a bare sabre, a Bible, and a Confederate cap, with the angel of peace ascending, pointing heavenward; and on the pinnacle of

the arch, just above this, was a pennant bearing the cross, as the emblem of Christianity. This picture, with the emblem above, was a beautiful design figurative of the blissful rest which our departed hero has long since enjoyed.

The setting might have been that of a popular outdoor religious drama. . . .

. . . Almost 50,000 people had gathered for the occasion. Stonewall Jackson was the quintessential Confederate martyr-hero to Southern ministers, so when the first statue to him was dedicated they helped make the occasion a religious one. The procession had included representatives from the Baptists' Richmond College and from denominational societies. Seated on the platform were several clergymen: Robert Lewis Dabney, the unreconstructed Presbyterian theologian who had served on Jackson's staff; the Reverend J. D. Smith, also of the General's staff; Methodist Bishop D. S. Doggett, who gave the invocation; and the day's orator, the Reverend Moses Drury Hoge.

The ceremonies began with Doggett's prayer, which was significant in affirming God's benevolence and omnipotence despite the Confederate defeat. Doggett acknowledged that God always acted in the best interests of His subjects and to the glory of His name, and he thanked Providence for gifted men who fulfilled the "benevolent purposes" of the Creator. Jackson, said Doggett, was such a man. At the heart of Doggett's prayer was a passage relating the day's events directly to religious concerns:

> Grant that the monument erected on this spot, to the honor of thy servant, may ever stand as a permanent memorial to thy praise, and a perpetual incentive to a high and holy consecration to thy service, in all the avocations of life. May it silently and effectually inculcate noble ideas and inspire lofty sentiments in all spectators for all time to come. Above all, may it teach the youth of the land the solemn lesson of thy word, that the foundation of true greatness is fidelity to thee.

Governor James L. Kemper then delivered a short address, in which he referred to Jackson as a "Christian warrior," and noted that for all mankind Jackson's career would be an "inspiration, teaching the power of courage and conscience and faith directed to the glory of God." The day's religious rhetoric was obviously not limited to the clergy.

To give the featured oration, the Virginia legislature had unanimously chosen Moses Drury Hoge, pastor of Richmond's Second Presbyterian Church. Tall, lean, and muscular, Hoge stood erect, with the bearing of a military man. . . . He [had] played an important role in the Confederacy, which he believed was waging a war for "civil and religious freedom." While continuing to preach to his Richmond congregation, Hoge at the same time [had] served as a spiritual adviser to many Confederate leaders; he [had] led the daily opening prayer at the Confederate Congress, and [had] served as a volunteer chaplain at the training camp outside Richmond. In that latter position he [had] preached at least three times a week, and sometimes daily, to a total of 100,000 soldiers just before they embarked on their first combat experiences. . . . The Southern defeat crushed Hoge. In May, 1865, one month after Appomattox, he wrote to his sister that "God's dark providence enwraps me like a pall." Shattered were his dreams of "a gospel guarded against the contamination of New England infidelity"; as a result, he felt "like a shipwrecked mariner thrown up like a seaweed on a desert shore." His depression and accompanying illness continued for a year or so, but eventually he reassured himself that, despite defeat, the South had not been wrong in the war.

On this October day in 1875, then, his own history had prepared Hoge to address the issue of the abiding meaning of the Confederacy. . . .

After considering the hero himself, Hoge grappled with the central, precipitating factor of the Lost Cause—the meaning of Southern defeat in the Civil War. Success was always pleasant, conceded Hoge, but pleasure was not everything. In a sentence that summed up the Southern religious interpretation of the Confederacy's defeat, Hoge said, "Defeat is the discipline which trains the truly heroic soul to further and better endeavors." Hoge saw hope for the future, and he praised the Southern people, especially the Confederate veterans, for their postwar behavior. Hoge ended his oration with an obligatory statement of the South's willingness to accept defeat, and of its desire for a fair reconciliation with the North; he noted, however, that the federal union was no longer the same as it had been in 1787. He then verbalized the fear of a catastrophe that haunted many Southerners, especially Southern preachers accustomed to thinking in apocalyptic terms:

> And if history teaches any lesson, it is this, that a nation cannot long survive when the fundamental principles which gave it life, originally, are subverted. It is true republics have often degenerated into despotisms. It is also true that after such transformation they have for a time been characterized by a force, a prosperity, and a glory, never known in their earlier annals, but it has always been a force which absorbed and obliterated the rights of the citizen, a prosperity which was gained by the sacrifice of individual independence, a glory which was ever the precursor of inevitable anarchy, disintegration, and ultimate extinction.

When Hoge finished, to the applause of the audience, soldiers hauled in the halyards attached to the canvas covering the statue, unveiling the monument to the accompanying sounds of musket and artillery blasts. After a brief pause the members of the Richmond Philharmonic Association performed a hymn of Luther's, "A Castle of Strength Is Our Lord." . . .

The sacred ceremony of October 26, 1875, was the ritualistic expression of the religion of the Lost Cause. Ritual is crucial to the emergence of a religion, because, as Clifford Geertz has argued, it is "out of the context of concrete acts of religious observance that religious conviction emerges on the human plane." "The primary phenomenon of religion is ritual," says Anthony F. C. Wallace. In a chaotic world, ritual embodies a symbol system that is "simple and orderly." The Lost Cause ritual celebrated a mythology which focused on the Confederacy. It was a creation myth, the story of the attempt to create a Southern nation. According to the mythmakers, a pantheon of Southern heroes, portrayed as the highest products of the Old South civilization, had emerged during the Civil War to battle the forces of evil, as symbolized by the Yankee. The myth enacted the Christian story of Christ's suffering and death, with the Confederacy at the sacred center. In the Southern myth the Christian drama of suffering and salvation was incomplete: the Confederacy lost a holy war, and there was no resurrection. But the clergy still insisted, even after defeat, that the Confederacy had been on a righteous crusade. . . .

. . . [T]he Confederate myth reached its true fulfillment after the Civil War in a ritualistic structure of activities that represented a religious commemoration and celebration of the Confederacy. One part of the ritualistic liturgy focused on the religious figures of the Lost Cause. Southern Protestant churches have been sparse in iconography, but the Southern civil religion was rich in images. Southern ministers and other rhetoricians portrayed Robert E. Lee, Stonewall Jackson, Jefferson Davis, and many other wartime heroes as religious saints and martyrs. They were said to epitomize the best of Christian and Southern values. Their images pervaded the South and were especially aimed at children. . . . Lee's birthday, January 19, became a holiday throughout the South, and ceremonies honoring his birth frequently occurred in the schools. Lee's picture on the wall was the center, the altar, for the event. The effect of these images could be seen in an anecdote concerning Father Abram Ryan, the poet-priest who wrote elegies about the Confederacy. He saw his young niece standing before a painting of the death of Christ, and he asked her if she knew who the evil men were who had crucified her Lord. "Instantly she replied, 'O yes I know,' she said, 'the Yankees.' " . . .

Of special significance was the hymn "Let Us Pass Over the River, and Rest Under the Shade of the Trees," which was officially adopted by the Southern Methodist church. The words in the title were the last words spoken by the dying Stonewall Jackson. Two other hymns, "Stonewall Jackson's Requiem" and "Stonewall Jackson's Way," made similar appeals. At some ceremonial occasions choirs from local churches, or a joint choir representing all the town's denominations, sang hymns. In 1907 Southerners organized the United Confederate Choirs of America, and soon young belles from Dixie, clad in Confederate gray uniforms, were a popular presence at ritual events.

These liturgical ingredients appeared in the ritualistic expressions of the Lost Cause. In the years immediately after the war, Southern anguish at Confederate defeat was most apparent during the special days appointed by the denominations or the states for humiliation, fasting, prayer, or thanksgiving. These special days could be occasions for jeremiads calling prodigals back to the church, prophesying future battles, or stressing submission to God's mysterious providence in the face of seemingly unwarranted suffering. Although Southerners usually ignored the national Thanksgiving Day, complaining that Northerners used that day to exploit the war issue and to wave the bloody shirt, they did celebrate thanksgiving day designated by their own denominations. In general, however, the days of humiliation, fasting, and prayer were more appropriate to the immediate postwar Southern mood.

Southern reverence for dead heroes could be seen in the activities of another ritual event, Confederate Memorial Day. Southern legend has it that the custom of decorating the graves of soldiers arose in Georgia in 1866, when Mrs. Charles William, a Confederate widow, published an appeal to Southerners to set apart a day "to be handed down through time as a religious custom of the South to wreathe the graves of our martyred dead with flowers." Like true Confederates, Southern states could not at first agree among themselves on which day to honor, but in 1916 ten states had designated June 3, Jefferson Davis's birthdate, as Memorial Day. . . .

The dedication of monuments to the Confederate heroes was a fourth ritualistic expression of the Lost Cause. In 1914 the *Confederate Veteran* magazine revealed that over a thousand monuments existed in the South; by that time many battlefields had been set aside as pilgrimage sites containing holy shrines. Preachers converted the innumerable statues dotting the Southern countryside into religious objects, almost idols, that quite blatantly taught Christian religious and moral lessons. "Our cause is with God" and "In hope of a joyful resurrection," among the most directly religious inscriptions on monuments, were not atypical. El Dorado, Arkansas, erected a marble drinking fountain to the Confederacy; its publicity statement said—in a phrase culled from countless hymns and sermons on the sacrificial Jesus—that the water in it symbolized "the loving stream of blood" shed by the Southern soldiers. Drinkers from the fount were thus symbolically baptized in Confederate blood. . . .

If religion pervaded the United Confederate Veterans, it saturated the United Daughters of the Confederacy. The importance of Christianity to the Daughters could be seen in the approved ritual for their meetings. It began with an invocation by the president:

> Daughters of the Confederacy, this day we are gathered together, in the sight of God, to strengthen the bonds that unite us in a common cause; to renew the vows of loyalty to our sacred principles; to do homage unto the memory of our gallant Confederate soldiers, and to perpetuate the fame of their noble deeds into the third and fourth generations. To this end we invoke the aid of our Lord.

The members responded, "From the end of the earth will I cry unto Thee, when my heart is overwhelmed; lead me to the rock that is higher than I." After similar chanted exchanges, the hymn "How Firm a Foundation" was sung, followed by the reading of a prayer composed by Episcopal Bishop Ellison Capers of South Carolina, himself a Confederate general before entering the ministry. After the prayer, the president then read the Lord's Prayer, and the meeting or convention began its official business.

The Daughters provided an unmatched crusading zeal to the Lost Cause religion. A typical local chapter motto was that of the Galveston, Texas, group: "With God Everything, Without God Nothing." . . .

The second organizational focus for the Southern civil religion was the Christian churches. The religion of the Lost Cause and the Christian denominations taught similar religious-moral values, and the Southern heroes had been directly touched by Christianity. The God invoked in the Lost Cause was distinctly biblical and transcendent. Prayers at veterans' gatherings appealed for the blessings of, in J. William Jones's words, the "God of Israel, God of the centuries, God of our forefathers, God of Jefferson Davis and Sidney Johnston and Robert E. Lee, and Stonewall Jackson, God of the Southern Confederacy." Prayers invariably ended in some variation of "We ask it all in the name and for the sake of Christ our dear Redeemer." . . . The references to Christ and the Holy Ghost clearly differentiated the Southern civil religion from the more deistic American civil religion. The latter's ceremonies rarely included such references because of the desire to avoid potential alienation of Jews, who were a small percentage of the Southern population. In Dixie, the civil religion and Christianity openly supported each other. To Southern preachers, the Lost Cause was useful in keeping Southerners a Christian people; in turn, Christianity would support the values of society. . . .

The close connection between the churches and the Confederate organizations could be seen in terms of the central experience of Southern Protestantism—evangelism. Confederate heroes were popular choices to appear at Southern revivals. The most influential Southern evangelist, the iconoclastic Georgia Methodist Sam Jones, was a master at having Confederates testify to the power of Christianity in their lives, preferably its inspirational effect on the battlefield. At the same time, a significant feature of the religious rhetoric of the reunions was the insistence on a response from the veterans. The invitation to follow Christ, which was made during the memorial services, was also an invitation to follow once again Robert E. Lee, Stonewall Jackson, and Jefferson Davis. Some of these reunions thus resembled vast revivals, with tens of thousands of listeners hearing ministers reminding them of the imminence of death for the aged veterans, and of the need to insure everlasting life.

🔖 *F U R T H E R   R E A D I N G*

Armstrong, Warren. *For Courageous Fighting and Confident Dying: Union Chaplains in the Civil War* (1988).

Brock, Peter. *Pacifism in the U.S. From the Colonial Era to the First World War* (1968).

DeBoer, Clara Merritt. *His Truth Is Marching On: African-Americans Who Taught the Freedmen* (1995).

DeMallie, Raymond J. *Sioux Indian Religion: Tradition and Innovation* (1987).

Evans, Eli. *Judah P. Benjamin: The Jewish Confederate* (1988).

Faust, Drew. *The Creation of Confederate Nationalism* (1988).

Fredrickson, George. *The Inner Civil War: Northern Intellectuals and the Crisis of the Union* (1965).

Goen, C. C. *Broken Churches, Broken Nation: Denominational Schisms and the Coming of the Civil War* (1985).

Harrison, Barbara G. *Visions of Glory: A History and Memory of the Jehovah's Witnesses* (1978).

Harvey, Paul. *Redeeming the South: Religious Cultures and Racial Identities Among Southern Baptists, 1865–1925* (1997).

Josephy, Alvin. *Wounded Knee* (1993).

Laderman, Gary. *Sacred Remains: American Attitudes Towards Death, 1799–1883* (1996).

Lincoln, C. Eric, and Lawrence H. Mamiya. *The Black Church in the African-American Experience* (1990).

Miller, Randall, H. Stout, and C. R. Wilson, eds. *Religion and the American Civil War* (1998).

Mooney, James. *The Ghost Dance and the Sioux Outbreak of 1890* (1991).

Paludan, Philip Shaw. *A People's Contest: The Union and the Civil War, 1861–1865* (1988).

Peden, Creighton. *Civil War Pulpit to World's Parliament of Religion: The Thought of William James Potter, 1829–1893* (1996).

Phillips, Kevin. *The Cousins' Wars: Religion, Politics, and the Triumph of Anglo-America* (1999).

Romero, Sidney. *Religion in the Rebel Ranks* (1983).

Shattuck, Gardiner H. *A Shield and a Hiding Place: The Religious Life of the Civil War Armies* (1987).

———. *This Great Day of Suffering: God, History, and the Civil War, 1865–1915* (1992).

Silver, James. *Confederate Morale and Church Propaganda* (1964).

Sobel, Mechal. *Trabelin' On: The Slave Journey to an Afro-Baptist Faith* (1979).

Thurow, Glen. *Abraham Lincoln and the American Political Religion* (1976).

Walker, Clarence E. *A Rock in a Weary Land: The African Methodist Episcopal Church During the Civil War and Reconstruction* (1982).

Wolf, William J. *The Almost Chosen People: A Study of the Religion of Abraham Lincoln* (1959).

CHAPTER
8

The New Immigration and Urban Reform: 1880–1925

In the decades after the Civil War the pace of American industrialization accelerated. Immigrants continued to pour in from Britain, Germany, and the Scandinavian countries (Norway, Denmark, and Sweden), with most settling in the booming cities. In addition, growing populations from such southern and eastern European countries as Italy, Poland, Greece, the Slavic lands of the Austro-Hungarian Empire, Russia, Rumania, and Turkey arrived, bringing with them strange folkways and religious customs that aroused fear and suspicion in the established American groups.

Even when people shared a religion, they did not necessarily see each other as brethren. For example, Irish Catholics, many of whom had been in America since the 1830s and 1840s, sometimes regarded the Italian, Slavic, and Polish Catholics as intruders with alien customs. They tried to ensure that American Catholicism followed a style of life and worship familiar to the Irish but unknown to most of the newcomers, and often tried to prevent the creation of distinctive "ethnic" Catholic parishes. Similarly, some members of the older German-Jewish population, mostly from the Reform tradition, feared that Orthodox Jews from Eastern Europe and Russia, with their strange clothes, hairstyles, dress, and religious observances, would create an upsurge of anti-Semitism in the Protestant population. These suspicions were offset, however, by a sense of fellow-feeling among other older immigrants who, remembering the difficulties of their own early days in America, established charities to help the "greenhorns."

The West Coast states of California, Oregon, and Washington meanwhile saw an influx of Japanese, Chinese, and Indian immigrants, bringing Buddhism, Hinduism, and Shinto to America. The Chicago World's Parliament of Religions in 1893, held as part of the festivities to celebrate the 400th anniversary of Christopher Columbus's discovery of America, was the first ever meeting of representatives from all the major religious groups on the planet, each of whom had the chance to explain his own tradition. By 1900 the United States was the most religiously diverse country in the world.

The older Protestant population, meanwhile, sought to keep control of the rapidly swelling cities and their polyglot population. Reforms of poor housing, nutrition, and sanitation were coupled with pleas for the reform of city government and an end to the corrupt "machines," such as New York's notorious "Tweed Ring," run by a group of second-generation Irish immigrants. The single most popular of all reform proposals among Protestants was for the prohibition of alcohol. If men were denied the temptation of drink, said temperance advocates, they would bring all their wages home, stop beating their wives and children, make their families prosper and be happy, and prevent industrial accidents. Thousands of Protestant women had their first experience of political work in the Women's Christian Temperance Union under the leadership of Frances Willard. For some, including Willard herself, working for the temperance movement led to the recognition of the disadvantages women faced so long as they were denied the vote. Thus, temperance became a training ground for suffragism. The campaigns for prohibition and women's suffrage both achieved their objectives at the end of the First World War, in constitutional amendments of 1919 and 1920.

Other women (and men, too) took consolation from spiritualist or idealist movements. One rapidly growing movement of the late nineteenth century was Christian Science, whose founder Mary Baker Eddy, rather than trying to change the material world, denied its reality altogether. She regarded sin, suffering, and death as no more than false mental projections that, with the right frame of mind, could be demonstrated as unreal.

While Frances Willard energized middle-class Protestant reformers against drink and Mrs. Eddy founded a church based on new forms of urban Christianity, including mental healing, the Salvation Army, imported from Britain, headed into the worst of the industrial slums. With members brightly attired in pseudo-military uniforms, it tried to adapt popular working-class habits and music to its gospel message of moral and religious reform. It was more likely to attract "fallen" Protestants—immigrants from the American countryside—than members of the new ethnic immigrant groups.

 # D O C U M E N T S

Document 1 (c. 1890), from an Italian immigrant's oral-history memoir, contrasts her own piety with her husband's anticlericalism and describes her inability to gain church approval for her remarriage after he deserted and divorced her. Document 2 (1886) is a tribute to temperance leader Frances Willard by one of her closest allies in the Protestant fight to rid America of alcohol. Document 3, from Mary Baker Eddy (1887), explains her view that God knows no such thing as sin, sickness, or death. In Document 4 (1893) the Swami Vivekananda writes to a friend back in India about the Americans' curious mix of wealth, hospitality, and religious naivete, and describes the World's Parliament of Religions, where his speech about Hinduism made him a spiritual celebrity. He later founded the Vedanta Society, an Americanized version of his faith. Document 5 (1900) describes the Salvation Army's origins in England, its spread to America, and its "soldiers'" efforts to evangelize in the worst slum districts and saloons of the American cities.

Documents 6 and 7 both come from superb novels about the Jewish immigrant experience in New York. Abraham Cahan's character, David Levinsky (1917), comes from Russia with plans for rabbinical study but is drawn by pressure of circumstances into the city's clothing business. Materially successful, he knows he has failed to realize his original religious ambitions. Anzia Yezierska's *Bread Givers* (1925) describes how a holy man from the Old World could become a patriarchal tyrant in the transformed conditions of the New World.

1. Rosa, an Immigrant, Contrasts Her Italian Catholicism with the American Version, c. 1890

When the coffee was on the table Gionin sat down with the others and started telling Francesca the plans he had made for her. Until she and Orlando were married on Sunday she was going to stay with an old Sicilian woman, Angelina, who was like a mother to all the young girls in camp. But after Sunday she and Orlando would live in a shack by themselves and she would do the cooking for another bunch of men. She was going to be married in a little village four miles down the tracks. But before then, on Saturday night, she must go to confession. Enrico, the boss of the iron mine, would go with her and interpret.

"*Santa Maria!* I have to tell my sins to a man not a priest? Better I don't get married!" Francesca was so comical she made everyone die laughing.

Gionin was laughing too and teasing Orlando about choosing a wife with sins so black that only a priest could hear them. But then he explained. He told how Enrico went in the priest's house with the girls and stood one side of the priest and the girl the other. Then the girl put her hand in the priest's hand and the priest asked the questions in English and Enrico said them in Italian. If the girl *did* make the sin—she did not go to mass on Sunday, or she stole something worth more than a penny—she must squeeze the priest's hand. Enrico couldn't see if she did or didn't. And in the end the priest gave her the penance and that was all.

"God is a dog," muttered Santino. "I'd burn in hell before I'd squeeze the hand of one of those black crows!"

"Listen to Santino!" laughed Pep. "Every Saturday night he's pinching the backside of his fat Annie or of some of those other bad women over Freddy's saloon. But he wouldn't squeeze the hand of a man—even to keep out of hell."

"Man, bah! I spit on all those black crows that wear dresses!"

As soon as I could I went into the bedroom and opened my chests. I had never expected to see them again. And there inside I found the featherbed and sheets Mamma Lena and Zia Teresa had put in. And I found the little Madonna and the crucifix Don Domenic had blessed. I kissed the bleeding feet of Jesus and said a little prayer. With that crucifix over my bed I would not feel so alone—so afraid. God would help me to be meek. I went into the other room to find a nail and Gionin came back and nailed the crucifix up for me. "Tomorrow, Rosa," he said, "I'll make you a shelf for the little Madonna." . . .

When everyone else had gone Santino blew out the lamp in the big room and came looking for me. Just inside the door he stopped. It was the crucifix over the bed that stopped him. He started cursing: "God is a dog! God is a pig! Can't a man sleep with his own wife without God watching him from the wall? Take it down, I tell you! Take it down!"

A wife doesn't have to obey her husband when he wants her to do something against God or the Madonna. I held my rosary tighter, waiting for him to come after

Marie Hall Ets, *Rosa, the Life of an Italian Immigrant* (Minneapolis: University of Minnesota Press, 1970).

me and watching for him to tear the crucifix down himself. But he didn't do either. He stood for a while just staring at it. Then without moving his eyes he backed away to the lamp and blew out the light. He was afraid—I could tell by the way he acted—afraid to have Jesus on the cross looking down at him. (But I have to leave that man out of this story. The things he did to me are too bad to tell! I leave him out, that's all!) . . .

So after Santino had the divorce Gionin and me went to the court in Chicago and got married together. The priest said he couldn't marry us in the church because I had that first husband living—only when he died we could be married in the church. Me, I was crying with tears coming down my eyes and praying God, "Oh God, why do You make it a sin for me to live with this good man Gionin? He's so good and so religious! My children will starve if he doesn't take care! Why do You make that a sin? How can that be a sin?"

Once a long time after, when Father Alberto came to America, I went by him and told him how I didn't say yes that time I was married with Santino in Bugiarno. I told him the priest was deaf but the people knew it that I didn't say yes. He said, "Well, if you can find all the people who were at your wedding and they sign their names on the paper that you didn't say yes, then I can marry you in the church."

But how am I going to find all those people? I can't, that's all!

(After Gionin and me were married together about ten years and have already three children, a missionary from Italy came in our church. He preached so strong against the divorce—what a sin it is against God, and the punishment God is going to give these people, and all and all—that Gionin got the scare and he went away and left me. About three months he left me alone to take care for all those children. Nobody but me knew why he went away that time, but I knew it was all the *missionario*'s doing. So then one day he went to confession to Father Alberto and Father Alberto told him it's a sin to leave me alone like that with those children. Oh, Gionin was glad to hear that, so he could come back! He said he only left me because he didn't want to go to hell.)

My husband he was many months carrying the bricks and the mud for that new church. But then those other *Toscana* people—that little bunch of *Toscani* were all very friends together—they said to him, "Oh you're foolish, Gionin. Why you don't get the horse and wagon and sell the bananas like us?"

So he did it—he got the horse and the wagon and he used to peddle the bananas. And when the cranberries came he sold the cranberries too. . . .

My husband when he was young was a beautiful man—nice teeth, nice hair, nice face, and big and strong. So all those ladies on Franklin Street, they liked him. And one woman, Dina, she loved him. And she all the time sent for him. But I don't think he did anything with her—he was just a very friend of her husband because they both sold bananas and would go together to buy them. I was brokenhearted, but I never said anything about it.

Well then one day a *Toscana* woman she came by me and said, "Oh Rosa, I saw your husband go in Dina's house and stay all night last night."

And sure, I knew he didn't come home till one o'clock. I was crying by myself and asking myself what am I going to do. So after that *Toscana* woman left me I said, "I know what I'm going to do to get happy again!"

I took my new baby in my arms—my Visella was just two or three weeks old at that time—and I walked way to State and Superior Street to the Holy Name Church. I don't know if it's there anymore, but there used to be a crucifix in the front hall of that church with Jesus about nine feet tall. It made you shiver to look at Him. I kneeled down saying all the prayers and crying for about one hour. And then I was looking up at the face. When you go here that face looks at you, and when you go there it looks. Where you are makes no difference—those eyes look at you anyway.

So then I took my little baby in my arms and started home. And all at once I was happy—I didn't have that worry no more in my heart. . . .

So then when my husband came home that night he was so sleepy. I said, "Sure you're sleepy. Why not when you come home one o'clock night?"

He said, "Yes, I went by Cesca's and I was playing cards."

So then I began weeping and I told him all that I had done.

He said, "Why Rosa, I have no intentions with those other women—they're jolly, that's all. Do you think I can put the beauty of you with that Dina and her rotten teeth?" And the tears were coming down from his eyes too. He said, "Rosa, I tell you, I'll never again walk in Dina's house! Never!" And he surely never did. And he even stopped buying bananas with Dina's husband.

Those other *Toscani* they were not religious. Only Gionin had the strong religion. And that husband of Dina's was terrible. When he and Gionin took their wagons and went together to peddle bananas and they came near a church he would say, "Hey, Gionin, hurry up and move away from this bad-luck place!" He wouldn't go near the churches and he hated the priests. He'd say, "Those blackbirds in there make me sick. If they put God alive in *my* mouth I will spit Him out! I will chew God up and spit Him out!" That man was so bad I was glad when Gionin stopped peddling bananas with him. It was only because they were *Toscani* together that they were friends like that. They had only a little bunch of *Toscani* in Chicago. The other Italians around there came later and they were Sicilian.

2. Mary Lathbury Pays Tribute to Frances Willard, Temperance Activist, 1886

In October, 1874, a voice that had been thrilling [Frances Willard] strangely wherever she heard a sound of it, came to her with a personal appeal. It was from the Woman's Christian Temperance Union, and the invitation to work with them was gladly accepted. She saw, with the clear intuition which is peculiar to her, that the little "root out of dry ground" was His promise of that which was to cover the land with a banyan-like growth. Said she, later: "I was reared on a western prairie, and often have helped kindle the great fires for which the West used to be famous. A match and a wisp of dry grass were all we needed, and behold the magnificent spectacle of a prairie on fire, sweeping across the landscape, swift as a thousand

Mary Lathbury, "Frances Willard of Illinois," in *Women and Temperance or The Work and Workers of the Women's Christian Temperance Union* (1883). (Chicago: Women's Temperance Publication Association, 1886), 28–32.

untrained steeds, and no more to be captured than a hurricane! Just so it is with the Crusade. . . . When God lets loose an idea upon this planet, we vainly set limits to its progress; and I believe that Gospel Temperance shall yet transform that inmost circle, the human heart, and in its widening sweep the circle of home, and then society, and then, pushing its argument to the extreme conclusion, it shall permeate the widest circle of them all, and that is, government."

So closely identified had she become with the womanhood of our country, that the question came very distinctly to her as a representative woman, "Who knoweth if thou be come into the kingdom for such a time as this?" The old feeling of being born to a work, a "destiny," had passed over from her own personality to the sex with which she is identified, as it is now passing over to the race, the "woman question" becoming the "human question."

There is much to be written from this point which cannot be brought within the limits of this sketch. It would be an unnecessary re-writing of the history of the Woman's Temperance Movement. This seed of the kingdom, after its wonderful planting in Ohio during the winter and spring of 1873–4, was beginning to bear fruit through the Middle and Western States. In August of that year, at Chautauqua, the "birthplace of grand ideas," the Women's Christian Temperance Union was born. A convention was called for November of the same year, at Cleveland, Ohio, and the National W. C. T. U. was then organized, with Miss Willard as Corresponding Secretary. It was at this Convention that she offered the resolution which, springing from the inspirations and the aspirations of the hour, has proved to be, in its spirit, a glory and a defence: "Realizing that our cause is combated by mighty and relentless forces, we will go forward in the strength of Him who is the Prince of Peace, meeting argument with argument, misjudgment with patience, and all our difficulties and dangers with prayer." Her work grew with the growth of the Union, and that growth was largely due to the tireless pen and voice and brain of its Corresponding Secretary.

While holding this office there occurred two episodes—apparent digressions—which did not, however, sever her connection with the Temperance work. In 1876–7, on invitation from Mr. Moody, she assisted him in the Gospel work in Boston for several months. Her hope in undertaking this enterprise was that the Temperance work might be united with the Gospel work, and brought with it to the front. The meetings for women, filling Berkeley and Park Street churches, and her words before the thousands gathered in the great Tabernacle, are memorable.

Says one who lives "in the Spirit" as few women do, "I have never been so conscious of the presence of the Divine power, the unction of the Holy One, in the ministry of the Word, as under the preaching of Miss Willard."

In this connection we are tempted to quote from a published statement recently made by Miss Willard:

"The deepest thought and desire of my life would have been met, if my dear old Mother Church had permitted me to be a minister. The wandering life of an evangelist or a reformer comes nearest to, but cannot fill, the ideal which I early cherished, but did not expect ever publicly to confess. While I heartily sympathize with the progressive movement which will ere long make ecclesiastically true our Master's words, 'There is neither male nor female in Christ Jesus'; while I steadfastly believe that there is no place too good for a woman to occupy, and nothing too sacred for her to do, I am not willing to go on record as a misanthropic complainer against the church which I prefer above my chief joy."

3. Mary Baker Eddy, the Founder of Christian Science, Denies the Reality of Suffering, Sin, and Death, 1887

Perhaps no doctrine of Christian Science rouses so much natural doubt and questioning as this, that God knows no such thing as sin. Indeed, this may be set down as one of the "things hard to be understood," such as the apostle Peter declared were taught by his fellow-apostle Paul, "which they that are unlearned and unstable wrest . . . unto their own destruction." (2 Peter iii. 16.)

Let us then reason together on this important subject, whose statement in Christian Science may justly be characterized as *wonderful.* . . .

The Scriptures declare that God is too pure to behold iniquity (Habakkuk i. 13); but they also declare that God pitieth them who fear Him; that there is no place where His voice is not heard; that He is "a very present help in trouble."

The sinner has no refuge from sin, except in God, who is his salvation. We must, however, realize God's presence, power, and love, in order to be saved from sin. This realization takes away man's fondness for sin and his pleasure in it; and, lastly, it removes the pain which accrues to him from it. Then follows this, as the *finale* in Science: The sinner loses his sense of sin, and gains a higher sense of God, in whom there is no sin.

The true man, really *saved,* is ready to testify of God in the infinite penetration of Truth, and can affirm that the Mind which is good, or God, has no knowledge of sin.

In the same manner the sick lose their sense of sickness, and gain that spiritual sense of harmony which contains neither discord nor disease.

According to this same rule, in divine Science, the dying—if they die in the Lord—awake from a sense of death to a sense of Life in Christ, with a knowledge of Truth and Love beyond what they possessed before; because their lives have grown so far toward the stature of manhood in Christ Jesus, that they are ready for a spiritual transfiguration, through their affections and understanding.

Those who reach this transition, called *death,* without having rightly improved the lessons of this primary school of mortal existence,—and still believe in matter's reality, pleasure, and pain,—are not ready to understand immortality. Hence they awake only to another sphere of experience, and must pass through another probationary state before it can be truly said of them: "Blessed are the dead which die in the Lord." . . .

God is All-in-all. Hence He is in Himself only, in His own nature and character, and is perfect being, or consciousness. He is all the Life and Mind there is or can be. Within Himself is every embodiment of Life and Mind.

Mary Baker Eddy, *Unity of Good* (1887; reprint, Boston: Allison V. Stewart, 1912), 2–8.

If He is All, He can have no consciousness of anything unlike Himself; because, if He is omnipresent, there can be nothing outside of Himself.

Now this self-same God is our helper. He pities us. He has mercy upon us, and guides every event of our careers. He is near to them who adore Him. To understand Him, without a single taint of our mortal, finite sense of sin, sickness, or death, is to approach Him and become like Him. . . .

Let us respect the rights of conscience and the liberty of the sons of God, so letting our "moderation be known to all men." Let no enmity, no untempered controversy, spring up between Christian Science students and Christians who wholly or partially differ from them as to the nature of sin and the marvellous unity of man with God shadowed forth in scientific thought. Rather let the stately goings of this wonderful part of Truth be left to the supernal guidance.

"These are but parts of Thy ways," says Job; and the whole is greater than its parts. Our present understanding is but "the seed within itself," for it is divine Science, "bearing fruit after its kind."

Sooner or later the whole human race will learn that, in proportion as the spotless selfhood of God is understood, human nature will be renovated, and man will receive a higher selfhood, derived from God, and the redemption of mortals from sin, sickness, and death be established on everlasting foundations.

The Science of physical harmony, as now presented to the people in divine light, is radical enough to promote as forcible collisions of thought as the age has strength to bear. Until the heavenly law of health, according to Christian Science, is firmly grounded, even the thinkers are not prepared to answer intelligently leading questions about God and sin, and the world is far from ready to assimilate such a grand and all-absorbing verity concerning the divine nature and character as is embraced in the theory of God's blindness to error and ignorance of sin. No wise mother, though a graduate of Wellesley College, will talk to her babe about the problems of Euclid.

Not much more than a half-century ago the assertion of universal salvation provoked discussion and horror, similar to what our declarations about sin and Deity must arouse, if hastily pushed to the front while the platoons of Christian Science are not yet thoroughly drilled in the plainer manual of their spiritual armament. "Wait patiently on the Lord;" and in less than another fifty years His name will be magnified in the apprehension of this new subject, as already He is glorified in the wide extension of belief in the impartial grace of God,—shown by the changes at Andover Seminary and in multitudes of other religious folds.

Nevertheless, though I thus speak, and from my heart of hearts, it is due both to Christian Science and myself to make also the following statement: When I have most clearly seen and most sensibly felt that the infinite recognizes no disease, this has not separated me from God, but has so bound me to Him as to enable me instantaneously to heal a cancer which had eaten its way to the jugular vein.

In the same spiritual condition I have been able to replace dislocated joints and raise the dying to instantaneous health. People are now living who can bear witness to these cures. Herein is my evidence, from on high, that the views here promulgated on this subject are correct.

Certain self-proved propositions pour into my waiting thought in connection with these experiences; and here is one such conviction: that an acknowledgment of the perfection of the infinite Unseen confers a power nothing else can. An incontestable point in divine Science is, that because God is All, a realization of this fact dispels even the sense or consciousness of sin, and brings us nearer to God, bringing out the highest phenomena of the All-Mind.

4. Swami Vivekananda Describes His Life as a Hindu Celebrity in America, 1893

CHICAGO,
2nd November, 1893.

DEAR ALASINGA,

At a village near Boston, I made the acquaintance of Dr. Wright, Professor of Greek in the Harvard University. He sympathized with me very much and urged upon me the necessity of going to the Parliament of Religions, which he thought would give me an introduction to the nation. As I was not acquainted with anybody, the Professor undertook to arrange everything for me, and eventually I came back to Chicago. Here I, together with the oriental and occidental delegates to the Parliament of Religions, were all lodged in the house of a gentleman.

On the morning of the opening of the Parliament, we all assembled in a building called the Art Palace, where one huge, and other smaller temporary halls were erected for the sittings of the Parliament. Men from all nations were there. From India were Mazoomdar of the Brâhmo Samâj, and Nagarkar of Bombay, Mr. Gandhi representing the Jains, and Mr. Chakravarti representing Theosophy with Mrs. Annie Besant. Of these, Mazoomdar and I were, of course, old friends, and Chakravarti knew me by name. There was a grand procession, and we were all marshalled on to the platform. Imagine a hall below and a huge gallery above, packed with six or seven thousand men and women representing the best culture of the country, and on the platform learned men of all the nations of the earth. And I, who never spoke in public in my life, to address this august assemblage!! It was opened in great form with music and ceremony and speeches; then the delegates were introduced one by one, and they stepped up and spoke. Of course my heart was fluttering and my tongue nearly dried up; I was so nervous and could not venture to speak in the morning. Mazoomdar, made a nice speech. Chakravarti a nicer one, and they were much applauded. They were all prepared and came with readymade speeches. I was a fool and had none, but bowed down to Devi Sarasvati and stepped up, and Dr. Barrows introduced me. I made a short speech. I addressed the assembly as "Sisters and Brothers of America," a deafening applause of two minutes followed, and then I proceeded, and when it was finished, I sat down, almost exhausted with emotion. The next day all the papers announced that my speech was the hit of the day, and I became known to the

Letters of Swami Vivekananda (Calcutta: Advaita Ashrama, 1986), 53–56.

whole of America. Truly has it been said by the great commentator Shridhara—
"Who maketh the dumb a fluent speaker." His name be praised! From that day I
became a celebrity, and the day I read my paper on Hinduism, the hall was
packed as it had never been before. I quote to you from one of the papers:
"Ladies, ladies, ladies packing every place—filling every corner, they patiently
waited and waited while the papers that separated them from Vivekananda were
read," etc. You would be astonished if I sent over to you the newspaper cuttings,
but you already know that I am a hater of celebrity. Suffice it to say, that whenever I went on the platform a deafening applause would be raised for me. Nearly
all the papers paid high tributes to me, and even the most bigoted had to admit
that "This man with his handsome face and magnetic presence and wonderful
oratory is the most prominent figure in the Parliament," etc., etc. Sufficient for
you to know that never before did an Oriental make such an impression on American society.

And how to speak of their kindness? . . .

I am now out of want. Many of the handsomest houses in this city are open to
me. All the time I am living as a guest of somebody or other. There is a curiosity
in this nation, such as you meet with nowhere else. They want to know everything, and their women—they are the most advanced in the world. The average
American woman is far more cultivated than the average American man. The men
slave all their life for money, and the women snatch every opportunity to improve
themselves. And they are a very kind-hearted, frank people. Everybody who has a
fad to preach comes here, and I am sorry to say that most of these are not sound.
The Americans have their faults too, and what nation has not? But this is my sum-
ming up: Asia laid the germs of civilization, Europe developed man, and America
is developing women and the masses. It is the paradise of the woman and the
labourer. Now contrast the American masses and women with ours, and you get
the idea at once. The Americans are fast becoming liberal. Judge them not by
the specimens of *hard-shelled Christians* (it is their own phrase) that you see in
India. There are those here too, but their number is decreasing rapidly, and this
great nation is progressing fast towards that spirituality which is the standard
boast of the Hindu.

The Hindu must not give up his religion, but must keep religion within its
proper limits and give freedom to society to grow. All the reformers in India made
the serious mistake of holding religion accountable for all the horrors of priestcraft
and degeneration, and went forthwith to pull down the indestructible structure, and
what was the result? Failure! Beginning from Buddha down to Ram Mohan Roy,
everyone made the mistake of holding caste to be a religious institution and tried to
pull down religion and caste all together, and failed. But in spite of all the ravings
of the priests, caste is simply a crystallized social institution, which after doing its
service is now filling the atmosphere of India with its stench, and it can only be
removed by giving back to the people their lost social individuality. Every man
born here knows that he is a *man*. Every man born in India knows that he is a slave
of society. Now, freedom is the only condition of growth; take that off, the result is
degeneration. With the introduction of modern competition, see how caste is disap-
pearing fast! No religion is now necessary to kill it. The Brâhmana shopkeeper,

shoemaker, and wine-distiller are common in Northern India. And why? Because of competition. No man is prohibited from doing anything he pleases for his livelihood under the present government, and the result is neck and neck competition, and thus thousands are seeking and finding the highest level they were born for, instead of vegetating at the bottom.

5. Booth Tucker Describes the Salvation Army's Social and Gospel Work in Slums and Saloons, 1900

The mudpools of society possess a peculiar interest for the sociologist, be he humanitarian or statesman. Hunger amounting to positive starvation, destitution that means the actual lack of the most common necessaries of existence, misery that represents a Niagara of tears, intertangled with a ghastly profusion of blasphemy, vermin, vice and crime, constitute a dark background to what would indeed be a loathsome picture, but for the fact that it is illumined with lightning flashes of love, piety and patient endurance, whose existence might least be suspected amid such sad surroundings. Here the dividing line between earth and hell becomes so hard to locate that those who inhabit this sombre shadowland of woe ofttimes feel and seem as though they had already passed from the one to the other.

Into this desolate region the Salvation army flung itself, nay from its very vortex of misery it may be said to have originated. The international developments and multitudinous outgrowths of the movement were represented at its inception by two solitary individuals, whom Providence had first linked together, and then plunged into the midst of this maelstrom of sin and sorrow. Singlehanded, unsupported by material resources of any kind, William and Catherine Booth planted the standard of salvation as near the gates of hell as they could reach.

It was in July, 1865, on Mile End Waste, in the east end of London, amid vice, degradation and squalor probably without parallel in any corner of the globe, that they commenced their work of spiritual and social reform.

They adapted their methods to the savage hordes of semi-barbarians to whom they had consecrated their lives. Their first citadels were planted in the heart of sindom and slumdom. Over the doorway of one of these was written the strange inscription: "No respectable people admitted." The sinners they were after gloried in their savagery. Their Bible was the "penny dreadful," their place of worship the saloon, their god their unbridled appetites, their prayer hideous blasphemy. No church-door was ever darkened with their shadow. They were neither expected, nor wanted. The sight of their unkempt condition would have driven away the usual worshippers.

But the dime museums and "penny gaffs," which these misfits of humanity had been accustomed to frequent, were pressed into service by this Prophet of the poor. They were quickly crowded to the doors with the rowdy element he sought to

Commander Booth Tucker, *The Social Relief Work of the Salvation Army in the United States* (Albany, NY: J. B. Lyon, 1900). Reprinted in *The Salvation Army in America: Selected Reports, 1899–1903* (New York: Arno Press, 1972), 3, 6, 18–20.

reach. Amongst the earliest converts were prize-fighters, pigeon-flyers, gamblers, drunkards, criminals, many of them notorious for their wickedness. . . .

As its name signifies, the Salvation army was originally started with the sole aim of reaching the non-church-going masses with the Gospel. Here was the appalling statement made by those who had given the matter years of patient study, that 90% of the working classes in the older civilizations of Europe habitually neglected public worship and had practically cut themselves loose from even the outward profession of religion. It was to remedy this condition of affairs that William and Catherine Booth set to work.

As evangelists they could crowd the largest buildings with the vast crowds who flocked to their meetings. Their converts were numbered by thousands. Yet they could not fail to notice and mourn over the fact that those who came were mostly church-goers and professors of religion. The godless multitudes drifted past their doors. To reach them, other methods must be pursued. Their habits must be studied and they must be followed to their haunts and hiding-places.

When, however, this had been done, it became daily more and more evident that the evils to be combated were of a temporal as well as of a spiritual character. Churchlessness was with these classes the natural outcome of homelessness, worklessness and worthlessness. To combat the evil, its causes must be radically dealt with. The task was truly a gigantic one. But General Booth was not the man to shrink from it. Cautiously and experimentally at first, and finally with the confidence that was the natural outcome of repeated success, he grappled with the problem.

In traversing and transforming these melancholy wastes of woe, root principles were discovered and laid down for the guidance of the legion of well-trained workers who had been rapidly enrolled.

The poor were to be treated with love, and not with suspicion or contempt.

They were to be classified, not as the worthy and unworthy, but as those who were willing to work out their own regeneration, and the unwilling.

They were to be encouraged in every possible way to become their own deliverers.

Each institution was to aim at self-support by the labor or payments of its inmates.

Social reform to be complete must include the soul as well as the body. In other words the man himself must be changed and not merely his circumstances.

To save a man for this world should be but a stepping-stone toward saving him for the next. . . .

Who has not heard of "Hell's Kitchen," "The Bowery," "The Tenderloin," or "Cherry street?" The very names have become world-famous, as synonyms for debauchery, slumdom and crime. In the very heart of these citadels of sin the Salvation army has planted its outposts. The girl-warriors who have dared to storm these "forts of darkness" have done so in the first instance at the risk of their lives. Pelted with refuse, treated with ignomiy, threatened with violence, they have persisted in their noble work, till a permanent footing has been gained.

Now, how different is their position. They are known by the name of "slum angels." At any hour of the day or night they can walk down streets or alleys where the police will only pass in twos. If a fight is going on, they will make straight for the center of the crowd, as the recognized peacemakers of the poor, and woe betide the man who lays a finger upon them. The worst dives and saloons are open to their ministrations.

"There are only two saloons," says the officer in charge of our Chicago slum-work, "where our girls are not admitted, and these two are visited by them regularly every week. When the boss says, 'Did I not tell you not to come here any more?' the captain replies, 'Yes, sir! But I have come to see whether you have changed your mind!'"

In the city of Cleveland one of the most notorious saloon-keepers and criminals was converted and has stood faithful for some years past. When his saloon was first visited by our women officers, he poured a schooner of beer down their backs as they knelt to pray! This man was popularly known as "The Ferret." His picture hangs in the Rogues' gallery of the United States, but the face has been turned to the wall, since the police are well aware that Fred Ford is converted and is earning an honest living.

Our slum officers live in the heart of slumdom, and minister day and night to the sick and suffering. In order to make themselves more one with the people they have adopted an even simpler and humbler garb than that worn by our ordinary officers. A poke bonnet would appear too respectable, and even extravagant, to those whose lives are spent in one long desperate struggle with poverty.

In New York alone we have 20 slum officers entirely set apart for work of this character, while other slum posts have been opened in Boston, Chicago, Philadelphia, Providence, Cincinnati, Cleveland and St Louis.

Not the least important feature of the slum officer's work is her nightly meeting. Gathered together in her hall is an intensely interesting collection of the toughest characters in the city. With wonderful skill and patience she handles them. Strange to say, although the meetings are of a strictly religious character, they possess for these wastrels of society a peculiar fascination. The greatest punishment that can be inflicted for a serious breach of discipline is exclusion from the meetings for a time. To see the girl captain march off a disturber of the peace, maintain order and go on with the meeting, as if nothing particular had happened, is in itself a marvel of spiritual conquest and control.

These Jeanne d'Arcs of the slums are filled with a sense of their divine mission and are accepted by their rough hearers as the modern apostles of "Poverty Row."

It was found by our slum officers in the course of their visitations that in many families where the mother was the breadwinner, she would go forth in the morning, locking the door on her babe, till she returned home in the evening. What else could she do? It was impossible for her to take the baby with her to her work.

Hence a slum creche soon became a necessary adjunct to this portion of our work. The mother brings her baby in the morning, leaves it for the day, and fetches it away in the evening. Wonderful reformations have thus been wrought in the way of cleanliness and health, as well as moral surroundings.

The little ones learn to sing the army songs and carry back to their miserable garrets an atmosphere of joy and brightness which has hitherto been unknown. A small charge of five cents is made to cover the cost of milk and food.

Occasionally the mother, who called in the morning, appears no more to claim the child, and then it becomes necessary to find some permanent home. But kind friends seldom fail to return a ready response to our appeal.

6. Abraham Cahan Shows How American Business Life and Religious Pluralism Shattered a Russian Jewish Immigrant's Traditional Faith, 1916

The great emigration of Jews to the United States, which had received its first impulse two or three years before, was already in full swing. It may not be out of order to relate, briefly, how it had all come about.

An anti-Semitic riot broke out in a southern town named Elisabethgrad in the early spring of 1881. Occurrences of this kind were, in those days, quite rare in Russia, and when they did happen they did not extend beyond the town of their origin. But the circumstances that surrounded the Elisabethgrad outbreak were of a specific character. It took place one month after the assassination of the Czar, Alexander II. The actual size and influence of the "underground" revolutionary organization being an unknown quantity, St. Petersburg was full of the rumblings of a general uprising. The Elisabethgrad riot, however, was not of a revolutionary nature. Yet the police, so far from suppressing it, encouraged it. The example of the Elisabethgrad rabble was followed by the riffraff of other places. The epidemic quickly spread from city to city. Whereupon the scenes of lawlessness in the various cities were marked by the same method in the mob's madness, by the same connivance on the part of the police, and by many other traits that clearly pointed to a common source of inspiration. It has long since become a well-established historical fact that the anti-Jewish disturbances were encouraged, even arranged, by the authorities as an outlet for the growing popular discontent with the Government.

Count von Plehve was then at the head of the Police Department in the Ministry of the Interior.

This bit of history repeated itself, on a larger scale, twenty-two years later, when Russia was in the paroxysm of a real revolution and when the ghastly massacres of Jews in Kishineff, Odessa, Kieff, and other cities were among the means employed in an effort to keep the masses "busy."

Count von Plehve then held the office of Prime Minister.

To return to 1881 and 1882. Thousands of Jewish families were left homeless. Of still greater moment was the moral effect which the atrocities produced on the whole Jewish population of Russia. Over five million people were suddenly made to realize that their birthplace was not their home. . . . Then it was that the cry "To

Abraham Cahan, *The Rise of David Levinsky* (1917; reprint, New York: Harper Colophon, 1966), 110–111.

America!" was raised. It spread like wild-fire, even over those parts of the Pale of Jewish Settlement which lay outside the riot zone.

This was the beginning of the great New Exodus that has been in progress for decades.

My native town and the entire section to which it belongs had been immune from the riots, yet it caught the general contagion, and at the time I became one of Shiphrah's wards hundreds of its inhabitants were going to America or planning to do so. Letters full of wonders from emigrants already there went the rounds of eager readers and listeners until they were worn to shreds in the process.

I succumbed to the spreading fever. It was one of these letters from America, in fact, which put the notion of emigrating to the New World definitely in my mind. An illiterate woman brought it to the synagogue to have it read to her, and I happened to be the one to whom she addressed her request. The concrete details of that letter gave New York tangible form in my imagination. It haunted me ever after.

The United States lured me not merely as a land of milk and honey, but also, and perhaps chiefly, as one of mystery, of fantastic experiences, of marvelous transformations. To leave my native place and to seek my fortune in that distant, weird world seemed to be just the kind of sensational adventure my heart was hankering for.

When I unburdened myself of my project to Reb Sender he was thunderstruck.

"To America!" he said. "Lord of the World! But one becomes a Gentile there."

"Not at all," I sought to reassure him. "There are lots of good Jews there, and they don't neglect their Talmud, either." . . .

[Later, from New York] I wrote long, passionate letters to Reb Sender, in a conglomeration of the Talmudic jargon, bad Hebrew, and good Yiddish, referring to the Talmud studies I pursued in America and pouring out my forlorn heart to him. His affectionate answers brought me inexpressible happiness.

But many of the other peddlers made fun of my piety and it could not last long. Moreover, I was in contact with life now, and the daily surprises it had in store for me dealt my former ideas of the world blow after blow. I saw the cunning and the meanness of some of my customers, of the tradespeople of whom I bought my wares, and of the peddlers who did business by my side. Nor was I unaware of certain unlovable traits that were unavoidably developing in my own self under these influences. And while human nature was thus growing smaller, the human world as a whole was growing larger, more complex, more heartless, and more interesting. The striking thing was that it was not a world of piety. I spoke to scores of people and I saw tens of thousands. Very few of the women who passed my push-cart wore wigs, and men who did not shave were an exception. Also, I knew that many of the people with whom I came in daily contact openly patronized Gentile restaurants and would not hesitate even to eat pork.

The orthodox Jewish faith, as it is followed in the old Ghetto towns of Russia or Austria, has still to learn the art of trimming its sails to suit new winds. It is exactly the same as it was a thousand years ago. It does not attempt to adapt itself to modern conditions as the Christian Church is continually doing. It is absolutely inflexible. If you are a Jew of the type to which I belonged when I came to New York and you attempt to bend your religion to the spirit of your new surroundings, it breaks. It falls to pieces. The very clothes I wore and the very food I ate had a fatal effect on my religious habits. A whole book could be written on the influence of a starched collar and a necktie on a man who was brought up as I was. It was inevitable that, sooner or later, I should let a barber shave my sprouting beard.

7. Anzia Yezierska Confronts an Orthodox Jewish Father over Changing Patterns of Religion and Women's Work, 1925

When we came to America, instead of taking along feather beds, and the samovar, and the brass pots and pans, like other people, Father made us carry his books. When Mother begged only to take along her pot for *gefülte* fish, and two feather beds that were handed down from her grandmother for her wedding presents, Father wouldn't let her.

"Woman!" Father said, laughing into her eyes. "What for will you need old feather beds? Don't you know it's always summer in America? And in the new golden country, where milk and honey flows free in the streets, you'll have new golden dishes to cook in, and not weigh yourself down with your old pots and pans. But my books, my holy books always were, and always will be, the light of the world. You'll see yet how all America will come to my feet to learn."

No one was allowed to put their things in Father's room, any more than they were allowed to use Mashah's hanger.

Of course, we all knew that if God had given Mother a son, Father would have permitted a man child to share with him his best room in the house. A boy could say prayers after his father's death—that kept the father's soul alive for ever. Always Father was throwing up to Mother that she had borne him no son to be an honour to his days and to say prayers for him when he died.

The prayers of his daughters didn't count because God didn't listen to women. Heaven and the next world were only for men. Women could get into Heaven because they were wives and daughters of men. Women had no brains for the study of God's Torah, but they could be the servants of men who studied the Torah. Only if they cooked for the men, and washed for the men, and didn't nag or curse the men out of their homes; only if they let the men study the Torah in peace, then, maybe, they could push themselves into Heaven with the men, to wait on them there.

And so, since men were the only people who counted with God, Father not only had the best room for himself, for his study and prayers, but also the best eating of the house. The fat from the soup and the top from the milk went always to him.

Mother had just put the soup pot and plates for dinner on the table, when Father came in.

At the first look on Mother's face he saw how she was boiling, ready to burst, so instead of waiting for her to begin her hollering, he started:

"Woman! when will you stop darkening the house with your worries?"

"When I'll have a man who does the worrying. Does it ever enter your head that the rent was not paid the second month? That to-day we're eating the last loaf of

Anzia Yezierska, excerpt from *Bread Givers* (1925; reprint, New York: Persea Books, 1975).

bread that the grocer trusted me?" Mother tried to squeeze the hard, stale loaf that nobody would buy for cash. "You're so busy working for Heaven that I have to suffer here such bitter hell."

We sat down to the table. With watering mouths and glistening eyes we watched Mother skimming every bit of fat from the top soup into Father's big plate, leaving for us only the thin, watery part. We watched Father bite into the sour pickle which was special for him only; and waited, trembling with hunger, for our portion.

Father made his prayer, thanking God for the food. Then he said to Mother:

"What is there to worry about, as long as we have enough to keep the breath in our bodies? But the real food is God's Holy Torah." He shook her gently by the shoulder, and smiled down at her.

At Father's touch Mother's sad face turned into smiles. His kind look was like the sun shining on her.

"Shenah!" he called her by her first name, to show her he was feeling good. "I'll tell you a story that will cure you of all your worldly cares."

All faces turned to Father. Eyes widened, necks stretched, ears strained not to miss a word. The meal was forgotten as he began:

"Rabbi Chanina Ben Dosa was a starving, poor man who had to live on next to nothing. Once, his wife complained: 'We're so good, so pious, you give up nights and days in the study of the Holy Torah. Then why don't God provide for you at least enough to eat?' . . . 'Riches you want!' said Rabbi Chanina Ben Dosa. 'All right, woman. You shall have your wish.' . . . That very evening he went out into the fields to pray. Soon the heavens opened, and a Hand reached down to him and gave him a big chunk of gold. He brought it to his wife and said: 'Go buy with this all the luxuries of the earth.' . . . She was so happy, as she began planning all she would buy next day. Then she fell asleep. And in her dream, she saw herself and her husband sitting with all the saints in Heaven. Each couple had a golden table between themselves. When the Good Angel put down for them their wine, their table shook so that half of it was spilled. Then she noticed that their table had a leg missing, and this is why it was so shaky. And the Good Angel explained to her that the chunk of gold that her husband had given her the night before was the missing leg of their table. As soon as she woke up, she begged her husband to pray to God to take back the gold he had given them. . . . 'I'll be happy and thankful to live in poverty, as long as I know that our reward will be complete in Heaven.' "

Mother licked up Father's every little word, like honey. Her eyes followed his shining eyes as he talked.

"Nu, Shenah?" He wagged his head. "Do you want gold on earth, or wine of Heaven?"

"I'm only a sinful woman," Mother breathed, gazing up at him. Her fingers stole a touch of his hand, as if he were the king of the world. "God be praised for the little we have. I'm willing to give up all my earthly needs for the wine in Heaven with you. But, *Moisheh*"—she nudged him by the sleeve—"God gave us children. They have a life to live yet, here, on earth. Girls have to get married. People point their fingers on me—a daughter, twenty-five years already, and not married yet. And no dowry to help her get married."

"Woman! Stay in your place!" His strong hand pushed her away from him. "You're smart enough to bargain with the fish-peddler. But I'm the head of this family. I give my daughters brains enough to marry when their time comes, without the worries of a dowry."

"*Nu,* you're the head of the family." Mother's voice rose in anger. "But what will you do if your books are thrown in the street?"

At the mention of his books, Father looked up quickly.

"What do you want me to do?"

"Take your things out from the front room to the kitchen, so I could rent your room to boarders. If we don't pay up the rent very soon, we'll all be in the street."

"I have to have a room for my books. Where will I put them?"

"I'll push my things out from under the bed. And you can pile up your books in the window to the top, because nothing but darkness comes through that window anyway. I'll do anything, work the nails off my fingers, only to be free from the worry for rent."

"But where will I have quiet for my studies in this crowded kitchen? I have to be alone in a room to think with God."

"Only millionaires can be alone in America. By Zalmon the fish-peddler, they're squeezed together, twelve people, in one kitchen. The bedroom and the front room his wife rents out to boarders. If I could cook their suppers for them, I could even earn yet a few cents from their eating."

"Woman! Have your way. Take in your boarders, only to have peace in this house." . . .

[The next day] from the kitchen came Father's voice chanting:

"When the poor seek water, and there is none, and their tongue faileth for thirst, I, the Lord, will hear them. I, the God of Israel, will not forsake them."

Mother put her hand over Muhmenkeh's mouth to stop her talking. Silent, breathless, we peeked in through the open crack in the door. The black satin skull-cap tipped on the side of his head set off his red hair and his long red beard. And his ragged satin coat from Europe made him look as if he just stepped out of the Bible. His eyes were raised to God. His two white hands on either side of the book, his whole body swaying with his song:

"And I will bring the blind by a way that they know not; I will lead them in paths that they have not known; I will make darkness light before them, and crooked things straight. These are things I will do unto them and not forsake them."

Mother's face lost all earthly worries. Forgotten were beds, mattresses, boarders, and dowries. Father's holiness filled her eyes with light.

"Is there any music on earth like this?" Mother whispered to Muhmenkeh.

"Who would ever dream that in America, where everything is only business and business, in such a lost corner as Hester Street lives such a fine, such a pure, silken soul as Reb Smolinsky?"

"If he was only so fit for this world, like he is fit for Heaven, then I wouldn't have to dry out the marrow from my head worrying for the rent."

His voice flowed into us deeper and deeper. We couldn't help ourselves. We were singing with him:

"Sing, O heavens; and be joyful, O earth; and break forth into singing, O mountains; for the Lord hath comforted his people."

Suddenly, it grew dark before our eyes. The collector lady from the landlord! We did not hear her till she banged open the door. Her hard eyes glared at Father.

"My rent!" she cried, waving her thick diamond fingers before Father's face. But he didn't see her or hear her. He went on chanting:

"*Awake! Awake! Put on strength, O arm of the Lord: Awake, as in ancient days, in the generations of old. Art thou not he that hath cut Rahab and wounded the dragon?*"

"*Schnorrer!*" shrieked the landlady, her fat face red with rage. "My rent!"

Father blinked his eyes and stared at the woman with a far-off look. "What is it? What do you want?"

"Don't you know me? Haven't I come often enough? My rent! My rent! My rent I want!"

"Oh-h, your rent?" Father met her angry glare with an innocent smile of surprise. "Your rent? As soon as the girls get work, we'll pay you out, little by little."

"Pay me out, little by little! The cheek of those dirty immigrants! A fool I was, giving them a chance another month."

"But we haven't the money." His voice was kind and gentle, as hers was rough and loud.

"Why haven't you the money for rent?" she shouted.

"The girls have been out of work." Father's innocent look was not of this earth.

"Hear him only! The dirty do-nothing! Go to work yourself! Stop singing prayers. Then you'll have money for rent!" She took one step towards him and shut his book with such anger that it fell at her feet.

Little red threads burned out of Father's eyes. He rose slowly, but quicker than lightning flashed his hand.

A scream broke through the air. Before we had breath enough to stop him, Father slapped the landlady on one cheek, then on the other, till the blood rushed from her nose.

"You painted piece of flesh!" cried Father. "I'll teach you respect for the Holy Torah!"

Screaming, the landlady rushed out, her face dripping blood as she ran. Before we knew what or where, she came back with two policemen. In front of our dumb eyes we saw Father handcuffed, like a thief, and taken away to the station house.

✎ *E S S A Y S*

Religious historians have always found it difficult to gain insight into the minds of people involved in religious practices and rituals. Robert Orsi of Indiana University has pioneered the use of anthropological techniques in an attempt to solve the problem. In his book *The Madonna of 115th Street* (1985), already a classic, from which the following passage is taken, he recreates the lost world of Italian Harlem in the first decades of the twentieth century and "reads" the rituals of the annual *festa*, when the statue of the Virgin Mary was paraded through the streets and the inhabitants prayed, feasted, processed, and sacrificed to their patroness. He investigates each of the rituals, including such seemingly grotesque actions as tongue-dragging along the church floor, linking them to the people's Italian rural traditions and their abrupt transition to the densely populated urban world of New York. In Orsi's work, description is followed by analysis of what these rituals meant to the participants and he draws extensively on interviews with elderly survivors from early-twentieth-century festivals.

Lillian Taiz, like Orsi, is a social historian interested in recovering the religious lives of ordinary people even if they left few written records. Her study of the Salvation Army in American cities led her to realize that it deliberately sought out sinners in the places most churches regarded as enemy terrain: the saloons, cheap theaters, and vaudeville houses. Its leaders had the psychological acuity to see that working people had fun in these "dens of vice." Borrowing the musical styles and the bright, vulgar, and sentimental habits of its target audience, the Salvation Army scored surprising successes in converting urban workers and slum dwellers to Christianity.

An Italian-American Street Festival to Honor the Virgin Mary

ROBERT ORSI

Shortly after midnight on July 16, the great bell high in the campanile of the church of Our Lady of Mount Carmel on 115th Street announced to East Harlem that the day of the festa had begun. It was a solemn moment; the voice of the bell seemed more vibrant and sonorous on this night. The sound touched every home in Italian Harlem. It greeted the devout already arriving from the other boroughs and from Italian communities in Connecticut, New Jersey, Pennsylvania, and even California. The sound filled Jefferson Park, where pilgrims who were not fortunate enough to have *compari* or family in East Harlem were camping out. In the church, the round of masses had begun and would continue until the following midnight, each mass expressing either gratitude for a grace bestowed or a plea for comfort and assistance. Italian Harlem was ready and excited. . . .

The Italians of East Harlem had been preparing for the festa for weeks. They had a special responsibility to host friends and relatives who came from out of town. The homes of Italian Harlem had been scrubbed clean, the windows had been washed and the floor polished. Residents had bought and cooked special foods in anticipation of the arrival of their guests. One participant described the scene in the homes like this:

> I remember my father, every year, people came from Paterson, New Jersey, there was a group of these people from our *paese* who lived there, they would come every time, they would sleep in our house, and eat and drink for four days, five days, going on. And everybody in the neighborhood had to clean their house that week, the week before, new curtains, and everything; it was the feast of Mount Carmel.

The time of the festa was long and undefined. Some people say it lasted two or three days, other say a week, even two weeks. It was a celebration that knew no time. As one participant expressed this, "It started July 16th and went on for about a week. . . . These things went on and on, for hours and hours."

Italian Harlem slept little during the days of the festa. Children played with their cousins from New Haven and Boston and then fell asleep in the laps of the adults, who stayed up all night talking and eating. People went out into the crowded

Robert Orsi, "The Days and Nights of the Festa," in *The Madonna of 115th Street: Faith and Community in Italian Harlem* (Yale University Press, 1985), 1–13.

streets at two or three in the morning to go to confession or to attend a special mass at the church that had been offered to *la Madonna* for the health of their mother or in the hope of finding a job. When they returned, there was more eating and talking and visiting.

Then sometime in the early afternoon of July 16, people would begin walking over to the church. They were dressed in their finest clothes, particularly the children, whose new outfits their families had bought at considerable sacrifice but also with the fierce determination that the family should make *bella figura* in the community and show proper *rispetto* for the Virgin on her feast day. . . .

Italian popular faith in both Italy and America sought the streets to express itself, and the street life of the festa was dense. Men stood in groups in front of storefront regional social clubs, getting ready to march in the procession, proud of their regional identification and secure in the company of their fellows. Boys from the different neighborhoods within East Harlem went to the church in groups. . . .

Vendors of religious articles set up booths along the sidewalks, competing for business with the thriving local trade in religious goods. The booths were filled with wax replicas of internal human organs and with models of human limbs and heads. Someone who had been healed—or hoped to be healed—by the Madonna of headaches or arthritis would carry wax models of the afflicted limbs or head, painted to make them look realistic, in the big procession. The devout could also buy little wax statues of infants. Charms to ward off the evil eye, such as little horns to wear around the neck and little red hunchbacks, were sold alongside the holy cards, statues of Jesus, Mary, and the saints, and the wax body parts.

The most sought-after items were the big and enormously heavy candles that the faithful bought, carried all through the blistering July procession, and then donated to the church. . . . The weights of the candles chosen by the people corresponded to the seriousness of the grace they were asking, and this was carefully specified in the vows made to the Madonna. A bad problem or a great hope required an especially heavy candle and weights could reach fifty or sixty pounds or more. . . .

The most characteristic sensuous facts of the Mount Carmel festa were the smell and taste of food. In the homes, in the streets, and in the restaurants, the festa of Our Lady of Mount Carmel had a taste. Big meals, *pranzi,* were cooked in the homes, and after the festa, family, friends, and neighbors would gather for long and boisterous meals. . . . Beer and wine were drunk, to the horror of those who came from New York's better neighborhoods to watch the lower classes at play.

The crowds slowly made their way to the Church of Our Lady of Mount Carmel on 115th Street between First and Pleasant avenues. The front of the church was decorated with colored lights that traced the outline of the facade and spelled out "Nostra Signora del Monte Carmelo." It was on the steps of the church that the intensity and diversity of the day were at their extreme. Penitents crawled up the steps on their hands and knees, some of them dragging their tongues along the stone. Thousands of people were jammed onto 115th Street in front of the church in the crushing July heat and humidity. Nuns and volunteers from the parish moved through the crowd to help those who succumbed. Many of the pilgrims stood barefoot on the scalding pavement; many had walked barefoot to the shrine through the night from the Bronx and Brooklyn—a barefoot and wearying trek through the long hours of the morning. They took off their shoes as an act of penance, as a demonstration of rispetto for the Virgin, and because they considered the place holy. The crowd had been gathering since midnight, and as the time of the procession neared—la Madonna would soon leave the church and come out among her people—the excitement sizzled like the heat.

There were outsiders in the crowd in front of the church. Irish and German Catholics, who dominated the neighborhood in the early days of the festa and still maintained a presence in East Harlem during the years of Italian ascendency, came to watch. . . . Irish police kept the peace.

In the afternoon, after the solemn high mass, parish and neighborhood societies began to take their places in front of the church in preparation for the procession. The members of the Congregation of Mount Carmel were there, together with the women of the Altar Sodality and the girls of the Children of Mary. . . . [A] large statue of the Madonna —not the one from the high altar, which left the church only on very special occasions, but a second statue—was mounted on a float which had been decorated with flowers and white ribbons. An honor guard of little girls and young unmarried women clothed in white surrounded the Madonna. Dressed in their best suits or, later in the history of the devotion, in rented tuxedos, the young men from the Holy Name society who would be pulling the float through the streets of East Harlem—a task that was viewed as a great honor and privilege— lined up in front of the Madonna. When everyone was in place, the banner of the Congregazione del Monte Carmelo was carried out by male members of the congregation. Then, at a signal from the priests and with an explosion of music and fireworks, the procession began.

The great Mount Carmel parade, with thousands of marchers, several bands, trailing incense and the haunting sounds of southern Italian religious chanting, made its way up and down every block in the "Italian quarter" of Harlem. . . .

As la Madonna slowly made her way through the streets of East Harlem, the devout standing on the sidewalks in front of their tenements kicked off their shoes and joined the procession. Fireworks that had been strung along the trolley tracks were lit as la Madonna approached, making a carpet of noise and smoke for her. In the days before the community was powerful enough to make arrangements, the procession was forced to stop while the trolley cars rumbled past. Above the procession, as it moved down Third Avenue, the thunder of the elevated train drowned out the music. Pushcart vendors saluted as the Madonna was carried past the great outdoor Italian market on First Avenue. Women and girls shouted entreaties over the heads of the crowd to their patroness; others cried aloud, arms outstretched, fingers spread. Noise, smoke, people shoving to get closer, the city's public transportation bearing down on them, children lighting firecrackers—all this, and men and women were still able to kneel on the gritty sidewalk as the statue or banner passed and, pulling a shawl of silence and respect around themselves, bow to la Madonna.

From time to time la Madonna was forced to stop in the street by her faithful. Lapolla tells of one woman who threw herself at the base of the "wandering shrine" to beg help for her family. Before the community, she identified her need, described the details of the situation that had brought her to the feet of la Madonna, and made her request. Others pushed their way through the crowd, or pushed their children through the crowd, to pin money onto the banner. In front of the image was a small box into which people threw money and jewelry. The contributions of the faithful on the day of the festa, even in the days of poverty, were considerable; it was this money that permitted the frequent beautification of the church.

At the very rear of the procession walked the penitents. All of them walked barefoot; some crawled along on their hands and knees; many had been walking all night. . . . Women bore huge and very heavy altars of candles arranged in tiered circles . . . and balanced on their heads with the poise that had enabled them and their mothers to carry jugs of water and loaves of bread on their heads in southern Italy. Sometimes white ribbons extended out from the tiered candles and were held by little girls in white communion outfits. Some of the people in the rear had disheveled hair and bloodied faces, and women of all ages walked with their hair undone. Some people wore special robes—white robes with a blue sash like Mary's or Franciscan-style brown robes knotted at the waist with a cord; they had promised to wear these robes during the procession, though some had promised to wear their *abitini* for several months, or even a year. Although the rear of the procession was the area designated for these practices, a penitential motif characterized the entire procession and, indeed, the entire day.

This behavior was governed by the vows people made to la Madonna. The seriousness with which these promises were made and kept simply cannot be overemphasized. All my East Harlem sources told me, matter-of-factly, that people did all this, that they came to East Harlem—and kept coming even when Italians grew frightened of Spanish Harlem and knew that the neighborhood was no longer theirs—because they made a vow. One of my sources described the promise like this:

> You see, these elderly women would make a vow, you know, they would pray for something, say, if I ever get what I'm praying for . . . you know, a son was sick or someone had died [at this point, another former East Harlem resident interjected, "Like some kind of a penance"], and they would make a vow . . . they'd say, maybe for five Mount Carmels we would march with the procession without shoes. In other words, do some sort of a penance to repay for the good that they'd gotten.

In later years, as the older generation passed away or became too sick to come to the festa, their children came and kept their promises for them.

When the tour of Italian Harlem was over, the procession returned to the doors of the church, where la Madonna was greeted with a round of fireworks and, in the earlier days, gunshot. Then the people lined up to wait for hours for their turn to enter the sanctuary and present their petitions or express their gratitude to their protectress, who waited for them on her throne on the altar of the downstairs church until 1923 and then in splendor on the main altar of the newly built sanctuary. Around her, hundreds of candles blazed and, until the late 1930s, the altar was piled high with wax body parts melting in the heat.

The people had come to be healed. The mood in the sanctuary was tense and charged, the crowd dense but quiet, the heat overpowering. Frequently the pilgrims broke spontaneously into hymns and prayers in the Virgin's honor. One man who witnessed this moment of the festa in 1939 wrote that the people were weeping when they came to the altar and they spoke "with incomprehensible words and deep sighs." Others laughed at the altar in joyful and uncontrollable gratitude for a grace received. The lame were carried in and the old were helped to the front. Men and women lit vigil lights for the intentions of their family and friends, in the United States and in Italy.

When, after the long wait outside and then the difficult passage to the altar, the pilgrims, predominantly women, were able to push through to la Madonna's throne, they lay at her feet the burdens they had been carrying during the procession. They gave the heavy candles and the body parts to the priests and nuns waiting at the altar; they also gave gifts of money and gold. . . .

Occasionally the following scene would be enacted. A woman . . . would begin crawling on her hands and knees from the back of the church toward the main altar, dragging her tongue along the pavement as she went. If she got tired or was unable to bend over far enough to lick the floor, members of her family would come and carry her along. The clergy discouraged this practice, and it seems to have disappeared for the most part by the 1920s. . . .

. . . [V]olunteers also accepted the small bundles of clothing thrust over the altar rail by women. In the earliest years of the devotion, it was customary for a woman who had had a child healed by the Madonna to bring that child to the festa dressed in the best clothes she could afford, often straining family resources to buy a new outfit especially for the occasion. Sometime during the day, the woman would find a private place in the church and change the child into more ordinary clothes, which she had carried along with her. Then she would make her way to the altar and offer the new clothes as a gesture of gratitude to the Madonna and an offering to be distributed to the poor of the parish.

The pilgrims had only a moment at the altar because others were pushing behind them. From the priests on the altar they received a scapular, which they valued as protection from all harm. They paused for a brief moment to say a prayer to la Madonna, and then they made their way back outside. The line waiting in the July night stretched down 115th Street to First Avenue, where it went along for blocks. . . .

At the heart of this joy and longing was the figure of la Madonna del Carmine. The statue that still stands high above the main altar is a lifelike representation of a young Mediterranean woman holding a small child. The Madonna's first gown, which she wore until her coronation in 1904, was decorated with rings, watches, earrings, and chains, all given to her by men and women who believed she had helped them in a moment of terrible difficulty or pain; and her statue, until it was moved into the upper church, was surrounded by canes, crutches, braces, and wax body parts left there as signs of their gratitude by people she had healed.

The Salvation Army Adapts Popular Culture in Spreading Its Gospel

LILLIAN TAIZ

Forty-eight hours after they landed in New York City in 1880, a small contingent of the Salvation Army held their first public meeting at the infamous Harry Hill's Variety Theater. The enterprising Hill, alerted to the group's arrival from Britain by newspaper reports, contacted their leader, Commissioner George Scott Railton, and offered to pay the group to "do a turn" for "an hour or two on . . . Sunday evening."

Lillian Taiz, "Applying the Devil's Work in a Holy Cause," *Religion and American Culture* 7 (Summer 1997): 195–223. © 1997 by the Center for the Study of Religion and Popular Culture.

In nineteenth-century New York City, Harry Hill's was one of the best known concert saloons, and reformers considered him "among the disreputable classes" of that city. His saloon, they said, was "nothing more than one of the many gates to hell."

In his advertising for Sunday's performance, Hill announced that "the Salvation Army will attract [attack?] the Kingdom of the Devil in Harry Hill's Variety Theater on Sunday, March 14, 1880, commencing at 6:30 p.m. sharp, after which the panorama of 'Uncle Tom's Cabin.' Admission 25c." Commissioner Railton was somewhat troubled by the fact that his little group would be "tak[ing] part in a Sunday entertainment for the people for which admission money was charged," and local friends had warned him that respectable people would reject the Army if they went "to such a den to begin with." He confessed, however, to feeling "a savage satisfaction in having this notorious sinner open his door to us before any church did so." That Sunday, Railton and the seven Salvation Army Lasses who made up the group climbed onto Harry Hill's stage, formed a semicircle (in minstrel show style), and then, with Railton kneeling and the Lasses surrounding him in "various and curious positions" (reminiscent of a tableau vivant), proceeded to sing hymns (including one to the tune of "Rosalie, the Prairie Flower"), exhort the audience, recite "obviously memorized" testimonies, and pray. While unanimously rejecting the invitation to repent, the audience reportedly applauded the effort, perhaps entertained by the Salvationists' use of the minstrel show idiom and music hall venue for religious ends.

Fifteen years before Railton and the Salvation Seven made their debut at Harry Hill's Variety Theater in New York City, William and Catherine Booth had organized what would eventually become the Salvation Army in Britain. During the 1870's, the group had evolved from a loosely organized extradenominational urban home mission known as the East London Christian Mission to a somewhat more structured revivalistic movement. In 1878, the organization adopted military symbolism and discipline and renamed itself the Salvation Army. . . .

In the late nineteenth century, when the Salvation Army entered the crowded American religious marketplace, it attracted its primarily working-class members by providing new ways for them to experience and express religiosity. When the eight Salvation Army officers ascended the music hall stage to sing, pray, and strike curious poses before an audience of sinners, they put working-class forms of popular culture in service to evangelical religion. Throughout the late nineteenth century, the Salvation Army in the United States would hold raucous indoor and open-air meetings at which both men and women worshiped God with their bodies as well as their souls. To the alarm of mainstream Christian society, Salvationists combined the culture of the saloon and music hall with a camp-meeting style and took it into the streets, where it successfully marketed itself and its religion to working-class men and women in America.

The Salvation Army emerged in an era of heightened concern about the religious life of the urban working class. In the United States, middle-class Protestants fretted that "[t]he faith on which the nation was founded . . . has almost no place among the working-class." The Salvation Army was one of a growing number of . . . movements established in the late nineteenth century in order to bring the gospel to the "heathen masses." The growth of these movements suggests that middle-class churches failed to offer the kind of religious experience desired by many working-class people. . . .

... [The] Salvation Army developed a relatively unique approach to working-class irreligion: working-class Army converts used working-class cultural forms to promote and market Salvationism to men and women of their own class. Wrote the *Christian at Work* in 1883:

> It ought not to be forgotten that the Army is composed of a very peculiar class, drawn from the lower strata of society, and that it is on this same class they are striving to operate. The methods they use and the language they employ may not commend themselves to more refined and intellectual Christian minds, but they are just such as seem to be appreciated and to reach the class they are intended for.

The Salvation Army's marketing of their religion proved fairly successful in the late nineteenth century. In the United States, the organization experienced a significant rate of growth throughout this period. Beginning with the "pioneer" corps opened in Philadelphia by the Shirley family in 1879, the Army grew to 735 corps by 1898. The geographical distribution of the corps also broadened. In 1880, only three eastern cities (Philadelphia, New York, and Newark) hosted twelve Salvation Army corps. Eight years later, however, two hundred and forty-six corps could be found in twenty-seven states across the nation.

New corps opened at an average rate of twenty-nine per year between 1879 and 1899, and the numbers of officers grew from sixteen in 1880 to nearly twenty-five hundred by the turn of the century. Increases in the numbers of rank-and-file members also reflected a pattern of growth. In 1880, the Army reported four hundred and twelve "privates" in the United States. By 1884, that number increased to five thousand, and, by 1896, the Salvation Army claimed twenty-five thousand soldiers across the nation. While the Army's rate of growth reflected significant expansion in the late nineteenth century, the group never really became a mass movement. Thousands reportedly attended its special services, but much smaller numbers actually joined the organization.

As the Army grew in the United States, it also underwent a religious evolution. During its first years in the United States, the group operated as an evangelical Christian revivalist organization that stressed the role of individual holiness in bringing about the millennium. Gradually, however, the Army evolved until, by the early twentieth century, it successfully combined evangelical Christianity and the social gospel in a single religious movement. In its amended millennial vision of societal as well as individual salvation, social service joined sanctification as a sign of true faith. ...

Theologically, the Salvation Army fell within a larger holiness movement that gained new momentum in the United States and Britain in the late nineteenth century. The Army was one of several "radical" holiness denominations whose teachings stressed "a profound personal experience of consecration, a filling with Spiritual power, and a dedication to arduous Christian service." In contrast to the premillennialism of most late-nineteenth-century evangelicals, however, the Army was post-millennialist and believed that, during the present era, "the Holy Spirit would be poured out and the Gospel spread around the world. Christ would return after this millennial age . . . and would bring history to an end." Salvationists served Christ as nineteenth-century heralds and foot soldiers of the millennium.

The roots of the Army's holiness theology lay . . . in the perfectionism of John Wesley in the eighteenth century. Wesley believed that God could free men and women "not only from particular sinful acts, but also from the disease of sinful motives and the 'power' of sin." In the nineteenth century, Phoebe Palmer helped to revive holiness teaching among Methodists. She suggested that the experience of holiness was both an "event in time" and "a way of life." By the late nineteenth century, holiness advocates "identif[ied] inward purity with decorous conduct" and rejected tobacco and alcohol as part of a regime that "does away with all that is hurtful to the soul, body or influence, and places before us the highest ideal of perfect manhood and womanhood."

Like other holiness denominations, the Salvation Army advocated abstention from sinful behaviors, which included the consumption of alcohol and, to a lesser degree, the smoking of tobacco, as a "witness" to potential converts of their submission to a holy life. "The purity and uprightness of [one's] outward conduct," wrote General Booth, was a public demonstration of one's salvation. "People will say, 'let us see the proofs of it [salvation] in his daily life'; and if they do not, they will conclude that he is either mistaken, or a willful deceiver." While it may be tempting to regard this working-class organization's advocacy of abstention as an effort to achieve a middle-class standard of respectability, it would be a mistake to do so. "The Salvation Army," according to one historian, "did not provide a route to bourgeois respectability." Although the Army rejected the "alcohol, sexuality and assertive masculinity" characteristic of working-class saloons and music halls, the group encouraged its members to adapt the boisterous camaraderie and an "atmosphere of conviviality . . . relaxed sociability, comfort and pleasure" that characterized these spaces to express religious experience and market Salvationism.

The Salvation Army, like many labor organizations in the late nineteenth century, understood the role of sociability in working-class subculture. This world, according to one labor historian, "demanded both individual commitment and group solidarity." Working-class leisure activities helped to "maintain the commitment of members through sociability rather than wait to test solidarity in the crucible of a strike." Similarly, sociability allowed the Salvation Army "to compete for the allegiance of workers" and maintain group solidarity. However, in stark contrast to the male world of labor unions and working-class leisure culture that circumscribed "participation from women and children," sociability Army-style was heterosocial. Like the women who mounted the stage at Harry Hill's Variety, female Salvationists participated along with their men in the Army's use of lively and often rowdy working-class leisure forms. . . .

Salvationists promoted all of their meetings with lively campaigns that exploited the power of spectacle to attract public attention and rally the troops. Seizing every opportunity to emphasize its similarity to other kinds of popular street performances, the organization at times even referred to itself as the "Hallelujah Circus." The Salvation Army in San Jose, California, for example, attached itself to the coattails of a genuine circus by having handbills distributed in town falsely announcing twice as many performances as were actually scheduled. After the real performers departed, the Salvationists set up their own tent and went on to hold "a monster open air on circus grounds," not only "netting souls" but also reportedly accumulating "[t]he largest offerings received in any one day since we opened fire here." That the audience / congregation not only failed to object to the Army's bait-and-switch technique but expressed its satisfaction with larger than usual donations suggests that the people found the Army nearly as entertaining as the circus.

Like circuses, the Salvation Army regularly used parades to promote meetings and literally lure people to its religious performances. In 1879, a Philadelphia newspaper described a small parade led by Salvationists Eliza and Anne Shirley, who "walk[ed] backward . . . down German Town road, singing a rousing hymn, and keeping step to the air." The march reportedly attracted a great deal of attention as "windows and doorways . . . filled with spectators [and the group was] . . . followed by almost everything that had legs." The crowd then piled into the Salvation Factory, wrote the reporter, filling the small building to capacity. . . .

Like Railton's first performance, Salvation Army religious services resembled a cross between a minstrel show and a religious service and consisted of songs, music, exhortation, and personal testimonies. While the delivery of personal testimonies was not unique to the Army, those of Salvationists often injected high melodrama or comic relief into the service. A particularly chilling example came in 1898, at the Higginsville Salvation Army corps, when a man who had murdered the brother of a Salvationist spoke out about his experience. Reported the brother of the murdered man: "This man . . . said no matter where he went, whether he was going to sleep or waking up, or whether he was working or resting—no matter what he did, everywhere he went and everything he did reminded him of my brother, and the fact that he had in a temper taken his life." The man went on to testify that the Salvation Army showed him God's willingness "to forgive even so base a sin as he had committed."

Not all testimonies were quite as dramatic. Indeed, some "experiences" sounded more like bad burlesque routines. One "comrade" claimed:

> I once went into a public house and saw some pickles so I asked the landlady to give me some, but she refused after I had spent all my money . . . so I went to the Salvation Army instead. Here I soon got into a pickle, for God shook me on account of my sins; these I at once forsook. Now thank God, I am saved and a soldier, and mean to fight for God, and I buy my own pickles. . . .

In addition to snappy testimonies, exhortation also borrowed from working-class popular culture in order to deliver religion and to entertain. At a particularly spectacular meeting, "the devil and his works were burned in effigy." After a parade through the streets and some hellfire preaching by Mrs. Staff-Captain Winchell, her husband proceeded to dramatize her argument. As the audience watched, Winchell held up one after another of the devil's works, preaching the dangers of each in turn.

> 1st: The devil of pride—a large over-trimmed women's bonnet, such as can be seen in any church or theatre; 2nd: The devil of unbelief, infidelity, higher criticism, Bob Ingersoll, book and papers; 3d: The theatrical devil—a huge bill-board poster; 4th: The political devil; 5th: The tobacco devil—cigarettes, pipes, etc.; 6th: The whiskey devil, which included politics, gambling, the sin of scarlet.

After the "lecture," the lights were dimmed, and the devil's works were placed in a pile topped with an effigy of the devil himself. Before a spellbound audience, the pile was set aflame, and, within a few seconds, not a trace of the devil remained. . . .

Even Salvation Army weddings captured the flavor of working-class entertainment culture. In contrast to the private style of middle-class weddings, which brought together family and friends, the Army often used weddings between officers as another form of special meeting and invited the public (for a modest admission price) to join in the celebration. The Hallelujah Weddings themselves often opened with a colorful parade.

> There were large numbers of flaring torches, banners and bannerettes and hundreds of smiling soldiers . . . but the great[est] attraction of all was the forty bridesmaids all dressed alike with white dresses, Stars and Stripes sashes and red liberty caps, with the Salvation Army red band around them. These lasses caused such an attraction that traffic was completely stopped.

Not only did Salvationists adapt the form of their religious performances from working-class popular culture, but the halls in which they held their services often struck outsiders as having the look and feel of working-class entertainment spaces. Wrote the *Chicago Tribune* in 1886, "[T]he Princess Rink was well filled yesterday afternoon. . . . The sawdust-covered floor, the chinese [*sic*] lanterns, and noisy band suggested the circus as much as anything else, and the exercises were some-what on that order." . . .

Of course, officers did not always appreciate the extent to which their audience made themselves "at home." To the discomfort of one young officer, some men and women who came to meetings at his corps treated the meeting hall as if it were the infamous "third tier." He recalled later that prostitutes sometimes used his Decatur, Illinois, hall as a place to meet with potential customers. "There were about a dozen prostitutes and street walkers . . . and there were possibly twenty-five or thirty men who were interested in such folks, and they seemed to make the Salvation Army hall a rendezvous for an opportunity to make dates and meet up with each other." . . .

Where "talent" and the availability of instruments permitted, musical accom-paniment also played an important part in Army services. In the early years, the Salvation Army relied heavily on easily mastered percussion instruments like bass drums, cymbals, and tambourines and did not demand much in the way of melody from brass horns. The *Chicago Inter-Ocean,* reporting on the "musical" conse-quences, noted:

> The blare of the trumpet, the "umtra-umtra" of the trombone, and the "biff biff boom" of a particularly corpulent bass drum filled the auditorium . . . with a delirious uproar last night, shook the rafters, and set the windows rattling like a grip car off the track. Melody got twisted into weird noises resembling the blended symphony that the lonely donkey sings at the moon, the Wagnerian strains evoked from a battered tin-pan by a small boy and the soul-stirring agony of a violin student's first attempt.

For Salvationists, boisterous singing, music, prayers, and exhortations made worship "a physical sensation" or "a tactile experience" and fostered a loss of con-trol over bodies and voices. . . .

In his memoirs, Salvationist James Price recalled that, on one Saturday night during a "hallelujah wind-up," he nearly passed out. "I seemed to be lifted out of myself," he said, "and I think that for a time my spirit left my body." While he did not faint, "mentally, for a time I was not at home." When he regained awareness, he found himself "on the platform among many others singing and praising God."

> [S]uddenly finding myself in the midst of a brotherhood with whom I was in complete accord; without the shadow of a doubt regarding its divine mission, and then the great meetings climaxing in scores being converted, all this affected me like wine going to my head. . . .

. . . "Many of the soldiers," wrote the *National Baptist,* "rock[ed] themselves backwards and forwards waving and clapping their hands, sometimes bowing far forward and again lifting their . . . faces, heavenward. The singing was thickly interlarded with ejaculations, shouts [and] sobs." Salvationists had created an urban working-class version of the frontier camp meeting style.

The Salvation Army institutionalized "enthusiasm" or the physical expression of a "continuous revival of feeling." Beginning with conversion, Salvationists experienced their religion with striking physical intensity. When an iron miner came "under conviction" and approached the altar to pray for forgiveness, according to Salvationist Arthur Jackson, "he prayed on his knees at the altar for a while, then he sat down on the floor in front of the altar and prayed, and then he lay down on his back on the floor and prayed, and then he seemed to get into a sort of convulsion or an agony. He turned over and lay on his stomach and prayed." Jackson also recalled an elderly woman who, when saved, "jumped from her seat like a jack out of a box and began to shout. . . . She pounded the back of the bench in front of her with her hands and screamed for joy."

While one might expect that the initial conversion experience would be intensely felt and expressed, even daily prayer in the Salvation Army was a loud physical experience. While dining with a captain at a Salvation Army training garrison, a visitor was startled by "a roar, as of thunder, and noise as if fifty sledge-hammered men were pounding on the floor over our heads." Creeping upstairs, the guest discovered "fifteen stalwart, hearty, powerful-lunged fellows upon their knees at prayer. They prayed with their voices, their feet, and both hands, and each one possessed of a pair of hands and feet, which were going for all they were worth." Leading prayer was also a physical experience. One young captain reportedly "would lean away over to one side, then lean the other way and wave his arms, throw back his head, putting his whole body into the exercise." . . .

To a Chicago judge in 1885, the Army's activities were tantamount to blasphemy. He described the Army as "a monkey show" and complained that the organization "gather[ed] together all the worst types of people." He was particularly appalled by the Army's "[r]idiculous street parades, blatant discourses before gatherings of hoodlums, and [their] . . . imitation of religious rites." These sacrilegious "parod[ies of] religious ceremonies," he said, "made the organization more than just a nuisance" because they fostered among "the ignorant and unthinking, a contempt for the religion these street performers profess."

Middle-class Christians also feared that the group would unleash civil disorder. . . . Prompted by these criticisms, city officials regularly dispatched police to arrest the Salvationists for disturbing the peace and obstructing the streets as they held open-air services and marched to their hall. Said one police officer in 1888, "They disturb the peace with their drums and tom-toms. They cause teams to break loose on the streets. . . . They drive simple-minded people crazy with their singing and praying and shouting. They are a public nuisance."

Concerns for order were not entirely without merit. When the Army attempted to "open fire" in some neighborhoods, the response could include beatings, theft of members' belongings, threats to tar and feather the officers, and arson. The emphasis on temperance in Army campaigns regularly provoked angry and violent responses from saloon owners and their working-class customers. On one occasion, locals invaded a corps hall and proceeded to wreak havoc by "taking up the chairs and breaking them over the heads of the soldiers, and then turning over the stove with the fire in it. The mob barricaded the doors and refused to let anybody go in or out." On another occasion, "the devil's agents got on the top of the hall, and first threw a keg full of ashes and herrings through the skylight on the platform then followed this up with a can full of kerosene, no doubt hoping to set the hall on fire." Open-air marches were particularly dangerous, and Salvationists could not count on police protection. Since municipal governments often had close political ties to saloons, the police generally made little effort to protect the soldiers and officers as they waged their campaigns against alcohol. Salvationists reported that "[s]tones, blows, pushing and profanity was heaped upon us. Ash boxes were opened and the contents thrown upon our soldiers, and this under the glaring lights of electric lamps and police all along the line of march." . . .

Fears that this "motley" group would either provoke or be unable to prevent civil and possibly sexual disorder were heightened by the fact that both male and female Salvationists exercised spiritual and administrative leadership within the organization. As early as 1878, the Salvation Army made itself one of the few mixed-sex organizations that officially allowed a woman to "hold any position of authority or power in the Army, from that of a local officer to that of the General." As officers and soldiers, the Army encouraged women to undertake duties usually left to men. Such behavior must not be regarded as "unwomanly," argued Army leaders, for a "lass who is led of the Spirit will not be wrong, even if it is beyond the bounds of what the world considers propriety." Filled with the Holy Spirit, "leather-lunged and iron-eared" female Salvationists paraded through the streets, entered the male world of the saloon in order to preach the gospel, shouted, sang, and "jumped in the air and screamed with joy," shocking the tender sensibilities of middle-class American Christians. . . .

By the turn of the century, the Salvation Army had gone through a religious evolution that combined evangelical Christianity with a form of the social gospel. In its new incarnation, the organization relied increasingly on the new technologies of mass commercial culture. Like the changed world of the nineteenth-century theater and variety shows, once highly participatory religious meetings now included stereopticon slide shows and films. Street parades, which were once spontaneous, boisterous, and rowdy events representing the religious fervor of the Salvationists, now included mechanical floats representing the increasingly important social work carried out by the organization.

✎ *F U R T H E R   R E A D I N G*

Blumberg, Leonard. *Beware the First Drink! The Washington Temperance Movement and Alcoholics Anonymous* (1991).
Bordin, Ruth. *Frances Willard: A Biography* (1986).
Curtis, Susan. *A Consuming Faith: The Social Gospel and Modern American Culture* (1993).
Dorsett, Lyle. *Billy Sunday and the Redemption of Urban America* (1991).
Ellis, John Tracy. *The Life of James Cardinal Gibbons, Archbishop of Baltimore, 1834–1921* (1952).

Findlay, James F. *Dwight L. Moody, American Evangelist, 1837–1899* (1969).

Higginbotham, Evelyn Brooks. *Righteous Discontent: The Women's Movement in the Black Baptist Church, 1880–1920* (1993).

Higham, John. *Strangers in the Land: Patterns of American Nativism, 1860–1925* (1955).

Hunter, Jane. *The Gospel of Gentility: American Women Missionaries in Turn-of-the-Century China* (1984).

Kane, Paula. *Separatism and Subculture: Boston Catholicism: 1900–1920* (1994).

McDannell, Colleen. *The Christian Home in Victorian America, 1840–1900* (1986).

Magnuson, Norris. *Salvation in the Slums: Evangelical Social Work, 1865–1920* (1977).

May, Henry. *Protestant Churches and Industrial America* (1949).

O'Brien, David. *American Catholicism and Social Reform* (1968).

O'Connell, Marvin. *John Ireland and the American Catholic Church* (1988).

Parot, John Joseph. *Polish Catholics in Chicago: 1850–1920* (1981).

Seager, Richard H. *The World's Parliament of Religions: The East-West Encounter, Chicago, 1893* (1995).

Sernett, Milton. *Bound for the Promised Land: African American Religion and the Great Migration* (1997).

Sizer, Sandra. *Gospel Hymns and Social Religion: The Rhetoric of 19th Century Revivalism* (1978).

Tomasi, Silvano. *Piety and Power: The Role of Italian Parishes in the New York Metropolitan Area, 1880–1930* (1975).

White, Ronald C. Jr. *Liberty and Justice for All: Racial Reform and the Social Gospel* (1990).

White, Ronald, Jr., and C. Howard Hopkins. *The Social Gospel: Religion and Reform in Changing America* (1976).

CHAPTER
9

Intellectual Controversies: 1860–1925

Religious Americans confronted a series of intellectual challenges in the late nine-teenth and early twentieth centuries. First the publication of Darwin's On the Origin of Species *(1859) intensified a debate about whether the Genesis account of the creation of the world could any longer be regarded as historically reliable, something nearly everyone had previously assumed. Some liberal Protestants believed that evolution was a superior explanation and that human society and religion, like the many species in the natural world, evolved, changed, and pro-gressed. They tried to reconcile a modified form of Christianity with evolutionary science. Conservative Protestants denied that this reconciliation was possible. In their view the Bible was God's word, delivered infallibly and absolutely truthfully once and for all. Christians, they said, are not free to pick and choose which parts of the Bible they will accept and which to reject. If they do so they are setting up their own judgment as superior to God's.*

Along with the evolutionary controversy, however, developments in historical study were also casting doubt on the Bible's uniqueness as a divinely inspired book. Textual critics began comparing biblical stories about creation, men and women, sin, the origins of language, and the flood to the myths of other Near Eastern cul-tures. Their findings showed common or comparable stories in all of them, and raised the unsettling possibility that the Hebrew Bible was just one among many collections of ancient tales that a series of historical coincidences had caused to become one of the foundations of Western civilization. Archaeologists and scholars in ancient history also made discoveries that cast doubt on some biblical narratives. Here again, conservative Protestants continued to have faith in the absolute truth of the Bible, whereas liberal Protestants, confident that faith and reason could not conflict, tried to bring them into harmony. In this discussion the significance of Jesus also changed. Liberal Protestants in particular shifted their concentration away from his death and resurrection and toward the events of his life. Some even began to treat him more as a great man than as the embodiment of God.

A third intellectual problem, related to the effects of industrialization exam-ined in Chapter 8, was the question of reconciling faith and wealth. Christians had always debated and disputed about money, but the issue took on a new urgency as the richest Americans made immense fortunes while the poorest spent their lives in squalor. Certain passages of the New Testament enabled Christian Socialists to make a good case for Jesus as a socialist—after all, his father was a working carpenter and Jesus in his parables and teachings often denounced great wealth. On the other hand, Christian capitalists could also produce plausible texts to suggest that Jesus had no objection to their favored economic system.

These disputes, over history, science, the Bible, and Christian wealth, found articulate spokesmen on every side. It would be wrong to assume that, for instance, the Christian opponents of Darwinian science were obtuse or anti-intellectual. Often the internal coherence and sophistication of their arguments is striking, even to readers who cannot share their first premises. The debaters' moral anxieties are apparent, too—biblical fundamentalists like William Jennings Bryan were afraid that if the Bible fell into question, so too would the nation's entire moral code.

 ## D O C U M E N T S

Charles Hodge, a professor of theology at Princeton Seminary and one of the fathers of modern Fundamentalism, admired Darwin's intellectual powers but in this extract from 1874 (Document 1) he argues that evolutionary theory leads to atheism and is therefore unacceptable. Lyman Abbott, one of the most famous turn-of-the-century liberal Protestants, speaks for the opposite point of view in Document 2 (1892), in which he argues that Christianity is itself the *product* of evolution. Document 3, from Harold Frederic's wonderfully acute novel *The Damnation of Theron Ware* (1896), depicts an undereducated rural Methodist minister suddenly awakening to the fact that his religion has complicated historical implications that he has never seriously considered. Documents 4 and 5 illustrate the two sides of the Christian controversy over biblical criticism. Washington Gladden (1894) defends the position that all of our energy should be dedicated to explaining and contextualizing the Scriptures, a job that he says will strengthen faith. William Jennings Bryan (1924), by contrast, warns against the intellectual pride and the moral dangers that result from a personal interpretation of God's words. In Document 6 (1895), Elizabeth Cady Stanton, a pioneer advocate of women's suffrage, reinterprets famous passages from Genesis to argue that God had no intention of making men superior to women but, rather, believed in gender equality right from the moment of creation. Documents 7 and 8 show two sides of the Christian dispute over wealth, with George Herron (1899) taking the Christian socialist position and Russell Conwell (1915) arguing that anyone can, with God's full approval, be rich, and that poverty is usually a matter of willful stupidity or idleness.

1. Charles Hodge Denounces Darwin's Theory of Evolution as Atheistic, 1874

Mr. Darwin is not a Monist, for in admitting creation, he admits a dualism as between God and the world. Neither is he a Materialist, inasmuch as he assumes a supernatural origin for the infinitesimal modicum of life and intelligence in the primordial animalcule, from which without divine purpose or agency, all living things in the

Charles Hodge, *What Is Darwinism?* (New York: Scribner, Armstrong, 1874), 168–178.

whole history of our earth have descended. All the innumerable varieties of plants, all the countless forms of animals, with all their instincts and faculties, all the varieties of men with their intellectual endowments, and their moral and religious nature, have, according to Darwin, been evolved by the agency of the blind, unconscious laws of nature. This infinitesimal spark of supernaturalism in Mr. Darwin's theory, would inevitably have gone out of itself, had it not been rudely and contemptuously trodden out by his bolder, and more logical successors.

The grand and fatal objection to Darwinism is this exclusion of design in the origin of species, or the production of living organisms. By design is meant the intelligent and voluntary selection of an end, and the intelligent and voluntary choice, application, and control of means appropriate to the accomplishment of that end. That design, therefore, implies intelligence, is involved in its very nature. No man can perceive this adaptation of means to the accomplishment of a preconceived end, without experiencing an irresistible conviction that it is the work of mind. No man does doubt it, and no man can doubt it. Darwin does not deny it. Haeckel does not deny it. No Darwinian denies it. What they do is to deny that there is any design in nature. . . . But in thus denying design in nature, these writers array against themselves the intuitive perceptions and irresistible convictions of all mankind,—a barrier which no man has ever been able to surmount. . . .

It is impossible for even Mr. Darwin, inconsistent as it is with his whole theory, to deny all design in the constitution of nature. What is his law of heredity? Why should like beget like? Take two germ cells, one of a plant, another of an animal; no man by microscope or by chemical analysis, or by the magic power of the spectroscope, can detect the slightest difference between them, yet the one infallibly develops into a plant and the other into an animal. Take the germ of a fish and of a bird, and they are equally indistinguishable; yet the one always under all conditions develops into a fish and the other into a bird. Why is this? There is no physical force, whether light, heat, electricity, or anything else, which makes the slightest approximation to accounting for that fact. . . .

It is further to be considered that there are innumerable cases of contrivance, or evidence of design in nature, to which the principle of natural selection, or the purposeless changes effected by unconscious force, cannot apply; as for example, the distinction of sex, with all that is therein involved. But passing by such cases, it may be asked, what would it avail to get rid of design in the vegetable and animal kingdom, while the whole universe is full of it? That this ordered Cosmos is not from necessity or chance, is almost a self-evident fact. Not one man in a million of those who ever heard of God, either does doubt or can doubt it. Besides how are the cosmical relations of light, heat, electricity, to the constituent parts of the universe, and especially, so far as this earth is concerned, to vegetable and animal life, to be accounted for? Is this all chance work? Is it by chance that light and heat cause plants to carry on their wonderful operations, transmuting the inorganic into the organic, dead matter into living and life sustaining matter? Is it without a purpose that water instead of contracting, expands at the freezing point?—a fact to which is due that the earth north of the tropic is habitable for man or beast. It is no answer to this question to say that a few other substances have the same peculiarity, when no good end, that we can see, is thereby accomplished. No man is so foolish as to deny that his eye was intended to enable him to see, because he cannot tell what the spleen was made for. It is, however, useless to dwell upon this subject. If a man denies that there is design in nature, he can with quite as good reason deny that there is any design in any or in all the works ever executed by man.

The conclusion of the whole matter is, that the denial of design in nature is virtually the denial of God. Mr. Darwin's theory does deny all design in nature, therefore, his theory is virtually atheistical; his theory, not he himself. He believes in a Creator. But when that Creator, millions on millions of ages ago, did something,—called matter and a living germ into existence,—and then abandoned the universe to itself to be controlled by chance and necessity, without any purpose on his part as to the result, or any intervention or guidance, then He is virtually consigned, so far as we are concerned, to non-existence. It has already been said that the most extreme of Mr. Darwin's admirers adopt and laud his theory, for the special reason that it banishes God from the world; that it enables them to account for design without referring it to the purpose or agency of God. . . .

[As the American naturalist Asa Gray has written:] "Let us hope, and I confidently expect, that it is not to last; that the religious faith which survived without a shock the notion of the fixedness of the earth itself, may equally outlast the notion of the absolute fixedness of the species which inhabit it; that in the future, even more than in the past, faith in an *order*, which is the basis of science, will not—as it cannot reasonably—be dissevered from faith in an *Ordainer*, which is the basis of religion.". . .

We have thus arrived at the answer to our question, What is Darwinism? It is Atheism. This does not mean, as before said, that Mr. Darwin himself and all who adopt his views are atheists; but it means that his theory is atheistic; that the exclusion of design from nature is, as Dr. Gray says, tantamount to atheism.

2. Lyman Abbott Argues That Christianity and Evolutionary Theory Are Compatible, 1892

All scientific men to-day are evolutionists. That is, they agree substantially in holding that all life proceeds, by a regular and orderly sequence, from simple to more complex forms, from lower to higher forms, and in accordance with laws which either now are or may yet be understood, or are at all events a proper subject of hopeful investigation. The truth of this doctrine I assume; that is, I assume that all life, including the religious life, proceeds by a regular and orderly sequence from simple and lower forms to more complex and higher forms, in institutions, in thought, in practical conduct, and in spiritual experience. It is my purpose not so much to demonstrate this proposition as to state, exemplify, and apply it.

As "evolution" is the latest word of science, so "life" is the supreme word of religion. All religious men agree that there is a life of God in the soul of man. . . . The Christian religion, then, is the perception of that manifestation of God, historically made in and through Jesus Christ, which has produced the changes in the moral life of man whose aggregate result is seen in the complex life of Christendom, past

Lyman Abbott, *The Evolution of Christianity* (1892; reprint, Garden City, N.Y.: Doubleday, Page, 1926), i–vi, 1–7.

and present. As all scientific men believe in evolution,—the orderly development of life from lower to higher forms,—so all Christians believe that there has been a manifestation of God in Jesus Christ which has produced historical Christianity. As I assume the truth of evolution, so I assume the truth of this fundamental article of the Christian faith. With the scientific believer, I believe in the orderly and progressive development of all life; with the religious believer, I believe in the reality of a life of God in the soul of man. It is not my object to reconcile these two beliefs, but, assuming the truth of both, to show that this divine life is itself subject to the law of all life; that Christianity is itself an evolution. Applying this law to the history of the Christian religion, it is my object to show that the manifestation of God in Jesus Christ has been a gradual and growing manifestation, and that the changes wrought thereby in the moral life of man have been gradual and growing changes, wrought by spiritual forces, or a spiritual force, resident in man. . . .

. . . Christianity has been, not a fixed and unchanging factor, but a life, subject to a continuous progressive change; this change has been, not lawless, irregular, and unaccountable, but according to certain laws, which, though by no means well understood, have never been either suspended or violated; and the cause of this change, or these changes, has been a force, not foreign to man himself, but residing in him. Thus Christianity, whether regarded as an institutional, an intellectual, a social, or a moral life, has exemplified the law of evolution. . . .

The doctrine of evolution . . . makes no attempt whatever to explain the nature or origin of life. It is concerned, not with the origin, but with the phenomena of life. It sees the forces resident in the phenomena, but it throws no light on the question how they came there. . . .

Making no attempt to explain the origin of life, the evolutionist insists that the processes of life are always from the simple to the complex: from the simple nebulæ to the complicated world containing mineral substances and vegetable and animal life; from the germinant mollusk through every form of animate creation up to the vertebrate mammal, including man; from the family, through the tribe, to the nation; from the paternal form of government, through the oligarchic and the aristocratic, to the democratic; from slavery, —the patriarchal capitalist owning his slave on terms hardly different from those on which he owns his wife,—to the complicated relationship of modern society between employer and employed. In this movement, notwithstanding apparent blunders, false types and arrested developments, the evolutionist sees a steady progress from lower to higher forms of life. The Christian evolutionist, then, will expect to find modern Christianity more complex than primitive Christianity. . . . And he will expect to find that the Christianity of the nineteenth century, despite its failures and defects, is better, intellectually, organically, morally, and spiritually, than the Christianity of the first century.

The doctrine of evolution is not a doctrine of harmonious and uninterrupted progress. The most common, if not the most accurate formula of evolution is "struggle for existence, survival of the fittest." The doctrine of evolution assumes that there are forces in the world seemingly hostile to progress, that life is a perpetual battle and progress a perpetual victory. The Christian evolutionist will then expect to find Christianity a warfare—in church, in society, in the individual. . . . He will remember that the divine life is resident in undivine humanity. He will not be surprised to find the waters of the stream disturbed; for he will reflect that the divine purity has come into a turbid stream, and that it can purify only by being itself indistinguishably combined with the impure. When he is told that modern Christianity is only a "civilized paganism," he will reply, "That is exactly what I supposed it to be; and it will continue to be a civilized paganism until the civilization has entirely eliminated the paganism." He will not be surprised to find pagan ceremonies in the ritual, pagan superstitions in the creed, pagan selfishness in the life, ignorance and superstition in the church, and even errors and partialisms in the Bible. For he will remember that the divine life, which is bringing all life into harmony with itself, is a life resident in man. He will remember that the Bible does not claim to be the absolute Word of God; that, on the contrary, it declares that the Word of God was with God and was God, and existed before the world was; that it claims to be the Word of God, *as perceived and understood by holy men of old*, the Word as spoken to men, and understood and interpreted by men, who saw it in part as we still see it, and reflected it as from a mirror in enigmas. He will remember that the Church is not yet the bride of Christ, but the plebeian daughter whom Christ is educating to be his bride. . . .

3. Harold Frederic's Fictional Methodist Preacher Discovers His Ignorance of Biblical History, 1896

"I am going to begin my book this afternoon," he remarked impressively. "There is a great deal to think about."

It turned out that there was even more to think about than he had imagined. After hours of solitary musing at his desk, or of pacing up and down before his open book-shelves, Theron found the first shadows of a May-day twilight beginning to fall upon that beautiful pile of white paper, still unstained by ink. He saw the book he wanted to write before him, in his mental vision, much more distinctly than ever, but the idea of beginning it impetuously, and hurling it off hot and glowing week by week, had faded away like a dream.

This long afternoon, spent face to face with a project born of his own brain but yesterday, yet already so much bigger than himself, was really a most fruitful time for the young clergyman. The lessons which cut most deeply into our consciousness are those we learn from our children. Theron, in this first day's contact with the offspring of his fancy, found revealed to him an unsuspected and staggering truth. It was that he was an extremely ignorant and rudely untrained young man, whose pretensions to intellectual authority among any educated people would be laughed at with deserved contempt.

Strangely enough, after he had weathered the first shock, this discovery did not dismay Theron Ware. The very completeness of the conviction it carried with it saturated his mind with a feeling as if the fact had really been known to him all along. And there came, too, after a little, an almost pleasurable sense of the importance of the revelation. He had been merely drifting in fatuous and conceited blindness.

Harold Frederic, *The Damnation of Theron Ware* (1896; reprint, New York: Penguin, 1986), 67–71.

Now all at once his eyes were open; he knew what he had to do. Ignorance was a thing to be remedied, and he would forthwith bend all his energies to cultivating his mind till it should blossom like a garden. In this mood, Theron mentally measured himself against the more conspicuous of his colleagues in the Conference. They also were ignorant, clownishly ignorant: the difference was that they were doomed by native incapacity to go on all their lives without ever finding it out. It was obvious to him that his case was better. There was bright promise in the very fact that he had discovered his shortcomings.

He had begun the afternoon by taking down from their places the various works in his meagre library which bore more or less relation to the task in hand. The threescore books which constituted his printed possessions were almost wholly from the press of the Book Concern; the few exceptions were volumes which, though published elsewhere, had come to him through that giant circulating agency of the General Conference, and wore the stamp of its approval. Perhaps it was the sight of these half-filled shelves which started this day's great revolution in Theron's opinion of himself. He had never thought much before about owning books. He had been too poor to buy many, and the conditions of canvassing about among one's parishioners which the thrifty Book Concern imposes upon those who would have without buying had always repelled him. Now, suddenly, as he moved along the two shelves, he felt ashamed at their beggarly showing.

"The Land and the Book," in three portly volumes, was the most pretentious of the aids which he finally culled from his collection. Beside it he laid out "Bible Lands," "Rivers and Lakes of Scripture," "Bible Manners and Customs," the "Genesis and Exodus" volume of Whedon's Commentary, some old numbers of the "Methodist Quarterly Review," and a copy of "Josephus" which had belonged to his grandmother, and had seen him through many a weary Sunday afternoon in boyhood. He glanced casually through these, one by one, as he took them down, and began to fear that they were not going to be of so much use as he had thought. Then, seating himself, he read carefully through the thirteen chapters of Genesis which chronicle the story of the founder of Israel.

Of course he had known this story from his earliest years. In almost every chapter he came now upon a phrase or an incident which had served him as the basis for a sermon. He had preached about Hagar in the wilderness, about Lot's wife, about the visit of the angels, about the intended sacrifice of Isaac, about a dozen other things suggested by the ancient narrative. Somehow this time it all seemed different to him. The people he read about were altered to his vision. Heretofore a poetic light had shone about them, where indeed they had not glowed in a halo of sanctification. Now, by some chance, this light was gone, and he saw them instead as untutored and unwashed barbarians, filled with animal lusts and ferocities, struggling by violence and foul chicanery to secure a foothold in a country which did not belong to them—all rude tramps and robbers of the uncivilized plain.

The apparent fact that Abram was a Chaldean struck him with peculiar force. How was it, he wondered, that this had never occurred to him before? Examining himself, he found that he had supposed vaguely that there had been Jews from the beginning, or at least, say, from the Flood. But, no, Abram was introduced simply as a citizen of the Chaldean town of Ur, and there was no hint of any difference in race between him and his neighbors. It was specially mentioned that his brother,

Lot's father, died in Ur, the city of his nativity. Evidently the family belonged there, and were Chaldeans like the rest.

I do not cite this as at all a striking discovery, but it did have a curious effect upon Theron Ware. Up to that very afternoon, his notion of the kind of book he wanted to write had been founded upon a popular book called "Ruth the Moabitess," written by a clergyman he knew very well, the Rev. E. Ray Mifflin. This model performance troubled itself not at all with difficult points, but went swimmingly along through scented summer seas of pretty rhetoric, teaching nothing, it is true, but pleasing a good deal and selling like hot cakes. Now, all at once Theron felt that he hated that sort of book. *His* work should be of a vastly different order. He might fairly assume, he thought, that if the fact that Abram was a Chaldean was new to him, it would fall upon the world in general as a novelty. Very well, then, there was his chance. He would write a learned book, showing who the Chaldeans were, and how their manners and beliefs differed from, and influenced———

It was at this psychological instant that the wave of self-condemnation suddenly burst upon and submerged the young clergyman. It passed again, leaving him staring fixedly at the pile of books he had taken down from the shelves, and gasping a little, as if for breath. Then the humorous side of the thing, perversely enough, appealed to him, and he grinned feebly to himself at the joke of his having imagined that he could write learnedly about the Chaldeans, or anything else. . . .

[He visits the local Catholic priest and meets the learned Doctor Ledsmar.] . . . [T]he reading-stand, the mass of littered magazines, reviews, and papers at either end of the costly and elaborate writing-desk—seemed to make it the easier for him to explain without reproach that he needed information about Abraham. He told them quite in detail the story of his book. . . .

[Ledsmar answers:] . . . "I daresay I can help you. You are quite welcome to anything I have: my books cover the ground pretty well up to last year. Delitzsch is very interesting, but Baudissin's 'Studien zur Semitischen Religionsgeschichte' would come closer to what you need. There are several other important Germans— Schrader, Bunsen, Duncker, Hommel, and so on."

"Unluckily I—I don't read German readily," Theron explained with diffidence.

"That's a pity," said the Doctor, "because they do the best work—not only in this field, but in most others. And they do so much that the mass defies translation. Well, the best thing outside of German of course is Sayce. I daresay you know him, though."

The Rev. Mr. Ware shook his head mournfully. "I don't seem to know anyone," he murmured.

The others exchanged glances.

"But if I may ask, Mr. Ware," pursued the Doctor, regarding their guest with interest through his spectacles, "why do you specially hit upon Abraham? He is full of difficulties—enough, just now, at any rate, to warn off the bravest scholar. Why not take something easier?"

Theron had recovered something of his confidence. "Oh, no," he said, "that is just what attracts me to Abraham. I like the complexities and contradictions in his character. Take for instance all that strange and picturesque episode of Hagar: see the splendid contrast between the craft and commercial guile of his dealings in

Egypt and with Abimelech, and the simple, straightforward godliness of his later years. No, all those difficulties only attract me. Do you happen to know—of course you would know—do those German books, or the others, give anywhere any additional details of the man himself and his sayings and doings—little things which help, you know, to round out one's conception of the individual?"

Again the priest and the Doctor stole a furtive glance across the young minister's head. It was Father Forbes who replied.

"I fear that you are taking our friend Abraham too literally, Mr. Ware," he said, in a gentle semblance of paternal tones which seemed to go so well with his gown. "Modern research, you know, quite wipes him out of existence as an individual. The word 'Abram' is merely an eponym—it means 'exalted father.' Practically all the names in the Genesis chronologies are what we call eponymous. Abram is not a person at all: he is a tribe, a sept, a clan. In the same way, Shem is not intended for a man; it is the name of a great division of the human race. Heber is simply the throwing back into allegorical substance, so to speak, of the Hebrews; Heth of the Hittites; Asshur of Assyria."

"But this is something very new, this theory, isn't it?" queried Theron.

The priest smiled and shook his head. "Bless you, no! My dear sir, there is nothing new. Epicurus and Lucretius outlined the whole Darwinian theory more than two thousand years ago. As for this eponym thing, why Saint Augustine called attention to it fifteen hundred years ago."

4. Washington Gladden Explains Higher Criticism, 1894

[T]he Bible is not an infallible Book, in the sense in which it is popularly supposed to be infallible. When we study the history of the several books, the history of the canon, the history of the distribution and reproduction of the manuscript copies, and the history of the versions,—when we discover that the "various readings" of the differing manuscripts amount to one hundred and fifty thousand, the impossibility of maintaining the verbal inerrancy of the Bible becomes evident. We see how human ignorance and error have been suffered to mingle with this stream of living water throughout all its course; if our assurance of salvation were made to depend upon our knowledge that every word of the Bible was of divine origin, our hopes of eternal life would be altogether insecure.

The book is not infallible historically. It is a veracious record; we may depend upon the truthfulness of the outline which it gives us of the history of the Jewish people; but the discrepancies and contradictions which appear here and there upon its pages show that its writers were not miraculously protected from mistakes in dates and numbers and the order of events.

It is not infallible scientifically. It is idle to try to force the narrative of Genesis into an exact correspondence with geological science. It is a hymn of creation, wonderfully beautiful and pure; the central truths of monotheistic religion and of modern

Washington Gladden, *Who Wrote the Bible?* (Boston: Houghton Mifflin, 1894), 351–355.

science are involved in it; but it is not intended to give us the scientific history of creation, and the attempt to make it bear this construction is highly injudicious.

It is not infallible morally. By this I mean that portions of this revelation involve an imperfect morality. Many things are here commanded which it would be wrong for us to do. This is not saying that these commands were not divinely wise for the people to whom they were given; nor is it denying that the morality of the New Testament, which is the fulfillment and consummation of the moral progress which the book records, is a perfect morality; it is simply asserting that the stages of this progress from a lower to a higher morality are here clearly marked; that the standards of the earlier time are therefore inadequate and misleading in these later times; and that any man who accepts the Bible as a code of moral rules, all of which are equally binding, will be led into the gravest errors. It is no more true that the ceremonial legislation of the Old Testament is obsolete than that large portions of the moral legislation are obsolete. The notions of the writers of these books concerning their duties to God were dim and imperfect; so were their notions concerning their duties to man. All the truth that they could receive was given to them; but there were many truths which they could not receive, which to us are as as plain as the daylight.

Not to recognize the partialness and imperfection of this record in all these respects is to be guilty of a grave disloyalty to the kingdom of the truth. With all these facts staring him in the face, the attempt of any intelligent man to maintain the theoretical and ideal infallibility of all parts of these writings is a criminal blunder. Nor is there any use in loudly asserting the inerrancy of these books, with vehement denunciations of all who call it in question, and then in a breath admitting that there may be some errors and discrepancies and interpolations. Perfection is perfection. To stoutly affirm that a thing is perfect, and then admit that it may be in some respects imperfect, is an insensate procedure. Infallibility is infallibility. The Scriptures are, or they are not, infallible. The admission that there may be a few errors gives every man the right, nay it lays upon him the duty, of finding what those errors are. Our friends who so sturdily assert the traditional theory can hardly be aware of the extent to which they stultify themselves when their sweeping and reiterated assertion that the Bible can *never* contain a mistake is followed, as it always must be, by their timid and deprecatory, "hardly ever." The old rabbinical theory, as adopted and extended by some of the post-Reformation theologians, that the Bible was verbally dictated by God and is absolutely accurate in every word, letter, and vowel-point, and that it is therefore blasphemy to raise a question concerning any part of it, is a consistent theory. Between this and a free but reverent inquiry into the Bible itself, to discover what human elements it contains and how it is affected by them, there is no middle ground. That it is useless and mischievous to make for the Bible claims that it nowhere makes for itself,—to hold and teach a theory concerning it which at once breaks down when an intelligent man begins to study it with open mind—is beginning to be very plain. The quibbling, the concealment, the disingenuousness which this method of using the Bible involves are not conducive to Christian integrity. This kind of "lying for God" has driven hundreds of thousands already into irreconcilable alienation from the Christian church. It is time to stop it.

How did this theory of the infallibility of the Bible arise? Those who have followed these discussions to this point know that it has not always been held by the

Christian church. The history of the canon, told with any measure of truthfulness, will make this plain. The history of the variations between the Septuagint and the Hebrew shows, beyond the shadow of a doubt, that this theory of the unchangeable and absolute divinity of the words of the Scripture had no practical hold upon transcribers and copyists in the early Jewish church. The New Testament writers could not have consistently held such a theory respecting the Old Testament books, else they would not have quoted them, as they did, with small care for verbal accuracy. They believed them to be substantially true, and therefore they give the substance of them in their quotations; but there is no such slavish attention to the letter as there must have been if they had regarded them as verbally dictated by God himself.

5. William Jennings Bryan Defends Biblical Infallibility, 1924

Is the Bible true? That is the great issue in the world to-day, surpassing in importance all national and international questions. The Bible is either true or false; it is either the Word of God or the work of man. If the Bible is false, it is the greatest impostor that the world has ever known. . . .

As there can be no civilization without morals, and as morals rest upon religion, and religion upon God, the question whether the Bible is true or false is the supreme issue among men. As the Bible is the only book known to the Christian world whose authority depends upon inspiration, the degradation of the Bible leaves the Christian world without a standard of morals other than that upon which men can agree. As men's reasons do not lead them to the same conclusion, and as greed and self-interest often overthrow the reason, the fixing of any moral standard by agreement is impossible. If the Bible is overthrown, Christ ceases to be a Divine character, and His words, instead of being binding upon the conscience, can be followed or discarded according as the individual's convenience may dictate.

If, on the contrary, the Bible is true—infallible because divinely inspired,—then all the books that man has written are as far below the Bible in importance as man is below God in wisdom. The only ground upon which infallibility or inerrancy can be predicated is that the Book is inspired. Man uninspired cannot describe with absolute accuracy even that which has already happened. . . .

The Bible not only gives us history, and that, too, written in many cases long after the events transpired, but it gives us prophecy which was fulfilled centuries later. The language of the Bible cannot be explained by environment, for environment, in most instances, was entirely antagonistic. It cannot be explained by the genius of the writers, for they were largely among the unlettered. The Bible could not have lived because of favouritism shown to it, because it has been more bitterly attacked than any other book ever written. The attacks upon it probably outnumber the attacks made upon all other books combined, because it condemns man to his face, charges him with being a sinner in need of a Saviour, indicts him as no other

William Jennings Bryan, "The Inspiration of the Bible," in *Seven Questions in Dispute* (New York: Fleming Revell, 1924).

book does, holds up before him the highest standard ever conceived, and threatens him as he is threatened nowhere else.

And yet the Book stands and its circulation increases. How shall we account for its vitality, its indestructibility? By its inspiration and by that alone. Those who accept the Bible as true, inerrant, and infallible believe that the original autograph manuscripts which, through copies, are reproduced in the Old and New Testaments, were true, and true because divinely inspired—"holy men of God spake as they were moved by the Holy Ghost" (2 Peter 1:21). Because they were moved by the Holy Spirit, they spoke with accuracy and with the truth of God Himself. . . .

Orthodox Christians believe in plenary inspiration; that is, that all of the Bible was given by inspiration. They believe in verbal inspiration; that is, that the words used in the original manuscripts were the actual words of God as spoken by holy men of God "as they were moved by the Holy Ghost." They accept the Bible as true and divinely inspired, beginning with belief in God as Creator of all things, continuing Ruler of the universe which He made, and Heavenly Father to all His children. They believe that God is a personal God, who loves, and is interested in, all His creatures. They believe that He revealed His will unto men, and they accept the testimony of the writers of the Bible when they declare that the Holy Ghost spoke through them or through those whom they quote. . . .

The real conflict to-day is between those, on the one hand, who believe in God, in the Bible as the Word of God, and in Christ as the Son of God, and those, on the other hand, who believe in God but who believe that the Bible is inspired only in part—differing among themselves as to how much of it is inspired and as to what passages are inspired. The latter set up standards of their own, and there are nearly as many different standards as there are believers in partial inspiration. When they deny the infallibility of the Bible, they set up a standard that they regard either as infallible or as more trustworthy than the Bible itself. They really transfer the presumption of infallibility from the Bible to themselves, for either they say, "I believe this part of the Bible to be untrue because my own reason or my own judgment tells me that it is untrue," or they say, "I believe it untrue because So-and-So, in whose judgment I have confidence, tells me it is untrue." Whether one trusts in his own judgment as to the truthfulness of a passage, or trusts the judgment of some one else who denies the truthfulness of a passage, he is, in fact, trusting his own judgment, because if he does not rely on his own judgment in rejecting the passage it is his own judgment that substitutes the authority of the individual selected by him for the authority of the Bible.

It need hardly be added that such a rejection of the Bible, however the objector tries to limit it, is equivalent to a total rejection of the Bible as an authority, because an authority which is subject to be overruled on any point on any subject by anybody who cares to take the responsibility of overruling it, ceases to be of real value. . . .

A sophomore in a Georgia college informed me, at the conclusion of an address in Atlanta, that in order to reconcile Darwinism and Christianity, he only had to discard *Genesis!* Only *Genesis!* And yet there are three verses in the first chapter of *Genesis* that mean more to man than all the books of human origin: the first verse, which gives the most reasonable account of creation ever advanced; the twenty-fourth verse, which gives the only law governing the continuity of life on earth; and the twenty-sixth, which gives the only explanation of man's presence here.

6. Elizabeth Cady Stanton Finds Feminist Implications in Genesis, 1895

Genesis i: 26–28.

And God said, Let us make man in our image, after our likeness: and let them have dominion over the fish of the sea, and over the fowl of the air, and over the cattle, and over all the earth, and over every creeping thing that creepeth upon the earth.

So God created man in his *own* image, in the image of God created he him; male and female created he them.

And God blessed them, and God said unto them, Be fruitful, and multiply, and replenish the earth, and subdue it; and have dominion over the fish of the sea, and over the fowl of the air, and over every living thing that moveth upon the earth.

The first step in the elevation of woman to her true position, as an equal factor in human progress, is the cultivation of the religious sentiment in regard to her dignity and equality, the recognition by the rising generation of an ideal Heavenly Mother, to whom their prayers should be addressed, as well as to a Father.

If language has any meaning, we have in [the Genesis creation texts] a plain declaration of the existence of the feminine element in the Godhead, equal in power and glory with the masculine. The Heavenly Mother and Father! "God created man in his *own image, male and female*." Thus Scripture, as well as science and philosophy, declares the eternity and equality of sex—the philosophical fact, without which there could have been no perpetuation of creation, no growth or development in the animal, vegetable, or mineral kingdoms, no awakening nor progressing in the world of thought. The masculine and feminine elements, exactly equal and balancing each other, are as essential to the maintenance of the equilibrium of the universe as positive and negative electricity, the centripetal and centrifugal forces, the laws of attraction which bind together all we know of this planet whereon we dwell and of the system in which we revolve.

In the great work of creation the crowning glory was realized, when man and woman were evolved on the sixth day, the masculine and feminine forces in the image of God, that must have existed eternally, in all forms of matter and mind. . . .

. . . All those theories based on the assumption that man was prior in the creation, have no foundation in Scripture.

As to woman's subjection, on which both the canon and the civil law delight to dwell, it is important to note that equal dominion is given to woman over every living thing, but not one word is said giving man dominion over woman.

Genesis ii: 21–25.

And the Lord God caused a deep sleep to fall upon Adam, and he slept; and he took one of his ribs, and closed up the flesh thereof.

And the rib which the Lord God had taken from man, made he a woman, and brought her unto the man.

Elizabeth Cady Stanton, *The Women's Bible* (1895; reprint, New York: Arno Press, 1972), 14–15, 20–21.

> And Adam said, This *is* now bone of my bone, and flesh of my flesh: she shall be called Woman, because she was taken out of man.
>
> Therefore shall a man leave his father and his mother, and shall cleave unto his wife; and they shall be one flesh.
>
> And they were both naked, the man and his wife, and were not ashamed.

As the account of the creation in the first chapter is in harmony with science, common sense, and the experience of mankind in natural laws, the inquiry naturally arises, why should there be two contradictory accounts in the same book, of the same event? It is fair to infer that the second version, which is found in some form in the different religions of all nations, is a mere allegory, symbolizing some mysterious conception of a highly imaginative editor.

The first account dignifies woman as an important factor in the creation, equal in power and glory with man. The second makes her a mere afterthought. The world in good running order without her. The only reason for her advent being the solitude of man.

There is something sublime in bringing order out of chaos; light out of darkness; giving each planet its place in the solar system; oceans and lands their limits; wholly inconsistent with a petty surgical operation, to find material for the mother of the race. It is on this allegory that all the enemies of women rest their battering rams, to prove her inferiority. Accepting the view that man was prior in the creation, some Scriptural writers say that as the woman was of the man, therefore, her position should be one of subjection. Grant it, then as the historical fact is reversed in our day, and the man is now of the woman, shall his place be one of subjection?

The equal position declared in the first account must prove more satisfactory to both sexes; created alike in the image of God—The Heavenly Mother and Father.

Thus, the Old Testament, "in the beginning," proclaims the simultaneous creation of man and woman, the eternity and equality of sex; and the New Testament echoes back through the centuries the individual sovereignty of woman growing out of this natural fact. Paul, in speaking of equality as the very soul and essence of Christianity, said, "There is neither Jew nor Greek, there is neither bond nor free, there is neither male nor female; for ye are all one in Christ Jesus." With this recognition of the feminine element in the Godhead in the Old Testament, and this declaration of the equality of the sexes in the New, we may well wonder at the contemptible status woman occupies in the Christian Church of to-day.

All the commentators and publicists writing on woman's position, go through an immense amount of fine-spun metaphysical speculations, to prove her subordination in harmony with the Creator's original design.

It is evident that some wily writer, seeing the perfect equality of man and woman in the first chapter, felt it important for the dignity and dominion of man to effect woman's subordination in some way. To do this a spirit of evil must be introduced, which at once proved itself stronger than the spirit of good, and man's supremacy was based on the downfall of all that had just been pronounced very good. This spirit of evil evidently existed before the supposed fall of man, hence a woman was not the origin of sin as so often asserted.

7. George Herron Depicts Jesus as a Revolutionary Socialist, 1899

We are in the habit of saying that Jesus had nothing to do with institutions or with politics; that he went about appealing to individuals to "be saved." We have a fatal way of viewing Jesus apart from his history and social perspective, apart from the human facts which form the setting of his career. . . .

It is absurd to suppose that Jesus was put to death for going about healing sick people and appealing to individuals to "be saved," or to "be good," as we understand these terms. He was crucified for disturbing the existing national order of things; crucified as a national menace, because he was aiming at the wrong at the heart of the nation. His avowed purpose was to make the Jewish people a messianic and redemptive nation to the world. When he was rejected, it was a governmental as well as an ecclesiastical rejection. His death was brought about by the politicians, who were also the priests, or belonged to the priestly party. The chief actors in the drama of the crucifixion were such as we call the "good people," or "judiciously progressive," whose plans Jesus spoiled, and to whom he seemed altogether unamenable to reason. . . .

. . . But there is a fact of greatest significance, which the critics seem to me to have scarcely touched. It is the fact that the four extremely antagonistic parties concerned in Jewish politics—parties which had never been able to unite on anything else—found a meeting-ground and common interest in the putting to death of Jesus. There were the Pharisees, or Puritan party; there were the Sadducees, or party of the national aristocracy; there were the Herodians, or party of the existing and usurping dynasty; there were the Romans, interested in maintaining their conquest, and in subjecting all parties to the perpetuation of their power. These parties watched each other with bitterest hatred, and day and night plotted for each other's destruction. Yet each party believed itself driven by self-interest to destroy Jesus. All parties alike, whether social or religious, economic or political, agreed that there was no safety for their interests so long as Jesus was left alive. . . .

. . . We have only to read the Gospels, with even a little historic sense, to see that the career of Jesus was as certainly political, in relation to his times and nation, as the career of Joseph Mazzini in Italy, or that of Joan of Arc in France. His words reveal him in closest touch with the political situation and the economic and social facts of his day. He planted his feet amidst the actual conditions and problems of Jerusalem, spending a large part of his ministry there in vain before he turned into Galilee. His hands were always in the human clay, and he went about his work with a knowledge of the complications and forces with which he had to deal. He was no pietist or mere dreamer, but a re-maker of men and of the conditions that make men. . . .

There is one instance of Jesus' political action which has been a subject of much dispute. According to John, the first public act of his ministry was to go up to Jerusalem and clean out the Capitol. Whatever attitude we take towards this action,

George Herron, *Between Caesar and Jesus* (New York: Thomas Crowell, 1899), 143–149.

whether we place it at the beginning or the end of Jesus' ministry, it has a significance which we have too long evaded. The Jewish temple, which Jesus purged, was the political Capitol of the nation. He did precisely what one of us would do if we should go up to Washington, and suddenly drive from the Senate chamber the lobbyists, the chief of whom are our elected senators—elected to represent the corporations for which they are paid attorneys. . . . [A]ccording to the beloved apostle, his public introduction was at the capital of his nation, in the Capitol building, through what seemed to the authorities a high-handed act of political and economic outrage. He was finally put to death by the supreme court of his nation, on the ground that he endangered the nation's existence by doing the things he was doing, by saying the things he was saying. . . .

I can never understand the bald and persistent statement that Jesus had nothing to do with politics or economics, except on the ground that we are anxious to keep him out of politics and economics. It is only an apostate Christianity that asserts that the Christ has nothing to do with politics. The reign of Christ will never be unless it comes as a political reign. The notion that it can come otherwise is the accursed fruit of that worst and blackest of all heresies,—the heresy that religion is one thing and life another. The kingdoms of this world belong to Christ; and the Christianity that says that the preaching of Christ must be kept separate from politics and economics is simply the betrayer of Christ into the hands of his enemies. The price paid for this treason is the money of political and economic self-interests, as it ever has been and ever will be, until we have the revival that shall show forth Christ as the giver of economic and political law.

8. Russell Conwell Squares Christianity with Worldly Success, 1915

Now then, I say again that the opportunity to get rich, to attain unto great wealth, is here in Philadelphia now, within the reach of almost every man and woman who hears me speak tonight, and I mean just what I say. I have not come to this platform even under these circumstances to recite something to you. I have come to tell you what in God's sight I believe to be the truth, and if the years of life have been of any value to me in the attainment of common sense, I know I am right; that the men and women sitting here, who found it difficult perhaps to buy a ticket to this lecture or gathering to-night, have within their reach "acres of diamonds," opportunities to get largely wealthy. There never was a place on earth more adapted than the city of Philadelphia to-day, and never in the history of the world did a poor man without capital have such an opportunity to get rich quickly and honestly as he has now in our city. I say it is the truth, and I want you to accept it as such; for if you think I have come to simply recite something, then I would better not be here. I have no time to waste in any such talk, but to say the things I believe, and unless some of you get richer for what I am saying to-night my time is wasted.

Russell Conwell, *Acres of Diamonds* (New York: Harper and Bros., 1915).

I say that you ought to get rich, and it is your duty to get rich. How many of my pious brethren say to me, "Do you, a Christian minister, spend your time going up and down the country advising young people to get rich, to get money?" "Yes, of course I do." They say, "Isn't that awful! Why don't you preach the gospel instead of preaching about man's making money?" "Because to make money honestly is to preach the gospel." That is the reason. The men who get rich may be the most honest men you find in the community. . . .

For a man to have money, even in large sums, is not an inconsistent thing. We preach against covetousness, and you know we do, in the pulpit, and oftentimes preach against it so long and use the terms about "filthy lucre" so extremely that Christians get the idea that when we stand in the pulpit we believe it is wicked for any man to have money—until the collection-basket goes around, and then we almost swear at the people because they don't give more money. Oh, the inconsistency of such doctrines as that!

Money is power, and you ought to be reasonably ambitious to have it. You ought because you can do more good with it than you could without it. Money printed your Bible, money builds your churches, money sends your missionaries, and money pays your preachers, and you would not have many of them, either, if you did not pay them. I am always willing that my church should raise my salary, because the church that pays the largest salary always raises it the easiest. You never knew an exception to it in your life. The man who gets the largest salary can do the most good with the power that is furnished to him. Of course he can if his spirit be right to use it for what it is given to him.

I say, then, you ought to have money. If you can honestly attain unto riches in Philadelphia, it is your Christian and godly duty to do so. It is an awful mistake of these pious people to think you must be awfully poor in order to be pious.

Some men say, "Don't you sympathize with the poor people?" Of course I do, or else I would not have been lecturing these years. I won't give in but what I sympathize with the poor, but the number of poor who are to be sympathized with is very small. To sympathize with a man whom God has punished for his sins, thus to help him when God would still continue a just punishment, is to do wrong, no doubt about it, and we do that more than we help those who are deserving. While we should sympathize with God's poor—that is, those who cannot help themselves— let us remember there is not a poor person in the United States who was not made poor by his own shortcomings, or by the shortcomings of some one else. It is all wrong to be poor, anyhow.

ESSAYS

George Marsden of the University of Notre Dame is probably the greatest living American religious historian. *Fundamentalism and American Culture,* which he published in 1980, revolutionized historians' understanding of Fundamentalism. Far from being an insignificant nineteenth-century remnant, as most historians had supposed since the "Scopes Monkey Trial" of 1925, Marsden showed that it was in fact a movement with a distinguished pedigree, intellectually rigorous, and of lasting significance for America past and present. In the following difficult but closely reasoned passage from his book, Marsden explains the philosophical aspects of Charles Hodge's theology. As Marsden shows, Hodge, whose arguments against Darwinism are included in the documents of this chapter, was himself working in the rich tradition of Scottish Common Sense philosophy—then one of the dominant strains of American intellectual life.

The second essay, by Patrick Allitt of Emory University, surveys a few of the dozens of biographies of Jesus written by Americans in the late nineteenth and early twentieth centuries. The details of Jesus's life had earlier seemed less important than his death and resurrection, but liberal Christians, some of whom were beginning to doubt certain supernatural aspects of their religion, treated him primarily as a great man. This view, together with the era's fascination with biography, led many of them to "fill in the gaps" of his life. Sometimes ingenious, sometimes wildly implausible, they strike contemporary readers as unintentionally comical. Certainly they tell us much more about the life and times of their authors than about Jesus's life in Roman Palestine.

Presbyterian Ideas About Truth

GEORGE MARSDEN

A number of factors had converged in shaping the conservative Presbyterian ethos. Ethnically it represented the continuation of a Scottish and Scotch-Irish heritage which in the early twentieth century still had considerable force. This ethnic identity, however, had been preserved largely by the perpetuation of a highly articulated and heavily theological religious tradition. The symbols of this tradition were the *Confession of Faith* and *Catechisms* of the Westminster Assembly. The "Shorter" and the "Larger" catechisms (the "Shorter" being shorter only relative to the "Larger") were carefully engraved upon the minds of the young through arduous and awesome processes of memorization. Children of ten years were commonly taught to memorize such *Shorter Catechism* answers as:

> God having, out of his mere good pleasure, from all eternity, elected some to everlasting life, did enter a covenant of grace, to deliver them out of the estate of sin and misery, and to bring them into an estate of salvation, by a Redeemer.

In the Kentucky home where Benjamin Warfield was raised the memorization of the 107 answers was ordinarily completed by one's sixth year. Literacy was a virtual prerequisite for such faith, although sophisticated education was not essential.

Equally important was the *Confession of Faith*, which summarized and systematized Biblical teaching. . . .

. . . Old School Presbyterians had preserved a distinctive view of truth. They tended to view truth in its purest form as precisely stated propositions. This applied not only to the *Confession*, but also to the infallible Scriptures that the *Confession* summarized. In either case truth was a stable entity, not historically relative, best expressed in written language that, at least potentially, would convey one message in all times and places.

This view of things was particularly compatible with the Scottish Common Sense philosophy. No doubt it was not coincidental that this philosophy developed in Scotland where Presbyterianism was strong. Certainly in America some of its most ardent and persistent supporters, especially of the Scotch-Irish party, were those who emphasized the importance of traditional Reformation dogmatic statements.

These affinities were reinforced by direct connections. Just before the American Revolution, Princeton College secured as president an outstanding Scottish clergyman and educator, John Witherspoon, who made the college the center for Scottish Realism in America. By 1812 when the Presbyterian Church established its own seminary at Princeton, Scottish Realism was likewise what the faculty taught. It would be difficult to exaggerate its influence on Princeton theology in the nineteenth century.

Many Americans during the first half of the century employed the Common Sense categories, but at Princeton the appeal had especially to do with their conscious preservation of the classic Protestant emphasis on *scriptura sola*. Combating Roman Catholic apologists, the defenders of the Reformation in the sixteenth and seventeenth centuries had to stress the sufficiency of Scripture as the only rule of faith and practice. This position implied a corollary, "the perspicuity of Scripture." If, as the Protestants argued against the Catholics, neither the church nor tradition was essential to understanding the Biblical message, then it was necessary to claim that even simple Christians could understand the essential message of the Bible on their own. "The Scriptures are so perspicuous in things pertaining to salvation," affirmed Francis Turretin, the seventeenth-century theologian whose Latin text was used at Princeton, "that they can be understood by believers without the external help of an oral tradition or ecclesiastical authority." This meant that in interpretation of the essentials of Scripture the common sense perceptions of the common man could be relied upon. "The Bible is a plain book," said Charles Hodge. "It is intelligible by the people. And they have the right and are bound to read and interpret it for themselves; so that their faith may rest on the testimony of the Scriptures, and not that of the Church."

At Princeton, as well as in much of the rest of nineteenth-century Protestant America, the idea that a person of simple common sense could rightly understand Scripture was grounded in the more general affirmation of the Scottish philosophy that in essentials the common sense of mankind could be relied upon. . . . Any sane and unbiased person of common sense could and must perceive the same things.

Here and in other Common Sense statements we find the affirmation that basic truths are much the same for all persons in all times and places. This assumption is crucial to an understanding of the view of Christianity at Princeton and in fundamentalism generally. At nineteenth-century Princeton, unlike the situation among most later fundamentalists, the underlying philosophical basis for this assumption was frequently articulated in opposition to the currents of the day that threatened to erode it. The formidable *Princeton Review*, long under the editorship of Charles Hodge, repeatedly presented detailed and laudatory expositions of the Common Sense position. . . .

Such eternal truth, whether revealed in Scripture or in nature, was best refined by the scientific method. . . . The Princeton theologians saw themselves as champions of "impartiality" in the careful examination of the facts, as opposed to "metaphysical and philosophical speculations" such as those of German Biblical critics. . . . They often drew an analogy between theology and the hard sciences. As Charles Hodge said in introducing his *Systematic Theology*:

> If natural science be concerned with the facts and laws of nature, theology is concerned with the facts and the principles of the Bible. If the object of the one be to arrange and systematize the facts of the external world, and to ascertain the laws by which they are determined; the object of the other is to systematize the facts of the Bible, and ascertain the principles or general truths which those facts involve.

Using the analogy to natural science, Hodge considered truth adequately supported only when it was based on the exact apprehensions of intellect, and not on indefinable feelings. In answer to Friedrich Schleiermacher, who argued that true religion was grounded on feelings, Hodge insisted that "intellectual apprehension produces feelings, and not feeling intellectual apprehension." Although certainly not opposing religious feelings per se Hodge attacked all the trends of his day which based knowledge of Christian truth on such experiences. When Christianity becomes, as the Germans said, "the life of the soul," then, said Hodge, "the word of God is made of none effect." . . .

Genuine religious experience, Hodge was convinced, grew only out of right ideas; right ideas, in turn, could only be expressed in words. Hodge developed this point in relation to the doctrine of the inspiration of Scripture, which was an increasingly embattled position in the Princeton line of defense as the century wore on. Writing in 1857, Hodge observed that some interpreters suggested that "inspiration" applied to the thoughts of the sacred writers, but not to their exact words. To Hodge this was sheer nonsense. "No man can have a wordless thought, any more than there can be a formless flower," he said. "By a law of our present constitution, we think in words, and as far as our consciousness goes, it is as impossible to infuse thoughts into the mind without words, as it is to bring men into the world without bodies." The purpose of inspiration was to communicate a "record of truth." For such a record "accuracy of statement" and an "infallible correctness of the report were essential." These would not be assured if the selection of words were left to humans, whose memories were faulty. Although the method of inspiration was not merely mechanical dictation, the Holy Spirit could guarantee the accuracy of the reports only by inspiring the authors to select correct words. . . .

This view of truth as an externally stable entity placed tremendous weight on the *written* word. If truth were the same for all ages, and if truth was apparent primarily in objective facts, then the written word was the surest means permanently and precisely to display this truth. Religious experiences, rituals, traditions, even unrecorded words spoken by God or Jesus, as essential as all of these were, nonetheless were transitory. Unassisted, none could guarantee that sure facts would be objectively apprehended in all ages. "The Bible is to the theologian," said Charles Hodge in his *Systematic Theology*, "what nature is to the man. It is his store-house of facts. . . ." At Princeton it was an article of faith that God would provide nothing less than wholly accurate facts, whether large or small. Common Sense philosophy assured that throughout the ages people could discover the same truths in the unchanging storehouse of Scripture.

Another important element in this view of Scripture was tied to the Common Sense tradition. Common Sense philosophy, in contrast to most philosophy since Descartes and Locke, held that the immediate objects of our perceptions were not *ideas* of the external world, but (as the *Princeton Review* put it) "we are directly conscious of the external objects themselves." The same principle applied to memory; what we remember is not the *idea* of a past event, but the past event itself. So, for example, we do not remember the *idea* of Rome (which is in the present) but Rome itself, which is in the past. For such knowledge of the past, we must furthermore rely on the testimony of honest witnesses, else we could not know the past at all, which would be contrary to common sense.

This view that the past could be known directly through reliable testimony meant that Scripture was not regarded as representing the *points of view* of its authors respecting the past, but it was rather an infallible representation of the past itself. This distinction was intimately connected with the demand at Princeton that Scripture be accepted as without error, even in historical detail. Increasingly, modern thought suggested that the point of view of the observer stood between the facts and his report of the facts. This would suggest that even the most honest and authoritative accounts of the past would be altered in detail by the observer's point of view. At Princeton, however, the ideal for truth was an objective statement of fact in which the subjective element was eliminated almost completely. In their view, Scripture did just that. Although they did not deny the human element, divine guidance was thought to produce accounts where the warp from point of view had been virtually eliminated.

The whole Princeton view of truth was based on the assumption that truth is known by apprehending directly what is "out there" in the external world, not a function of human mental activity. The mind discovers objective truth, which is much the same for all people in all ages.

Yet, if truth is so objective and common sense so reliable, how does one account for the wide prevalence of error? This was the great obstacle to the whole Common Sense philosophy and the rock against which in the nineteenth century it repeatedly foundered, until all but its most stubborn exponents were dislodged. How is it that there are so many rational and upright people of good will who refuse to see the truth which consists of objective facts that are as plain as day? As the nineteenth century wore on, Americans were confronted with a bewildering diversity of ethnic and religious groups, and the Anglo-Saxon Protestant religious and moral consensus was breaking down. Questions concerning why others did not see the truth became increasingly acute. The Princeton and fundamentalist Common Sense explanations of why individuals accepted error has, of course, a great deal to do with understanding the fundamentalist reaction to modern ideas.

The Common Sense view of truth and error stood in a relationship to the prevailing modern views that was closely analogous to the relationship between Ptolemaic and Copernican accounts of the universe, and the difficulties in relating one view to the other were just as insuperable. As in the Ptolemaic astronomy the earth was regarded as a fixed point with the heavenly bodies all revolving around it, so in the Common Sense view of knowledge there was one body of fixed truth that could be known objectively, while around it revolved all sorts of errors, speculations, prejudices, and subjective opinions. Most other modern schemes of thought have tended toward the view that all observers, like all bodies in the Copernican universe, are (as it were) in motion—caught in historical processes. Rather than seeing truth as objectively existing at one fixed point, they have viewed knowledge as at least to a considerable degree relative to a person's time and point of view.

For B. B. Warfield, the greatest champion of the Princeton cause, during the critical period of the shipwreck and breaking apart of the Common Sense consensus in America, between the Civil War and World War I, accounting for the immense growth of error from a Common Sense position was a crucial concern. Like his predecessors, Warfield emphasized that faith must be grounded in right reason. . . . Reason is as necessary to faith, said Warfield, as light is to photography. Warfield indeed wrote as though he had unbounded confidence in the apologetic power of the rational appeal to people of common sense. . . .

With this opinion of the power of unaided reason in demonstrating the truth of Christianity, it was essential to Warfield's position to maintain that intellectually the believer and the non-believer stood on common ground. This common-ground approach eliminated from Warfield's apologetics the use of a venerable line of explanation for the failures of reason. In the traditions of Augustine, Calvin, and Jonathan Edwards the Fall was often regarded as having so blinded the human intellect that natural knowledge of God had been suppressed and therefore no one could have true understanding without receiving the eyes of faith. . . . Warfield, . . . was utterly mystified by this approach to apologetics which he described as "a standing matter of surprise." True to the demands of Common Sense, Warfield saw the effects of the Fall on human consciousness as pervasive but quite limited. "The science of sinful man is thus a substantive part of the abstract science produced by the ideal subject, the general human consciousness, though a less valuable part than it would be without sin."

How then, if Christian and non-Christian reason are essentially part of one human consciousness, does one explain the undeniable fact that human inquiry so often leads to totally wrong conclusions. Among traditional explanations were moral error, faulty reasoning, speculative hypotheses, metaphysical fancies, and the prejudices of unbelief or false religions. It was disturbing, however, in the latter decades of the nineteenth century to find that scientists who had been reared as Christians, morally upright, and certainly reasonable, were abandoning the faith as a consequence of their scientific studies. Warfield was particularly concerned with the case of Charles Darwin. Part of the explanation of Darwin's rejection of Christianity, he observed, was that he placed too much weight on speculation and hypothesis so that he developed an "invincible prejudice" or "predilection for his theory of the origin of species." In addition, Warfield saw a more basic issue, which he feared might be a widespread problem in the scientific community. Concentrating so intensely on their narrow scientific investigations, they were losing their capacity to deal with spiritual, moral, or ethical matters. "We can only account for Mr. Darwin's failure to accept the guidance of his inextinguishable conviction here," concluded Warfield, "by recognizing that his absorption in a single line of investigation and inference had so atrophied his mind in other directions that he had ceased to be a trustworthy judge of evidence."

Early in the twentieth century Warfield confronted the manifestation of this same problem in the growing rejection of the miraculous, not only by scientists, but even among theologians. In this case he saw a bias in their first principles. "Mere unreasonable dogmatism" prejudiced the opponents of miracles. The solution, however, was not to set one worldview or set of premises against another as competing hypotheses. Rather it was the Baconian method of setting a body of facts, objectively knowable by unbiased and dispassionate observers, against the eccentric and prejudiced biases of all competing worldviews. "In other words," Warfield concluded triumphantly, "are the facts that are to be permitted to occur in the universe to be determined by our precedently conceived world-view or is our world-view to be determined by a due consideration of all the facts that occur in the universe?" . . .

The Presbyterian furor reached its peak in the 1890s. Early in the decade moderately liberal leaders attempted a revision of the Confession of Faith, which was defeated in 1893. In the meantime conservatives counterattacked by bringing in succession formal action against three of the most famous of the progressive seminary professors, Charles A. Briggs, Henry Preserved Smith, and Arthur Cushman McGiffert. By the end of the decade all three had left the Presbyterian church as a result of these actions. Union Theological Seminary in New York severed its ties with the denomination in 1892 in response to the General Assembly's actions against Professor Briggs. Although some broad issues of departure from Calvinist orthodoxy were involved, in each case the specific allegations concerned the narrow issue of inerrancy. On several occasions during the decade the General Assembly declared that the doctrine of inerrancy was a fundamental teaching of the church.

As in other denominations, something of a truce seemed to prevail during most of the first two decades of the twentieth century; yet conservative Presbyterians were using the time to retrench themselves in the positions they had committed themselves to and successfully defended during the intense battles of the 1890s. This defensive strategy had an important bearing on the larger fundamentalist movement. For one thing it seemed to establish a precedent for the successful restraint of liberalism by formal ecclesiastical action. For another, it helped to characterize the movement as committed to defending a few fundamentals of faith. This latter effect, which was ironic in view of the elaborate confessionalism of conservative Presbyterians, apparently was not entirely intended. In 1910 the Presbyterian General Assembly, in response to some questions raised about the orthodoxy of some of the graduates of Union Theological Seminary, adopted a five-point declaration of "essential" doctrines. Summarized, these points were: (1) the inerrancy of Scripture, (2) the Virgin Birth of Christ, (3) his substitutionary atonement, (4) his bodily resurrection, and (5) the authenticity of the miracles. These five points (which included both the narrow issue of inerrancy and some of the broad issues concerning the supernatural in Christianity) were not intended to be a creed or a definitive statement. Yet in the 1920s they became the "famous five points" that were the last rallying position before the spectacular collapse of the conservative party. Moreover, because of parallels to various other fundamentalist short creeds (and an historian's error), they became the basis of what (with premillennialism substituted for the authenticity of the miracles) were long known as the "five points of fundamentalism."

As the issues broadened in the decades of relative peace at the beginning of the century, so apparently did conservative Presbyterians' willingness to cooperate with others who had a strict view of Scripture and were adamant against compromise on the essential supernatural elements in Christianity. With these increasingly important criteria in mind, the dispensationalist and Kewsick Bible teachers, with whom the Princeton party had many disagreements, looked more and more like worthwhile allies. The conservative wing of the Presbyterian church, of which Princeton was only the leading edge, already included some prominent leaders from the more evangelistically oriented movement. Although Princeton and the interdenominational Bible teachers' movement developed their views of Scripture and of the essential importance of the supernatural for independent reasons, they had much in common philosophically, and therefore spoke the same language and defended the faith in similar fashion.

The emergence of this alliance is most clearly perceptible in the foundation in 1903 of the Bible League of North America. This organization, with its journal, *The Bible Student and Teacher,* was initially dedicated to semipopular scholarly defense of the faith. It had the leadership predominantly of prominent conservative professors at Northern and Southern Presbyterian seminaries. Soon, however, dispensationalists became active in the movement, regular contributors to the journal (on non-dispensationalist themes), and board members. By 1913 board membership of the journal had been expanded well beyond the alliance of conservative Presbyterians and dispensationalists, with the editorship in the hands of a Methodist. The journal's name was changed to the *Bible Champion,* which signalled a more militant and popular stance. This anti-modernist coalition had one principal goal—"to maintain the historic faith of the Church in the divine inspiration and authority of the Bible as the Word of God." The outlines of a broad fundamentalist alliance were emerging.

Popular Versions of Jesus

PATRICK ALLITT

The two most popular novels in late-nineteenth-century America were Lew Wallace's *Ben Hur* (1880) and Charles Sheldon's *In His Steps* (1896). . . . Although the first of these two books is set in ancient Palestine and the second takes place in the contemporary American Midwest, they are dominated by the same central character, Jesus. Wallace's Judah Ben-Hur is a wealthy Jew. At first he intends to throw off the yoke of Roman rule by leading an insurrection, but when his mother and sister are healed of leprosy by Jesus, Ben Hur turns from the ways of war to the Christian promise of peace and love. The actions of Sheldon's characters spring from a scene early in the novel in which a Midwestern minister, Henry Maxwell, pledges that before he makes any decision or takes any action, he will ask himself: "What would Jesus do?" Just as Ben Hur's life is transformed by Jesus' message of love, so too is the life of Maxwell's city. Prostitution, drunkenness, and political corruption are gradually replaced by Christian faith, simplicity, and honesty.

Patrick Allitt, "The American Christ," *American Heritage*, November 1988, 128–141. Reprinted by permission of American Heritage Magazine, a division of Forbes, Inc. Copyright Forbes, Inc., 1988.

Between them *Ben Hur* and *In His Steps* sold more than ten million copies, were translated into twenty languages, and were adapted for the stage and screen. These two novels are the most famous examples of an abundant and well-circulated literature on Jesus written in the United States during the last two centuries. Novelists, biographers, reformers, poets, and businessmen joined theologians and ministers in the attempt to explain what Jesus was really like, hoping that Christianity could be understood in modern terms. Some were sincere, others disingenuous, but they almost invariably described a Jesus sympathetic to their own concerns. Bruce Barton, a businessman, wrote that Jesus was really an early advertising genius and his disciples a group of marketing executives; Eugene Debs, the American Socialist party leader, declared that "Comrade Jesus" was a hardworking carpenter who came to the rescue of the Galilean working class; and Robert Ingersoll, the most famous self-proclaimed agnostic of his day, argued that Jesus, like himself, had come to save the world from the tyranny of organized religion. Clearly, most of these self-serving portraits of Jesus tell us more about the lives and times of their American authors than they do about Palestine two thousand years ago.

It is a powerful advantage in a predominantly Christian nation to believe that Jesus approves of one's way of life. By identifying oneself with Jesus, one stands a good chance of seizing the American moral high ground. The ambiguous character of the four Gospels made it possible for each of these authors to find the Jesus and the idealized vision of themselves that they were looking for. The Gospels are short, they sometimes contradict one another, and they leave a great deal unsaid about the life of Jesus. Two of the evangelists, Matthew and Luke, describe the miracles surrounding Jesus' birth, but the other two start with his ministry at about the age of thirty. Apart from a single reference in Luke to Jesus as a twelve-year-old boy questioning the priests in the temple, none of the Gospels speak of his early life. But where the Gospels were silent, the American biographers of Jesus rushed in with a spectacular variety of explanations of what he was doing for all those undescribed years.

Biographers continued to differ on the significance even of those portions of Jesus' life that *are* recorded in the Gospels. They disputed whether Jesus saw himself as the promised Messiah of the Old Testament and whether his greatest work was his teaching, the healing miracles, or the inspiration he provided for social reforms. . . .

Books about Jesus, written by men and women with no pretensions to biblical scholarship, showed up with increasing regularity in the 1860s and 1870s. At first many authors hoped to combine full descriptions of Jesus' life with strict historical accuracy. They regarded their books—which appear fictitious to us—as biographical. For example, Henry Ward Beecher, one of the most eminent clergymen of his day, wrote *The Life of Jesus, the Christ* in 1871. He said that he was worried about the scholarly controversy in Germany. Although modern New Testament studies "may lead scholars from doubt to certainty, they are likely to lead plain people from certainty into doubt and leave them there."

Beecher, who came from a distinguished theological family, had been deeply influenced by reading Charles Darwin's *On the Origin of Species* soon after its publication in 1859. Some ministers regarded Darwin's evolutionary theory as a terrible threat to their faith, but Beecher welcomed it. He came to believe that religious thought was subject to the same evolutionary processes as were human beings themselves and that, accordingly, the Gospels needed to be rewritten to take advantage of recent progress: "There are reasons deeper yet why the Life of Christ should be rewritten for each and every age. The life of the Christian Church has . . . been a gradual unfolding and interpretation of the spiritual truths of the gospels. The knowledge of the human heart, of its yearnings, its failures, its sins and sorrows, has immensely increased in the progress of the centuries. . . ."

Beecher declared that his advantageous position down the evolutionary chain from the evangelists made it possible for his life of Jesus to be *better* and more illuminating than theirs. It is no surprise after this preparation to find that Beecher's Jesus turns out to be an evolutionary theorist: " 'Think not that I am come to destroy the law, or the prophets: I am not come to destroy, but to fulfil.' Jesus would reform the world not by destroying but by developing the germs of truth already existing. He accepted whatever germs of truth and goodness had ripened through thousands of years. He would join his own work to that already accomplished, bringing to view the yet higher truths of the spiritual realm."

By the 1870s tensions in America were becoming aggravated by the rise of the industrial cities, and Beecher's *Life of Jesus, the Christ* refers to several social problems of the day, including the issue of temperance. Evangelical Christians were then at the forefront of a campaign to prohibit the sale and consumption of alcohol. What were they to do with passages in the New Testament that describe Jesus drinking wine, or the first miracle at Cana, where he changed water into wine? The Reverend William Thayer had tried to solve the problem by arguing in *Communion Wine and Bible Temperance* (1869), that the Bible actually spoke of two different kinds of wine, of which Jesus drank only the type that was an unfermented grape juice. Beecher, in his narrative of Jesus' life, spent several pages discussing the merits of Thayer's view but finally rejected it, though he did note that the wine of Palestine was "light," not at all the "fiery spirits" that caused such havoc in American city slums.

Turning aside for a moment from what Jesus actually did, Beecher argued: "Had Jesus, living in our time, beheld the wide waste and wretchedness arising from inordinate appetites, can any one doubt on which side he would be found? Was not his whole life a superlative giving up of his own rights, for the benefit of the fallen? Did he not teach that customs, institutions and laws must yield to the inherent sacredness of man? In his own age, he ate and drank as his countrymen did, judging it to be safe to do so. But this is not a condemnation of the course of those who, in other lands and under different circumstances, wholly abstain from wine and strong drink, for their own good and for the good of others."

By making this argument, Beecher established one of the techniques that have persisted in the Jesus literature ever since. If Jesus did something of which an author approves, he is cited as authority for doing likewise. But if Jesus did the opposite of what the author requires, an argument about changed social context can always explain away the difficulty: Jesus *would* have acted this way had he been alive now.

Beecher's sister Harriet Beecher Stowe was already one of the most famous women in America; her best seller of 1852, *Uncle Tom's Cabin*, had done much to arouse antislavery sentiment in the North in the years before the Civil War. In 1877 Stowe wrote a life of Jesus, *Footsteps of the Master*. The degree to which Jesus was malleable in the hands of different authors becomes apparent when we find Stowe arguing that Jesus was "one of those loving, saintly mothers." Although she doubted some of the miraculous stories in the Gospels, Stowe was determined that the virgin birth of Jesus should not be rationalized away; so long as it was preserved, Jesus remained exclusively the child of a woman, and thus more capable of sympathy toward women than any other famous man in history.

From that time on many women writing about Jesus made the same case. Elizabeth Stuart Phelps wrote, in *The Story of Jesus Christ* (1897), that Jesus had an unrivaled sensitivity to the needs of sick and elderly women. She described Jesus as a reforming visionary in his treatment of women as the equals of men: "He seemed almost unconscious of the social revolution of which he was laying the foundations. He went straight on with serene and beautiful indifference, always treating women with respect, always recognizing their fettered individualism, their force of character . . . their undeveloped powers, their terrible capacity for suffering, their superiority in spiritual vigor. He boldly took . . . the stand . . . that . . . men and women stood before God upon the same moral plane, and that they ought so to stand before human society."

In the case of Phelps, an autobiographical element entered into her description of Jesus. She made a considerable fortune by writing sentimental novels, the most renowned of which, *The Gates Ajar* (1868), told of the Heaven to which dying Victorians could aspire. Her husband, younger than she, lived off her earnings, refused to comfort her in a long sickness, and failed to return from a yachting trip when she lay dying. Phelps's Jesus is the sort of caring husband she would doubtless have preferred.

Phelps, Stowe, and many other women of the late nineteenth century depicted a nurturing and feminized Jesus. But all other Jesus literature of the era was overshadowed by *Ben Hur*, Lew Wallace's hymn to muscular and manly Christianity. Wallace himself was a colorful man: a major general in the Union Army during the Civil War, a state senator in his home state of Indiana and later governor of the New Mexico Territory, a part-time novelist, and ultimately America's minister to Turkey. He finished *Ben Hur* during his tenure at Santa Fe, breaking off at one point to pursue the Apache rebel Victorio. At first *Ben Hur* was not particularly well received. One San Francisco reviewer wrote: "Governor Lew Wallace is a 'literary feller' chiefly given to writing novels of an uncertain sort. He is following up *The Fair God* with *Ben Hur: A Story of the Christ*. I protest, as a friend of Christ, that He has been crucified enough already without having a Territorial Governor after Him." After a slow start *Ben Hur*'s popularity and sales began to soar, and translations and adaptation for the stage soon followed. After reading an Italian translation, Pope Leo XIII commended Wallace for his contributions to Christian understanding.

Ben Hur, for all its fame, has many faults . . . : its melodramatic Victorian plot is full of unexplained gaps, and the story advances with the help of a series of wildly improbable coincidences and strokes of good fortune. Of these, perhaps the most noteworthy is that the hero, Judah Ben-Hur, has an unrivaled talent for acquiring wealth without working. He survives five years as a Roman galley slave, rescues his admiral in the heat of battle, and receives a fortune as a reward. He then travels to Antioch, where he discovers that the richest man in the world, Simonides, is none other than an old family slave. Moreover, Simonides has made the money not for himself but for his "young master," and he begs to be allowed to serve as slave to the house of Hur once again, as does his comely daughter Esther (who ends the book as Mrs. Hur).

Wallace mixed high adventure with Christianity by having his chief character act as an alter ego to Jesus. Jesus makes contact with Ben Hur at crucial turning points in the book, once to save the hero from despair as he trudges to the galleys, later to cure Ben Hur's mother and sister of their hideous leprosy, and finally at the crucifixion, when Ben Hur realizes that Jesus is dying in order that he and all other mortals might live. Between these brief but crucial appearances of Jesus, Ben Hur leads a vigorous and unreflective life. He wins a chariot race against his arch-enemy Messala, plots the overthrow of Rome by secretly training an army of Jewish malcontents, and almost falls into the clutches of a beautiful but treacherous Egyptian temptress.

While the ostensible theme of the book is that the temptation of worldly affairs is overcome in Christianity, Wallace actually revels in the worldly adventures of Ben Hur. . . .

Some Americans of the 1880s still regarded novels as morally corrupting and refused to permit them into their homes. But as the reputation of *Ben Hur* spread, this book, with its blending of fiction and religious uplift, was admitted to homes previously free of novels. Wallace, in later years, said that the idea of making his novel a vindication of Christianity came to him after a chance encounter on a train with Robert Ingersoll, whose lecture tours in the late nineteenth century delighted free-thinkers and scandalized the orthodox. It is remarkable to find that the agnostic Ingersoll, no less than his Christian contemporaries, had a great deal to say about Jesus and that, like them, he found a Jesus rather like himself: "For the man Christ I have infinite respect . . . [and] to that great and serene man I gladly pay . . . the tribute of my admiration and my tears. He was a reformer in his time. He was regarded as a blasphemer and his life was destroyed by hypocrites, who have in all ages done what they could to trample freedom and manhood out of the human mind. Had I lived at that time, I would have been his friend and should he come again he will not find a better friend than I will be." Ingersoll recognized that it was not enough simply to discount the traditional religious interpretation of Jesus. Rather, in a society where Jesus was almost universally honored, he had to show how closely his own views and those of Jesus agreed. He, no less than his Christian rivals, was trying to lay claim to "the real Jesus."

America was a dynamic, commercially expanding society in the Gilded Age of the late nineteenth century, and its people must have found reassuring the coexistence of Christianity with immense wealth in *Ben Hur*. Charles Sheldon, with *In His Steps* (1896), did little to disturb the picture. At first it seems that the people of the city of Raymond (modeled on Sheldon's hometown of Topeka, Kansas) are going to be financially ruined by pledging to ask at every turn of their lives, "What would Jesus do?" In the short run there are many difficulties. The citizen who discloses corruption on the railroad loses his job, the newspaper whose editor refuses to print descriptions of a prizefight loses circulation, and the dry-goods merchant who decides to treat his work force as one big happy Christian family surrenders his steady profits. All endure temporary reversals. But as the book moves to its climax, we discover that Christian honesty is the best policy and that the people are thriving commercially as never before. . . .

In His Steps is a fascinating guide to the social reform priorities of American Protestants in the depression decade of the 1890s. It is, above all, a temperance novel, arguing that the woes of poor Americans spring principally from the temptations of drink. The middle-class characters in the novel devote themselves to contesting the political privileges of the saloonkeepers and to rescuing the "fallen women" who lurk in the shadows of their taverns. "Was not the most Christian thing they could do to act as citizens in the matter, fight the saloon at the polls, elect good men to the city offices, and clean the municipality?"

Sheldon was also interested in the settlement-house movement. In the slums of Chicago and New York, progressive reformers like Jane Addams and Lillian Wald had established settlements of middle-class volunteers to help poor immigrants adapt to urban life and to improve conditions of public health and sanitation. One of the characters in *In His Steps*, Felicia Sterling, relinquishes her soft and privileged existence to do likewise, and Sheldon remarks of the settlement-house movement: "It was not a new idea. It was an idea started by Jesus Christ when He left His Father's House and forsook the riches that were His in order to get nearer humanity and, by becoming a part of its sin, helping to draw humanity apart from its sin. The University Settlement idea is not modern. It is as old as Bethlehem and Nazareth." . . .

In His Steps . . . is different from *Ben Hur* and the Jesus biographies in that Jesus himself never actually appears but is, rather, contained within the minds of the characters. Another literary sensation of the 1890s using the same device of an implicit Jesus was William T. Stead's *If Christ Came to Chicago* (1893). Stead was an English urban reformer with a particular ardor for stamping out prostitution, and he scandalized Chicago by printing a list of all the businessmen and local dignitaries who were implicated in the prostitution trade. He went on to claim that Jesus would do the same thing were he to reappear in Chicago. "If Christ came to Chicago, it seems to me that there are few objects that would more command His sympathy and secure His help than efforts to restore the sense of brotherhood to man and to reconstitute the human family on a basis adjusted to modern life." Stead, more than Sheldon or Wallace, preached a hard lesson on the basis of Jesus' example, and he exhorted his readers and fellow reformers: "Be a Christ. The more you disbelieve in Christianity as it is caricatured, the more earnestly you should labor to live the life and manifest the love and, if need be, to die the death, of Jesus of Nazareth."

Many late-nineteenth-century reformers believed that cities threatened the republican spirit of the American people, and they looked with suspicion at the Italians, Jews, Slavs, and other immigrants flowing into them. For biographers of Jesus living in these surroundings, it became highly significant that Jesus lived in the country village of Nazareth, gathered his disciples in the countryside of Galilee, and came to grief only when he went to the big city of Jerusalem.

The title of Mary Austin's biography of Jesus, *A Small Town Man* (1915), emphasized this point. She presents a Jesus who would have been at home in upstate New York or downstate Illinois in the early twentieth century: "One finds him going about with other householders, decent folk owning their own businesses, employing hired servants, paying their own scores, and obliged to ask no man's leave if they chose to lay aside their work for a season and go a-proselyting." It was no surprise to Austin that Jesus should be destroyed by the wicked leaders of the big city of Jerusalem. She believed that Jesus was crucified because he was in danger of breaking up the corrupt city and temple oligarchy, which was as brazen in its administration as the Tweed Ring of New York or the cases that Lincoln Steffens had recently exposed in *The Shame of the Cities*. "The constant flow of tribute into Jerusalem had begotten a ring of grafters as invincible and corrupt as ever controlled a modern municipality. . . . Altogether the temple rake-off amounted to forty thousand dollars yearly."

Like many progressive reformers, Mary Austin had an optimistic view of humanity and believed that if the corrupt ringleaders of the government could be removed, decency would be restored. Once again, the parallels between her own times and those of Jesus were apparent: "The difficulty was that the chief reason why Jesus must be put out of the way—his interference with the temple traffic—nobody dared mention. Evidently not all the Sanhedrin shared or approved of the buying and selling within the sanctuary. Here we have a thoroughly modern situation: a representative body in the main well-intentioned, manipulated by a group within the group whose spring of action was illegitimate profit."

This theme of conflict between country and city persisted well into the twentieth century. In Fulton Oursler's bestselling biography of Jesus, *The Greatest Story Ever Told* (1949), there is again a juxtaposition of the simple, honest country folks going into the lion's den of a corrupt city and trying to preserve their independence and pride as they go: "Oh yes, he [Joseph] knew that in Jerusalem sophisticates looked down on the countrified Nazarenes, yokels with a ridiculous northern accent. . . . But Joseph, with all his fellow townsmen, felt that the people of Jerusalem were unnatural and overcivilized. Anyway, he was proud of his home town."

Joseph and his fellow villagers are impressed by the magnitude of the city despite themselves: " 'I think Nazareth is a very much pleasanter place,' Mary answered. With this the others agreed. They said that Jerusalem was a great place to visit but they would never want to live there."

Although the development of giant cities gave rise to this literary protest, few Americans wanted to abandon the source of their growing prosperity. An alternative solution was offered by American socialists, who accepted industrialization but sought a more equitable distribution of its profits, putting their faith in the future rather than in the past. Just as the advocates of rural simplicity had found a Jesus to their liking, so too did the socialists.

In Europe the socialist movement was anticlerical and usually hostile to religion as an "opiate of the masses." Karl Marx and Friedrich Engels wrote that "Christ was a man as we are, a prophet and a teacher, and his Eucharist is a mere commemoration meal wherein bread and wine are consumed without any mystic garnishing."

Inclined to revere Jesus and to see in his ministry a precursor of their own struggle, American socialists were often more sympathetic to religion than their European counterparts. After all, Jesus was a carpenter, sprung from the simple working people, and a man who detested exploitation of the weak by the strong. Socialist magazines such as *The Masses* ran cartoons of Jesus, wearing overalls and carrying his carpenter's tools, speaking at union meetings and participating in the life of the working class.

The Socialist party leader and perennial presidential candidate Eugene Debs was also a biographer of Jesus. In *Jesus, the Supreme Leader* Debs argued that Jesus "organized a working class movement . . . for no other purpose than to destroy class rule and set up the common people as the sole and rightful inheritors of the earth." The heroic days of the early church, said Debs, had been true to Jesus' message, but then Christianity was co-opted by the Roman Empire and became the religion of the oppressing classes: "The dead Christ was then metamorphosed from the master revolutionist who was ignominiously slain, a martyr to his class, into the pious abstraction, the harmless theological divinity who died that John Pierpont Morgan [a prominent banker] could be 'washed in the blood of the lamb.' " Another socialist depiction of Jesus was Upton Sinclair's *They Call Me Carpenter* (1922). Lew Wallace and Charles Sheldon had smoothed over the awkward matter of Jesus' teaching against great wealth; Sinclair seized on it. "Mr. Carpenter," a modern transfiguration of Jesus, lives with strikers, socialists, and the impoverished Mexican inhabitants of Los Angeles. Sinclair emphasizes Jesus' wrathful sermons against hypocrites and Pharisees (updated as Hollywood entrepreneurs and the established churches) and has Carpenter declare: "The days of the exploiter are numbered. The thrones of the mighty are tottering, and the earth shall belong to them that labor." . . .

. . . The vitality of American business during the 1920s played a part [in the decline of socialism] and it is no coincidence that two biographies of Jesus from that decade are celebrations of capitalism. The more flagrant is Bruce Barton's *The Man Nobody Knows* (1924). Barton was a partner in the advertising agency Batten, Barton, Durstine and Osborn, and it seemed to him that he was doing for the twentieth century what Jesus had done for the first. His lead quotation, "Wist ye not that I must be about my father's *business,*" set the tone for the book, in which Barton presents Jesus as an advertising genius.

The hard-hitting, straightforward language of the parables, the bluntly effective managerial style, and the man's sheer energy won Barton's praise. Some people think of Jesus as effeminate and weak, said Barton, but in fact, he was "a great outdoorsman," "the most popular dinner guest in Jerusalem," and an unrivaled entrepreneur. "Every one of his conversations, every contact between his mind and others, is worthy of the attentive study of any sales manager." What were his twelve apostles but a marketing organization that set forth and conquered the world? Why were they so successful? Because they believed in the quality of the product! *The Man Nobody Knows* sold half a million hardback copies, and it is still in print, not just as a historical curiosity but as an inspirational guide.

Defenders of capitalism usually emphasize that theirs is not solely a system designed to facilitate the piling up of fortunes. They stress instead that it provides money for the protection of families and a higher quality of workmanship than can be found under any other economic system. These themes are stressed in another capitalist-Jesus biography from the 1920s, Robert Norwood's *The Man Who Dared to Be God* (1929). Solving the mystery of what Jesus did up to the age of thirty, Norwood tells us that he was a successful boatbuilder on the Sea of Galilee. On leaving home, he tells his mother: "Let me go to Capernaum and build boats. It is a good business. The lake towns are prosperous. . . . There ought to be a fine chance for a handy man to lead some of that prosperity hither to Nazareth."

Norwood writes that Joseph has died young, leaving the family threatened with poverty. Jesus steps in and builds up his boat business for his brothers and acquires money for his sisters' dowries before setting out on his mission: "He had toiled to lift the shadow of poverty from the door of his father's house. He had left nothing undone. His brothers were prosperous. His mother was happy."

FURTHER READING

Allitt, Patrick. *Catholic Converts: British and American Intellectuals Turn to Rome* (1997).

Appleby, R. Scott. *Church and Age Unite: The Modernist Impulse in American Catholicism* (1992).

Carey, Patrick, ed. *American Catholic Religious Thought: The Shaping of a Theological and Social Tradition* (1987).

Cort, John. *Christian Socialism: An Informal History* (1988).

Fuller, Robert C. *Naming the Antichrist: The History of an American Obsession* (1995).

Hart, D. G. *Defending the Faith: J. Gresham Machen and the Crisis of Conservative Protestantism in Modern America* (1994).

Hoeveler, David J. *James McCosh and the Scottish Intellectual Tradition: From Glasgow to Princeton* (1981).

Hutchison, William. *The Modernist Impulse in American Protestantism* (1976).

Kuklick, Bruce. *Churchmen and Philosophers from Jonathan Edwards to John Dewey* (1985).

———. *Puritans in Babylon: The Ancient Near East and American Intellectual Life, 1880–1930* (1996).

Livingstone, David N. *Darwin's Forgotten Defenders: The Encounter Between Evangelical Theology and Evolutionary Thought* (1987).

McDannell, Colleen. *Heaven: A History* (1988).

Marsden, George. *The Soul of the American University: From Protestant Establishment to Established Non-Belief* (1994).

Moore, James R. *The Post-Darwinian Controversies: A Study of the Protestant Struggle to Come to Terms with Darwin in Great Britain and America, 1870–1900* (1979).

Roberts, Jon. *Darwinism and the Divine in America: Protestant Intellectuals and Organic Evolution, 1859–1900* (1988).

Sandeen, Ernest. *The Roots of Fundamentalism: British and American Millenarianism, 1800–1930* (1970).

Szasz, Ferenc. *The Divided Mind of Protestant America, 1880–1930* (1982).

Turner, James. *Without God, Without Creed: The Origins of Unbelief in America* (1985).

Weber, Timothy. *Living in the Shadow of the Second Coming: American Premillennialism, 1875–1925* (1979).

Wells, David, ed. *Reformed Theology in America: A History of Its Modern Development* (1985).

Assimilation and Adaptation: 1920–1960

American participation in the First World War in 1917 and 1918 led to intense pressure for "Americanization." The several million German-Americans who still spoke and worshiped in German hastily converted their public meetings into English, while members of other ethnic groups adopted American ways to demonstrate their own "100% Americanism." In 1921 and 1924 Congress passed laws restricting immigration from southern and eastern Europe. From then on, through the middle decades of the twentieth century, the number of immigrants arriving in America was relatively small. As a result the ethnic communities that had welcomed each new wave of immigrants began to break up. Assimilated members of the second and third generations, familiar with American customs and the English language, moved away from old neighborhoods, often taking their religions with them but leaving most of their grandparents' foreign characteristics behind.

Sociologists and journalists then, and historians since, have debated the extent of assimilation. Was there a real American "melting pot" out of which the descendants of immigrants came as generic Americans? Or was there, as religious sociologist Will Herberg suggested in the 1950s, a "triple melting pot," in which Protestantism, Catholicism, and Judaism, each sharing core American values and speaking English, became the three acceptable ways of expressing one's Americanness? Internal variations within Protestantism, Catholicism, and Judaism did not disappear, but antagonists within all three generally conformed to what another sociologist, Robert Bellah, called America's "civil religion."

The early through mid-twentieth century was also a period of immense scientific and technological progress. As larger numbers of Americans gained access to higher education, the colleges and universities lost much of the distinctive religious character they had once exhibited. Most had begun as Protestant seminaries, but by 1960 the best ones advocated an intellectual ideal of scientific impartiality, where appointment to a faculty position relied on expertise rather than religious orthodoxy. Jewish intellectuals, no longer excluded for ethnic and religious reasons and sympathetic to the scientific ideal, became important players among the American intellectual elite.

In other ways, too, Protestant influence was declining. The great Protestant-Progressive reform movements of the early twentieth century were incorporated by trade unions or secular branches of government. Prohibition, a reform movement to which several generations of Protestants had dedicated themselves, proved to be a disastrous failure. It provoked such a wave of organized crime, evasion, and cynicism in the 1920s that President Franklin Roosevelt directed Congress to repeal it in 1934. While the Protestant "mainline" felt acutely the waning of its influence, Catholic and Jewish commentators worried that too much assimilation would eviscerate their traditions altogether. Their objective, expressed in various ways between the 1920s and the 1960s, was to make themselves "different, but not too different" from their neighbors of other faiths.

 D O C U M E N T S

Clara Grillo, a Cleveland schoolteacher from an Italian family, describes in Document 1 (c. 1920) how a Protestant settlement house, by offering practical help and advice to immigrants, began to lure them away from their traditional Catholicism. In Document 2 (c. 1920), Jacob Sonderling, an immigrant rabbi, describes his dismay at finding American Jews abandoning venerable practices such as the segregation of men and women in the synagogue, and tells how some of them manipulated Prohibition and the kosher food laws to their own advantage. In Document 3 (1927), Sinclair Lewis, the first American to win a Nobel Prize for literature, describes skeptically the religious atmosphere of a small midwestern Protestant community in which his scoundrelly character Elmer Gantry grew up. Walter Lippmann, author of Document 4, was one of the most influential journalists and commentators of the 1920–1960 era. His book *A Preface to Morals* (1929), excerpted here, points to the dilemma of a world where confident faith is declining and shows that the fundamentalist author Gresham Machen has seen and analyzed the issue more clearly than his liberal Protestant adversaries. Mordecai Kaplan, founder of Jewish Reconstructionism, argues in Document 5 (1948) that Judaism is as much a form of civilization as a religion, and that it must constantly evolve to meet new cultural conditions. Document 6 is a passage from sociologist Will Herberg's pioneering book *Protestant, Catholic, Jew* (1955), in which he makes the case for a generically American faith subdivided into three main categories, rather than a miscellaneous "melting pot." Donald Thorman, author of Document 7 (1962), is a Catholic journalist eager to see his coreligionists get out of the religious ghetto and assimilate into the mainstream of American life, but anxious lest they lose their distinctiveness in the process.

1. Clara Grillo Recalls Protestant-Catholic Tensions in Cleveland, c. 1920

My father's attachment to the old country lasted only while his mother was alive. When she died, he really abandoned things Italian since he spoke enough English to get along. When he was nearing 80 years of age, however, he became lonesome for his Italian friends and family and he even returned to church services. He had

Salvatore J. LaGumina, *The Immigrant Speaks* (New York: Center for Migration Studies, 1977), 118–119, 122–133.

no membership in clubs although I still maintain the old ties with "Little Italy" via correspondence and visits.

The first house rented by my parents was about two doors away from the Mayfield Theater. It was the front house, the backyard of which housed the local wine press. Among the important institutions in the neighborhood was the Holy Rosary Church, established in 1860, whose priest called personally for donations.

Not long after we moved there, we discovered the Alta House located on the corner of E. 125th Street and Mayfield Road. . . . Being illiterate both my father and mother never went there. Both were obsessed with work. . . . They had no time for socials or recreation or education. The church, Alta Settlement House (said to be named after a member of John D. Rockefeller's family) and Murray Hill School, all offered much help to the newcomers. The Alta House was a settlement home established by the Rockefellers under Protestant direction. As such, the Holy Rosary Catholic Church priests did not approve but a number of Italians went there despite this. Alta tried to Americanize immigrants, stressing health, cleanliness, nutrition, crafts, sports, and American citizenship. Since the old rickety, clapboard houses in Little Italy had only the most basic plumbing, and were without bathtubs or showers, many used the Alta facilities. Our boarders, for example, bathed at the Alta House on Saturdays. For ten cents they received a clean towel, soap, and a shower. . . .

In Alta House women learned to sew, embroider and care for themselves when pregnant in prenatal clinics after which they later attended the baby clinics there. For school children the settlement house provided tonsil clipping clinics, sports, swings and baseball. Dancing parties and even citizenship preparation classes and English classes met there. All tended to "Americanize" recent arrivals—the vogue of social workers then.

There was also in Cleveland a Citizenship Bureau, the International Institute branch of the Y.W.C.A. and the Cleveland Board of Education which conducted bilingual classes to help immigrants become citizens. Immigrant women were provided with interpreters when applying for charity, specialized clinics for eyecare and rare diseases or for welfare. Americanization was intended to make us forget our Italian roots since anything "foreign" was suspect. Yet, nobody bothered to stop and explain to us what was wrong or right. Consequently, we were seldom welcome in established communities. Social workers played a prominent role in our Americanization although the oldest Italian population was not easily influenced.

The Catholic Church was the most important influence although a Protestant church existed near the Murray Hill school. The latter's progress was unheralded. Everything centered around the Holy Rosary parish. . . .

The religious services available to us during our early years were adequate. We availed ourselves only of church attendance and priests' services for special religious holidays and what I term vital statistics. That is, we were baptized soon after birth, made our First Communion after proper instruction, took on an additional name for Confirmation, were married in the Church and buried with a High Mass and/or grave rites.

Those who were not regular in church attendance were denied the glory of the central aisle for their marriages or funerals. These reprobates were ushered into the side entrance of the church for burial. The godparents for confirmees were denied the privilege of being godparents if their answers to the priest's probing sounded too liberal. Personally, I was told I was a good Christian and not a good Catholic. I had doubly sinned: once by teaching the *Parables of Jesus* at the University Baptist Church in Austin, Texas; and second by being a missionary in a black Protestant community during my freshman and sophomore years. Oh yes, and in Cleveland, Ohio, I was a Boy Scout temporary leader in 1926 (after I had obtained my Bachelor of Science degree in Education from Ohio State University). I had overheard the Italian Baptist minister complain of lack of leadership in the community so I volunteered, was accepted and stayed on until a male was found to take over. This was interpreted as "crazy" by the neighbors. They blamed it on too much reading.

The clergy available to us were good, kind, but sometimes limited. They helped the poor, comforted the bereaved, and counseled the confused women of the community. The Irish priests in Little Italy were sometimes arrogant but largely respected. Father Francis Haley was a patient home visitor, confessor, and helper. The Trivisonos and other families mentioned in the *Church History of Holy Rosary Church* labored hard to pay off the mortgage, establish a parochial school and acquire their own social hall to offset the hated Protestant influence of their rival— the Alta House. In the early days one had to choose either the Church or the settlement house. Now, however, I understand that this schism has been healed through the valiant efforts of the enlightened Church and settlement house leaders. There was also a Protestant church on Murray Hill Road and one later in the Collinwood, "Five Points" (spin-off of Little Italy) on Kipling Road, which numbered many Italians in their congregations.

In later years native American clergy were assigned to our parishes. They seemed more attractive than their somber Italian trained confreres. I remember getting to know one jolly younger Italian priest who had a real *joie de vivre*. Basically, it was the attitudes of the older, "ex-monks" that repelled me as a youngster.

2. Jacob Sonderling, Immigrant Rabbi, Observes American Jewish Life, c. 1930

In 1923, a new life opened to me—America. The *Manchuria* left Antwerp—the last city in Europe I had seen—and went out on the high seas towards an unknown tomorrow. . . .

I had with me two bottles of cognac. The *Manchuria*, an American boat, suffered from prohibition, but there were a number of people on that boat who loved a drink; so, the rabbi turned into a bartender—one cigar, one small glass of cognac— and we managed beautifully until we arrived in New York.

One afternoon, there was that picture, so strange for European eyes—skyscrapers next to little houses, and at the pier the Statue of Liberty. One Jewish woman told me that the inscription on that statue was made by Emma Lazarus, a Jewess.

From the Hotel Commodore, I rushed early in the morning over to Forty-third Street and Fifth Avenue to see Temple Emanu-El—which some years before had

Jacob Sonderling, "Casual Notes for an Autobiography," *American Jewish Archives* 16 (November 1964): 107–123. Reprinted by permission of the American Jewish Archives, Cincinnati Campus, Hebrew Union College, Jewish Institute of Religion.

cost me, or rather the Hamburg Temple, one million marks. When the Hamburg Temple set out to raise funds for a new building, Mr. Henry Budge, a very rich New York banker who had returned to Europe and lived in Hamburg, had been my first target for a contribution. My president had sent me to him, and I had told him about our plan to build a new temple in Hamburg. Budge had asked me how much it was going to cost. We had figured one million marks. I expected him to give us 5,000 or 10,000 marks. "You can have the million," he said, "under one condition. I would like to have a service like Temple Emanu-El in New York—men and women sitting together, men without hats and without *talesim* (prayer shawls)."

"I have to refuse your generous offer, Herr Budge—we are building a Temple for Hamburg Jewry, not for you."

Returning to my board, I had offered my resignation as their rabbi. Having refused so generous a gift, I could not, I felt, hold on to my pulpit. My board, however, agreed with me, and in the Hamburg Temple, the cradle of Reform, men and women remained separated up to the last moment.

It took me years to accustom myself to seeing men and women sitting together. . . .

I shall never forget those first days in New York. Here I was—lost in the colossus of houses, streets, faces, a babel of languages—a replica of the Wandering Jew. How often I stood, looking at Hebrew letters like *Bosor Kosher* (kosher meat), which gave me a feeling of nostalgia! . . .

. . . The first Friday evening I went to a synagogue and at eight o'clock in the evening came to a Jewish restaurant on Broadway. The place was dark. I tried the door—it opened; the man was about to leave.

"What's the matter?" I asked.

"*Shabbos* (the Sabbath)," he said.

"Can you let a Kosher Jew starve?"

"No, I'll give you something to eat," and he was about to go to the kitchen.

I stopped him.

"Wait, it's Shabbos. I have no money." (I had money.)

"It doesn't matter," he said. He brought me a full dinner, waited on me, and I left the place without paying. I simply could not understand it. Two days later I returned there for lunch. The man was behind the counter—I took my check, with a five dollar bill—the man did not deduct for my Friday night dinner.

"Don't you remember that I was here Friday night?"

"Yes, I do remember."

"Suppose I didn't come back?"

The man got angry: "Are you going to prevent me from doing a *mitzvah* (a good deed)?"

Outside I stood, very much bewildered. I saw a little bit of a place, the restaurant—a man working perhaps twelve hours a day to make a living, resenting my not giving him a chance for a *mitzvah*. For the first time, I realized the beauty of the expression that "to show hospitality is more precious than to see God." . . .

An old friend of mine, Shmarya Levin, met me at 111 Fifth Avenue, the Zionist headquarters.

"What are you doing here?" he cried. "Go back to Europe—this is no place for you."

It was not very encouraging to hear that from so clever a man. There, too, I met Louis Lipsky, the leader of American Zionism, Maurice Samuel, and others, who took me to a Zionist meeting. Called upon, I spoke in German. The next morning I received a telegram from the Zionist Organization of America, offering me an engagement for a series of talks on Zionism throughout the country, and I began to bring the message of Theodor Herzl to American Jewry. One of the first communities I visited was Chicago. Everything was new to me. I was what was called a "greenhorn." . . .

. . . "We are officers of a congregation, and listening to you last night, we decided that you have to become our rabbi."

"But I cannot speak English!"

"You will learn."

"What kind of congregation are you?"

"We are Orthodox."

"I'm not Orthodox."

"We are semi-Orthodox."

I didn't know what it meant. They did not argue—they just took out a contract and asked me to sign it. With the help of a dictionary, I found out that they had offered me a decent salary and obligated themselves to bring my family over from Europe and to furnish me with an apartment. I signed. They left, and here I was sitting in my hotel room, believing that I had dreamed it. So, four weeks after my arrival in a new continent, I had a congregation. Another four weeks passed by, and they asked me whether I would agree that they amalgamate with another congregation. That was new to me.

"How do you do that?"

"Oh, we sell our synagogue."

"Whom do you sell it to?"

"In our neighborhood there is a Negro congregation—they want to buy the building."

I was bedeviled and bewildered. The next Saturday I went to my pulpit and said: "I have found a new interpretation for a Bible text. First came the Irish, who built the church; they left and sold the sanctuary to the Italians; then came the Jews, and now the Jews have sold it to the Negroes—now I understand what the Bible says: 'My house shall be a house of prayer for all peoples (Isaiah 56:7).' "

The two congregations married—mine was Hungarian; the other Lithuanian. The honeymoon lasted four weeks. The fifth week started, and there was trouble: on one side the Hungarians, and on the other the Litvaks. Finally I suggested: "Gentlemen, goulash, herring, and sauerkraut do not mix."

Something else happened. A member of my congregation's board brought me the newest list of our membership and asked me to sign it.

"What do you need my signature for?"

In all innocence he explained: "Every synagogue member, according to American law, is entitled to five gallons of sacramental wine. The congregation is buying that wine from the Government at a cheap price, selling it afterwards at a very high price to all the people, and doing great business."

Of course, I refused to do that, and my congregation was upset, believing that its rabbi was queer. My friend Levin, whom I mentioned before, said once that Orthodox rabbis, doing big business in those days in sacramental wine, had changed the *Tilim*

(Psalms); Psalm 121 says, "From whence (*me-ayin*) does my help come?" Levin suggested: "Instead of *me-ayin* ('from whence'), read *miyayin* ('from wine')!" . . .

[He returned to New York.] Another two years passed by, and I moved from Manhattan Beach to Washington Heights. Members of the new congregation approached me with a request: "The butchers in Washington Heights are selling *treffa* (non-kosher) meat—something has to be done!" I refused. I told them that I was not Orthodox and that the Vaad Hakashruth (the representative board overseeing Kashruth matters) of Greater New York was in charge. People came again and again. Finally, they approached Dr. Louis Ginzberg, of the Jewish Theological Seminary, who lived opposite me in Washington Heights, to induce me to do something. . . .

I worshipped him. When it was raining on *Shabbos,* he would not go to the Seminary synagogue, but, together with his wife, he would come to my synagogue in Washington Heights. They were sitting together, when one day I asked him: "Mr. Ginzberg, how can you?" And here is his answer: "When you live long enough in America, you will realize that the status of womanhood has changed so much that separating women from men has become obsolete." That convinced me, and today, in my synagogue, our men and women sit together—with one exception, which I regret: My wife protests at being seated on the platform!

So, to pick up my story, Professor Ginzberg approached me and urged me to take over the supervision of Kashruth. I called eighteen butchers together and told them that—only out of respect for Professor Ginzberg—I would be willing to supervise Kashruth under two conditions. First, the *mashgiach* (inspector) and I myself had to have the right to inspect their places twenty-four hours a day. That was accepted. Second, if I found it necessary to take back a butcher's certificate of Kashruth, that butcher should have no recourse to the law. About that they argued—I remained adamant. There was still another condition. The *mashgiach* could neither be hired nor fired by the butchers. His salary was to be paid by the butchers into a special fund.

So we started. The *mashgiach* would report to me every day. Once he came and told me that one of the butchers had a chicken market elsewhere and kept it open on the Sabbath. When I called the offender in, he told me that his partner was not Jewish and gave me a talmudical analysis that, in this case, his place could be open. I refused to follow his thought. "You make your living selling kosher meat to people who believe in Kashruth. I have lost my confidence in you—give me back my certificate." I finally got it. A month later, another certificate appeared in his window, signed by an Orthodox rabbi on the Lower East Side; the butcher had gotten it for $50. I was finished with the supervision of Kashruth.

3. Sinclair Lewis Satirizes the Narrowness of Midwestern Baptists, 1927

For years the state of sin in which dwelt Elmer Gantry and Jim Lefferts had produced fascinated despair in the Christian hearts of Terwillinger College. No revival but had flung its sulphur-soaked arrows at them—usually in their absence. No prayer at the Y. M. C. A. meetings but had worried over their staggering folly. . . .

Sinclair Lewis, *Elmer Gantry* (New York: New American Library, 1980), 31–34. Copyright 1927 by Harcourt, Inc. Renewed in 1955 by Michael Lewis. Reprinted by permission.

Now, Eddie Fislinger, like a prairie seraph, sped from room to room of the elect with the astounding news that Elmer had publicly professed religion, and that he had endured thirty-nine minutes of private adjuration on the train. . . .

. . . Elmer had always been in danger of giving up his favorite diversions—not exactly giving them up, perhaps, but of sweating in agony after enjoying them. But for Jim and his remarks about co-eds who prayed in public and drew their hair back rebukingly from egg-like foreheads, one of these sirens of morality might have snared the easy-going pangynistic Elmer by proximity.

A dreadful young woman from Mexico, Missouri, used to coax Jim to "tell his funny ideas about religion," and go off in neighs of pious laughter, while she choked, "Oh, you're just too cute! You don't mean a word you say. You simply want to show off!" She had a deceptive sidelong look which actually promised nothing whatever this side of the altar, and she might, but for Jim's struggles, have led Elmer into an engagement.

The church and Sunday School at Elmer's village, Paris, Kansas, a settlement of nine hundred evangelical Germans and Vermonters, had nurtured in him a fear of religious machinery which he could never lose, which restrained him from such reasonable acts as butchering Eddie Fislinger. That small pasty-white Baptist church had been the center of all his emotions, aside from hell-raising, hunger, sleepiness, and love. And even these emotions were represented in the House of the Lord, in the way of tacks in pew-cushions, Missionary Suppers with chicken pie and angel's-food cake, soporific sermons, and the proximity of flexible little girls in thin muslin. But the arts and the sentiments and the sentimentalities—they were for Elmer perpetually associated only with the church.

Except for circus bands, Fourth of July parades, and the singing of "Columbia, the Gem of the Ocean" and "Jingle Bells" in school, all the music which the boy Elmer had ever heard was in church.

The church provided his only oratory, except for campaign speeches by politicians ardent about Jefferson and the price of binding-twine; it provided all his painting and sculpture, except for the portraits of Lincoln, Longfellow, and Emerson in the school-building, and the two china statuettes of pink ladies with gilt flower-baskets which stood on his mother's bureau. From the church came all his profounder philosophy, except the teachers' admonitions that little boys who let garter-snakes loose in school were certain to be licked now and hanged later, and his mother's stream of opinions on hanging up his overcoat, wiping his feet, eating fried potatoes with his fingers, and taking the name of the Lord in vain.

If he had sources of literary inspiration outside the church—in McGuffey's Reader he encountered the boy who stood on the burning deck, and he had a very pretty knowledge of the Nick Carter Series and the exploits of Cole Younger and the James Boys—yet here too the church had guided him. In Bible stories, in the words of the great hymns, in the anecdotes which the various preachers quoted, he had his only knowledge of literature—

The story of Little Lame Tom who shamed the wicked rich man that owned the handsome team of grays and the pot hat and led him to Jesus. The ship's captain who in the storm took counsel with the orphaned but righteous child of missionaries in Zomballa. The Faithful Dog who saved his master during a terrific conflagration (only sometimes it was a snowstorm, or an attack by Indians) and roused him to give up horse-racing, rum, and playing the harmonica.

How familiar they were, how thrilling, how explanatory to Elmer of the purposes of life, how preparatory for his future usefulness and charm.

The church, the Sunday School, the evangelistic orgy, choir-practice, raising the mortgage, the delights of funerals, the snickers in back pews or in the other room at weddings—they were as natural, as inescapable a mold of manners to Elmer as Catholic processionals to a street gamin in Naples.

The Baptist Church of Paris, Kansas! A thousand blurred but indestructible pictures.

Hymns! Elmer's voice was made for hymns. He rolled them out like a negro. The organ-thunder of "Nicæa":

> Holy, holy, holy! all the saints adore thee,
> Casting down their golden crowns around the glassy sea.

The splendid rumble of the Doxology. "Throw Out the Lifeline," with its picture of a wreck pounded in the darkness by surf which the prairie child imagined as a hundred feet high. "Onward, Christian Soldiers," to which you could without rebuke stamp your feet.

Sunday School picnics! Lemonade and four-legged races and the ride on the hay-rack, singing "Seeing Nelly Home."

Sunday School text cards! True, they were chiefly a medium of gambling, but as Elmer usually won the game (he was the first boy in Paris to own a genuine pair of loaded dice) he had plenty of them in his gallery, and they gave him a taste for gaudy robes, for marble columns and the purple-broidered palaces of kings, which was later to be of value in quickly habituating himself to the more decorative homes of vice. The three kings bearing caskets of ruby and sardonyx. King Zedekiah in gold and scarlet, kneeling on a carpet of sapphire-blue, while his men-at-arms came fleeing and bloodstained, red blood on glancing steel, with tidings of the bannered host of Nebuchadnezzar, great king of Babylon. And all his life Elmer remembered, in moments of ardor, during oratorios in huge churches, during sunset at sea, a black-bearded David standing against raw red cliffs—a figure heroic and summoning to ambition, to power, to domination.

Sunday School Christmas Eve! The exhilaration of staying up, and publicly, till nine-thirty. The tree, incredibly tall, also incredibly inflammable, flashing with silver cords, with silver stars, with cotton-batting snow. The two round stoves red-hot. Lights and lights and lights. Pails of candy, and for every child in the school a present—usually a book, very pleasant, with colored pictures of lambs and volcanoes. The Santa Claus—he couldn't possibly be Lorenzo Nickerson, the house-painter, so bearded was he, and red-cheeked, and so witty in his comment on each child as it marched up for its present. The enchantment, sheer magic, of the Ladies' Quartette singing of shepherds who watched their flocks by nights . . . brown secret hilltops under one vast star.

And the devastating morning when the preacher himself, the Rev. Wilson Hinckley Skaggs, caught Elmer matching for Sunday School contribution pennies on the front steps, and led him up the aisle for all to giggle at, with a sharp and not very clean ministerial thumb-nail gouging his ear-lobe.

And the other passing preachers: Brother Organdy, who got you to saw his wood free; Brother Blunt, who sneaked behind barns to catch you on Halloween;

Brother Ingle, who was zealous but young and actually human, and who made whistles from willow branches for you.

And the morning when Elmer concealed an alarm clock behind the organ and it went off, magnificently, just as the superintendent (Dr. Prouty, the dentist) was whimpering, "Now let us all be particularly quiet as Sister Holbrick leads us in prayer."

And always the three chairs that stood behind the pulpit, the intimidating stiff chairs of yellow plush and carved oak borders, which, he was uneasily sure, were waiting for the Father, the Son, and the Holy Ghost.

He had, in fact, got everything from the church and Sunday School, except, perhaps, any longing whatever for decency and kindness and reason.

Even had Elmer not known the church by habit, he would have been led to it by his mother. Aside from his friendship for Jim Lefferts, Elmer's only authentic affection was for his mother, and she was owned by the church.

She was a small woman, energetic, nagging but kindly, once given to passionate caresses and now to passionate prayer, and she had unusual courage. Early left a widow by Logan Gantry, dealer in feed, flour, lumber, and agricultural implements, a large and agreeable man given to debts and whisky, she had supported herself and Elmer by sewing, trimming hats, baking bread, and selling milk. She had her own millinery and dressmaking shop now, narrow and dim but proudly set right on Main Street, and she was able to give Elmer the three hundred dollars a year which, with his summer earnings in harvest field and lumber-yard, was enough to support him—in Terwillinger, in 1902.

She had always wanted Elmer to be a preacher. She was jolly enough, and no fool about pennies in making change, but for a preacher standing up on a platform in a long-tailed coat she had gaping awe.

Elmer had since the age of sixteen been a member in good standing of the Baptist Church—he had been most satisfactorily immersed in the Kayooska River. Large though Elmer was, the evangelist had been a powerful man and had not only ducked him but, in sacred enthusiasm, held him under, so that he came up sputtering, in a state of grace and muddiness. He had also been saved several times, and once, when he had pneumonia, he had been esteemed by the pastor and all visiting ladies as rapidly growing in grace.

But he had resisted his mother's desire that he become a preacher. He would have to give up his entertaining vices, and with wide-eyed and panting happiness he was discovering more of them every year. Equally he felt lumbering and shamed whenever he tried to stand up before his tittering gang in Paris and appear pious.

4. Walter Lippmann Traces the Fading of Religious Confidence, 1929

By the dissolution of their ancestral ways men have been deprived of their sense of certainty as to why they were born, why they must work, whom they must love, what they must honor, where they may turn in sorrow and defeat. They have left to

Walter Lippmann, *A Preface to Morals* (1929; New York: Macmillan, 1935), 21–36. Copyright 1929 by Macmillan Publishing Company; copyright renewed 1957 by Walter Lippmann. Reprinted with permission of Simon & Schuster, Inc.

them the ancient codes and the modern criticism of these codes, guesses, intuitions, inconclusive experiments, possibilities, probabilities, hypotheses. Below the level of reason, they may have unconscious prejudice, they may speak with a loud cocksureness, they may act with fanaticism. But there is gone that ineffable certainty which once made God and His Plan seem as real as the lamp-post.

I do not mean that modern men have ceased to believe in God. I do mean that they no longer believe in him simply and literally. I mean that they have defined and refined their ideas of him until they can no longer honestly say that he exists, as they would say that their neighbor exists. Search the writings of liberal churchmen, and when you come to the crucial passages which are intended to express their belief in God, you will find, I think, that at just this point their uncertainty is most evident.

The Reverend Harry Emerson Fosdick has written an essay, called "How Shall We Think of God?", which illustrates the difficulty. He begins by saying that "believing in God without considering how one shall picture him is deplorably unsatisfactory." Yet the old ways of picturing him are no longer credible. We cannot think of him as seated upon a throne, while around him are angels playing on harps and singing hymns. . . .

Having said that this picture is antiquated, Dr. Fosdick goes on to state that "the religious man must have imaginations of God, if God is to be real to him." He must "picture his dealing with the Divine in terms of personal relationship." But how? "The place where man vitally finds God . . . is within his own experience of goodness, truth, and beauty, and the truest images of God are therefore to be found in man's spiritual life." I should be the last to deny that a man may, if he chooses, think of God as the source of all that seems to him worthy in human experience. But certainly this is not the God of the ancient faith. This is not God the Father, the Lawgiver, the Judge. This is a highly sophisticated idea of God, employed by a modern man who would like to say, but cannot say with certainty, that there exists a personal God to whom men must accommodate themselves.

An Indefinite God

It may be that clear and unambiguous statements are not now possible in our intellectual climate. But at least we should not forget that the religions which have dominated human history have been founded on what the faithful felt were undeniable facts. . . .

The popular gods are not indefinite and unknowable. They have a definite history and their favorite haunts, and they have often been seen. They walk on earth, they might appear to anyone, they are angered, they are pleased, they weep and they rejoice, they eat and they may fall in love. The modern man uses the word "supernatural" to describe something that seems to him not quite so credible as the things he calls natural. This is not the supernaturalism of the devout. They do not distinguish two planes of reality and two orders of certainty. For them Jesus Christ was born of a Virgin and was raised from the dead as literally as Napoleon was Emperor of the French and returned from Elba.

This is the kind of certainty one no longer finds in the utterances of modern men. . . .

. . . In other ages there was no acknowledged distinction between the ultimate beliefs of the educated and the uneducated. There were differences in learning, in religious genius, in the closeness of a chosen few to God and his angels. Inwardly there were even radical differences of meaning. But critical analysis had not made them overt and evident, and the common assumption was that there was one God for all, for the peasant who saw him dimly and could approach him only through his patron saint, and for the holy man who had seen God and talked with him face to face. It has remained for churchmen of our era to distinguish two or more differ-ent Gods, and openly to say that they are different. . . .

The Protest of the Fundamentalists

Fundamentalism is a protest against all these definitions and attenuations which the modern man finds it necessary to make. It is avowedly a reaction within the Protes-tant communions against what the President of the World's Christian Fundamentalist Association rather accurately described as "that weasel method of sucking the mean-ing out of words, and then presenting the empty shells in an attempt to palm them off as giving the Christian faith a new and another interpretation." In actual practice this movement has become entangled with all sorts of bizarre and barbarous agitations, with the Ku Klux Klan, with fanatical prohibition, with the "anti-evolution laws," and with much persecution and intolerance. This in itself is significant. For it shows that the central truth, which the fundamentalists have grasped, no longer appeals to the best brains and the good sense of a modern community, and that the movement is recruited largely from the isolated, the inexperienced, and the uneducated. . . .

Not all the fundamentalist argument, however, is pitched at this level. There is also a reasoned case against the modernists. Fortunately this case has been stated in a little book called *Christianity and Liberalism* by a man who is both a scholar and a gentleman. The author is Professor J. Gresham Machen of the Princeton The-ological Seminary. It is an admirable book. For its acumen, for its saliency, and for its wit this cool and stringent defense of orthodox Protestantism is, I think, the best popular argument produced by either side in the current controversy. We shall do well to listen to Dr. Machen. . . .

. . . "From the beginning Christianity was certainly a way of life. *But how was the life to be produced?* Not by appealing to the human will, but by telling a story; not by exhortation, but by the narration of an event." Dr. Machen insists, rightly I think, that the historic influence of Christianity on the mass of men has depended upon their belief that an historic drama was enacted in Palestine nineteen hundred years ago during the reign of the Emperor Tiberius. The veracity of that story was fundamental to the Christian Church. For while all the ideal values may remain if you impugn the historic record set forth in the Gospels, these ideal values are not certified to the common man as inherent in the very nature of things. Once they are deprived of their root in historic fact, their poetry, their symbolism, their ethical significance depend for their sanction upon the temperament and experience of the individual believer. There is gone that deep, compulsive, organic faith in an exter-nal fact which is the essence of religion for all but that very small minority who can live within themselves in mystical communion or by the power of their understand-ing. For the great mass of men, if the history of religions is to be trusted, religious experience depends upon a complete belief in the concrete existence, one might almost say the materialization, of their God. The fundamentalist goes to the very heart of the matter, therefore, when he insists that you have destroyed the popular foundations of religion if you make your gospel a symbolic record of experience, and reject it as an actual record of events. . . .

. . . Modernism, which in varying degree casts doubt upon the truth of that [the Jesus] story, may therefore be defined as an attempt to preserve selected parts of the experience after the facts which inspired it have been rejected. The orthodox believer may be mistaken as to the facts in which he believes. But he is not mistaken in thinking that you cannot, for the mass of men, have a faith of which the only foundation is their need and desire to believe. . . .

If it is true that man creates God in his own image, it is no less true that for religious devotion he must remain unconscious of that fact. Once he knows that he has created the image of God, the reality of it vanishes like last night's dream. It may be that to anyone who is impregnated with the modern spirit it is almost self-evident that the truths of religion are truths of human experience. But this knowledge does not tolerate an abiding and absorbing faith. For when the truths of religion have lost their connection with a superhuman order, the cord of their life is cut. What remains is a somewhat archaic, a somewhat questionable, although a very touching, quaint medley of poetry, rhetoric, fable exhortation, and insight into human travail. . . .

. . . [W]hat would be the plight of a lover, if we told him that his passion was charming?—though, of course, there might be no such lady as the one he loved.

5. Mordecai Kaplan Defends Jews' Life in Two Civilizations, 1948

It may be asked: How can a community, which permits diversity of religious belief and practice, claim religious status? What would entitle us Jews to be designated as a religio-cultural instead of merely a cultural group? The answer is to be found in a proper understanding of what we mean by "religion." If, for example, we were to accept the popular notion of religion and maintain that for a group to be called "religious" it must lay claim to having originated with some supernatural event or person, we would have to exclude from the category of "religious" eighty-three per cent of the rabbinate who, according to a recent study, no longer believe in the supernatural origin of the Jewish people. The only way in which it is possible to determine whether we are entitled to designate our communal status "religious" is to ascertain whether that status will fulfill the function that is generally meant by religion.

The function of a religion is to enable those who live by it to achieve salvation, or life abundant. If the indivisible peoplehood of the Jews is as indispensable a means to the salvation of the Jew, as the Church is to that of the Christian, it serves a religious function. Since the Jewish community is the medium through which

Mordecai Kaplan, "Living in Two Civilizations Calls for a Redefinition of Religion," in *The Future of the American Jew* (New York: Macmillan, 1948), 99–104. Reprinted by permission of the Reconstructionist Press.

that peoplehood would enable the Jew to achieve his salvation, it is entitled to all the privileges and immunities that the modern democratic state confers upon all religious bodies. To be sure, salvation would not consist, as it did in the past for all Jews, in a feeling of confidence in the coming of a personal Messiah, who would gather all Jews back to Eretz Yisrael, and in eternal bliss to be enjoyed by each Jew in the hereafter. It would consist rather in the cultivation of basic values like faith, patience, inner freedom, humility, thankfulness, justice and love which enable a man to be and do his best, and to bear uncomplainingly the worst that may befall him. A religio-cultural community that can help its members achieve that kind of salvation is invaluable to a democratic state, whose strength consists in a citizenry of self-reliant and self-respecting men and women.

What seems to trouble some people, when the idea of living in two civilizations is suggested to them, is that it would necessitate splitting our personalities, and giving, as it were, one half to each civilization. This mechanical notion is as groundless as imagining that we cannot be as proficient in two languages as we can be in one. The very contrary is the case. They who know English only, do not even know English. Those whose life horizon is limited to their one native civilization do not know even that one as well as they should, if they are to be citizens of the world. Moreover, they cannot elicit from it all the good that is latent in it.

The vicissitudes of history have brought it about that the average human being has to draw upon two civilizations to obtain all those values which he requires for his self-realization as a human being. It is a need to which Christians are no less subject than Jews. . . .

. . . Why . . . should the efforts of Jews to live by Biblical law, as embodied in Jewish civilization, be an evidence of segregationism? If it is legitimate for the Irish to parade on St. Patrick's day, in glorification of the patron saint of a non-American nation, why would it be less legitimate for Jews to carry the *Sefer Torah* in procession through the streets on *Simhat Torah*? On Palm Sunday, the streets are thronged with Christians bearing palm branches, but on *Sukkot*, Jews, if they must carry a *lulav* through the streets usually wrap it in paper to conceal its identity, because they assume that any flaunting of a distinctively Jewish culture trait will expose them to the charge of ghettoism. Why is it American to go about on All-Saints Eve in masquerade, and an exotic practice to do the same on *Purim*? Why should Jews consider it a good American practice for Christians to display Christmas trees and sing Christmas carols in public, while feeling too inhibited to display the *Hanukkah* lights publicly and to sing Hebrew hymns in the streets?

In the Diaspora, Jews are bound to identify themselves spiritually as well as culturally with the nations among which they live. *Judaism, to evoke American Jews' loyalty, must be not only compatible with their loyalty to America but also corroborative of it.* . . .

Judaism, or the religious civilization of the Jewish people, in its present effort to arrive at a *modus vivendi* in the midst of other civilizations has the opportunity of making an important contribution to the recognition of a far-reaching social principle, namely, that *any civilization which has no aggressive purpose or "mission" has an intrinsic right to live either by itself, or in symbiosis with any other civilization.*

The commonwealth status which the Jewish people seeks to achieve in Eretz Yisrael is the expression of the desire on the part of the Jewish civilization to live by itself. As a civilization, it is the product of a particular land, and, so long as it survives, it is entitled to live in that land. Having been driven out by *force majeure* did not deprive it of that right. The argument that the modern Italians have a claim on Britain or France analogous to that of the Jews on Eretz Yisrael is the height of absurdity. The Italian civilization has no roots in either country, whereas the Jewish civilization is inconceivable without Eretz Yisrael.

Moreover, *a civilization has a right to live cooperatively with another civilization in any one country so long as it has no intentions of competing with the latter, much less dominating it.* Such cooperative living may be interpreted in terms of group equality, as in countries where minorities as such are granted political rights, or in terms of individual equality, as in the United States. In the latter case, the individual has only one set of religious values to live by. . . .

The undertaking to live in two civilizations simultaneously is, to be sure, a new experiment in the art of living. But for us Jews to try out better ways of human living should be nothing new. It may be that we have in us the kind of stuff which, having remained unconsumed in the iron furnace of Egypt, cannot be liquefied in any of the modern national melting pots. Being loyal to two civilizations is as ethical as being loyal to father and mother. "The serving of two masters," said Harry Wolfson, "is not a moral anomaly, unless, as in the original adage, one of the masters be satanic."

Sometimes nature, instead of waiting for chance to bring new species into existence has the same living creature undergo changes in structure and function. The slowly crawling caterpillar, for example, is transformed into the winged butterfly. In such creatures, life seems to be too impatient of evolution's slow course. Driven by some overpowering creative urge, life leaps far ahead of the stage in which it happens to be. The result is a new type of being that emerges from one continuing life. This process is known as metamorphosis.

We would do well to read the meaning of human development in the light of this extraordinary phenomenon in nature. Physically, man is subject to the slow process of evolution which has to be measured with the yardstick of geological eons. But mentally and spiritually, man finds natural evolution too slow. His irresistible urge to be more than what he is may be regarded as a yearning to achieve metamorphosis into a higher order of being. It has somehow fallen to our lot as a people to herald and incarnate this principle of human metamorphosis. With our messianic ideal, we Jews have awakened in the human heart that discontent which is the forerunner of a regenerated humanity. If we can reinterpret our messianism as future-mindedness, then, by all means, let us retain it. Some one well said: "Perhaps, unless we can learn to think of ourselves as we might be a hundred thousand years hence, we shall destroy each other one hundred months hence. Perhaps only the Utopians can help us survive."

From the standpoint of this interpretation of human history and of Israel's place in the world, the circumstances which have made it necessary for Jews to live in two civilizations are part of the metamorphosis which the human race is undergoing at the present time. This necessity is a challenge to the Jewish people. It compels the Jewish people to reconstitute itself into a different kind of people from that which it was in the past. It must assume a new incarnation.

6. Will Herberg Analyzes Religion and Assimilation, 1955

[T]he immigrant was not expected to change his faith upon arrival in this country, not because Americans were indifferent to religion or were committed to theological views which called for non-interference in religious matters, but because almost from the beginning, the structure of American society presupposed diversity and substantial equality of religious associations.

Of the immigrant who came to this country it was expected that, sooner or later, either in his own person or through his children, he would give up virtually everything he had brought with him from the "old country"—his language, his nationality, his manner of life—and would adopt the ways of his new home. Within broad limits, however, his becoming an American did not involve his abandoning the old religion in favor of some native American substitute. Quite the contrary, not only was he expected to retain his old religion, as he was not expected to retain his old language or nationality, but such was the shape of America that it was largely in and through his religion that he, or rather his children and grandchildren, found an identifiable place in American life.

I

As soon as the immigrant family arrived in the New World it became involved in a far-reaching double process. On the one hand, . . . the conditions of American life made for the emergence of the ethnic group, in terms of which the immigrant identified himself and was located in the larger community. On the other hand, however, the formation of the ethnic group at the center of immigrant life was from the very beginning accompanied by its dissolution at the periphery. The ethnic group emerged to define and express the immigrant's curious combination of foreignness and Americanness; but his children, the moment they entered school, the moment even they were let out on the street to play with children of other tongues and origins, began to escape the ethnic-immigrant life of their parents. Their language, their culture, their system of values, their outlook on life, underwent drastic change, sometimes obviously, sometimes imperceptibly; they were becoming American, assimilated, acculturated, no longer fully at home in the immigrant family and ethnic group, though neither as yet fully at home in the America to which they belonged. Though this double process was operative from the very beginning, the "negative" aspect was not visible so long as large-scale immigration continued; all phases of ethnic life flourished, societies spread and increased in membership, foreign-language publications grew in scope and circulation, cultural institutions prospered. But this prosperity and expansion at the center could not halt the disintegration of ethnic group life that came with the growing Americanization of the second generation.

These conflicting forces drove the second generation into a difficult position and engendered an acute malaise in the sons and daughters of the immigrants. Frequently, though not always, the man of the second generation attempted to resolve his dilemma by forsaking the ethnic group in which he found himself. "He wanted to forget everything," this man of the second generation, "the foreign language . . . the religion [of his immigrant parents] . . . the family customs. . . . The second generation wanted to forget, and even when the ties of family affection were strong, wanted to lose as many of the evidences of foreign origin as they could shuffle off." The great mobility of American society encouraged this process, and was in turn spurred by it. As the second generation prospered economically and culturally, and moved upward in the social scale, assimilation was speeded; the speeding of assimilation stimulated and quickened the upward movement.

First to go was the foreign language and the culture associated with it, for the foreign language was the manifest symbol of foreignness and a great impediment to advancement. Religion too was affected, though not so explicitly. The second generation developed an uneasy relation to the faith of their fathers: sometimes this meant simply indifference; in other cases, relatively few, a shift to denominations regarded as more "American." In most cases, however, the ties with the old religion were never entirely broken.

The immediate reaction of many of the second generation was escape. But enough of this generation always remained in the ethnic group to provide a permanent nucleus around which the incoming masses of immigrants could gather and organize their lives in the New World. Through the nineteenth and well into the twentieth century, the ethnic group throve and flourished.

Then came the stoppage of immigration, first as a consequence of the World War, and later, more definitively through the legislation of the 1920s. Almost at once the picture changed drastically, for the hitherto hidden effects of the assimilative process became evident. "The total halt to immigration after 1924 severed the last remaining ties [of the immigrants and their children] to the Old World. Without additions from across the ocean, memories of transatlantic antecedents faded. As the second, and in time, the third generation grew to maturity, affiliations based upon some remote immigrant ancestor became ever less meaningful. The old customs grew unfamiliar in the bustle of American life." The various and multiform activities of the ethnic group began to shrivel and disappear; the ethnic group itself, in its older form at least, became less and less intelligible and relevant to American reality. It was the end of an era. . . .

Marcus Hansen has graphically formulated what he calls the "principle of third-generation interest" in these terms: "what the son wishes to forget, the grandson wishes to remember." "After the second generation," Hansen points out, "comes the third. . . . [The members of the third generation] have no reason to feel any inferiority when they look around them. They are American-born. Their speech is the same as that of those with whom they associate. Their material wealth is the average possession of the typical citizen." . . . They were Americans, but what *kind* of Americans? ". . . They wished to belong to a group." But what group could they belong to? The old-line ethnic group, with its foreign language and culture, was not for them; they were Americans. But the old family religion, the old ethnic religion, could serve where language and culture could not; the religion of the immigrants— with certain necessary modifications, such as the replacement of the ethnic language by English—was accorded a place in the American scheme of things that made it at once both genuinely American and a familiar principle of group identification. The connection with the family religion had never been completely broken, and to religion, therefore, the men and women of the third generation now began to turn to define their place in American society in a way that would sustain their Americanness and yet confirm the tie that bound them to their forebears, whom they now no longer had any reason to reject, whom indeed, for the sake of a "heritage," they now wanted to "remember." Thus "religion became the focal point of ethnic affiliations. . . . Through its institutions, the church supplied a place where children could learn what they were. . . ." Religious association now became the primary context of self-identification and social location for the third generation, as well as for the bulk of the second generation, of America's immigrants, and that meant, by and large, for the American people.

But in thus becoming the primary context of social location, religious association itself underwent significant change. All of the many churches, sects, and denominations that characterize the American religious scene were still there, and indeed continued to thrive. But "increasingly religious activities fell into a fundamental tripartite division that had begun to take form earlier in the century. Men were Catholics, Protestants, or Jews, categories based less on theological than on social distinctions." A new and unique social structure was emerging in America, the "religious community."

In the early 1940s, Ruby Jo Kennedy undertook an investigation of intermarriage trends in New Haven from 1870 to 1940. . . .

"The large nationality groups in New Haven," Mrs. Kennedy found, "represent a triple division on religious grounds: Jewish, Protestant (British-American, German, and Scandinavian), and Catholic (Irish, Italian, and Polish) . . ." In its early immigrant days, each of these ethnic groups tended to be endogamous; with the years, however, people began to marry outside the group. . . . Members of Catholic stocks married Catholics in 95.35 per cent of the cases in 1870, 85.78 per cent in 1900, 82.05 per cent in 1930, and 83.71 per cent in 1940; members of Protestant stocks married Protestants in 99.11 per cent of the cases in 1870, 90.86 per cent in 1900, 78.19 per cent in 1930, and 79.72 per cent in 1940; Jews married Jews in 100 per cent of the cases in 1870, 98.82 per cent in 1900, 97.01 per cent in 1930, and 94.32 per cent in 1940. "Future cleavages," in Mrs. Kennedy's opinion, "will therefore be along religious lines rather than along nationality lines as in the past. . . . Cultural [i.e., ethnic] lines may fade, but religious barriers are holding fast. . . . When marriage crosses religious barriers, as it often does, religion still plays a prominent role, especially among Catholics," in that such marriages are often conditioned upon, and result in, one of the partners being brought into the religious community of the other. "The traditional 'single melting pot' idea must be abandoned, and a new conception, which we term the 'triple melting pot' theory of American assimilation, will take its place, as the true expression of what is happening to the various nationality groups in the United States. . . . The 'triple melting pot' type of assimilation is occurring through intermarriage, with Catholicism, Protestantism, and Judaism serving as the three fundamental bulwarks. . . . The different nationalities are merging, but within three religious compartments rather than indiscriminately. . . . A triple religious cleavage, rather than a multilinear nationality cleavage, therefore seems likely to characterize American society in the future." . . .

Just as sociologically we may describe the emerging social structure of America as one great community divided into three big sub-communities religiously defined, all equally American, so from another angle we might describe Protestantism, Catholicism, and Judaism in America as three great branches or divisions of "American religion." The assumption underlying the view shared by most Americans, at least at moments when they think in "nonsectarian" terms, is not so much that the three religious communities possess an underlying theological unity, which of course they do, but rather that they are three diverse representations of the same "spiritual values," the "spiritual values" American democracy is presumed to stand for (the fatherhood of God and brotherhood of man, the dignity of the individual human being, etc.). That is, at bottom, why no one is expected to change his religion as he becomes American; since each of the religions is equally and authentically American, the American is expected to express his religious affirmation in that form which has come to him with his family and ethnic heritage.

7. Donald Thorman Assesses New Roles for Catholic Laity, 1962

American Catholics are facing problems unknown to their forefathers. Today's laymen have little past experience on which to base their future actions, so they stand apprehensively and hesitantly before the present and the future.

Some laymen, unable to cope with attempting to live a full Christian life in pagan surroundings, have drifted out of the Church and have adopted a lowest-common-denominator kind of secularism as an easy solution; they do not reject God, but they live and act as if He did not exist. Others, fearful of their irreligious surroundings, have built up what has come to be called a "ghetto mentality," and have sought to withdraw from much of modern society, erecting a kind of barricade between themselves and the world.

This pluralistic society, . . . is a new experience without historical precedent for most American Catholic laymen who are only a few generations removed from an immigrant background. Frequently, their parents or grandparents, upon arrival in the United States, sought out their own former countrymen. Italian, Polish, German, Irish and other nationality groups set up their own little communities within the American cities in which they settled. They found economic, political, cultural, and religious stability and security in these little reproductions of the old country. It helped make the transition easier and generally proved to be a good thing.

These communities served as kind of a compression chamber in which the new immigrant could gradually become acclimatized and adjusted to a new way of life within the framework of friendly and familiar surroundings. They also helped preserve the faith of the immigrants who frequently brought their own priests with them to minister to their spiritual needs.

Donald Thorman, *The Emerging Layman: The Role of the Catholic Layman in America* (Garden City, N.Y.: Doubleday, 1962). Copyright © 1962 by Doubleday. Used by permission of Doubleday, a division of Random House, Inc.

But, of course, the inevitable happened. The first and second generation children of these immigrants, for a variety of reasons which have been widely discussed in many books, began to leave their immigrant homes and move on to other parts of the city or nation. The sociological processes of assimilation and accommodation were hard at work making them into full-fledged Americans. . . .

Since the end of World War II, however, two new historical facts have coalesced to place today's American Catholic layman in a position of crisis which he must resolve without the aid of any past history on which to draw for assistance. For the problems he faces are unique and he will find little in ancient or modern history to supply him with the answers he needs.

World War II itself helped tear millions of young men from their social and cultural roots and throw them, unprotected, into close and prolonged contact with other young men of every cultural, religious, political, and economic background. Then, from 1946 on, as young Catholics returned from the wars, married, and established families, the housing shortage made it necessary for many of them to scatter far from their origins to find adequate living quarters. For the first time, many found themselves uprooted not only from their socio-cultural moorings but from their religious roots as well. The dramatic growth of groups such as the Christian Family Movement at about this time is an indication of the strong desire on the part of many couples to solve this problem by seeking out like-minded religious couples who would help them reinforce their religious values.

But about the same time the voice of the Church grew more and more insistent—we must withdraw from the ghetto and penetrate modern society with the principles of Christ. For too long have we ignored the secular world. It is the layman's job to restore that world to Christ. And the only way to do this is to become a part of it. . . .

Religion aside, our open, pluralistic society makes it very difficult for the family life of any distinctive minority to survive. For the norms and values of such minorities are usually so different from the norms and values of the majority that they require a conscious and sustained effort on the part of the minority to maintain itself. This is particularly true of the Catholic minority, where the standards and requirements—easily seen, for example, in the case of contraception—are much more demanding than those of the majority culture. . . .

The family, the school, and the Church are the traditional means by which "adequate knowledge of its family standards" is passed on to each new generation of the Catholic minority. Unfortunately, the current trend is for parents to abdicate their role as religion teachers and to turn this over to the school; and making the situation even more serious is the fact that the growth of the Catholic population is making it more and more difficult for Catholic children to get a Catholic education from kindergarten to college. . . .

I, for one, do not fear our problems so much as I do the kind of malaise I sometimes detect on the part of some Catholics who shrug their shoulders and halfheartedly ask, "Yes, but what can we do about it?" We are developing a defeatist attitude that is more concerned with problems than with opportunities. We sometimes seem to be so worried about plugging the holes on what appears to be a sinking ship that we forget to maintain the vessel on its course and keep moving ahead. We are neglecting the essential Christian virtues of hope and fortitude in the face of tribulations. . . .

One of the most immediate challenges is how to counter secularism. As Catholic parents, we are especially concerned about the effect of a pagan atmosphere on the spiritual formation of our children. Because our society is one characterized by religious pluralism, we simply have to face up to the fact that we and our children will always be associating with many different groups with widely varying sets of values and religious ideas. We do not live in a society that strongly reinforces the religious life of the family.

Parents know well what this means. They have to make certain minimal demands on their children—attendance at Mass at least on Sunday, time for confession on Saturdays, possibly some family devotions or other religious activities. If they are living in a neighborhood of secularists, or even among Catholics who don't make these similar demands, their children may rebel or they may be inclined to think that religion can't be too important because the other people they know don't take it seriously. When an individual Christian family is isolated in the midst of a nonreligious society, it is difficult to rear the children properly. . . .

. . . [W]hat can we do to avoid the problem of being isolated in a pagan atmosphere? One thing we all certainly can do is to seek out the companionship of like-minded Christian families with whom our children may associate. This will help give the children the balance they need to see that many other families share their parents' views and ideas.

There is also the possibility in these days of frequent moves to the suburbs for concerned Catholic families to buy homes near each other so they can form their own little community within the larger community. The important thing is for families who share the same ideals to join together so they give each other and their children the mutual support and encouragement that comes with unity of purpose.

Note carefully that this is not fostering a ghetto mentality, which is essentially a negative, defeatist withdrawal from the majority culture. Instead, what I am suggesting is a positive protection on the level of ideals and religious practices. This is an essential for the Catholic minority to survive the assaults of what has been called our post-Christian society.

I am not saying that the Catholic family owes nothing to society or that we can withdraw our Christian influence from the larger community. I believe the exact opposite to be true. What I am saying, however, is that we cannot throw the doors of our homes open indiscriminately to the avalanche of pagan ideas and customs that prevail in most areas today. If our homes are to become true nurseries of the Faith, little churches in which the Holy Family dwells, we cannot allow them to be infiltrated and penetrated by paganism.

❧ *E S S A Y S*

The essays in this chapter address various aspects of assimilation and Americanization. Edward Kantowicz of Carleton University, Ottawa, explains how a generation of powerful urban bishops centralized the administration of Catholicism in their dioceses during the first half of the twentieth century and tried to ensure that the members of their flocks, after abandoning their old ethnic particularism, became exemplary Americans. He shows how artfully George Mundelein, his principal example, negotiated two sets of hazards in this work: reassuring the Catholic authorities in Rome that he was strictly orthodox in his faith, but simultaneously reassuring his non-Catholic neighbors in Chicago that he too was a full-blooded American. Nowhere was this double-act more apparent than in the seminary library he built, modeled outside on Jefferson's University of Virginia and inside on the Roman Barberini Palace.

American Jews lacked Catholicism's strong centralizing principle, and as the twentieth century progressed, American Jews undertook a vigorous and far-ranging debate about exactly what it meant to be Jewish. As Jenna Weissman Joselit of New York, a skillful historian of material culture, recounts in the second essay, many Jews who had abandoned the more strenuous aspects of observant Judaism maintained their traditions by adapting kosher food rules to the American scene. For some, their motivation was strictly religious; for others, observance was more a sentimental issue. As Joselit shows, in an American consumer world preoccupied with gourmet food and cookbooks, kosher food advocates also had to allay fears that their offerings were tasteless and lacked nutrition. To the contrary, they declared that kosher is appetizing, tasty, and nutritious.

In the third essay, David Hollinger of the University of California, Berkeley, investigates the "de-Christianization" of American higher education in the early twentieth century and the role that cosmopolitan Jewish intellectuals such as Walter Lippmann played in that trend. Such people were opposed to their own families' form of particularism, favoring instead universal ideals of objectivity and science, and they flourished in a setting where dogmatic Christian confidence had already been undermined by a generation of liberal Protestants leaning toward agnosticism. Hollinger's explanation of this process reminds readers to consider a puzzling question: Should we not be as surprised by the persistence of American Christianity throughout most of the population as we are by its decline in the lives of public intellectuals?

Catholic Assimilation

EDWARD R. KANTOWICZ

When George Cardinal Mundelein of Chicago built his massive major seminary of St. Mary of the Lake in the 1920s, he designed its facades on early American, neoclassic lines, but he molded the seminary rules from Roman models. The exterior of the seminary library resembled Thomas Jefferson's University of Virginia, but the interior was an exact replica of the Barberini Palace in Rome. American on the outside, but Roman to the core—this had been the goal of the American Catholic church from the days of John Carroll's consecration as first bishop in 1789. The leaders of the Catholic minority tried to forge a community that was different in values from the American norm, but not too foreign, a community separate but equal.

Remaining separate was not difficult for a church composed largely of immigrants. Builder bishops and brick-and-mortar priests raised enough churches and parochial schools in the nineteenth century to ensure a separate institutional base for Catholics. Doctrinal intransigence and puritanical morals also kept Catholics distinctive in a Protestant but increasingly secular nation. Yet until well into the

Edward Kantowicz, "Cardinal Mundelein of Chicago and the Shaping of Twentieth Century American Catholicism," *Journal of American History* 68 (June 1981): 52–68.

twentieth century, American Catholics did not feel equal to other Americans or even to other Catholics elsewhere in the world.

Though the Catholic community was the largest American religious denomination as early as 1850, it lacked status and respect, both in Rome and in America. Rome considered the United States a mission territory as late as 1908, and in its mediation of various church disputes in the nineteenth century, the Roman Congregation of the Propaganda, which administered the church in mission lands, consistently misunderstood events in America. American Protestants, for their part, feared and mistrusted the Catholic church as an un-American invader of the Republic. . . .

. . . American Catholics remained too Roman for the native Protestants and too American for Rome. It fell, then, to the leaders of twentieth-century American Catholicism to make the separate Catholic community feel equal, fully Catholic, and fully American.

In the years surrounding World War I, a generation of American-born but Roman-trained bishops came to power in the largest urban dioceses of the United States. These men—such as Cardinal Mundelein in Chicago, William Cardinal O'Connell in Boston, Denis Cardinal Dougherty in Philadelphia, John Cardinal Glennon in St. Louis, and, at a somewhat later date, Francis Cardinal Spellman in New York—were "consolidating bishops" who, like their counterparts in American business and government, saw the need for more order and efficiency in their bailiwicks. Despite its hierarchical structure and theological dogmatism, the Catholic church in the United States had been decentralized and disorganized. The consolidating bishops of the first half of the twentieth century centralized and tightened the administrative structure of the church in the largest dioceses and tied American Catholicism more closely to headquarters in Rome. They also gained new respect for the American Catholic church, both in Rome, where their financial support became the mainstay of the "prisoner in the Vatican," and in the United States, where their business ability and political influence bolstered the self-image of their American subcommunity. . . .

Mundelein can serve as a case study of these episcopal leaders who shaped the twentieth-century Catholic experience in America. His life reads like an American success story. Born in 1872 and raised in the oldest German parish in New York City, he turned down a bid to the Naval Academy in 1889 and entered instead upon priestly studies for the Brooklyn diocese. Ordained in 1895, he became chancellor of the diocese two years later, a monsignor at age thirty-four, and an auxiliary bishop at thirty-seven. In 1915, when Rome appointed him to head the Chicago archdiocese, one of the three largest in the country, he became the youngest archbishop in America. Mundelein administered the Catholic church in Chicago from 1916 until his death in 1939, becoming a cardinal in 1924. Churchmen and laymen alike esteemed him primarily for his business acumen. One of his secular admirers flattered him: "There was a great mistake in making you a Bishop instead of a financier, for in the latter case Mr. Morgan would not be without a rival in Wall Street." . . .

. . . [I]n the large cities of the Northeast and Midwest, Catholic leaders visibly threw their weight around in an attempt to instill self-confidence in their flocks. The activities of big city bishops to gain prestige and raise Catholic self-esteem can be considered under five headings: giantism, "going first class," businesslike administration, Americanism, and advising presidents and politicos.

Like any insecure class of outsiders, the Catholic bishops began with the assumption that bigger is better. Building on a massive scale proclaimed Catholic importance. This impulse had been present in the American church for a long time, as St. Patrick's Cathedral, built on Fifth Avenue in New York in the nineteenth century, illustrates. In the twentieth century, both the National Shrine of the Immaculate Conception in Washington, D.C., and Cardinal Glennon's new cathedral in St. Louis were designed in the eclectic style that can best be described as Babbit Byzantine or simply Catholic Big. In Chicago, Mundelein showed better architectural taste; he attempted to restrain individual pastors who wanted to memorialize themselves with massive piles of masonry. Yet he was not immune to the virus of giantism. An instinctive adherent to the Chicago philosophy of Daniel Burnham—"Make no little plans"—Mundelein showed his giantism most clearly in the building of Chicago's seminaries. . . .

. . . He envisioned a Catholic University of the West to rival and perhaps surpass the struggling Catholic institution in Washington, D.C. The country property he had bought would house the divinity school and a central administration for the university. Individual religious orders, such as the Jesuits and the Dominicans, would be invited to locate their own houses of divinity studies around St. Mary's Lake, making this institution the most high-powered theological center outside of Rome. . . .

. . . The plans envisioned nine major buildings for the divinity school aligned along the arms of a Latin cross, with the main chapel, a monumental plaza, and a ceremonial dock and boathouse forming the upright of the cross. . . . All the buildings were to be in red brick, early-American, neoclassic design, with the main chapel an enlarged copy of a Congregational meetinghouse in Old Lyme, Connecticut. . . .

. . . St. Mary of the Lake seminary was finally completed with the dedication of its auditorium in 1934. By considerable arm-twisting at the Vatican, Cardinal Mundelein obtained from Rome the status of pontifical university for St. Mary of the Lake in 1929, an honor that permitted the conferring of doctoral degrees in theology.

. . . [T]he seminary and its extensive campus gave him a showcase. Visiting cardinals or other dignitaries were inevitably driven the forty miles out into the country for a grand tour or, in the early days, a cornerstone laying. Lake County, where the seminary was located, was heavily Protestant, and the archdiocese even had to fight off a local court challenge to St. Mary's tax exempt status. Nevertheless, the citizens of the nearby town of Area, like good boosters everywhere, recognized the importance of their institutional neighbor. In 1925 they voted to rename their town Mundelein. . . .

The secluded acres of Mundelein, Illinois, formed a backdrop for the most spectacular example of giantism during the cardinal's regime, the Twenty-eighth International Eucharistic Congress of 1926. . . . Though most of the events of the 1926 congress were conducted in Chicago churches or in the lakefront Soldiers' Field, some 800,000 pilgrims went by auto or by interurban rail to St. Mary of the Lake for the final day's procession. . . . The Chicago Catholic weekly newspaper, the *New World*, cautioned its readers: "Let there be no mistaking the fact that the Eucharistic Congress is no endeavor to demonstrate strength. There is no thought behind it of a flaunting of vast numbers before non-Catholics. . . . It is distinctly a religious manifestation."

Nevertheless, a "flaunting of vast numbers before non-Catholics" is precisely what the Eucharistic Congress was, a once-in-a-lifetime media event for the Catholic church in Chicago. . . .

Giantism and a flaunting of numbers were basic parts of the church's drive for status in the twentieth century. A more subtle form of the same impulse could be described as "going first class" whenever possible. Mundelein's seminary again illustrates the point. At a time when nearly all Catholic seminaries comprised a single building with spartan dormitory accommodations for the students, St. Mary's was a sprawling, multibuilding complex. Each seminarian had a private room and bath, a luxury that scandalized many older priests and one that many of the immigrant-bred students certainly did not enjoy at home. Eighty acres of the grounds were laid out as a golf course for the seminarians and for the priests of the archdiocese. On major holidays, the cardinal tried to devise unique surprises for the seminarians. He once flew in fresh lobsters for the entire student body, but most of the midwestern boys had never seen such a strange meal before and returned it to the kitchen untouched.

"Going first class" was the rule in other areas besides seminary training. . . .

. . . As a cardinal prince of the church, Mundelein affected the style of a Renaissance prince in public. He clearly loved ceremony both for its own sake and for the reflected glory it shone on his church. . . . In 1930, [Joseph W.] McCarthy, by then Mundelein's personal architect, completed a villa for the cardinal across the lake from the major seminary buildings. This house, a close copy of George Washington's Mount Vernon, became Mundelein's principal residence, even though the archdiocese already owned a handsome episcopal mansion in the city just off Lincoln Park.

"Going first class" as a prince of the church was a calculated risk for Mundelein. It could, and perhaps did, evoke Protestant fears of the church's foreign and antirepublican connections. On the other hand, Americans love a show, and they frequently fawn over royalty with all its ceremony. Mundelein shrewdly gambled that a magnificent display of Catholic power and self-confidence would do more good than harm to the American Catholic image, and he carefully included American trappings, such as the Mount Vernon model for his villa, in the display.

In the 1920s, the "business of America was business"; so going first class meant, above all, cultivating a businesslike image. The cardinal formed close friendships with the local financiers on LaSalle Street, such as Walter Cummings and William Reynolds of the Continental Bank and Harold L. Stuart of the Halsey-Stuart brokerage firm, upon whom he often called for short-term loans. He also retained enough connections in New York circles so that he could occasionally do an end run around the local banks and obtain more favorable rates on Wall Street. . . .

Mundelein's own reputation as a fundraiser was well merited. During the 1920s, Chicago Catholics contributed annually, on the average, about $120,000 to Peter's Pence, over $200,000 to the work of the missions, and almost $750,000 for local Catholic charity work. The Chicago cardinal employed numerous publicity gimmicks in the course of fund raising. One year he sponsored a contest among parishes for the greatest support of the missions, figured on a per capita basis, and rewarded the three winning parishes with sacred relics and church vessels blessed by the pope. When soliciting from business establishments, Mundelein employed what he called "the methods of our Jewish friends" by pointing out the advertising value of the diocese's lists of contributors. . . .

Mundelein was even more successful at administering money than at raising it. . . .

In order to shift capital internally within the archdiocese, Mundelein used his corporate bonding power to create a central banking mechanism. Legally constituted as a corporation sole, the Catholic Bishop of Chicago had the power to issue bonds. Mundelein's predecessors had occasionally used this power to sell Catholic Bishop of Chicago (CBC) bonds on the open market. . . .

Both in fundraising and in administration Mundelein applied modern American business techniques to an archaic institution. Money management was at the heart of the American Catholic drive for status, as Rome became increasingly dependent on American largesse. . . . As France in the nineteenth century had defended the Papal States militarily and protected the Catholic missions in colonial lands, American Catholics now sustained both the Vatican and its worldwide missions with money.

Businesslike management earned the respect of American businessmen as well. The Archdiocese of Chicago never had any problems marketing its CBC bonds; even during the depression of the 1930s these bonds rarely dropped below par. Ordinarily the archbishop was able to borrow from the banks at a percentage point below the market rate of interest. . . .

Mundelein and his colleagues also strove to earn respect and approval in the non-Catholic community by a policy of vigorous, 100 percent American patriotism. . . . They plunged headfirst into symbolic and emotional bursts of American patriotism on issues they knew would not irritate Rome.

Mundelein, for example, aligned himself with the "100 percent" attitude toward ethnic assimilation in America. In his first interview after being appointed to the Chicago archdiocese, he stated firmly that he did not believe in hyphens: "The people of the United States must be Americans or something else. They cannot serve two masters." He believed that the transitional phase of immigrant accommodation in ethnic parishes had lasted long enough and that new immigrant groups should be nudged toward full assimilation. In the very first months of his administration in Chicago, Mundelein appointed a new central school board which decreed that all instruction in Catholic schools be carried on in English, with the exception of some classes in catechism and reading which might be presented in an immigrant language. The "English only" order earned widespread praise outside the church, though it was resented by immigrant Catholics. . . .

World War I elicited an even greater outpouring of American patriotism from Catholic leaders. Within days of the United States declaration of war in 1917, the American archbishops hurriedly assembled and pledged unequivocal church support to the president and the war effort. Back in Chicago, Mundelein reiterated this support. . . .

Mundelein backed up his words with action, suspending temporarily some of his own ambitious fund-raising and building plans. When the first liberty loan was solicited in June 1917, the Chicago archbishop announced his personal purchase of $10 thousand worth of bonds. He instructed every pastor to invest at least $100 of parish funds in the liberty loan, even if they had to borrow the money to do so. . . .

This outpouring of wartime patriotism, as well as the efforts toward ethnic assimilation, showed clearly the deep longing for social acceptance on the part of American Catholic leaders. . . . Mundelein prided himself on his third-generation

Americanism and frequently alluded publicly to his grandfather who had died in the Civil War. His choice of Early-American architecture for the seminary was a deeply felt symbolic statement, and the Congregational church after which he modeled his main chapel was one he had visited as a boy on a New England vacation. . . .

A final factor that raised the Catholic church's self-image in America was the role of Mundelein and other leading bishops in advising presidents and politicos. Political influence was a necessity for the leaders of an extensive institution like the Catholic church. The church had many interests—a separate school system, tax privileges, the welfare of its largely immigrant membership—to protect from political assaults. Naturally, political ties were closest with the Irish-dominated local Democratic party. In the early years of Mundelein's administration, the bishop's personal representative in the state legislature was the speaker of the House, an Irish Democrat named David Shanahan, who buried many bills threatening Catholic schools. . . .

Mundelein played a very minor role in national politics until the Great Depression. Then, during the New Deal years, he became widely known as the most liberal Catholic bishop in America and Franklin Roosevelt's staunchest Catholic supporter. . . .

Mundelein and Franklin Roosevelt established an immediate rapport and a genuine friendship. The fact that both were devoted collectors gave them an initial point of contact, and both came to respect the other's abilities. . . .

The Mundelein-Roosevelt relationship was a useful one for both parties. The president needed prominent Catholic support, particularly in the late 1930s when Alfred E. Smith, Charles E. Coughlin, and other Catholics began to attack the New Deal as communistic and when many churchmen suspected the administration of sympathy for Spanish loyalists and Mexican anticlericals. Mundelein provided such support enthusiastically. . . . The cardinal, for his part, wanted reassurance that federal welfare funds would be equitably distributed to the unemployed, great numbers of whom were Catholic, and also wanted to ensure some institutional role for the church in making the distribution. . . . The cardinal could not be unaware, either, of the prestige which a close relationship with the president would bring to his church. Certainly Chicago Catholics swelled with pride when Franklin Roosevelt lunched at the cardinal's residence after delivering his "quarantine address" in Chicago on October 5, 1937. . . .

The careers of O'Connell, Mundelein, and Spellman spanned the entire period from the turn of the century to Vatican II. Their leadership and that of similar bishops in other cities, plus the growing numbers and wealth of American Catholics, achieved separate but equal status for the Catholic church in the United States. Inheriting a strong institutional base and a morally intransigent faith, the twentieth-century bishops "put the Church on the map" and "got it out of the catacombs" by providing highly visible leadership and instilling pride and confidence in American Catholics. Winthrop Hudson has pointed out in his popular history of American Protestantism that by the 1950s it was impossible to imagine that the death of any national Protestant leader could command the attention that accompanied the death of an American cardinal. With money, morals, and masonry, Cardinal Mundelein and his contemporaries raised the status of the American Catholic church so that it could command such attention.

Jewish Food and Jewish Identity

JENNA WEISSMAN JOSELIT

Recently, the front page of a well-regarded metropolitan newspaper, the *New York Observer,* carried a headline that read, "Many Jews in the City Forgo Temple; Rabbi Says Zabar's Does the Job." Explaining that Jewish New Yorkers do not feel they have to go to synagogue to express their Jewishness, the article acknowledged that "in New York City, Zabar's [the renowned Upper West Side food emporium] does that job for you." Nominally about synagogue attendance, the article underscored the relationship between food and identity characteristic of American Jews.

Whether reference is made to "kitchen," "culinary," or "gastronomic Judaism," the notion that food is a powerful vehicle by which Jews (or, for that matter, any group) express a religious, cultural, or ethnic identity has a long and popular history in both the Old World and the New. Heinrich Heine, in fact, was among the first to popularize the concept of *fressfrömmigkeit,* the expression of piety through the eating of holiday foods. The popularity of that concept, loosely rendered in English as "kitchen Judaism," was especially marked in the New World, where the American Jewish laity excelled in creating all sorts of inventive gastronomic alternatives to more traditional modes of Jewish identification. One Conservative rabbi in the mid-1940s even went so far as to propose a brand-new denominational model of American Jewry in which he substituted such new categories of affiliation as "A" Jews, or "Jews by Accident," "B" Jews, or "Bar Mitzvah Jews," and "G" Jews, or "Gastronomic Jews," for the standard typology of Reform, Conservative, and Orthodox. Not surprisingly, the "gastronomic Jewish" community boasted the greatest number of adherents. "Gastronomically considered, we do have 100% a religious community," he concluded wryly. Delmore Schwartz's aunt put it even more revealingly when asked about the extent of ritual attentiveness within her own second-generation American Jewish family. Searching about for a concise and accurate definition, she instinctively drew on the vocabulary of food to make her point: the family is proudly Jewish, she reported, "but not Jewish in dishes or anything."

When it comes to being "Jewish in dishes," the centrality of kashrut, the dietary laws, to Jewish cuisine complicates the relationship between food and culture still further. The Jewish case is a particularly complex one because of the way ritual restrictions define and shape both the preparation and the consumption of food. "The simple act of eating has become for us a complicated ceremony, from the preparatory phases of ritual slaughter through *milchigs* and *fleishigs, kosher* and *treif* . . . what Sacred Communion is to Catholics, the everyday meal is to Orthodox Jews." What is more, as the history of "kosher-style" cooking and dining suggests, American Jews could successfully detach from and disregard the ritual of kashrut while actively maintaining an affinity for and a commitment to Jewish cuisine. Improvising on tradition, American Jews fashioned a unique culinary phenomenon, remarkable for its blend of innovation and nostalgia. "'Delicious home-cooked

Jenna Weissman Joselit, "Jewish in Dishes: Kashrut in the New World," in *The Americanization of the Jews,* ed. Robert Seltzer and Norman Cohen (New York: NYU Press, 1995), 247–266.

meals, kosher style, like mother used to make' is a sign featured in most deli-catessens today," observed Ruth Glazer in 1946, noting the growing popularity of the distinction between "Jewish" and "kosher." "Uncertain, in a precarious world, of the articles of their faith, the Jews of the neighborhood," she continued, "could make one affirmation unhesitatingly. Jewish food was good." . . .

The study of kashrut in America touches on a wide range of issues: the rela-tionship between domesticity, gender roles, and ethnicity; the Americanization of diet; the cultural improvisation of religious tradition; and distinctions between pub-lic and private realms of behavior. The focus here is on the *ideology* of kashrut or, to put it differently, on how American Jewish cultural authorities—which I define broadly to include rabbis, sisterhood presidents, cookbook authors, as well as commercial manufacturers of kosher food—understood and promoted the Jewish dietary laws in the years between the first and second world wars.

Harnessing such trappings of modernity as advertising, cookbooks, and com-mercial food products, they promoted an ancient ritual. Advocates of the dietary laws drew on a wide range of arguments and artifacts in their campaign for kashrut. Science, reason, emotion, domesticity, gender, aesthetics—each was pressed into the service of the sacred, as were recipes, manuals, advertisements, scientific ex-periments, and iconography. "It is indeed desirable," wrote one kashrut adherent, "to inoculate the appreciation of the [dietary] laws through every means possible," through "historical, physiological, hygienic, scientific, or any channel of investiga-tion." From the pulpit and the printed page, in sermons and in pamphlets like "Yes, I Keep Kosher," the affinity of kashrut with the modern world was repeatedly and imaginatively emphasized. Theological imperatives or, for that matter, such touch-stones as God, the Bible, or the Talmud were conspicuously absent.

What united these disparate interpretations, apart from any mention of the divine, was the fact that in the America of the interwar years kashrut was no longer a given, a cultural assumption, or an intrinsic part of the modern Jewish experience. What earlier generations took for granted had now to be explained, interpreted, ac-tively championed, and, to succeed, thoroughly modernized as well. American Judaism, observed a leading Conservative rabbi, has become an "optional Judaism. *Everything* has now become optional," he noted, pointing to the abandonment of He-brew, Sabbath observance, and especially the dietary laws. American Jewry, he con-cluded, is "rapidly becoming denuded of all Jewish religious practices." Another rabbi observed that the "philosophy which prevails [among American Jews] is conve-nience. If there be no inconvenience involved in the observance of religious custom, good and well. The American Jew will relish the knadlach, homentashen, gefilte fish but would strenuously object if you will interfere with his gastronomic inclinations."

Statistical evidence, though admittedly slight, bears out these observations. Between 1914 and 1924, the consumption of kosher meat in the New York area fell by 25 to 30 percent. Elsewhere throughout the nation, the decline was equally pro-nounced. A Minneapolis rabbi in 1948 estimated that less than 15 percent of the Jews in his city kept kosher; including those Jews who kept kosher at home but not outside, he wrote, "brings the number to less than half of this number." Meanwhile, sociological studies of ritual behavior in the postwar era revealed an even more precipitous falling-off in the observance of kashrut: where an estimated 46 percent of second-generation American Jews followed the dietary laws, less than 10 percent of their children maintained the practice in its fullest, traditional sense. "During the war I decided not to buy kosher meat any more because it was very difficult with the ration points. So we gave up keeping a kosher house," a suburban informant told sociologist Marshall Sklare. "But in many ways we do keep the Jewish customs nevertheless," she continued, "and I could never buy pork or serve butter with meat at meals."

It is against this background of a growing optional or selective American Judaism during the interwar years that active propagandizing on behalf of kashrut became more pronounced. As the number of adherents fell off, explanations multiplied: kashrut was variously sanitized, domesticated, aestheticized, commodified, and reinterpreted. In most instances, these interpretations were designed expressly to inspire and encourage the continued practice of kashrut by emphasizing its consonance with modernity. "Kashruth need not be a burdensome affair," explained the editor of the *Jewish Examiner Prize Kosher Recipe Book* in 1937. "The substance of kashruth needs only to be made available in terms that are *understandable* to the young American Jewish housewife, to gain for the Biblical dietary laws the allegiance to which they are entitled." Latently, though, these latter-day interpretations served an altogether different function: to challenge and undermine the critique of kosher food as poorly prepared, inadequate, tasteless, and at once socially and gastronomically inferior, a critique rooted in a mix of theological, cultural, and nutritional concerns. As Mrs. Levy's *Jewish Cookery Book,* the first American Jewish cookbook ever published, insisted as far back as 1871, "without violating the precepts of our religion, a table *can be* spread, which will satisfy the appetites of the most fastidious. Some have, from ignorance, been led to believe that a repast, to be sumptuous, must unavoidably admit of forbidden food. We do not venture too much when we assert that our writing clearly refutes that false notion."

Modern-day champions of kashrut frequently drew on science for legitimation, hoping to endow the ancient practice with a rational, dispassionate "stamp of approval." Hailing the dietary laws as among the "first public health rulings," a wide range of voices, including those of cookbook authors, rabbis, anthropologists, and pharmacologists, insisted that when subjected to the "searchlight of science," kashrut made sense empirically, medically, and nutritionally. "Whoever made the Jewish dietary laws, whether given by Hammurabi in his code, or by Moses in the Thora, or by Joseph Karo in the Shulchan Aruch, . . . each and every one of them was, as you might say, a bacteriologist, a pathologist," commented one doctor in 1903, interjecting a rare note of comparative religion into the discussion. Still other texts affirmed that "medical science reveals, after exhaustive research, that the Dietary Laws have sound, practical knowledge behind their religious significance."

In many instances, this "sound, practical knowledge" was based on insights derived from the increasingly popular fields of nutrition and medical anthropology. "In short, 'kosher' means wholesome and sanitary," one writer on the topic observed categorically in 1912, "while *'treife'* conveys the idea of anything that is either directly unhealthy, malign, poisonous, or inefficient for the needs of the human body." . . .

Nutrition and anthropology were by no means the only sciences to which kashrut champions looked for support. Contemporary findings derived from zoology, chemistry, toxicology, biochemistry, and pharmacology were also enlisted and then widely popularized in monographs such as *The Jewish Dietary Laws: From a Scientific Standpoint* and "The Scientific Aspects of the Jewish Dietary Laws." The first text, published in 1912 by Bloch Publishers, was based on the research conducted by a Detroit physician, N. E. Aronstam, and presented at the International Exhibition of Hygiene a year earlier in Dresden. Drawing on Darwinian theories of evolution, he sought to validate and ratify the biblically mandated choice of ritually permissible foods in contemporary scientific terms. Forbidden foods like reptiles, mollusks, and crustaceans, Aronstam argued, were less complex anatomically and hence "insufficient as articles of diet"; they also contained various poisonous microorganisms. Fish with scales, he added, "stand higher on the ladder of evolution," and as a result are more digestible and "of greater nutritive value" than piscatory creatures without them. After placing each category of forbidden food within a comparative evolutionary context, the good doctor concluded forcefully that the precepts of kashrut "are in accordance with the doctrines of modern sanitation and its regulations compatible with the dictates of hygiene. The Bible is the pioneer of the sanitary sciences of to-day." . . .

Commercial purveyors of kosher food products also championed the notion that kosher food was healthy food by emphasizing the sanitary, controlled conditions under which it was manufactured. During the interwar years, the number of available mass-produced kosher foodstuffs grew enormously: by 1945, more than thirty-seven companies, including national companies like Heinz and Procter & Gamble and smaller Jewish concerns like Rokeach, Horowitz Bros. & Margareten, and Goodman & Sons, produced close to two hundred kosher food products, skillfully integrating kashrut into their mass-marketing strategies. "The Hebrew Race had been waiting 4000 years for Crisco," the maker of vegetable shortening exuberantly proclaimed in 1912 when it first introduced the product to the kosher market. Crisco's imaginatively designed marketing campaign, which invoked both tradition and modernity, stressed that its newfangled product carried not only a traditional rabbinic imprimatur but also a laboratory seal of approval. . . .

Mordecai M. Kaplan was perhaps the keenest exponent of the "constructive" view of kashrut. Pronouncing the scientific approach to kashrut as "gratuitous," he urged his followers not to overstate the practical importance of the dietary laws. "By giving them a utilitarian purpose, their function as a means of turning the mind to God is bound to be obscured," he wrote in his seminal *Judaism as a Civilization*. Instead, Kaplan preferred to think of kashrut as a "Jewish folkway" that enhanced the quality of modern Jewish life. "But if Jews are not to exaggerate the importance of the dietary practices," he cautioned, "neither should they underestimate the effect those practices can have in making a home Jewish. If the dietary folkways are capable of striking a spiritual note in the home atmosphere, Jews cannot afford to disregard them." By turns instrumental and emotional in his views on kashrut, Kaplan squarely situated its observance within a contemporary framework: by his lights, kosher food, along with Jewish artwork and Jewish bric-a-brac, infused the middle-class Jewish home with an appropriately Jewish sensibility. Inasmuch as the preparation and consumption of kosher food added Jewish atmosphere to the home, the practice was to be encouraged but by no means was it obligatory.

Interestingly enough, the founder of Reconstructionism also localized the practice of kashrut, restricting its observance to the home. "Moreover, since the main purpose of these practices is to add Jewish atmosphere to the home, there is no reason for suffering the inconvenience and self-deprivation which result from a rigid adherence outside the home. . . . By this means," he continued, "dietary practices would no longer foster the aloofness of the Jew, which, however justified in the past, is totally unwarranted in our day." As much a reflection of the times as its creation, Kaplan's geography of kashrut highlighted the extent to which "eating *out*" developed into a normative American Jewish practice. Comments on the order of "well, I keep a kosher home as far as possible . . . but when I go out I eat all sorts of things I don't have at home," emerged, in due course, as a standard refrain.

Jewish Intellectuals and Secularization

DAVID HOLLINGER

"Any large number of free-thinking Jews" is "undesirable" if one wants to maintain or develop a society in which a Christian tradition can flourish, said T. S. Eliot in 1934. He was right. At least he was right if the standard for a flourishing Christian tradition is the one Eliot took for granted. This conception of an ideal, racially and religiously homogeneous society Eliot illustrated with his ancestral New England. . . . It was an inauspicious time for a sophisticated and internationally minded intellectual to send off to the press a suggestion that there might be any context at all in which Jews should be declared undesirable: a full year had passed since Hitler had begun his notorious purge of Jews from German universities. Amid the dismay now routinely registered about Eliot's anti-Semitism, we risk losing touch with two insights embedded in this, his most lamented public utterance. Eliot was right to suggest that community building and maintenance involves at least some drawing of social boundaries. And he was correct to single out Jews, especially freethinking Jews, as a unique threat in the 1930s to the realization in the United States of a Christian community of the sort in which Eliot—and not Eliot alone— would have preferred to live.

Religious and nonreligious Jews were far from the only agents and referent points in the story of American Protestantism's encounter with diversity and the consequent attraction of Protestantism's leaders to "pluralism." But this story will not be accurately told until the role of Jews is explored more extensively than it has been in previous tellings. Although Catholics had long been a more numerous non-Protestant presence in the United States, and a more formidable threat to Protestant religious leaders, these Catholics were, after all, Christians. The challenge they presented to Protestant hegemony was less absolute than the one presented by an entirely non-Christian demographic bloc, even if this non-Christian bloc was made up of "People of the Book." Despite the existence of the American Jewish Committee and the several councils of rabbis. Jews were not so easily categorized as a single religious entity. Jews threw themselves more directly into American cultural life and embraced the public schools with enthusiasm, while Catholics developed their own

David Hollinger, "Jewish Intellectuals and the De-Christianization of American Public Culture in the Twentieth Century," in *Science, the Jews, and Secular Culture* (Princeton, N.J.: Princeton University Press, 1996), 17–41. Reprinted by permission of the author.

comprehensive educational system supervised by a single network of organizations ultimately responsible to the Vatican. Moreover, substantial segments of the Jewish population were in possession of greater capital holdings, higher class position, and stronger technical skills than were the bulk of their Catholic counterparts. Although Catholics developed effective political bases in some urban localities, the political visibility of Jews within the circles of the nation's old Protestant elite was signaled by the appointment of Louis Brandeis to the United States Supreme Court in 1916. This Jewish presence was also concentrated to a large extent in the most conspicuous of places: New York City, the closest thing to an American cultural capital. By 1920, nearly one-third of New York's population was Jewish.

In addition, there arose from within the Jewish population an articulate and energetic minority of intellectuals—the "free-thinking Jews" of Eliot's most pointed concern—who took little interest in Judaism but did not become Christians and who, even more portentously, brought a skeptical disposition into the American discussions of national and world issues that had been the all but exclusive domain of Protestants and ex-Protestants. To these freethinking Jews there was virtually no Catholic equivalent. Even if Protestants managed to mentally shoehorn religious Jews into the categories of religious particularism—another peculiar "denomination" like the Mormons or the Seventh-Day Adventists—the cosmopolitan, Enlightenment-inspired Jews refused to stay put. It was not adherence to some un-American "tribal" faith that created a problem here; rather, what made these intellectuals special was their manifest failure to be Jewish parochials. This applied to many of the Zionist as well as the non-Zionist intellectuals in the group. Their transcending of conventional religious categories rendered them a problem for Protestants quite distinct from the challenge presented by Orthodox, Conservative, and Reform Jews. Like their European prototypes Marx, Freud, and Durkheim, these emancipated Jews engaged the same "universal" discourses that American professors and authors had reproduced in terms more distinctly Protestant than would be widely acknowledged until later. This Protestant matrix was cast into bold relief first by Jews, then by Catholics who had long resented it but did not confront it very directly until the era of John Courtney Murray and Vatican II, and eventually by a third, very different set of critics: the multiculturalists of our own time, for some of whom the exposure of the parochially Anglo-Protestant character of earlier American intellectual life has become an almost sacred calling. Before the role of Jews in this process can be properly assessed, however, it is important to clarify the question to which American Jews are part of a satisfactory answer.

No one doubts that the public culture of the United States was more decisively Protestant at the beginning of the twentieth century than it is today. The point is not simply that the overwhelming majority of religiously affiliated Americans had always been identified with one or another of a host of Protestant denominations. Nor is it that American ecclesiastical institutions were dominated in the early and middle decades of this century by a loose "Protestant Establishment" consisting of the recognized leaders of the most socially prominent of these denominations (especially Congregationalists, Baptists, Methodists, Presbyterians, Disciples, Episcopalians, and Lutherans). The question is not thus situated in "religious history," narrowly conceived. The starting point for the inquiry lies instead in the larger history of the United States itself, and in the influence there of a generic Protestantism for which the ecclesiastical "Protestant Establishment" was assumed to be a reliable voice. This generic, transdenominational Protestantism had come by the end of the nineteenth century to be taken for granted by nearly all of the Americans in a position to influence the character of the nation's major institutions, including those controlling public education, politics, the law, literature, the arts, scholarship, and even science. This confident spiritual proprietorship lay behind the continued currency well into the century of the idea that the United States was a "Christian nation." In recent decades Protestants, increasingly aware that the old, generic Protestantism is taken for granted by fewer and fewer of the people running the relevant institutions, have tended to acknowledge that the religious character of the nation is contested. They have been inclined to describe themselves as but one of a variety of parties to a "pluralism" that accepts the legitimacy within the American nation not only of Catholics and Jews, but, more recently, of a vast expanse of cultural units defined by ethnoracial as well as religious principles. What accounts for this transition from "Protestant culture" to the acceptance, however gradual and in some cases grudging, of a pluralism in which Christianity is acknowledged to be but one of several legitimate religious persuasions in America? This is the question.

The place to begin is with a recognition that this question should be nested within another one that lies beyond the scope of this essay. "Why is there so much Christianity in the United States in the twentieth century? What most needs to be explained is surely not the decline of Protestant cultural hegemony in one of the most socially diverse and highly literate of the industrialized nations of the North Atlantic West, but rather its persistence in such a setting. It would be implausible to expect the generic Protestantism of 1900 to be able to maintain its authority for long against the aggressive expansion of scientific culture, against the pluralizing force of massive migrations of Catholics and Jews down to 1924, and against the particularizing pressures of social diversity within the ranks of American Protestants. The relative slowness and limited extent of de-Christianization in modern American history even down to the present is an event of the same order as the failure of the American Left to develop social democratic movements comparable to those of Great Britain, France, and Germany. The historiography of twentieth-century America has wrought many variations on the classic question "Why is there no socialism in the United States?" but this relative "failure of the Left" has a less widely addressed counterpart in the relative "failure of secularization." Why, indeed, is there so much Christianity in America today? . . .

Cognitively, refinement of the critical tradition of the Enlightenment created structures of credibility within which many of Christianity's truth-claims looked highly suspect. This sharpening of Enlightenment-inspired critique was visible in the historical study of the Bible, in the Darwinian revolution in natural history, in the development of materialist analyses of the human self and of society, and in a multitude of efforts to substitute "science" for other authorities in a variety of specific contexts. Throughout the nineteenth century most of the Americans who welcomed and helped to advance the Enlightenment in these respects were, of course, Christians, many of whose descendants were in turn able to retain or to reconstitute their faith in relation to the increased cultural authority of science. But some were not. By the turn of the century many of the leading intellectuals whose professional work was most associated with the defense of a religious sensibility—Josiah

Royce and William James are convenient examples—knew better than to count biblical evidence as among the reasons for accepting a given idea as true. Careers like those of Margaret Mead, David Riesman, and Daniel Bell indicate the extent to which social scientists replaced the clergy as the most authoritative public moralists for educated Americans. The simple notion that the Enlightenment diminished the place of Christianity in the West may be banal, but it is also true. It applies in an arena stretching far beyond twentieth-century America, but it applies there too, and formidably so. . . .

. . . [A]s Protestant leaders worried more about secularism, one cohort after another of Protestant leaders came around to recognizing in their Catholic coreligionists a force that could be mobilized against religious indifference and even against the de-Christianizing influence of secular intellectuals and, some felt, of Hollywood. The same alliance was extended, with some theological adjustments, to religious Jews through the popularization of the idea of a "Judeo-Christian Tradition." . . .

. . . The difficulty of establishing Christianity's superiority to other religions—once they were really scrutinized with a modicum of honest sympathy—bedeviled many in the wake of the 1893 World's Parliament of Religions. And foreign missionary experience, too, sometimes had the effect of undermining a confidence more easily maintained within the confines of a small town in rural America. Moreover, it was the secular intellect's claim to be able to handle any experience that came along that most distinguished it from its apparently more parochial rivals. All methods of "fixing belief" other than science will eventually fail, Charles Peirce explained in the pages of *Popular Science Monthly,* because of the social world's diversity: the tenaciously faithful may try to hide from the diversity of human testimony about the world, but they will be unable to ignore it forever. . . .

. . . Jews who managed to find a place for themselves in the public intellectual life of the nation—rather than speaking to a distinctly Jewish constituency—reinforced the most de-Christianized of the perspectives already current among the Anglo-Protestants. If lapsed Congregationalists like [John] Dewey did not need immigrants to inspire them to press against the boundaries of even the most liberal of Protestant sensibilities, Dewey's kind were resoundingly encouraged in that direction by the Jewish intellectuals they encountered in urban academic and literary communities. Franz Boas was among the earliest of these Jewish intellectuals to achieve prominence. He founded a tradition of relativist anthropology that exercised enormous deprovincializing influence through both Gentile (Margaret Mead, Ruth Benedict) and Jewish (Edward Sapir, Melville Herskovitz) followers. Boas himself was the only prestigious American scientist to campaign actively against the ostensibly scientific racism used to justify the immigration exclusion act of 1924. The biologist Jacques Loeb also became a celebrity well before World War I. Loeb was a forthright atheist whose rejection by New York's Century Association led the Columbia psychologist J. McKeen Cattell to mount a public protest. Loeb became a symbol for the ethical austerity of science and served as a model for Max Gottlieb, the Jewish scientist-hero Sinclair Lewis contrasted to the priggishly moralistic Reverend Ira Hinkey in Lewis's most acclaimed novel, *Arrowsmith.* . . .

. . . Gentiles in the New York of this era produced a number of testimonies to the cosmopolitan influence of Jewish intellectuals. The most famous of these testimonials is "The Intellectual Preeminence of Jews in Modern Europe," written by Thorstein Veblen shortly after his 1918 arrival in New York. Veblen treated Jewish intellectuals—with whom the "rootless" and "marginal" Veblen, a son of Norwegian immigrants, clearly identified—as "the vanguard of modern inquiry." . . .

. . . Jews were suspect in academia partly because many Anglo-Protestants thought them socially crude and aggressive, and politically radical. But religion was a very large part of it, as is revealed by patterns in the location and intensity of suspicion of a Jewish presence. The barriers to Jews in business, engineering, medicine, and law—where technical skills rather than responsibility for constituting and transferring culture were central—were not as high, nor as entrenched. Intellectually ambitious Jewish undergraduates of the teens, twenties, and thirties were routinely counseled to give up on the idea of becoming philosophers or historians and were encouraged to pursue, instead, a career in one of the service professions. . . . The social snobbery that victimized Jews was thus the most potent when allied with the defense of a generic, if theologically inconspicuous, Protestantism. . . .

By the midcentury mark, intellectuals of Jewish origin were no longer systematically excluded from even the teaching of English and philosophy. It is not easy to separate cause from effect in the ethnodemographic transformation of American academia during the midcentury decades. Did Jews find their way into this sector of American life because of a prior de-Christianization well advanced among intellectuals of Anglo-Protestant origin, or because these Jews, themselves, had helped by their very presence and by their pressure against the old exclusionary system to de-Christianize the space they were gradually entering? Both were surely true, but there was an additional factor, more easily isolated.

Hitler was a major agent of this transformation in two respects. His example—horrifying to many Americans even before the full dimensions of the "Final Solution" became known—rendered anti-Semitism of even the genteel sort more difficult to defend. If this helped American Jews beginning careers in the late 1940s and early 1950s, a second of Hitler's acts made a more dramatic and immediate impact: he pushed from Central Europe to a relatively welcoming America a distinctive cohort of Jewish scholars, scientists, and artists that attracted extensive notice within the American academic and literary worlds. This cohort included not only Albert Einstein and a substantial percentage of the physicists who built the atomic bomb, but a galaxy of distinguished humanists and social scientists. The fame and prestige of some of these men and women enabled this migration to have a symbolic impact far beyond the specific, local communities into which these refugee intellectuals were absorbed.

American academia expanded rapidly in the postwar era, and a larger and larger portion of faculties turned out to be Jews, the descendants, in most cases, of the East European Jewish immigration of 1880–1924. . . .

The de-Christianization that accompanied these changes in the ethnodemographic base of American intellectual life was indirect but not necessarily trivial. Gentiles could take pride in the creation of a collegial environment in which Jewish colleagues would not feel marginalized. Religion was increasingly private, and public discussion was increasingly secular. It is worth considering, in juxtaposition to one another, two widespread perceptions concerning the elite college and university faculties of the last quarter-century. One perception is that the prevailing culture of these faculties is more secular than is the rest of the society and even the rest of the American academy, and that within these faculties the open profession of Christian belief in the course of one's professional work is uniquely discouraged.

Most investigators trying to answer the question "Why is there so much Christianity in the United States?" would squander little time interviewing the citizens of Cambridge, New Haven, Ann Arbor, Hyde Park, Madison, and Berkeley. The second perception is that these same faculties are disproportionately Jewish. The first of these two perceptions may be impressionistic in foundation, but the second has been confirmed by a report of the Carnegie Commission on Higher Education. This 1969 study found that while Jews constituted only about 3 percent of the American population, they accounted for 17 percent of the combined faculties of the seventeen most highly ranked universities.

✎ F U R T H E R   R E A D I N G

Blumhofer, Edith. *Aimee Semple McPherson: Everybody's Sister* (1993).
Brown, Dorothy, and Elizabeth McKeown. *The Poor Belong to Us: Catholic Charities and American Welfare* (1997).
Cox, Harvey. *The Secular City: Secularization and Urbanization in Theological Perspective* (1965).
Feldman, Egal. *Dual Destinies: The Jewish Encounter with Protestant America* (1990).
George, Carol V. *God's Salesman: Norman Vincent Peale and the Power of Positive Thinking* (1993).
Glazer, Nathan. *American Judaism,* 2nd ed. (1974).
Gleason, Philip. *Contending with Modernity: Catholic Higher Education in the Twentieth Century* (1995).
————. *Keeping the Faith: American Catholicism, Past and Present* (1987).
Glenn, Susan. *Daughters of the Shtetl: Life and Labor in the Immigrant Generation* (1990).
Halsey, William. *The Survival of American Innocence: Catholicism in an Era of Disillusionment* (1980).
Heinze, Andrew. *Adapting to Abundance: Jewish Immigrants, Mass Consumption, and the Search for American Identity* (1990).
Higginbotham, Evelyn B. *Righteous Discontent: The Women's Movement in the Black Baptist Church, 1880–1920* (1993).
Howe, Irving. *World of Our Fathers* (1976).
Hutchison, William R. *Between the Times: The Travail of the Protestant Establishment in America, 1900–1960* (1989).
Joselit, Jenna Weissman. *The Wonders of America: Reinventing Jewish Culture, 1880–1950* (1994).
Kantowicz, Edward. *Corporation Sole: Cardinal Mundelein and Chicago Catholicism* (1983).
Keyser, Les and Barbara. *Hollywood and the Catholic Church: The Image of Roman Catholicism in American Movies* (1984).
Lotz, David W. *Altered Landscapes: Christianity in America, 1935–1985* (1985).
Marcus, Jacob Rader. *United States Jewry, 1776–1985,* 3 vols. (1989).
————. *The American Jewish Woman: A Documentary History* (1981).
Marty, Martin. *Modern American Religion,* Volume 2, *The Noise of Conflict, 1919–1941* (1991).
Meyer, Michael. *Response to Modernity: A History of the Reform Movement in Judaism* (1988).
Moore, Deborah Dash. *To the Golden Cities: Pursuing the American Jewish Dream in Miami and L.A.* (1994).
Orsi, Robert. *Thank You Saint Jude: Women's Devotion to the Patron Saint of Hopeless Causes* (1996).
Raphael, Marc Lee. *Profiles in American Judaism: The Reform, Conservative, Orthodox and Reconstructionist Traditions in Historical Perspective* (1985).

CHAPTER
11

War and Religion:
1914–1985

*The twentieth century witnessed a succession of catastrophic wars. When they
entered these conflicts, Americans wanted to be confident that they were justified in
fighting, and they drew on their religious heritage to find evidence of God's blessing
for their actions. A growing chorus of pacifists and antiwar advocates answered
that a God of peace, justice, and mercy would never approve their participation.*

*Just as in the Civil War both sides had claimed to be fighting a godly war (see
Chapter 7), so now the religious advocates quoted chapter and verse of the Bible to
prove either that God was warlike or that he was not. The Bible mentions many
godly warriors—Goliath, Saul, David, Samson, Moses, Joshua, and others—but
the prophet Isaiah and Jesus himself are inspirational figures for pacifists. Here, as
elsewhere, biblical evidence proved ambiguous. Christian warriors noted that Jesus
had said: "I come to bring not peace, but a sword" and that he had angrily overturned the tables of the moneylenders in the temple. Pacifists countered by reminding readers that Jesus healed the soldier's ear in Gethsemane when Peter cut it off,
and that Jesus declared, "My kingdom is not of this world."*

*American clergy overwhelmingly supported intervention in the First World
War because they accepted the propaganda portrait of the Germans as brutal
"Huns," who had committed such atrocities as the mass rape of Belgian nuns.
After the war, when these tales proved to be false, many clergy reacted with embarrassment and shame, and promised that they would never again accept such a
demonic caricature of the enemy. Clergy played a dominant role in the Fellowship
of Reconciliation and other pacifist movements in the 1920s and 1930s, and took to
heart President Woodrow Wilson's pledge that the events of 1914–1918 had been
the "war to end all wars."*

*In 1939, World War II began in Europe. When stories of the Holocaust began
to filter out of Europe, they sounded so similar to the wild tales from twenty years
before that many Christians conscientiously refused to believe them. Tragically, they
were wrong twice—the first time for being too credulous, the second time for being
too skeptical. Hitler's "final solution" for exterminating the Jews of Europe (along
with Gypsies, communists, and members of Christian resistance groups) was really
happening. American Jewish groups urged U.S. intervention in Europe, but*

President Franklin Roosevelt hesitated until the Japanese attack on Pearl Harbor in December 1941 brought America into the war against both Germany and Japan. Even then the Holocaust could not be stopped until the death camps were liberated by Allied troops in 1944 and 1945. The fact of the Holocaust has played a large role in Jewish and Christian theological discussions of war and the nature of evil ever since.

The controversial use of atomic bombs by the United States to end the war against Japan in 1945 and the forty-four-year Cold War standoff with the Soviet Union that followed presented new challenges to religious Americans. Was it morally responsible to threaten using weapons of mass destruction in the name of preserving "the Christian West"? Those who saw the Soviet Union as a demonic threat to the survival of Judeo-Christian civilization said yes. However, the Vietnam era (roughly 1965–1975) engendered a great revulsion against American militarism. By the 1980s, a growing number of Christians and Jews were arguing that, politically and morally, a defense policy based on the threat of nuclear annihilation was impermissible.

The peaceful conclusion of the Cold War in 1989–1990 ended a long, anxious confrontation, but the subsequent Gulf War (1990–1991), the long crisis in Yugoslavia throughout the 1990s, and wars elsewhere in the world showed that the great questions linking war, religion, and the human conscience remained unsettled.

❧ D O C U M E N T S

John Haynes Holmes, a progressive New Yorker and Unitarian minister, believed that humanity had evolved beyond the point of needing war. He had looked forward confidently to an era of Christian peace and brotherhood under a benign form of socialism. These visions were shattered by the outbreak of World War I in 1914, and in Document 1 (1916), before America became a direct participant in the war, he pleaded for Christian pacifism. Document 2, by Virginian minister Edward Leigh Pell (1917), answers that Jesus was always a fighter and would have joined eagerly in the war effort with a clear conscience. In Document 3, written in 1966 regarding events of the late 1930s, Reinhold Niebuhr, the foremost Protestant theologian of twentieth-century America, explains why he came to see American intervention in World War II as part of his Christian duty and why he founded the journal *Christianity and Crisis* to advocate it. Dorothy Day was leader of the Catholic Worker Movement, whose Houses of Hospitality, in the worst districts of American cities, took care of destitute workers, the homeless, and the mentally ill. Day was an absolutely uncompromising Christian pacifist. In Document 4 (1942), she denies allegations of cowardice and asserts that the class war within America is more important than the antifascist war in Europe. Document 5, a 1945 editorial from the *Christian Century* (a leading liberal Protestant journal), surveys the shattered world after Hitler's defeat and the incineration of Hiroshima by atomic bombs; it pleads for Christian unity as a first step to the great rebuilding. Jesuit theologian John Courtney Murray, in Document 6 (1960), makes a classic statement of the Cold War idea that the Soviet Union embodies anti-Christian forces of evil, and that it must be opposed at all costs. Twenty years later, however, his own Catholic church was religious leader of the antinuclear movement, and its pastoral letter "The Challenge of Peace" (1983) signaled the Catholic bishops' refusal any longer to accept the American government's nuclear-based defense policy. It and similar statements are explained by James Wood, editor of the *Journal of Church and State,* in Document 7 (1983).

1. John Haynes Holmes Appeals for Christian Pacifism in World War I, 1916

When the Great War burst upon the world in August 1914, it was natural that affrighted and outraged men should regard this disaster as a final demonstration of the failure of Judaism, Christianity, the organised peace propaganda, and international socialism. The tradition of Israel reaches back to a period antedating the advent of Christianity by more than seven centuries; the gospel of love, associated with the name of Jesus, has been known to humanity for nearly two thousand years; the peace movement, led by able and distinguished men, backed by abundant resources, well-organised and persistently aggressive, has had three generations to impress its doctrines upon the modern mind; and during the last half-century or so, we have seen a massing of the forces of labour, in all countries, under the banner of socialism, which seemed to constitute a sure protection against war. And yet, when the crisis came, no one of these great forces proved of any avail. The tide of conflict swept across Europe, Asia, Africa, and the seven seas as swiftly and terribly as though no bulwarks had ever been raised against it. What wonder that men in their disappointment and fear, declared religion a failure, the peace movement a farce, and socialism an arrant sham!

That this indictment is rightly to be levelled against Jews and Christians, pacifists and socialists, is to my mind undeniable. Never has humanity been called upon to witness a more tragic spectacle than that of the millions of Germans, Austrians, French, Russians, English—all of them pledged in one way or another to the cause of peace—marching away to the battlefront, at the first sound of alarm, not only without protest, but with enthusiasm. There were some Jews and Christians, we may well believe, who revolted inwardly, if not outwardly, against the call to arms; there were some peace advocates, we know, who were distraught and ashamed; the attempt of the socialists, before the declarations of war were made, to stay the flood of madness then threatening the race, stands out as one of the few glorious episodes of the dreadful days of July and August, 1914. But that, when the actual moment of dread decision came, these millions of religionists, pacifists, internationalists, abandoned their spiritual professions and clung to patriotism as the one sure passion of their souls, is a sober fact. Everywhere they gave way at the very moment when, if ever, they should have stood fast, and thus failed!

That this failure of individuals, however, involves any failure of the various churches or movements, to which these individuals had pledged allegiance, is, to my mind, the unfairest of charges. Judaism, Christianity, the peace propaganda, socialism, a failure? When, let me ask, has the world ever put into practical effect, in the form of laws and social institutions, the moral principles of Judaism or the spiritual ideals of Christianity? . . . Christianity, pacifism, socialism—when and where and how have these had any chance? All have been professed, but not one has been practised. Lip-service is the uttermost of reverence which ever has been paid to them. Other forces, of a wholly different character, have controlled the movements and fashioned the organisations of society—and these forces it is which have led us

John Haynes Holmes, *New Wars for Old* (New York: Dodd, Mead, and Co., 1916).

to the horror of the present cataclysm of universal disaster. . . . This hour marks perhaps the hour of darkest failure in all of human history. But it is the failure not of Christianity but of civilised barbarism, not of Christ but of Cæsar, not of love but of blood and iron! . . .

. . . We have even been called upon to witness, during the last few months, the spectacle of a group of men, gathered self-consciously in Independence Hall, in the brave attempt to organise a movement for the establishment of *peace by force!* . . . [W]e forget that, in attempting to destroy Germany and to protect our-selves by force against the menace that Germany represents, we are ourselves tak-ing up her weapons, reproducing her system, doing her work. So that humanity actually finds itself face to face with the very excellent probability that German arms, in due course, will be destroyed, but that, by the very process of victory, the German spirit will find itself triumphant in France, England, Russia, America. . . .

It is this situation which makes imperative an unfaltering reaffirmation of the true gospel of peace, which is none other than the gospel of righteousness preached by Isaiah, the gospel of love proclaimed by Jesus, the gospel of goodwill main-tained by all the pacifists of the ages, the gospel of democracy and co-operation set forth by socialists everywhere—in one word, the gospel of non-resistance!

2. Edward Leigh Pell Justifies Christian Warfare, 1917

For a hundred years and more millions of people have been thinking of Jesus as a dear, saintly, harmless soul, of quiet mien and gentle speech, who likes to think up kind things to say about the devil and who never protests against anything except the cruel custom of killing flies.

This is the Christ of our Sunday afternoon dreams.

The Christ of history was the bravest fighter the world has ever known.

I do not say that he was not gentle and kind and tender-hearted. I have seen some gentle and kind and tender-hearted women who were tremendous fighters. And Jesus, though the gentlest and kindest and most tender-hearted of men, was a tremendous fighter. . . .

. . . If we are fighting we know perfectly well whether we are right or wrong, and we know it not by what is going on on the surface but by what is going on in our hearts. We know that the thing that counts with God is not what our fists are doing, but what our hearts are doing. If I were fighting to deliver a poor fellow from the hands of a cruel oppressor I would have a sense of exaltation as strong and pure as that which comes at the moment of supreme sacrifice; but if I should sud-denly discover that I was not really concerned about the poor fellow at all, but had jumped on the oppressor because he was my enemy and I wanted to get even with him, my spirit would fall into the bottomless pit of degradation and shame.

It is not fighting that counts against us; it is the hating that is back of most of our fighting. To say that all fighting is wrong because it is impossible to fight

Edward Leigh Pell, *What Did Jesus Teach About War?* (New York: Fleming Revell, 1917), 34–35, 63–4, 94–5.

without hate is not only puerile, but it gives the lie to every noble character that has ever lived. History does not record, so far as I can recall, a single noble life that was not filled with fighting. I am sorry for the man who says he cannot fight without hate, just as I am sorry for the man who cannot punish a child until he gets "mad." Any brute can whip his child when he is mad: it takes a real man to whip his child when he is not beside himself. And it takes a real man to fight when there is not a trace of hate in his heart. A real man cannot fight without fire, but he can fight without hate. He must burn with wrath—wrath against wrong—but that is a different matter; a very different matter. . . .

Can a Christian Be a "Slacker"?

The kingdom of Christ is a kingdom of peace, but you cannot establish a kingdom without war. And the army of Christ is still on the fighting line. The moment we enlist in his service we find ourselves face to face with forces of evil which call for all the fighting spirit we have and more. And what we lack he will supply. There are teachings of Jesus which cannot get into the blood without turning the veriest "slacker" into a hero. If a man is a Christian he is bound to fight. It is in his blood. He cannot retreat. He cannot surrender. He cannot hide his head in the sand. He must fight.

Christianity means war. It doesn't necessarily mean this or that kind of a war, but it means war. We cannot follow Christ and not fight. We must fight individually and we must fight as a people. We must fight with our spirits—heaven only knows how we have to fight with our spirits! We must fight with our intellects. And so long as savagery remains in the world—so long as there are human beings who are not susceptible to moral appeal—it may be necessary once in a long while to fight with our bodies. We may cut war out of our hymns and our rituals and our school histories and our ethical culture societies, but we cannot cut it out of the Christian life. A Christian is no "slacker." A Christian is every inch a fighter.

3. Reinhold Niebuhr Explains the Christian Case for Fighting Nazism (c. 1939), 1966

As one of the midwives of CHRISTIANITY AND CRISIS, I have been asked to reminisce about its past and speculate on its future. I can begin by stating that the name was given spontaneously because there was no question about the crisis that prompted the birth of this new Protestant journal.

It was quite simply the crisis of Western civilization, posed by the Nazi threat to its moral and religious foundations. Hitler's Fascist movement combined a pagan philosophy with a racialism and anti-Semitism that threatened the very existence of the Jewish minority in the whole of Europe. Some of us suspected the degree of this evil even before millions of Jews perished in the terrible gas chambers of Auschwitz. The paganism and racialism was related to and a product of an extravagant

Reinhold Niebuhr, "A Christian Journal Confronts Mankind's Continuing Crisis," *Christianity and Crisis* 26 (February 21, 1966): 11–13. Reprinted by permission of the Estate of Reinhold Niebuhr.

nationalism, which threatened all the non-German nations of the Continent with slavery. The fabled militarism of Germany, developed from the days of Frederick the Great to Bismarck and the Kaiser, was the instrument of this planned subjugation of Europe to the "master race."

When our founders used the word "crisis," however, they were referring not only to the perils confronting Western culture but also to the moral and religious crisis in our own nation. This was manifested in the complacency and irresponsibility of American neutralism in the face of the Nazi threat to a common religious, moral and political culture.

This irresponsibility had both political or national roots and religious roots, which we must analyze in turn. Nationally our traditions bred self-righteousness because—from Jefferson to Wilson—we were under the illusion that we were a "chosen" democratic nation and, therefore, free of the European vices of national egotism and aggression. . . .

Closely related to the idealistic reaction in the nation was the crisis in the Church. American Protestantism was influenced by the radicalism of the sects, which had had only a minor influence in Europe. But on the frontier they combined sectarian millenarianism with secular utopianism, and thus imparted an atmosphere of political sentimentality to our religious and moral life. De Tocqueville, writing about nineteenth-century America, thought that both our religious and political life were informed by a self-righteous and complacent assumption that the Kingdom of God had been established in the new nation, as distinguished from the sin-tainted old nations of Europe. Thus it could be truthfully observed that "spiritually we are all Quakers."

The religious pacifism that grew up after World War I was a combination of the old perfectionism and an idealistic reaction to the horrendous international realities revealed in the Treaty of Versailles. I was one of those new perfectionists who swore never again to participate in a war. Ours was a rather simple solution to the complex problems of the morality of sovereign nations living in a state of international anarchy.

Some of the founders of CHRISTIANITY AND CRISIS were perfectionists of this type. But they disavowed their earlier pacifism when they recognized that our neutralism in the face of the Nazi threat posed the problem of guarding our virtue by irresponsibly ignoring the dangers facing other nations. . . .

Most of the founders, however, were never bitten by the perfectionist illusions of radical Protestantism. They were, on the whole, the children of the orthodox or Anglican Reformation, and included priests and bishops of the Episcopal Church, ministers of Presbyterian and other churches, and some idealists turned realist, such as the present author. . . .

. . . In addition to the political crisis, we were concerned by the crisis in the Church's relation to the political and international order. This was occasioned by the absence of discriminate responsibility toward all the complex problems of social existence in an increasingly technical culture, culminating ultimately in the fantastic nuclear dilemma.

Our nation was cured of irresponsible neutralism by the measure of its power after World War II. We were, in fact, one of the two great nuclear powers of the world, involved in a struggle with Russia on the edge of a nuclear abyss. Though saved from our irresponsibility, we were still tempted to self-righteousness. Were we not the appointed guardians of the "free world" against "Communist despotism"?

The two forms of crisis were constantly changing. In the world nazism was displaced by communism. But this change merely emphasized the other form of crisis in the Church, namely the need for perceptive judgment in relating the absolutes of the Gospel to the various challenges of justice, order and peace—domestically in a technical culture and internationally in an era of nuclear terror. Our most recent domestic crisis was to help the nation to take belated steps toward racial justice for a Negro minority long defrauded of its rights as citizens and of its dignity as human beings.

The problem of indiscriminate pacifism in a community in which order and justice are attained not by pure love or pure reason but by an equilibrium of various forms of economic and political power has given way to the problem of curbing pure force in the international realm. Thus we seek to persuade our nation that Chinese communism cannot be contained or restrained purely by military violence, particularly when we regard ourselves as the appointed saviors of the world and do not consult the consensus of the nations. We also need to be more astute in rejecting all false analogies, particularly the flagrant ones that equate Nazi and Communist despotism and that fail to distinguish between Russian and Chinese communism, the one partly domesticated and the other in its original revolutionary fervor.

Thus a survey of past history in both Church and State, and possibly a projection of that history into the future, reveals that the social life of mankind is in a perpetual crisis of community and conflict on various levels—tribal, national, imperial and universal. History also reveals that such diverse instruments as language, religion, racial identity, political power and military force can be used as instruments both of community and of conflict.

The moral crisis is ever changing, but all changes reveal one constant factor. The moral life of man is continually in the embarrassment of realizing that the absolutes of biblical and rational norms—which enjoin responsibility for the neighbor's welfare—can never be perfectly fulfilled, either by the use of or abstention from any of the instruments of community or conflict. Therefore, religious and moral guides must teach the necessity of discriminate judgment. As long as this journal combines moral imperatives with moderate moral discrimination, it will have a creative future in both Church and Nation.

4. Dorothy Day Compares World War II to the Class War, 1942

"[W]e are at war," people say. "This is no time to talk of peace. It is demoralizing to the armed forces to protest, not to cheer them on in their fight for Christianity, for democracy, for civilization. Now that it is under way, it is too late to do anything about it." One reader writes to protest against our "frail" voices "blatantly" crying

Dorothy Day, editorial from *Catholic Worker,* February 1942, reprinted in *By Little and Little,* ed. Robert Ellsberg (New York: Knopf, 1983), 263–266. Copyright 1983, 1992 by Robert Ellsberg and Tamar Hennessey. Published in 1992 by Orbis Books, Maryknoll, New York 10545. Used by permission.

out against war. . . . Another Catholic newspaper says it sympathizes with our sentimentality. This is a charge always leveled against pacifists. We are supposed to be afraid of the suffering, of the hardships of war.

But let those who talk of softness, of sentimentality, come to live with us in cold, unheated houses in the slums. Let them come to live with the criminal, the unbalanced, the drunken, the degraded, the perverted. (It is not [the] decent poor, it is not the decent sinner who was the recipient of Christ's love.) Let them live with rats, with vermin, bedbugs, roaches, lice. . . .

Let their flesh be mortified by cold, by dirt, by vermin; let their eyes be mortified by the sight of bodily excretions, diseased limbs, eyes, noses, mouths.

Let their noses be mortified by the smells of sewage, decay, and rotten flesh. Yes, and the smell of the sweat, blood, and tears spoken of so blithely by Mr. Churchill, and so widely and bravely quoted by comfortable people.

Let their ears be mortified by harsh and screaming voices, by the constant coming and going of people living herded together with no privacy.

Let their taste be mortified by the constant eating of insufficient food cooked in huge quantities for hundreds of people, the coarser foods, so that there will be enough to go around; and the smell of such cooking is often foul.

Then when they have lived with these comrades, with these sights and sounds, let our critics talk of sentimentality. As we have often quoted Dostoevsky's Father Zossima, "Love in practice is a harsh and dreadful thing compared to love in dreams."

Our Catholic Worker groups are perhaps too hardened to the sufferings in the class war, living as they do in refugee camps, the refugees being, as they are, victims of the class war we live in always. We have lived in the midst of this war now these many years. It is a war not recognized by the majority of our comfortable people. They are pacifists themselves when it comes to the class war. They even pretend it is not there.

Many friends have counseled us to treat this world war in the same way. "Don't write about it. Don't mention it. Don't jeopardize the great work you are doing among the poor, among the workers. Just write about constructive things like Houses of Hospitality and Farming Communes." "Keep silence with a bleeding heart," one reader, a man, pro-war, and therefore not a sentimentalist, writes us.

But we cannot keep silent. We have not kept silence in the face of the monstrous injustice of the class war, or the race war that goes on side by side with this world war. . . .

Read the letters in this issue of the paper, the letter from the machine-shop worker as to the deadening, degrading hours of labor. Remember the unarmed steel strikers, the coal miners, shot down on picket lines. Read the letter from our correspondent in Seattle who tells of the treatment accorded agricultural workers in the Northwest. Are these workers supposed to revolt? These are Pearl Harbor incidents! Are they supposed to turn to arms in the class conflict to defend their lives, their homes, their wives and children?

Last month a Negro in Missouri was shot and dragged by a mob through the streets behind a car. His wounded body was then soaked in kerosene. The mob of white Americans then set fire to it, and when the poor anguished victim had died, the body was left lying in the street until a city garbage cart trucked it away. Are the

Negroes supposed to "Remember Pearl Harbor" and take to arms to avenge this cruel wrong? No, the Negroes, the workers, in general are supposed to be "pacifist" in the face of this aggression.

Perhaps we are called sentimental because we speak of love. We say we love our President, our country. We say that we love our enemies, too.

"Greater love hath no man than this," Christ said, "that he should lay down his life for his friend."

"Love is the measure by which we shall be judged," St. John of the Cross said.

"Love is the fulfilling of the law," St. John, the beloved disciple, said.

Read the last discourse of Jesus to his disciples. Read the letters of St. John in the New Testament. And how can we express this love—by bombers, by blockades?

Here is a clipping from the *Herald Tribune,* a statement of a soldier describing the use of the bayonet against the Japanese:

"He [his father] should have been with us and seen how good it was. We got into them good and proper, and I can't say I remember much about it, except that it made me feel pretty good. I reckon that was the way with the rest of the company, by the way my pals were yelling all the time."

Is this a Christian speaking?

Love is not the starving of whole populations. Love is not the bombardment of open cities. Love is not killing, it is the laying down of one's life for one's friends. . . .

. . . [The] accusation "holier than thou" is . . . made against us. And we must all admit our guilt, our participation in the social order which has resulted in this monstrous crime of war.

We used to have a poor, demented friend who came into the office to see us very often, beating his breast, quoting the Penitential Psalms in Hebrew, and saying that everything was his fault. Through all he had done and left undone, he had brought about the war, the revolution.

That should be our cry, with every mouthful we eat—"We are starving Europe!" When we look to our comfort in a warm bed, a warm home, we must cry, "My brother, my mother, my child is dying of cold.

"I am lower than all men, because I do not love enough. O God, take away my heart of stone and give me a heart of flesh."

5. *Christian Century* Editors Urge Christian Unity in an Era of Total War, 1945

The apocalyptic end of the war lays upon the Christian church a responsibility which it cannot evade. It must preach to modern man the good news of possible salvation. It must breathe upon the remaining embers of his ancient faith and fan them into flaming hope that the abyss into which he has stared in horror is not inevitably to engulf him. It must also, . . . proclaim "the good news of damnation," since it is a gain to know without doubt that continuation in the course which we

"The Church's Responsibility," *Christian Century,* August 22, 1945, 953. Copyright 1945 by the Christian Century Foundation. Reprinted by permission from Christian Century.

have followed is a certain road to extinction. It is the mission of the church to face man with his present inescapable choice between life and death and to bring him to a decision in favor of the unsearchable riches of life in a world whose energies all derive from God.

There is reason to believe that the conscience of the church is awakening to this responsibility. In the chaplaincy, among the men at the front, in the ranks of scientists and in the general membership of the churches there is a growing realization that there is simply no alternative to the Christian faith except destruction. No other religious faith can provide an answer to the ultimate questions which crowd the modern mind. No other has the slightest chance of laying the spiritual basis for world community. If the first planetary civilization does end in unbelievable violence almost at the moment of its birth, the Christian church cannot plead innocent of the responsibility.

To realize this is immediately to recognize how appallingly unequal the church now is to its high responsibility. The Church of Rome extols peace but unceasingly probes every fissure in the political and social structure in the interest of clerical power. Eastern Orthodoxy has emerged from the fires of a persecution unparalleled in diabolical severity bound hand and foot by the will of the Soviet state. European Protestantism has survived the war with a magnificent record of resistance to totalitarian bondage, but its contribution to world Christianity must be limited by the tragic exhaustion of its resources. American Protestantism has maintained its freedom but has used it to create and extend denominational divisions which had little relevance in the prewar world and have become a scandal in the world of today. And throughout the non-Christian world the younger churches confront older religions and the new paganism, both fired to fresh zeal by the second demonstration in a generation of the powerlessness of followers of the Prince of Peace to shape the policy of nations which have called themselves Christian.

By every standard of human judgment the church is unequal to the responsibility which rests upon it. Measuring its shortcomings against either the task which confronts it at the end of the war or its own ancient but now imperative mission, it might justifiably yield to despair. If this is our only hope, it might be said, then indeed we are doomed. But such reasoning leaves out of account the one factor which has caused the church to survive not only epochs but civilizations. It forgets the secret of renewal which has not only given the church longevity in a world where institutions rise and fall but has made it a recurrent source of revolutionary change in the societies in which it has taken root. That secret is found not in its own strength but in the power which surges into the church again and again from its living head, the Lord Jesus Christ.

That power is available only to a church on its knees. The first mandate which the present crisis lays upon men and women of faith is to confess the justice of the judgment which hangs like the sword of Damocles over Western civilization including the Christian church itself. More than that, we must acknowledge that our condemnation is greater because we have proved ourselves to be faithless trustees of the divine word, fractious exponents of the brotherhood of the family of God, harsh advocates of redeeming love.

But the responsibility of the church does not end at the altar. It must set its own house in order. Every ecumenical tie must be greatly strengthened, beginning in the communities in which the churches stand. In this country local churches have accumulated out of the blood money of war prosperity immense funds for postwar building construction. These edifices will set the pattern of community relationships for more than a generation. Upon these buildings may rest the curse of continuing our unhappy divisions. They may also symbolize a denial of the spiritual community which is the basic reality of the Christian revelation.

The denominations, as such, must also face their responsibility for this building expansion and for their use of the great funds which they are now piling up. Every large denominational project should be held in suspension until there is evolved an ecumenical plan which will eliminate competition on the community level, insure maximum cooperation among the churches of the nation and strengthen the world witness of the Christian faith. A national council of churches which is representative of the principal functions of the churches as well as of their peripheral interests is an immediate necessity. So also is a World Council of Churches which reaches beyond Europe and whose mission of redemption is so clearly universal that it can no longer be accused of being simply the religious arm of Anglo-American imperialism.

Underlying all this is the responsibility of the church for the spiritual regeneration of mankind. The accumulating hatreds of successive wars will never be dissipated short of the collective destruction of the race unless a way can be found to make Christian repentance, forgiveness and reconciliation operative in the minds and the affairs of men. The church must find that way. Nobody else will even make the attempt.

6. John Courtney Murray, S.J., Argues That the Cold War Is a Spiritual Confrontation, 1960

A Fourfold Uniqueness

Russia is unique as a state or a power. For the first time in history it has brought under a single supreme government the 210,000,000 people scattered over the 8,600,000 square miles of the Euro-Asiatic plain, the great land-mass that stretches from the River Elbe to the Pacific Ocean. This gigantic power is a police state of new proportions and unique efficiency. Within it there is no such thing as the "rule of law"; there is only the thing called "Soviet legality." Power is used according to certain forms; but there is no concern for justice and no sense of human rights. The Soviet Union has not adopted the Western concept of law nor has it evolved a comparable concept of its own. Its theory of government is purely and simply despotism. In this respect Sir Winston Churchill was right in viewing the Russians . . . as a "formless, quasi-Asiatic mass beyond the walls of European civilization." These walls, that contain the Western realization of civility, were erected by men who understood the Western heritage of law—Roman, Greek, Germanic, Christian. The Soviet Union has no such understanding of law.

John Courtney Murray, S.J., "Doctrine and Policy in Communist Imperialism" from *We Hold These Truths* (New York: Sheed & Ward, 1960). Reprinted by permission of Sheed & Ward, an Apostolate of the Priests of the Sacred Heart, Franklin, Wis.

Moreover, through a novel set of institutions the Soviet Union has succeeded in centralizing all governmental power to a degree never before achieved. The ultimate organ of control is the Communist party, a small group of men who think and act under an all-embracing discipline that has likewise never before been achieved. Under its historically new system—a totally socialized economy—the Soviet Union has become an industrial and technological power whose single rival is the United States. . . .

Second, Russia is unique as an empire, as a manner and method of rule, as an *imperium.* It is organized and guided in accordance with a revolutionary doctrine. For the first time in history this doctrine has consciously erected an atheistic materialism into a political and legal principle that furnishes the substance of the state and determines its procedures. Soviet doctrine is exclusive and universal in its claim to furnish, not only an account of nature and history, but also a technique of historical change. It is therefore inherently aggressive in its intent; and it considers itself destined to sole survival as an organizing force in the world of politics. . . .

Third, Russia is unique as an imperialism. The Soviet Union is essentially an empire, not a country. Nearly half her subjects should be considered "colonial peoples." . . .

It has exhibited a new mastery of older imperialistic techniques—military conquest, the enduring threat of force, political puppetry, centralized administration of minorities, economic exploitation of "colonial" regions. It has expanded the old concept of the "ally" into the new concept of the "satellite." But perhaps its newness is chiefly revealed in the creation of the historically unique imperialistic device known as "Soviet patriotism." This is not a thing of blood and soil but of mind and spirit. It is not born of the past, its deeds and sufferings, borne in common; it looks more to the future, to the deeds yet to be done and to the sufferings still to be borne. It is a "patriotism of a higher order," and of a more universal bearing, than any of the classic feelings for *das Vaterland, la patrie,* my country. It is a loyalty to the Socialist Revolution; it is also a loyalty to the homeland of the Revolution, Russia. Its roots are many—in ideology, in economic facts, and in the love of power; in a whole cluster of human resentments and idealisms; and in the endless capacities of the human spirit for ignorance, illusion, and self-deception. This higher patriotism claims priority over all mere national loyalties. . . .

Finally, the Soviet Union is unique as the legatee of a longer history. It is the inheritor both of Tsarist imperialism and of mystical panslavist messianism. It carries on, at the same time that it fundamentally transforms, the myth of Holy Russia, the "spiritual people," the "godbearing children of the East," whose messianic destiny is to rescue humanity from the "Promethean West." Communism, whether in theory or in practice, is not a legacy of Western history, nor is it a "Christian heresy" (the pernicious fallacy popularized by Prof. Toynbee). Essentially, it came out of the East, as a conscious apostasy from the West. It may indeed be said that Jacobinism was its forerunner; but Jacobinism was itself an apostasy from the liberal tradition of the West, as well as from Christianity, by its cardinal tenet (roundly condemned by Pope Leo XIII) that there are no bounds to the juridical omnipotence of government, since the power of the state is not under the law, much less under God. In any case, Communism has assumed the task at which Jacobinism failed—that of putting an end to the history of the West. Communism has undertaken to inaugurate a new history, the so-called Third Epoch, that will abolish and supplant what are called the two Western epochs, feudalism and capitalism. . . .

. . . It is an *imperium,* a mode of rule, guided in its internal and external policy by a comprehensive systematic doctrine that contradicts at every important point the tradition of the West. Soviet theory and practice stand in organic interdependence. Only Soviet doctrine makes Soviet power a threat to the United States. Only Soviet doctrine explains the peculiar nature of Soviet imperialism and shows it to be unappeasable in its dynamism. Only Soviet doctrine illumines the intentions of the new messianism that has come out of the East, fitted with an armature of power, and organized implacably against the West. . . .

In his book, *The Illusion of the Epoch: Marxism-Leninism as a Philosophical Creed,* Prof. H. B. Acton makes this concluding statement: "Marxism is a philosophical farrago." Other scholars, within the Academy and within the Church, after even more extensive studies have likewise stigmatized the Soviet dogma as scientific, historical, philosophical, and theological nonsense. But what matters for the statesman is not that the dogma is nonsense but that the Soviet leaders act on the dogma, nonsense though it be. . . .

. . . It would be almost impossible to set limits to the danger of Communism as a spiritual menace. It has induced not simply a crisis in history but perhaps the crisis of history. Its dream of the Third Epoch that will cancel Western and Christian history and the major institutions of that history (notably the rule of law and the spiritual supremacy of the Church) has gone too far toward realization over too wide a sweep of earth to be lightly dismissed as a mere dream. On the other hand, as a sheerly military menace Communism is strictly limited. It is limited in the first instance by its own doctrine. This doctrine has always assigned to military force a real role in the advancement of the World Revolution. Nevertheless, the role of force has always been ancillary, subordinate, supportive of political, economic, and ideological initiatives. Force is to be employed only when the historical moment is right and the military or political risk is minimal. Moreover, there is every reason to believe that in the nuclear age, in which all risks are enhanced most horribly, Communist doctrine has set a still more diminished value on the use of force. By a sort of perverse genius, proper to the children of darkness, it has at the same time set a higher value on the sheer threat of force.

7. James E. Wood Surveys Church Protests Against Nuclear Weapons, 1983

For the main line churches, the nuclear arms race has become a matter of particular importance and for many of them the most crucial single issue in public affairs. The escalation and proliferation of the nuclear arms race have had a sobering impact on the churches, both Catholic and Protestant, even on those American churches that traditionally have not been known for their peace witness. The threat of nuclear war

James E. Wood, "The Nuclear Arms Race and the Churches," *Journal of Church and State* 25 (Spring 1983): 219–230.

has brought the churches to a new awareness of the urgency for peace and the imperative need for a peace witness on behalf of the churches. Clearly the nuclear age has given to the churches a new dimension to war and peace and a new challenge of involvement in both national and international affairs.

Nationalism and militarism engulf the world. Whatever else may be said about the twentieth century, including its scientific and technological achievements, it has been a century repeatedly marred by the most devastating civil and international wars in human history and the systematic mass annihilation of millions by a variety of governments around the world. More than 25 million people have died in more than forty wars since World War II. At the same time, this century has been marked by the unprecedented development of military arms, culminating in nuclear arms, the potential use of which defies human comprehension and description. Notwithstanding the painful lessons of two world wars and unresolved military conflicts of long duration in various parts of the world since 1945, the threat of war, even nuclear war, far from being lessened has become an ever present reality. The imminent possibility of nuclear war is undeniable, made all the more so with the escalation and proliferation of the nuclear arms race. By the next decade it is projected that at least fifty countries will have the capability of developing nuclear weapons. Already, nuclear arsenals of the world are estimated to possess a combined destructive force equivalent to four tons of TNT for every man, woman, and child in the world. . . .

Opposition to the nuclear arms race has been voiced by the majority of America's major national religious groups, including: African Methodist Episcopal Church, American Baptist Churches in the U.S.A., American Jewish Congress, Christian Church (Disciples of Christ), Church of the Brethren, Church Women United, Episcopal Peace Fellowship, Evangelicals for Social Action, Lutheran Council in the U.S.A., National Conference of Catholic Bishops, National Council of Churches in the U.S.A., Presbyterian Church in the U.S., Progressive National Baptist Convention, Reformed Church in America, Southern Baptist Convention, Union of American Hebrew Congregations, Unitarian-Universalist Association, United Church of Christ, United Methodist Church, and United Presbyterian Church in the U.S.A. During 1979 and 1980, more than one hundred fifty religious leaders and over forty national religious organizations founded a coalition to give firm support for the ratification of SALT II, not because the treaty was worthy in itself, but rather because a failure to ratify it was viewed as "the far greater evil." This spring eighteen national Christian and Jewish groups, in a joint statement released at the Capitol, denounced the administration's proposed increases in military spending and charged that the budget for 1984 "in the name of national defense . . . equates peacekeeping with firepower and thereby increases our insecurity as more and more destabilizing weapons systems are added to an already bloated arsenal." In addition, the joint statement called for Congress to reduce military spending and to cancel "dangerous or unnecessary" weapons systems, specifically the MX missile and B-1 systems.

These views, while broadly representative of America's main line denominations, are not shared by the New Religious Right, which soundly denounces such views as rooted in political liberalism and moral weakness. Financed by the Moral Majority, full page ads in major American newspapers recently featured "an open letter from Jerry Falwell," who there opposed a nuclear freeze and strongly endorsed substantial increases in military spending, including the production of MX missiles and B-1 bombers. The virtually unqualified support given by the New Religious Right to the present military buildup and the group's intense opposition to SALT II reenforce the incompatibility present between main line churches and the New Religious Right on nuclear arms reduction and a nuclear freeze.

By all odds, the single most important development in the involvement of the churches in the nuclear arms race is the pastoral letter on war, armaments, and peace, by the National Conference of Catholic Bishops. Entitled "The Challenge of Peace: God's Promise and Our Response," the first draft was presented at the 1981 general meeting of Catholic bishops. A second draft of 110 pages, with seventy-three footnotes, was submitted at the bishops' annual meeting on 15–18 November 1982 and provoked a storm of controversy. Within a short time the pastoral letter became the most important single religion news story of the year. A third and final draft of the pastoral letter has been prepared for presentation and final action by the bishops at their forthcoming meeting on 2–3 May 1983 in Chicago.

Already the document is being heralded for the debate that it has generated on the proposed nuclear arms buildup both within the churches and in society at large. Even more important is the long-range potential influence of the document in articulating, on behalf of the Catholic bishops of America, their unalterable opposition to any first use of nuclear weapons, their specific condemnation of the MX missile, and their categorical rejection of the stated U.S. policy of retaliation against Soviet cities in the event of an attack by the Soviet Union. "We write this letter," the bishops declared, "because we agree that the world is at a moment of supreme crisis" and "because nuclear war threatens the existence of our planet."

Written in the context of a theology of peace, the document affirms the bishops' unequivocal rejection of nuclear war. "To say 'no' to nuclear war," the bishops affirmed, "is both a necessary and a complex task. . . . We see with clarity the political folly of a system which threatens mutual suicide." This no to nuclear war must, in the end, "be definitive and decisive." Americans are warned not to be "so paralyzed in their efforts at peacemaking by a form of anti-Sovietism" that they fail "to grasp the central danger of a superpower rivalry." As alternatives to present U.S. nuclear policy the bishops recommend: "immediate, bilateral verifiable agreements to halt the testing, production and deployment of new strategic systems"; "negotiated bilateral deep cuts in the arsenals of both superpowers, particularly of those weapon systems which have destabilizing characteristics"; "a comprehensive test ban treaty"; and "removal by all parties of nuclear weapons from border areas and the strengthening of command and control over tactical nuclear weapons to prevent inadvertent and unauthorized use." . . .

With 51 million members, the Roman Catholic Church is, of course, the largest single religious denomination in the United States. For the first time in the history of this nation, the Catholic Church hierarchy has found itself in confrontation with the government on key issues of national policy and in fundamental disagreement with an administration's priorities in domestic and foreign policy. While the views of the bishops have been and will continue to be challenged by those within and without the Catholic Church, "The Challenge of Peace" clearly represents a milestone in Catholic church-state relations in the United States. Of even more significance is the document's contribution to the role of churches in their peace witness and in advancing the cause of peace throughout the world.

With the escalation and proliferation of the nuclear arms race, time is running out. Without arms limitation and arms reduction, both subject to existing systems of verification, the nuclear arms race will continue unabated, and the chance of a nuclear war virtually becomes inevitable. There has never been a military weapon developed that was not eventually used. The consequences of a nuclear war are far too grave to be ultimately decided on the basis of nationalism or military strategy. As the leading nuclear powers of the world, the United States and the Soviet Union have a special responsibility on behalf of all mankind to engage continually in serious bilateral negotiations that will result in a systematic limitation of arms and a deescalation of the present arms race. There must also be an international agreement, with appropriate verification, to halt the production and deployment of all first-strike nuclear weapons. On these questions, the churches cannot remain silent. Rather, as the National Conference of Catholic Bishops affirmed, "Because the nuclear issue is not simply political but also a profoundly moral and religious question, the church must be a participant in the process of protecting the world and its people from the spectre of nuclear destruction."

ESSAYS

Ray Abrams's *Preachers Present Arms* (1933) is a grand old classic. Abrams studied the prowar excesses of the American clergy during the First World War and the way in which they helped mobilize public opinion in 1917 and 1918. Abrams prided himself on being an "objective" social scientist, one who stands above the disputes he is studying, to explain them logically, systematically, and impartially. No reader can doubt, however, that he is furiously angry with the clergy for their role in promoting war fever and hatred of the enemy.

The second essay comes from a biography of Reinhold Niebuhr, written in 1985 by Richard W. Fox of Boston University. Niebuhr, a German-American minister's son from Missouri, became a Detroit pastor in the 1920s and then a professor at Union Seminary in New York. Sympathetic at first to the utopian, antiwar, prosocialist mood of many liberal Protestants, he changed rapidly in the 1930s, becoming an outspoken advocate of "neo-orthodox" theology, which insisted on the inevitable sinfulness of mankind and our tendency, especially in groups, to commit evil. His book *Moral Man and Immoral Society* (1932) was his classic statement of this theme; it is still widely read and admired by theologians and ethicists today. Niebuhr asked repeatedly: what is the nature of Christian responsibility in a sinful world? It seemed clear to him in the crisis of the late 1930s and early 1940s that this responsibility had to include fighting the evil that Nazism represented. He agitated for it, in writings, speeches, and organizational work with the Union for Democratic Action, and he founded *Christianity and Crisis* to advocate it while denouncing a Christian pacifism that seemed to him irresponsible.

The third essay traces the history of the concept of a "Judeo-Christian tradition." Mark Silk, a Harvard Ph.D. in history and now a journalist with the *Atlanta Journal-Constitution,* shows that the threat of Nazism and the World War II crisis gave rise to the idea that Jews and Christians had more things in common than points of separation. The phrase became a handy rallying point, first against the Nazis, and then, by an easy transfer of antagonist, against the "godless communism" of the Soviet Union. Niebuhr helped popularize it, and Will Herberg, a section of whose book *Protestant, Catholic, Jew* is included in Chapter 10, became one of its leading Jewish advocates.

Preachers and the Great War Euphoria

RAY H. ABRAMS

Immediately following the severance of diplomatic relations with Germany, with the sending home of Count Von Bernstorff, the churches held patriotic services, passed resolutions promising to support the President to the limit. Many urged war at once. By the time Congress got around to carrying out these desires, one looks in vain for protests. All the church organizations and nationalistic groups vied with each other in flowery resolutions of patriotism—the Jews, the Catholics, the Protestants, the various Irish, German, Lutheran societies and the Mormons.

The Methodists of New England, assembled, pledged themselves "and all that we have—our fortunes, our lives, our prayers, and our sacred honor—to the cause of our country, in this, her critical hour of peril and need," while the presidents of three Lutheran bodies sent out a call to the members to prove their loyalty to the President and Congress. . . .

While this analysis is concerned primarily with the churches and the clergy, it is to be remembered that other groups and individuals were affected as deeply by the *Zeitgeist*. If the most noted social scientists, who had spent all their days in scholarly research and in critical analysis and judgment of world events, lost possession of their reasoning faculties, it is not surprising that the most intelligent of the clergy, as well as the lesser lights, did likewise.

In fact, cold intelligence seems to have had relatively little chance in those days. People were guided by their emotional reactions and those were basically the same for all men. Radicals, liberals, conservatives, atheists, infidels, agnostics, advanced theologians, modernists, and fundamentalists, all alike were swept off their feet by the mass movement. The war was heartily endorsed and scriptural reasons furnished by representatives of such extreme points of view as Isaac Haldeman and Frank M. Goodchild, premillenarians and defenders of the faith on the one hand, and such heretics within the Baptist fold as Dean Shailer Mathews of the Divinity School of the University of Chicago, and Harry Emerson Fosdick of the Union Theological Seminary, New York, on the other.

What happened to the pacifists who were so opposed to war in the preparedness era? Most of them also succumbed. Rabbi Stephen S. Wise, who had scolded the war-like clergy and called the preparedness movement "unchristian," now lost his detachment and led in the cry for the "slaughter of the Boche." In his estimation the Germans should be made to pay to the uttermost farthing. Frank Oliver Hall who had "preached for peace and worked for peace for thirty years" was soon calling for a fight to the finish and asking men and women to serve their country "to the last penny in their purses and the last drop of blood in their veins."

Frederick Lynch, one of the founders of the Church Peace Union, and editor of *Christian Work*, was one of the most ardent peace men in America, if not in the world. In 1915 he had recommended the "excommunication" of "every man that takes up the sword." He worked against our entrance into the war up to the very

Ray H. Abrams, *Preachers Present Arms* (1933; reprint, Scottsdale, Ariz.: Herald Press, 1969). All rights reserved.

last. But once in the fray he was calling the Germans "Huns" and "baby-killers" with gusto. The president of the Church Peace Union, Bishop David Hummell Greer of the Cathedral of St. John the Divine, New York, after some mental and spiritual struggle, came around to thanking God for the two great nations. England and America, "standing hand in hand, shoulder to shoulder in the great crusade against tyranny and aggression." . . .

How did the molders of religious opinions in the churches justify our entrance into the war? This question has been answered in part, for, . . . the process of rationalization of the struggle in terms of light versus darkness, virtue versus sin, humanity versus autocracy, civilization versus chaos and God versus the devil had been going on in many a pulpit for at least two years prior to April, 1917. The legend of the "holy war," concocted in England, had grown to be almost universally accepted by the idealists in the churches over here. America had now entered the holy crusade on the side of the Allies. Nothing was more natural than for Randolph H. McKim to proclaim from his pulpit in Washington that

> It is God who has summoned us to this war. It is his war we are fighting. . . . This conflict is indeed a crusade. The greatest in history—the holiest. It is in the profoundest and truest sense a Holy War. . . . Yes, it is Christ, the King of Righteousness, who calls us to grapple in deadly strife with this unholy and blasphemous power [Germany]. . . .

. . . [C]ivilization was the creation and the expression of Christianity. The destruction of one meant the annihilation of the other. Since civilization now hung in the balance, Christianity was thereby fighting for her life. God would not stand by and countenance such a catastrophe. America had been chosen as his loyal servant to take the leading part in punishing the ruthless Germans and to save Christianity. Thus with such a divine calling victory would be ours. The fight for righteousness, justice, liberty and to make the world safe for democracy simply meant defending the principles for which Christ himself had died. Hence the war itself was a holy war to promote the Kingdom of God upon earth. To give one's life for his country was to give it for God and His Kingdom. God and country became synonymous.

Joseph Fort Newton, leaving the Church of the Divine Paternity, New York, to accept the call from the City Temple, London, had carried with him an American flag presented in an appropriate farewell service by Frank Oliver Hall to "entwine it with the British." Dr. Newton, theologian and mystic, expressed his convictions:

> Think it all through, and at bottom, the war is religious. If our enemies are right, our religion is wrong, our faith a fiction, our philosophy false—yes, justice a dream, and righteousness a delusion. Then might is right, the battle is to the strongest and the race to the swiftest, and the more ruthless and unscrupulous we are the better. By the same token, if our religion is right, if God is a reality, and the order of the world is moral, our enemies are wrong! The very stars in their courses are against them. . . .

Samuel McCrea Cavert, assistant secretary of the General War-Time Commission of the Churches, saw in America's participation in the war a profound "missionary enterprise as the moral equivalent of war."

> In the last analysis the ultimate issues of the war are moral and religious. It is simply to say that we are in the war because we believe that thereby we are somehow serving God—taking a step in the direction of a society that is more in accord with his will and the spirit and principles of Jesus Christ. For, whatever may have been the origins of the war, it is rapidly becoming clearer every day that it is now developed into a conflict

between forces that make for the coming of the Kingdom of God and forces that oppose it. Hence when as Christians we give our support to the cause now presented by the war, we are simply doing, in a restricted way, a small part of what as "good soldiers of Jesus Christ" we are all the while aiming to do.

James A. Francis (Baptist) of California put it succinctly, "I look upon the enlistment of an American soldier as I do on the departure of a missionary for Burma." . . .

In this Crusade against the powers of darkness, it was necessary to convince the mothers and fathers who were making a sacrifice that they were not offering up their sons to Baal. So, it was reasoned, the soldiers, in fighting, found salvation itself. "They who offer up their lives for a high ideal of justice and humanity walk side by side with the world's Savior and King," assured Ernest M. Stires of St. Thomas's Church, New York. Moreover, he argued, their training as troops is but

> the preparation for the higher level to which they will climb on the consecrated fields of France, where the baptism of fire will cleanse and inspire. This is no dream of a visionary. . . . The calm judgment of reasonable leaders declares that invaluable results have already been gained, and that vastly greater results are not far away.
>
> They will find God. They will discover their souls.

For Dr. Stires the war made soldiers Christian in a way that all the preaching of nearly two thousand years had failed to accomplish. The historian, he believed, would record when the war ended, "the very faces of the victorious soldiers were ennobled by the beauty of the ideals for which they fought." . . .

Confronted with the necessity of every Sunday facing a congregation composed of Christians spiritually troubled and anxious about not only the physical well-being but the spiritual aspects of the lives of their sons, ministers were under compulsion to reenforce the hopes and faith of the fathers and mothers, the brothers and sisters, wives and sweethearts. What else could they have preached other than that the boys in the trenches had found God? To have remained silent or to have pointed out the spiritually devastating effect of warfare would have cost them their leadership and their jobs. The churches demanded ministers who gave comfort and dogmatic assurance, and they received it, for clergy and laity alike could not continue to believe in the orthodox God and face reality—the possibility of their sons going to war for a holy cause and losing their faith in God on the way. The psychological factors at work were, of course, extremely powerful. The churches and the Y. M. C. A., the Catholic and Jewish organizations sensed this great spiritual need and tried to meet it. . . .

To ask men to enlist in a "holy war" meant that the interpreters of the mind of Christ had to convince their followers that Jesus was not a pacifist, that he approved of the war and that he would fight himself, if he were here upon earth. . . .

. . . [M]ost of the theologians had no difficulty whatsoever in placing Jesus in the forefront of the thickest fighting leading his troops on to victory.

Was Jesus a pacifist? In answer to that critical question J. Wesley Johnston, of the John Street Methodist Episcopal Church, New York, affirmed: "Christ was the greatest fighter the world has ever seen." He was "the Lion of the Tribe of Judah," and "surely every believer in Christ . . . will unsheathe his sword and gladly give his life . . . to help win the fight against the forces of cruelty, abomination and hell."

Edward Leigh Pell, of Richmond, Virginia, wrote: "We will fight pacifism not only because it is contrary to the teachings of Christ, but because its whole tendency is to make a yellow streak where you want a man." "Jesus was just as truly a fighter as Moses, Joshua, David, Washington, Lee or the fighting parsons of the gold-fever days in the far West." "The fact that Jesus never used it [physical force] proves nothing except that he never needed it . . . he had higher forces." . . .

There were, of course, plenty of texts and incidents to support the view that Christ could be a mighty warrior. There was the driving out of the money-changers. There was the injunction, "Render unto Cæsar, the things that are Cæsar's." Further-more, since Jesus of Nazareth had never come out with his opinion about war as had General Sherman, his very silence seemed to give consent.

But the texts that were being used by the pacifists to justify their position had either to be proved spurious or shown to have been misinterpreted. This task of ex-plaining away the favorite pacifist texts of the New Testament turned out to be simply a matter of exegesis. A text, for instance, that presented difficulties was the command to turn the other cheek. Dr. Pell insisted Jesus "could not have meant it literally, for the Master always practiced what he preached and you know he never turned the other cheek." . . .

. . . Take, for instance, the use of the one weapon of warfare which seemed more hideous and barbarous than all the others—the bayonet. To ignore its use Christians could not; defend it they ultimately must; glorify it they frequently did.

A Y. M. C. A. physical director, A. E. Marriott of Camp Sevier, supplied the soldiers with an "invaluable little manual" on *Hand-to-Hand Fighting*. The chief points of attack were minutely explained:

> Eyes. Never miss an opportunity to destroy the eyes of the enemy. In all head holds use the finger on the eyes. They are the most delicate points in the body and easy to reach. The eye can easily be removed with the finger.

George W. Downs, speaking in the Asbury Methodist Episcopal Church in Pittsburgh, in November, 1917, regretted that he was not at the front. He explained how he felt about the matter. His "blood boiled" when he heard men say "their relig-ion forbids the killing of men with guns and bayonets." He is also reported to have declared: "I would have gone over the top with other Americans, I would have driven my bayonet into the throat or the eye or the stomach of the Huns without the slight-est hesitation and my conscience would not have bothered me in the least."

According to the Boston *Herald*, Herbert S. Johnson, pastor of the Warren Avenue Baptist Church of that city, likewise contributed to the education of the church people on the technique of bayoneting the enemy. Pointing to the location of his vital organs, he explained: "Three inches are not enough, seven inches are too many and twelve inches are more than too many, for while you are pulling out the bayonet you are losing the opportunity to drive it into another man five inches."

Albert C. Dieffenbach, editor of *The Christian Register* (Unitarian), was proud of the part that Jesus would play in the war. In an editorial he wrote:

> As Christians, of course, we say Christ approves [of the war]. But would he fight and kill? . . . There is not an opportunity to deal death to the enemy that he would shirk from or delay in seizing! He would take bayonet and grenade and bomb and rifle and do the work of deadliness against that which is the most deadly enemy of his Father's kingdom in a thousand years. . . . That is the inexorable truth about Jesus Christ and this war; and we rejoice to say it.

Reinhold Niebuhr in World War II

RICHARD W. FOX

Niebuhr's oversimplification certainly had its political uses. It was vintage pamphleteering, as was the collection *Christianity and Power Politics*, which Scribners brought out in the fall of 1940. It contained several of his recent *Nation* pieces, including "An End to Illusions," and a number of other occasional papers published as early as 1934. Together they formed a polemical barrage against the "vapid" character of liberal Christian culture—a culture whose "will-to-live has been so seriously enervated by a confused pacifism, in which Christian perfectionism and bourgeois love of ease have been curiously compounded, that our democratic world does not really deserve to survive." In unacknowledged debt to Nietzsche, Niebuhr blasted the Christian tendency to reduce "love" to the mere avoidance of conflict, to equate self-assertion with evil, and self-sacrifice with good. "Civilized life" was sickly, impotent before the steely hordes of "barbarism." Christians had to be tough, to adapt to "the rough stuff of politics," to redefine love not as the "negative perfection of peace in a warring world," but as "responsibility for the weal and woe of others." . . .

. . . [T]he Protestant press was up in arms. The controversy solidified [Niebuhr's] place as the primary Christian advocate of intervention: rallying point for some, symbol of Antichrist for others. Christian pacifists bordered on verbal violence in their denunciations of him—a fact he did not hesitate to use in accusing them of abandoning their principles. With C. C. Morrison, one of his earliest boosters, his relations became irreconcilably bitter. . . . He reconciled himself to a state of war with his former friends, a state not of hate but of the love of enemies: "something more transcendent than friendship, . . . namely the spirit of forgiveness in the 'body of Christ' which exists at least for fleeting moments when self-righteous combatants cease to be self-righteous and stand under a common divine judgment and know themselves in need of a common divine mercy." Loving one's enemies did not mean one had to like them, only that one recognized their ultimate sanctity as children of God.

Morrison had been much on Niebuhr's mind in late 1939 and 1940 as he mulled over the idea of a new journal of Christian opinion with Pit Van Dusen and Francis Miller. All three were devoted friends of Britain (Van Dusen's wife was a Scot), and Van Dusen and Miller were longtime leaders in the world student and ecumenical movements. They agreed on a journal that would unite Christian interventionists of all political stripes, and quickly assembled an impressive board of thirty sponsors: Niebuhr intimates John Bennett, Sherwood Eddy, and William Scarlett, along with such ecclesiastical stars as Henry Sloane Coffin, William Adams Brown, John R. Mott, Francis J. McConnell, Robert E. Speer, his old Detroit model Lynn Harold Hough, and his summertime neighbor Howard Chandler Robbins. When the first number of *Christianity and Crisis* came out in February, 1941—with

Richard W. Fox, "Wiser in Their Generation," chap. 9 in *Reinhold Niebuhr, A Biography* (San Francisco: Harper and Row, 1985). Reprinted by permission of Richard Wrightman Fox.

the lead editorial by Miller and lead article by Niebuhr—it was plain to all that Morrison's *Christian Century* was both target and model. From the alliterative double *C* of the title to the familiar layout—opening editorials, substantive articles, closing news of the Christian world—*Christianity and Crisis* was the *Century*'s conscious clone, except that it appeared biweekly, not weekly, and could not afford as many pages. The likeness of a blood relative, but the animus of a rebellious child: Niebuhr set out to discredit Morrison's Christian isolationism. *Christianity and Crisis*, which attracted seven thousand subscribers in the first six weeks, quickly deprived the *Century* of its longtime monopoly at the apex of the liberal, interdenominational press. But it delivered no mortal blow; Morrison's ideas were too deeply rooted in the northern and especially midwestern church. . . .

. . . [Niebuhr's] literary efforts were concentrated in *Christianity and Crisis* and the *Nation*, just as his day-to-day organizational work shifted from the Fellowship of Socialist Christians to the new group he helped found in 1941, the Union for Democratic Action.

The UDA sprang up out of the disgust many New York leftists felt at the isolationism of the Socialist Party. After the Socialist convention in April, 1940, Niebuhr joined Murray Gross and Lewis Corey of the International Ladies' Garment Workers' Union, George Counts of the American Federation of Teachers, John Childs of Columbia's Teachers College, and Freda Kirchwey and Robert Bendiner of the *Nation* in a major recruiting effort. The goal was to gather those interventionists who were actively pro-labor—unlike the Henry Luces and James Conants of William Allen White's Committee to Defend the Allies and the Henry Coffins and Pit Van Dusens of *Christianity and Crisis*. Conservatives were excluded by definition; Communists were kept out by practical calculation. The UDA was zealous in barring party members, and as a result drew the scorn of the *Daily Worker* and many non-Communist progressives. . . .

If the UDA's influence in the wider political world cannot be precisely measured, Niebuhr's own influence within the UDA can: he held it together by charismatic force. Also by the example of tireless devotion. He rarely missed presiding over weekly evening policy meetings at the office, and rarely refused to address fund-raisers in other cities. He worked closely with Loeb in drafting the UDA rating of Congressional voting records—ratings published in the *New Republic*—and took charge of defending the UDA against Congressman Martin Dies's charge that it was Communist inspired. Dies was troubled by the organization's tolerance for former Communists (Lewis Corey, for example, had under his real name Louis Fraina been a founder of the American Communist Party) and also by its campaign against conservative Congressmen like himself. It was politically advantageous to label the UDA "red." Niebuhr had to expend valuable energy in a defensive counterattack.

He also labored to goad the Roosevelt administration in 1943 to allow more European Jews to emigrate to the United States. While his friend Rabbi Stephen Wise struggled to make Americans comprehend the reality of mass murder, Niebuhr gathered the signatures of "fifty prominent persons" on an "Open Letter" from the UDA to the President and secretary of state. The letter did not mention the death camps themselves or call for American military action to save the Jews in Germany or Poland. It stuck to the more modest—and politically obtainable—goal of increasing European immigration totals. "In view of Hitler's campaign of extermination against the Jews," it read,

> we believe that the United States ought to follow a more liberal immigration policy within the limits of the present law. There are many Jews and other anti-Nazis in Spain, North Africa, Portugal, whose country of origin is some Axis or occupied nation and who are eligible under the respective quotas. Some Axis partners, such as Roumania and Hungary, contain many racial and other anti-Nazis who could come to us via Turkey. Since practically empty ships are coming back from North Africa, Spain and the Near East, transportation offers no difficulties for a more generous immigration policy.

The Roosevelt administration did make a gesture in the direction of a more generous policy a few months later when it created the War Refugee Board. But the President did little to empower it. Niebuhr continued to toil on this issue—he and columnist Dorothy Thompson were two major exceptions to the rule of studied apathy among American intellectuals about the plight of the Jews. And he slogged on for the UDA on one issue after another. Bruce Bliven, editor of the *New Republic* and active in the UDA during the war, remembered his work a quarter-century later. "I recall at meeting after meeting seeing Reinhold looking as tired as I felt, but struggling on, like a man walking in thick sand."

As if his labors for the UDA and *Christianity and Crisis* were not enough to overwhelm him, he also took charge of the American Friends of German Freedom. It had begun informally in the late 1930s when Niebuhr undertook fund-raising for exiled German Socialist Karl Frank (alias Paul Hagen), founder of the Neue Beginnen left-wing Socialists after Hitler's destruction of the Social Democrats. Hagen was in and out of Germany until the outbreak of the war, smuggling literature, helping comrades across the border, keeping up contacts with the underground labor movement and with other exiled Socialists in Lisbon and Stockholm. . . .

Niebuhr's stature as a spokesman for the American Friends of German Freedom, the UDA, and *Christianity and Crisis*—and as a much sought after sponsor for countless other groups—was enormously increased by the release in March, 1941, of the first volume of . . . *The Nature and Destiny of Man: Human Nature*. If the secular press ignored *Christianity and Power Politics*, they hailed *The Nature and Destiny of Man* as an epochal work. "Sin Rediscovered," announced *Time*'s upbeat review of what it took to be a downbeat thesis. "The religious book-of-the-year was published last week," *Time* reported breezily, "and it puts sin right back in the spotlight." Niebuhr, "the high priest of Protestantism's young intellectuals," was leading "his legions back to an almost medieval emphasis on the basic sinfulness of man." *Time*'s reviewer Whittaker Chambers, until recently a Communist and still a fierce opponent of liberalism, lauded Niebuhr as a "belligerent" antagonist of the liberal doctrine of the goodness of man. . . .

The first volume of *The Nature and Destiny of Man* accepted the monumental challenge of surveying the history of classical and modern thought about man and expounding a "Biblical" perspective that did more justice to the observed facts of human existence. The fundamental structure of the work was already laid out in Niebuhr's BD thesis written at Yale almost three decades before. A succession of "naturalisms" and "idealisms" in western thought had tried to make sense of human nature, and they had always failed.

The naturalist sees human freedom as little more than the freedom of *homo faber* and fails to appreciate to what degree the human spirit breaks and remakes the harmonies and unities of nature. The idealist, identifying freedom with reason and failing to appreciate that freedom rises above reason, imagines that the freedom of man is secure, in the mind's impetus toward coherence and synthesis. Neither naturalism nor idealism can understand that man is free enough to violate both the necessities of nature and the logical systems of reason.

Neither naturalism nor idealism comprehended man "in a dimension sufficiently high or deep to do full justice to either his stature or his capacity for both good and evil." As a Christian apologist Niebuhr was arguing that the Biblical view was contingently necessary since it was better than any alternative. It could encompass man in all his manifestations. "Man does not know himself truly except as he knows himself confronted by God. Only in that confrontation does he become aware of his full stature and freedom and of the evil in him." . . .

The final paradox of human nature was that man remained ultimately free as a moral agent despite the inevitability of his own sin. Indeed, "man is most free in the discovery that he is not free." Only those aware of the depth of their own sinfulness could be truly free, only they could act responsibly, in full appreciation of their limits. Only they could eschew the fanaticisms of the thirties and take one careful step at a time in the social and political arena. The dilemma of human life was the perpetual war of the self against itself, deluding itself, losing itself alternately to pride or despair, yet always capable of—indeed, "called" to—responsible action in the world. Human achievements, even human progress, were possible, but they always contained the seeds of their own destruction. The higher the good attained, the greater the potential for evil.

Robert Calhoun, historical theologian at Yale . . . made the most trenchant critiques of *The Nature and Destiny of Man.* He rightly observed that it was a prophetic, not a scholarly, work. "No cautious weigher of evidence here," he wrote, "but a preacher expounding the Word in line with his private revelation. . . . Other authors, Christian and nonChristian . . . are swiftly divided into sheep and goats. The former are treated with enthusiasm and insight, the latter dismissed as not worth much bother. Swiftness is the word always." . . .

Niebuhr did not appreciate Calhoun's published judgment that "on its historical side this book cannot be taken seriously." He supposed that Calhoun was skewering him because of their disagreements on other issues (Calhoun was a pacifist). Calhoun replied that his critique was a purely professional judgment: "Your account of Christian and secular thought shows clearly that at various points you have lacked either time, equipment, or inclination to study the relevant data." . . . Yet even Calhoun went out of his way to praise the book for its insight into the human condition. "The real ground of the author's doctrine is not what he has read but what has happened to him as a struggling self"; his reflections on the mysteries of selfhood "must become a permanent part of any reader's thinking." Niebuhr had managed the uncommon feat of dissecting the intricacies of the self while communicating his own sense of wonder at its secrets. Analysis framed by amazement. He marveled at the capacity of the self to step back and examine itself; he shook his head at the thought of "a spirit who can set time, nature, the world and being *per se* into juxtaposition to himself and inquire after the meaning of these things." The book displayed the wisdom of one who knew what it meant to pass beyond knowledge and see again with the eyes of a child. He found the prophetic voice he had been seeking: authoritative and humble. Understanding human nature meant probing its paradoxes—the creaturely creator, determined yet free, sinful but responsible—and reveling in its mysteries. . . .

Pearl Harbor put an abrupt and shocking end to the interventionist–isolationist debate. Nearly three thousand sailors were dead and the nation was nearly unanimous in joining the Allies. It was not until six months later that the Nazis began to suffer the reverses that gave the Allies assurance of ultimate victory in Europe. But from the very start of American involvement Niebuhr was preoccupied with imagining the peace that would follow victory. His first foray into postwar planning addressed the fate of the Jews, whose plight had been for him one of the key arguments for intervention. "Jews After the War" offered *Nation* readers—many of them anti-Zionist Jews like contributing editor I. F. Stone—an eloquent statement of the Zionist case: the Jews had rights not just as individuals, but as a people, and they deserved not just a homeland, but a homeland in Palestine. Niebuhr had come a long way in two decades. As a thirty-year-old Detroit pastor in 1923 he was still in favor of converting Jews to Christianity, and blamed the tiny number of converts on both "the unchristlike attitude of Christians" and "Jewish bigotry." By 1926 he was ready to jettison missionizing altogether: liberal Jews like Rabbi Stephen Wise were speaking appreciatively of Jesus, and Christians themselves needed the leaven of pure Hebraism to counteract the Hellenism to which they were prone. After his move to New York in 1928 he was drawn to Zionist currents of thought, though Jewish leader Judah Magnes's commitment to a binational Palestine gave him pause. Niebuhr's "personal pacifistic bias in favor of an end which can be carried out without the use of coercion" inclined him toward Magnes. "Yet the ideal of a political homeland for the Jews is so intriguing that I am almost willing to sacrifice my convictions for the sake of it." By the early thirties he had made the ethical leap to coercion, and grasped that Hitler was bent on the cultural annihilation of the Jews. From that time on he was a firm, though sometimes qualified, backer of the Zionist cause.

The American Palestine Committee, a Zionist support group, reprinted tens of thousands of copies of "Jews After the War," and by April Niebuhr had over two hundred invitations to speak to Jewish groups around the country. . . .

Creating a Jewish homeland would require the forthright exercise of American and British power: "The Anglo-Saxon hegemony that is bound to exist in the event of an Axis defeat will be in a position to see to it that Palestine is set aside for the Jews." Justice for the Jews depended on what Niebuhr soon began calling "imperialistic realism," the determination of the major Allied powers to assume responsibility for the reorganization of the world. Superior power bestowed greater responsibility; the victors alone could enact the peace. American and British "idealists" erred in supposing that the moral course was to surrender excess power, to seek equal participation by all nations in a world government. Yet "balance-of-power realists" were also wrong in mocking the whole notion of international organization and preaching a perpetual standoff between power blocks. As he did in theology, Niebuhr fought a two-front war against those he termed sentimentalists and cynics: his projected middle ground drew from both the cynics' grasp of power relations and the sentimentalists' dream of equality and fellowship.

The Idea of a Judeo-Christian Tradition

MARK SILK

In 1952 . . . a few days before Christmas, President-elect Eisenhower gave a speech before the Freedoms Foundation in New York in which he called attention to the foundations of democracy. "Our form of government," he explained, "has no sense unless it is founded in a deeply felt religious faith, and I don't care what it is. With us of course it is the Judeo-Christian concept but it must be a religion that all men are created equal."

As of 1952 good Americans were supposed to be, in some sense, committed Judeo-Christians. It was a recent addition to the national creed.

In the beginning, "Judeo-Christian" had served only to designate connections between Judaism and Christianity in antiquity. Its first appearance, according to the Supplement to the *Oxford English Dictionary*, occurred in the *Literary Guide* in 1899: a "Judeo-Christian 'continuity' theory" postulated the development of Church ritual out of the practices of the Second Temple. Not until some decades later did the term begin to be used to refer to values or beliefs shared by Jews and Christians, to a common western religious outlook. Writing in 1934, the American communist Joseph Freeman spoke of "Judeo-Christian asceticism" and of seeing "Greek paganism . . . through Judeo-Christian spectacles." George Orwell, in a 1939 book review, remarked that not acting meanly was "a thing that carries no weight in the Judaeo-Christian scheme of morals." The dates and the politics of the authors are significant, for what brought this usage into regular discourse was opposition to fascism. Fascist fellow-travelers and anti-Semites had appropriated "Christian" as an identifying mark; besides Father Coughlin's Christian Front, there were such organizations as the Christian American Crusade, Christian Aryan Syndicate, Christian Mobilizers, and Christian Party, and publications like the *Christian Defender* and *Christian Free Press*. "Judeo-Christian" thus became a catchword for the other side. In its 1941 handbook, *Protestants Answer Anti-Semitism,* the left-liberal *Protestant Digest* described itself (for the first time) as "a periodical serving the democratic ideal which is implicit in the Judeo-Christian tradition."

Carl Friedrich, introducing a 1942 volume of essays on anti-Semitism, asserted that the Jews might "well perish unless the Gentile world comes to see in truer perspective the vital part the Jews constitute in the total pattern of Judeo-Christian world culture." He went on to ask, "What justifies the expression Judaeo-Christian culture? Are not Judaism and Christianity fundamentally opposed to each other?" To the contrary. Friedrich paid tribute to the French Catholic philosopher Jacques Maritain, who in *A Christian Looks at the Jewish Question* (1939) had advanced the "highly persuasive" proposition that in striking at the Jews anti-Semites were striking at Christ and Christianity. Maritain, whose wife Raïssa came from a Russian-Jewish family, himself wrote an essay while in the United States in 1942 in which he praised "la tradition judéo-chrétienne" as a source of the West's enduring values.

Mark Silk, "Notes on the Judeo-Christian Tradition," *American Quarterly* 36 (Spring 1984): 65–80.

Antifascist affirmation of a shared religious basis for western values was nowhere more evident than at the large convocations of liberal academics and intellectuals held annually from 1940 by the Conference on Science, Philosophy and Religion in Their Relation to the Democratic Way of Life, Inc. Organized by Lyman Bryson of the Columbia Teachers College and Louis Finkelstein of the Jewish Theological Seminary, the Conference originated, in Friedrich's words, "essentially as a rallying point for Judeo-Christian forces in America against the threat presented to them by the Axis ideology and actions." During the war and in the years immediately after it, participants denoted the spiritual underpinnings of democracy with "Judeo-Christian" and a family of related terms: "Hebraic-Christian," "Hebrew-Christian," "Jewish-Christian," "Judeo-Christianity," even "Judaistic-Christian." ("Totalitarianism is the historical result of the weakening of the Greek and Hebraic-Christian traditions we have described." "Tyranny can never tolerate the cultivation of the Hebrew-Christian tradition." "Beneath all other contributing factors . . . modern democracy is rooted in the Hebrew-Christian heritage of faith in God." "To deal effectively with the present crisis of civilization we must recognize that most of the cherished ideals are rooted unseverably in the Jewish-Christian faith.")

The Judeo-Christian forces were not always precise about the meaning of their rallying cry. As Harvard's Douglas Bush commented after a particularly effusive talk by the theologian Amos Wilder, "One could wish for fuller hints of what the Hebraic-Christian tradition, to which all pay at least vague lip service, actually does or can mean in modern terms for modern men of good will. . . ." Yet greater precision might have provoked unwanted disagreement when the idea was to invoke a common faith for a united democratic front. Bush to the contrary, not everyone concerned with the fate of the West was prepared to leap onto the Judeo-Christian bandwagon. . . .

Judeo-Christian enthusiasm came under fire . . . in 1943, when the Jewish publicist Trude Weiss-Rosmarin issued a tract criticizing statements by the president of Reform Judaism's Hebrew Union College, Julian Morgenstern. Speaking in the dark days of the war, Morgenstern had called for a partnership between Judaism and Christianity: it would be based, he claimed, on close genetic ties.

> Today we realize, as never since Christianity's birth, how intimate are the relations of the two religions, so intimate and insoluble that they are truly, basically one, that they have a common descent, a common vision, hope, mission, face a common foe and a common fate, must achieve a common victory or share a common death. We speak now, with still inadequate but steadily expanding understanding, of the Judeo-Christian heritage. We comprehend, as we have not comprehended in all of nineteen hundred years, that Judaism and Christianity are partners in the great work of world-redemption and the progressive unfolding of the world-spirit.

Separately, each faith was unequal to the task: each had its own unique and necessary contribution to make "to what we may truthfully call Judaeo-Christianity, the religion of tomorrow's better world." This, to Weiss-Rosmarin, was dangerous nonsense. Making Jewish-Christian amity depend on a shared religious identity was "a totalitarian aberration" fundamentally at odds with the pluralistic principles of democracy. Judaism and Christianity were *not* basically one; her book sought to spell out the profound differences between them. She was not the last Jewish writer to perceive in "Judeo-Christian" a syncretizing threat to the survival of Judaism.

On the rhetorical front, however, "Judeo-Christian" and its companion terms were unstoppable. After the revelations of the Nazi death camps, a phrase like "our Christian civilization" seemed ominously exclusive: greater comprehensiveness was needed for proclaiming the spirituality of the American Way. "When our own spiritual leaders look for the moral foundations for our democratic ideals," observed Cornell's Arthur E. Murphy at the 1949 Conference on Science, Philosophy and Religion, "it is in 'our Judeo-Christian heritage,' the culture of 'the West,' or 'the American tradition,' that they tend to find them."

For his part, Murphy was contrasting America's spiritual leaders with the leaders of the Soviet Union, who proclaimed high-flying moral ideals of their own. President-elect Eisenhower made his remarks on the "Judeo-Christian concept" in a similar context: while describing the difficulty he once experienced explaining democracy to the Soviet commander, Marshall Zhukov.

> And since at the age of 14 he had been taken over by the Bolshevik religion and had believed in it since that time, I was quite certain it was hopeless on my part to talk to him about the fact that our form of government is founded in religion.

At the National Federation of Temple Brotherhoods convention in October of 1951, Roger Straus, the federation's honorary president, declared that the "greatest peril" confronting the western world was "the world-wide clash of two divergent beliefs: the Judeo-Christian philosophy and the crass materialism of communism." In July of the following year, at the convention of the Military Chaplains Association of the United States, Daniel Poling, the president of the association, warned, "We meet at a time when the Judeo-Christian faith is challenged as never before in all the years since Abraham left Ur of the Chaldees." In an *American Mercury* article of July 1953, J. B. Matthews, executive director of Senator Joseph McCarthy's Permanent Sub-Committee on Investigations, described the communist conspiracy as aiming "at the total obliteration of Judeo-Christian civilization." Having proved itself against the Nazis, the Judeo-Christian tradition now did duty among the watch-fires of the Cold War.

On February 7, 1954, with President Eisenhower in attendance, Reverend George M. Docherty of the New York Avenue Presbyterian Church devoted his sermon to urging inclusion of the phrase "under God" in the country's Pledge of Allegiance. In ruminating over the pledge, said Docherty, he had found something missing,

> and that which was missing was the characteristic and definitive factor in the American way of life. Indeed, apart from the mention of the phrase, "the United States of America," it could be the pledge of any republic. In fact, I could hear little Moscovites repeat a similar pledge to their hammer-and-sickle flag in Moscow with equal solemnity. Russia is also a republic, that claims to have overthrown the tyranny of kingship. Russia also claims to be indivisible.

The sermon stirred Congress into action, and Congressional speeches on behalf of the change recurred again and again to the importance of "under God" in differentiating America from its ideological adversary. "Judeo-Christian" served the same purpose, highlighting, in a way that included Americans of all faiths, the godliness of the United States against the godlessness of the USSR.

Yet the hot and cold wars of mid-century do not alone account for the rise of Judeo-Christian attitudes. There was a theological dimension as well. Since the late thirties, some American Protestant thinkers had begun to emphasize the ground that Christianity shared with Judaism. These were not, as might have been expected, liberal divines disposed to winnow Christian doctrine down to love of God and neighbor. Theirs, rather, was the darker vision of the Continental theology of crisis. They followed Karl Barth and Emil Brunner in scorning the optimistic image of man and his works that had prevailed in nineteenth-century Protestantism. The fundamental facts were man's sinfulness and his obligation to transform himself through faith in the absolute. Theology based on categories derived from ancient Greek and modern secular philosophy was denigrated in favor of a "biblical" theology that could better convey the personal relation between God and man pictured in Scripture. . . .

America's leading Protestant theologian, Reinhold Niebuhr, was also the foremost Christian "Hebraist." The Hebrew prophets provided the essential inspiration for Niebuhr's great theme of the moral complexity of historical existence. "I have," he wrote in 1944, "as a Christian theologian, sought to strengthen the Hebraic-prophetic content of the Christian tradition." In fact, in the postwar period, Niebuhr's conception of the nature of Christianity evolved increasingly towards the Hebraic. . . .

. . . Paul Tillich, whose systematic theology relied on secular philosophical categories, took his friend and colleague to task for what he considered an over-emphasis on Christianity's Hebraism. Tillich nonetheless endorsed the Judeo-Christian outlook in Hebraist terms. "The Church," he wrote, was "always in danger of losing her prophetic spirit," and it therefore needed "the prophetic spirit included in the traditions of the synagogue . . . as long as the gods of space are in power, and this means up to the end of history. . . ." In "Is There A Judeo-Christian Tradition?," written in 1952 for the journal *Judaism*, Tillich argued the affirmative by asserting that the two religions shared faith in an exclusive and righteous God, an understanding of man's historical existence, and the need to wrestle with "a legalistic and utopian interpretation of righteousness."

Neo-orthodoxy insisted on the limited and historically conditioned character of all earthly institutions. The great sin, endemic to humanity, lay in absolutizing the contingent; this was idolatry. The great virtue, embodied in the prophetic tradition, was constantly to question society's false absolutes in the name of the only true absolute, the God who transcended history. Among the false absolutes were the Church and its theology. Christianity as an institution embedded in history needed to be modest about its exclusive claims to truth—especially vis-à-vis Judaism. Tillich held that Christianity could be seen as a Jewish heresy and Judaism as a Christian one, a position adopted by Niebuhr as well: "At best, the two can regard themselves as two versions of one faith, each thinking of the other as an heretical version of the common faith." . . .

Jewish writers did not fail to grasp the outstretched hand. . . .

. . . The foremost Jewish proponent of Jewish-Christian Hebraism . . . was Will Herberg. Herberg had been a leading communist activist and theoretician, but in the late thirties his Marxist faith collapsed and he turned to religion—as a result of reading Niebuhr. He struggled with the possibility of becoming a Christian but was dissuaded by Niebuhr himself, who told him he could not become a good Christian until he was first a good Jew. (In a paper read in 1958 before a joint meeting of the Jewish and Union Theological Seminaries, Niebuhr described Judaism and Christianity as "sufficiently alike for the Jew to find God more easily in terms of his own religious heritage than by subjecting himself to the hazards of guilt feeling involved in a conversion to a faith, which whatever its excellencies, must appear to him as a symbol of an oppressive majority culture.") Returning to Judaism, Herberg began to write theology, and in 1955 was named Professor of Judaic Studies and Social Philosophy at (Methodist) Drew University. . . .

One religious reality did not mean one religion. The differences between a Christ-centered Christianity and a Judaism centered on God's covenant with Israel were real and irreducible, and must persist "until the final clarification." American society would evidently persist as the "triple melting pot" portrayed by Herberg in his widely-read *Protestant, Catholic, Jew* (1955). Yet while setting a stamp of approval on the country's plural religious order, that book too ends with an impassioned avowal of "Jewish-Christian faith." In the final analysis this was the real thing, the authentic faith needed "to transform the inner character of American religion." . . .

Yet for all its usefulness to ideological combat and consensus during the fifties, the Judeo-Christian enterprise of neo-orthodoxy had its recusants. The Catholics, especially, withheld the hem of their garment. The *philosophia perennis* required no Hebraic infusion to save it from liberalism, and as for undergirding anticommunism with religion, American Catholicism was sufficient unto the day. "Hebraic faith," moreover, contained much that was repugnant to Rome. . . .

Under the circumstances even John Courtney Murray, American Catholicism's lonely champion of religious pluralism, could have no use for the Jewish-Christian faith of Niebuhr and company. In *We Hold These Truths,* a collection of essays that adds up to a defense of natural law against its neo-orthodox critics, Murray held that Protestantism, Catholicism, and Judaism were "radically different" styles of religious belief, none of which "is reducible, or perhaps even comparable, to any of the others." The best that might be hoped for was "creeds at war intelligibly" under "the articles of peace which are the religion-clauses of the First Amendment." . . .

. . . [B]y the mid-sixties a certain Hegelian twilight was beginning to settle over the Judeo-Christian tradition: writers pro and con became conscious of it as a historically conditioned concept. . . .

In 1970 Arthur A. Cohen published a collection of his articles under the title *The Myth of the Judeo-Christian Tradition.* In freshly written introductory and concluding essays, Cohen asserted that the Judeo-Christian tradition was no *tradition* at all: the history of Jewish-Christian relations was fundamentally a history of social and theological antagonism, not of common cause. As for the idea of the tradition, its roots lay in the Enlightenment, which, hostile to all revealed religion, had linked Judaism and Christianity as sharing a common untruth.

✎ *F U R T H E R   R E A D I N G*

Adeney, Bernard T. *Just War, Political Realism, and Faith* (1988).

Au, William. *The Cross, the Flag, and the Bomb: American Catholics Debate War and Peace* (1985).

Barish, Louis. *Rabbis in Uniform: The Story of the American Jewish Military Chaplain* (1962).

Bush, Perry. *Two Kingdoms, Two Loyalties: Mennonite Pacifism in Modern America* (1998).

Ernst, Eldon G. *Moment of Truth for Protestant America: Interchurch Campaigns Following World War I* (1974).

Fisher, James T. *Doctor America: The Lives of Thomas Dooley* (1997).

McNeal, Patricia. *The American Catholic Peace Movement, 1928–1972* (1978).

Miller, William D. *Dorothy Day: A Biography* (1983).

Murray, John Courtney. *We Hold These Truths: Catholic Reflections on the American Proposition* (1960).

Niebuhr, Reinhold. *The Irony of American History* (1952).

Piehl, Mel. *Breaking Bread: The Catholic Worker and the Origin of Radical Catholicism in America* (1979).

Piper, John F. *American Churches in World War I* (1985).

Sittser, Gerald. *Expanding Democracy on the Home Front: Religion in World War II* (1995).

Vaux, Kenneth. *Ethics and the Gulf War: Religion, Rhetoric, and Righteousness* (1992).

Weigel, George. *Tranquillitas Ordinis: The Present Failure and Future Promise of American Catholic Thought on War and Peace* (1987).

Zahn, Gordon. *War, Conscience, and Dissent* (1967).

C H A P T E R
12

Religion and Protest
Movements, 1955–1990

Martin Luther King, Jr., a Baptist minister, led the Montgomery bus boycott in 1955–1956 and succeeded in forcing the bus company to desegregate. Meetings of the Montgomery Improvement Association were held in black churches and King, a genius with the media, early learned how to arouse the consciences of white as well as black Americans through his command of biblical language. Ministers were prominent figures in segregated black communities in the early and mid-twentieth century—often the most highly educated and highly paid people in the community not dependent on whites' good will. It is no surprise, therefore, that many civil rights movement leaders, like King, were also ministers, including Ralph Abernathy, Andrew Young, and Jesse Jackson.

King, borrowing from Mohandas "Mahatma" Gandhi, the Indian independence leader, insisted on nonviolence and on the value of using the oppressor's own bad conscience as a weapon against him. In the 1960s, however, younger civil rights advocates became dissatisfied with the self-denial implied in nonviolence. As segregationists' attacks on civil rights workers increased—one 1963 bombing of a Birmingham, Alabama, church killed four Sunday school children—advocates of a more forceful response challenged King's methods. Radical black activists, some of them also ministers, began to demand "black power" and even payment of "reparations" from white churches as compensation for centuries of oppression. This new militancy scared off some white supporters of the civil rights movement and contributed to bitter conflicts in the late 1960s.

Also during the mid-1960s, the American military presence in Vietnam escalated. As discussed in Chapter 11, war had been a divisive issue in the churches earlier in the century; it became even more divisive now. With no vital American interest under attack in remote Vietnam, many Americans believed the United States was morally and politically unjustified in fighting there. Some clergy continued to support the war policy as a painful but necessary obligation in America's anticommunist struggle. Others, convinced that it was wrong, created the ecumenical alliance "Clergy Concerned Against Vietnam," bringing together Protestant ministers, Catholic priests, and Jewish rabbis to protest against the war. Two brothers, Philip and Daniel Berrigan, both Catholic priests, went further. They

denounced the Americans as warmongers, enacted a series of theatrical demonstrations against offices of the Selective Service (which organized the military draft for
the war), and suffered arrest and imprisonment.

   *Other religious protest groups in the 1970s and 1980s also used a repertoire
of techniques first developed in the black freedom struggles of the 1950s and early
1960s, including nonviolent demonstration—deliberately undergoing arrest as a
form of "witnessing" against injustice and standing firm against the government.
The sanctuary movement of the 1980s, for example, helped illegal immigrants
who were fleeing from wars in Central America to get into the United States and
avoid deportation by the Immigration and Naturalization Service. It was dominated by Christian activists, many of whom had earlier worked in civil rights and
who, in turn, faced arrest and imprisonment for their actions. The anti-abortion
movement also considered itself in the lineage of the civil rights movement and
used many of the same techniques. In its view, the Supreme Court's decision in*
Roe v. Wade *(1973), legalizing first trimester abortions, confronted the unborn
with an even more severe form of discrimination than African-Americans had
suffered in the days of segregation—a threat to life itself. Many were willing to
sacrifice themselves to oppose and overturn the policy. This movement, like some
of its predecessors, eventually developed a violent fringe that disavowed the initial
philosophy of nonviolence. Through all these protest movements runs a strain
of Christian militancy, a biblical idiom, and a sense of gospel-inspired strength
and righteousness.*

 D O C U M E N T S

Document 1 (1963) is a sermon in which Martin Luther King, Jr., preaches one of the
main themes of his ministry: that hatred must be overcome by the power of love, and
that reconciliation occurs only when we recognize the good in everyone. It may not
seem practical, he admits, but living according to "practical" principles has proved
disastrous. Ironically, he concludes, the Christian way of love is *more* practical than
the alternatives. The African-American novelist James Baldwin was a boy-preacher in
New York's Harlem ghetto, a traumatic period of his life recalled in *The Fire Next Time*
(Document 2, 1963). Unlike King, he depicts religion as a "racket," and ultimately,
despite the exhilaration he gained from it, as something false. In Document 3 (1966),
the National Conference of Black Churchmen declares that white and black Christians
will be able to resolve their religious differences only when they are equally powerful.
The new assertiveness implied by this posture, especially when it coincided with the
slogan "Black Power" used by some black leaders, dismayed many white religious
leaders and led to a waning of their support for the civil rights movement in the late
1960s. This more critical mood is apparent in Document 4, an editorial from the moderate evangelical journal *Christianity Today* (1969).

   Richard Hein, author of Document 5 (1968), explains his role as a military chaplain
in Vietnam. Despite the decade's great upheavals, he continues to focus on a minister's
traditional tasks: protecting the soldiers from immorality and trying to convert them. He
makes no judgments on the war itself. In the same year, the Catholic journal *Commonweal*
(Document 6) commented on the demonstrations of the Berrigan brothers and justified
their unusual form of "witnessing" against a war they considered immoral and un-Christian.
Document 7 (1986) shows how techniques of Christian civil disobedience, developed in the

civil rights and antiwar movements, were later used in the church-led sanctuary movement of the 1980s, and Document 8 (1988) observes similar methods adopted by the anti-abortion group Operation Rescue.

1. Martin Luther King, Jr., Preaches on the Power of Love, 1963

Probably no admonition of Jesus has been more difficult to follow than the command to "love your enemies." Some men have sincerely felt that its actual practice is not possible. It is easy, they say, to love those who love you, but how can one love those who openly and insidiously seek to defeat you? Others, like the philosopher Nietzsche, contend that Jesus' exhortation to love one's enemies is testimony to the fact that the Christian ethic is designed for the weak and cowardly, and not for the strong and courageous. Jesus, they say, was an impractical idealist.

In spite of these insistent questions and persistent objections, this command of Jesus challenges us with new urgency. Upheaval after upheaval has reminded us that modern man is travelling along a road called hate, in a journey that will bring us to destruction and damnation. Far from being the pious injunction of a Utopian dreamer, the command to love one's enemy is an absolute necessity for our survival. Love even for enemies is the key to the solution of the problems of our world. Jesus is not an impractical idealist: he is the practical realist.

I am certain that Jesus understood the difficulty inherent in the act of loving one's enemy. He never joined the ranks of those who talk glibly about the easiness of the moral life. He realized that every genuine expression of love grows out of a consistent and total surrender to God. So when Jesus said "Love your enemy," he was not unmindful of its stringent qualities. Yet he meant every word of it. Our responsibility as Christians is to discover the meaning of this command and seek passionately to live it out in our daily lives.

Let us be practical and ask the question, *How do we love our enemies?*

First, we must develop and maintain the capacity to forgive. He who is devoid of the power to forgive is devoid of the power to love. It is impossible even to begin the act of loving one's enemies without the prior acceptance of the necessity, over and over again, of forgiving those who inflict evil and injury upon us. . . .

Second, we must recognize that the evil deed of the enemy-neighbour, the thing that hurts, never quite expresses all that he is. An element of goodness may be found even in our worst enemy. Each of us is something of a schizophrenic personality, tragically divided against ourselves. A persistent civil war rages within all of our lives. . . .

. . . [W]e love our enemies by realizing that they are not totally bad and that they are not beyond the reach of God's redemptive love.

Third, we must not seek to defeat or humiliate the enemy but to win his friendship and understanding. At times we are able to humiliate our worst enemy. Inevitably, his weak moments come and we are able to thrust in his side the spear of defeat. But this we must not do. Every word and deed must contribute to an understanding with the enemy and release those vast reservoirs of goodwill which have been blocked by impenetrable walls of hate.

The meaning of love is not to be confused with some sentimental outpouring. Love is something much deeper than emotional bosh. . . .

Now we can see what Jesus meant when he said, "Love your enemies." We should be happy that he did not say, "Like your enemies." It is almost impossible to like some people. "Like" is a sentimental and affectionate word. How can we be affectionate toward a person whose avowed aim is to crush our very being and place innumerable stumbling blocks in our path? How can we like a person who is threatening our children and bombing our homes? That is impossible. But Jesus recognized that *love* is greater than *like*. . . .

Let us move now from the practical *how* to the theoretical *why: Why should we love our enemies?* The first reason is fairly obvious. Returning hate for hate multiplies hate, adding deeper darkness to a night already devoid of stars. Darkness cannot drive out darkness; only light can do that. Hate cannot drive out hate; only love can do that. . . .

Another reason why we must love our enemies is that hate scars the soul and distorts the personality. Mindful that hate is an evil and dangerous force, we too often think of what it does to the person hated. This is understandable, for hate brings irreparable damage to its victims. We have seen its ugly consequences in the ignominious deaths brought to six million Jews by a hate-obsessed madman named Hitler, in the unspeakable violence inflicted upon Negroes by bloodthirsty mobs, in the dark horrors of war, and in the terrible indignities and injustices perpetrated against millions of God's children by unconscionable oppressors.

But there is another side which we must never overlook. Hate is just as injurious to the person who hates. . . .

A third reason why we should love our enemies is that love is the only force capable of transforming an enemy into a friend. We never get rid of an enemy by meeting hate with hate; we get rid of an enemy by getting rid of enmity. By its very nature, hate destroys and tears down; by its very nature, love creates and builds up. Love transforms with redemptive power.

Lincoln tried love and left for all history a magnificent drama of reconciliation. . . .

We must hasten to say that these are not the ultimate reasons why we should love our enemies. An even more basic reason why we are commanded to love is expressed explicitly in Jesus' words, "Love your enemies . . . *that ye may be children of your Father which is in heaven.*" We are called to this difficult task in order to realize a unique relationship with God. We are potential sons of God. Through love that potentiality becomes actuality. We must love our enemies, because only by loving them can we know God and experience the beauty of his holiness.

The relevance of what I have said to the crisis in race relations should be readily apparent. There will be no permanent solution to the race problem until oppressed men develop the capacity to love their enemies. The darkness of racial injustice will be dispelled only by the light of forgiving love. For more than three centuries American Negroes have been battered by the iron rod of oppression, frustrated by day and bewildered by night by unbearable injustice, and burdened with the ugly weight of discrimination. Forced to live with these shameful conditions, we are tempted to become bitter and to retaliate with a corresponding hate. But if this happens, the new order we seek will be little more than a duplicate of the old order. We must in strength and humility meet hate with love.

Of course, this is not *practical.* Life is a matter of getting even, of hitting back, of dog eat dog. Am I saying that Jesus commands us to love those who hurt and oppress us? Do I sound like most preachers—idealistic and impractical? Maybe in some distant Utopia, you say, that idea will work, but not in the hard, cold world in which we live.

My friends, we have followed the so-called practical way for too long a time now, and it has led inexorably to deeper confusion and chaos. Time is cluttered with the wreckage of communities which surrendered to hatred and violence. For the salvation of our nation and the salvation of mankind, we must follow another way. This does not mean that we abandon our righteous efforts. With every ounce of our energy we must continue to rid this nation of the incubus of segregation. But we shall not in the process relinquish our privilege and our obligation to love. While abhorring segregation, we shall love the segregationist. This is the only way to create the beloved community.

To our most bitter opponents we say: "We shall match your capacity to inflict suffering by our capacity to endure suffering. We shall meet your physical force with soul force. Do to us what you will, and we shall continue to love you. We cannot in all good conscience obey your unjust laws, because non-co-operation with evil is as much a moral obligation as is co-operation with good. Throw us in jail, and we shall still love you. Send your hooded perpetrators of violence into our community at the midnight hour and beat us and leave us half dead, and we shall still love you. But be ye assured that we will wear you down by our capacity to suffer. One day we shall win freedom, but not only for ourselves. We shall so appeal to your heart and conscience that we shall win *you* in the process, and our victory will be a double victory."

2. James Baldwin Becomes a Boy Preacher in Harlem (c. 1936), 1963

To defend oneself against a fear is simply to insure that one will, one day, be conquered by it; fears must be faced. As for one's wits, it is just not true that one can live by them—not, that is, if one wishes really to live. That summer, in any case, all the fears with which I had grown up, and which were now a part of me and controlled my vision of the world, rose up like a wall between the world and me, and drove me into the church.

James Baldwin, *The Fire Next Time* (New York: Dell, 1963). Reprinted by permission of the James Baldwin Estate.

As I look back, everything I did seems curiously deliberate, though it certainly did not seem deliberate then. For example, I did not join the church of which my father was a member and in which he preached. My best friend in school, who attended a different church, had already "surrendered his life to the Lord," and he was anxious about my soul's salvation. (I wasn't, but any human attention was better than none.) One Saturday afternoon, he took me to his church. There were no services that day, and the church was empty, except for some women cleaning and some other women praying. My friend took me into the back room to meet his pastor— a woman. There she sat, in her robes, smiling, an extremely proud and handsome woman, with Africa, Europe, and the America of the American Indian blended in her face. She was perhaps forty-five or fifty at this time, and in our world she was a very celebrated woman. My friend was about to introduce me when she looked at me and smiled and said, "Whose little boy are you?" Now this, unbelievably, was precisely the phrase used by pimps and racketeers on the Avenue when they suggested, both humorously and intensely, that I "hang out" with them. Perhaps part of the terror they had caused me to feel came from the fact that I unquestionably wanted to be *somebody's* little boy. I was so frightened, and at the mercy of so many conundrums, that inevitably, that summer, *someone* would have taken me over; one doesn't, in Harlem, long remain standing on any auction block. It was my good luck—perhaps—that I found myself in the church racket instead of some other, and surrendered to a spiritual seduction long before I came to any carnal knowledge. For when the pastor asked me, with that marvellous smile, "Whose little boy are you?" my heart replied at once, "Why, yours."

The summer wore on, and things got worse. I became more guilty and more frightened, and kept all this bottled up inside me, and naturally, inescapably, one night, when this woman had finished preaching, everything came roaring, screaming, crying out, and I fell to the ground before the altar. It was the strangest sensation I have ever had in my life—up to that time, or since. I had not known that it was going to happen, or that it could happen. One moment I was on my feet, singing and clapping and, at the same time, working out in my head the plot of a play I was working on then; the next moment, with no transition, no sensation of falling, I was on my back, with the lights beating down into my face and all the vertical saints above me. I did not know what I was doing down so low, or how I had got there. And the anguish that filled me cannot be described. It moved in me like one of those floods that devastate counties, tearing everything down, tearing children from their parents and lovers from each other, and making everything an unrecognizable waste. All I really remember is the pain, the unspeakable pain; it was as though I were yelling up to Heaven and Heaven would not hear me. And if Heaven would not hear me, if love could not descend from Heaven—to wash me, to make me clean— then utter disaster was my portion. Yes, it does indeed mean something—something unspeakable—to be born, in a white country, an Anglo-Teutonic, antisexual country, black. You very soon, without knowing it, give up all hope of communion. Black people, mainly, look down or look up but do not look at each other, not at you, and white people, mainly, look away. And the universe is simply a sounding drum; there is no way, no way whatever, so it seemed then and has sometimes seemed since, to get through a life, to love your wife and children, or your friends, or your mother and father, or to be loved. The universe, which is not merely the stars and the moon and the planets, flowers, grass, and trees, but *other people,* has evolved no terms for your existence, has made no room for you, and if love will not swing wide the gates, no other power will or can. And if one despairs—as who has not?—of human love, God's love alone is left. But God—and I felt this even then, so long ago, on that tremendous floor, unwillingly—is white. And if His love was so great, and if He loved all His children, why were we, the blacks, cast down so far? Why? In spite of all I said thereafter, I found no answer on the floor—not *that* answer, anyway—and I was on the floor all night. Over me, to bring me "through," the saints sang and rejoiced and prayed. And in the morning, when they raised me, they told me that I was "saved."

Well, indeed I was, in a way, for I was utterly drained and exhausted, and re-leased, for the first time, from all my guilty torment. I was aware then only of my relief. For many years, I could not ask myself why human relief had to be achieved in a fashion at once so pagan and so desperate—in a fashion at once so unspeak-ably old and so unutterably new. And by the time I was able to ask myself this question, I was also able to see that the principles governing the rites and customs of the churches in which I grew up did not differ from the principles governing the rites and customs of other churches, white. The principles were Blindness, Loneli-ness, and Terror, the first principle necessarily and actively cultivated in order to deny the two others. I would love to believe that the principles were Faith, Hope, and Charity, but this is clearly not so for most Christians, or for what we call the Christian world.

I was saved. But at the same time, out of a deep, adolescent cunning I do not pretend to understand, I realized immediately that I could not remain in the church merely as another worshipper. I would have to give myself something to do, in order not to be too bored and find myself among all the wretched unsaved of the Avenue. And I don't doubt that I also intended to best my father on his own ground. Any-way, very shortly after I joined the church, I became a preacher—a Young Minister—and I remained in the pulpit for more than three years. My youth quickly made me a much bigger drawing card than my father. I pushed this advantage ruthlessly, for it was the most effective means I had found of breaking his hold over me. That was the most frightening time of my life, and quite the most dishonest, and the resulting hysteria lent great passion to my sermons—for a while. I relished the attention and the relative immunity from punishment that my new status gave me, and I relished, above all, the sudden right to privacy. It had to be recognized, after all, that I was still a school-boy, with my schoolwork to do, and I was also expected to prepare at least one sermon a week. During what we may call my hey-day, I preached much more often than that. This meant that there were hours and even whole days when I could not be interrupted—not even by my father. I had immobilized him. It took rather more time for me to realize that I had also immobilized myself, and had escaped from nothing whatever.

The church was very exciting. It took a long time for me to disengage myself from this excitement, and on the blindest, most visceral level, I never really have, and never will. There is no music like that music, no drama like the drama of the saints rejoicing, the sinners moaning, the tambourines racing, and all those voices coming together and crying holy unto the Lord. There is still, for me, no pathos quite like the pathos of those multicolored, worn, somehow triumphant and transfigured faces, speaking from the depths of a visible, tangible, continuing despair of the goodness of the Lord. I have never seen anything to equal the fire and excitement that sometimes, without warning, fill a church, causing the church, as Leadbelly and so many others have testified, to "rock." Nothing that has happened to me since equals the power and the glory that I sometimes felt when, in the middle of a sermon, I knew that I was somehow, by some miracle, really carrying, as they said, "the Word"—when the church and I were one. Their pain and their joy were mine, and mine were theirs—they surrendered their pain and joy to me, I surrendered mine to them—and their cries of "Amen!" and "Hallelujah!" and "Yes, Lord!" and "Praise His name!" and "Preach it, brother!" sustained and whipped on my solos until we all became equal, wringing wet, singing and dancing, in anguish and rejoicing, at the foot of the altar. It was, for a long time, in spite of—or, not inconceivably, because of—the shabbiness of my motives, my only sustenance, my meat and drink. I rushed home from school, to the church, to the altar, to be alone there, to commune with Jesus, my dearest Friend, who would never fail me, who knew all the secrets of my heart. Perhaps He did, but I didn't, and the bargain we struck, actually, down there at the foot of the cross, was that He would never let me find out.

He failed His bargain. He was a much better Man than I took Him for. It happened, as things do, imperceptibly, in many ways at once. I date it—the slow crumbling of my faith, the pulverization of my fortress—from the time, about a year after I had begun to preach, when I began to read again. I justified this desire by the fact that I was still in school, and I began, fatally, with Dostoevski. By this time, I was in a high school that was predominantly Jewish. This meant that I was surrounded by people who were, by definition, beyond any hope of salvation, who laughed at the tracts and leaflets I brought to school, and who pointed out that the Gospels had been written long after the death of Christ. This might not have been so distressing if it had not forced me to read the tracts and leaflets myself, for they were indeed, unless one believed their message already, impossible to believe. I remember feeling dimly that there was a kind of blackmail in it. People, I felt, ought to love the Lord *because* they loved Him, and not because they were afraid of going to Hell. I was forced, reluctantly, to realize that the Bible itself had been written by men, and translated by men out of languages I could not read, and I was already, without quite admitting it to myself, terribly involved with the effort of putting words on paper. Of course, I had the rebuttal ready: These men had all been operating under divine inspiration. *Had* they? *All* of them? And I also knew by now, alas, far more about divine inspiration than I dared admit, for I knew how I worked myself up into my own visions, and how frequently—indeed, incessantly—the visions God granted to me differed from the visions He granted to my father. I did not understand the dreams I had at night, but I knew that they were not holy. For that matter, I knew that my waking hours were far from holy. I spent most of my time in a state of repentance for things I had vividly desired to do but had not done. The fact that I was dealing with Jews brought the whole question of color, which I had been desperately avoiding, into the terrified center of my mind. I realized that the Bible had been written by white men. I knew that, according to many Christians, I was a descendant of Ham, who had been cursed, and that I was therefore predestined to be a slave. This had nothing to do with anything I was, or contained, or could become; my fate had been sealed forever, from the beginning of time.

3. National Conference of Black Churchmen Demands Equal Power, 1966

The fundamental distortion facing us in the controversy about "black power" is rooted in a gross imbalance of power and conscience between Negroes and white Americans. It is this distortion, mainly, which is responsible for the widespread, though often inarticulate, assumption that white people are justified in getting what they want through the use of power, but that Negro Americans must, either by nature or by circumstance, make their appeal only through conscience. As a result, the power of white men and the conscience of black men have both been corrupted. The power of white men is corrupted because it meets little meaningful resistance from Negroes to temper it and keep white men from aping God. The conscience of black men is corrupted because, having no power to implement the demands of conscience, the concern for justice is transmitted into a distorted form of love, which, in the absence of justice, becomes chaotic self-surrender. Powerlessness breeds a race of beggars. We are faced now with a situation where conscienceless power meets powerless conscience, threatening the very foundations of our nation. . . .

It is of critical importance that the leaders of this nation listen also to a voice which says that the principal source of the threat to our nation comes neither from the riots erupting in our big cities, nor from the disagreements among the leaders of the civil rights movement, nor even from mere raising of the cry for "black power." These events, we believe, are but the expression of the judgment of God upon our nation for its failure to use its abundant resources to serve the real well-being of people, at home and abroad. . . .

We deplore the overt violence of riots, but we believe it is more important to focus on the real sources of the eruptions. These sources may be abetted inside the ghetto, but their basic causes lie in the silent and covert violence which white middle-class America inflicts upon the victims of the inner city. The hidden, smooth and often smiling decisions of American leaders which tie a white noose of suburbia around their necks, and which pin the backs of the masses of Negroes against the steaming ghetto walls—without jobs in a booming economy; with dilapidated and segregated education systems in the full view of unenforced laws against it; in short: the failure of American leaders to use American power to create equal opportunity *in life* as well as *in law*—this is the real problem and not the anguished cry for "black power."

From the point of view of the Christian faith, there is nothing necessarily wrong with concern for power. At the heart of the Protestant reformation is the belief that ultimate power belongs to God alone and that men become most inhuman when concentrations of power lead to the conviction—overt or covert—that any nation, race or organization can rival God in this regard. At issue in the relations between whites and Negroes in America is the problem of inequality of power. Out of this imbalance grows the disrespect of white men for the Negro personality and community, and the disrespect of Negroes for themselves. This is a fundamental root of

National Conference of Black Churchmen, "Black Power Statement," July 31, 1966, in *Black Theology: A Documentary History, 1966–1979,* ed. Gayraud Wilmore and James H. Cone (Maryknoll, N.Y.: Orbis Books, 1979), 23–30. First published in the *New York Times,* July 31, 1966.

human injustice in America. In one sense, the concept of "black power" reminds us of the need for and the possibility of authentic democracy in America. . . .

As black men who were long ago forced out of the white church to create and to wield "black power," we fail to understand the emotional quality of the outcry of some clergy against the use of the term today. It is not enough to answer that "integration" is the solution. For it is precisely the nature of the operation of power under some forms of integration which is being challenged. The Negro Church was created as a result of the refusal to submit to the indignities of a false kind of "integration" in which all power was in the hands of white people. A more equal sharing of power is precisely what is required as the precondition of authentic human interaction. We understand the growing demand of Negro and white youth for a more honest kind of integration; one which increases rather than decreases the capacity of the disinherited to participate with power in all of the structures of our common life. Without this capacity to *participate with power*—i.e., to have some organized political and economic strength to really influence people with whom one interacts—integration is not meaningful. For the issue is not one of racial balance but of honest interracial interaction.

For this kind of interaction to take place, all people need power, whether black or white. We regard as sheer hypocrisy or as a blind and dangerous illusion the view that opposes love to power. Love should be a controlling element in power, not power itself. So long as white churchmen continue to moralize and misinterpret Christian love, so long will justice continue to be subverted in this land. . . .

. . . "Black power" is already present to some extent in the Negro church, in Negro fraternities and sororities, in our professional associations, and in the opportunities afforded to Negroes who make decisions in some of the integrated organizations of our society.

We understand the reasons by which these limited forms of "black power" have been rejected by some of our people. Too often the Negro church has stirred its members away from the reign of God in *this world* to a distorted and complacent view of *an otherworldly* conception of God's power. We commit ourselves as churchmen to make more meaningful in the life of our institution our conviction that Jesus Christ reigns in the "here" and "now" as well as in the future he brings in upon us. We shall, therefore, use more of the resources of our churches in working for human justice in the places of social change and upheaval where our Master is already at work.

4. *Christianity Today* Criticizes Black Americans' Intimidation of White Churches, 1969

A small group of anti-American black revolutionaries began a campaign of open persecution this month against white churches and synagogues. In a 2,500-word "Black Manifesto" they vowed church seizures, disruptions, and demonstrations and demanded half a billion dollars in "reparations" from the American Christian-Jewish community.

Editorial, "Black Manifesto Declares War on Churches," *Christianity Today,* May 23, 1969, 29. Used by permission of Christianity Today.

"To win our demands we will have to declare war on the white Christian churches and synagogues and this means we may have to fight the total government structure of this country," the manifesto said.

The initial confrontation came May 4 when James Forman, reputed author of the manifesto, stopped a Sunday-morning worship service at New York's fashionable Riverside Church. Forman stood in the altar area after the opening hymn and began to read a series of demands. The Rev. Ernest T. Campbell led the choir out, and the service never did resume.

The same day, the manifesto's demands were read during a similar disruption by blacks at the First United Presbyterian Church of San Francisco.

Two days earlier, Forman had appeared before the General Board of the National Council of Churches to air the manifesto. The board had expressed its thanks to Forman and agreed to send the document to its constituent denominations for "study." . . .

Forman's manifesto was adopted by a vote of 187–63. In an introduction, he called the United States "the most barbaric country in the world," adding flatly that "we have a chance to help bring this government down."

Forman has been the director of international affairs for the Student Non-Violent Coordinating Committee in Atlanta. His introduction also declared that "our fight is against racism, capitalism and imperialism and we are dedicated to building a socialist society inside the United States where the total means of production and distribution are in the hands of the state. . . . We work the chief industries in this country and we could cripple the economy while the brothers fought guerrilla warfare in the streets."

The manifesto confined itself to overturning churches. The $500 million to be gleaned from the churches has already been budgeted: $200,000,000 for a Southern land bank to establish cooperative farms; $10,000,000 each to set up publishing industries in Detroit, Atlanta, Los Angeles, and New York; $10,000,000 each to "audio-visual networks" in Detroit, Chicago, Cleveland, and Washington, D.C.; $30,000,000 for a black research skills center; $10,000,000 for a communications training center; $10,000,000 for the already existing National Welfare Rights Organization, a lobby for welfare recipients; $20,000,000 for a black labor strike fund; $20,000,000 for an International Black Appeal to produce more capital; and $130,000,000 for a black university.

The money is demanded as "only a beginning of the reparations due us as people who have been exploited and degraded, brutalized, killed, and persecuted." To extract the funds the manifesto calls for "total disruption of selected church sponsored agencies. . . ."

The manifesto concluded: "Our objective in issuing this manifesto is to force the racist white Christian church to begin the payment of reparations which are due to all black people, not only by the church but also by private business and the U.S. government. We see this focus on the Christian church as an effort around which all black people can unite. Our demands are negotiable, but they cannot be minimized."

Two Episcopal bishops met newsmen in New York after issuance of the demands. They said they agreed that their denomination and others were racist, and that the demands for money were just. "You're not wrong in asking," said the Rev. J. Brooke Mosley, "you're asking the wrong people."

At the headquarters of the Lutheran Church in America in New York, Forman posted the demands on the front door. He said he did so "in the spirit of Martin Luther."

5. Richard Hein Describes His Work as a Military Chaplain in Vietnam, 1968

The role of Army chaplains is a threefold role, no matter where they are sent. Be it a training center, an airborne division, or overseas in Korea or Vietnam, or wherever, the chaplains serve as pastors to their men, as ambassadors for Christ, and as representatives of the church. Actually I got the idea for this article while I was riding on a helicopter, on my way in to make a combat assault with Company "C" of the 2nd Battalion of the 327th Airborne Infantry. Then as we hiked, slipped, slid, and climbed our way through jungles, down ravines, up mountains and through rice paddies and streams, the germ of the idea began to develop and take shape in my mind. The more my feet and back ached, the more I thought, "Just what am I doing here, for heaven's sake?" But that is just the very answer! I'm here for heaven's sake, or more specifically, for our Lord Jesus Christ's sake. I would like to explain why by developing these three points. . . .

. . . We conduct church services on the Lord's day. Of course when my battalion is out in the field on combat operations, services may have to be given on Saturday, Sunday, and Monday, or have to wait until the tactical situation will permit. It is nothing unusual to have four services on Saturday and four services on Sunday, and not preach to the same men twice. Also whenever practical and possible we administer the sacraments. Thus far I have not had the opportunity to baptize anyone, but some of my fellow chaplains report many wonderful experiences of baptizing men on confession of faith, using streams, ponds, or perhaps even the South China Sea as a baptistry. I've been privileged, however, to administer the Bread and the Cup in the field; and believe me, I haven't words to describe the sacredness of that holy moment when, perhaps amid the rubble and debris and smoke of war, men gather at our Lord's table to feast spiritually upon his broken Body and shed Blood "as a seal of his coming again." . . .

The counseling ministry is a very important part of the chaplain's pastoral relationship with his men. I've been awakened at an unearthly hour of the night by a man about to go into combat. I've had to help men struggle with family problems from the disadvantageous point of 7,000–10,000 miles from the problem. Due to the fact that our battalion is out on combat operations, I don't have the luxury of office hours so that my men can come to see me when they want to discuss a problem. Therefore my counseling ministry is often included in my pastoral calling ministry. . . .

. . . [I]t is the chaplain's duty to act as an adviser to the command in the areas of religion, morals, and morale. The commander is, by Army regulations, held responsible for all matters pertaining to his command. But he counts on his chaplain to carry out the religious program and to keep him advised in these specific areas. The chaplains endeavor to have and maintain a good relation between themselves and the "Old Man," as well as his staff.

Richard Hein, "What Am I Doing Here?" *The Chaplain*, January–February 1968, 14–18.

Secondly, we try to bring the Christian perspective to bear in any and all situations. This is a far less dramatic aspect of the ministry than going into combat with the troops, but it is just as important. For example, in our brigade we have movies fairly regularly; a good proportion of soft drinks and beer come our way; also mail is delivered regularly. If the soft drinks were not made available, we chaplains would be up in arms immediately. In fact, for a while after the brigade first got here, only beer was being distributed. A loud and long protest from all the brigade chaplains forced a hasty re-evaluation and now we get an adequate supply of soft drinks.

As far as our battalion is concerned our commander has a strict policy with regard to passes into town. This helps to keep the prostitutes poor, but it aids our men in the long run. Chance remarks by my predecessor and me, made on the basis of a good relationship between commander and chaplain, may have helped the commander make up his mind.

Finally, we chaplains serve as a living reminder of the link with the church back home. . . . Certainly I would be the first to say that some chaplains, unfortunately, are not fit representatives of the church. But I've met very few. The few have been atrociously bad examples, but their influence is nil. The men soon spot a phony. In most cases the chaplains have been and are concerned and dedicated pastors. The Roman Catholic chaplains have been real brothers and the respect we Protestant clergy have for the Roman Catholic is equally matched by their respect for us.

In the final analysis, the chaplain will probably only represent to the men that image of the church to which they are accustomed. Therefore it is up to the church to teach, train, and prepare its young men for total commitment to Christ, and a life of dedicated discipleship in fellowship with Christ and his church. We chaplains can help by taking the place of the home pastor through a very significant time in a man's life. And often we can send back to the churches men that were never reached by the churches. But what really matters is that, wherever we are called to serve, we serve effectively for the glory of the Lord Jesus, and "as your servants for Jesus' sake." To that end we Army chaplains in Vietnam are dedicated, and for that purpose may we continue to covet an interest in your prayers.

6. *Commonweal* Supports Symbolic Attacks on the Vietnam Draft Board, 1968

Even keen partisans of the Berrigan brothers are having difficulty understanding their newest protest against the war in Vietnam: the seizing of files from a Catonsville, Md., Selective Service office and the incineration of these with homemade napalm.

Wasn't the point made a couple of months ago when Father Phil Berrigan poured duck's blood into a Baltimore draft office's files, and Father Dan Berrigan publicly endorsed the action?

Only partially, obviously.

Editorial, *Commonweal*, June 7, 1968, 346. Copyright Commonweal Foundation.

For reasons that are probably psychological, and most certainly religious and humanitarian, a term in jail has become essential to the Berrigan brothers for the fullness of their witness. And what surer way for them to win jail than for the two to be accomplices in a raid on a draft office—Father Phil Berrigan while he is free on his own recognizance, awaiting sentence for a conviction on a similar charge of mutilating government property; and Father Dan Berrigan while espousing a commitment to radical action until jailed.

The whole business doesn't make sense to most people, but it does to those who know the Berrigan brothers intimately and grasp the anguish which is theirs over the enormity of the evil of the Vietnam war. These people can not only give intellectual assent to the radicalism of the Berrigan brothers, but can so frame the existential logic of the Berrigans that an action such as that in Catonsville becomes a gentle, not violent, gesture, a defendable means to a positive end—imprisonment.

There is undoubtedly a measure of romance and rationalization in this thinking, but it is not to be dismissed contemptuously. The world would be better off with more rather than fewer Berrigans, and it will profit from their witness, impractical though this may occasionally appear to be.

An idea of what motivates the Berrigans will be conveyed in the book (*Night Flight to Hanoi*) which Dan Berrigan has written for publication next September, and the manuscript of which he mailed to Macmillan just an hour or two before the torch was set to the napalm in Catonsville. The book discusses Berrigan's recent trip to North Vietnam as intermediary in the release of two captured Americans; its foreword, which Berrigan circulated to a few intimates, anticipated the events in Catonsville. It provides what seems to be intentional documentation of the "purpose and forethought" of that action, (perhaps to make it easier for the law to convict him), and opens insight into the intensity of the man's feelings. Dan Berrigan writes:

> Our apologies, good friends, for the fracture of good order, the burning of paper instead of children, the angering of the orderlies in the front parlor of the charnel house. We could not, so help us God, do otherwise. For we are sick at heart; our hearts give us no rest for thinking of the Land of Burning Children. And for thinking of that other Child, of whom the poet Luke speaks.

Passionate? Yes . . . Foolhardy? Don't be too sure.

It is very easy to write off Catonsville and similar incidents as serving little beyond the satisfaction of the religious and psychological impulses of those protesting. This is unfair. Such actions have high purpose and call attention to a bevy of injustices; economic and racial, as well as military.

So it was with the demonstrators at Catonsville. Their aim was not only to protest the war (though they are aware here of new urgencies, with the popular delusion that because there are talks in Paris there is peace in Vietnam). It was also to protest American "economic oppression" across the world; to protest the imbalance of wealth aggravated by U.S. enterprise; and to dramatize the neglect at home to the poor, particularly poor blacks.

This is written as though there were the Berrigans at Catonsville and no others. There were, of course, nine colleagues. Dan Berrigan speaks of himself and them in his foreword: "Our record is bad; trouble-makers in church and state, a priest married despite his vows, two convicted felons. We have jail records, we have been turbulent, uncharitable, we have failed in love for the brethren, have yielded to fear and despair and pride, often in our lives. Forgive us."

But of forgiveness there is no need. Better there be gratitude.

7. Renny Golden Describes Religious Women's Work in the Sanctuary Movement, 1986

The hot desert wind unfurled the banners painted with signs of hope. Women of Conscience, a small group from the Los Angeles religious community gathered outside El Centro detention center near the Mexican border in Southern California. Hundreds of Central American refugees are imprisoned there in the desert behind ten-foot high cyclone fences topped with spirals of barbed wire, guarded by the United States Immigration and Naturalization Service. As the women kept their vigil outside, the imprisoned men, awaiting deportation and possible death or torture upon their return, threw a sheet over the barbed wire. The sheet pointed north and bore the words, "*En el nombre de Dios, ayudanos,*" ("In the name of God, help us"). The bright red letters were painted with a mixture of punch and their own blood.

"In the name of God, help us." That sign, sticking on the barbs of a desert prison, symbolizes the cry of a people, rising from Central America, written, not only in the blood of the men at El Centro, but in the blood of tens of thousands of the poor. The imprisoned, the fugitive, the deported, the *campesinos* organized and struggling for freedom, even the dead cry out.

This is the story of women on both sides of the conflict, those in the North American religious community who heard that cry and have chosen to stand with the dispossessed by proclaiming their communities of faith public sanctuaries for refugees from El Salvador and Guatemala, and the women of Central America whose lives bear witness to hope in the midst of atrocity. Scores of religious communities have sheltered undocumented refugees in direct defiance of the United States government's interpretation of the Immigration and Naturalization Act of 1980. The United States government calls the act of sanctuary criminal, punishable by a $2,000 fine and up to five years in prison. By declaring sanctuary, white, mostly middle-class congregations took on a portion of the risk that the popular church of Central America and the clandestine church of Mexico have endured for years. Sanctuary has become one of the first acts of authentic solidarity for the North American religious community—a solidarity of defiant love.

Sanctuary provides a place where refugees can speak the truth. Even in the refugee camps, the desperation to tell their story is evident to visitors. The refugees offer quickly scrawled notes to North Americans who visit there, pleading with them to share the refugees' stories. They write, "We cannot leave these camps. It is

Renny Golden, "Sanctuary and Women," *Journal of Feminist Studies in Religion* 2 (Spring 1986): 131–150.

up to those who visit to share the truth." Suzanne Doerge, a leader in the sanctuary movement in Cincinnati, relates this story from the Honduran camps:

> Five worn figures huddled with us around the wooden table in the priest's tent. One gas lamp created a circle of light that brought us together for a few brief hours blocking out the constant danger of U.S. helicopters hovering over us. They gave us the gift of their stories animated by their hands, scarred by sudden mountain escapes. A soft voice with no hint of revenge, told of her papa cut to pieces and the heads of her brothers stuck on sticks. Her mother had cried out for her children, but the soldiers gunned her down in the street. The daughter crossed the Lempa River wearing only her underwear and traveled that way for fifteen days. Their village was bombed and their houses burned. Why?—Because they were catechists.

The United States government calls women like this one who fled illegal aliens who come here solely for economic reasons. Since 1980 only 341 Salvadorans have gained political asylum out of nearly thirty thousand applicants. Those in the sanctuary movement call them refugees with the right to live here. Over seventy thousand United States citizens have actively participated in breaking United States law as interpreted by the government, in order to "feed the hungry, shelter the homeless and welcome the alien." Most sanctuary churches knew from the beginning that it was insufficient to merely bind the wounds of the victims without trying to stop the cause of those wounds. Welcoming services for refugee families at the sanctuary sites became occasions to decry United States foreign policy and mobilize the community to stop the flow of arms from the United States to Central America. Telling the truth was coupled with stopping the horror of that truth.

The sanctuary movement was born in an encounter between North Americans and Central Americans—an encounter not around a conference table, but on the road, in the desert, along the barbed wire of a border crossing. Through that face-to-face encounter, the religious community was confronted with a grave moral problem. Central Americans were fleeing their homelands because of violence and terror and were being met in the United States by official government policy that deported them directly back to that violence. In 1981 and 1982, as the sanctuary movement was beginning, the United States, the only country in the world sending Salvadorans directly back to their country, deported on the average of one thousand per month. Out of the fifty-five hundred who had applied for political asylum in 1981 only two received it.

At first the religious community near the border responded with food and shelter and help in working through the legal process set up by the Immigration and the Naturalization Service. They bonded refugees out of detention camps, putting up their cars and homes as collateral, but the best they could do was buy some time. After two years of such work none of the fourteen hundred refugees had gained political asylum. It became clear that the hearing process was not designed to gain justice for immigrants, but only to carry out the executive branch's foreign policy, which insisted that all Central Americans were economic refugees.

Authentic help finally came, exactly as the refugees had asked—in the name of God. On March 24, 1982, on the second anniversary of the assassination of Archbishop Oscar Romero of El Salvador, California and Arizona churches declared themselves public sanctuaries for Guatemalan and Salvadoran refugees. They told the INS quite bluntly to stay out or risk breaking sacred law. The sanctuary movement was born.

When Southside Presbyterian of Tucson and five churches in the East Bay declared the first sanctuary, they were drawing on scriptural tradition. The sacred law they referred to came from Moses' proclamation that certain Canaanite cities were places of sanctuary where people could seek asylum from blood avengers (Numbers 35). The concept of sanctuary was so compelling that it was recognized in Roman law, medieval canon law and English common law. In the 1600s in England, every church was a potential sanctuary. During the seventeenth century the whole North American continent was seen as a sanctuary from the political and religious persecutions of Europe. Pennsylvania and Rhode Island were exceptional examples of tolerance and shelter for the outcast. Sanctuary became a part of the accepted understanding of what it meant to be American by people here and around the world. That sentiment was finally engraved on the Statue of Liberty, "Give me your tired, your poor, your huddled masses, yearning to breathe free."

Two of the most heroic periods of the sanctuary tradition date from the 1850s in the United States, and the Second World War in Europe. After the passage of the Fugitive Slave Act in 1850 made it illegal to harbor or assist a slave in gaining freedom, religious people and churches became stations on the underground railroad, in defiance of federal law. More recently, monasteries hid Jews fleeing the Holocaust, providing food, false documents and shelter. In southern France, a Protestant parish named Le Chambon, under the leadership of its pastor Andre Trocme, collectively decided to be a sanctuary, specifically citing the law of Moses. The parish hid over three thousand Jews, and throughout the underground became known as the safest place for Jews in all of Europe.

While the declaration at Tuscon and Berkeley could draw on a heroic history, it was framed as an immediate response to an urgent situation. In three years, the movement has grown beyond the imaginations of its originators. Over two hundred twenty churches, synagogues, and Quaker meeting houses have publicly declared themselves sanctuaries. Sanctuary has touched the consciences of sisters in Concordia, Kansas; workers in Ohio; farmers in Iowa; and Catholic bishops in Seattle and Milwaukee. What was so compelling about the sanctuary movement that it attracted and emboldened so many people, even when it meant defying the government's interpretation of the law and risking a fine and imprisonment?

For the first time in this century, the war victims, the people on the other end of our bombs and artillery fire and covert actions, were not an anonymous enemy that could be labeled "gooks" or "chinks." Instead, they were Juan, Jose, Albertina, Angelica and Ramon. The wreckage, the carnage of United States foreign policy arrived on our shores as living or half-living people. The majority of the refugees who flee are women trailing, carrying and cajoling children to continue to walk a terrible journey. . . .

. . . By 1984, however, the United States government increased repression of the movement with the first arrests of sanctuary workers on the Texas border. The sanctuary movement had moved from initial acts of charity to acts of liberation which challenged government policy. In early February of 1984, Stacey Merkt, a worker from Casa Romero refugee assistance center, was arrested coming out of the Rio Grande Valley with Salvadoran Brenda Sanchez-Galan, her eighteen-month-old infant, Bessie, and Mauricio Valle. . . .

In January of 1985, a year after the arrest of Stacey Merkt . . . the government "cracked down" on another border by indicting twelve Arizona/Mexican sanctuary workers after a ten-month investigation. The government charged the sanctuary workers with seventy-one counts of "conspiracy to aid illegal aliens" by shielding, harboring and transporting them.

The government gathered most of the evidence in the indictment through informers wearing bugging devices who had infiltrated church meetings. Sanctuary workers called the surveillance a threat to civil liberties and unnecessary considering that the sanctuary movement has always been open. . . .

Many in the sanctuary movement feel it is the government that should be standing trial. Sister Julie Sheatzley, CSJ, a member of the Cincinnati Sanctuary Coalition said, "It is not these people of faith who should be indicted. It is the United States government that should be indicted on charges of inducing refugees to flee El Salvador and Guatemala by sending millions of dollars of military aid to those oppressive governments. The United States government should be indicted on charges of [deporting] tens of thousands of refugees back to harrassment, torture and possible death."

Sanctuary congregations have resolved to continue and even expand their work. Since the indictments, there have been demonstrations at INS facilities around the country, declarations of sanctuary in Vermont, Chicago and Houston, and examples of commitment like that of Sister Anna Priester, BVM. Sister Anna of Phoenix symbolized the attitude of those indicted. She has Hodgkins disease, and right after the indictment was handed down went into the hospital to have her spleen removed. The judge on the case moved to drop the charges against her because of her physical condition. The operation was successful but Sr. Anna did not want the charges dropped. She sent her lawyer to inform the prosecutor that if charges were dropped she would be out helping the refugees again as soon as her recovery was complete. She added that if the judge wanted to show compassion, he should do it for the refugees. . . .

[The movement's] hope and determination was best summarized in a statement made by another indictee, Sister Darlene Nicgorski. The following statement was published before Darlene was indicted:

> We cannot "legitimate" our involvement with refugees—it is impossible. As we begin to walk with them, some of the marginalization, oppression and repression will come to us . . . The message of the prophets from the South is often hard for us to hear—we who love so much and live in a sense of righteousness and with the illusion of power and control. The spirit is moving in the church, but it is now a movement from the South to the North. Again it comes in forms hard to recognize—another language, culture, experience. It is all changed—what appears to be religion is politics, what appears to be political is faith lived in the public forum. Sanctuary is one of the clearest ways the North American church has to identify with the spirit, life, and the future. In solidarity with those struggling, we are asked to risk the traditional concept of church—peace and neutrality. Do we know where this leads? Do we trust that this is not just another North American white middle-class, male, clerical, paternalistic program of compassion trying to seek approval of the institution or is it something we do in solidarity with the church of the South—with the thousands suffering in the camps

in southern Mexico, in the church camps in San Salvador or with those hiding in the mountains of Guatemala? The refugees in public sanctuary are following the example of the saints of Latin America—they are the voice of the voiceless.

8. Tina Bell Joins an Anti-Abortion Demonstration, 1988

The symbol of anti-abortion civil disobedience is the stubborn, lonely figure of Joan Andrews. In prison since 1986—for trying to rip an electrical cord out of a suction-abortion machine—she has refused to cooperate with the "authorities" or obey prison rules, for which she has been subjected to harsh privations during an unjustly long sentence. Her identification with the unborn ("Reject them, Reject me,"), with its strong overtones of Christian martyrdom, has made her a heroine to a large segment of the anti-abortion movement. But she is a heroine difficult to emulate, more useful as a symbol of voluntary sacrifice than as a model of political effectiveness.

Not so with Operation Rescue which, though inspired by activists like Joan Andrews, works for political victory *via* large-scale, organized defiance of the law. During the first week of May, it mobilized almost a thousand people who came to New York City for the purpose of getting themselves arrested.

The pamphlet advertising Operation Rescue (which was to be a series of non-violent sit-ins at New York abortion clinics) offered a vision of leadership to inspire anti-abortionists frustrated by 15 years of futile opposition to legalized abortion. It's a vision of "hundreds and hundreds of people around an abortion mill, praying and singing. . . . Imagine huge banners unfurled in the wind, declaring 'Operation Rescue' and 'No More Dead Children' . . . Imagine a rescue mission so well-organized . . . so well managed, with the participants so calm, free of hateful or bitter words . . . participants so decent and upright the American people are forced to consider the reasons for their actions and the merits of their arguments."

Randall Terry, the 29-year-old evangelical minister who heads Operation Rescue, argues that moral—even political—victory is possible if his followers are willing to get arrested and, if necessary, spend time in jail in numbers large enough to attract media attention. The New York sit-ins were intended to initiate a "heroic uprising."

By the time Operation Rescue got to New York, Terry had refined the crowd-control techniques of previous efforts, such as in Cherry Hill, New Jersey (outside Philadelphia), where 210 activists were arrested at a single abortion-clinic sit-in. He had also managed to attract some prominent anti-abortionists to his cause. By the end of the New York operation, he had also "achieved" more than 1,600 arrests (and re-arrests) of his disciplined, nonviolent troops. Among them were some 50 clergy and religious, including several rabbis, evangelical ministers, priests, nuns, and Bishop Austin Vaughan, an auxiliary to New York's Cardinal John O'Connor. Also arrested were Mrs. Adele Nathanson, whose husband, Dr. Bernard Nathanson, is the now-famous ex-abortionist who has become a leading figure in the "Pro-life"

Tina Bell, "Operation Rescue," *Human Life Review* 14 (Summer 1988): 37–52. Reprinted by permission.

movement. And Mark Bavaro, the All-Pro football star (of the New York Giants), who is vice-chairman of something called Athletes for Life. No doubt about it, anti-abortion activists are everywhere nowadays. . . .

How did young Randall Terry get almost a thousand Americans from across the political spectrum to come to New York City (the belly of the beast, if you're an evangelical Christian) for anti-abortion "direct action"? If you have an abortion mill in your home town, New York isn't any more "evil" than a quiet, middle-American community. The answer lies in the character of the participants and the nature and purpose of the sit-ins.

The participants are enthusiasts who've inherited the political legacies of the sixties. Many of the people I met both at rescues and evening rallies were young evangelical Christians who—with their blue-jeans, T-shirts and long hair—looked like the kind of people I saw when I went to Woodstock 20 years ago. Woodstock, in fact, makes a good comparison. The music was the unifying principle there, and its mood was intensified by the use of drugs which made Woodstock utopianism (Three Days of Peace and Music, remember?) easier to believe in. The unifying principle at Operation Rescue was religious fervor, an *internal* music. The Quakers, another group of politically-active enthusiasts, claimed that they were moved by a God-given "inner light." The young evangelicals I met seemed moved by some-thing similar, accessible only to initiates—those who were willing to be, or had been, arrested.

And Randall Terry fits very well Ronald Knox's definition of an enthusiast: "He expects more evident results from the grace of God than we others. He sees what effects religion can have, does sometimes have, in transforming a man's whole life and outlook; these exceptional cases (so we are content to think) are for him the average standard of religious achievement. He will have no 'almost-Christian,' no weaker brethren who plod and stumble, who (if the truth must be told) would like to have a foot in either world, whose ambition is to qualify, not to excel."

This religious enthusiasm translates well into the spirit of Operation Rescue, where total commitment is the unspoken requirement for membership. Even Bap-tism has its analog in the rescue movement: getting arrested. . . .

The rescuers being mostly evangelicals, the rally had a born-again flavor to it. I wondered what some of the other neophytes, conservative Catholics like myself who probably preferred Gregorian chant to "Rock of Ages," thought of it? The speeches were really sermons, punctuated with "Alleluias" and prayers. When a ser-mon really got going people would even stand up and shout "Alleluia!" in a chorus. Randall Terry, a very clean-cut young man who began in humorous self-deprecation, built up to a fiery crescendo, speaking of martyrdom, sacrifice, and the blood of in-nocent children. He is a young man gifted with the ability to condemn sin without making his listeners feel guilty. We felt, rather, that we were his accomplices in a war against evil.

Bishop Austin Vaughan, of Newburgh, New York, was more moderate in tone; but he concluded by saying that his episcopal ring had three names inscribed on it—Christ, and Sts. Peter and Paul—and each man had been executed by a govern-ment. . . . The Battle Hymn of the Republic was sung militantly, not hesitantly, as it's sung in most churches. . . .

Randall Terry was only 14 when *Roe* v. *Wade* legalized abortion. The claim cannot be made that the members of Operation Rescue—many of whom would have been undistinguishable in a crowd of '60's anti-war demonstrators—are protesting the demise of a *familiar* moral order. They grew up in the sixties and seventies! They are trying to *resurrect* a moral order (based on Judaeo-Christian laws) they never knew. They lean on no political or theological traditions; no institutions support them directly. This is the attraction they hold, and the danger they present.

Why do rescues strike a jarring note in society? Because abortionists like to work behind closed doors, and society lets them. None of the abortion clinics targeted for sit-ins had the words "Abortions Performed Here" posted over their doors. Even those who defend abortion don't defend *abortion*—they defend "choice" and, lately, "constitutional rights." But rescues really do show the truth of it. Part of the impact of a rescue is its revelatory nature. The rescuers were always singing and praying—often for the abortionists and their supporters as well as the mothers and unborn babies. Their faces reflected the positive truths which move them. The angry, contorted faces of the "pro-aborts," who just wanted the rescuers to go away, radiated hatred.

☞ E S S A Y S

David Garrow of Emory University is a biographer of Martin Luther King, Jr., and a leading scholar of the civil rights movement. In the first essay he examines the nature of King's leadership and traces it to an episode during the Montgomery bus boycott when threats against his life and his family brought on a crisis of confidence. The intense feeling of God's presence and help, at that moment, enabled King to regain his composure and provide decisive leadership to the movement. As King told it in *Stride Toward Freedom,* his 1958 book about the boycott, God then addressed him as "Martin Luther," emphasizing his link to one of the great European church reformers. Garrow shows that King's rhetoric in the face of death threats and a failed murder attempt in 1957 closely paralleled his speech in Memphis eleven years later, immediately before his assassination. In both cases he compared himself to Moses, on the "mountaintop," able to see into "the Promised Land" but not to lead his people there in person. As his leadership broadened to become nationwide in the 1960s, King began to emphasize the cross he had to bear, a comparison with Christ just before his crucifixion. As Garrow makes plain, King's sustaining vision throughout the movement was religious, not political.

John McGreevy of the University of Notre Dame studies the relationship between several things that at first glance seem unconnected: the Second Vatican Council (Vatican II) among Roman Catholics (1962–1965), the civil rights movement, and the changing character of urban neighborhoods in northern cities. As he shows, however, the council helped to widen a split in the Catholic ranks, between liberals who supported and tried to promote racial integration, on the one hand, and conservatives who resisted it on the other hand. The conservative Catholics' resistance was not simply a matter of barefaced racism. Rather, says McGreevy, these descendants of Irish, Italian, Slavic, and Polish immigrants had built strong Catholic neighborhoods around their churches. They believed that the arrival of black residents would lead to a "white flight" and shatter these neighborhoods, which over the years had become a kind of sanctified ground. When they demonstrated against integration they were horrified to see priests and nuns, whom they had grown up revering, leading pro-integration demonstrations against them. They linked Vatican II's liturgical reforms to racial reforms, often switching back and forth between the two issues when they voiced their anxieties. McGreevy's exceptional skill, like that of Eugene Genovese and Elizabeth Fox-Genovese in Chapter 6, lies in his ability to take readers, provisionally, into the minds of people whose racial ideas they would otherwise deplore, but not to endorse their actions.

Martin Luther King, Jr.'s Leadership

DAVID J. GARROW

Martin Luther King, Jr., began his public career as a reluctant leader who was drafted, without any foreknowledge on his part, by his Montgomery colleagues to serve as president of the newly created Montgomery Improvement Association (MIA). Montgomery's black civic activists had set up the MIA to pursue the boycott of the city's segregated buses called by the Women's Political Council (WPC) immediately after the December 1, 1955, arrest of Rosa Parks.

King was only twenty-six years old and had lived in Montgomery barely fifteen months when he accepted that post on Monday afternoon December 5. Two years later King explained that "I was surprised to be elected . . . both from the standpoint of my age, but more from the fact that I was a newcomer to Montgomery." On December 5, however, King was as much anxious as surprised, for his new post meant that he would have to deliver the major address at that evening's community rally, which had been called to decide whether a fabulously successful one-day boycott would be extended to apply continuing pressure on bus company and city officials to change the bus seating practices. King later explained that he had found himself "possessed by fear" and "obsessed by a feeling of inadequacy" as he pondered his new challenge, but he turned to prayer and delivered a superb oration at a jam-packed meeting that unanimously resolved to continue the protest. . . .

By mid-January 1956, as the ongoing boycott received increased press coverage, King became the focal point of substantial public attention. That visibility made King a particular target when Montgomery's city commissioners adopted new, "get tough" tactics against the MIA. On Thursday, January 26, while giving several people a lift as part of the MIA's extremely successful car pool transportation system, King was pulled over by two policemen and carted off to the city jail on the fallacious charge of going thirty miles per hour in a twenty-five-mile-per-hour zone. . . . King was fingerprinted and jailed for the first time in his life, thrown into a filthy group cell with a variety of black criminals. In a few moments' time, Abernathy and other MIA colleagues began arriving at the jail, and white officials agreed to King's release. His trial would be Saturday.

That arrest and jailing focused all the personal tensions and anxieties King had been struggling with since the first afternoon of his election. The increased news coverage had brought with it a rising tide of anonymous, threatening phone calls to his home and office, and King had begun to wonder whether his involvement was likely to end up costing him, his wife, Coretta, and their two-month-old daughter,

David J. Garrow, "Martin Luther King, Jr., and the Spirit of Leadership," *Journal of American History* 74 (Sept. 1987): 438–47.

Yolanda, much more than he had initially imagined. The next evening, January 27, King's crisis of confidence peaked. . . . "The first twenty-five years of my life were very comfortable years, very happy years," King later recalled.

> I didn't have to worry about anything. I have a marvelous mother and father. They went out of their way to provide everything for their children . . . I went right on through school; I never had to drop out to work or anything. And you know, I was about to conclude that life had been wrapped up for me in a Christmas package.
>
> Now of course I was religious, I grew up in the church. I'm the son of a preacher . . . my grandfather was a preacher, my great grandfather was a preacher . . . my daddy's brother is a preacher, so I didn't have much choice, I guess. But I had grown up in the church, and the church meant something very real to me, but it was a kind of inherited religion and I had never felt an experience with God in the way that you must . . . if you're going to walk the lonely paths of this life.

That night, for the first time in his life, King felt such an experience as he thought about how his leadership of the MIA was fundamentally altering what had until then been an almost completely trouble-free life. . . . Then, in what would forever be, in his mind, the most central and formative event in his life, Martin King's understanding of his role underwent a profound spiritual transformation.

"It was around midnight," he explained years later. "You can have some strange experiences at midnight." That last threatening phone call had gotten to him. "Nigger, we are tired of you and your mess now, and if you aren't out of this town in three days, we're going to blow your brains out and blow up your house." . . .

> I sat there and thought about a beautiful little daughter who had just been born. . . .
>
> And I started thinking about a dedicated, devoted and loyal wife who was over there asleep. . . .
>
> And I discovered then that religion had to become real to me, and I had to know God for myself. And I bowed down over that cup of coffee. I never will forget it . . . I prayed a prayer, and I prayed out loud that night. I said, "Lord, I'm down here trying to do what's right. I think I'm right. I think the cause that we represent is right. But Lord, I must confess that I'm weak now. I'm faltering. I'm losing my courage. And I can't let the people see me like this because if they see me weak and losing my courage, they will begin to get weak."

Then it happened.

> And it seemed at that moment that I could hear an inner voice saying to me, "Martin Luther, stand up for righteousness. Stand up for justice. Stand up for truth. And lo I will be with you, even until the end of the world." . . . I heard the voice of Jesus saying still to fight on. He promised never to leave me, never to leave me alone. No never alone, no never alone. He promised never to leave me, never to leave me alone.

That experience, that encounter in the kitchen, gave King a new strength and courage to go on. "Almost at once my fears began to go. My uncertainty disappeared."

The vision in the kitchen allowed King to go forward with feelings of companionship, of self-assurance, and of mission that were vastly greater spiritual resources than anything he had been able to draw on during the boycott's first eight weeks. It also allowed him to begin appreciating that his leadership role was not simply a matter of accident or chance, but was first and foremost an opportunity for service—not an opportunity King would have sought, but an opportunity he could not forsake. His new strength also enabled him to conquer, thoroughly and permanently, the fear that had so possessed him that Friday night in his kitchen, while allowing him to appreciate that although his calling might be unique, it was the calling, and not himself, that was the spiritual centerpiece of his developing role.

That strength and dedication remained with King throughout the Montgomery protest, which ended in success, with the integration of the city's buses just prior to Christmas 1956. In the wake of that achievement, however, some whites directed repeated acts of violence against the newly desegregated buses, and in mid-January, a series of bombings struck several black churches and the homes of MIA leaders. The violence weighed heavily on a very tired King. Then, on Sunday morning, January 27—the first anniversary of King's kitchen experience—twelve sticks of dynamite, along with a fuse that had smoldered out, were found on the porch of King's parsonage.

The murder attempt deeply affected King. In his sermon later that morning to his Dexter Avenue Baptist Church congregation, he explained how his experience one year earlier had allowed him to resolve his previous fears about the question of his own role and fate. "I realize that there were moments when I wanted to give up and I was afraid but You gave me a vision in the kitchen of my house and I am thankful for it." King told his listeners how, early in the boycott, "I went to bed many nights scared to death." Then,

> early on a sleepless morning in January 1956, rationality left me. . . . Almost out of nowhere I heard a voice that morning saying to me, "Preach the gospel, stand up for truth, stand up for righteousness." Since that morning I can stand up without fear.
>
> So I'm not afraid of anybody this morning. Tell Montgomery they can keep shooting and I'm going to stand up to them; tell Montgomery they can keep bombing and I'm going to stand up to them. If I had to die tomorrow morning I would die happy because I've been to the mountaintop and I've seen the promised land and it's going to be here in Montgomery.

Those remarks, uttered in January 1957, and so clearly presaging the very similar comments that King made in Memphis, Tennessee, on the evening of April 3, 1968, bring home a simple but crucial point: that Martin Luther King, Jr.'s mountaintop experience did not occur in April 1968, nor even in August 1963, but took place in the kitchen at 309 South Jackson Street in Montgomery on January 27, 1956. King's understanding of his role, his mission, and his fate was *not* something that developed only or largely in the latter stages of his public career. It was present in a rather complete form as early as the second month of the Montgomery boycott.

Appreciating King's own understanding of his role and responsibilities is really *more* crucial than anything else, I would contend, to comprehending the kind of leadership that Martin Luther King, Jr., gave to the American black freedom struggle of the 1950s and 1960s. By 1963–1964, as that role and those responsibilities grew, King thought increasingly about his own destiny and what he termed "this challenge to be loyal to something that transcends our immediate lives." "We have," he explained to one audience, "a responsibility to set out to discover what we are made for, to discover our life's work, to discover what we are called to do. And after we discover that, we should set out to do it with all of the strength and all of the power that we can muster." As his close confidant Andrew Young later expressed it, "I think that Martin always felt that he had a special purpose in life and that that purpose in life was something that was given to him by God, that he was the son and grandson of Baptist preachers, and he understood, I think, the scriptural notion of men of destiny. That came from his family and his church, and basically the Bible."

The revelation in the kitchen gave King not only the ability to understand his role and destiny, but also the spiritual strength necessary to accept and cope with his personal mission and fate. Its effect was more profoundly an ongoing sense of companionship and reassurance than simply a memory of a onetime sensation. "There are certain spiritual experiences that we continue to have," King stated, "that cannot be explained with materialistic notions." One "knows deep down within there is something in the very structure of the cosmos that will ultimately bring about fulfillment and the triumph of that which is right. And this is the only thing that can keep one going in difficult periods."

King's understanding of his life underwent a significant deepening when he was awarded the 1964 Nobel Peace Prize. The prize signaled the beginning of a fundamental growth in King's own sense of mission and in his willingness to accept a prophetic role. "History has thrust me into this position," he told reporters the day the award was announced. "It would both be immoral and a sign of ingratitude if I did not face my moral responsibility to do what I can in this struggle."

More and more in those years King thought of his own life in terms of the cross. It was an image he invoked repeatedly, beginning as early as his 1960 imprisonment in Georgia's Reidsville State Prison. He focused particularly on it, and on the memory of his experience in the kitchen, at times of unusual tension and stress. In mid-September 1966, amid a deteriorating intramovement debate about the "Black Power" slogan, King talked about how his sense of mission was increasingly becoming a sense of burden.

> We are gravely mistaken to think that religion protects us from the pain and agony of mortal existence. Life is not a euphoria of unalloyed comfort and untroubled ease. Christianity has always insisted that the cross we bear precedes the crown we wear. To be a Christian one must take up his cross, with all its difficulties and agonizing and tension-packed content, and carry it until that very cross leaves its mark upon us and redeems us to that more excellent way which comes only through suffering.

More than anything else, the Vietnam War issue brought King face to face with what was becoming a consciously self-sacrificial understanding of his role and fate. He had spoken out publicly against America's conduct of the war as early as March 1965 and had stepped up his comments during July and August 1965, but he had drawn back in the face of harsh criticism of his views stimulated by the Johnson administration. Throughout 1966, King largely had kept his peace, reluctant to reignite a public debate about the propriety of the nation's leading civil rights spokesman becoming a head-on critic of the incumbent administration's uppermost policy. Then, in early 1967, King resolved to take on Lyndon B. Johnson's war publicly as never before.

King knew full well that his new, aggressive stance on the war would harm him politically and might well damage the civil rights movement financially. Those considerations, however, were not enough to shake King from his resolve. "At times you do things to satisfy your conscience and they may be altogether unrealistic or wrong, but you feel better," King explained over wiretapped phone lines to his longtime friend and counselor, Stanley Levison. America's involvement in Vietnam was so evil, King explained, that "I can no longer be cautious about this matter. I feel so deep in my heart that we are so wrong in this country and the time has come for a real prophecy and I'm willing to go that road."

King's attacks on the war, and particularly his April 4, 1967, antiwar speech at New York's Riverside Church, brought down a flood of public criticism on his head. Even some of King's most trusted advisers, including Levison, reproached him for the tone of that speech. King, however, rejected the complaints. "I was politically unwise but morally wise. I think I have a role to play which may be unpopular," he told Levison. "I really feel that someone of influence has to say that the United States is wrong, and everybody is afraid to say it."

In late May 1967, King spoke to his aides about how he had come to see the war issue in terms of his understanding of the cross.

> When I took up the cross, I recognized its meaning. . . . The cross is something that you bear and ultimately that you die on. The cross may mean the death of your popularity. It may mean the death of a foundation grant. It may cut down your budget a little, but take up your cross, and just bear it. And that's the way I've decided to go.

No longer did he suffer from any indecision on the question of Vietnam.

> I want you to know that my mind is made up. I backed up a little when I came out in 1965. My name then wouldn't have been written in any book called *Profiles in Courage.* But now I have decided that I will not be intimidated. I will not be harassed. I will not be silent, and I will be heard.

King's determination to forge ahead in the face of discouraging political circumstances also manifested itself during the late 1967–early 1968 planning of the Poor People's Campaign, Washington protests intended to be so "dislocative and even disruptive" that the federal government would launch a full-scale program to eliminate poverty in America. On March 28 King's determination to pursue the campaign faltered and turned to despair when a protest march that he had helped lead in Memphis, Tennessee, ended in widespread violence. . . .

King's expectations proved largely correct. The *New York Times,* terming the Memphis violence "a powerful embarrassment to Dr. King," recommended he call off the Poor People's Campaign since it probably would prove counterproductive to his cause. King, however, did not give up, and on Wednesday, April 3, he returned to Memphis to aid in the preparations for a second march. That evening, at the cavernous Mason Temple church, before a modest-sized but emotionally enthusiastic crowd, King vowed that both the Memphis movement and the Poor People's Campaign would go forward. Then he turned to an emotional recapitulation of his own involvement in the preceding thirteen years of the black freedom struggle, expressing how happy and thankful he was that he had been given the opportunity to contribute to and to live through its many significant events. Then he closed with the same ending he had used more than eleven years earlier in Montgomery when he had first explained how the vision in the kitchen had given him the strength and the courage to keep going forward.

I don't know what will happen now. We've got some difficult days ahead. But it really doesn't matter with me now, because I've been to the mountaintop. And I don't mind. Like anybody, I would like to live a long life. Longevity has its place. But I'm not concerned with that now. I just want to do God's will. And he's allowed me to go up to the mountain, and I've looked over, and I've seen the promised land. I may not get there with you. But I want you to know tonight that we, as a people, will get to the promised land. And so I'm happy tonight. I'm not worried about anything. I'm not fearing any man. Mine eyes have seen the glory of the coming of the Lord.

In conclusion, then, I want to reiterate that the key to comprehending Martin King's own understanding of his life, his role, his burden, and his mission lies in that spiritual experience that began for him in his Montgomery kitchen on January 27, 1956. Martin King's awareness that his calling was to devote and ultimately to sacrifice his own individual life in the service of a great and just cause ennobled him as a human being, strengthened him as a leader, and allowed him to accept the symbolic role and accompanying fate that helped propel forward a struggle he rightfully recognized would be never ending.

Urban Catholics and the Civil Rights Movement

JOHN T. McGREEVY

Catholic participation in the southern civil rights movement culminated at Selma in March 1965. As was customary in much of the South, Selma's Catholic churches were strictly segregated, with the priests in charge of the African American "mission" parish ignored by the city's other clergy. (One attempt at integration of the city's "white" parish by a group of African American Catholic teenagers met with fierce resistance.) In addition, the bishop of Montgomery, Thomas Toolen, attempted to prevent northern Catholics from responding to the pleas of civil rights activists for assistance, maintaining that outsiders were "out of place in these demonstrations— their place is at home doing God's work. . . ." Regardless, priests from fifty different dioceses, lay people, and nuns flocked to Alabama to join in the marches.

One participant observed that many speakers at the headquarters of the Selma campaign "pointed out with happiness and gratitude that this was the first time that so many Catholic priests, acting with their bishops' permission, had joined them on the front lines of the movement." Ralph Abernathy congratulated one priest on the Catholic turnout, jocularly adding that "the only ones they hate more than Negroes down here are Roman Catholics, especially Monsignors." Newspapers across the country, including the *New York Times* and the *Washington Post,* carried front-page photos of nuns in full-habit striding down Dallas County roads. One editorial concluded that "For a great many Catholics . . . the pictures of demonstrating clergymen and religious, flashed on TV screens or bannered across front pages, spoke more clearly and directly than any conciliar decree could ever do about the effective presence of the Church in the world of today." A nun marching down Selma's Highway 80 made the same point more emphatically: "We are the Church," she declared. . . .

John T. McGreevy, "Radical Justice and the People of God," *Religion and American Culture* 4 (Summer 1994): 221–54. © 1994 by Center for the Study of Religion and American Culture.

Significantly, debates provoked by the civil rights movement echoed more sophisticated discussions occurring in Rome. Even as Daniel Berrigan asked at Selma, "What is the Church anyway? Is it where we came from, or is it here, being created by Negroes and their white acolytes?" the world's bishops were formulating answers to precisely the same questions. By the time of the council's conclusion in December 1965, the bishops had authorized a series of changes more sweeping than any since the Reformation.

The council's impact on American Catholicism was particularly profound. Before 1960, in contrast to their Western European counterparts, American Catholic leaders had been able to point with pride to the continuing faithfulness of most of their charges, numerous religious vocations, a vast educational effort, and financial generosity. These genuine accomplishments, however, masked theological rigidity. With few exceptions, American leaders and theologians toed a narrow line on doctrinal matters, persistently reiterating established principles on moral and sexual matters, along with occasional references to a vaguely defined "social doctrine." With little dissent, the energy of the church in America focused on the construction of parishes and schools and on Catholic professional societies and social organizations—an American religious subculture of unparalleled depth and scope.

This highly disciplined religious climate created a people and a clergy unprepared for sweeping changes. "The faithful," as one theologian observed, "had been kept . . . carefully sheltered from any suggestion that certain issues were under discussion." The most emotional alterations were the new aesthetics and guidelines: the priest facing the congregation, the replacement of Latin liturgies with the vernacular, an end to the ban on Friday consumption of meat, folk guitars on the altar, and churches constructed in the round.

Underlying these changes were new conceptions of church and community. For American Catholics interested in racial issues, three themes proved central. First, the bishops reframed conceptions of the nature of the church. In place of more traditional hierarchical and juridical definitions, the bishops repeatedly described the church by using a biblical image, the "people of God." Instead of a building or structure, the church itself had to be a "sign and instrument . . . of communion with God and of unity among all men."

Second, the bishops repeatedly emphasized that a truly Catholic church would awaken its members "to the drama of misery and to the demands of social justice made by the Gospel and the Church." The first lines of the Pastoral Constitution on the Modern World, quoted fervently by American Catholic liberals during the rest of the decade, declared that "the joys and the hopes, the griefs and the anxieties of the men of this age, especially those who are poor or in any way afflicted, these too are the joys and hopes, the griefs and anxieties of the followers of Christ." Bereft of "earthly ambition," the people of God were enjoined to carry forth the work of Christ, who entered the world "to bear witness to the truth, to save and not to judge, to serve and not to be served."

Finally, both the proceedings and the outcomes of the council suggested the formation of a global church. At the council itself, for the first time, native bishops from Africa, Asia, and Latin America joined their European and American colleagues. The abandonment of Latin—a language obviously tied to Western Christendom—and the unprecedented tolerance of new liturgical forms implied a union of churches as well as promoting an exchange of ideas between North and South. Indeed, one of the indirect thrusts of the council was to remind Catholics that the demographic future of the church lay not in the industrial West but in the less developed world.

The cumulative impact of these shifts in emphasis—from a hierarchical to a servant church, from an institution set apart from the world to one intimately concerned with modern anxieties and fears, from a reliance on Roman theology to a more pluralistic concern with the "signs of the times"—was enormous. In particular, a renewed focus on social justice reshaped the relationship between religious and civil authorities in much of the developing world. . . .

At precisely this moment, as American Catholics reevaluated their roles in contemporary society, the national focus on racial issues and urban poverty provided a mechanism for engagement with the world. Understandably, then, as American Catholics attempted to implement the principles they interpreted from the council, they placed enormous stress on the problems surrounding them in the northern cities. Editors of the *National Catholic Reporter* pledged in their first issue to focus on the "events that really matter—the Vatican Council, for example, or the civil rights movement." In reply to a query about the racial issue in Boston from local church members, Matthew Ahmann of the National Catholic Council for Interracial Justice (NCCIJ) emphasized that nothing is "as intimate to the renewal of Christ's Church as the removal of racial discrimination in the Church and our relevant witness to the equality of all men in contemporary society." . . .

. . . [D]ramatic changes occurred in communities of religious women. Convent life in the pre-Vatican II era only infrequently included participation in activities outside the parish, but women religious throughout the North did become involved in tutoring and education programs related to racial discrimination in the early 1960's. Nuns from several Chicago convents began "discussions about the problems of the area in which they were living," discussions which became the genesis of an archdiocesan-approved Urban Apostolate of the Sisters in which nuns tutored disadvantaged students and visited parishioners' homes. "These nuns now must realize," one priest commented, "that the great foreign mission apostolate of the Church is in their own backyard." . . .

These efforts merged with the excitement of the Second Vatican Council. More than any other group of American Catholics, women religious took seriously papal commands to reexamine all religious work in light of council teachings. Inevitably, nuns extended their vision to urban and racial questions. Sr. M. Charles Borromeo Muckenhirn, for example, argued soon after the conclusion of the council that "it is the city near or in which a convent exists which is the church, the people of God in that area." She added that "although many were shocked at the events in Selma, there has evolved more clearly the awareness that the Christian, most of all the religious, belongs with those who have no power in this world." Again, racial issues provided a useful metaphor. One nun maintained that "the habit has become a kind of 'skin coloring' so that prejudices and stereotypes have to be broken down before the person can gain the response due to a person and not to 'one of the good sisters.' " . . .

For many Catholic liberals, criticisms of traditional attitudes toward African Americans routinely merged with a distaste for the institutions—parishes, schools, and religious societies—that had shaped so much of the Catholic past. Until the 1960's, specifically Catholic organizations were presumed superior; in the context of the Vatican Council and the civil rights movement, Catholic liberals pleaded with fellow communicants to develop a more ecumenical outlook. "[T]here is no reason," concluded one theologian, "why the Church should maintain and, what is worse, continue to build institutions of health, education, and welfare." One sociologist concluded that the primary "challenge to Christianity" in the modern era was the "building of community without walls," while the editors of the *National Catholic Reporter* worried that Catholics "kept in [Catholic] ghettos long after they should have been assimilated" would develop a "permanent inferiority complex which they can cope with only by staying in the ghetto. . . ." In fact, the editors concluded, "it is legitimate to ask whether national parishes really foster a vibrant Christianity or merely preserve ethnic identities (and thereby promote racial discrimination)."

To many Catholics sitting in the pews of those churches, however, these criticisms came as if in another language. . . . [L]arge numbers of American Catholics continued to labor, socialize, and worship in patterns barely distinguishable from those developed by their immigrant ancestors. Communicants still answered with a parish name when asked, "Where are you from?" Pastors managed the parish "plant"; nuns oversaw the schools.

Especially to Catholics who remained in the northern cities, discussions of "social evil" paled beside the fear of plummeting property values and the abandonment of traditional communities. Indeed, Catholic parishes had sanctified particular neighborhoods, fostering a territorial sense of community throughout the urban North. Now, representatives of the very institution that had instilled a sacramental template onto the idea of "neighborhood" seemed willing to sacrifice these same neighborhoods on the altar of integration. In areas where the church itself had named the local community and helped define the meaning of its parishioners' lives—through nationality, the parish school, and the spires of the church building towering over the neighborhood skyline—the anger by the mid-1960's was palpable. A Cleveland woman addressed her bishop in 1964: "These people," she wrote, "are concerned about their homes, their children, and the parishes that they worked so hard for. The Catholics have been more than willing to sacrifice for all the building programs you have thought necessary, but when these are at stake, after all their efforts, you are going to see the resentment. . . ." She then listed relatives robbed or mugged in the neighborhood. "My folks and my husband's are in the St. Thomas area. 18 to 20 years ago, it was possible to live with the first ones that came around, and the priest encouraged people to stay. The ones that moved were the smart ones. Now those that are left live in constant fear for the safety of their families."

Reactions to the participation of priests and nuns in the Selma marches suggest the depths of this division. To Catholic liberals, the demonstrations at Selma were a triumph. "We made the Church visible," proclaimed one St. Louis nun, "illustrating that the twentieth century church has a social conscience." . . .

That other Catholics drew different conclusions is evident from the same diocesan newspaper. One woman professed herself "sick at heart" from viewing pictures of marching nuns in the newspaper. Instead of public protests, she argued, the nuns "should be down on their knees . . . praying. . . ." She continued, "I was taught that the habit is blessed to help in prayer and obedience, not public demonstrations. I feel the superiors of these nuns should be punished just as we mothers should be punished for any neglect towards our children." Another Cleveland reader maintained that coverage of events in Selma allowed "communist leaders . . . to divide the Catholic population." Indeed, "[s]egregation, birth control and civil rights are issues that are held up especially to draw the expression of different Catholic spokesmen in order to destroy unity."

Catholics in Chicago reacted with equal vehemence to the arrest of five nuns and seven priests in a protest against public school segregation. (The daily papers splashed photos of the nuns stepping into police paddy wagons across the front page.) A statement issued by the priests argued that "it is an appropriate and religious act for priests and nuns" because of the "moral and religious issues" involved. One African American priest maintained that the arrests of the nuns proved that "Chicago is worse than Selma" since "for the first time in the history of this country, Catholic nuns were arrested." . . .

Other Catholics condemned the protests. "Certainly," argued one letter writer, "there are more effective ways of working for racial justice than associating with a group of unwashed beatniks in breaking the laws of the city." A Mrs. Dorgan protested:

> [T]his show of nuns and priests marching for this and that. . . . We can accept the changes in the liturgy or theology, but these peacemakers stirring up trouble because of their conscience, God forbid. I have all I can do to keep my faith in God the ways things are going in this world. What has happened to the beautiful Catholic Church's unity, togetherness, same belief. . . ?

Mrs. Dorgan's plaintive plea for Catholic unity correctly identified the central development of the era. Scholars have recently begun to recognize the waning of denominational unity during the 1960's as a harbinger of a cultural shift that would shape American politics and society through the 1980's. Alliances on issues as diverse as abortion, school busing, and censorship, in other words, became predicated less on denominational affiliation than on perceptions of authority, historical change, and social justice. By the mid-1960's, then, the shared political and theological concerns that drew Protestant, Jewish, and Catholic liberals together in the civil rights movement also pushed some working-class Catholics apart from their putative religious leaders. Moreover, racial issues brought to the fore divisions on the nature of authority, questions about the relationship of religion to political concerns, and tensions between parochial institutions and an increasingly cosmopolitan theology. . . .

Participation by priests and nuns in civil rights marches, as well as in attempts to calm angry white neighborhoods, provided the most vivid evidence of divisions among the people of God. In Cleveland's heavily Italian Murray Hill area, twelve priests attempted to calm angry crowds protesting the integration of the local public school through forced busing. The crowd's response was to throw garbage on the street and jeer the clerics. "Mind your own business, Father," yelled a few bystanders, while others started a mocking chant, "Pray for us, Father." One priest from the local parish tolled his church bells for a prayer service, but only fifty people chose to attend.

Members of Philadelphia's archdiocesan commission on human relations spent several tense evenings moving through crowds in the city's Kensington area after an African American family moved beyond an informal neighborhood boundary line. Following initial disturbances, all children in the local parochial school took home letters to their parents asking them to ensure quiet streets. Since parochial schools enrolled roughly half of the area's students, priests from both the parishes and Northeast Catholic High School attempted to spot pupils and order them away from the scene. Generally, the priests were treated with respect. At one point, however, a local priest spoke to the crowd from a bullhorn, asking that "the parents . . . take their little children home." He added, "I hope all the Catholics in the crowd will go home." In response, many in the crowd booed. . . .

. . . [In the summer of 1966 Martin Luther] King authorized the first in what became a series of protest marches focusing on segregationist real estate practices [in Chicago]. Inevitably, these marches threw into sharp relief the chasms that separated various groups within the Catholic church. The first marches and prayer vigils occurred in Gage Park where, out of 28,244 residents in what one observer called the most heavily Catholic neighborhood in the city, precisely two were African American.

Because of its location to the west of the African American ghetto, the area had become home to many of the roughly 400,000 Catholics displaced by the expanding ghetto in the 1940's and 1950's. Already, crowds of whites had harassed representatives from the freedom movement who had gathered beneath a twenty-foot cross on the grounds of St. Gall's Church in Gage Park for two prayer vigils. Large groups of priests, nuns, and Catholic lay people joined the marches, and, while a few marches produced only verbal confrontations, huge mobs of whites tossed stones and bricks at the marchers during several of the demonstrations.

Initial police efforts to halt the violence were tentative enough to cause one observer to note that "it was obvious that some officers were torn between their duty and their identity with their friends and neighbors in the crowd." The crowds screamed with such unrelenting fury that King, after one march in which he had been briefly felled by a rock, declared he had "never seen anything so hostile and so hateful. . . ." A Catholic high school student recalled seeing "people I went to church with, screaming 'Nigger!' and throwing rocks and dirt at King—these nice people I knew all my life. I couldn't believe it."

Eventually, movement activists, Mayor Daley, and civic leaders (including [Archbishop] Cody) negotiated an open-housing agreement that ended the formal protests. Many Catholic liberals emerged from the protests with their commitment to a more cosmopolitan, ecumenical community affirmed. A Catholic instructor at a local inner-city community college asked Archbishop Cody whether "any member of the Church in Chicago has thought about the wisdom of fostering in Chicago our past and present 'tribal' social system. I can understand how much of a consolation it must have been for a Pole to live in a neighborhood with other Poles, but is this sort of thing needed any longer?" Only Martin Luther King's example, wrote one Chicago nun, enabled her to learn what "Christianity is all about. . . ." When she returned to the African American section of the city after one perilous journey, the hugging and crying made her realize "what a community was in a way I have never known at even the most beautiful of Catholic Masses."

Much of the city's liberal Catholic community, however, continued to lick its wounds. The fury of the crowds, and their particular hostility to priests and nuns, had stunned Catholic activists. "The scores of nuns and priests who marched," noted John McDermott, "became a special target. Spectators yelled 'You're not a real priest' and 'Hey Father, are you sleeping with her?' " During a July 31 march, a rock struck one suburban nun, Sr. M. Angelica, O.S.F., who was working in a summer volunteer program. When she fell, the crowd cheered. ("For the first time in history of this city," the archdiocesan newspaper thundered, "a nun was attacked on the streets of Chicago in a public demonstration. And the attack came from a mob of howling Catholics.") A number of priests from local parishes moved through the crowds, attempting to persuade area residents to leave the scene, but they learned that "the sight of a Roman collar incited [the crowd] to greater violence and nastier epithets."

Unsurprisingly, liberals repeatedly referred to their inability to pierce barriers in local communities and, at times, even their own families. "For [those still in the neighborhood]," noted one commentator, "the civil rights issue may . . . represent the possible loss of a home, the transformation of a familiar neighborhood into a ghetto—a threat to family, community and, not least of all, to the Church itself." John McDermott noted that "they consider themselves good Catholics, yet utterly reject integration. And they are particularly bitter toward priests, bishops and organizations who tell them they are in conflict with their religion. 'Since when?' they retort." Unfortunately, another cleric concluded, "In no sense do they [liberals] represent the people. They speak another language and, it now seems very clear, practice a different religion."

Echoes of these tensions reverberated over the next year. In January, Msgr. Edward Burke, a pastor on the city's northwest side, the former chancellor of the archdiocese, and a longtime supporter of activist Saul Alinsky, poured out his frustrations in a parish bulletin article entitled "Let's Do Some Thinking for a Change." "When we fight for the rights of the Negro," Burke maintained, "we cannot overlook the rights of the white person. He has been forced to support, unaided, himself and his family. If he owns property, he purchased it by the sweat of his brow and is a true Christian when he asks that his possessions be not disturbed." Burke readily conceded that "the Negro has God-given rights—equal to the rights of the white," but he also argued that his "reasons for opposing integration are based on the conviction that proponents of civil rights possess a superficial viewpoint of what integration really is." Integration, in Burke's view, did not equal "physical proximity." Why do "Catholic newspapers who continuously urge the whites to love the minorities, never fight the landlord, who [is] responsible for the slum . . . [?]" If Catholic liberals found his remarks unpalatable, Burke warned, he would simply resign his post.

A few of Burke's supporters also expressed their position. "Why should we give money to priests that are buying property to GIVE to the colored?" asked one Berwyn correspondent. "Look at what happened to Blessed Sacrament . . . or Our Lady of Sorrows, did the colored keep them up? I love Father Burke for his stand." A Chicago resident recommended to Archbishop Cody that "the church preach the neighborhood policy in housing and schooling." One woman responded:

> I'm all for Msgr. Burke and I'm sure I can speak for all of Cicero and Berwyn. I have three cousins that are priests and two that are nuns and thank God none of them think like you do. How can anyone have respect for a priest when he makes a monkey of himself by marching down the street with a bunch of nitwits or sits on a curb to demonstrate[?] I tried living with them when they moved into our neighborhood in Chicago. . . .

I worked all my life and still have a mortgage for what I lost. . . . Now I live in Cicero and Msgr. Burke knows exactly what he is talking about when he says Negroes must learn to accept obligations, *including respect for property.* . . .

In short, "race" helped mark the cultural changes sweeping through both the church and American society. Between 1964 and 1967, two distinctly Catholic visions of church, community, and authority clashed in the streets, parishes, and Catholic schools of the northern cities. More traditional Catholics resisted what they perceived as the destruction of their communities—once fostered by the church and now seemingly threatened by the church's own representatives. Catholic liberals, on the other hand, questioned traditional parochial structures while becoming active participants in local civil rights coalitions.

The prolonged Catholic encounter with racial issues also provoked basic questions of faith. A remarkable facet of the pre-conciliar, twentieth-century church had been the range and depth of popular religious practices—the parades through the parish on feast days, the endless, well-attended rosary crusades, the seventy thousand Catholics who might pack into a single church during one week for a novena, and the traveling statues of Mary.

The most important project of Catholic liberals in the 1940's and 1950's had been to refocus attention on the celebration of the Mass and away from these less structured, individualistic acts of piety and petition. To liberals, the parishioner saying the rosary during Mass and the statues of saints drawing attention away from the altar destroyed the communal and social meaning of the liturgy. This social meaning (particularly the theme of "unity") drew many Catholic interracial activists into programs of liturgical reform. As early as the 1940's, liturgical conferences included discussions of the connections between liturgical reform and racial issues. Chicago interracial pioneer Msgr. Daniel M. Cantwell, for example, gave frequent retreats for activists on a farm in rural Wisconsin. There Cantwell celebrated the avant-garde "dialogue Mass," with the priest facing the congregation and the worshipers allowed to respond at certain points of the liturgy. In 1963, the annual liturgical conference took place in Philadelphia just days before the March on Washington. Hundreds of participants placed small "March on Washington" buttons next to their conference badges and made plans to stop in the capital on the way home from the conference. Listeners continually interrupted Benedictine Godfrey Diekmann's keynote address with ovations. "[W]e trumpet the blasphemous triumph of Satan," Diekmann thundered, "if we eat of the Bread and drink the cup, and refuse to accept the Negro as our daily table guest."

The Vatican Council ratified and extended these notions. Virtually no mention was made of the pious practices so evident in Catholic life. Moreover, relatively little mention was made of the ecumenically suspect Mary. Priests now faced the congregation, worshipers were encouraged to participate through responses and music, and the entire liturgy was in the vernacular. Again, liturgical reformers connected these changes to social issues. "No Christian who understands the liturgical renewal," wrote one Pittsburgh priest in 1964, "can be indifferent to the interracial situation in our country today." . . .

. . . The same priests, nuns, and lay people marching through heavily Catholic neighborhoods also pushed for the reformation (and occasionally abandonment) of the traditional rituals that structured so much of Catholic spiritual life. In Chicago, a bitter fight broke out between parents and clergy when parents discovered that a new religion textbook for third graders contained the sentence "Dr. Martin Luther King is like Jesus." Debates on the matter often lurched into attacks on the withdrawal of vigil lights from the church building or the lack of emphasis in Catholic schools on praying the rosary. Parents in a Detroit parish who considered the local nuns too liberal on racial issues added in the same breath that they also disapproved of new catechetical strategies.

Both the outward forms—the various Catholic institutions, the cohesiveness of the neighborhoods—and the rituals that endowed those forms with meaning came under siege. For Catholic liberals, the question often became whether any genuine faith could escape the confining structures (both physical and moral) of the parochial system. . . .

By contrast, some parishioners asked whether such individuals could be trusted to lead the institution that had helped orient their lives. One woman told interviewer Robert Coles of her concerns. "They're talking as if we did something wrong for being white. . . . Priests never used to talk about the Negro when I was a child. Now they talk to my kids about them all the time. I thought the Church is supposed to stand for religion and eternal things."

Internecine battles over these issues became passionate. Already, Catholic liberals, inspired by both Selma and the Second Vatican Council, had begun to apply a language of "freedom" and "rights" to what they perceived as oppressive structures within the church, even as more conservative co-religionists recoiled from the theological and social implications of this new parochial world. In no other era in American history would the notion of "authority" come under such scrutiny, and this scrutiny inevitably extended to perhaps America's most authoritative institution. In retrospect, previously isolated priests, seminarians, nuns, and laypeople became fully engaged with American society at a moment of tremendous flux. In this way, the crisis within the church both mirrored and shaped the reorientation of American culture during the late 1960's.

✎ *F U R T H E R   R E A D I N G*

Baer, Hans A., and Merrill Singer. *African-American Religion in the Twentieth Century: Varieties of Protest and Accommodation* (1992).

Bergsma, Herbert. *Chaplains with the Marines in Vietnam* (1985).

Blanchard, Dallas. *The Anti-Abortion Movement and the Rise of the Religious Right* (1994).

Branch, Taylor. *Parting the Waters: America in the King Years, 1954–1963* (1988).

Cleague, Albert. *The Black Messiah* (1968).

Cone, James. *Martin and Malcolm and America* (1991).

Coutin, Susan B. *The Culture of Protest: Religious Activism and the U.S. Sanctuary Movement* (1993).

Cunningham, Hilary. *God and Caesar at the Rio Grande: Sanctuary and the Politics of Religion* (1995).

Davis, Cyprian. *The History of Black Catholics in the United States* (1990).

Fauset, Arthur H. *Black Gods of the Metropolis* (1944).

Fisher, James T. *The Catholic Counterculture in America: 1933–1962* (1989).

Frazier, E. Franklin. *The Negro Church in America* (1963).

Garrow, David. *Bearing the Cross: Martin Luther King and the Southern Christian Leadership Conference* (1986).

Haley, Alex. *The Autobiography of Malcolm X* (1965).

Jacoby, Kerry N. *Souls, Bodies, Spirits: The Drive to Abolish Abortion Since 1973* (1998).

Lincoln, Eric. *The Black Muslims in America* (1961).

Lischer, Richard. *The Preacher King: Martin Luther King, Jr., and the Word That Moved America* (1995).

McGreevy, John. *Parish Boundaries: The Catholic Encounter with Race in the Twentieth Century Urban North* (1996).

Meconis, Charles. *With Clumsy Grace: The American Catholic Left, 1961–1975* (1979).

Novak, Michael, Robert M. Brown, and Abraham Heschel. *Vietnam: Crisis of Conscience* (1967).

Ochs, Stephen. *Desegregating the Altar: The Josephites and the Struggle for Black Priests, 1871–1960* (1990).

Risen, Jim. *The Wrath of Angels: The American Abortion War* (1998).

Robinson, Jo-Ann. *The Montgomery Bus-Boycott and the Women Who Started It* (1987).

Tomsho, Robert. *The American Sanctuary Movement* (1987).

Weisbrot, Robert. *Father Divine* (1992).

Wilmore, Gayraud. *Black Religion and Black Radicalism* (1972).

Zaroulis, Nancy, and G. Sullivan. *Who Spoke Up? American Protest Against the War in Vietnam* (1984).

CHAPTER
13

Religion and Counterculture:

1970–1995

The social upheavals of the 1960s and 1970s included the civil rights movement, the anti–Vietnam War movement, the New Left, the women's liberation movement, the gay liberation movement, the hippies, yippies, and a flourishing drug scene. Compare photographs of college students taken in 1960 and in 1970 to get a sense of just how drastically young people's appearance changed during that decade. Radical changes in values and beliefs often accompanied the switch from trim haircuts and suits or dresses to tie-dyed psychedelic shirts, unisex jeans, and flowing locks. Journalists and sociologists as well as hippies and radicals used the term "counterculture" to describe the era's communal living experiments, new sexual expressiveness, dress idiom, drugs, and music.

These changes made a strong impression on American religious life. Asian religions, particularly Zen Buddhism, had already enjoyed a vogue among the 1950s' "Beat Generation," appearing, for example, in Jack Kerouac's novel The Dharma Bums. *Variations on Indian religion surged in popularity when the Beatles, the sixties' great pop music phenomenon, went in search of enlightenment from an Indian guru. The shave-headed Hare Krishnas became a fixture of the American urban scene, especially in college towns and at major airports, wearing their distinctive saffron and yellow robes, dancing to tambourines, and chanting "Hare Krishna, Hare Rama!" with monotonous enthusiasm.*

Some Christians tried to adapt to changing times by evangelizing among spiritually restless drug addicts and hippies. In the time-honored American way of arguing that one's way of life was really just like that of Christ himself, the "Jesus Freaks" depicted Jesus as a man who had "dropped out" of conventional society way back in Roman Palestine. The stage musical and Hollywood film Jesus Christ, Superstar *(1973) took the same approach but inadvertently made Judas Iscariot seem much more interesting than the Messiah himself.*

Meanwhile the women's movement subjected traditional American religion to searching criticisms. Women began to lobby for inclusion in the ministry of churches that had previously excluded them, and succeeded in many, though they were unable to broach the Roman Catholic tradition of a male-only, all-celibate priesthood. Radical religious feminists took the view that Judaism and Christianity

394

were inherently sexist. One classic statement of this view was Mary Daly's Beyond God the Father *(1973). Daly and many other women began to seek spiritual alternatives that, as they saw it, validated their experience as women instead of marginalizing it. Among their new creations (albeit making claims of an ancient lineage) were goddess-worship, witchcraft, and spiritual eco-feminism.*

Countercultural religion in the 1960s, 1970s, and 1980s was extremely diverse, giving rise to hundreds of movements, many of which lasted only a few years. They ranged from the hedonistic to the severely ascetic, but they all shared a sense of dissatisfaction with mainstream American life and religion, a fascination with self-realization, and a boldly experimental approach to new forms of communal living.

✎ D O C U M E N T S

Jacob Needleman, author of Document 1 (1970), describes his migration from the East Coast to the West as the 1960s came to an end and his discovery of the rich, experimental world of alternative religions that he found there, mostly of Asian origin and all, implicitly, feeding the spiritual hunger of an America in psychological and social turmoil. Document 2, a passage from Hal Lindsey's bestseller *The Late Great Planet Earth* (1970), uses current events such as the first moon landing (1969) and the "mind-expanding" drug cult as packaging for familiar premillennialist claims about the imminent "Rapture" (disappearance into heaven) of those whom Christ has saved, to be followed by seven years of suffering, Christ's return, and the millennium that brings history to an end. Document 3 (1974) explains why bewildered young Americans found solace among the Hare Krishnas, while Document 4 (1988) narrates the rise of Jim Jones's cult-church, the People's Temple, and its catastrophic finale (mass suicide) in the Guyanese jungle. Documents 5, 6, and 7 illustrate some of the countercultural directions taken in women's spirituality in the same years. Starhawk (1979) describes and defends the witchcraft she has re-created, Carol Christ (1987), a professor of religious studies, baptizes herself into goddess religion at a Greek temple of Aphrodite, and eco-feminist Mary Ann Flaherty (1994) finds spiritual strength and comfort in the embrace of Mother Earth.

1. Jacob Needleman Discovers the Appeal of Eastern Religions, 1970

What, then, have they found, these followers of the new, religious teachings? It is possible that a serious look at them, and at the people involved in them, will change our whole idea of religion.

Who will deny that some such change is necessary? When God was recently pronounced dead it was not because people were no longer asking fundamental questions about life and death, human identity, suffering, and meaninglessness. On the contrary. Never before have men been more desperate about these questions.

True, our established religions are alive to this desperation. They are in agony because of it. We see them twisting and turning, seeking to change form without

---

Jacob Needleman, *The New Religions* (New York: Pocket Books, 1972), 9–13. Reprinted by permission of the author.

altering their essence. They wish to become *relevant* to the times, for the times are torturing us all.

But how are they, how is religion, to do this? We are tortured—agreed. The scientific world-view, recently so full of hope, has left men stranded in a flood of forces and events they do not understand, far less control. Psychiatry has lost its messianic aura, and therapists themselves are among the most tormented by the times. In the social sciences, there exists a brilliant gloom of unconnected theories and shattered predictions. Biology and medicine promise revolutionary discoveries and procedures, but meanwhile we suffer and die as before; and our doctors are as frightened as we.

And we cling violently to forms of life which, perhaps, were not even meaningful to us in quieter times.

So, when religion, in the name of relevance, seeks to adjust itself to the times, the question is bound to arise: is the leader being led? As church and synagogue turn to psychiatry, the scientific world-view, or social action, are they not turning toward what has failed and is failing? And has not the very failure of these non-religious enterprises shifted the common mind back to a renewed interest in the religious?

Men turn to religion and find, to their ultimate dismay, that religion turns to them, to their sciences, their ideas of action and accomplishment, and their language. This is what is known as secularization: the effort by religion to be "relevant," to "solve" human problems, to make men *"happy."* . . .

Most of [the new religions] are sourced in Asia. Therefore, if we wish to know what they have brought to America, we have to begin by understanding something about Eastern religion.

Almost all the religions of Asia have one thing in common: "self-centeredness." Their goal is always release from suffering, *my* suffering as well as the suffering of humanity. Their cosmology and metaphysics, their imperatives to act morally or to serve God, are almost always instrumental toward this goal. What is true or good is what helps me out of my suffering; what is false or evil is what locks me in it. . . .

What is this suffering? And how is this goal any different from the contemporary Western effort to make men happy, which we have just characterized as "secularization"? The answer to this question involves an idea that is markedly alien to our modern minds: *the satisfaction of desire is not happiness.*

Because human desires are so multiform and contradictory, the satisfaction of one is always at the expense of another. And even if it were possible to satisfy all our desires, it would still be a contradictory and chaotic satisfaction corresponding to the contradictory and chaotic condition of the desires themselves. Contradictory satisfaction is what we call inner conflict, and the modern man experiences inner conflict as suffering.

In religious literature the desires—physical as well as emotional and mental, the wishes, hopes, fears, and so forth—are often symbolized by animals. It is as though within man there were a thousand animals each seeking its own food and comfort. Some of these animals are, moreover, the very food that the others seek. *What is called "pleasure" or satisfaction is the feeding of one or another of these animals.*

Thus, in this view, man's suffering is based on the mistake of identifying his whole self with these animals as they appear in him and make their wants known by howling for their food. No sooner is one fed than another appears, hungrier than ever, and sometimes hungry for the very food that has just been given his predecessor—and is therefore no longer available. By identifying himself with these animals, man forfeits the possibility of inner unity and wholeness, a possibility which represents another level of existence for him.

In these traditions, this level is variously spoken of as "higher" or "deeper" or "inner." It is that level from which consciousness can control and care for the animals in a way that corresponds to their true needs as part of a whole. In its function as master, this level of consciousness is spoken of as a special force; as guardian it is called knowledge; as action in the world it is known as love or service. It is *able, conscious,* and *beneficent:* i.e., "divine."

According to Eastern psychology, there is something in man which he squanders by understanding himself to be no more than these animals, a sort of energy or life which he ignorantly gives to them, and which they really do not need or use. To turn that energy to its proper use, to direct it toward the work of integration and awareness is one of the primal functions of religious discipline. But it is much, much harder to do than one thinks, for there is always an animal in man, a kind of monkey, perhaps, which imitates the real work and which wants to *feel* whole rather than *be* whole.

In this perspective, religion becomes "secularized" when its main concern is more to feed than to control the animals—that is, when its concern is primarily with the external conditions of human life. In this sense what we ordinarily call happiness is the exact opposite of what the Eastern traditions understand by release from suffering.

In Eastern thought these animals, these desires, are much more various than we might suspect. Physical desires—for ordinary food and drink, warmth, sexual gratification, etc.—comprise only a small fraction of the total. Some others are: the desire for praise and recognition, the wish to be superior, the fear of pain, the desire for security, the wish to control others, the desire to be desired, the desire to express oneself, the fear of the unknown, etc., etc. The list is very long, and relatively few religions become secularized in the sense of seeking to gratify only the basic physical desires. The difficulty is that certain non-physical desires are identified and officially sanctioned as corresponding to the inner or divine in man, whereas in reality they are merely "animals" on a level with all the others.

When this happens all the other animals go hungry, and when they are hungry enough they go crazy. . . .

. . . The main point here is that the central thrust of Eastern religion is toward the *transformation of desire,* not satisfaction of desires. At its purest, it is a radical and constant movement inward, into the "self." Thus, the contemporary idea of "relevance"—which by and large has to do with the satisfaction of certain desires, or the allaying of certain fears—is antagonistic to the sense of Eastern religion. And thus the revolution in religion that is brewing among these new teachings in America is one that may run directly counter to the direction of contemporary religious reform.

2. Hal Lindsey Foresees the Millennial "Rapture," 1970

One small step for a man—one giant leap for mankind.

Apollo 11 Commander Neil Armstrong
20 July 1969

The Ultimate Trip

Science fiction had prepared man for the incredible feats of the astronauts, but when the reality of the moon landing really hit, it was awesome.

On that historic Sunday in July we watched TV, laughing as Armstrong and Buzz Aldrin loped on the moon's surface. We walked out the front door and looked up at the Old Man and said, "It's really happening—there are a couple of guys walking around up there right now. Amazing."

Astounding as man's trip to the moon is, there is another trip which many men, women, and children will take some day which will leave the rest of the world gasping. Those who remain on earth at that time will use every invention of the human mind to explain the sudden disappearance of millions of people.

Reporters who wrote the historic story of Apollo 11 told how the astronauts collected rocks which may reveal the oldest secrets of the solar system. Those who are alive to tell the story of "Project Disappearance" will try in vain to describe the happening which will verify the oldest secrets of God's words. . . .

Someday, a day that only God knows, Jesus Christ is coming to take away all those who believe in Him. He is coming to meet all true believers in the air. Without benefit of science, space suits, or interplanetary rockets, there will be those who will be transported into a glorious place more beautiful, more awesome, than we can possibly comprehend. Earth and all its thrills, excitement, and pleasures will be nothing in contrast to this great event.

It will be the living end. The ultimate trip.

If you are shaking your heads over this right now, please remember how many "impossibles" you have said in your lifetime—or how many "impossibles" men throughout the ages have said to many things God has revealed through His spokesmen. And yet they were possible, because nothing is impossible for God.

We have been examining the push of world events which the prophets foretold would lead the way to the seven-year countdown before the return of Jesus Christ to earth. The big question is, will you be here during this seven-year countdown? Will you be here during the time of the Tribulation when the Antichrist and the False Prophet are in charge for a time? Will you be here when the world is plagued by mankind's darkest days?

It may come as a surprise to you, but the decision concerning your presence during this last seven-year period in history is entirely up to you.

God's Word tells us that there will be one generation of believers who will never know death. These believers will be removed from the earth before the Great

Tribulation—before that period of the most ghastly pestilence, bloodshed, and starvation the world has ever known. . . .

According to all the Scriptures we are told that the place He is preparing for us will be utterly fantastic. Eternal life will surpass the greatest pleasures we have known on earth. . . .

. . . [I]n eternity we are going to recognize people we knew here on earth. If you're not too satisfied with the face or body you now have, you will have a glorious new body. However, you will be recognizable, just as you will recognize others.

We won't have to eat to be sustained, but the Scripture says we can eat if we want to—and enjoy it. For those who have a weight problem, that sounds rather heavenly in itself. Our eternal bodies will not be subject to aging, or pain, or decay.

Just think how excited a woman can get about a new wardrobe. How much more excited we should be about acquiring a new body!

When the Scripture says, "the dead will be raised imperishable" and "for this perishable must put on the imperishable," it refers to the Christians who have died physically. They will be resurrected to meet Christ in the air.

However, when it says, "this mortal must put on immortality," it is referring to those who are alive at the coming of Christ. That's the mystery, the Rapture or translation. That is the hope that Paul offered for the generation which will be alive when Christ returns.

The Thessalonians were evidently worried about something that might be concerning you also. They wondered if those who had died and would be resurrected when Christ returned might be in some separate part of God's Kingdom. No Christian would want to miss seeing their loved ones throughout eternity.

However, the apostle Paul assured them that God's plan was perfect: those who had "fallen asleep in Jesus," or the Christians who had died, will join the Lord first. Then the Christians who are alive at that time will be caught up "together with them in the clouds" to meet the Lord in the air (I Thessalonians 4:13–18).

What a great reunion that will be!

The world will not know what has happened, because it occurs in an atom of time. . . .

The largest descriptive volume of the Tribulation is found in Revelation 6 through 19. Here is a fascinating revelation about Revelation. In the first five chapters of this book, the church is mentioned thirty times. In fact, in chapters 2 and 3, at the end of each letter to the churches, John says "let him hear what the Spirit saith unto the churches." This is repeated seven times. Then we have the beginning of the description of the Tribulation, and there is not one mention of the churches. The church is conspicuous by its absence. Why? Because the church will be in heaven at that time.

If you are a believer, chapters 4 and 5 of Revelation describe what you will be experiencing in heaven. Talk about mind expansion drugs! We are told we shall expand in understanding and comprehension beyond that of any earthbound genius.

When will the Rapture occur? We don't know. No one knows. But God knows. However, we believe that according to all the signs, we are in the general time of

His coming. "But you, brethren, are not in darkness, that the day should overtake you like a thief" (I Thessalonians 5:4 NASB).

In other words, you shouldn't be surprised when Christ returns to take you with Him. Unfortunately, this does not refer to all believers. We may have to go over to some of them and say, "I told you so, friend." It will be a surprise because they don't study the prophetic word. What an exciting time they may have missed on earth! The study and understanding of prophecy is an experience we pray all Christians will have. . . .

Have you ever found an electric train, or a bedraggled doll that belonged to you as a child and remembered how terribly important it was to you years ago? When we meet Christ face to face we're going to look back on this life and see that the things we thought were important here were like the discarded toys of our childhood.

What a way to live! With optimism, with anticipation, with excitement. We should be living like persons who don't expect to be around much longer.

3. J. Stillson Judah Explains Why Hippies Join the Hare Krishnas, 1974

Chanting and dancing Hare Krishna devotees have become familiar sights on the streets of many of our metropolitan cities. These devotees are witnessing to their faith and trying to spread the message of Krishna Consciousness, but the unfamiliarity of this type of religious ritual to the American people has caused varied reactions in many cities. . . .

The mayors of New York and San Francisco have commended the Movement for its work with youth, who comprise about 85 percent of its membership. These cities and many others have recognized the transformations in thousands of youths who might otherwise be drug addicts and adding further to the increasing crime rates in our cities. Each year the San Francisco Police Department has given its co-operation in blocking traffic on the city streets where the Movement parades its huge image-bearing carts during its famous Ratha-yātrā Festival. Mayor Warren Widener of Berkeley has also expressed his approval of the Hare Krishna Movement for having given a purpose in life to so many alienated youth.

An Alternative Life Style in Communal Living

The Hare Krishna devotees are persevering. They continue in the face of opposition, just as members of other religions have done under similar conditions. Feeling that they have found a purpose and meaning they had been seeking when they left their homes, families, and traditional organized religions, they have separated themselves from the culture of the establishment. They have also separated themselves from the drug scene of the counterculture, in which most of them had been involved. The majority of the devotees live together at the temple where they form

J. Stillson Judah, *Hare Krishna and the Counter Culture* (New York: John Wiley, 1974). Reprinted by permission of the author.

their own alternative society. . . . They now follow a spiritual master who has given them a discipline and teaching that they follow without question. This could not contrast more sharply with the "hang loose" ethic of "doing one's own thing" that had characterized the former countercultural philosophy of many.

When asked what type of person makes the best devotee, one devotee replied:

> The Movement has appealed mainly to youngsters who have led the hectic . . . hippie type of life, divorcing themselves from their families, living through the knocks of life, living on their own under all . . . adverse conditions until they find Krishna Consciousness. It not only provides them with a wonderful faith, but it is also providing them with a community that they can feel a part of, that is divorced from the society within which they lived.

Stability of the Hare Krishna Life Style

Although the counterculture has produced many types of communal living, evidence, including some from Hare Krishna devotees who had lived in communes before, seems to indicate that there is greater stability in the Hare Krishna temples than in other communes. Six reasons can be given. First, there is a unity of purpose, in this case Krishna Consciousness, which is interpreted by a strong charismatic authority like Swāmi Bhaktivedanta. One devotee who had been a member of an unsuccessful commune said:

> Prior to coming to Krishna Consciousness, my wife and I were searching . . . studying all different forms of religion, trying this and that as if in a supermarket. Finding nothing, frustrated, and in despair, we left the country, gave up our jobs, our home, everything we had. We went to British Honduras . . . there were fifteen of us altogether. We formed a commune. We were going to try to search for God in our own ways, but couldn't do it. It was evident after a couple of weeks. Everybody was doing his own thing—into sense gratification. Once in a while we'd try meditating on the impersonal aspect of the supreme which got us simply nowhere. A few tried *yoga* . . . all in all nothing was accomplished. I was into drugs, heavy into alcohol, and after a few weeks everybody started leaving, until after four months the only ones left in the jungle was my family and I. It dawned on me that I needed a spiritual master, because I wasn't going to make it on my own . . . So we gave up our land and everything we owned . . . I had just enough to make it here to this temple . . . and it changed my life so much.

Second, there is a common discipline. This is a discipline that requires those living in the temples to concentrate on Krishna with all their thoughts and actions during their waking hours; its importance can be seen in the preceding quotation. The process is designed to strengthen faith in Krishna and in an entire way of living. Devotees are continually increasing their faith by reading about Krishna and discussing him with others in the temple, by reciting the *mahāmantra* to themselves, by listening to taped lectures of their spiritual master, by witnessing to their faith on the streets in their *kīrtans,* and by preaching his message to all who will listen.

Third, there is a similarity in age and background. All devotees interviewed have shown some sympathy with countercultural ideas; they are all antiestablishment to varying measures. Although there are exceptions, similarity in ages has often been a factor in closer fellowship. . . .

Fourth, there is a common ritual that offers the possibility of religious experience, as we shall later see. Together with the rest of the discipline, this ritual validates and internalizes their philosophy, culture, and way of life.

Fifth, its business enterprises offer the Movement a financial stability that further ensures its continuation.

Sixth, the Movement offers under one discipline, authority, and purpose a variety of alternative life styles. One may live in the outside world and carry on a business, profession, or trade for Krishna. Or he may devote his full time to the religious life associated with just the temple, while having the secure feeling that Krishna will take care of him. The latter alternative is especially attractive to those who have found fault with the establishment's principle of the competitive life. . . .

. . . [T]he devotees follow definite rules concerning who is accepted to live in the temple.

First, only those who are seriously interested in developing Krishna Consciousness are welcomed. This excludes those who have no intention of following the minimum rules of the discipline, such as those who seek only to find shelter and food.

Second, the devotees give counsel to hippies, or others, who are on drugs. They invite them to chant the *mahāmantra* and follow the regulative rules as a way to drug release. They will not allow them to live in the temple while continuing the use of narcotics, however. I remember the example of an obviously stoned hippie who visited the Berkeley temple. He was too loaded to do anything but sit in the corner during the service. Although invited to return and to chant, he was not permitted to stay the night, and I finally drove him to a drug care hostel in Oakland. The autobiographical and statistical information later introduced confirms that chanting and following the regulative rules have given release from drugs in many cases.

Third, although former homosexuals may be found among the membership of the Society, their life style is strictly forbidden. This includes transvestites. The case of "Winifred" is an example. When I first met him he told me his story. It had included the use of drugs, being busted, a brief incarceration at Santa Rita Prison, and trying to get along in society dressed as a woman. Dissatisfied, frustrated, and failing in a suicide attempt, he had sought entry into the Hare Krishna temple as a woman. He was refused, since female and male devotees' sleeping quarters are kept strictly separate, but was advised to return to a male role. After a short period the change was made. The last time I saw him, he had a shaven head and was wearing Vaishnava male attire. For a time he succeeded in making the change and finding his place in the Society.

The Alternative Hindu Culture of the Society

These devotees have protested against the American mode of the establishment in definite ways. Having rejected it, they have found the answers they had been seeking in a form of Hindu religion and culture. The change has been radical, and their spiritual master has been their interpreter.

Most of them wear Hindu style clothing. Although some married devotees who have secular positions do not follow this practice, I have yet to see an exception among the youthful followers of Krishna living in the temples. The unmarried men wear flowing saffron colored cloths (*dhoties*), which distinguish them from the yellow-robed married devotees. The women follow similar patterns of dress by wearing *sāris.*

The men generally shave their heads except for a slender tuft of hair (*śikhā*), which denotes that they have surrendered themselves to the spiritual master. Each day upon arising they ornament themselves with *tilaka,* a wet mixture of clay that they paint on their faces and on eleven other places of their bodies. This is done for "sanctification and protection." These markings denote that they are Vaishnavas and that their bodies are temples of Vishnu, their Supreme Lord. . . . Conformity is important, if not an absolute requirement.

After following the discipline carefully for six months or longer, the new convert becomes eligible for initiation when the spiritual master comes to the area. Devotees living in temples that he does not have time to visit will travel to the closest place where he is staying. When Swāmi Bhaktivedanta accepts a devotee, he gives him a Sanskrit name, and accepts the responsibility of guiding him to Krishna Consciousness. The student on his part is expected to take the spiritual master's orders as his own "life and soul," and to honor him as he would God, since he is to be considered as God's representative. . . .

After one or two years spent in the first and celibate student stage (*brahma-chārī*), the devotee is allowed to marry and become a householder (*grihastha*). Marriage has only two purposes in the Society: to raise Krishna Conscious children, and to help one another to deepen Krishna Consciousness. A married man generally moves out of the temple with his wife to occupy a separate dwelling. Marriage is by arrangement rather than by courtship. . . .

The Society has its own marriage ceremony, which is a sacrament of the faith. Instead of primarily denoting a relationship between husband and wife, it signifies the surrender of both parties to Krishna. It teaches that one can only really love another if he or she loves Krishna first, by no matter what name one designates the deity. But since Krishna must be regarded as the Supreme Personality of Godhead, a good part of the ceremony consists in chanting, dancing, and giving devotion to Krishna.

4. David Chidester Traces the People's Temple to Its Mass Suicide in Guyana (1978), 1988

On November 18, 1978, a sudden outburst of violence occurred in Guyana that crystallized in the American media and popular imagination as the Jonestown event. A congressional delegation was ambushed at the Port Kaituma airstrip leaving five dead and nine wounded; a mother and three children died by having their throats cut at the Lamaha Gardens apartment headquarters of the Peoples Temple; and 914 residents of the Peoples Temple Agricultural Project, Jonestown, Guyana, died in a mass murder-suicide. The Jonestown event became an emblem of horror and tragedy, a single image of madness and deception, a curious mixture of religion, politics, and violence that defied imagination. . . .

David Chidester, *Salvation and Suicide* (Bloomington, Ind.: Indiana University Press, 1988).

James Warren Jones was born May 13, 1931, in the small midwestern town of Lynn, Indiana, a town whose major industry was casket making, in a region of the country divided by racial segregation and imbued with Christian fundamentalism. . . .

[As a teenager and student, Jones rebelled against the conventions of his environment by becoming a socialist and an advocate for racial integration. But he retained an ardent Christian faith.]

The Methodist social creed of 1952, dedicated among other things to the civil rights of all racial groups, provided an impetus for Jones to accept a position as student pastor at Somerset Methodist Church. There he sponsored a youth center for "children of all faiths." By 1953 Jones began to recognize the potential in Pentecostal-style, evangelical faith healing for attracting crowds, raising money, and serving as a pretext for integrating churches. . . .

Beginning in the late 1950s, Jones was attracted to the Peace Mission movement of Father Divine, which provided an exemplary model of the marriage of religion and racial equality. Father Divine's Peace Mission emerged from the depression of the 1930s to provide social welfare programs, food, and housing for the poor, an organized campaign for racial equality, and a religious movement revolving around the leadership of the enigmatic M. J. Divine, who claimed to be a living, embodied god. In tones that would later be echoed in the sermons of Jim Jones, Father Divine announced, "Because your god would not feed the people, I came and I am feeding them. Because your god kept such as you segregated and discriminated, I came and I am unifying all nations together." While he was struggling to build an interracial ministry in Indianapolis, Jim Jones first visited the Peace Mission headquarters in Philadelphia in 1956. Discovering a successful interracial, communal, supportive environment in the Peace Mission, Jones declared at a banquet speech on a return visit in 1958, "I came and saw the reality of things I had known for years." Based on the model of Father Divine's Peace Mission, Jones established soup kitchens, a free grocery store, the distribution of free clothing, and other community services in Indianapolis under the auspices of the Peoples Temple Full Gospel Church. Eventually, Jones would attempt more than simply an imitation of the communal, social service oriented example set by the Peace Mission; he would claim the mantle of Father Divine as a living god in a body. . . .

. . . During 1964 assistant ministers Ross Case, Jack Beam, and Archie Ijames moved to northern California; in July of the following year Jones and perhaps as many as 140 of his followers moved to the town of Ukiah in the Redwood Valley area above San Francisco. Jones would later claim that they moved to Ukiah because it was the farthest they could get from Indianapolis without falling into the ocean. The motive of avoiding the devastation of an imminent nuclear war, however, was definitely present, and it remained a prominent theme in the subsequent sermons of Jim Jones as his ministry became based in California. . . .

During the rapid expansion of the movement in the early 1970s the Peoples Temple encountered a number of problems. One event that may not have seemed problematic at the time, but which eventually became a pivotal issue in the destruction of the movement, was the birth to Grace Stoen, wife of Jones's legal advisor Timothy Stoen, of the child John Victor Stoen on January 25, 1972. The child's birth certificate may have listed Timothy Stoen as father, but on February 6, 1972, Stoen signed a document specifying that in April of the previous year he had entreated his beloved pastor, James W. Jones, to sire a child by his wife. This document, countersigned by Marceline Jones, had Timothy Stoen state: "I wanted my child to be fathered, if not by me, by the most compassionate, honest, and courageous human being the world contains." It was apparently customary during this period of the Peoples Temple's history for members to sign a variety of incriminating, obligatory documents in order to seal their loyalty to the movement. Five years later this particular document would be at the center of a custody dispute that would act as a catalyst in the destruction of the Peoples Temple.

A more immediate source of concern during the early 1970s, however, was the first negative media coverage the Peoples Temple received through a series of articles in the *San Francisco Examiner* by Reverend Lester Kinsolving. Beginning September 17, 1972, the Kinsolving articles attacked Jones's messianic pretensions, his claims to have raised forty-three people from the dead, and began to explore the authoritarian structure of the Peoples Temple. Originally planned as a series of eight articles, the Kinsolving series was stopped after four had appeared, apparently through the lobbying efforts of the Peoples Temple at the *Examiner* offices. . . .

During the early 1970s the Peoples Temple membership rose to between three thousand and five thousand members; the Temple claimed a total membership of twenty thousand, which would have made it one of the largest Protestant congregations in America; and Timothy Stoen has estimated that during this period as many as one hundred thousand people came to hear the sermons of Jim Jones. In addition to this expanding religious ministry, Jones became increasingly involved in local San Francisco politics. Placing Temple support behind the successful mayoral candidacy of George Moscone in 1975, Jones was rewarded by being appointed to the San Francisco Housing Authority in October 1976, and he soon became chairman. Social service programs of the Peoples Temple attracted considerable attention during this period, and Jones was acknowledged for his ostensibly humanitarian work by a number of awards. . . .

Having resolved in October 1973 to establish a Peoples Temple mission in the South American country of Guyana, Jim Jones visited Guyana two months later to open negotiations for the lease of twenty-seven thousand acres in the Matthew Ridge area, near the Venezuelan border. . . .

By 1975 about fifty members of the Peoples Temple were stationed in Jonestown, clearing the dense jungle, building houses, and carving out a space in the wilderness for the Peoples Temple Agricultural Project. The American embassy in Guyana was impressed by these American pioneers; they were well organized, adequately financed, and dedicated to creating a viable community in the jungle. The Peoples Temple was not the only religious movement of American origin working to establish a place in Guyana. A small group that called itself The East, under the leadership of former civil rights activist Les Campbell, who took the name Jitu Weusi, lived about fifty miles from Georgetown; Hashabah Yisrael, a group started by two former New York City school teachers, had as many as one hundred members by 1977 living in five homes and on a fifty acre farm outside Georgetown; and a large, influential movement, the House of Israel, under the leadership of civil rights activist and fugitive from American justice David Hill, who adopted the name Rabbi Edward Emmanuel Washington, claimed as many as seven thousand members owing their allegiance to Rabbi Washington and Prime Minister Burnham. Like the House of Israel, the Peoples Temple appeared in

Guyana as a black liberation movement, dedicated to a socialist, communal program and loyal to the Burnham government. In his sermons Jim Jones referred to Guyana as the "Promised Land" where blessed places were being prepared for the Peoples Temple's exodus from America.

Exodus to Guyana became an increasingly attractive option for the Peoples Temple during 1977, as journalists Marshall Kilduff and Phil Tracy prepared to publish an exposé on the movement in *New West* magazine. Based on allegations by former members, including Grace Stoen, who defected in July 1976, and some of the members who had defected in 1973, the article finally appeared in the August 1, 1977, issue of *New West*. It suggested that the Peoples Temple should be investigated for certain financial misdealings, coercive practices, alleged beatings of members, and questionable involvement in local San Francisco politics. . . .

In May 1977 there were still only about fifty members of the Peoples Temple in Jonestown; but by September nearly one thousand had been transplanted from California to the jungles of Guyana. Accommodating such a sudden influx of residents placed a severe strain on the limited facilities of Jonestown, but through disciplined hard work, the community managed to sustain itself and create an impressive communal village in the jungle. . . . Jonestown was designed as a utopian heaven on earth, a socialist paradise in the jungle where racism, sexism, ageism, and classism would be eliminated, and people who had been deprived, discriminated against, and persecuted in America could live in peace and freedom. Obviously, no community could live up to the glowing public statements and progress reports that emanated from Jonestown during the last eighteen months of its existence. But most of the residents seemed happy with their new life in the Peoples Temple Agricultural Project in Guyana.

Beginning in September 1977, the Jonestown community came under direct attack from former members. . . . During 1978 the Stoens and other defectors, who formed the Committee of Concerned Relatives, pursued custody cases against the Peoples Temple, issued a statement on "Human Rights Violations" at Jonestown, circulated an affidavit of former member Deborah Blakey that described rehearsals for mass suicide at Jonestown, and lobbied in Congress for an official investigation of the Jonestown community. In their attacks on Jonestown the Concerned Relatives depicted the community as a concentration camp, patrolled by armed guards with automatic weapons and even a bazooka, and as a prison in which residents were subject to brainwashing, coercion, forced labor, food and sleep deprivation, torturous punishments, and denial of any contact with the outside world. The Concerned Relatives sought congressional assistance in forcing Jones to meet their demands for a governmental investigation of Jonestown, around-the-clock inspection of the community, and repatriation of their relatives. If he refused to abide by those demands, the Concerned Relatives insisted that concerted steps be taken by the United States and Guyanese governments to expel Jim Jones from Guyana.

Congressman Leo Ryan, representing the San Mateo district of northern California, took up the challenge of mounting an official congressional investigation of Jonestown. The visit of Ryan, reporters, and relatives, entering Jonestown on November 17, 1978, for an inspection of the facilities, interviews with residents, and an assessment of the charges against the community, ended in disaster. When the delegation tried to take fourteen dissatisfied residents back to America the following day, it was ambushed by the Jonestown security force. Ryan, one of the defectors, and three newsmen were killed. Even more shocking than those murders, however, was the mass murder-suicide of the entire Jonestown community, beginning about 6:00 P.M. on November 18, 1978, in which Jonestown was transformed into a region of death. All life was extinguished: dogs, fish, farm animals, the community's pet chimpanzee Mr. Muggs, and 914 men, women, and children.

5. Starhawk Advocates Witchcraft, 1979

Writers, teachers, nurses, computer programmers, artists, lawyers, poets, plumbers, and auto mechanics—women and men from many backgrounds come together to celebrate the mysteries of the Triple Goddess of birth, love, and death, and of her Consort, the Hunter, who is Lord of the Dance of life. The religion they practice is called *Witchcraft.*

Witchcraft is a word that frightens many people and confuses many others. In the popular imagination, Witches are ugly old hags riding broomsticks, or evil Satanists performing obscene rites. Modern Witches are thought to be members of a kooky cult, primarily concerned with cursing enemies by jabbing wax images with pins, and lacking the depth, the dignity and seriousness of purpose of a true religion.

But Witchcraft is a religion, perhaps the oldest religion extant in the West. Its origins go back before Christianity, Judaism, Islam—before Buddhism and Hinduism, as well, and it is very different from all the so-called great religions. The Old Religion, as we call it, is closer in spirit to Native American traditions or to the shamanism of the Arctic. It is not based on dogma or a set of beliefs, nor on scriptures or a sacred book revealed by a great man. Witchcraft takes its teachings from nature, and reads inspiration in the movements of the sun, moon, and stars, the flight of birds, the slow growth of trees, and the cycles of the seasons.

According to our legends, Witchcraft began more than 35 thousand years ago, when the temperature of Europe began to drop and the great sheets of ice crept slowly south in their last advance. Across the rich tundra, teeming with animal life, small groups of hunters followed the free-running reindeer and the thundering bison. They were armed with only the most primitive of weapons, but some among the clans were gifted, could "call" the herds to a cliffside or a pit, where a few beasts, in willing sacrifice, would let themselves be trapped. These gifted shamans could attune themselves to the spirits of the herds, and in so doing they became aware of the pulsating rhythm that infuses all life, the dance of the double spiral, of whirling into being, and whirling out again. They did not phrase this insight intellectually, but in images: the Mother Goddess, the birthgiver, who brings into existence all life; and the Horned God, hunter and hunted, who eternally passes through the gates of death that new life may go on.

Male shamans dressed in skins and horns in identification with the God and the herds; but female priestesses presided naked, embodying the fertility of the Goddess. Life and death were a continuous stream; the dead were buried as if sleeping in a womb, surrounded by their tools and ornaments, so that they might awaken to a new life. . . .

The primary symbol for "That-Which-Cannot-Be-Told" is the Goddess. The Goddess has infinite aspects and thousands of names—She is the reality behind many metaphors. She *is* reality, the manifest deity, omnipresent in all of life, in each of us. The Goddess is not separate from the world—She *is* the world, and all things in it: moon, sun, earth, star, stone, seed, flowing river, wind, wave, leaf and branch, bud and blossom, fang and claw, woman and man. In Witchcraft, flesh and spirit are one.

. . . Goddess religion is unimaginably old, but contemporary Witchcraft could just as accurately be called the New Religion. The Craft, today, is undergoing more than a revival, it is experiencing a renaissance, a re-creation. Women are spurring this renewal, and actively reawakening the Goddess, the image of "the legitimacy and beneficence of female power." . . .

The importance of the Goddess symbol for women cannot be overstressed. The image of the Goddess inspires women to see ourselves as divine, our bodies as sacred, the changing phases of our lives as holy, our aggression as healthy, our anger as purifying, and our power to nurture and create, but also to limit and destroy when necessary, as the very force that sustains all life. Through the Goddess, we can discover our strength, enlighten our minds, own our bodies, and celebrate our emotions. We can move beyond narrow, constricting roles and become whole.

The Goddess is also important for men. The oppression of men in Father God-ruled patriarchy is perhaps less obvious but no less tragic than that of women. Men are encouraged to identify with a model no human being can successfully emulate: to be minirulers of narrow universes. They are internally split, into a "spiritual" self that is supposed to conquer their baser animal and emotional natures. They are at war with themselves: in the West, to "conquer" sin; in the East, to "conquer" desire or ego. Few escape from these wars undamaged. . . .

Magic is the craft of Witchcraft, and few things are at once so appealing, so frightening, and so misunderstood. To work magic is to weave the unseen forces into form; to soar beyond sight; to explore the uncharted dream realm of the hidden reality; to infuse life with color, motion, and strange scents that intoxicate; to leap beyond imagination into that space between the worlds where fantasy becomes real; to be at once animal and god. Magic is the craft of shaping, the craft of the wise, exhilarating, dangerous—the ultimate adventure.

The power of magic should not be underestimated. It works, often in ways that are unexpected and difficult to control. But neither should the power of magic be overestimated. It does not work simply, or effortlessly; it does not confer omnipotence. "The art of changing consciousness at will" is a demanding one, requiring a long and disciplined apprenticeship. Merely waving a wand, lighting a candle, or crooning a rhymed incantation do nothing in and of themselves. But when the force of a trained awareness is behind them, they are far more than empty gestures.

Learning to work magic is a process of neurological repatterning, of changing the way we use our brains. So, for that matter, is learning to play the piano—both processes involve the development of new pathways for neurons to follow, both require practice and take time, and both, when mastered, can be emotional and spiritual channels for great beauty. Magic requires first the development and then the integration of right-hemisphere, spatial, intuitive, holistic, patterning awareness. It opens the gates between the unconscious and the conscious mind, between the starlight and flashlight vision. In so doing, it deeply influences an individual's growth, creativity, and personality.

The language of the old belief, the language of magic, is expressed in symbols and images. Images bridge the gap between the verbal and nonverbal modes of awareness; they allow the two sides of the brain to communicate, arousing the emotions as well as the intellect. Poetry, itself a form of magic, is imagic speech. Spells and charms worked by Witches are truly concrete poetry.

A spell is a symbolic act done in an altered state of consciousness, in order to cause a desired change. To cast a spell is to project energy through a symbol. But the symbols are too often mistaken for the spell. "Burn a green candle to attract money," we are told. The candle itself, however, does nothing—it is merely a lens, an object of focus, a mnemonic device, the "thing" that embodies our idea. Props may be useful, but it is the mind that works magic.

Particular objects, shapes, colors, scents, and images do work better than others to embody particular ideas. Correspondences between colors, planets, metals, numbers, plants, and minerals make up a great body of magical lore. . . . But the most powerful spells are often improvised, out of materials that feel right or that simply happen to come to hand. . . .

Sensing the energy climate is a matter of intuition and experience. Some Witches make a detailed study of astrology in an effort to plan their magical workings at the optimum times. Personally, I prefer simply to work when I feel the time is right. Of all the planets, the moon's influence on subtle energies is the strongest. Subtle power increases as the moon waxes, so the time of the waxing moon is best for spells involving growth or increase, such as money spells. The power peaks when the moon is full, and that is the best time for workings of culmination and love. During the waning moon, power subsides and turns inward: the waning period is used for banishing, binding, and discovering hidden secrets.

Spells can be adjusted to fit the time. For example, if you are obsessed with the need to do a money spell on the waning moon, focus on banishing poverty. A friend of mine whose business had been limping along for two years did precisely that and realized soon afterward that most of his problems stemmed from his partner's miscalculations and lack of management. At the same time, his partner decided to quit. The waning moon had done its work. By the next full moon, the business had begun to turn around.

6. Carol Christ Is Initiated into Goddess Worship, 1987

In European history, relationship with the Goddesses was severed by the forced closing and officially sanctioned razing of the Goddess temples during the reign of Theodosius I (known as "the Great") between 379 and 395 C.E., and by the subsequent persecution and murder of those who continued to follow ancient practices in Christianized Europe.

Carol Christ, "Initiation into the Symbols of the Goddesses," *Journal of Feminist Studies in Religion* 3 (Spring 1987): 57–66. Reprinted by permission of the author.

Many of us today whose contemporary experiences impel us "in search of Her" . . . know neither the prayers, the rituals, the places, nor the stories as preserved in an ongoing community. Yet we can piece together fragments of stories, rituals, and prayers, and learn the places, from the surviving archaeological and historical records, from the fragments of pre-Christian images, symbols, and rituals which have survived in Christianity. In addition we can trust our own desires, and listen for the echoes of the still resounding voices of ancestors, of the Goddesses.

My initiation into the symbols and rituals of the Goddesses began a number of years ago when my own experiences of the silencing of the voice of my experience and perception within patriarchal religious and academic structures led me to desire female God-language which would validate me. In the early 1970s this longing became so powerful that I could no longer participate in the Christian worship of Father and Son that had sustained me through much of my life. Whenever I set foot in church, I would find myself developing headaches, neck and shoulder aches, and stomachaches, as the enormity of the power of my exclusion from Christian worship sunk deeply into my bones.

Some years later . . . I found myself engaged in a dialogue with God inspired by [Elie] Wiesel's story of God and Man changing places, the epilogue to *The Town beyond the Wall*. As I retold Wiesel's story from a woman's point of view, I changed places with God and began to reproach him for allowing women's voices to be silenced in history, and in churches and synagogues called his. I asked him why he hadn't sent a messiah or at least a prophet to relieve our suffering, our beatings, our rape. My energy spent, I fell silent in my room. After a bit, I heard, what I described as a "still small voice" saying, "In God is a woman like yourself. She shares your suffering. She too has had her power of naming stolen from her. First she was called an idol of the Canaanites, and then she ceased to exist as God." In retrospect, I would name that night as the beginning of my initiation into the Goddess. At that time I knew almost nothing of her history, and I did not know that many other women were experiencing similar revelations. Though I was not at that time engaging in a "spiritual practice," my struggles to understand the meaning of Wiesel's stories for myself and for God could be viewed as a kind of spiritual discipline. Wiesel could be viewed as my "teacher," even though he probably would not have recognized or validated the words that came to me in that night. (I think of [Saint] Teresa telling her visions to her confessor, and writing only of those he approved.)

In the next several years I met Starhawk, Z Budapest, Hallie Iglehart, and others. I learned that the Goddess had made her presence felt in their lives as well. In the succeeding years, I began to read and teach about the history of the Goddesses and also began creating and participating in rituals that celebrated the Goddess in her connection to the cycles of the moon and the seasons. . . . I went to Greece and have been going back ever since: without my choosing them, the Greek Goddesses have chosen me. . . .

. . . Because coming to terms with my mother and understanding the bonds I shared with women had been an important part of my feminist journey, I had done some research on the Eleusinian mysteries and had created and celebrated a spring equinox ritual focused on Demeter and Persephone. When we arrived at Eleusis, I was overwhelmed with sadness, for the site is devastated and scarcely visited. The words, "so much has been lost, so much has been destroyed," echoed in my mind.

Yet when we drew our hands together in a circle on the ruins of the telesterion, the site where the initiations had been performed, I felt an enormous surging of energy: it was as if the place were waiting for us to come to sanctify it again, to draw up its energies for ourselves, for our work for women. In the five years I have been visiting Eleusis, I have felt my dedication to the Goddess confirmed as I have participated with other women in rituals in which we told stories about our mothers and daughters, and re-enacted the mysteries of separation and reunion, life and death, in relation to Demeter and Persephone.

On Lesbos, the Greek island where I have spent much time, there is an ancient temple to Aphrodite at Mesa (which means Inside), in the marshy ground at the mouth of a large womblike bay. There my initiation continued. . . . Though Aphrodite has been trivialized as Goddess of Love and Beauty, she comes from the prehistoric Goddesses of life, death, and renewal, of which sexuality is a powerful manifestation.

In my class at the Aegean Women's Studies Institute, we read the chapter on Aphrodite from Downing's *The Goddess*. Downing wrote of Aphrodite as Goddess of transformation, noting that her temples often stood in the marshy ground where sea and dry land meet, or on cliffs where mists rise from the sea. She is often imaged rising from the sea on a shell, and she is known as the golden one because she prefers the sunlight. Downing also mentioned Aphrodite's laughter. Inspired by Downing and Aphrodite, the class shared stories of sexual transformation, of life and death. One of the other women and I spoke of going to Aphrodite's temple to reclaim the sexuality we each had lost touch with after the endings of particularly powerful love affairs. The tension built within each of us until we knew that we would visit the temple. While wandering around town agitatedly before the time we were to meet, I noticed a white gauze dress with golden threads and golden shawl I had admired the night before. I would go to Aphrodite's temple in white, symbolizing my desire to be initiated into her mysteries. The golden shawl would honor her goldenness and my own. When I met my friend she too was wearing a white dress. We bedecked ourselves in golden bronze jewelry from our Greek friend's tourist shop, found another golden shawl, bought a handmade pottery pitcher and bowl, white with rose and indigo flowers. We stopped to buy red wine and golden retsina, golden biscuit cookies, milk and honey, and yogurt. On impulse we each picked out a pair of double shells which became a central symbol in our ritual.

The temple is at the far end of a farm road. No sign marks it. It is deserted. The temple is small, and though none of its columns still stand, its grey stone floor is clearly exposed, and fragments of columns are strewn about the site. Two trees grow at the center of the temple. We scrambled over a barbed-wire fence and found ourselves standing amidst thorns in what must have been the temple's forecourt. We filled our pitcher with red wine and the bowl with water. Ready to enter the temple, we were excited and apprehensive. As we paused at the threshold, I poured out the water and wine. All of a sudden I heard what I can only describe as the laughter of Aphrodite. The sound was clear and vivid. I heard Aphrodite saying through her golden laughter, "Who ever told you you could know sexual ecstasy without pain?" And then she began to laugh again, saying, "What can you do but laugh?" I laughed with her. When I looked at my friend, I knew that she had heard the laughter too.

When we stepped into the temple we saw her everywhere. We found womblike spirals and vaginal roses carved in stone. We began to make an altar on one of the broken columns, but I felt myself drawn to the space between the two trees, at the center of the temple. I went to the spot and sat between the trees opening my body to the midday sun. I anointed myself with milk and honey and poured milk and honey into my shells. The sun warmed and transformed my body. Alone with the Goddess in her sacred space, I felt myself opening, becoming whole. I became Aphrodite. Later my friend performed her own ritual in the sacred space, and then we sat together beneath the trees, drinking retsina, eating milk and honey from our shells, and sharing stories. When we left the temple, we each filled one of our shells with milk and honey, offered it to Aphrodite and poured out a libation of retsina.

My initiation deepens each time I visit the sacred spaces. During one of the rituals at Eleusis, I was profoundly challenged when I expressed my desire to give birth to a daughter. Completely unexpectedly one of the women in the group, a Jungian analyst who had been deeply influenced by my work, but whom I had just met, stepped into the center of the circle, looked me in the eyes, and said, "I don't know whether or not you will ever have a physical daughter, but you have many spiritual daughters, and I don't think you're taking responsibility for that." I felt as if I had been addressed by Demeter.

7. Mary Ann Flaherty Sympathizes with Planet Earth Under the Threat of War, 1994

Under my feet, the muffled crunch of fall's half-rotten leaves played the rhythm for my song of celebration. Homework and parents behind, I approached the familiar rise a half-mile down the wooded path from our house, where three tall trees had fallen so as to form a near perfect triangle. I swung a leg over one of the logs, stopped to wrap my arms around the cool ridges of the knotty, rounded beam, and hugged my strong and enduring companion. With my cheek pressed to the skin of the log, I could smell its breath—damp, sweet, enticing. As I rolled off the log into the bed of leaves below, my imagination had already begun to swirl. Here, in my wooded sanctuary, I was free to read, write, draw, and dream, until the clanging of the distant dinner bell bade me back to my other life.

For many of us, childhood was a time of intimacy with our creative source. Creative expression and exploration were as natural as breathing. In times of trouble or joy, we had access to power—the power to create—a fantasy, a drawing, a song, a mudpie. We could express our voices, if only in solitude. Creating and living were one and the same. We breathed in the world and breathed out our response. . . .

. . . [Now, as adults do] we give voice to our yearnings for creative expression or do we muzzle them for fear of rejection? When we have touched the Earth, our home, and breathed with it, yelled into the wind and listened in silence to its rhythms, the choice becomes easier and more compelling.

When the war in the Persian Gulf began in January of 1991, on the event of my fifth wedding anniversary, I was overcome with hopelessness. Having marched in

Mary Ann Flaherty, "Creation's Heartbeat," *Creation Spirituality* 10 (Spring 1994): 20–23.

Washington in several Vietnam war protests twenty years ago, I had held onto the possibility of seeing the world at peace. The voice of the news reporter announcing that the United States, the country I call home, had begun dropping bombs on Iraq, dropped an iron curtain between my dream for peace and its fulfillment. The swiftness and ease with which the destruction was wrought and my feeling of powerlessness made a mockery of my conviction in the power of creativity. It was hard to touch anything life-giving in myself or in anybody else. . . .

As in past times of crisis, I found myself drawn to the woods. Here, I lay on brown hillsides and waded in the icy stream. I sat on cold rocks and studied silver fish darting through crystal currents. I knelt on the damp grass and marveled at tiny, sprouting snowdrops. I spent hours absorbing the Earth's pulse—vibrant, rhythmic, dependable—and breathing in its healing presence. The Earth and I listened to each other.

In this communion of quiet beauty, I imagine that I can hear the shrieks and screams of death as U.S. bombs fall on creatures of all sizes and species, on land and in the sea and I am angry. I am angry at the unbearable unfair contrast of my life at that moment and the lives of those whose screams I hear. I am angry at the monumental injustice of the slaughter of so many voiceless creatures. I am angry at the rape of the Earth which so faithfully nurtures me. I am angry to be a member of the species that is wreaking such havoc, angry at feeling so helpless against the vast machinery of war. And I am angry that the fate of the Earth and all its species hangs on the choices of the very creatures who kill. At this moment, it is hard to believe that creation, not destruction, will be chosen, and I am afraid.

When I was young, the Earth spoke to me. I heard its power in ocean waves, in massive mountains, in sculpted canyons and dense forests, and I believed that the Earth was immortal, invincible, and always available for my enjoyment. Today I hear a different message from the Earth. Lying at eye level with new born snowdrops and shimmering, diamond dewdrops, I hear of Earth's fragility. The spider's web, the ripples from a stone thrown in the pond, and the ephemeral colors of the rainbow teach me that Creation is vulnerable. The uncertainty of my future, the sudden death of tens of thousands of unsuspecting Iraqis, and my powerlessness to stop the bulldozing destruction of the U.S. war machine speak to me of human fragility. The Earth and I are bound by our vulnerability to human choices.

I hear the Earth calling me to choose life; to choose Creation; to acknowledge my connection to this planet that sustains me. I want to choose for survival and for beauty. I want to return the gift of life to my parent, the Earth. If I do not so choose I am an ungrateful child. . . .

Give me strength again, sustainer Earth, that I might choose wisely. Let me know with every cell in my body, of our connection so that I might resist the choices of destruction.

You call me to a muddy creek in summer and invite me to play. I smear the dripping mud on arms, legs, chest, and face. I am caressing your skin and I remember. I rub crushed grittiness across my face and I remember rocks grinding rocks. Cool wetness seeps into my pores and I remember hydrogen atoms connecting with oxygen atoms for the first time. The odor I inhale awakens every cell to ancient memories of strength, for this lifegiving mud holds the molecules of universal birthings— minerals, bacteria, protoplasm—all the ancient ones and I now share the story.

Today this fertile, oozing slime will become the stuff of my Creation story. I will make a bowl or a castle or a snake, not only because it is fun, but because I must enact my union with the creating Earth. I must remember the beat:

> Ebb, flow—the rhythms of Creation
> Summer, fall, winter, spring—the process of Creation
> Life, death, decay, rebirth—the cycles of Creation
> Fertility, harvest, abundance—the fruits of Creation
> Blood, cells, heartbeat—the energy of Creation
> Iron molecules existing in the stars before the birth of planet Earth now pulse
> through my hemoglobin—the continuity of Creation

The Earth and I create to the beat of the same drum and I am strengthened. Yes, I will rise up from the mud and answer the call to create a future for the Earth and all its wondrous creatures.

 E S S A Y S

In this chapter and the next there is a certain amount of overlap between documents and essays because the movements involve people still alive, reflecting on their own experiences. Among the interpretive problems arising from the religious counterculture are the following: who is attracted to these new movements, why, and what causes some to stay while others move on restlessly in search of something new? In the first essay, Ted Mann of York University, Toronto, applies sociological techniques to analyze the membership of the Rajneesh cult, which originated with an Indian guru but grew rapidly in Germany, Britain, and Canada and at Rajneeshpuram (Antelope), Oregon. Mann provides a social portrait of the members and goes on to explore their psychological motivations—an exercise that religious historians have traditionally found difficult. Another central problem for the study of countercultural religions is the degree to which they are either continuous with the American past or unique to the new conditions and crises of affluent America in recent decades. In the second essay, J. Gordon Melton of the University of California, Santa Barbara, shows that the "New Age" religious movement of the 1980s had links to nineteenth- and early-twentieth-century spiritualism and theosophy despite such new characteristics as "channeling" and the use of crystals. New Age religiosity was so diverse, decentralized, and ephemeral that it was always difficult to define, but Melton isolates its central characteristics to show how they shaped the movement and how, after its demise, they continue to influence religious Americans who were never directly involved.

Social Psychology of the Rajneesh Cult

TED MANN

During a bus trip at the Oregon commune I was chatting rather vivaciously with an American sannyasin in his thirties whom I had just met. Passing by sannyasins on the road, our attention became directed to the strange assortment of people there and on the bus. He suddenly turned to me, remarking, "All the misfits from around the world are gathered together here." I had to agree. This sannyasin didn't *appear* to be a misfit, but his work, doing past life regressions, is hardly a conventional

Ted Mann, "The Crazies: Who Follows Rajneesh and Why," in *The Rajneesh Papers: Studies in a New Religious Movement* (Delhi: Motilal Banarsidass, 1993), 17–46.

occupation. Quite a few others in sight did not appear misfits, but judging from mannerisms, conversation, and some objective evidence, they were loners; outside the commune setting they often would not "fit in."

My research judgement suggested most members of the Oregon commune and the great majority of Rajneesh's followers were socially marginal, i.e. they lived and functioned on the periphery of our society's major institutions. They were not strongly affiliated with established organizations, either professional or occupational, or with unions, traditional religions, political parties, nor with accepted voluntary associations or conventional family groupings. . . .

A couple of generalizations from author Sally Belfrage who visited Poona around 1980 and briefly became a sannyasin, expand on the above. She says the Rajneeshees are:

> . . . inevitably well-off, if only in the post-hippy flower-child sense of caring little for cash but always able to summon up enough to fly halfway around the world; they have the kind of money "that seems to breed in its owners dissatisfactions requiring extreme measures to put right." [She adds that] "through with radical politics, drugs, communal living, feminism, psychoanalysis, encounter groups, they're seeking still more exotic solutions for problems that are luxuries in the first place. Now it's 'who am I?'"

In effect, Belfrage suggests, and the evidence is plentiful, that a majority of Rajneeshees have had a connection with the counter culture, and many with the human potential or growth movement. British sociologist Mullan adds: "I would argue that the 'average' Rajneeshee is middle class, well educated, professionally qualified . . . divorced at least once, has suffered a 'personal crisis,' has been through mysticism, drugs, politics, feminism and is 'thirtyish'; in short, the counter cultural-ist brought up to date." . . .

The term counter-culture is a sociological abstraction and open to a variety of definitions. I prefer to conceive of it as a rather amorphous grouping of generally urban, middle class youth sharing a sub-culture with a specific value set. This sub-culture favours expressive as against instrumental values and leans towards impulse gratification as against its inhibitions; i.e., patterns normally confined to the lower class. Its members devalue or scorn mechanical and non-creative work and, conversely, highly value an expressive outlook that favours lively or ecstatic type experiences typically gained through LSD, dope, sex and/or meditative states. Life is to be experienced not rationalized, feelings are more important than logic and logical analysis. Harvey Cox, the noted theologian, says the members of the counter culture have a "longing for what the consumer culture cannot provide, a community of love and a capacity to experience things deeply." The counter culture's social posture is basically rebellious, strongly scornful of established bourgeois work, family and money values. In a lecture, Rajneesh once called his followers "the Crazies"—partly a tongue-in-cheek remark, but it also signified that, from a bourgeois and worldly standpoint, their actions seemed to be crazy: they would work for nothing (for the Master) and make no effort (any longer) to become established or accepted in the "straight" world.

Counter cultural signatures were somewhat more predominant in Poona than in Oregon. At Oregon in September 1982, when I visited the commune, long hair and beards—a trademark of the counter culture—predominated. Most of the women, too, had long hair. Perhaps 10% of the males had short hair and no beard. But when

I asked one of these if he didn't feel conspicuous, he replied, "There's been a new ruling by Bhagwan that short hair is now in." Sheela and Arup had short hair, though Rajneesh sported longish hair and a beard. Another objective mark of the counter culture is smoking dope. While not officially approved of, this was common among Rajneeshees, many of whom had smoked dope or tripped acid before becoming sannyasins.

Other eastern religious movements have attracted large numbers of counter culture types. Among these are the 3HO, the Sikh movement, whose followers dress in white, and the Divine Light Mission of Maharaj-ji.

Equally common in the background of Rajneeshees is experience with encounter, primal and Gestalt therapies, the stock in trade of the human potential movement. It is significant that Rajneesh early attracted to Poona leaders or enthusiasts from growth or body therapy centres like Quaesitor in London, England, and Radix in California. The human potential movement participant's interest is in self-realization and self expression. The goal is to achieve an ever greater amount of awareness, creativity, empathy, intuitive insight and the capacity to express one's essence. Of the 13 life stories of Rajneeshees summarized in Mullan's book, 10 had previously investigated one or more human potential therapies. This percentage accords with my observations of the cult's following in four countries.

One noted writer on the human potential movement is John Rowen. He claims that the movement has three main principles: the salience of an intense and profound group experience in which certain break-throughs and insights occur; "the existential experience of being totally alone and totally responsible for oneself; and the ecstatic peak experience where for a (brief) moment the pattern and unity of everything and everybody . . . can be glimpsed."

In the Poona ashram, according to interviews, many sannyasins underwent intense group identifications and/or ecstatic experiences. This occurred either in therapy groups or during active meditations like kundalini, or while dancing in the Music Group. Thus, one sannyasin, commenting on the cathartic effects of the dynamic meditation said, "Bhagwan invented a lovely way to wash away your crazies." Another added, "I can let out just about anything . . . [in the dynamic]. Through it I can make my inner being free of everything." Many full-time ashramites, i.e. those living in the ashram, experienced profound feelings of close identification with the group and with Rajneesh. Such highs functioned to hook sannyasins to the movement, often for years. These ecstasies were seen by many as steps on the way to enlightenment. For growth therapists and habitues of human potential therapies the hazy, mystical notion of enlightenment often functioned as a very powerful carrot. Once enlightened, it was expected that one would live in a state of permanent bliss, or euphoria. Those who had experienced even brief moments of an oceanic merging or other form of mystical fusion were often too easily seduced by hopes of making these states regular and permanent. . . .

. . . In religious affiliation before age 18, 27% reported being Catholic, 30% Protestant and 20% Jewish: 14% had no such affiliation. Gordon, who is a Jew, notes that Jews, who have drifted away from their faith in large numbers, were touched by Rajneesh's commentaries on Hasidic tales and Hasidism. "Hasidism," he explained, "is the core of Judaism, its heart, just as Zen was the core of Buddhism." In political background, 51% of Rajneeshpuram's sannyasins characterized themselves as liberal, and 11% as formerly radical. Gordon remarks that "people like Deeksha, who had been active in the radical political movements of the sixties and early seventies found themselves agreeing with Rajneesh's critiques of politics . . . even those who still wanted to change society felt the need for an internal change . . . a detachment that would protect them from the temptations to egoism and hypocrisy that political activity would inevitably bring." . . .

. . . [M]y observations at Poona, at the London, England Centre, and in Toronto and Vancouver Centres suggests that a sizeable percentage of Rajneeshees were rootless drifters or gypsy types, who moved from job to job and place to place, and seemed unable to settle down long in one place. Thus, for example, one Toronto sannyasin admitted, "I never really had a clear sense of direction. I would move around frequently, when finances dried up, and take whatever job opportunities arose." Again an interview with the head of the Toronto Centre in April 1983 revealed that it had an annual turnover of almost 100% in those living in the Centre. "We're always having to adjust to a new bunch," she added, underlining the restless character of its resident membership. Many of these were younger, probably below 30 years of age.

In another category are the fairly-to-quite successful persons discontented with the fruits of the "rat race." This group included many like Devaraj, Rajneesh's personal physician and the author of a pro-Rajneesh book, who expressed a strong distaste with careerism and from time to time took a holiday from medical practice. These are well established middle class persons, but had a restless seeker predilection and wanted more meaning and fun out of life. Some of these persons may not have been heavily involved in growth groups prior to taking sannyas, but others were.

Various students of Rajneeshism including Mullan emphasize the number of professionals in the membership. My observations and interviews indicate this comment needs elaboration. First, it is the lower status and newer professions that are more common among Rajneeshees:—nurses, masseurs, social workers, teachers, therapists, actors, dancers and the like. . . . What are absent from these lists are occupations . . . in which the main tasks are routine and highly bureaucratic . . . former business people, accountants and civil servants . . . are a minority and do not by any means set the tone. Wallis amplifies this important point, confirmed by my researches, noting that "the typical follower chose specifically not to be located in the industrial, commercial or bureaucratic core of the modern world. Rajneeshees, by and large, and *before* they had become sannyasins, had already rejected the routine predictability of corporate life, its impersonality and rationalization, to pursue a course more concerned with creativity and the imagination, with human contact and with more spiritual values. Those drawn to Rajneesh . . . had identified themselves with the pursuit of the *expressive* life. Although many . . . were materially comfortable . . . this did not constitute their primary definition of the ideal human condition . . . it was precisely this group . . . who could concentrate their attention upon the pursuit of the ideal self." . . .

Seekers—The Process of Seeking

Sociological experts on the cults describe the most common type of follower as the spiritual seeker. These are numerous among Rajneeshees. Gordon notes, speaking of the sannyasins at Poona, "most of them have the edgy discomfort of the seeker, the itch of the rebellious and unfulfilled, the apprehensive self-absorption of the narcissistic." In interviews some describe themselves in precisely these terms. Thus, one sannyasin told me, "I am a seeker: I am always looking for new experiences and relationships." Another sannyasin said, "I was following the spiritual scent, but (previously) something was lacking." A third emphasized: "I was searching for something to fulfil me . . . I never did find it, so I was going on, moving, searching, from one city to another, but not really knowing what it was."

Specifically Rajneeshees may be classified as mostly freshman seekers. This means they are under 40, are seeking with great eagerness and are often willing to make a strong commitment. The contrary sociological type, veteran seekers, are typically over 40, predominantly women and tend to flit, without settling down, from one unconventional religious group to another. Rajneesh's sannyasins have made a commitment, though a considerable percentage did leave within a year or two. A good many who did leave were still seeking. Gordon describes two of these and I met others. Many, as noted earlier, had previously belonged to other religious or para-religious groups and, after being disillusioned, moved into Rajneeshism. For example, a number were attached to Transcendental Meditation, a few having even risen to trainer status therein.

There appears to be a definable pattern in this process of drifting from one movement to another. It has been uncovered by Professor Metta Spencer, sociologist at the University of Toronto, . . . at a conference entitled, Sub-cultures of Psychotherapy. Studying a large number of therapists and their patients in the Metro Toronto area, she discovered that when clients shifted from one therapist to another, usually because he/she was not meeting their expectations, they frequently shifted to someone a bit more unconventional or unorthodox. From her data, she constructed a continuum of therapists and patients, extending from psychiatry and conventional psycho-analysis on the right end, to the more unorthodox on the left; i.e. Primal, neo-Reichian, and on the far left, therapies based on past life exploration. The pattern she observed in studying scores of respondents was that both clients and therapists, when dissatisfied, typically shifted one or two degrees or "steps" from right to left on this continuum. In short, they chose an approach just a little more unconventional or unorthodox but seldom made a big leap from an orthodox to a quite unorthodox far left therapy.

Preliminary work by Professor Spencer now suggests the same principle holds for persons leaving new religious movements. When these shift allegiance, they tend to change to a group a little more unusual or unorthodox than the one previous. This is exemplified by sannyasins doing TM. Typically, they may have gone from TM to a Yoga group or to someone like Swami Muktananda and then on later to Rajneesh. . . .

The appeal of Rajneeshism may be analyzed in several different ways. On the one hand, a certain specific experience such as the dynamic meditation seems to draw individuals into the cult. Such individual items have been described by sociologists Bromley and Shupe as "hooks." On the other hand, there is the total or overall appeal of the large communes like Poona, Oregon or Medina, which caters to a wide spectrum of human growth or "happiness industry" interests.

The draw of the large commune stems first from its provision of something for everyone. It is the same marketing principle that animates the modern service university, which offers courses on just about anything; or the American big city drugstore that sells not just drugs, but groceries, shoes, tobacco, candles; in fact, almost everything the public wants. Rajneeshism latched onto this principle in the late 70's. In essence, it meant offering any and all kinds of activities, therapeutic, educational, mystical, sexual, that promised to meet a consistent, reliable consumer demand. So by 1977–78, Poona offered over a dozen therapies, various meditations, music and dancing, daily arts and crafts, so-called university courses and seminars, a variety of massages, the isolation or tranquillity tank, etc., etc. Here for almost the first time was available a broad range of the conventional growth therapies along with the promise of ecstatic or mystical experiences and the possible attainment of the ultimate in self-realization, i.e. enlightenment. The offerings expanded up to 1981. . . .

The message seemed to be do what comes easy for you, do what comes naturally and let it all hang out. Sannyasins into dope or easy sex or whatever were allowed to maintain their lifestyle. Male disciples were given the honorific title of Swami. The women were called Ma, which symbolized mother, but had none of the heavy or tiresome duties of being a real mother. Both genders could easily feel part of a special and avant garde community. These aspects would appeal to drifters, the deviant, the undisciplined, the creative, etc.

In another sense the emphasis on group experience and self-realization meant Rajneesh meditation centre or commune life resembled a dream factory or utopia. Anything now seemed possible. Moreover, one could, without serious criticism, come and go from the Poona ashram or from the participation in any given Rajneesh Centre. . . .

The sexually repressed or hungry could get hooked and/or kept in the movement by the easy accessibility of sex without guilt. All around in the communes were eager and attractive partners. One could change partners quickly with no group sanctions. Also those longing for ecstatic or intense experiences as a way of validating a change of lifestyle, were hooked by cathartic experiences while doing a kundalini, or a dynamic meditation. Once hooked, they probably soon sought other more intense experiences. It is instructive that wherever I've visited Rajneesh Centres, in Europe or North America, the majority of participants were non-sannyasins. Sannyasins had gone through that type of experience and were interested in something else.

Participants in growth therapies do get hooked into taking more groups. This is a well known phenomenon in the human potential movement. In certain groups they experience a sense of greater inner freedom, or personal power, or energy and they return, looking for more. After ten or twelve, however, the experience begins to wear thin. . . .

It is important as well that for the intellectually rebellious, whether it be political or religious, Rajneesh's ideas made a strong appeal. They called for a radical transformation of society and their revolutionary sweep was calculated to draw in avant garde types or advanced intellectuals who felt strongly about society's evils. Rajneesh repeated anti-authoritarian themes that counter-cultural types or the political radicals felt strongly about and he said it all with such poetic style and distinction that he touched the hearts of many in these categories. . . .

Transference

A variety of observers at Poona, . . . emphasized Rajneesh's role and appeal as a father figure. There is evidence that many if not a majority of sannyasins did not get along well with their father or with both parents. This was supported by the results of numerous interviews. Ex-sannyasin Anna Forbes, quoted frequently by Gordon, has told me that she has yet to meet a sannyasin or ex-sannyasin who got along well with his/her parents. Thus, it is reasonable to assume that some of these sannyasins, lacking the emotional security provided by a loving parental relationship, might unconsciously gravitate to an authority figure on whom to lean and to whom to surrender their autonomy. Such a figure must, of course, be prepared to take responsibility for their lives. Rajneesh filled this need. He talked with great authority, claimed enlightenment, was an eminently successful and mature person and presented himself as wise, benevolent and trustworthy. His writings and communes presented a clear life style, with an answer to every question. The many glamorized photographs of him in each commune conveyed a sense of his immediate presence, spiritual power and ready availability for those who needed or wanted such an authority figure. Cult literature, too, encouraged sannyasins to ask for answers to personal questions from Rajneesh by talking to him in their heads as if praying to a deity. In addition, in Oregon, the fuss attending his daily drive-by in a Rolls cast him in the style of an Emperor bestowing loving care on all his subjects. As long as he made this daily drive-by, the impression was left that nothing really can go wrong with the commune and its members.

Rise and Fall of the New Age Movement

J. GORDON MELTON

The New Age Movement, which emerged to prominence in the late 1970s, represents to a large extent the metaphysical/occult phase of the spread of new religious movements (NRMs) during the past generation. It is of considerable interest in that it brought together a number of older metaphysical organizations, such as the Arcane School founded in the 1920s by the British theosophist Alice A. Bailey, with other groups which had emerged since World War II. During the 1960s, several of these groups which shared a basic theosophical world-view were first linked together in a self-conscious network around a new millennial vision: the coming of a New Age, sometimes called the Aquarian Age.

During the 1970s, members of the network, primarily British metaphysical teachers, spread the New Age millennial vision throughout Great Britain, continental Europe, North America, and former countries of the British Empire such as South Africa and Australia. By the 1980s, the efforts of the initial prophets of the New Age bore fruit and the vision of the Coming Era of Peace, Love, and Light captured the imagination of the established metaphysical and psychic organizations

J. Gordon Melton, "The Future of the New Age Movement," in *New Religions and New Religiosity,* ed. Eileen Barker and Margit Warburg (Aarhus, Denmark: Aarhus University Press, 1998), 133–149.

and brought millions of people into a broad social movement. After flourishing through the 1980s, by the end of the decade, the movement was obviously on the decline and today we can confidently pronounce its obituary. As of 1994, it is difficult to locate anyone who professes allegiance to the New Age vision.

However, *the New Age Movement did not simply arrive and depart like the latest fashion fad.* It made a significant impact upon metaphysical thought, brought occultism to a new level of respectability, led many new people into the metaphysical community, and caused the formation of a number of new metaphysical, psychic, and occult groups which have assumed a more or less permanent place on the religious landscape. Coming to some overview of the New Age Movement will assist us in filling out our understanding of the nature of the impact of NRMs during the last half century, as well as highlighting a major European contribution to contemporary pluralism.

The Origin and Nature of the New Age Movement

The New Age Movement, as its name might suggest, was a social movement built around the belief that during the next generation, human society was going to undergo a massive social transformation that would bring into existence a "new age" of peace and harmony. Banished would be all the major problems which beset humanity such as war, political oppression, racism, hunger, and poverty. Such a vision has its roots in the millennial yearnings of the Theosophical Society as espoused by Annie Besant and Charles W. Leadbeater.

That initial vision was developed through the 1920s and 1930s by Alice A. Bailey and culminated in one of her last books, *The Reappearance of the Christ,* published in 1948. Bailey suggested that the New Age would come towards the end of the twentieth century and would include the appearance of a new world saviour, generally referred to as Christ or Maitreya (the Buddhist figure viewed as the coming enlightened one). She founded the Arcane School, with headquarters in New York, London, and Geneva, to prepare the way for the New Age and the reappearance of the Christ. Possibly more important, she established a means by which the school members could actively participate in bringing in the New Age. Through their meditation, adherents could receive the energies from the spiritual hierarchy, the illuminated and evolved beings who guided the course of humanity, and radiate those energies to the surrounding community and the world. She pictured the world as illuminated by many "points of light," people and groups scattered around the globe who engaged in the energy work. She further grounded the ideas by initiating the Triangles programme that brought people together in groups of three who covenanted to unite daily in radiating spiritual energy.

While Bailey's ideas were studied and acted upon by the Arcane School and the several additional Baileyite groups which emerged after her death, they also reached into many smaller independent theosophical and metaphysical groups. Bailey had received the essential core of her teachings from her channelled sessions with one of the masters of the spiritual hierarchy. Leaders in some of the independent groups, like Bailey, had become channels and regularly received and circulated channelled materials from an entity they described as either a master, the Great White Brotherhood (i.e., another name for the spiritual hierarchy) or God. This channelling activity somewhat alienated the independent groups from the orthodox Bailey groups that relied solely on her books. In the 1960s, these independent groups linked together and initially began to project what would become the New Age vision.

The first international network was called the Universal Link. During the 1960s and 1970s it had its headquarters in London. Originally, it centred upon the prediction of a cataclysmic event to occur in 1967. That event did not occur, but was later reinterpreted as having occurred on a spiritual level, a new release of God's energy in the world beginning the transition into the New Age. In 1970, an American, David Spangler, came to England and began to move among the groups of the Universal Link. He was led to visit one in northern Scotland, the Findhorn Community. His brief planned visit stretched into a three-year stay. While there, he developed a perspective of the New Age which he presented in a series of books beginning with *The New Age Vision* (1973). Upon his return to the United States in 1973, through his writing, speaking and networking, he became one of the major architects of the new movement.

Spangler argued that the present generation was a special time in history when an increased amount of spiritual energy was available to human kind. A New Age was becoming present. It was humanity's duty to take the free flow of energy and use it to become co-creators in the building of the New Age that was dawning. Spangler represented what was to become the dominant voice in the New Age community. Previously, for example, the leaders at Findhorn had argued that the New Age would be brought in by a cataclysmic event, an approach that assumed that people were essentially passive observers of what God and the hierarchy were doing. At best they could announce it. Spangler, in contrast, suggested that humanity had to cooperate with the powers if the New Age was to occur.

Spangler also gave emphasis to the second great truth of the New Age movement as it was being constituted. The movement into the New Age could be partially experienced now in the transformation of the individual. The nature of the transformation could be quite varied. The sick could be healed. The poor could attain some degree of financial success. The bored and lost could find a life of spiritual meaning. The mundane could be lifted up to the transcendental realm. In any case, while waiting for the larger transition into the New Age, a foretaste was available for individuals in their own personal alteration. By the end of the 1970s, the New Age swept through the metaphysical/occult community in both Europe and North America. The response to the New Age overwhelmed those who had created it, and it took on a life of its own.

The New Age in the 1980s

During the 1980s, the New Age Movement became a mass social movement involving people throughout the world. Besides Northern and Western Europe and North America, it spread through South and Central America and to a lesser extent to all the major urban centres except in Muslim and Marxist dominated countries. As the New Age became a mass movement, two important components, channelling and crystals, were developed.

Central to the New Age movement was channelling, what we had in previous generations termed mediumship. The older mediumship, however, had a much narrower focus. It was limited primarily to a single movement, Spiritualism, and referred primarily to contact with spirit entities generally thought of as spirits of the deceased. The purpose of mediumship was also primarily to demonstrate survival of bodily death.

Channelling was distinct from mediumship in several ways. Primary contact was not with the dead, though the dead were by no means excluded. The entities who spoke through New Age channels were believed to be extraterrestrials, ascended masters, master teachers, deities, Jesus Christ, God, or the channel's higher self. Ramtha was conceived as a master teacher who had lived on earth 35,000 years ago, but never died. He founded the means to ascend. St. Germain is an ascended master. Sananda is another name for Jesus in the theosophical hierarchy. Channelling also had a different purpose. While mediums contacted the dead and dealt primarily with persons going through the grief process, channelling concentrated on teaching cosmology and theology, and based upon that cosmology laying out a life course for New Agers. It worked from an inspirational model. Channelling was compared to the inspiration of musicians and the intuition of poets. And, of course, channelling was not a new phenomenon. It was at least as old as the Bible. The Book of Revelation is a classic channelled work:

> I was in the spirit on the Lord's Day, said John, and I heard behind me a great voice as of a trumpet saying, "What you see, write in a book and send it to the seven churches . . . "

Through the late nineteenth century, channelling was established in Spiritualism through the work of such men as John Ballou Newbrough (1828–1891), who authored and published in 1882 a massive channelled work, *Oahspe,* subtitled *A New Age Bible.* A short time later, Levi Dowling channelled *The Aquarian Gospel of Jesus Christ. Oahspe* became the basis of a new religious movement, the Universal Faithists of Kosmos, while the *Aquarian Gospel* was accepted by many Spiritualists as a supplement to the Bible, filling in the events of the so-called lost years of Jesus and giving support to a metaphysical Bible interpretation. Channelling became integral to the Flying Saucer contactee movement in the 1950s, and a number of the early New Age channels had been nurtured among the flying saucer enthusiasts. . . .

Among the products of channelling was the great fad of the New Age, crystals. There was, of course, an old teaching about the occult significance of crystal stone that had been the almost exclusive property of the occult elite, the ritual magicians. Then it was placed on the popular metaphysical agenda again by Edgar Cayce, the great channel of the mid-twentieth century, and one of the precursors of the New Age. But not until 1982 and the publication of the three-volume channelled work by Frank Alper, *Exploring Atlantis,* did crystals have any place in the New Age. Alper had begun a series of channelling sessions on Atlantis in 1980/81, at the request of some of the entities who spoke through him. Surprisingly, the entities began to describe the power source for the mythical Atlantean culture in crystal power. They described the crystal's power to store and release energy, and in an important twist, mentioned its power to heal. This topic caught the interest of those who participated in the sessions, and the entities went on to describe in a rather minute and elaborate manner, the nature of crystal energy, the differences between crystals and their relation to various diseases, and the techniques for placing crystals on the body for therapeutic effects. Crystals could be worn as jewellery or placed in patterns on a reclining body. Larger crystals could be left in prominent positions around one's domicile.

For whatever reason, Alper's work, initially published privately and informally, caught on with New Agers and became the source of what for a decade became a growth industry. It is of more than passing interest in that the use of crystals rested entirely on channelled material. As crystals gained popularity, there was an attempt to justify their use with scientific data, and several very lengthy and carefully argued apologies appeared by people who obviously knew their crystallography. However, in the end the more honest had to admit that there was no science behind the use of crystals; it was entirely a matter of a belief in a "spiritual" energy possessed by crystals. The internal critique of crystals by New Age believers became crucial to the demise of the New Age.

At the beginning of 1990, so quickly that numerous small investors were left with large supplies of crystals, the bottom suddenly fell out of the market. The New Age soon followed.

The Demise of the New Age

By the end of the 1980s, it became evident that the New Age Movement was in its last stages. Like all popular social movements from the Millerite apolcalyticism [sic] of the 1840s to the Red Scare of the 1950s to the Civil Rights Movement of the 1960s, the New Age Movement was doomed to pass from the scene. The New Age, of course, has experienced the heavy criticism of conservative Christian voices as well as the scepticism of academics who question the existence of any occult realities. As a whole, these did little to change the course of the movement. With hindsight, we can see that the Christian critique was too late. The great majority of Christian books appeared after most New Agers began to abandon the position which the Christian literature attacked. The sceptical literature was simply ignored. Without reference to either source, New Age leaders, including David Spangler, began to question and then abandon the New Age vision itself.

The New Age Movement seems to have peaked at the end of 1987 with the airing of the movie version of Shirley MacLaine's popular book *Out on a Limb* as a mini-series on American television. The series gave the movement new life and, at least briefly, made MacLaine a star in a new arena. However, it also appears that the enthusiasm that greeted MacLaine obscured the equally significant events which can be traced to the spring of 1988 when the important intellectual leaders of the movement began to announce their abandonment of the New Age vision. . . .

However, the loss of faith in the New Age itself did not mean that people simply walked away from the movement and returned to their pre–New Age life and stance. Just as the Millerites in 1844 did not return to their position prior to their encounter with William Miller, and survive to this day in the various branches of Adventism, so too the New Age Movement did not throw away everything it had acquired. It refocused and has continued, though with a quite varied appearance.

One aspect of the New Age included visions of social change, crystals, the Harmonic Convergence and planetary alignments—all elements in the hope for social transformation. However, there was a second very important teaching in the movement, a corollary to the New Age vision. The logic ran something like this:

For the New Age to arrive, many individuals have to be transformed. Just as society will be transformed, so you too—individually—can be transformed. And having experienced a personal transformation, you will come to know the truth of the possibility of social transformation. Ultimately, your commitment to the social vision will be grounded in your experience of a personal transformation and the change and growth to follow.

Taken over by the New Age movement, the older metaphysical, psychic and occult means for individual growth and development were recast into tools for personal transformation and evolution. Many of these methodologies, the prominent one being meditation, most of which have a venerable history both inside and outside metaphysical circles, and both inside and outside the Christian Church, worked as they always have. Millions of people have experienced a personal transformation in their life. Some have been healed of physical diseases, some report a new integrated personality, some rejoiced in discovering a way out of various negative situations from loneliness and poverty to meaninglessness and boredom.

Having lost faith in the social vision, leaders of the New Age fell back on a variation of an old argument. The personal transformation, they argued, was really the heart of the movement all along. Through the New Age, people have discovered a new consciousness, and living out of that new consciousness is inherently a better way of life. Holistic health is better than modern medicine. A diet built around vegetarianism and whole food is better than one built around animal fat and processed substances. A life in touch with the larger spiritual reality of the inner self is a more positive and vivifying way to live than the limited scientism of Western culture. The spiritual life is better than boring Christian religiosity. A life affirming ethic is superior to a Christian ethic which has sanctioned war, racial and ethnic prejudice, political oppression, and religious persecution from the Inquisition to the present anti-cult movement. An appealing argument. And over the last few years we have discovered just how appealing.

While surveys vary, they have all indicated that 20 to 30 percent of Westerners believe in reincarnation, either practise or have practised meditation, and follow their horoscope to some degree, the three bellwethers of the growth of an alternative consciousness in the face of a still dominant Christian faith. Many have, of course, found a way to integrate these beliefs in a somewhat traditional Christian belief structure. After all, most Christians do something called *meditation* regularly, and for centuries astrology was seen as compatible with Christianity. We forget that the first great Lutheran theologian, the author of the Augsburg Confession, was also an astrologer, and that when Philip Melancthon initially addressed his new colleagues at Wittenberg University he spoke on the dignity of astrology. Reincarnation, of course, is theological heresy in the extreme, but that has not kept people from trying to integrate it into their Christian perspective.

Thus while the New Age has died, the community of people affected by its vision and transformed by its teachings remain. Many have found the acceptance of a personal spiritual world-view sufficient. Others have returned to mainline churches much vivified by their experience. . . .

Conclusion

The New Age movement has passed into history. Just as there are some people who are still fighting the American Civil War, at least in their heads, there are a few who still await the imminent New Age, but they have shrunk to a minuscule number. However, the people brought into the metaphysical/psychic/occult world as a result of the New Age movement remain. It is unfortunate that we do not have some of the hard data about public opinion and the content of religious commitments from the earlier decades of this century from which we could see the pattern of development of such beliefs as reincarnation and astrology to the significant level they have attained today. I suspect there has been a steady growth throughout this century, but we know that (1) the existence of a large popular body of dissent from mainstream perspectives (Christian and secular) provided a base upon which the New Age movement could grow and that (2) the successes of the New Age community enlarged that base of dissent to its present level. We just do not know how big the original body of dissent was and, hence, how much of the present high level of dissent can be attributed to it.

In our assessment of the New Age movement, possibly the most important fact to keep before us is the numbers. In considering NRMs, we often are talking about hundreds of adherents, in a minority of cases about thousands of members, and in a very few cases of tens of thousands. When it comes to the New Age, we are talking about hundreds of thousands of adherents—millions, in the United States alone, who accept the broad New Age world-view, and tens of millions who accept several basic ideas which, though not necessarily definitive of the New Age (astrology, reincarnation), are closely associated with it. While the New Age movement has died and fragmented into a multitude of competing organizations, those figures have not decreased in the least.

Once we begin to think in terms of 20 to 30 percent of the population, we are no longer dealing with a marginal phenomenon. The dissenting opinions symbolized by the New Age movement are now strongly entrenched in Western society, and in the near future we can expect to see it offering a more direct challenge to more familiar modes of thinking and acting.

✎ *F U R T H E R   R E A D I N G*

Adler, Margot. *Drawing Down the Moon: Witches, Druids, Goddess-Worshippers, and Other Pagans in America Today* (1986).
Anderson, Walter. *The Upstart Spring: Esalen and the American Awakening* (1983).
Bellah, Robert, and Charles Glock. *The New Religious Consciousness* (1976).
Brown, Karen McCarthy. *Mama Lola: A Voudou Priestess in Brooklyn* (1992).
Clecak, Peter. *America's Quest for the Ideal Self: Dissent and Fulfillment in the 60s and 70s* (1983).
Cox, Harvey. *Turning East: The Promise and Peril of the New Orientalism* (1977).
Daly, Mary. *Beyond God the Father: Toward a Philosophy of Women's Liberation* (1973).
Ellwood, Robert. *Alternative Altars: Unconventional and Eastern Spirituality in America* (1979).
———. *The Sixties Spiritual Awakening* (1994).
Feinsod, Ethan. *Awake in a Nightmare: Jonestown, the Only Eye-Witness Account* (1981).

Fowler, Robert Booth. *The Greening of Protestant Thought* (1995).

Furlong, Monica. *Zen Effects: The Life of Alan Watts* (1986).

Graham, Dom Aelred. *Zen Catholicism* (1963).

Kerouac, Jack. *The Dharma Bums* (1958).

Knott, Kim. *My Sweet Lord: The Hare Krishna Movement* (1986).

Leary, Timothy. *Flashbacks, An Autobiography* (1985).

Meyer, Donald. *The Positive Thinkers: Religion as Pop Psychology from Mary Baker Eddy to Oral Roberts* (1980).

Moore, R. Laurence. *In Search of White Crows* (1977).

Niehardt, John G. *Black Elk Speaks: Being the Life Story of a Holy Man of the Oglala Sioux* (1979).

Palmer, Susan J. *Moon Sisters, Krishna Mothers, Rajneesh Lovers: Women's Roles in New Religions* (1994).

Perry, Charles. *The Haight-Ashbury: A History* (1984).

Roof, Wade Clark. *A Generation of Seekers: The Spiritual Journeys of the Baby Boom Generation* (1993).

Roszak, Theodore. *The Making of a Counterculture* (1969).

Starhawk. *Truth or Dare: Encounters with Power, Authority, and Mystery* (1990).

Strelley, Kate. *The Ultimate Game: The Rise and Fall of Bhagwan Shree Rajneesh* (1987).

Watts, Alan. *The Way of Zen* (1957).

Weaver, Mary Jo. *New Catholic Women: A Contemporary Challenge to Traditional Religious Authority* (1985).

New Immigrants and
Religious Multiculturalism:
1970–2000

*After a lull between the 1920s and the 1950s, immigration to America accelerated
in the 1960s and continues today at a rate of more than half a million per year.
This new wave of immigration was facilitated by revised immigration laws from
1965 (no longer favoring northwestern Europe's ethnic groups), by the Refugee Act
of 1980, and by further immigration reform laws in 1986 and 1990. It consisted of a
massive emigration (legal and illegal) from Mexico and other parts of Latin America
and the Caribbean, mainly of poor people in search of work and economic opportunities, and an influx of Asian refugees, including many displaced by the Vietnam
War. Many of the characteristic experiences of the European immigrants depicted in
Chapters 6, 8, and 10 are being repeated among these groups. Will Herberg noted
(Chapter 10) that immigration sometimes* strengthened *Europeans' religious identification in the New World, and there are signs of the same phenomenon among
some Hispanic and Asian immigrants.*

*Hispanic immigrants' religion was Catholicism but of a different style than
that practiced in most American Catholic churches. Hispanic Catholics' presence
rose rapidly after 1960; so did their representation among the clergy and bishops.
At the same time, the development of liberation theology in the 1970s and 1980s,
which is based on the idea of God and the church taking a "preferential option
for the poor," made war-torn Latin America an arena of intense concern to American theologians.*

*Asian immigrants brought a variety of religious cultures with them. Vietnam
had been a French colony until the mid-1950s and many of the refugees came from
families that had converted to Catholicism in the colonial era. However, elements of
an older Confucianism were mixed with their Catholicism, which, like that of the
Hispanic newcomers, did not blend easily with the dominant American-Catholic
style. Buddhists from China, Tibet, and Japan, Hindus from India, and Muslims
from Middle Eastern nations further added to the blend of new religious groupings
in the United States.*

Cultural encounters always affect both parties. Immigrants certainly felt the shock of living in an alien land, even when they tried to build institutions to preserve their old heritage. Their children learned English, went to American schools, and were exposed to the dangers as well as the benefits of their new surroundings. At the same time, Asian religious teachings had a radiance to some Americans that they could no longer find in the churches and synagogues of their upbringing. Hence the phenomenon of white Buddhists and black Muslims, each giving themselves a religious identity deliberately remote from the American mainstream.

 D O C U M E N T S

This selection of documents relies more heavily than those in previous chapters on the observations of sociologists and anthropological fieldworkers, because there is not yet a good supply of religious narratives in English from inside the new immigrant groups. The social scientists are themselves often older immigrants from the same background who are sympathetic to the plight of the people they are observing, and their observations are illuminated with direct quotations from new immigrants. Jesse Nash and Elizabeth Trinh Nguyen, in Document 1 (1995), describe the courtship rituals that take place in a Vietnamese community in New Orleans, and the paradoxical blending of Catholic and Confucian elements they reveal. Charles Munzy, in Document 2 (1989), also studies a Vietnamese community, this time in Oklahoma City, and its changing funeral customs. In Document 3, a fragment of Richard Rodriguez's autobiography *Hunger of Memory* (1981), a young man traces the interplay of his parents' Mexican Catholicism with the Irish variety he encounters in Sacramento, California. Documents 4 (1997) and 5 (1994) explain the challenges awaiting Muslims, both immigrant and African-American, as they deal with America's secular and hedonistic culture. Several informants note, however, that there are some clear advantages for Muslims living in America—that while some friends and neighbors are critical, others actively help them to maintain their religious obligations. In Document 6 (1998), Prema Kurien explains how Hindu immigrants from south India to southern California have created new institutions to soften the impact of migration and uphold their religious tradition.

1. Jesse Nash and Elizabeth Trinh Nguyen Observe Vietnamese Immigrants Courting at Church in New Orleans, 1995

As if on cue, dusk gives way to an ebon nightfall. Except for the occasional flicker of a cigarette lighter, the moon supplies the only light. Then someone lights the candles on the altar, and the priest begins his homily.

A gentle breeze carries hints of whispers and mocking giggles, disclosing to the ear what the dark hides from the eye and offering competition of sorts to the homiletic comments of the priest. Appropriately enough, that time of night can evoke both religious awe and romantic longing, religious faith and romantic desire,

Jesse Nash and Elizabeth Trinh Nguyen, *Romance, Gender, and Religion in a Vietnamese-American Community* (Lewiston, N.Y.: Edwin Mellen Press, 1995).

the two sides of traditional Vietnamese society and Vietnamese-American existence in the United States.

The Vietnamese refugee community of New Orleans had gathered outside their, at that time, unfinished church building. A stage had been erected, a program devised, and a band formed. All this activity is focused on the young people of the parish and their participation in CCD, the religious education program. It is the end of another year, one more step in the religious maturation of the young and the perfect opportunity to warn the young that religious faith is not merely studied but lived out, especially in the vacation time of the approaching summer, summers having been the occasion of more than one flirtation with temptation and subsequent capitulation to desire. The priests and sisters congratulate the students on having successfully completed their religion classes, and they promise an even better series of classes in the fall. The students then sing religious songs and perform religiously-inspired skits for the rather large audience thronged throughout the future parking lot.

All this under a romantic moon.

And the moon works its own peculiar magic.

Younger people, teenagers and budding adults, drift to the back and the sides of the assembled community. Boldly, a young girl chases a boy making faces at her. Elsewhere, more genteel, traditional Confucian manners prevail: groups of boys talk in low voices to groups of girls. A young fisherman, more boisterous than others, surveys the young women and announces his approval, calling out a taunt and bringing a blush to a young feminine cheek with an undisguised wink. As the night progresses and the dark deepens, the noise of flirting increases, but no one seems outraged or surprised. In this section of the audience, romance competes with religion, and the religious gathering has become an occasion for romance.

Practically every religious ceremony of this very Catholic and Confucian community is also an occasion for young men and women to meet each other, size up the competition, and make a good impression. In one sense, these occasions are arranged with the full knowledge of the elders and clergy of the community. It is as if religion conspires with romance to provide an appropriate public arena for desire. At these occasions, parents are also watching and sizing up the young people. Who will make an appropriate mate for their child? Is she beautiful enough? Does he have a good enough job? Does he or she have a good family? Sometimes the priests complain that every religious gathering, festival, pilgrimage, ceremony, or retreat runs the risk of becoming a fashion show or beauty pageant, and yet the priests themselves are involved in the matchmaking, suggesting some matches and cautioning against others. Religion, within the Vietnamese-American community, cannot help but sponsor romance, even though the priests and parents often complain mightily that romance is unnecessary.

Because they are Catholic and Confucian, the Vietnamese are obsessed with marriage, families, and making matches. Romance is as natural to them as their religion, although the two cultural domains are often understood to be in bold opposition to each other. Their Catholicism, as their priests tell them, demands that they give the altar their whole-hearted attention. Their Confucianism, as their priests and parents tell them, demands that marriage be a no-nonsense affair; romantic feelings are often understood to be antithetical to a good and proper marriage. Because they are also becoming American, the Vietnamese are more interested in exploring unfettered romantic love. And there is also another fact that must be remembered. In spite of their Catholicism and Confucianism, and, perversely perhaps, because of their religious traditions, romantic love has always been highly valued among the Vietnamese.

Without working out the contradictions, the Vietnamese habitually mix religion and romance. This curious and seemingly contradictory mixing of romance and religion is clearly present during the yearly Vietnamese-American community's pilgrimage to Carthage, Missouri for a week devoted to the celebration of the Virgin Mary's role in their religion, family life, and personal self-cultivation. This religious festival too is an opportunity for the younger folks to meet each other and look for possible future mates, for parents to size up the available mates, and for everyone, parents, young adults, and clergy, to sing traditional sad love songs.

At this pilgrimage, a curious series of oppositions of a sort is at play. The explicitly religious exercises, such as the mass and the recitation of rosaries, essentially use desire as a foil—to be holy, desire for a human being must be extinguished, and God alone be desired.

Yet desire forms the basis of the family and is recognized as necessary if the marital bonds are to be sustained. Desire can also be the enemy of the marital bond and familial obligations. At the religious activities and parades, however, female participants are chosen because of their beauty, decorum, mien, and youthfulness, in short, their desirability. Desirable women, it seems, draw attention to the deity as well as to themselves, giving rise to the oft-quoted proverb that "God too likes beautiful women."

2. Charles Munzy Attends Vietnamese Funerals in Oklahoma City, 1989

Unlike Vietnamese weddings which were observed to sometimes conform to the traditional ceremonies, funerals resembled those of the host society. . . . In Vietnam the death of a family member necessitated elaborate preparations for food and drink to accommodate visiting family, neighbors, and even the whole village. It was preferred practice for the person to die at home. After this the family would prepare the body; send for a coffin; entertain visitors; organize a wake; and conduct the funeral ceremony.

> In Vietnam at a funeral all the family comes to the house. All the neighbors will also come to the house to see the family. They would cook and bring food, and they came and brought money to give to their neighbor to help them. In Oklahoma City they do nothing like this.
>
> When my father died in Vietnam, we bought a cow and a pig and killed them and made a big party for the whole village who attended the funeral. It was busy because the whole family had to discuss about organizing the funeral. We kept the body at home

Charles Munzy, "Funerals," in *The Vietnamese in Oklahoma City* (New York: AMS Press, 1989), 155–160.

for one week. Then we had the funeral. Everyone came to eat, drink wine and have a party. Some brought money, flowers, incense, candles and other things. We put the coffin in the house in front of the altar and set up a small altar in front of the coffin. It was like a small table with a picture of the dead, candles, incense container, incense, some fruit, and some food like one bowl of rice. Usually they put one boiled egg on top of the rice with only one pair of chopsticks around the egg. In Vietnamese if you say "I almost ate the egg in the rice bowl" it means I almost died. Everyday we had a ceremony at the altar and everyone who came had to lai. In Vietnam after three years my family dug up the coffin, washed the bones with wine and put them in a smaller ceramic coffin and re-buried them in another place forever.

[But in America], one must adhere to the laws of the land in certain aspects of private sector behavior. The Vietnamese must follow the larger state laws concerning embalming and exhumation. According to these laws, embalming is a required procedure, if burial is not within twenty-four hours. The practice of the family digging up the remains in three years for reburial is no longer possible for Vietnamese in Oklahoma. In addition to the regulations that govern the treatment of the dead, the Vietnamese preference to die at home is not shared by the host culture. In America people are usually not allowed to die at home, and are primarily taken to the hospital when they become gravely ill. In Vietnam people were rushed home from the hospital as they approached death.

Keeping a sick or dying person home could now result in charges of neglect by family members. Vietnamese must also follow the American practices for the treatment of the ill. Many of the Vietnamese preferences concerning death and dying are prohibited by law. The majority of Vietnamese now also die in the hospital in the U.S. The hospital then sends the body directly to a funeral home, where routine procedures are followed. The Vietnamese family is more excluded from the death of family members in the United States, and they closely follow the established American patterns.

> In the United States the Vietnamese funeral practices are just like the Americans, with only one thing different, the religion. If you are a Buddhist, the monk will come to hold the prayer ceremony at the funeral home. If you are a Protestant, then the minister will come. If you are Catholic then the priest will come. In Vietnam it was very different. They never go to the funeral home and they don't embalm the dead.
>
> The Vietnamese accept the American way for the funeral. The family comes to the funeral home and everyone else comes there to pray for the dead and to see the family. The Buddhist monk will come to the funeral home to pray for the funeral ceremony. Then they take the body to the cemetery for burial. After one week we had a ceremony at the pagoda to pray for the dead.
>
> The Vietnamese must do like the Americans because we come to this country and we must follow the customs and laws about the funerals. When someone dies some families still make an altar in the home but the coffin is in the funeral home. After the funeral they take down the altar. Then about forty days after the death they bring the picture of the dead to the pagoda and leave it there.

Catholic and Protestant Vietnamese follow the established church procedures in their funeral arrangements. The Catholics have a rosary at the funeral home and a funeral mass the following day. For Protestants, the minister conducts the service at the mortuary or at the church. Traditionally, Buddhists' family members wore white robes or mourning clothes during the funeral in Vietnam. In Oklahoma this has also been modified. During the Buddhist prayer service at the funeral home or at a memorial service at the temple, immediate family members were observed to only wear white cloth head bands. After the ceremony the cloth strip was removed and discarded. Very little variation from the American funeral practices were found among the Vietnamese.

At the first Buddhist funeral I attended, I noticed that the funeral director was quite uncomfortable and unaccustomed to Vietnamese practices. This was his first Vietnamese funeral and he had never seen a Buddhist monk burning incense and chanting prayers before in Oklahoma City. The most outstanding occurrence of minor difference in behaviors was observed at a later funeral. Two of my students were hit by a train on their way home after night school, and both were killed instantly. The same funeral director now had a double Vietnamese Buddhist funeral to contend with. The second time he was more experienced and knew what to expect at a Vietnamese Buddhist funeral. At the grave sites he quietly stood by the hearses and watched the eldest sister conduct the ceremonies. She burned incense and assisted each family member to pray (lai) at the foot of each coffin.

As the coffins were lowered into the graves the crowd of almost one hundred mourners began to tear flowers from the arrangements and throw them into the graves. I distinctly remember watching the director panic and try to quietly deter the Vietnamese from doing this. Finally, he gave up and watched all the flower arrangements torn apart and thrown into the graves. Shortly after this the family produced a big tray of Vietnamese stuffed dumplings from a nearby car. The oldest sister began to serve food and drink to all the mourners. Other American teachers were also unaccustomed to this behavior and didn't know how to respond. Excluding these few observed differences, Vietnamese follow the dominant American etiquette for funerals. In Oklahoma City, Vietnamese funerals no longer resemble those elaborate and festive occasions which were common in Vietnam.

For the Vietnamese family, death and burial were only the beginning of a continuous series of ceremonies and observances throughout the mourning period. After this time, the death anniversary became an important day for the entire family. According to the Vietnamese tradition of mourning, the seventh day, the forty-ninth day and the one hundredth day after death required observances by the family. Offering food and prayers for the dead and then having a large meal for the living family members were the components of these Vietnamese ceremonial events. After one year a more elaborate celebration was organized to mark the end of the first year. . . .

A necessary element for the observance of death anniversaries and Tet ceremonies was the family altar in the home. According to Hickey, altars were found in Buddhist, Catholic, Confucian, and Cao Dai homes in Vietnam. At these altars family heads conducted the ceremonies which were attended by all family members. The traditional altar in the home has changed for the Vietnamese since their arrival in Oklahoma City.

> In Vietnam almost all families had an altar at home. Even the Catholic families always had an altar with a crucifix or a holy picture. Catholics had simple altars with pictures, candles and maybe some flowers. In Oklahoma City my wife has a picture of the Sacred Heart and two small candles on the mantle in the living room. (Catholic informant)

Most Vietnamese families in Oklahoma City no longer have an ancestor altar at home. The Vietnamese family in the U.S. usually does not have the altar in the home. I do, but very few people make a special altar at home. They are Buddhists or Ancestor Worshipers, but they don't do that any more. I would say that ninety percent of the Vietnamese don't have an altar in their home. (President of Buddhist Association)

We don't have an ancestor altar in our home. We did in Vietnam but not in Oklahoma. My father has a picture of his father on a book shelf with a small incense container, but we don't have an altar. We don't pray to the dead or observe the anniversary days since we came to the U.S. (Vietnamese Baptist)

We don't have an altar in our home any more. In Vietnam we did and we observed the death anniversaries of our family. I don't know why, but it is just different here. We changed this when we came to the U.S. Now we take the picture of the dead person to the pagoda and pray there on the anniversary.

3. Richard Rodriguez Recalls His Hispanic-Catholic Childhood, 1981

The steps of the church defined the eternal square where children played and adults talked after dinner. He remembers the way the church building was at the center of town life. She remembers the way one could hear the bell throughout the day, telling time. And the way the town completely closed down for certain feastdays. He remembers that the church spire was the first thing he'd see walking back into town. Both my parents have tried to describe something of what it was like for them to have grown up Catholic in small Mexican towns. They remember towns where everyone was a Catholic.

With their move to America, my mother and father left behind that Mexican Church to find themselves (she praying in whispered Spanish) in an Irish-American parish. In a way, they found themselves at ease in such a church. My parents had much in common with the Irish-born priests and nuns. Like my parents, the priests remembered what it was like to have been Catholic in villages and cities where everyone else was a Catholic. In their American classrooms, the nuns worked very hard to approximate that other place, that earlier kind of religious experience. For a time they succeeded. For a time I too enjoyed a Catholicism something like that enjoyed a generation before me by my parents.

I grew up a Catholic at home and at school, in private and in public. My mother and father were deeply pious *católicos*; all my relatives were Catholics. At home, there were holy pictures on a wall of nearly every room, and a crucifix hung over my bed. My first twelve years as a student were spent in Catholic schools where I could look up to the front of the room and see a crucifix hanging over the clock. . . .

When we were eleven years old, the nuns would warn us about the dangers of mixed marriage (between a Catholic and a non-Catholic). And we heard a priest say that it was a mortal sin to read newspaper accounts of a Billy Graham sermon. But the ghetto Catholic Church, so defensive, so fearful of contact with non-Catholics,

Richard Rodriguez, "Credo," in *Hunger of Memory: The Education of Richard Rodriguez* (Boston: David Godine, 1981). Reprinted by permission of David R. Godine, Publisher, Inc. Copyright 1982 by Richard Rodriguez.

was already outdated when I entered the classroom. My classmates and I were destined to live in a world very different from that which the nuns remembered in Ireland or my parents remembered in Mexico. We were destined to live on unhallowed ground, beyond the gated city of God. . . .

It was to be in college, at Stanford, that my religious faith would seem to me suddenly pared. I would remain a Catholic, but a Catholic defined by a non-Catholic world. This is how I think of myself now. I remember my early Catholic schooling and recall an experience of religion very different from anything I have known since. Never since have I felt so much at home in the Church, so easy at mass. My grammar school years especially were the years when the great Church doors opened to enclose me, filling my day as I was certain the Church filled all time. Living in a community of shared faith, I enjoyed much more than mere social re-enforcement of religious belief. Experienced continuously in public and private, Catholicism shaped my whole day. It framed my experience of eating and sleeping and washing; it named the season and the hour. . . .

I was *un católico* before I was a Catholic. That is, I acquired my earliest sense of the Church—and my membership in it—through my parents' Mexican Catholicism. It was in Spanish that I first learned to pray. I recited family prayers—not from any book. And in those years when we felt alienated from *los gringos*, my family went across town every week to the wooden church of Our Lady of Guadalupe, which was decorated with yellow Christmas tree lights all year long.

Very early, however, the *gringo* church in our neighborhood began to superimpose itself on our family life. The first English-speaking dinner guest at our house was a priest from Sacred Heart Church. I was about four years old at the time, so I retain only random details with which to remember the evening. But the visit was too important an event for me to forget. I remember how my mother dressed her four children in outfits it had taken her weeks to sew. I wore a white shirt and blue woolen shorts. (It was the first time I had been dressed up for a stranger.) I remember hearing the priest's English laughter. . . . He left a large picture of a sad-eyed Christ, exposing his punctured heart. (A caption below records the date of his visit and the imprimatur of Francis Cardinal Spellman.) That picture survives. Hanging prominently over the radio or, later, the television set in the front room, it has retained a position of prominence in all the houses my parents have lived in since. It has been one of the few permanent fixtures in the environment of my life. Visitors to our house doubtlessly noticed it when they entered the door—saw it immediately as the sign we were Catholics. But I saw the picture too often to pay it much heed.

I saw a picture of the Sacred Heart in the grammar school classroom I entered two years after the priest's visit. The picture drew an important continuity between home and the classroom. When all else was different for me (as a scholarship boy) between the two worlds of my life, the Church provided an essential link. During my first months in school, I remember being struck by the fact that—although they worshipped in English—the nuns and my classmates shared my family's religion. The *gringos* were, in some way, like me, *católicos*. Gradually, however, with my assimilation in the schoolroom, I began to think of myself and my family as Catholics. The distinction blurred. At home and in class I heard about sin and Christ and Satan and the consoling presence of Mary the Virgin. It became one Catholic faith for me.

Only now do I trouble to notice what intricate differences separated home Catholicism from classroom Catholicism. In school, religious instruction stressed that man was a sinner. Influenced, I suspect, by a bleak melancholic strain in Irish Catholicism, the nuns portrayed God as a judge. . . .

Unlike others who have described their Catholic schooling, I do not remember the nuns or the priests to have been obsessed with sexual sins. Perhaps that says more about me or my Mexican Catholicism than it says about what actually went on in the classroom. I remember, in any case, that I would sometimes hear with irony warnings about the sins of the flesh. When we were in eighth grade the priest told us how dangerous it was to look at our naked bodies, even while taking a bath—and I noticed that he made the remark directly under a near-naked figure of Christ on the cross.

The Church, in fact, excited more sexual wonderment than it repressed. I regarded with awe the "wedding ring" on a nun's finger, her black "wedding veil"— symbols of marriage to God. I would study pictures of martyrs—white-robed virgins fallen in death and the young, almost smiling, St. Sebastian, transfigured in pain. At Easter high mass I was dizzied by the mucous perfume of white flowers at the celebration of rebirth. At such moments, the Church touched alive some very private sexual excitement; it pronounced my sexuality important. . . .

In contrast to the Catholicism of school, the Mexican Catholicism of home was less concerned with man the sinner than with man the supplicant. God the Father was not so much a stern judge as One with the power to change our lives. My family turned to God not in guilt so much as in need. We prayed for favors and at desperate times. I prayed for help in finding a quarter I had lost on my way home. I prayed with my family at times of illness and when my father was temporarily out of a job. And when there was death in the family, we prayed.

I remember my family's religion, and I hear the whispering voices of women. For although men in my family went to church, women prayed most audibly. Whether by man or woman, however, God the Father was rarely addressed directly. There were intermediaries to carry one's petition to Him. My mother had her group of Mexican and South American saints and near-saints (persons moving toward canonization). She favored a black Brazilian priest who, she claimed, was especially efficacious. Above all mediators there was Mary, *Santa María,* the Mother. Whereas at school the primary mediator was Christ, at home that role was assumed by the Mexican Virgin, *Nuestra Señora de Guadalupe,* the focus of devotion and pride for Mexican Catholics. The Mexican Mary "honored our people," my mother would say. "She could have appeared to anyone in the whole world, but she appeared to a Mexican." Someone like us. And she appeared, I could see from her picture, as a young Indian maiden—dark just like me.

On her feastday in early December my family would go to the Mexican church for a predawn high mass. The celebration would begin in the cold dark with a blare of trumpets imitating the cries of a cock. The Virgin's wavering statue on the shoulders of men would lead a procession into the warm yellow church. Often an usher would roughly separate me from my parents and pull me into a line of young children. (My mother nodded calmly when I looked back.) Sometimes alone, sometimes with my brother and sisters, I would find myself near the altar amid two or three hundred children, many of them dressed like Mexican cowboys and cowgirls.

Sitting on the floor it was easier to see the congregation than the altar. So, as the mass progressed, my eye would wander through the crowd. Invariably, my attention settled on old women—mysterious supplicants in black—bent deep, their hands clasped tight to hold steady the attention of the Mexican Virgin, who was pictured high over the altar, astride a black moon.

The *gringo* Catholic church, a block from our house, was a very different place. In the *gringo* church Mary's statue was relegated to a side altar, imaged there as a serene white lady who matter-of-factly squashed the Genesis serpent with her bare feet. (Very early I knew that I was supposed to believe that the shy Mexican Mary was the same as this European Mary triumphant.) In the *gringo* church the floors were made not of squeaky wood but of marble. And there was not the devotional clutter of so many pictures and statues and candle racks. "It doesn't feel like a church," my mother complained. But as it became our regular church, I grew to love its elegant simplicity: the formal march of its eight black pillars toward the altar; the Easter-egg-shaped sanctuary that arched high over the tabernacle; and the dim pink light suffused throughout on summer afternoons when I came in not to pray but to marvel at the cool calm.

The holy darkness of church never frightened me. It was never nighttime darkness. Religion at school and at church was never nighttime religion like religion at home. Catholicism at home was shaped by the sounds of the "family rosary": tired voices repeating the syllables of the Hail Mary; our fingers inching forward on beads toward the point of beginning; my knees aching; the coming of sleep.

Religion at home was a religion of bedtime. Prayers before sleeping spoke of death coming during the night. It was then a religion of shadows. The last thing I'd see before closing my eyes would be the cheap statue of Mary aglow next to my bed.

But the dark at the foot of my bed billowed with malevolent shapes. Those nights when I'd shudder awake from a nightmare, I'd remember my grandmother's instruction to make a sign of the cross in the direction of my window. (That way Satan would find his way barred.) Sitting up in bed, I'd aim the sign of the cross against the dim rectangle of light. Quickly, then, I'd say the Prayer to My Guardian Angel, which would enable me to fall back to sleep.

4. Kambiz GhaneaBassiri Explains Muslims' Mixed Feelings About American Culture, 1997

Generally, the prevailing attitude of Muslims toward American culture, whether immigrant or indigenous, is one of ambivalence. This ambivalence is rooted in the age-old discussion of the extent to which individual freedoms should be limited in order to ensure the prosperity of the society as a whole. A conversation with virtually any Muslim will show that the omnipresence of alcohol, drug addiction, nudity on television and in movies, homosexuality, sexual intercourse outside marriage, and the constant drive for wealth in the United States are all viewed as signs of an immoral society and a decaying nation. One interviewee saw the presence of AIDS and the natural disasters that have occurred in California to be results of U.S. decadence. Another said, "They complain of AIDS and rape, but on 'Oprah' and 'Sally' they explicitly talk about sexual intercourse in ways I am too embarrassed to say." Another interviewee expressed a stronger point of view:

> I don't believe in economic depression. The depression they are suffering from is moral depression—prostitution, homosexuality, throwing children out of the home. . . . Here the dogs are in homes, the children are in the streets. This nation, I would say every nation in Europe, is culturally retarded. I wish, if not Islam, if they were good Christians they wouldn't have these problems. They don't care about religion. . . . They believe that money is everything.

On the other hand, immigrant Muslims have benefited from the opportunities found in the United States. They opted to immigrate to the United States to take advantage of the educational and economic opportunities available here. Others sought refuge from governments hostile to their political views. Surprisingly, one Turkish interviewee indicated that he came to the United States several decades ago "to live Islam" and escape from the secular Turkish government's persecution of practicing Muslims. Thus, while many Muslims speak of the prevalence of sin in the United States, they also realize that they can benefit from and be transformed by the opportunities and freedom found here. The critic of "Sally" and "Oprah" best manifested this attitude. Though he censured the content of these shows, he continued to watch them.

As the above examples suggest, immigrant Muslims' perceptions of American culture and society are often formed by the media rather than by close contact with non-Muslim Americans and their families. Many immigrant Muslims do not realize that much of what is seen on talk shows, sitcoms, and the news is just as shocking (and amusing at the same time) to most non-Muslims in the United States, and does not reflect the way they lead their daily lives. Few immigrants take the time to understand the underpinnings of American society. In an interview with journalist Steven Barboza, one Pakistani Muslim recounted a story of how his perception of life in the United States changed. Coming to this country to study, he admitted that his opinions had been shaped by what he had seen in movies and magazines. An alternative view was presented to him by U.S. ambassador to Pakistan at that time. The ambassador showed him and several other students who were coming to the United States a picture from *Playboy* magazine and admonished them, "Now I want you to get it through your thick skulls that in America this is not how all women are. They are like your sisters and your mothers." As a result of this experience, this gentleman indicated that he and his colleagues, unlike many other immigrant Muslims, gained a better understanding of and respect for Americans.

This ambivalent attitude toward the United States is also mirrored in the indigenous Muslim population. One interviewee spoke of the difficulties of keeping a "pure mind" when one comes across pictures of nude men and women and other forms of corruption on television. Another, pointing at a picture of a woman in a bikini on the front page of the classified section of a newspaper, sarcastically remarked, "And they call themselves a righteous nation." However, unlike immigrant Muslims, Muslims born in the United States are, for the most part, familiar with life in this society. Thus, while they may criticize the media, they do not see it as a reflection of real Americans' lives. Moreover, this is the only society most indigenous Muslims have come to know and to call home, hence, they are closely tied to it. And, in general, most appreciate their quality of life in the United States. An African-American woman, born into an Islamic family, expressed this appreciation, which for her involved gender equality, in the following way:

> As far as would I feel a bond to Islamic countries (Middle East, etc.)—no, because I can't accept the culture's treatment towards women. I plan to become a doctor and marry a man that will work with me as a team. I have only lived in the U.S. Unless I was born there I could never accept that culture.

Other American-born Muslims, in response to charges of corruption, have sought to defend their loyalties to the United States by stating that the freedom and democracy found in the United States are more in compliance with Islamic values than any social or governmental structure found in the so-called Islamic countries: "America, more than any other country, has demonstrated that it is trying to live up to that Qur'anic injunction, that everyone has the freedom to be whatever they want to be."

Muslims' ambivalent attitudes toward the United States and American culture were also noted in responses to the questionnaires. Fifty-one percent of all Muslims and 49 percent of indigenous Muslims surveyed stated that "the popular culture and values of the United States have caused" them to become more religious. This number rose to 67 percent among African-American Muslims. A significant number of Muslims are thus finding shortcomings in American culture and society, which in turn reinforces their own religiosity. When asked whether the popular culture of the United States has had any influence on Muslims' lives in the United States, an *imam* indicated, "I tell you there are Muslims who . . . gave up drinking alcohol and womanizing after they came here."

There are, of course, many Muslims whose religiosity is not defined in contrast to American culture. These Muslims believe that their religious life should not be influenced by the activities of their greater environment. Many believe that it is their duty to display their Islamic way of life to the corrupt American society so that others may come to realize "the glory of Islam." Needless to say, the success of these Muslims in isolating themselves from the influences of the greater community has been facilitated by the presence of various cultural and religious enclaves in which they can interact socially and in an exclusively Islamic context. . . .

. . . For most Muslims, the primary purpose of Islamic schools is not to teach Islam. Sixty-four percent of this study's sample indicated that they believe one or both parents are "most responsible for the religious instruction of children." One interviewee stated, "I don't want Islamic centers or any other [institutions] teaching my kids Islam. I want to teach them Islam." However, this interviewee advocated the creation of Islamic schools: "There should be some contact with other Muslims besides the family." Islamic schools, therefore, are intended to provide a social context for Muslims to reinforce their values by interacting with people of the same faith who, although not of the same culture or nationality, share in beliefs different from those found in non-Islamic schools or other non-Islamic environments. Hence, in the declaration of its philosophy, the New Horizon School states:

"Growth in social skills through positive peer and adult interaction, with emphasis on Islamic values, will help children develop self-esteem, positive self-image and Islamic identity." Many Muslims feel that the reinforcement of such values is impossible in non-Islamic schools.

5. Richard Wormser Describes Pressures on Muslim Teenagers in American High Schools, 1994

The rumor had spread around the school since Tuesday. A Muslim girl, no one knew who, had been walking home from school when a car suddenly pulled alongside her. A male student she didn't know jumped out and ripped the scarf off her head, blew his nose in it, threw it back at her, jumped back in the car, and drove off, leaving the poor girl in tears.

The problem was that nobody knew if the story was true. Anam, whose family had come to America from Pakistan, felt that even if it wasn't true, it could have been. The World Trade Center in New York had recently been bombed. People had been killed in the explosion and "Muslim fundamentalists" had been arrested and charged. The air was tense and Anam could sense that when people looked at her, their looks were not friendly. And so she made a major decision:

> As a Muslim woman, I am required to cover my hair. We do this to avoid attracting men and engaging in flirtations. It is a way of protecting us. In my parents' country, all women are covered, so none of us stand out. But in America, being covered makes you stand out. I am a very religious person, but I do not want to draw attention to myself. So I decided not to wear my hejab in public.

Anam's problem is one that is shared by many young Muslim women. While their religion requires them to be covered, they feel they need to make compromises for reasons of personal safety.

Although Muslim students are not usually bothered in school, harassment can suddenly escalate in times of crisis. Several Muslim students in southern high schools were slammed against lockers and walls during the Gulf War. Sadeck, a ninth-grade student in New Jersey, remembers how painful it was for her to go to public school after the World Trade Center bombing. "The kids would call me towel-head," she says, "and threaten to remove my hejab to see if I was bald." . . .

. . . In Michigan, a female student tried to pull a hejab off the head of a Muslim student and discovered, to her astonishment, that Muslim women are not necessarily pacifists. "She didn't mess with me anymore after that," the Muslim student recalls, adding, "We are taught to avoid fighting if we can, but if we can't, then we should avoid losing."

Most Muslim students learn to handle the petty annoyances from other students without too much difficulty if the behavior is childish and not vicious. Muhammad Jihad, a student in Ohio, says that after a bomb exploded on a Pan Am jet over Scotland, killing everyone on board, a fellow student asked him if he was the guy who

Richard Wormser, "High School," in *Growing Up Muslim in America* (New York: Walker and Co., 1994). Reprinted by permission of Walker and Co.

planted the bomb. "It was a stupid thing to say, and I felt as bad as anybody. In fact, I think I felt a lot worse than most." Another student says that when she first entered high school and wore a hejab, some students spread a rumor that she was receiving chemotherapy for cancer and that she covered her head because she had lost all her hair. "It was dumb, but that's the kind of thing you have to put up with if you're a Muslim." Tehani El-Ghussein recalls that she was friendly with a Jewish student who sat behind her in class: "I hadn't covered when I first was in class, so he didn't know I was Muslim. Then, when I decided to cover, he was shocked. He asked me if I was Muslim, and I said yes. 'Aren't we supposed to hate each other?' he said. He was kind of kidding, and we were friendly afterwards, but it was never the same."

Some students have problems with their teachers. A few teachers are openly hostile to Muslims. One student remembers how a teacher once remarked, "Your people are enemies of the United States." Other teachers, while not expressing their hostility openly, do so in subtle ways. Deena, who eventually left public school to attend a Muslim school, was denied permission to take advanced courses even though her grades made her eligible. "My teacher never said why he denied me," she says, "but I was sure that it was because of my religion."

Malal Omar, an honor student and an excellent basketball player, remembers how she and her friend Inayet had to overcome their coach's prejudices:

> We were both good enough to be starters. But we did not wear the usual basketball shorts and short sleeves that the other players wore because we are Muslims. Instead we kept our head covered and wore loose clothing when we played. Our coach, who was male, didn't understand this. When we went out on the court he said, "Come to the sidelines, what are you doing there?" At first he didn't play us. He kept us on [the] bench for a while, which was a downer, a blow to our egos . . . but when he saw that our dress didn't interfere with our playing, he was cool.

Some teachers perpetuate the stereotypes that all Muslims are rich oil sheiks and terrorists. Other teachers who discuss Islam or the Middle East in class often get the facts wrong. One student recalls sitting in class listening to the teacher giving incorrect information about Arab history: "I wasn't strong enough to speak out. So I sat there listening to all those distortions, burning inside." Another Muslim student, Mai Abdala, took the opposite position at her school: "When a teacher made a mistake, I spoke up—and said too much." Another student reports: "I had a teacher who called my religion Mohammedanism. I corrected him, and he got angry. He showed me a book in which the term was used. I said, 'Yes, but this book was written by a Western man a long time ago who didn't understand us. We don't worship Muhammad. He was a prophet, not a God. It offends us when somebody calls us Mohammadans.' The teacher accepted the criticism, but he wasn't happy about it. I had to work real hard to keep my A in his class." . . .

Many people believe that Muslim women are restricted if not oppressed by men. This is true in some countries where the patriarchal tradition is strong, modernization is limited, and religious fervor is high. Historically, Islam improved the condition of women at the time of the prophet Muhammad by guaranteeing them certain basic rights, and ending female infanticide, which some of the desert clans practiced. Today, middle-class women in most Muslim countries enjoy a wide variety of rights. (This isn't always the case for poorer women.) All of the young Muslim women interviewed for this book strongly denied they were oppressed in any way in the United States. Anjum Mir remarked: "People are very appearance-oriented. They don't understand it. They have to be educated. We don't feel subjugated. Separation makes us feel more equal. We feel men respect us as a person, not as a sexual object."

Qurat Mir gets annoyed when people judge her and her friends on the basis of her appearance and stereotypical notions:

> Just because we are covered and don't date and sit separately from men in the mosque or in class, people say we are oppressed. That's just not so. Just because a woman wears sexy clothing, does that make her free spirited? Just because we wear loose clothes and are covered, does that make us oppressed and sedated? The only true freedom for me is freedom of the mind. Not being trapped by your body frees the mind. By being covered the mind shows. People deal with you for what you are, not how you look.

Rania Lawendy, a college student who is invited to high schools to speak to students about this issue, shares Qurat's feelings:

> I don't feel Western women are free. Muslim women had the right to have property and vote long before Western women could. When a woman's money was her husband's in the West, Muslim women kept whatever they earned. I don't think it's freedom to show off your body. American women need to be educated. No one can tell me that they're more free than I am!

Another problem Muslim students have to contend with is charges of terrorism. Whenever there is a violent incident, some Muslims become tense. They try to explain to other students that the terrorism has nothing to do with them. Ibrahim Sidicki, a college student, has spoken to many students:

> I try to tell them that the overwhelming majority of Muslims living in the United States are Americans and America is now their country. Whatever people do to hurt this country, hurts us as well. Secondly, I say to judge us by the actions of a few terrorists is like us judging you on the basis of a few mass killers. We know serial killers exist in this country, but we don't look at all Americans as serial killers. So don't look at all of us as terrorists.

Homosexuality is another issue that often leads to some spirited debates with non-Muslims. Nizar Muhammed says that Muslims consider homosexuality to be a sin and as going against the natural order. He quotes the passages in the Quran in which Allah says the prophet Lot chastised his people: "Do you commit lewdness such as no people in creation ever committed before you? For you practice your lusts on men in preference to women: you are indeed transgressing beyond bounds" (7:80–81). According to the Quran, one of the main reasons God destroyed Sodom was homosexual activity. Muslims believe the purpose of sexual relations is to have children.

Even though their beliefs and behavior are different from those of non-Muslims, and despite the occasional problems that arise, Muslim students, for the most part, enjoy public school and make good friends there. Ayesha Kezmi recalls that her non-Muslim friends helped her assert her identity as a Muslim: "I did not cover my head until I was in high school. Although I felt myself a sincere Muslim, I did wonder about the kind of life other students were living. Interestingly, it was my non-Muslim friends who encouraged me to assert my identity as a Muslim. I strongly believe that you can't stay to yourself. You have to have both non-Muslim and Muslim friends."

Some students believe that their friends show them more respect because they're Muslim. . . . Rania was elected senior class president in her high school even though there were no other Muslim students in attendance. "I feel they elected me," says Rania, "because they know that as a Muslim, I don't lie, I don't cheat, and I can be trusted to keep my word." She finds that her girlfriends trust her with their secrets and talk to her about their fears: "Because I'm a Muslim, they know I won't try and steal their boyfriends and I could look at things objectively and tell them the truth." Kalil says that his classmates even help him to be a better Muslim: "I notice that during Ramadan, they try and help me keep my fast. They don't eat around me, and some of them even try to fast with me for a day or two. They try to keep me in check." Tehani El-Ghussein remembers that when she was about to enter high school, she felt a great deal of anxiety about covering her head. Her best friend, who was not Muslim, said, "Hey, do it! That's your religion. It's cool." . . .

Sometimes, Muslim students feel a certain degree of alienation from non-Muslim students, who are much less serious than they are. Qurat Mir found many of her fellow high school students to be "hollow. I really saw people around me only concerned with petty things, how they looked, about their dates, things like that. It bore no relevance to the kind of life I wanted for myself."

To give their children a fuller religious life and to avoid exposing them to the problems and temptations in public school, some Muslims send their children to a religious school rather than a public school. Throughout the United States there are only 165 full-time Muslim schools, and many of them go only as high as the eighth grade. As a result, only one of every ten Muslim children attends a Muslim school. While elementary school children are sent by their parents, some Muslim high school students ask to switch from public school to Islamic school. . . .

. . . Nadia, whose family comes from Turkey, hated her public school: "Nobody bothered me or anything like that. But it was hard practicing my religion in public school. Most kids didn't understand what we did or why we did it. I didn't like the language some of the kids used, or some of the music that preached violence. I am an American but I'm also a Muslim, and I want to be a good Muslim and a good American. In a Muslim school, I can be both."

Tariffa, a sophomore in an Islamic school in Ohio, voluntarily transferred from a public school to a Muslim school to avoid personal problems. She was aware that she was headed for serious trouble unless she changed her lifestyle:

> I was already getting in trouble in intermediate school. I was sneaking out for dates. I would try a drink once in a while. I liked boys and was attracted to them. I knew that if I went to high school, I would get in really serious trouble. So I asked my parents to send me to a Muslim school. Now I focus on my studies and being a good Muslim and doing something with my life.

Young men also find Muslim schools help them avoid temptation. Thomas, who is sixteen, says that "in public schools, it seemed like everyone was into drugs, stuff like crack cocaine, reefer, booze. It was hard not to do that, especially when you were out with your buddies and everybody else was doing it. So I decided to go to a religious school."

Most of the students who attend Islamic schools feel secure in their religious beliefs. They are able to enjoy their lives as Muslims, free from the pressures of socializing, smoking, and drinking that are found in most high schools. For Jeremy, the Muslim school offers him the chance for a better future: "In my regular high school, many kids drop out and don't go on to college. Here, just about everybody goes to college."

Muslim schools differ in many ways from the public schools. In larger schools, boys and girls are taught in separate classrooms. In smaller schools, they may sit in the same room but in separate sections. There is no socializing, which seems to bother the boys more than the girls. An eighth-grade male student says that the hardest part about being in a Muslim school "is you can't hang out with the girls."

Islamic schools, like all religious schools, must meet standards set by the state board of education. History, mathematics, sciences, and social studies are taught. But since Muslim schools are private, they are allowed to teach religion. Part of the school is used as a mosque. Arabic is a basic requirement because students are expected to eventually read the Quran in Arabic. Courses are also given in Islamic civilization.

Is there any conflict between secular education and Islamic religion? There can be, especially when dealing with the scientific explanations of how the world was created and how human beings evolved. Islam holds that God created the world and human beings. Scientific theory talks of creation and evolution as natural phenomena that can be explained without God. In Islamic schools, both views are presented. The contemporary theory of evolution is taught with the qualification that it presents what many modern scientists believe, if not what Islam believes. However, some Muslim schools tip the scales in favor of Quranic teaching and minimize other theories.

6. Prema Kurien Explains Hindus' Adjustments to American Life, 1998

Introduction

How to "fit in" but still maintain one's cultural and personal integrity is the challenge that most immigrants in the United States face in their transition from immigrants to ethnics. Indian immigrants from a Hindu background have achieved this end by using Hinduism, albeit a Hinduism that has been recast and reformulated to make this transition possible. Religion has conventionally defined and sustained ethnic life in this country, and thus while "becoming Hindu" may on the surface appear to be the antithesis of "becoming American," these Indian immigrants have made the transition from sojourners to citizens by developing a Hindu American community and identity. Asserting pride in their Hindu Indian heritage has also been their way of claiming a position for themselves at the American multicultural table. . . .

New Forms of Hindu Practice

Satsang.   It is a pleasant Saturday evening. In a suburban area, a row of expensive cars are parked in front of an upper-middle-class house. Shoes and sandals are placed

Prema Kurien, "Becoming American by Becoming Hindu: Indian Americans Take Their Place at the Multicultural Table," in *Gatherings in Diaspora: Religious Communities and the New Immigration,* ed. R. Stephen Warner and Judith G. Wittner (Philadelphia: Temple University Press, 1998). Excerpted and reprinted by permission of Temple University Press. © 1988 by Temple University. All rights reserved.

neatly outside on the porch. Inside, the furniture has been cleared from the large living room and sheets spread over the carpet. In the center is a makeshift shrine with
pictures of several Hindu deities arranged against the wall. Several of the deities are
adorned with fresh flower garlands. Tall brass oil lamps with flickering flames stand
on either side of the shrine. Baskets containing fruit and flowers have been placed in
front. A man dressed in traditional South Indian clothes is seated on the floor before
the shrine, his wife beside him in a silk saree. Around the couple are seated about
fifty people, the men and boys in casual Western clothes largely on one side of the
room, and the women and girls in rich and colorful Indian clothes on the other. This
is the monthly devotional meeting of the Organization of Hindu Malayalees (OHM),
a *satsang* (congregation of truth) of Hindu immigrants from the state of Kerala in
South India. The states in India have generally been formed on the basis of language,
and thus Kerala constitutes a distinct linguistic and cultural unit. Its people are
Malayalees, speaking the language Malayalam. The OHM, established in 1991, is a
religiocultural organization of around fifty to seventy-five Hindu Malayalee families.
Members meet on the second Saturday of the month in different locations (mostly in
people's houses) around the region for the *pooja* (worship) and *bhajans* (devotional
songs). Around forty to sixty people attend each *pooja.* Since the members are scattered over a wide area, except for the "regulars," it is a changing group that attends
each meeting, depending on the locality. The OHM meeting starts with the lay worship leader chanting an invocation (in Sanskrit) to the deities. This is followed by the
singing of *bhajans* accompanied by cymbals, played by the leader's wife. The leader
of the *bhajan* sings a line, and the rest of the group repeats it. Occasionally, there is a
brief lull, and the leader and his wife call for volunteers to start new *bhajans.* Different members of the group, including a teenage girl, take turns leading the singing.
Some fifteen to twenty *bhajans* are sung, each lasting around five minutes.

. . . [A] Gita discussion period was introduced toward the end of the *pooja,* where
two verses from the *Bhagavad Gita* were translated and explained by Mrs. Kala
Menon, a university professor, followed by a group discussion (in English). During
one such meeting, a member of the group wanted to know why bad things happened
to good people, and why people should bother to be good if that was the case. Mrs.
Menon's reply was that the bad thing may have been caused by something bad that
the person had done in a past incarnation. "Good deeds will be rewarded, if not in
this life, then at least in the next," she answered firmly. Two of the teenage girls in the
group also became involved in the discussion at this point, one pointing out that
the Hindu conception of good and evil is more complicated than the Christian, since
"good does not always give place to good." The other elaborated, "Yes, a person may
lead a good life and then be rewarded in the next life with a lot of money, but the
money may make him arrogant. So he will be punished in the following life."

After the teenagers complained that they felt alienated from the OHM meetings since they were largely Sanskrit-based and adult-oriented, the group has been
making special efforts to try to involve them through discussions and youth activities. If the participation in the Gita sessions is any indication, this effort seems to
be yielding results.

The two-and-a-half-hour worship concludes with further invocations and devotions by the lay priest and a group chant. A potluck vegetarian South Indian meal
follows, during which there is a lot of joking and teasing as people catch up on the
month's news. Relatives and jobs are enquired after, clothes and jewelry admired,

and recipes and professional information are traded, while those who have recently visited India regale the others with their accounts. Youngsters go off and form their own groups. In the adult clusters, children are discussed in great detail by the parents—their health, educational progress, extracurricular accomplishments, and, in the case of older children, parental concerns about finding appropriate marriage partners for them.

Bala Vihar.   On a Sunday afternoon in another suburban South Indian household in the same region, twelve Hindu families with school-age children from Tamil Nadu, another state in South India, get together for their monthly *bala vihar* (child development) meeting, also led by a lay leader, the father of two children in the group. After they sing some familiar *bhajans* and learn a new one, taught by one of the mothers, there is a discussion of Hindu philosophy and values (also in English) and how they can be practiced in everyday life in American society. The first issue discussed is the need for each individual to do his or her allotted tasks, however small, to the best of his or her ability, for the well-being and smooth functioning of society. Children and parents together discuss the problems involved in maintaining the delicate balance between working toward the good of the whole and achieving individual success. One of the young girls gives an example of this tension: "Like, you know, I may want all my friends to get good grades, but my effort is spent in studying to get a good grade for myself." The group nods in agreement. . . .

. . . One of the women adds, "Not getting the end that you think you deserve is very hard. I used to get very depressed when that happened to me and still do some-times, but over time I have tried to cultivate a certain detachment. You should try to recognize that your effort is the only thing that you have control over, so do your very best but then stop thinking about it, go out and have a good time to rejuvenate yourself"—she pauses and then explains—"for the next big effort." There is laughter at this. She continues, "But the effect of this attempt to better yourself is that it results in an expanding sphere of influence. Take Gandhi for instance. He was at first only trying to better himself, but soon that started affecting others, and finally it resulted in his having a major effect on the whole world."

After a snack break, the group divides into two for the Tamil language class. The junior class focuses on vocabulary, while the senior class is taught to appreciate the beauty of classical devotional Tamil poetry. The group reconvenes in the living room for the story session led by yet another woman. The stories are taken from the Hindu epics. Here again the moral of each story is expounded and discussed. One of the day's stories had a message about the sanctity of marriage and family, and the evils of extramarital sex. Particular Hindu practices deriving from the stories are explained, and the children are encouraged to follow them since they have been "time tested over thousands of years." The eagerly awaited crossword puzzle of the month is given out next. The puzzle has questions about Hinduism, Tamil vocabu-lary, and the history, geography, and culture of India. The three-and-a-half hour *bala vihar* concludes with the "host family time," when a child of that family makes a presentation to the group. This month the teenage daughter shows a video of the family's trip to South India, during which they made a pilgrimage to several temples that ended with their family temple. She gives an emotional account of the trip and its meaning for her, ending with a beautiful *bhajan* that she said was the favorite of the deity in their family temple. Several in the group are visibly moved. Finally, there is a lavish potluck meal to end the gathering.

Satsang groups and *bala vihars* have proliferated among the immigrant Indian community in the United States. They represent two different strategies adopted by Indian immigrants to re-create a Hindu Indian environment on foreign soil. The first, which largely targets adults, celebrates and reenacts religious practice. The second is directed at teaching the children about the religion. . . .

In this process of institutionalization, however, Hinduism is also "reinvented." Both *satsangs* and *bala vihars* are forms of religious practice that do not typically exist in India. In fact, group religious activity does not exist in "traditional" Hinduism. In India, Hindus worship largely as families or as individuals, in their homes or a temple. Larger groups at the temple may be present to witness the *pooja* performed by the priest on behalf of the community. Only festivals are celebrated communally by a village. At temple festivals, groups of devotees might sing songs, and individuals take turns to be part of the group so that the singing can be continued uninterrupted for the whole period. As an Indian woman I spoke to mentioned, "I grew up in India, I consider myself a good Hindu, but I'd never heard of many of these things [the *satsangs, bala vihars,* and Hindu youth camps] until I came here." . . .

The first-wave immigrants came in search of better economic prospects and often planned only a temporary stay. Thus, in the early years, they were generally preoccupied with building their careers and establishing an economic foothold. . . .

Most of the members of the OHM are first-wave immigrants, and its secretary offered a . . . poetic explanation about why the group was formed:

> Before we established OHM, many of the true lovers of Kerala heritage and culture were lost in the congested wilderness of Southern California without having any communication with other Kerala members who shared similar interests. Some of them felt lonely in the crowded streets of this faraway land, and hungry and thirsty, in this land of plenty, for company of people who recognized and understood them. They searched everywhere for some familiarity, to prove to their beloved children that the usual bedtime stories of their motherland and her heritage were not some fairy tales but existed in reality.

The teaching of Indian culture and values to the children was an important reason for the formation of the *satsangs* and the primary reason for the formation of *bala vihars.* Indian parents were concerned about the environment within which their children were growing up, which they perceived to be filled with unstable families, sexual promiscuity, drug and alcohol abuse, and violence. The attitudes and values that the children were picking up from school in many ways seemed completely alien to the parents, and created a frightening feeling that the second-generation was growing up to be total strangers with whom parents and other relatives could not even communicate. One of the members of the OHM told me about her friend, whose child came home from school one day and asked, "Why don't I have a white mommy like everyone does? I want a white mommy." Another described how her child, when younger, would dissociate herself from anything Indian and would refuse to walk with her father, acting like she didn't know him, when he wore Indian clothes.

ESSAYS

The best way to understand recent events is to study the history of the people involved. Each of the essays in this section discusses one of America's new religious groups from a longer historical perspective. In the first, Eldin Villafane of Gordon-Conwell Theological Seminary explains how the Spanish conquistadors of the sixteenth century brought the cross and the sword to Latin America. The apparition in 1531 of the Virgin Mary to a poor Aztec man near present-day Mexico City (the site of which became the shrine of Our Lady of Guadalupe) began the process by which the religions of the conqueror and the conquered blended to create the distinctive Hispanic Catholicism that immigrants now bring to the United States. Unfortunately, says Villafane, who is himself an advocate of liberation theology, the immigrants often feel that, in their new context, they have been "spiritually colonized."

In the second essay, John Voll of the University of New Hampshire shows how the long Muslim tradition provides a series of instruments to aid immigrants in adapting to their new home: *hijra* (emigration), *jihad* (exertion), and *da'wa* (mission or calling). In fact, as he argues, Islam has expanded through the world ever since the days of Muhammad by reacting creatively to new settings. In America the opportunity presents itself again in a "postmodern" setting. The third essay, by Rick Fields of Boulder, Colorado, applies equally to this chapter and to Chapter 13 on the religious counterculture. As Fields explains, what is exotic and countercultural to "white Buddhists" taking flight from mainstream America is home ground to "ethnic Buddhists" from China, Japan, and Tibet. The essay argues that white Buddhists, despite their great debt to Asian teachers, can sometimes be inadvertently racist in their assumptions about what Buddhism "really" is and how it should be adapted to American conditions. Fields, like Voll and Villafane, understands the importance of looking back to the earlier history of white and ethnic Buddhists' relations in America, and not confining himself just to present difficulties.

Latino Religion in the United States

ELDIN VILLAFANE

The Hispanic American is a "homo religiosus." There is no area of life, no matter how trivial, that is not "transmuted" by the religious sentiment. The depth of Hispanic religiosity cannot be fathomed by mere statistical quantification of church attendance, or for that matter, statistical surveys or religious profiles. The Hispanic culture and person cannot be understood apart from this religious dimension. . . .

In order to comprehend the enormous cultural, socio-political, and religious role played by the Roman Catholic Church among Hispanics one must do so within the framework of understanding the religio-cultural phenomenon of "Christendom." This complex phenomenon, which is so critical for understanding the role of the church in society, is succinctly defined by Orlando Costas:

> Christendom is *not* the sum total of Christians in the world. It is, rather, a "historical project" that has taken various shapes and forms from the time when it was introduced in the Edict of Milan (A.D. 313), when Constantine made Christianity the state religion. Whatever its form, however, Christendom is the vision of a society organized around Christian principles and values with the church as its manager or mentor. . . .

Eldin Villafane, "Hispanic-American Religious Dimension," in *The Liberating Spirit: Toward an Hispanic American Pentecostal Social Ethic* (Lanham, Md.: University Press of America, 1992). Reprinted by permission of the author.

The Spaniards arrived in the New World with "La Cruz y la Espada" [the cross and the sword]. They were imbued with zeal for "God, Gold and Glory," particularly after having just vanquished the Moors in their unifying of Spain in 1492. A partnership was formed by the Cross and the sword—a partnership that Mackay states was "... formed in the name of evangelism, in which the sword opened the way for the cross, and the cross sanctified the work of the sword, that constituted the originality of Spanish Christianity."

One should note the power of *Patronato Real* ("Royal Patronage") which the crown had over the church. Alexander VI granted the Spanish crown not only political but also religious authority over all lands discovered. According to Justo González, "The result was that the church in Spanish America had very few direct dealings with Rome, and became practically a national church under the leadership of the Spanish kings and their appointees." The conquest and eventual cultural domination of the Amerindians and later the Africans represented this "unholy alliance" of the Church and the State. . . .

. . . 1962 marked a new spirit in the Catholic Church—Vatican II. The "windows were opened" leading to the historic Medellin Conference and the Church's "preferential option for the poor," thus the beginning of the Liberation Movement. This movement injected a new spirit in the Catholic Church in siding with the poor and oppressed, and the recapturing of Christianity as a "Church" and not as "Christendom." In the words of [Enrique] Dussel:

> Christendom—that vast cultural, religious, and socio-political reality of the past—is on its way out. That is the reason behind all the critical problems we as Christians are now facing in Latin America. Some want to hold on to Christendom, but time spent on seeking to preserve Christendom is so much time lost for Christianity.

The historical development of the Catholic Church during these periods and its dominance of the culture of Latin America has been well documented. One cannot fathom the Latin American "mind and heart," for that matter the Hispanic American (who shares equally this cultural heritage), without noting the extent of this dominance:

> The Church was everywhere and with every individual all of his life and filled all of his days. The day began with early morning mass and ended with an Ave Maria, and every occasion, every sorrow, every joy, every holiday had its own special religious symbolism to be acted out in church. During the colonial period the Church was also the school, the university, the hospital, the home of the aged, the sick and the abandoned. It served the individual and the community in many ways. In the absence of newspapers, libraries, museums, theaters, the religious exercise and ritualism in the churches, the orders, the monasteries and the convents filled the role of giving the individual his place in an enchanted and meaningful world. And everything that happened from a bull fight to the arrival of a new Viceroy, an earthquake, or the King's birthday always required public manifestations, processions, prayers, masses and sermons in which the Church was active, perhaps the chief actor in the drama, or better, the chief embodiment of the symbolism that endowed every activity with meanings. It surrounded life at all turns and all times. The church or cathedral bell dominated the community, and daily life was disciplined and ordered to its sound.

It is within the framework of Christendom and its cultural dominance that we picture the conquistadores, friars and the early mission settlement in Florida, the

Southwest and California. Juan Ponce de Leon landed on April 2, 1513, in Florida, which according to Ricardo Santos dates the history of the Latin American Church in the U.S.A. In 1539 Franciscan Marcos de Niza and the black slave Estevan begin exploration in what is now New Mexico in search for the Seven Cities of Cibola and its stories of great riches. The zeal for "God, Gold and Glory" follows the settling of New Mexico in 1595 by Juan de Onate, the ill fated expedition into the territory of Florida by Panfilo de Narvaez and Juan Rodriguez Cabrillo's original exploration of California and the pathway, "El Camino Real" (The King's Highway).

The ceding by Spain of Florida to the U.S.A. in 1819, Texas Independence in 1836, and the treaty of Guadalupe-Hidalgo (1848), giving half of all territory of Mexico to the U.S.A., all led to the transfer of political power to U.S.A. in these conquered territories, leaving subsequently several thousand Spanish and Mexicans "captive strangers in their own land."

To complicate matters for these Hispanics the existing Catholic Church in the USA ousted the native Mexican clergy and bishops and replaced them with French and Spaniards. These were replaced in turn, in the twentieth century, by Irish and German Americans. This trend has continued to exist to this date, with attempts at redress beginning to appear in the late 1960's and early 1970's.

Andrés Guerrero, while writing about the physical and psychological colonization of the Chicano by the Anglos, also speaks strongly about their "spiritual colonization," which has been perpetuated by the USA Catholic Church since the conquest and colonization.

> The systematic denial of spiritual leadership to Chicanos constitutes a form of spiritual colonization. The leaders of the institutional church insured the occupation of the Southwest by denying Chicanos responsible representative leadership in our Catholic Church. Just as we are treated as strangers in our land, so we are also treated as strangers in our own church, which has existed in the Southwest since the 1500s. . . .

In my conceptualization of the socio-religious idea of "spiritual colonization" the religious "powers that be" (those aligned with the conquering forces—coming with them or already present in the society) exercise "spiritual colonization" when at least these three criteria are present:

1. Disenfranchisement of "native" clergy—The denial and lack of development and empowerment of indigenous leadership.
2. Real or attempted religious and cultural domination of a people—a domination over the linguistic and symbolic culture and religious expression, so critical for the identity and liberation of a people.
3. Sacramentalizing the ruling economic-political system—which ultimately means siding with the oppressors.

As a socio-religious concept, "spiritual colonization" can be a useful analytic tool, yielding valuable insight on the power relations of a church and a people, particularly of the same religious confession. . . .

The conquest and colonization of Puerto Rico (1898) by the USA also led to a trend of importing of American and foreign priests and religious personnel on the Island. This was in keeping with a history, first by the Spanish Catholic Church and then by the USA Catholic Church, of not developing and empowering "native" clergy. "Spiritual colonization" was thus perpetuated in Puerto Rico by the U.S. Catholic hierarchy.

According to Antonio M. Stevens-Arroyo, " . . . this practice of importing clergy and the inability to imbue Puerto Rican Catholicism with a nationalistic flavor carried over to the pastoral practice of the Church towards Puerto Ricans in the mainland of the United States."

It is one of the tragic notes of the Puerto Rican migration to the U.S.A. that "they came without their priest" and no "national parishes" received them. They were thus "received" in "integrated parishes"—again experiencing "spiritual colonization." The Hispanic Roman Catholic Church in the USA has indeed been "a people without clergy" and "invisible to the American Church." . . .

It has been only since the late 1960's and early 1970's that the Hispanic Roman Catholic Church has begun to make significant impact on the American Roman Catholic Church and to really begin to seriously challenge "spiritual colonization."

This challenge has been most noticeable in the movement to train more "native" clergy and in the appointment by August 1985 of seventeen Hispanic Bishops in mainland United States (the earliest, Patricio F. Flores, May 5, 1970). Virgilio Elizondo notes this emerging "native" leadership:

> We are also beginning to see the first stages of a native leadership within the Hispanic church. By "native" I mean born in the United States. Often in the past native-born American Hispanics have been oppressed and dictated to by U.S. taskmasters and by Latin Americans, who also took it for granted that we could not do our own thing. Today leadership is beginning to grow out of the Hispanic communities. We have learned much from Latin America but we have also learned much from our own U.S. experience. Today we are blending aspects of both to put together new models of thought and action.

Noteworthy in the emerging indigenous leadership is the development of the organization of PADRES (Priests Associated for Religious, Educational, and Social Rights); Las Hermanas; the Northeast Catholic Pastoral Center for Hispanics, in New York City; the Mexican American Cultural Center, in San Antonio; the establishment of the Office of the Secretariat for Hispanic Affairs, U.S. Catholic Conference; the issuing on December 12, 1983, of "A Pastoral Letter on Hispanic Ministry: The Hispanic Presence: Challenge and Commitment" by the National Conference of Catholic Bishops; and the growth of "Cursillo" and "Comunidades de Bases" throughout hundreds of Hispanic communities. These developments are some of the positive signs of hope and liberation among the Hispanic Roman Catholic Church in the U.S.A.

The religious symbols and images of a people in a given community, given an internalization development through their history, combine in the complex narrative known as myths. . . .

In the "evangelization" of the Americas no other myth or symbol has played such a dominant role as "the religious symbol of Guadalupe." . . . La Morenita's ("the brown lady") appearance to Juan Diego, an Aztec, on December 9, 1531, on the hill of Tepeyac, became such a strong religious symbol that eight million native Americans were baptized into the Catholic Church during the seven years after her apparition. Virgilio Elizondo states that:

> The symbolism of *la Morenita* opened up a new possibility for racio-cultural dialogue and exchange. The synthesis of the religious iconography of the Spanish with that of the indigenous Mexican people into a single, coherent symbol-image ushered in a new, shared experience. The missioners and the people now had an authentic basis for dialogue. What the missioners had been praying for had now come in an unexpected

(and for some, unwanted) way. The cultural clash of sixteenth-century Spain and Mexico was resolved and reconciled in the brown Lady of Guadalupe. In her the new *mestizo* people finds its meaning, its uniqueness, its unity. Guadalupe is the key to understanding the Christianity of the New World, the self-image of Mexicans, of Mexican-Americans, and of all Latin Americans.

Symbol systems are critical tools for religious affirmation and theological reflection. . . .

Guadalupe as a symbol of faith speaks to the Chicano Catholic in terms of God's motherly love for them, the oppressed—after all the mother of Jesus has taken on their color, their clothes, their cause. She is the symbol of trust and of the impossible.

Guadalupe as a symbol of identity provides a sense of meaning, a cultural sense of belonging and ultimately a reference point and glue, "that keeps the structures together: the politics, the kinship system, the mutual aid societies, modern-day association groups, and the church as an institution." . . .

Guadalupe as a symbol of hope is a symbol that is rooted deep in the consciousness of the Chicano, appealing to positive Amerindian and Spanish heritage and influence. According to Elizondo, "The power of hope offered by the drama of Guadalupe came from the fact that the unexpected good news of God's presence was offered to all by someone from whom nothing special was expected: the conquered Indian, the lowest of the low."

Guadalupe as symbol of woman against *machismo* "is important because she guarantees a place for womanhood . . . " and challenges the worst elements of machismo by reminding the *macho* that the "Chicana is not his scapegoat and that Our Lady of Guadalupe, a symbol of our mother, is against *machismo.*"

Guadalupe is also a symbol of liberation. Her inspirational role was graphically displayed in the banner and flags leading the Mexican Independence under Father Hidalgo and most recently Cesar Chavez's struggles with the exploitation of farm workers.

Guerrero asks, "What is Guadalupe saying to Chicanos about their church, which has no Chicano leadership? What is Guadalupe saying in terms of the educational deficiencies of Chicano children . . . in terms of Texas Chicano children having a health record worse than any other children in the other forty-nine states? . . . in terms of human rights issues? In terms of world solidarity?" His resounding response is loud and clear: "Guadalupe as a symbol of liberation is the Mother of the Oppressed. Like any mother, she does not abandon her children nor does she fail to respond to their cries."

Muslim Adaptation in America

JOHN O. VOLL

Muslims in the United States face a variety of challenges. Many of these are similar to those faced by other minority communities in America. However, Muslims also face challenges and opportunities that are tied to the character of Islam. The Islamic faith

John O. Voll, "Islamic Issues for Muslims in the United States," in *The Muslims of America*, ed. Yvonne Yazbeck Haddad (New York: Oxford University Press, 1991), 205–216. Copyright © 1991 Oxford University Press, Inc. Used by permission of Oxford University Press, Inc.

and its practice involve special obligations and responsibilities that shape the way Muslims as individuals and groups respond to the conditions of American society. Often people become involved in examining the "American" issues faced by distinctive and minority communities in the United States forgetting that the special characteristics of the community are also important. Significant Islamic issues are involved in the life of Muslims in the United States as well as important American issues.

These Islamic issues should not be viewed simply as special problems or difficulties. Some issues do involve problems, but others involve challenges that are significant opportunities as well. The ways that Muslims respond to changing conditions in the United States may provide important guidelines for Muslims elsewhere and for non-Muslims in the United States, since at the heart of Islamic issues there are universal concerns.

There are two different types of Islamic issues for Muslims in the United States. First are what might be thought of as the "classic" issues for Muslim minorities everywhere. In these, the "key concern is how to live an Islamic life in a non-Muslim country." Here the basic issues are maintaining Islam as a way of life in a context where that is difficult, and deciding the meaning and implications of community-faith concepts such as *hijra* (emigration), *jihad* (exertion), and *da'wa* (mission or calling) in the American context. In some ways these issues are similar to those faced by Muslim minority communities throughout the history of Islam.

A second type of Islamic issue also is directly related to the special conditions of the contemporary world. These are the issues involved in the great transformations of human society which have been taking place in the past decades. These changes have been described by some as the emergence of postindustrial society while others speak of the development of postmodern perspectives and institutions. Whatever descriptive title is given to the processes, the transformations of recent decades create the conditions within which special issues arise for Muslims and others living in the emerging "postmodern" society in the United States.

The Islamic issues facing Muslims in the United States are shaped by the basic nature of Islam. The worldview and guidance for behavior provided by Islam contain specific elements as well as general approaches that are specially affected by the nature of American society.

It is often noted that Islam is not "just a religion," but a total way of life. This observation is made by both non-Muslims and Muslims when they are discussing the nature of the Islamic faith, obligations, and experience. It refers to the comprehensive and inclusive nature of the Islamic ideal. Muslims have a guide and model that covers "the most mundane aspects of everyday life and behavior as well as the general principles directing the community."

All major religious traditions in some way attempt to guide humans in their lives. Christian and Jewish aspirations define "ways of life" and, in some contexts, have presented comprehensive ideals for believers. The worldview of medieval Western Christendom provides an example of a comprehensive Christian social ideal, as does the worldview of orthodox Judaism. However, in the modern era in Western societies the secularization of worldview has been a prominent development. This has meant that a growing proportion of society accepts a differentiation among the various sectors of life—religious, economic, political.

In many ways, the process of secularization became most widely accepted and most clearly implemented in the United States of the twentieth century. The separation of church and state became almost a political dogma. Similarly, "religion" in the United States has come to be seen by many as a "private" and individual matter rather than a public one. To a remarkable extent, social attitudes and political expectations in the United States are built on an assumption that the basic faith of an American will, in a significant way, be "just a religion." The expectation is that religion can be separated from politics and a sense that the United States is a secular society.

The context and basic social framework within which Muslims live in the United States is in some important ways secular. One of the major issues for Muslims is how Islam, which defines a comprehensive way of life, can function within such a secular context. . . . Muslims . . . face a special challenge of operating within a legal and social framework in which church-state relations have been defined primarily in relation to Judaism and Christianity. . . .

The issue of prayer in public schools can be used as an example of how American church-state issues relate to Islamic experiences. At the present time, the subject of whether or not prayer should be allowed in American public schools is hotly debated. The vigor of the debate shows that many Americans, possibly a growing proportion, do not accept the full implications of secularism for American society. . . .

None of the most visible or prominent groups involved in the debate has discussed the situation in a context within which a Muslim would be able to fulfill the obligation of *salat,* the prescribed five daily prayers. Much of the school prayer debate uses the basically Christian approach, which assumes prayer to be a private communication between the believer and God. As has often been pointed out, salat "are somewhat different from 'prayer' as used in the Christian sense, although personal supplication and glorification of God (known as *du'a*) are also a very important part of the Muslim worship."

The specific conditions requisite for the regular prescribed prayers are not readily available in American schools (or in offices and factories). In addition to the need for released time at the proper hours, the believer also needs facilities for the preliminary ablutions and an appropriate space. . . .

For Muslims to support the opponents of prayer in school would be for them to accept the assumptions of a secularized society. In particular, this position encourages the attitude that religion is a personal rather than a public matter and, therefore, its activities should not be practiced in public places. The issue thus challenges the sense of Islam as a total way of life. There are believers in Islam as well as in Judaism and Christianity who accept secularist assumptions, but they are challenged by more fundamentalist believers, as in the other religious traditions.

For the American Muslim, then, an important task is to redefine issues of religious life in America in such a way that an Islamic alternative is possible within the debate. Such an alternative would recognize in some way the special character of Islam as a total way of life, in both the public and private arenas. The prayer in school issue reflects the type of concern involved in such an effort. . . .

The situation of Muslims in the United States has many elements that are not unique in the history of Islam. In many different eras and areas, Muslims have found themselves in societies where they are not the controlling group or the majority. As a result, over the centuries certain concepts have developed which define modes of response to the situation of living within a non-Muslim majority. Some of the most important of these are hijra, jihad, and da'wa. Each of these concepts is important in defining a specific way of responding to the minority situation.

Hijra can be translated in a number of ways. The core of the meaning is the act of leaving one place and moving to another, often with the implication of seeking refuge but sometimes simply as a process of emigration. A "hijra experience" is at the heart of the historic development of the Islamic community during the lifetime of the Prophet Muhammad.

The hijra of the Prophet marks the beginning of the Islamic calendar era. It was a significant transition in the nature of the community of followers of Islam. Muhammad began his prophetic mission in Mecca, where he presented the revelations he received as a preacher in an already established community. The leaders and controlling elite in Mecca did not accept the message Muhammad preached and placed limitations on him and the small number of people who had accepted Islam. Then, in A.D. 622, Muhammad and the rest of the Muslim community moved to another town, which later became known as Medina. It is this movement from Mecca to Medina which is called the Hijra in Islamic tradition.

The Hijra of the Prophet represented a major transformation of the Islamic community. In Medina, Muhammad organized his followers into an effective community, and the Islamic message defined the full way of life of that community. In this historical context, hijra is an escape from persecution and unbelief, but it is also an emigration to a new context within which the Islamic community can flourish as a full way of life. . . .

The dynamic expansion of Islam in world history has, in fact, depended on Muslims who did not emigrate when they found themselves in non-Muslim societies. Muslim merchants and traveling teachers, for example, were important vehicles for the expansion of Islam in sub-Saharan Africa and Southeast Asia. In other contexts, Muslim minority communities have survived and adapted to non-Muslim societies in China, the Balkans, and now in the Soviet Union. In such situations, any hope for the conversion of the society as a whole to Islam is a long-term vision, but the communities have been able to maintain an authentic sense of Islamic identity. . . .

The experience of Muslims in Sub-Saharan Africa identifies the other alternatives: rather than hijra, Muslims should work to transform the societies in which they find themselves. This option includes two important concepts arising out of the Islamic tradition. They are related to each other and to a sense of hijra as well. These are da'wa, which can be translated in this context as mission or call or message, and jihad.

Despite the fact that many writers, both Muslim and non-Muslim, have tried to explain the broader meanings of jihad, it remains a very misunderstood term in the West. If average, non-Muslim Americans heard the statement that Muslims, even those in the United States, accepted the responsibility of jihad in the path of God, they would assume that this meant that those Muslims were obligated to engage in acts of violence in the name of their religion. *Jihad* is most frequently translated simply as "holy war." While jihad does, in certain contexts, mean holy war, it has a much broader meaning within Islamic consciousness. Jihad in the path of God is an active striving for righteousness. At times this may mean fighting for one's faith, but it also involves the more general sense of actively serving God in every way possible. It is jihad in this broader sense that becomes the responsibility of all Muslims, whether they are living in a Muslim or a non-Muslim society. There is, however, a special sense of the need for each Muslim actively to affirm Islam in non-Muslim contexts.

Muslims, wherever they are, are expected to strive for recognition of God's oneness through social justice and a properly ordered society. . . .

For Muslims in non-Muslim societies, this striving may take many different forms, both independently and in cooperation with other forces in society. In the struggle against drug sales and drug-related crimes in Brooklyn, for example, a mosque took an active role in cooperation with the police. Reports of this noted that Muslims "risked personal safety to defend the area against drug dealers" and resulted in local non-Muslims saying, "Thank God for the Muslims." A similar activist Muslim program has helped reduce drug dealing in some housing projects in Washington. Activities like these reflect a type of jihad that is working for the transformation of non-Muslim society. Elsewhere, programs for control of alcohol abuse and gambling and recreation programs for youth have a similar impact.

Related to this jihad effort is the active effort to present the message positively to the people in the non-Muslim society. This mission or call is da'wa. In the perspective of Islam as a total way of life, as one Muslim leader expressed it, "living in surrender to Allah cannot be actualized fully unless other people join us in our endeavor, unless the whole society lives in surrender. Hence, at least inviting others to join our venture, that is Da'wah, is an essential part of being a Muslim." . . .

. . . It is possible for Muslim communities to survive and thrive in a variety of contexts within American society. There certainly are problems in fulfilling Islamic obligations in the midst of a secular society, but these problems can be resolved in many ways.

It is, however, important to go beyond these observations to the long-term evolution of faith and religion in the United States (and, in fact, in the world in general). The major evolution is in the direction of what some people have called postmodern faith. There is a move away from the secularist perspective and a growing sense, in the major religious communities, of the public dimensions and obligations of their faiths.

Globally, major religious traditions have had an increasingly visible role in the political arena. The forces of the Islamic resurgence have been very important here, although the emergence of Liberation Theology in Latin America and the roles of the Roman Catholic Church in Poland and elsewhere show that this broadening of the sphere of religion is not simply an Islamic phenomenon. One important aspect of this has been in areas beyond the strictly political. The moral and ethical implications of science have become important topics of debate in societies where science has traditionally been considered a "value-free" activity.

Shortly after World War II, Arnold Toynbee identified special contributions that might be made by Islam to the social life of the emerging global "great society." Toynbee, writing in the late 1940s, felt that the race consciousness of modern Western society was a source of danger for humanity and that the message and achievements of Islam in this area were a source of possible strength that could "decide this issue in favour of tolerance and peace." Although it has been argued that the Muslim record was idealized by people like Toynbee, in the context of American society Islam has provided a way to move against at least some aspects of racism. The message of Islam provided a way for a Malcolm X to break away not only from the racism of American whites but also of the early Black Muslim movement, led by Elijah Muhammad. Islam has provided a new perspective for the emerging morality of identity and pluralism in the American context.

The Islamic ideal of informing the total way of life by divine revelation is in tune with the broader movements of moral awareness in the United States. Muslims in the United States have a special opportunity which has been articulated by Muslim activists in terms of da'wa (mission). Ismail Faruqi, for example, has said, "if you look upon this as an event in world history, you will see that Allah, *subhanahu wa ta'ala,* has prepared the course of history to welcome you in the West. . . . By bringing you here . . . Allah, *subhanahu wa ta'ala,* has carved out a vocation for you, a new mission, and this mission is to save the West." Suzanne Haneef, at the conclusion of her introduction to Islam, states, "As the number of indigenous and immigrant Muslims continues to increase in the Western world, it is hoped that they will make very significant contributions to the societies in which they live, side by side with other likeminded people, by making Islam's point of view known, and drawing upon the vast legacy of its teachings to work toward solutions of the many grave problems and dilemmas confronting mankind."

These statements point to two somewhat different types of Islamic issues facing Muslims in the United States. First, there are the classic issues of community survival in a minority context. Islam as a way of life requires certain things that are sometimes difficult to do in the context of a secular society. In that context, concepts such as emigration (hijra), religious exertion (jihad), and mission (da'wa) have special meaning and represent obligations for Muslims.

Second, there are the grand issues of the mission of Muslims in contemporary world history. As modern societies enter the postmodern era, new issues are raised and new approaches must be developed. In this, there is a move away from the old modernist-secularist approaches. Worldviews that see faith and practice as a total way of life may have a particular contribution to make. American Muslims are in a special position and have a special challenge of finding ways to have postmodern society in the United States reflect the Judaeo-Christian-Muslim tradition most Americans share.

Contrasting Immigrant Buddhists and "White Buddhists"

RICK FIELDS

Two very different events date the beginnings of the project of American Buddhism: first, the construction of America's first Buddhist temple in San Francisco's Chinatown in 1853 by the Sze Yap Company; and second, the taking of the Three Refuges Vow by a New York businessman, Charles Strauss, from the Sinhalese Anagarika Dharmapala in the aftermath of the World Parliament of Religions held in Chicago

Rick Fields, "Divided Dharma: White Buddhists, Ethnic Buddhists, and Racism," in *The Faces of Buddhism in America,* ed. Charles Prebish and Kenneth Tanaka (Berkeley, Calif.: University of California Press, 1998), 196–206.

in 1893. On the one hand, an Asian ethnic community builds a temple to protect and preserve its values, as well as to minister to the spiritual needs of its members. On the other hand, a mostly white and middle-class group adopts and adapts a Buddhism taught by a charismatic, or at least a compelling, missionary. These two very different beginnings, separated by forty years, symbolize the dual development of American Buddhism.

Today, more than a hundred years after the most recent of these two events, Buddhism in America has proliferated wildly. There are groups of mostly white middle-class students organized around missionary teachers from Japan, China, Korea, Burma, Sri Lanka, Vietnam, and Tibet. At the same time, there are communities of Asian Buddhist immigrants, or their descendants, organized around ethnic temples. The strong presence of both these groups indicates that late twentieth-century America has become not only a refuge for Buddhist immigrant communities but the staging area for an entirely new project in Buddhist history, the creation of something called American Buddhism. With all its diversity, it is not surprising that no one can claim to know with any accuracy the number of Buddhists in America as we approach the millennium, but a telephone survey in 1989–90 found that at least one million Americans identified themselves as Buddhists, while the number of people with no formal Buddhist affiliation who have attended Buddhist teachings or meditation retreats probably runs into the hundreds of thousands.

A few years ago, I attempted to write an essay for an American Buddhist journal as part of a special section titled "Dharma, Diversity and Race." Attempting a view from my own experience as a white middle-class American who had studied with teachers from Japan, Tibet, and Burma, I ran into a classificatory bramble. The term *American Buddhist* was far too broad to address the distinctions I was trying to uncover, and was descriptive only of a still unclear future. The reality, in any case, revealed a landscape of complex and bewildering variety: what might be called American Tibetan Buddhists, American Japanese Zen Buddhists, American Korean Buddhists, American Burmese (or Vipassana) Buddhists on one side; and immigrant Asian Buddhists and their often native-born bicultural children: Japanese American Buddhists, Korean American Buddhists, Vietnamese American Buddhists, Burmese American Buddhists on the other. . . .

. . . This definitional frustration led me to the term *white Buddhist*. This term was not without its problems, of course, but it had the virtue of bringing to light a situation that is so pervasive it is hardly noticed—the fact that the so-called missionary or Euro-American Buddhism, in all its bewildering variety, is largely white and middle-class. The term *white Buddhist* is admittedly somewhat arbitrary, as Americans of all races can be found scattered through some "white Buddhist" communities. . . .

As it turns out, the term *white Buddhist* also has a certain historical resonance. The term was first used in connection with Col. Henry Steel Olcott and Madame Blavatsky, the founders of the Theosophical Society. Blavatsky considered the mysterious masters to be "Esoteric Buddhists." In Ceylon, Olcott and Blavatsky (who had taken out American citizenship) became the first Americans to become Buddhists in a traditional sense. On May 25, 1880, both he and Blavatsky knelt before a Buddhist priest at a temple in Galle and performed the ceremony of taking *pansil*—the Five Precepts, a lay vow to undertake to refrain from killing, stealing, sexual misconduct, lying, and intoxicants. They recited the vows in Pāli, as well as the Triple Refuge in Buddha, Dhamma, and Sangha, before a large crowd. "When we had finished the last of the Silas," Olcott noted in his diary, "there came a mighty shout to make one's nerves tingle."

Olcott later campaigned vigorously in the anticolonial struggle of Sinhalese Buddhists, giving speeches and founding Buddhist schools and seven branches of the Buddhist Theosophical Society of Ceylon. Part of this work included mentoring a young Buddhist by the name of Anagarika Dharmapala, the same man who would give the Three Refuges to Strauss at the World Parliament of Religions in 1893.

Olcott's Buddhism has been criticized for contaminating Sri Lankan Buddhism with Protestant elements, thus giving rise to "Protestant Buddhism," a case in point being the popular (still in print) *Buddhist Catechism* (1871), used in the Buddhist schools he was instrumental in starting. Certainly there were Protestant elements in Olcott's rationalized approach, which encouraged Buddhists to adapt Christian missionary methods against the Christians, but Olcott was also an avid student. Before writing his *Buddhist Catechism,* he read some ten thousand pages on Buddhism in English and French translation, went over the Sinhalese version of the manuscript word by word with Sumangala, principal of the Vidyodaya College, and received Sumangala's imprimatur. In Olcott's introduction, he suggested that *Buddhism* was a Western term; the proper term was *Buddha Dharma.* Nor should it be thought of as a religion. "The Sinhalese Buddhists," he wrote, "have never yet had any conception of what Europeans imply in the etymological construction of the Latin root of this term. In their creed there is no such thing as a 'binding' in the Christian sense, a submission to or merging of self in a Divine Being." . . .

Unlike white Buddhists, ethnic Buddhist communities suffered the racism that has been the nightmare squatting at the heart of the American dream from the very beginning. Judge Charles T. Murray of the California Supreme Court laid bare the underlying pattern in 1854, just one year after the Sze Yap Company built America's first Buddhist temple in San Francisco's Chinatown, when he disallowed the testimony of a Chinese eyewitness to a murder involving two white men. Ever since the time of Columbus, said the judge, "the American Indian and the Mongolian or Asiatic were regarded as the same type of species," which is to say, less than human and without white rights. The same pattern repeated itself in the Chinese Exclusion Act of 1882, "the first departure from our official policy of open *laissez-faire* immigration to be made on ethnocultural grounds," as Stuart Creighton Miller points out in *The Unwelcome Immigrant.* This anti-Asian legacy culminated in Executive Order 9066, which relegated 110,000 Japanese Americans to internment camps in 1942.

It is true that white Buddhists are nearly all students of Asian Buddhist missionaries, and that many of them have adopted the customs of their teachers. However, though white Buddhists may go by Japanese, Chinese, Korean, Tibetan, Sinhalese, or Vietnamese Dharma names, wear robes and shave their heads, affect to speak with a Japanese or Tibetan accent, eat soba, kim-chee, or mo-mos, sip green tea or chai, they remain part of the mainstream white culture. To put it crudely in the lexicon of racism, "they can pass." . . . Asian Americans, be they recent immigrants or third-generation Sansei, are always in peril of being placed by color and race, no matter that they may be Christian (as perhaps more than half of Asian Americans are) or live an exemplary middle-American suburban life.

Racism at its deepest level is the power to define, which is always the paramount power in a racist society. It is hardly surprising, then, that in the ongoing discussion about the meaning of an emergent "American Buddhism" from the present and confusing plurality of Buddhisms in America, it is mainly white Buddhists who are busy doing the defining. Nor is it surprising that they are defining it in their own image. This image has been in large part formed by the countercultural movement of the sixties, which crested in a great wave of white Buddhist activity. The Beat Buddhism of the fifties had been largely literary, but beginning with the sixties, the dramatic rigors of Zen practice galvanized the most zealous white Buddhists. Psychedelics may have had more to do with this than most would like to admit these days, but I would suggest that the mind-blowing intensity of the psychedelic experience gave practitioners in the sixties a taste—at times a thirst—for extreme experiences. White Buddhists who came of age during the sixties wanted enlightenment, and they wanted it immediately. . . .

In Asia disciplined and regular meditation had been largely limited to monks. But in America, the monastic emphasis on meditation was practiced in coed Dharma centers and retreats. This has led to a worthy experiment, but one with certain inherent contradictions. As Suzuki Rōshi once said, scratching his head: "You Americans are not quite monks and not quite laypeople." Nevertheless, a bias toward hard-style monastic and yogic practice has remained the central focus of white Buddhists, and has become part of the founding legend of American Buddhism. Suzuki Rōshi, it is said, came to America to minister to the ethnic Sōtō Zen mission in San Francisco. But he found that the Japanese American Buddhist members of the temple were interested largely in social affairs and ritual. Only the young and wild Americans were willing to undergo the rigors of true Zen training. And so Rōshi left the Japanese American Sōtō Zen mission to forge the brave new world of American Zen. . . .

. . . Just what American Zen or American Buddhism might be is still unclear. Will it be some hybrid of all the Buddhisms now present, or will the various lineages maintain their boundaries (and, some might say, integrity)? . . .

Though the shape of this incipient white Buddhism in America is necessarily hazy at present, several general trends can be identified. The first is that it is largely a layperson's movement, at least as far as the majority of practitioners are concerned, though monks and nuns have certainly played a central role as teachers and leaders. Second, it is based on a strenuous practice of sitting meditation associated with Zen or *vipassanā*, especially mindfulness of breathing. Third, it welcomes Western psychology as a valid and useful, some argue necessary, adjunct. . . . Fourth, American Buddhism is increasingly shaped by feminist insights and critiques. There are women teachers in most traditions, conferences, journals, and the growing literature. Some teachers hold retreats solely for women, arguing that women's spirituality is different from men's. Fifth, it harbors an impetus toward social action. The Buddhist Peace Fellowship, which seeks to bring the teachings of Buddhism to the peace movement, and the peace movement to the attention of Buddhists, is one of the few viable pan-*sangha* organizations in existence. The Vietnamese Zen teacher Thich Nhat Hanh is also a powerful voice for a politically engaged Buddhism. And, sixth, it contains democratic and antiauthoritarian or antihierarchical sentiments; at least one *sangha* has limited the terms of its leaders, and other groups have devised codes of ethics, with special attention being drawn to abuses of sexuality and power.

All these trends, except for the second, are characteristically American components that seem to run counter to Asian norms. Many white Buddhists see these trends as natural adaptations, necessary and salutary correctives to out-of-date Asian hierarchies and patriarchies. Whether they prove helpful or damaging in the long run, only time will tell.

Ethnic Buddhism and Racism

Today there is a whole new wave of Asian immigrants: Vietnamese, Thais, Cambodians, Burmese, Taiwanese, Mainland Chinese, and most recently, even a few thousand Tibetans. Unlike the first Chinese and Japanese, these Asian immigrants are entering a country that has, for the first time in its history, an active if small Buddhist population. No doubt there have been many instances of fellowship and communication and help between Asian and white Buddhists. As early as 1899, for example, five white Californians joined Jōdo Shinshū Japanese missionaries to form an organization called the Dharma Sangha of Buddha, publishing an English-language journal called *The Light of Dharma.* In the thirties and forties Julius Goldwater was an important figure who worked to bring white Americans into the Buddhist Churches of America.

Whatever outreach that had occurred was derailed, however, by the traumatic experience of the internment camps. . . .

. . . There was, and still is, far less fellowship and communication between the two groups than one would expect. Much of this split stems no doubt from the natural ethnic fellowship of an immigrant community in which Buddhist temples have functioned as cultural and community centers above all else. Activities are conducted in a particular Asian language. Even when English is used at ethnic Buddhist temples, many white Buddhists are reminded of the empty and yet required religious rituals of their childhood, just what they fled from into Buddhism. "It's just like church" is a common reply when white Buddhists are asked why they don't have more contact with their fellow Asian American Buddhists.

Of course, there are many reasons for this situation. Some of them are obvious: by definition an ethnic Buddhism serves and protects the interests of a particular community within the bubbling cauldron we used to call a melting pot. And it is true, as well, that deep historical and ethnic animosities exist between various Asian immigrant and Asian American communities. Furthermore, there do seem to be very real differences in styles of practice; the division between white and ethnic Buddhists may be less racial and more the continuation of an ongoing sectarian dialectic about how best to realize liberation.

Whatever the tangled, tragic, interdependent chain of cause and effect may be, since racism remains such a powerful force, such a ubiquitous component of national ego, as unconscious on the national level as the notion of solid self is on the personal level, some white Buddhists have begun the task of deconstructing their racism under the hard bright light of meditative awareness. From this vantage point, racism turns out to be nothing less than the terrified apprehension of the other, which in itself is a reflection of the old Buddhist problem of self. . . .

When racism is brought fully into the light of meditative awareness, it may become evident that the "other Buddhism," as exemplified by new Asian immigrants as well as by the long-established Pure Land Buddhist Churches of America, holds an important clue to the creation and survival of American Buddhism. To begin with, the other Buddhism is inseparable from community. It is a Buddhism that is part of a culture and is not self-conscious. This in itself is a lesson well worth considering, especially by Buddhists exerting themselves to see through the delusion of self.

And if the Asian American Buddhists may seem to lack the bent-for-enlightenment zeal of some white Buddhists, they also lack the self-centered arrogance that all too often accompanies it. I remember the teaching offered by a Vietnamese woman when she felt my irritation that the weekend retreat had been delayed by a wedding at the temple. "Hey, take it easy," she said. "You're in the temple now."

Another characteristic of white Buddhism is, or certainly has been, its naïveté. Some of this naïveté may come from a bent for idealistic thinking, endemic to Judeo-Christian theism. Some comes from a simpler cause: this generation of white Buddhists are all first generation, at least as far as their Buddhism is concerned, and every first-generation experience is bound to lack a certain breadth. White Buddhists are just now beginning to have the opportunity to find out what all their talk about impermanence really means. Witnessing old age, sickness, and death in a way the young rarely can in contemporary society is doing much to deepen the practice of the white Buddhist community. A very practical result of this is involvement in hospice work. Indeed, one of the main correctives that Buddhism offers contemporary American society is in its skillful and straightforward teachings about dying and death. . . .

Conclusion

That aspect of Buddhism which is subsumed under the rubric of "faith," and the practices connected with it, are still a kind of a terra incognita for American Buddhists in general. One reason for this is that the practices such as prayer and other forms of devotion are, for many Americans, tarred with the sticky feathers of their Judeo-Christian past.

This suggests another interesting point of intersection, since the two aspects of faith and effort, of other and self-power as it is expressed in the Japanese tradition, are not as far apart as adherents of both traditions suppose. Indeed, anyone who has gone through the boot camp of a Rinzai Zen *sesshin,* for example, knows that at a certain point there is nothing to do but give up. Or to put it another way, at a certain point the seeking mind simply gives up, sometimes through what we might call grace but more often through nothing more miraculous than sheer exhaustion. When the compulsively seeking mind stops seeking, a great relaxation dawns. And along with it comes a tremendous feeling which manifests as compassion and gratitude. This is a great release, and relief, and can be found expressed quite fully in the Jōdo Shin tradition. If you really recognize that we are all already "saved" by virtue of Amida's vow, then you can finally (1) relax and (2) be grateful to everyone around you.

It may well be that certain aspects of Asian American Buddhism will provide the turning word for white American Buddhists caught in the dilemma of a lay practice based on monastic models. Shinran, the founder of Japanese Pure Land, was a revolutionary who insisted that the liberating insights of Dharma were fully available to the ordinary man and woman. And the teachers who continue to insist that this is so are neither monks nor priests nor rinpoches nor rōshis but married "ministers." This model, which has existed right in front of our noses, may be at least worth contemplating, both for its successes and failures. The community aspects of ethnic Buddhism have a great deal to offer a white Buddhism caught in the dilemma of a lay practice based on monastic models. A Zen practitioner writes in a recent issue of *Turning Wheel,* the journal of the Buddhist Peace Fellowship, on family:

> We Buddhist parents often believe we're making history, forging a family based Buddhism. In one sense, we are; most of our Asian teachers are from monastic traditions. But in the widest sense we are not. The Japanese branch of the Pure Land tradition, for instance . . . has family-based communities all over the country, complete with English-language services, dharma schools for children, festivals, rites and rituals and individual practice. . . . In many parts of Asia, lay people of strong spiritual inclination have recourse to formal daily practice, such as [to] mantra practice and to a teacher. And they raise families. Although we live in different cultural circumstances, I believe we still have much to learn from lay Buddhist parents and lay Buddhist traditions from other cultures.

FURTHER READING

Abalos, David. *Latinos in the United States: The Sacred and the Political* (1986).

Brown, Karen McCarthy. *Mama Lola: A Voudou Priestess in Brooklyn* (1991).

Dasgupta, Sathi. *On the Trail of an Uncertain Dream: Indian Immigrant Experience in America* (1989).

Davidman, Lynn. *Tradition in a Rootless World: Women Turn to Orthodox Judaism* (1991).

Deloria, Vine. *God Is Red: A Native View of Religion* (1994).

Diaz-Stevens, Ana Maria. *Oxcart Catholicism on Fifth Avenue: The Impact of the Puerto Rican Migration on the Archdiocese of New York* (1993).

Dolan, Jay P., and Gilbert M. Hinojosa, eds. *Mexican-Americans and the Catholic Church, 1900–1965* (1994).

Freeman, James. *Hearts of Sorrow: Vietnamese American Lives* (1989).

Georges, Eugenia. *The Making of a Transnational Community* (1990).

Gonzalez, Justo. *The Theological Education of Hispanics* (1988).

Gutierrez, Ramon. *Feasts and Celebrations in North American Ethnic Communities* (1995).

Haddad, Yvonne, ed. *Muslims in America* (1991).

Kelly, Gail. *From Vietnam to America: A Chronicle of the Vietnamese Immigration to the United States* (1977).

Leonard, Karen. *Making Ethnic Choices: California's Punjabi Mexican Americans* (1992).

Marin, Marguerite. *Social Protest in an Urban Barrio: A Study of the Chicano Movement, 1966–1974* (1991).

Naff, Alixa. *Becoming American: The Early Arab Immigrant Experience* (1985).

Sandoval, Moises. *On the Move: A History of the Hispanic Church in the United States* (1990).

———, ed. *The Mexican American Experience in the Church* (1983).

Tweed, Thomas. *The American Encounter with Buddhism, 1844–1912: Victorian Culture and the Limits of Dissent* (1992).

Waters, Mary. *Ethnic Options: Choosing Identities in America* (1990).

Williams, Raymond B. *Religions of Immigrants from India and Pakistan: New Threads in the American Tapestry* (1988).

Religion, Politics, and the Constitution: 1960–2000

One of the central problems of American religious history has been the difficulty of deciding where politics stops and religion starts. During the Cold War years, many influential Americans wanted to emphasize that America led the godly forces of the West against a godless Soviet communist rival. In the 1950s they added the phrase "under God" to the Pledge of Allegiance and "IN GOD WE TRUST" to U.S. banknotes.

But was America really godly? A succession of politically influential preachers, from Billy Graham in the 1950s and 1960s, to Jerry Falwell in the 1970s and 1980s, believed that the nation was sinking into sin and secularity, and could be purified and redeemed only by a Christian revival. In their view, the separation of church and state, safeguarded by the First Amendment to the Constitution, had gone too far. Such political coalitions as the Christian Anti-Communist Crusade in the 1960s and the Moral Majority in the 1980s campaigned for legislation to restore Christian values in American society.

Their mission was complicated by a Supreme Court that seemed to further the trend toward strict separation. In three decisions of the early 1960s, the Court, under Chief Justice Earl Warren, prohibited prayer and Bible reading in public schools. However, these decisions, lengthening the reach of the First Amendment's "No Establishment" clause, were accompanied by a more generous interpretation of the amendment's "Free Exercise" clause; another series of decisions tried to ensure that citizens' freedom of religion was as broad as possible.

In the 1970s and 1980s, a great shift took place in the political alliances made by religious groups—one that sociologist Robert Wuthnow referred to, in the title of a famous book, as The Restructuring of American Religion. *In 1960, several Protestant groups campaigned against John F. Kennedy, the Democratic candidate in that year's presidential election, on the grounds that as a Roman Catholic he would be unable to exercise his own political judgment but would make America subservient to the pope in Rome. Kennedy won and made no reference to Rome in his policies. His presidency eased such fears and never again did Catholics as a bloc find themselves in conflict with Protestants as a bloc over a political issue. From then on, conservative Catholics, conservative Protestants, and conservative Jews more often made common cause on such issues as prayer in school and opposition to abortion, whereas liberal Catholics, liberal Protestants, and liberal Jews joined hands to prevent the teaching of "creation science" in schools and to promote a broad spectrum of social policies. The proper relationship between religion and politics remained controversial up to the end of the twentieth century, and it was possible throughout the period to find some advocates of further separation and some who urged a greater integration of the two.*

 D O C U M E N T S

The first three of these documents come from the 1960s and the remainder from the 1980s—their approaches to the church-state controversy show some repetition but also some decisive shifts. Document 1 (1965), from one of Billy Graham's books, compares the sins of mid-century America to wild fires burning out of control. Graham's immense success as an evangelical preacher had by then made him one of the best-known men in the world. Document 2 describes the 1960 electoral efforts of Protestants United, a group that aimed to prevent what they thought of as improper Catholic influence over American political life. From the Catholic vantage point the group seemed to be keeping alive an old and ugly form of prejudice. Document 3, from the *Christian Herald* (1963), expresses dismay over the news that the Supreme Court had outlawed prayer in public schools— its author points to a long and venerable religious tradition in public education.

The year 1976 witnessed the presidential election victory of a "born again" Christian, Jimmy Carter. In the following four years political organization by evangelicals increased rapidly, generally in a conservative direction. Document 4, a statement from Evangelicals for Social Action, published two months before the election of 1980, reveals some of the characteristic political concerns of the "New Religious Right" and shows that they were neither so heartless nor so simple-minded as a hostile news media alleged.

Politicized religion characterized much of the 1980s. From the liberal side, theologian Langdon Gilkey (Document 5, 1985) explains why he worked for the American Civil Liberties Union (ACLU) against a creation science law in Arkansas. From the conservative side (Document 6, 1984), *Christianity Today* follows a legislative campaign whose goal is to restore religious group activities in public schools. In Document 7 social critic Wilfred McClay warns that America's national "civil religion," despite its benefits, can lead to the political contamination of solemn religious ceremonies. Finally, in Document 8 (1990), Michael McConnell, a lawyer, castigates the Supreme Court for decisions that, as he sees it, constrict American religious freedom.

1. Billy Graham Urges a Troubled Nation to Turn Back to God, 1965

A few years ago the trees on the mountains behind our home caught fire. The flames were discovered by forest rangers who keep a twenty-four-hour lookout from a nearby mountain. The fire was already out of control and moving rapidly toward our home when we were told to be ready to evacuate. Fire fighters came, and we fought the fire all night until it was brought under control.

Our world is on fire, and man without God will never be able to control the flames. The demons of hell have been let loose. The fires of passion, greed, hate, and lust are sweeping the world. We seem to be plunging madly toward Armageddon. . . .

The Bible teaches that sin is transgression of the law (I Jn. 3:4). This word "transgression" could be translated "lawlessness." Jesus indicated that as men approached the end of history there would be a worldwide rebellion against law and order. Rebellion and lawlessness are already present on a scale such as the world has never known. Children rebel against their parents until many parents are actually afraid of their children. Young people rebel against their teachers. University students rebel against administrative authorities. There is an organized attempt to downgrade the policeman, to make fun of him and despise him. All this is part of a general disrespect for law and order.

It ought to shock us that in many countries organized crime is the biggest business of all. In fact, one of America's leading racketeers casually boasted a short time ago: "Organized crime is bigger than the United States Government."

Crime grosses close to 10 percent of the American national income and forms virtually a state within a state. It costs us more than all our educational and welfare programs combined. Organized crime, with its syndicates, underworld, racketeering, and the Mafia, almost controls some of the world's major cities. In addition, there is unorganized crime, and it is just as bad if not worse.

Crime is increasing with such rapidity that we are now close to open rebellion and anarchy. It is dangerous to walk the streets of almost any city in America after dark. In some areas people live in fear and terror. It is as though some sinister, supernatural force were loose. Our city streets are turned into jungles of terror, mugging, rape, and death. The blight of criminality threatens to engulf our society; as the crime rates rise, the moral foundations of the nation crumble. . . .

Premier Chou En-lai of China said recently in an English broadcast from Peking: "The colored people of the world outnumber the white 12 to 1. Let's wipe them out." An eminent sociologist confided recently that he believes we will be involved in a bitter racial war within the next few years. Men of the stature of Dr. Martin Niemöller, one of the presidents of the World Council of Churches, and Sir Hugh Foote, a member of the British Labor Government, have joined in warning about the possibility of race war.

In New York City a Negro boy of seventeen was arrested recently for murder. He was called "Big Giant." His mother said he used to be such a wonderful boy, but that the black nationalists made him hate the white man. She said he was brainwashed.

There is no doubt that racial tension is increasing throughout the world. In some areas it is already flaming into underground warfare. . . .

There is so much hypocrisy on the subject of racial prejudice that it is difficult to know where to start. Christ has taught the dignity of man and the possibility of the brotherhood of man in Himself. Wherever there is discrimination, Christ is at work with His sword cutting out hatred and intolerance. The Bible says plainly that God is no respecter of persons. This cuts across the theory of racial supremacy and makes all men equal in the sight of God. This Biblical position tends to create dissatisfaction among those who feel they are discriminated against. It also creates a guilt complex among those who do the discriminating.

We are not told in the Bible where the various colors of skin began. There are some who think the races began from the three sons of Noah, but there is no proof as to which one of these sons was dark and which one was white. . . .

There is only one possible solution to the race problem and that is a vital personal experience with Jesus Christ on the part of both races. In Christ the middle wall of partition has been broken down. There is no Jew, no Gentile—no black, white, yellow, or red. We could be one great brotherhood in Jesus Christ. However, until we come to recognize Him as the Prince of Peace and receive His love in our hearts, the racial tensions will increase, racial demands will become more militant, and a great deal of blood will be shed. The race problem could become another flame out of control!

Communism is a dangerous threat, not only to the West but to Christianity everywhere. . . .

Whatever the method, Communism is real and it is dangerous! The Communists believe in, they plan toward, and they work for ultimate triumph. This is what we might call the eschatalogical aspect of Communism. It is the feature that binds them together and helps them endure the frowns and grimaces from the West. Their sense of destiny has almost a religious aura about it, a faith in their ability to triumph. Motivated by such a fanatical, burning desire to win, the Communists find no sacrifice too great to make for their cause.

Theirs is an "end justifies the means" philosophy. Wrong though they are, they have a goal, a purpose, and a sense of destiny. It is clear that we can never cope with Communism simply by fearing it and hating it. We must recapture our own national sense of purpose, our devotion to a great cause, and a vital faith, if we are to vie successfully with a foe who is making plans to bury us.

We speak of Communism being a great challenge to Christianity, and ideologically it is; but no system can be seriously threatened by an enemy "without" until it has been weakened by some enemy "within." While I am diametrically opposed to Communism *per se,* I am more concerned about the lack of zeal for Christianity than I am about the zeal and purposes of the Communists.

Communism can never succeed unless Christianity fails. . . .

The Communist's goal is to liquidate religion, for they hold the concept that religion is a product of the capitalist system. Here is another error of Communist reasoning. The Christian religion was begun by Jesus Christ, who was by no stretch of the imagination a wealthy American or European. He was a poor, Middle Eastern carpenter. The Bible says: "Though he was rich, yet for your sakes he became poor, that ye through his poverty might be rich" (II Cor. 8:9). He was born in a borrowed stable. He had no home to call His own. He said: "Foxes have holes, and birds of the air have nests; but the Son of man hath not where to lay his head" (Lk. 9:58). He celebrated His last supper in a borrowed room. He rode into Jerusalem on a borrowed donkey. He was crucified on a borrowed cross and buried in a borrowed tomb.

Although He refused to put class against class, we read that the common people heard Him gladly. Yet He was as concerned for the bourgeois as He was for the proletariat. He had as much time for the rich young ruler as He had for the blind beggar, and He was as concerned for Nicodemus as He was for the poor lame man at Siloam's pool. . . .

It is an ironic fact that science, dedicated to solving our problems, has itself become a problem. Science has given us the electric light, the automobile, the airplane, television, and the computer, but science has also given us the hydrogen bomb. We can use automobiles profitably for transportation and pleasure, but the other side of the coin is that tens of thousands of people in America alone die by automobile accidents every year. When scientists first split the atom and released the power of its nucleus, the first use of this great scientific achievement was to rain suffering and death on Hiroshima and Nagasaki.

The problem of science lies in its misuse. The blessing of knowledge becomes a curse when we pervert it. Because man is what he is, scientific achievements are often used destructively rather than constructively. Because our morality does not match our intellectuality, the misuse of science can be greater than the use. Not until man's moral progress catches up with his intellectual progress can we hope to solve the problems posed by science. While science has achieved the ultimate in destruction, it still lies prone and helpless before the really great problems of life. . . .

History speaks with thundering words to say that no state or government devised by man can flourish forever. It is also true, as Will Durant said: "No great nation has ever been overcome until it has destroyed itself." Republics, kingdoms, and empires all live their uncertain lives and die. In America we are now on the verge of seeing a democracy gone wild. Freedom has become license. Moral law is in danger of being abandoned even by the courts. To what degree can we expect immunity from the inevitable law of regress that sets in when nations defy the laws of God? . . .

Into this cacophony of the voices of doom comes the Word of God. The Bible says that it is *not* too late. I do not believe that we have passed the point of no return. I do not believe that all is black and hopeless. There is still time to return to the moral and spiritual principles that made the West great. There is still time for God to intervene. But there is coming a time when it will be too late, and we are rapidly approaching that time!

2. C. Stanley Lowell Explains His Fear of Catholics in 1960

The 1960 election campaign brought Americans United its days of greatest strain. At the same time this episode brought an unprecedented opportunity to educate the American public in regard to church-state separation. POAU had always opposed certain Roman Catholic policies on church and state but it had always insisted that no Catholic should be barred from public office merely because of his personal faith. The organization had never specifically supported or opposed any candidate for public office. What should be its attitude during the difficult period of the Nixon-Kennedy campaign, when, for the first time, a Roman Catholic seemed to be within striking distance of the White House?

C. Stanley Lowell, *Embattled Wall* (Washington, D.C.: Protestants and Other Americans United for Separation of Church and State, 1966).

The prospect of a Catholic candidate on one of the major tickets fired up religious antagonists. There were those who hated the idea of a Catholic—any Catholic at all—either on the ticket or in the White House. Such persons wanted to use Americans United as a weapon to defeat such a candidate. We could not lend ourselves to any such operation. There were those who wanted to use the campaign that eventually involved a Roman Catholic candidate, John F. Kennedy, as the occasion for an anti-Catholic crusade. This sort of thing had to be rigorously opposed. . . .

Paul Blanshard prepared for the board of Americans United a proposed policy statement for the campaign. After careful study and appraisal it was accepted with very few modifications. The statement was published in CHURCH & STATE, also in *The New York Times* and many other newspapers.

Unhappily, the POAU policy statement was published on the same day as a statement by a new group formed under the leadership of Dr. Norman Vincent Peale. . . . The Peale committee was so bitterly attacked in the press that Dr. Peale soon withdrew from it.

This incident called attention to the extremely difficult role of Americans United. There was a grave danger, which such an episode strengthened, that the entire church-state issue involving the candidacy of a Roman Catholic would be swept under the rug with the spurious plea of "intolerance" or "bigotry." We at Americans United headquarters were determined that this must not happen. Thus we were caught between the brotherhooders on the one hand, and the fanatics on the other. It was hard to say which were worse!

The statement authored by Paul Blanshard set a fair and proper course to which we meticulously adhered throughout the campaign. The statement warned against any display of religious prejudice in connection with the 1960 conventions and election. However, it pointed out with candor that Catholic candidates for President should be "scrutinized with particular care." The reason?—

> Because their church has taken a definite stand against the Supreme Court's interpretation of separation of church and state, and particularly against the denial of public money to sectarian schools. Their church leaders have also expressed opinions favorable to the appointment of an American ambassador to the Vatican. To challenge every Catholic candidate on these issues is a wise and necessary precaution designed to protect our American traditions.

Then came the crucial part of the statement—"Questions for a Catholic candidate." These questions were to become famous during the 1960 election campaign. . . . The . . . questions were:

> 1. The Canon Law of your church (Canon 1374) directs all American Catholic parents to boycott our public schools unless they receive special permission from their bishops. Do you personally approve or disapprove of this boycott rule?
> 2. The bishops of your church in an official statement in November 1948 have denounced the Supreme Court's interpretation of the religion clause of the First Amendment and have urged that the Constitution actually permits the distribution of public money on an equitable basis to sectarian schools and other sectarian institutions . . . What is your personal attitude toward your bishops' interpretation of the Constitution, and toward the new plan for financing parochial schools?
> 3. Many nations recognize your church as both a church and a state and send official ambassadors to the Holy See. If you become President what would be your policy concerning the appointment of an American ambassador or a personal representative to the Vatican?

Every conceivable effort was made by Catholic apologists to "bigot" their way out of the troublesome predicament in which the questions placed them. The Catholic press cried "bigot," "foul," "religious prejudice," "Ku Klux Klan" and strove eagerly to raise all the old goblins. Catholic leaders and political leaders as well sought the aid of a group called the Fair Campaign Practices Committee. This group had been organized to call attention to unfair tactics being used by any candidate or party.

In March 1960 a meeting was held in New York City under the auspices of the Fair Campaign Practices Committee with the idea of discussing the problem of unfair use of religion in the election campaign. No one from the staff of Americans United was invited, which appears odd in view of the fact that Americans United was a principal object of discussion. It soon became evident that a Catholic priest, Msgr. Francis J. Lally, editor of the *Boston Pilot,* hoped to secure from the committee some kind of public denunciation of Americans United. The *Boston Pilot* is one of the most reactionary of the Catholic diocesan publications, second only to the *Brooklyn Tablet.* But it is the Boston diocesan publication—the diocese of the Kennedys. It was rumored that Msgr. Lally had refused to attend the session if any member of the Americans United staff were invited. Whether or not this was the fact, the inclusion of Msgr. Lally and the exclusion of our staff were both accomplished. Msgr. Lally took a great deal of the committee's time attacking Americans United. He saw that a denunciation of the group by the Fair Campaign Practices Committee would not only promote the Kennedy candidacy via a "fair and free of prejudice" appeal but would also strike a heavy blow at Msgr. Lally's number one enemy, Americans United. . . .

Chief spokesman among Catholics in the attempted hush-hush of the religious issue was the late Gustave Weigel, S.J. Father Weigel sought to bury the matter once and for all in a widely quoted interview with the press. Fr. Weigel's strategy was to equate Roman Catholic clerical directives with "conscience" and plead for its inviolability. He failed to mention a single one of the specific questions that Americans United had raised. He insisted that the realms of political concern and religion were separate and distinct. Never did he address himself to the problem which occurs when a "moral directive" of an absolutist church conflicts with an official's civil duty.

A good example of the smear and dodge tactic was offered by Father John A. O'Brien of the Notre Dame University faculty and a long time consultant for the National Conference of Christians and Jews. In a story prepared for *Look* magazine, February 16, 1960, Father O'Brien was asked this question by the interviewer: "How do you explain the fear of some Americans that the separation between church and state will break down if a Catholic is elected President?" He replied:

> I believe this fear is chiefly the result of the 12-year propaganda campaign by an organization called Protestants and Other Americans United for Separation of Church and State, which follows the same line of attack on Catholics the Know-Nothings followed in the 1850's. The campaign has been intensified because a Catholic may be candidate for President this year. Of course, the current attacks have no more basis in fact than those of a century ago.

Fr. O'Brien's charge against Americans United was of course entirely false. It was a bit of McCarthyism with a double design—to damage the principal antagonist of Catholic demands on the state and to obscure the real "religious issue" which a Catholic candidate for President posed.

3. Joseph M. Hopkins Deplores the Supreme Court's Decision Against School Prayer, 1963

"Almighty God, we acknowledge our dependence upon Thee, and we beg thy blessings upon us, our parents, our teachers and our country."

This prayer, prepared by the Regents of New York State's public schools for voluntary use in classrooms, was last June declared unconstitutional by the U.S. Supreme Court. . . .

At stake is a larger question: the place of religion in the public schools and, indeed, in our national life. That the Supreme Court itself is not of one mind is evident from the divergent opinions delivered last June. Justice Hugo L. Black, in the majority opinion, objected to the prayer on the ground that "it is no part of the business of government to compose official prayers for any group of American people to recite." Superficially at least, this would seem to infer that *un*official prayers and other non-compulsory religious exercises would not be affected by the ruling. But Justice William O. Douglas, in a concurring opinion, read far more into the interpretation. The audience for a prayer in a school, court or legislature, he declared, is a "captive audience." Justice Potter Stewart, the Court's lone dissenter, said that he could not see how "an official religion" would be established by permitting the use of a non-sectarian prayer. He reminded his fellow jurists that the Supreme Court decreed ten years ago: "We are a religious people whose institutions presuppose a Supreme Being."

Perhaps much of the furor could have been averted had the Court been more explicit in setting forth the implications of its decision. If the extreme position advocated by Justice Douglas ultimately is adopted, the logical outcome will be the removal of "In God We Trust" from our coins, the cessation of prayers at sessions of Congress, the withdrawal of chaplains from the Armed Forces and the deletion of all references to America as a nation "under God" from our official documents.

Is this what our founding fathers intended? It has been well stated that, to the contrary, their concern was that American people enjoy freedom *of* religion, not freedom *from* it. Benjamin Franklin told the delegates to the Constitutional Convention, "We have been assured . . . that except the Lord build a house, they labor in vain that build it. I firmly believe this, and I also believe that without His concurring aid, we shall succeed no better in this political building than the builders of Babel."

The First Amendment states, "Congress shall make no law respecting an establishment of religion or prohibiting the free exercise thereof." In their zeal to safeguard minorities against *establishment,* civil-liberties groups and others would deny the majority *free exercise.* Surely it was not the purpose of the framers of the Constitution to discriminate against religious faith, but rather to protect minorities from diverse indoctrination by *particular* sects. Dr. Louis Evans has aptly observed, "The Constitution provides for free *exercise* of religion, not free *extermination* of it."

Yet in at least one school a plaque bearing the Ten Commandments was ordered removed from a classroom wall. In other communities the singing of Christmas carols by school choruses is forbidden. "Frosty the Snowman" and "Rudolph the Red-Nosed Reindeer" are acceptable, but "Silent Night" and "Joy to the World"

Joseph Martin Hopkins, "The Separation of God and State," *Christian Herald* 86 (July 1963). Reprinted by permission of Christian Herald Magazine, Christian Herald Associates, Inc.

are not. A few years ago a state university barred church-sponsored groups from holding campus religious meetings.

This turn of events is ironic in view of the fact that it was the Christian churches which gave education its first impetus in colonial America. Eight of the first nine colleges in this country were founded by churches. The motto of Harvard University, established in 1636, expressed the philosophy of them all—"For Christ and the Church." The primary consideration in the minds of the founders of these institutions was that there might be an educated ministry for the church.

The New England Primer, the McGuffey readers and other early textbooks abounded in quotations from the Bible and other religious material. The elimination of such content from public-school textbooks undoubtedly has had a great deal to do with the condition of religious illiteracy which prevails in America today.

Daily Bible reading is required in the public schools of 12 states, optional in 24 states, and prohibited in 11 others. The remaining three have no official policy. George W. Cornell, Associated Press religion writer, has reported that "prayers of some kind are used regularly in public schools in about 33 per cent of the nation's communities, and occasionally in another 17 per cent. Prayers evidently are used sometimes in about half of the country's 117,855 public schools—or about 58,927 of them. . . . Schools in about 41 per cent of the nation's communities also have regular Bible reading."

Pennsylvania's law requiring the reading of ten verses of Scripture without comment at the beginning of each school day was ruled unconstitutional in 1959 by a three-judge Federal Court in Philadelphia. The law was thereupon amended to provide that children may be excused from this exercise upon the request of their parents. But even with this "escape clause," the law was again ruled unconstitutional by the Philadelphia court on grounds that it constituted "the promotion of religiousness"! An appeal to the U.S. Supreme Court is now awaiting a ruling.

The Reverend Robert E. Merry, in a letter to the Pittsburgh *Post-Gazette,* has noted, "The only thing we can't teach our kids in public school is the only thing which can defeat Communism." To which the editors replied by saying that the proper place for religious instruction is "in the home and in the church or synagogue." This was substantially President Kennedy's response to the Supreme Court decision.

The difficulty with this widely held viewpoint is that it gives the child the impression that religion is something people do only on Sunday, that God and spiritual values are of secondary or peripheral importance. The effect, as William Ernest Hocking has put it, is to teach "atheism by omission," or if not atheism, then the blasphemy of isolating God from day-by-day living and learning.

4. Evangelicals for Social Action Offer Guidance on Voting Biblically, 1980

Christ is Lord of the world as well as the church. Our vote can become one of Christ's instruments for fostering the peace and justice he desires as Lord of the world.

. . . [But] there is no biblical text to tell us which candidate should be president. There is no chapter that contains an economic blueprint for the international

"Can My Vote Be Biblical?" *Christianity Today* 24 (September 19, 1980). Written by the board and staff of the Evangelicals for Social Action.

economic order in the 1980s. But that does not mean that Christians should derive their economic and political views entirely from secular theories. There are biblical principles that have profound importance for our politics.

Certainly the application of those biblical principles to concrete situations today is an extremely complex task. People equally committed to biblical principle disagree strongly over specific social programs. That disagreement among Christians is legitimate and healthy.

But Christians ought to be willing to regularly discuss these conflicting proposals with those who disagree with them in a spirit of prayer, openness to the Holy Spirit, and unconditional submission to God's Word. The more deeply our politics are grounded in biblical principles, the more Christian they are.

1. *The family is a divinely-willed institution.* The family, not the state, is the primary institution for rearing children. Christians must resist the growing tendency of the state to usurp the role of the family. It is God's will for one man and one woman to live together in lifelong commitment. Legislation such as tax rates should help create a climate conducive to the biblical understanding of marriage, family, and sexuality. Homosexual sinners, like adulterous sinners, have inalienable civil rights (e.g., jobs and housing). Nonetheless, legislation and public funds should not promote sinful lifestyles.

2. *Every human life is sacred.* Every person is created in the image of God. Since God "desires all to be saved" so much that he sent his Son to die "as a ransom for all," every person in the world is immeasurably valuable. The great value and worth of each individual is totally independent of his or her social usefulness. Biblical people cannot remain silent when modern society forgets the value of each individual human life—as when it neglects the retarded and aged, practices racial or sexual discrimination, or allows abortion on demand.

3. *Religious and political freedom are God-given, inalienable rights.* Throughout the Bible, we see that even though people rebel against God, he continues to provide the necessities of life. Not until the end does God separate the wheat and the tares. The state should not impose civil penalties for unbelief. The church and state should be separate. Every individual is valuable in God's sight. Further, sinful, selfish people regularly abuse power that lacks checks and balances. Therefore, freedom of expression and political liberty are crucial.

4. *God and his obedient people have a very special concern for the poor.* In literally dozens and dozens of places Scripture teaches that God has a very strong concern for justice for the poor and oppressed. Therefore, God also commands his people to have a deep concern for them. A genuine sensitivity to the poor and a strong commitment to seek justice for them ought to be a central concern of politicians who seek to be biblical. "If a king judges the poor with equity, his throne will be established forever."

5. *God requires just economic patterns in society.* The starting point of all biblical thinking on economics is that God is sovereign. God is the only absolute owner of all things. He wants the earth's resources to benefit everyone.

The Bible condemns both those who are lazy and those who become rich by oppressing others. Throughout the Scriptures, God has commanded and guided his people to implement programs of economic sharing that reduced extremes of both wealth and poverty. In fact, God cares so much about economic justice that he destroyed both Israel and Judah for two basic reasons: idolatry and economic oppression. The One who is sovereign over economics requires economic patterns that enable all people to earn a just living in fulfilling work.

6. *God requires Christians to be peacemakers.* Christians look forward to the time when "nation shall not lift up sword against nation, neither shall they learn war any more." Until the Lord returns, unfortunately, people persistently resort to wars and rumors of wars. Many Christians believe that as the lesser of two evils they should engage in just wars for the sake of preserving some order in a fallen world. Other Christians believe war is contrary to the teaching of Christ and that he calls us to overcome our enemies with suffering love rather than the sword. But all agree that Jesus' words, "Blessed are the peacemakers," are urgent in our time.

We must live out Jesus' call to peacemaking in a world that devotes to military expenditures each year an amount equal to the total annual income of the poorest one-half of the world's people. Because we know human life is sacred, Christians must do everything they can to reduce the growing danger of nuclear holocaust. President Eisenhower reflected a biblical concern when he said: "Every gun that is made, every warship launched, every rocket fired signifies, in the final sense, theft from those who hunger and are not fed."

7. *The Creator requires stewardship of the earth's resources.* The earth is the Lord's, and humanity is to exercise dominion over it. Such a high calling requires each generation to protect the environment and preserve the quality of life for future generations. We are stewards of God's good gift.

8. *Sin is both personal and social.* Consciously willed individual acts such as lying and adultery are sinful. So too, according to the Scriptures, is participating uncritically in social structures that are not just. In one breath the prophets condemn both kinds of sin. The Bible denounces laws that are unjust. Politicians with a biblical perspective will have a deep concern to correct social structures that are evil.

9. *Personal integrity is vital.* The Scriptures demand honesty and personal righteousness. Dishonesty in public affairs undercuts the democratic process. A politician's personal and family life should be a good model for the rest of society. Government leaders ought to be humble and honest enough to acknowledge mistakes. Knowing that we all err, we should forgive those who offer forthright confession. Personal religious belief that fosters a profound sense of God's sovereignty over all nations and sharp awareness of God's passion for justice helps prevent the abuse of political power for narrow personal or nationalistic purposes.

To proclaim Christ's lordship in politics means evaluating political candidates by their commitment to biblical principles, rather than by their pragmatism, patriotism, or personality.

That does not mean that Christians should only vote for Christians. Ironically, non-Christians sometimes have a deeper commitment to fundamental biblical teaching about society than do many Christians. Christians must resist the temptation to espouse simple prescriptions for complex problems, remembering that there is a mistaken zeal in politics as well as religion. There is undeniably a superficial appeal in the call to Christians to mobilize as a political force and elect "one of our own." But the Christian must resist all temptation to use the gospel for political purposes or to make the gospel hostage to any politician or political cause. The words of the apostle Paul, "Do not be conformed to this world," must continually ring in our ears.

Unfortunately, no candidate for public office will embody perfectly a commitment to all the biblical principles mentioned above. More likely, candidates will be strong in some areas, weak in others. One should strive to find candidates concerned about the whole range of concerns reflected in these principles. Biblically informed politics will reflect the balance of concerns revealed in God's Word.

5. Langdon Gilkey Opposes Creation Science, 1985

[L]et me summarize this law . . . and explain, again briefly, why I opposed it. The law in effect required in every class in science in the school system of Arkansas "balanced treatment" (Section 2) of the "two scientific models" concerning the origin of "the universe, earth, life and man." More precisely, it mandated that wherever one model is taught, the other model must be given roughly the same time and attention (Section 5). It characterized (Section 4) these two models as "creation science" and "evolution science" and then proceeded to define them each by means of six or seven propositions. Carefully it specified that no religious instruction was to be permitted, nor reference to religious sources or doctrines made (Sections 2 and 5); rather, only the "scientific evidences and the inferences therefrom" (Section 2) in favor of both scientific models were to be taught.

The first thing on which it was important for me to become clear was the reason for my public opposition, and that of all those of us on the ACLU team, to this law. This opposition was not directed against either fundamentalism or creation science in itself. I agree with neither one of these two interrelated interpretations or forms of the Christian religion. Nevertheless, both on the basis of my own religious convictions (which hold that each of us must be free in conscience to choose and to determine the form that characterizes our own faith) and on the basis of my interpretation of democracy (which holds to the importance of the non-establishment by the State of religion or of any particular form of religion), the creationists have, it seems to me, a right under God and under our Constitution to preach, teach, and practice their faith in freedom as long as they do not interfere with the similar rights held by others.

I do not agree with their doctrines; nevertheless, the only counter to them which I would either employ or support is the force of persuasion, and not the force of legislative, judicial, or executive authority of the State. My aim in challenging creation science in Little Rock was, then, not at all the goal of silencing either creation science or fundamentalism, or of challenging their right to express either one. It was simply and solely to defeat *their* effort, which I believed Act 590 represented, to advance their own particular religious viewpoint through legislation—that is, to require through legislation that this particular religious view of our origins be taught as a science (and as *the* alternative to evolution) in the public schools.

But was this not, one might ask, a particularly democratic and fair piece of legislation? So it seemed. On the face of it, Act 590 appeared innocent and virtuous enough. It stated as its major intentions the protection of academic freedom by

Langdon Gilkey, *Creationism on Trial: Evolution and God at Little Rock* (Minneapolis, Winston Press, 1985). Reprinted by permission of the author.

providing students genuine "choice," the protection of freedom of religious exercise and belief, and the prevention of the "establishment of religious instruction"—in fact, the very values we accused it of seeking to subvert. And it stated it would ensure these values of freedom, tolerance, and openness by a method long recognized in public affairs: that each side should have its adequate and fair "say," specifically the principle of balanced treatment in classroom discussion and in use of textbooks.

What, one might ask, could be more just or more "American" than to give the two models, or the two theories of origins, equal time in school, just as we give equal time to the two political parties and their candidates? So it seems to many.

During that initial reflection on the law, however, I came to the conclusion that this law and ones similar to it are, despite this appearance, in fact dangerous to the health of our society; and that through its wide enactment it would represent a disaster to our common life, especially our religious life. Further experience over the following weeks prior to, during, and after the trial would only deepen this conviction. Since for many it comes as a surprise that a theologian and a "believer" should resist this law, it may be well at the outset of this account to explain further the reasons for my own personal antipathy to it.

First of all, the enactment of this sort of law—especially if it were to be widely adopted—would represent a disaster for religion in our society. This was to me, and to each of us representing religion among the plaintiffs, the most important issue at stake. There can be, I believe, no healthy, creative, or significant religious faith in a modern society unless, as I have noted, the forms of that faith are free. A politically enforced or supported religious faith becomes corrupt, dead, and oppressive, encouraging inevitably in reaction a deep personal distaste and moral disdain at such spiritual imperialism. Enforced religion breeds precisely what it most fears: rebellion against religion, cynicism about religion, skepticism about its claims, and, as a consequence, indifference at best and outright antipathy at worst. The First Amendment is important not only to guarantee the rights of alternative religions and of nonreligious persons in society; it is also important in setting the only possible legal and social conditions for the creative health of serious religion itself. This my own tradition—the Baptist (as well as that of the Quaker and the Unitarian)—has held from its own early beginnings on this continent.

Freedom of religion in society, especially in any modern diversified culture, invariably means plurality of religious viewpoints and even of religions within society; and so it entails widely diverse opinions regarding all sorts of issues important to each set of religious beliefs. If each community or group is to be free religiously to develop itself, it must allow the others equal freedom, or else claim such freedom for itself alone, and be led thereby down the sinful slope of intolerance, inquisition, persecution, and, ultimately, the oppressive elimination of other religious groups. When society through its government, its public funds, or its public schools favors one form of religion, or identifies religion with that one form to the exclusion of others, it endangers all forms of religion. The First Amendment is the deepest constitutional or "worldly" base of whatever health our religious institutions and life may claim. This law, I was convinced—and this was my subsequent argument—would serve to establish a particular form of the Christian religion in the teaching program of the public schools; therefore, it represented a grave threat to the free religious life of our society.

So it was by no means accidental that most of the plaintiffs and one-half of the witnesses in this case represented religion. Many private individuals and a number of national and state-wide institutions who identified themselves as "religious" (that is, as concerned with the health of the Christian and the Jewish faiths) had hastened to stand up actively in opposition to this law. Specifically, twelve of the seventeen individuals who were plaintiffs were clergymen, and four of the six associations were religious associations (American Jewish Congress, e.g.). Among the ministers were representatives of the Presbyterian churches, the Disciples churches, the Methodist, Episcopal, and Roman Catholic bishops, and the Union of American Hebrew Congregations. Only one scientific group (The National Association of Biology Teachers) and one educational organization (the Arkansas Educational Association) joined these representatives of religion among the plaintiffs.

Although the media and most scientific commentators presented this trial as a continuation of the so-called "warfare between science and religion," the fact was, as the above shows, that in this case the legal defense of science and the legal opposition to fundamentalist control of education were instigated and executed largely by religious individuals and groups. When I asked as many of these staunch clerical plaintiffs as I could *why* they had so acted—often against their best interests in relation to their congregations—they all replied, "To save the Christian faith from an untrue and yet fatal identification with intolerant literalism on the one hand and an anti-scientific attitude on the other."

6. *Christianity Today* Describes Political Coalition-Building to Restore Religion in Schools, 1984

Equal-access legislation, ardently supported by almost all evangelical and mainline church organizations, has become federal law. It prevents public secondary schools from disbanding student religious groups that want to meet for prayer, Bible study, or discussions of religion. . . .

Heartfelt, sometimes rancorous, congressional debate about the measure hinged on a question that ordinarily lies dormant beneath the surface of national consciousness: May individual rights of free speech and assembly cross over the boundary between church and state?

In response, the U.S. Senate voiced a resounding yes, voting 88 to 11 in favor of the bill. The U.S. House of Representatives followed suit in July with a 337 to 77 vote. But on the same afternoon the House took its decisive vote, a U.S. Circuit Court of Appeals in Pennsylvania said no. The court overturned an earlier ruling in favor of Williamsport high school students who organized a Bible club called Petros.

To protect groups like Petros, the Equal Access Act makes it unlawful for any public secondary school to discriminate against student groups based on the subject matter they are discussing. It protects "religious, political, philosophical, or other"

"Congress Gives Student Religious Groups Access to Public Secondary Schools," *Christianity Today* 28 (September 7, 1984), 77–79. Used by permission of Christianity Today.

types of speech rather than singling out only religious speech. The law does not allow nonstudents to "direct, conduct, control, or regularly attend" such meetings.

The act does not authorize the government to withhold federal financial assistance to schools that do not comply, a provision earlier drafts included. It defines "noninstructional time"—during which extracurricular groups may meet—as occurring before or after the school day begins. It does not specifically prohibit religious meetings during free periods throughout the school day, but court decisions around the country, including the recent Williamsport ruling, have done so. . . .

An earlier version of the Equal Access Act failed to pass the House in June after it was blocked by the American Civil Liberties Union (ACLU), National Education Association (NEA), and several Jewish lobby groups. In the wake of that narrow defeat, Senate sponsor Mark O. Hatfield (R-Oreg.) redoubled his efforts to work out an acceptable compromise.

Drafting the bill and nudging it through Congress proved to be a grueling decathlon of unusual procedures, power plays, and negotiation. Hatfield's staff lawyer Randy Sterns met with strategists from the Christian Legal Society (CLS), National Association of Evangelicals, and Baptist Joint Committee on Public Affairs. They painstakingly weighed and measured the nuances of each phrase troubling the bill's opponents. Finally, the ACLU declared itself neutral toward the measure, and Hatfield attached it to a bill providing federal funds to upgrade math and science teaching—a program dear to the heart of the NEA. Once the ACLU declared a truce, "that broke the logjam and changed a lot of votes," Sterns said.

Hatfield's involvement with the issue began in 1981 after a court decision in Lubbock, Texas, prevented a student religious group from meeting at school. In response, Hatfield shaped a coalition of 24 senators who filed an unprecedented friend-of-the-court brief on behalf of the Lubbock students. "We built a strong basis of support from which to introduce this bill," Sterns said, including 50 cosponsors by the end.

After achieving Senate passage, the bill went to the House. It was promptly shelved by House Speaker Thomas P. O'Neill, who sent it to two committees from which he never expected it to emerge. But Democrats who supported the measure threatened to use an obscure confrontational tactic to upstage committee chairmen who tried to block the bill.

O'Neill backed down and agreed to suspend the usual rules of debate. That move was necessary to prevent opponents from choking off debate by offering hundreds of meaningless amendments.

Opponents voiced fears of cults infiltrating student meetings; of "student-initiated catechism or baptism or other religious services"; and of school districts "inundated by demands from students for religious meetings of various types of cults, fringe groups, and allegedly religious movements."

Throughout the congressional wrangling, equal-access supporters drew attention to the Williamsport case, a classic illustration of the type of discrimination they wanted to remedy. To their relief, the appeals court decision opposing the students came down after Congress approved the Equal Access Act.

The appeals court ruling acknowledges the students' right to free speech and the school's prerogative to allow clubs to meet in its classrooms. But the court applied a traditional three-part test of whether a religious activity is constitutional, and it gave the Petros club a failing grade because it would have the effect of "advancing" religion under the auspices of the state.

The majority said high school students are apt to be immature and impressionable, thus "less able to appreciate the fact that permission for Petros to meet would be granted out of a spirit of neutrality toward religion and not advancement." Some students may come to believe that the school endorses and encourages religious practice, the decision says, because "involuntary contact between nonparticipating students and religious groups is inevitable." The club is unconstitutional, according to the court, because "public schools have never been a forum for religious expression."

A strong dissent by one circuit court judge pointed out that Petros is the only club in the school's history to be denied the right to meet. This "selective exclusion," he said, raises a more pertinent question: Is the school officially hostile to religion? . . .

Court decisions have made school officials increasingly wary of allowing student religious groups to meet. But passage of the Equal Access Act trumpets a clear signal that these clubs are legitimate and acceptable. Even so, future court challenges are expected.

"We have no sense of smugness about resolving every issue that's going to come up," Sterns said. "The particulars will have to be worked out in case-by-case litigation." Meanwhile, it is up to students, parents, and schools to work out ways to exercise their equal-access rights.

7. Wilfred M. McClay Warns Against the Political Contamination of Religion, 1988

Not too many months ago, it seemed that 1988 would be the year that religion-in-politics came into its own.

To be sure, the 1980 and 1984 presidential campaigns had featured religion-in-politics galore, to an extent perhaps unrivaled since the days of William Jennings Bryan. Ronald Reagan was swept into the office partly on the wave of fervent support he had carefully built up for years among evangelical and fundamentalist Christians; and he was not bashful about acknowledging their support and speaking to their concerns. "I endorse you and everything you do," candidate Reagan enthused in August 1980 to a large political-action briefing assembled under the auspices of the Religious Roundtable; and much to the astonishment of pundits, this association not only did not hurt him politically, but gave him an enormous boost, even running against the born-again Jimmy Carter. Nor did Democratic attempts in 1984 to implicate Reagan in the premillennial-dispensationalist view of Armageddon do anything to revive the fortunes of the hapless Walter Mondale.

Thus, when televangelist Pat Robertson announced, after long consideration and innumerable straws in the wind, that he would be a candidate for the Republican nomination in 1988, it seemed a logical next step for this increasingly powerful movement—and increasing reason for concern among those who disliked or feared

Wilfred M. McClay, "Religion in Politics; Politics in Religion," *Commentary* (October 1988), 43–49. Reprinted by permission. All rights reserved.

it. In retrospect, however, the increasing power, like so much else in our public-relations-dominated politics, seems to have been more apparent than real.

The discrepancy began with Reagan himself, who, once elected, quickly made it clear that, although he liked to speak to conservative Christians' social and moral concerns, he had no intention of doing much about them. Rarely has a political pressure group been more effectively coopted, for the evangelicals' political clout was almost completely tied to Reagan; and Reagan would never risk his popularity by departing too far from the curve of mainstream public opinion. As if this were not ill fortune enough, the steady succession of fallen or besmirched televangelists made the entire movement look fraudulent and foolish. Nothing in the most lurid recesses of Sinclair Lewis's imagination could have surpassed the lurid spectacle provided by press accounts of Jimmy Swaggart's encounters in the seedy motels of Airline Highway, or of Jim Bakker's ambidextrous doings behind the closed doors of various Xanadus. In politics, nothing can long withstand the force of ridicule. Even if Robertson had been a more competent candidate than he turned out to be, his candidacy would have been doomed.

Perhaps, then, it is a fair indication of the national mood that each of the parties' 1988 nominees for President is a more or less nonideological, pragmatic, managerial type, who does not evince more than a faint tinge of religiosity, and who does not (and will not) have any deep appeal to the religious groups that found Reagan so attractive. In short, the issues of religion-in-politics are dormant, for now. But it would be a mistake to think that they are gone for good. Certainly the history of the subject would suggest otherwise. . . .

. . . [T]his country has . . . had a long tradition of civic piety—of a quasi-religious veneration of, for example, the Founders and of the Constitution—which has served to bring religious loyalties roughly into line with political ones. Of course, in its more extreme manifestations, such as the Puritan regime in Massachusetts Bay, or the crusading of 19th-century Protestants to Christianize the world at large, and extirpate the alien influences of Catholics and Jews at home, such adhesion could be a fearsome and intolerant thing. But in the more moderate, generalized, and pluralistic form dubbed "civil religion" by the sociologist Robert Bellah, it has not only helped to foster cohesion in a pluralistic society, but served the deeper purpose of legitimating the political order by relating it to transcendent purposes and ideals. One finds this tone struck preeminently in the rhetoric of Abraham Lincoln; but in fact nearly all effective American political oratory taps into classic civil-religious themes. . . .

. . . One could readily find in the rhetoric of Martin Luther King, Jr., repeated allusions to the key elements of the American civil religion. In his well-known Lincoln Memorial address, for example, biblical and patriotic allusions abounded; and in his "Letter from Birmingham Jail" he proclaimed that protesters "were in reality standing up for what is best in the American dream and for the most sacred values in our Judeo-Christian heritage . . . the sacred heritage of our nation and the eternal will of God are embodied in our echoing demands." Social activism and adhesion were not incompatible; King's rhetoric was very different, in this respect, from that of the decidedly non-adhesional Christian abolitionist, William Lloyd Garrison (1805–79), whose most famous public act was the burning of the Constitution.

The spirit of Garrison, however, was increasingly abroad in the land [in the 1960s], as openly adversarial religious leaders like the Berrigan brothers and

Bishop James Pike began coming to the fore, along with a counterculture that strove to decouple established faiths (when it did not disdain them altogether) from the existing political order. The postwar period of adhesional unity crumbled under the force of the period's social upheaval, and it remains unrestored, despite various efforts, including those of the religious New Right, to rediscover or rebuild it. . . .

. . . Most of the controversial issues that have roiled this country's spiritual politics in the past several decades—school prayer and other forms of public religious expression, abortion, tax-exemption for religious organizations, the proper provision of social welfare, nuclear strategy, and so on—have been responses to actions of the state, and have revolved around "the increasingly problematic boundary between church and state." . . .

[There are now] many organizations, large and small, with an explicitly political focus: Coalition for Religious Freedom, Moral Majority, National Federation for Decency, National Council of Churches, Christian Voice, Americans United for Separation of Church and State, Christian Law Association, World Conference on Religion and Peace, Society of Separationists, Americans for God, American Baptist Black Caucus, and so on, and on, list without end. There are organizations for gay Mormons, for disarmament, for the handicapped, for the divorced, for women's rights, for any and every cause. "Despite a formal wall of separation between church and state," [sociologist Robert] Wuthnow concludes, "a growing mass of religious organizations has come into being with the state very much a part of their specific objectives."

Wuthnow has used survey data to confirm something most observers would suspect: that some people may participate in more than one special-purpose group, and, more significantly, that there is a predictable pattern to their participation (and nonparticipation), a pattern that has little to do with their denomination. He has found two clusters of activity groupings, one "liberal" and one "conservative," and this liberal-conservative split cuts clearly across denominational lines, reflecting profound and growing intra-denominational divisions. Hence the frequently encountered phenomenon that, say, a conservative Methodist may feel and have far more in common with a conservative Catholic, or even a conservative Jew, than with a liberal of his own denomination. Three decades ago, such experiences were exceedingly rare; that they have now become commonplace does not augur particularly well for the denominations.

In one of the most interesting of Wuthnow's findings, the single best predictor of the category to which an individual will gravitate is level of education. Those who have been to college are far more likely to be, or to have become, religious liberals— liberal in their theological attitudes (for example, rejection of scriptural literalism), in their choice of causes (anti-nuclear coalitions rather than prison ministries; holistic health groups rather than Bible study groups), in their social attitudes (favorable view of social activism, homosexuality, feminism), and in their support for a specific political agenda (environmentalism, disarmament, affirmative action, Palestinian state). In the past, denominationalism correlated neatly with ethnicity, region, and class; think, for example, of all that "Episcopalian" once conjured up. Today the crucial distinctions are increasingly *political,* they exist within and across denominations, and they correlate more readily with educational levels than with any other single factor. . . .

In the 1940's and 1950's, differences were downplayed, and the American civil religion saw to it that there was a powerful sense of the nation's fundamental meaning—its legitimating myth, as Wuthnow puts it. Now, he says, we have not one but two legitimating myths in our civil religion: one to which conservatives appeal, and one to which liberals appeal. Religious conservatives are likely to point to the providential destiny of America, its special place in human history and the divine order, as validation of traditional American values and institutions. Religious liberals are more likely to disparage patriotism, and to speak in broad, universalistic tones of the country's moral responsibility to use its wealth to make the world a more just and equitable place; and they point for justification not only to biblical sources but also to the egalitarian rhetoric of the Declaration of Independence and the language of "human rights."

As the conflict between liberals and conservatives has become more heated, the common ground has shrunk. As a consequence, the civil religion has lost its cohesive force. . . .

Perhaps, after all these abstractions, I may be permitted a concrete personal example, which illuminates something of what is being lost, at least in the mainline Protestant environment most familiar to me. A couple of years ago, I attended a funeral service for a young woman, a secretary at the university with which I was then affiliated. She was an attractive, generous, incandescent soul, beloved by everyone she worked with, no mean feat in such a contentious setting. She had died, tragically, in giving birth to her second child—a death even more bitterly shocking than an automobile accident or a street-corner shooting, for it seemed almost too atavistic to be possible. How, in this day and age, in a major American city with all the most advanced medical technologies available, could such a thing still happen?

Evidently the same question was on the mind of the minister who stepped up to deliver the eulogy to the overflow crowd of mourners that day. But where the rest of us had been stunned into reflective silence, awed and chastened by this reminder of the slender thread by which our lives hang, the minister had other things in mind. He did not talk about the deceased, except to praise her laughter briefly and imprecisely, leaving one with the feeling that he had not even known her. (I later found out this was not so.) He did not try to comfort her family and friends. Nor did he challenge us to remember the hard words of the Lord's Prayer, "Thy Will be done." Instead, he smoothly launched into a well-oiled tirade against the misplaced priorities of our society, in which billions of dollars were being poured into "Star Wars" research while young women such as this one were being allowed to die on the operating table.

That was all the minister had to say. His eulogy was, in effect, a pitch for less federal spending on defense and more spending on the development of medical technology. There was also an unmistakable hint that the young woman's doctors might well have been guilty of malpractice, but would of course be insulated from the consequences of their mistakes by our corrupt system. The only thing omitted was an injunction that we write our Congressman, or Ralph Nader, about this outrage.

I could hardly believe my ears. Had the minister set out to desecrate her memory rather than honor it, he could hardly have done a better job. But leave aside the eulogy's unspeakable vulgarity, and its unintentional cruelty to the woman's family.

Leave aside the flabby and clichéd quality of language and speech. Leave aside the self-satisfied tone of easy moral outrage. Leave aside the fashionable opinions, too, since honorable and intelligent men and women can disagree about these things. I am even willing to concede, for the sake of argument, that the minister may have been right in everything he said. All these considerations are beside the point. Nothing can alter the fact that he failed us, failed her, and failed his calling, by squandering a precious moment for the sake of a second-rate stump speech, and by forcing us to hold our sorrow back in the privacy of our hearts, at the very moment it needed a common expression. That moment can never be recovered.

Nothing that religion does is more important than equipping us to endure life's passages, by helping us find meaning in pain and loss. With meaning, many things are bearable; but our eulogist did not know how to give it to us. All he had to offer were his political desiderata. For my own part, I left the funeral more shaken and unsteady than before. Part of my distress arose from frustration, that my deepest thoughts (and those of many around me, as I later discovered) were so completely unechoed in this ceremony and in these words. But another part of my distress must have stemmed from a dark foreboding that I was witnessing another kind of malpractice, and another kind of death.

8. Michael W. McConnell Fears for American Religious Freedom, 1990

Passage of the Religion Clauses of the First Amendment ("Congress shall make no law respecting an establishment of religion or prohibiting the free exercise thereof. . . .") was one of the first effective exertions of political muscle by minority groups in the United States. James Madison, usually credited with their authorship, initially found the idea of a Bill of Rights "highly objectionable." During the early months of 1788, he tried to persuade his fellow Virginians that inclusion of a Bill of Rights in the new Constitution would be unnecessary, maybe even dangerous. Madison began to reconsider, however, when he found himself under attack for this position among his constituents. Baptists, previously his enthusiastic supports, were opposing the Constitution and threatening to support his opponent, James Monroe, in the congressional elections of that fall. Madison prudently changed his mind, and wrote to Baptist minister George Eve that he would now support "specific provisions made on the subject of the Rights of Conscience." In return, the Baptists held an election rally at their church at which Pastor Eve took "a very spirited and decided part" for Madison and reminded the crowd of his "many important services to the Baptists." (Those who think that church involvement in electoral politics began with Jesse Jackson and Pat Robertson do not know their American history.) Madison was duly elected to Congress and he did not forget his pledge. He became the draftsman and floor leader for what would later be called the First Amendment.

The Baptists had good reason to be concerned about religious freedom. As late as the 1760s, Baptists in Virginia were attacked, horsewhipped, fined, and jailed

Michael W. McConnell, "Taking Religious Freedom Seriously," *First Things* 1 (May 1990), 30–33.

for preaching their faith. But they were not the only religious minority that felt threatened by the absence of a guarantee of religious freedom in the new Constitution. Some Quakers in Pennsylvania opposed the Constitution for fear that the new national government would not respect their conviction against military service. Representative Daniel Carroll of Maryland, one of only three Roman Catholics in the First Congress, spoke up for the proposed religion amendment, stating that "many sects have concurred in [the] opinion that they are not well secured under the present Constitution." It is symptomatic of the unusual religious circumstances of America that a Roman Catholic should become the spokesman for the diversity of religious sects. . . .

In any event, the struggle for addition of protections for religious freedom in the Constitution was led by evangelical Protestants. Once proposed by the First Congress, the First Amendment met with easy and widespread approval, not because the majority believed in religious freedom as a matter of principle—most did not—but because the sheer number of religious denominations made each feel vulnerable to the combined efforts of the others. . . .

That ought to tell us something about the purpose and original meaning of the Religion Clauses. They were not intended as an instrument of secularization, or as a weapon the non-religious or anti-religious could use to suppress the effusions of the religious. The Religion Clauses were intended to guarantee the rights of those whose religious practices seemed to the majority a little odd. . . .

Despite the origins of the Religion Clauses, the Supreme Court has not tended to interpret them in light of the concerns and fears of minority religions. In the first Religion Clause case decided on its merits, the Court in 1878 upheld conviction of a Mormon leader for carrying out his religious duty of polygamy. In the next case, a dozen years later, the Court upheld denial of the vote to anyone who supported polygamy, and that same year the justices sustained an Act of Congress abolishing the Mormon Church and expropriating its property. In the course of countenancing this, the most brutal act of official religious suppression in this country since adoption of the Bill of Rights, the Court added insult to injury by questioning whether any belief so bizarre as the Mormons' advocacy of polygamy could even be given the title of "religious" and thus claim the protections of the First Amendment. Only when the leaders of the Church received a revelation repudiating the practice of polygamy, thus conforming to the usual family structure of the United States, were the Mormons allowed to practice what was left of their religion in peace.

Over the course of time the Supreme Court became more sensitive to those who do not share the majority's religious outlook. It for example gave extensive protection to the often annoying practices of the Jehovah's Witnesses, guaranteed access to unemployment compensation to those who celebrate the sabbath on Saturday, allowed the Old Order Amish to remain separate from the secularizing influences of the upper grades of high school, and put an end to organized "nondenominational" prayer and Bible reading in the public schools. But the Court's record remained mixed. It has turned a blind eye to the claims of Orthodox Jews in two cases involving them as well as to plausible claims by Muslims, fundamentalists, Scientologists, practitioners of Native American religions, and others outside the religious mainstream.

On the Establishment Clause front, the Court also entered decisions that run counter to the interest of religious minorities in maintaining a separate identity. One of the major subjects of the Court's attention has been the issue of aid to religious schools. Private religious-school systems were formed by minority religious groups precisely to avoid assimilation into the majority religious culture, originally Protestant, now largely secular. These schools are a principal means for preserving corporate religious identity. The decisions of many states to extend to students attending these schools some fraction of the support they would receive if they went to public schools have, however, repeatedly been struck down by the Supreme Court under the Establishment Clause. The effect of these decisions has been to force children of lower and middle income families into the melting pot of public education.

The Supreme Court evinces little recognition of the central place of religious pluralism, hence minority religions, under the First Amendment. . . .

The Establishment Clause doctrine of the Court does not even give verbal support to religious pluralism. Under the so-called "*Lemon* test" (*Lemon v. Kurtzman,* 1971), government actions are condemned if they lack a secular purpose, if they "advance" religion, or if they threaten to "entangle" government with religion. It may well be that it is *Lemon* that is most responsible for the anemic enforcement of the Court's free-exercise doctrine, since a vigorous defense of the free exercise of religion is non-secular, advances religion, and often embroils government in issues of religion. To the degree we are serious about the *Lemon* test, we correspondingly downplay or ignore the free-exercise doctrine.

A recent case involving a Native-American religion illustrates the point. In *Lyng v. Northwest Indian Cemeteries Protective Association* (1988), members of the Yurok, Karok, and Tolowa Indian tribes of Northern California challenged the decision of the Forest Service to build a logging road through an area called the "High Country," in which the Indians practice their spiritual devotions. On the basis of a study commissioned by the Forest Service and the evidence presented in court, the lower courts concluded—and the Supreme Court accepted—that construction of the road would "virtually destroy the Indians' ability to practice their religion." Moreover, it was essentially conceded that the government's interest in building the road was less than compelling; to many, the road looked like an utter boondoggle. It should have been an open-and-shut case for the Free Exercise Clause.

Instead a majority of the Court rejected the Indians' claim on the theory that the government can do whatever it wants with "*its*" land." How the government's exercise of its property powers under Article IV, Section 3, Clause 2 somehow attained exemption from the Bill of Rights remains unexplained, but that was the Court's decision.

The significant point about the Indians' argument in *Lyng* is that they were asking the government to violate all three of the prongs of the *Lemon* test. The secular considerations favored building the logging road; the Indians asked that non-secular reasons be considered as well. That violates *Lemon*. To preserve the sacred area in its pristine form would surely advance the Indians' religion. That violates *Lemon*. And to ask the government to regulate its land use in accordance with the religious significance some place on particular areas is to ask the government to be deeply entangled in religious affairs and to make delicate religious judgments. That violates *Lemon* too. The government evidently was faced with a choice between violating *Lemon* and saving the Indians' religion, or saving their religion and violating *Lemon*.

This dilemma is the predictable result of a legal formula that does not distinguish between advancing *religion* and advancing *religious freedom*. The *Lemon* test prohibits the government from "advancing" religion. But it *necessarily* advances religion to accommodate the secular dictates of public policy to the spiritual needs and concerns of religious minorities. The *Lemon* test is therefore a serious impediment to a policy of religious pluralism. . . .

. . . By forbidding all government action that has the effect of "advancing religion"—even by preserving its free exercise—the *Lemon* test fosters secularism, not religious pluralism.

One Justice, Sandra Day O'Connor, has called for abandoning the *Lemon* test and has proposed a new formulation expressly oriented to the needs of religious minorities. Her approach warrants quotation at length:

> The Establishment Clause prohibits government from making adherence to a religion relevant in any way to a person's standing in the political community. Government can run afoul of that prohibition in two principal ways. One is excessive entanglement with religious institutions, which may interfere with the independence of the institution, give the institution access to government or governmental powers not fully shared by nonadherents of the religion, and foster the creation of political constituencies defined along religious lines. The second and more direct infringement is government endorsement or disapproval of religion. Endorsement sends a message to nonadherents that they are outsiders, not full members of the political community, and an accompanying message to adherents that they are insiders, favored members of the political community. Disapproval sends the opposite message.

While I do not think Justice O'Connor's proposed "endorsement" test will work as a practical test for deciding cases, it is significant, and hopeful, that she has addressed her attention to the religious "outsider," for whose protection the Religion Clauses were adopted. Perhaps this will mark a turning point for the Court as a whole.

Unfortunately, Justice O'Connor has gotten the matter only half right. She is correct that an important element of religious freedom is that those who maintain beliefs at variance with the mainstream should not be made to feel like "outsiders, not full members of the political community." But that is not all there is to religious freedom. It is equally important that those who maintain beliefs at variance with the mainstream should be *permitted* to act like outsiders, and to keep their distance from the mainstream. Assimilation and secularization are threats to religious pluralism equally as serious as intolerance and ostracism.

And this is where the Supreme Court is most prone to be insensitive. Overt official acts of intolerance are, thankfully, rare in this society, and would, I am confident, be squelched by the courts if they occurred. But America's secularized Protestant culture presses about us from all sides with subtle nudges to conform. It invites us, it tempts us, to become full insiders even when we are not.

ESSAYS

The essays in this section each look further back in history to find the origins of recent politico-religious controversies. James Reichley of the Brookings Institute traces the history of Supreme Court interpretations of the First Amendment. As he explains, the justices had no hesitation in the nineteenth century about condemning Mormon polygamy, which they considered an outrage to the decency of what they assumed to be a Christian nation.

The passage of the Fourteenth Amendment in the wake of the Civil War had long-term consequences. It enabled the Court eventually to apply the federal Constitution's Bill of Rights to intrastate issues. Reichley shows how events in the outside world (the Second World War, fear of communism) clearly affected the justices as they extended the free exercise principle and erected a "wall of separation" to uphold the Establishment clause. Passionate rhetoric has swirled around all these cases, but Reichley, in a coolly detached way, sheds more light than heat on the church-state issue.

Nancy Ammerman of Hartford Seminary, a religious sociologist, traces the history of modern Fundamentalism to the intellectual and religious controversies of the late nineteenth century. She explains how Fundamentalism got its name and how it defined itself vis-à-vis other evangelicals. It suffered a defeat at the "Scopes Monkey Trial" of 1925, but re-emerged as a politically powerful force in the late 1970s under the leadership of the Reverend Jerry Falwell's Moral Majority. Ammerman shows how political fundamentalists reacted energetically and skillfully to many of the issues noted in the documents of this and earlier chapters: changing gender relations and sexual mores, homosexuality, abortion, school prayer, and threats to the family. By the 1980s they had become, and they remain, important players in American political life.

The Supreme Court and the First Amendment

JAMES REICHLEY

One effect of the Civil War was rejection of the extreme states-rights position. The Fourteenth Amendment, approved by Congress in 1866 and ratified by the states in 1868, places three restrictions on the states: that they not "abridge the privileges or immunities of citizens of the United States"; that they not "deprive any person of life, liberty, or property without due process of law"; and that they not "deny any person . . . equal protection of the laws."

The chief immediate objective of the Fourteenth Amendment was to extend full rights of citizenship to the former slaves who had been freed under the Emancipation Proclamation or the Thirteenth Amendment. . . .

Some modern scholars and the Supreme Court itself since 1940 have found in the Fourteenth Amendment the much broader purpose of applying to the states all the restrictions placed on the federal government by the Bill of Rights, including the religion clauses of the First Amendment. Applying this interpretation, the Court has plunged boldly—some would say recklessly—into the thicket of complex relationships involving religion, civil society, and the individual. The result is a tangled body of law, reflecting both traditional standards and contemporary ideological pressures. . . .

In 1862, clearly with Mormon practice in mind, Congress outlawed polygamy in the territories. The federal government soon obtained conviction of a Mormon named Reynolds, who freely admitted that he had "married a second time, having a first wife living," but claimed First Amendment immunity on the grounds that he had entered the second marriage "in conformity with what he believed at the time

James Reichley, "Interpreting the First Amendment," in *Religion in American Public Life* (Washington, D.C.: Brookings Institute, 1985), 115–167.

to be a religious duty." (The question of whether the First Amendment applied to the states did not arise; Utah, where Reynolds lived, was a territory under the direct authority of the federal government.)

Reynolds appealed to the Supreme Court, and Chief Justice Morrison Waite delivered the Court's unanimous decision in 1878. "Polygamy," Waite observed, "has always been odious among the northern and western nations of Europe, and, until the establishment of the Mormon Church, was almost exclusively a feature of Asiatic and of African people." Congress, therefore, was operating within the main current of Western moral tradition when it acted to uphold monogamous marriage, upon which "society may be said to be built." Waite dismissed Reynolds' contention that prosecution for polygamy violated his right to free exercise of religion. Under the First Amendment, "Congress was deprived of all legislative power over mere opinion, but was left free to reach actions which were in violation of social duties or subversive of good order." Polygamy was an action, not an opinion and therefore was subject to legal prohibition.

While seeming to limit the reach of the First Amendment, Waite's judgment also created future ammunition for strict separationists by giving official recognition for the first time to Jefferson's view that the religion clauses require "a wall of separation between church and state." . . .

The Mormon cases had shown that the Court was not disposed to interpret the free exercise clause as placing much limit on the law enforcement powers of the federal government, at least when these were directed against an unpopular sect. In two cases decided at the turn of the century, the Court appeared equally loath to put a tightly restrictive reading on the establishment clause.

In 1899 the Court rejected a taxpayer's contention that expenditure of federal funds to build an isolation wing for a hospital operated by the Catholic Sisters of Charity in the District of Columbia constituted a "law respecting an establishment of religion." Since the hospital was open to everybody, the Court held, it was not a "religious or sectarian body," and therefore did not offend the establishment clause.

Eight years later the Court similarly decided that payment by the federal government of sums drawn from Indian treaty funds to support schools for Indians operated by the Catholic Church was permissible, because it was the right of the Indians "to choose their own school and to choose it frankly because the education therein is under the influence of the religious faith in which they believe . . . and to have the use of their proportion of tribal funds applied . . . to maintain such schools." Any other construction, the Court argued, would pervert the establishment clause "into a means of prohibiting the free exercise of religion."

Well into the twentieth century the religion clauses had virtually no effect on the numerous practices through which government gave broad acknowledgement to the value of religion: prayer and Bible-reading exercises in the public schools; various forms of financial aid, including exemption from taxation, by government to churches; enforced observance of religious holidays; and many others. . . .

[In *Pierce v. Society of Sisters* (1925) the Court] establish[ed] a right of parents to educate their children in religious schools. Oregon had passed a law through popular referendum requiring that all children between the ages of eight and fifteen attend public schools—in effect outlawing church-operated schools below the college level. An order of Catholic nuns operating a system of parochial schools challenged the law's constitutionality. The Court found for the nuns. "The fundamental theory of liberty upon which all governments in this Union repose excludes any general power of the State to standardize its children by forcing them to accept instruction from public teachers only. The child is not the mere creature of the State; those who nurture him and direct his destiny have the right coupled with the high duty, to recognize and prepare him for additional obligations."

Also in 1925 in the celebrated case of *Gitlow v. New York,* the Court explicitly found that the rights to free speech and freedom of the press established by the First Amendment had been extended to the states by the due process clause of the Fourteenth. . . .

The Free Exercise Clause

If the clauses of the First Amendment requiring freedom of speech and the press applied to the states, the clause protecting the free exercise of religion must surely do so as well. This finding was made explicit in 1940. Cantwell, a member of Jehovah's Witnesses, a personalist sect sprung from the same pietist branch of Protestantism that had earlier produced the Baptists and the Quakers, had been convicted of breaching the peace. His offense had been to play a record attacking the Catholic religion on a public street in a neighborhood of New Haven where the population was 90 percent Catholic. He had further been found guilty of violating a Connecticut law requiring a religious solicitor to obtain a state license.

The Supreme Court overturned both convictions on the finding that the man's rights under the First and Fourteenth Amendments had been violated. "The First Amendment declares that Congress shall make no law respecting an establishment of religion or prohibiting the free exercise thereof. The Fourteenth Amendment has rendered the legislatures of the states as incompetent as Congress to enact such laws." No matter how offensive Cantwell's utterances might be to Catholics or members of other denominations, he had the right to say (or play) what he pleased about rival faiths, without going through the licensing procedure established by Connecticut.

Besides extending the free exercise clause—and, almost in passing, the establishment clause—to the states, the decision in *Cantwell v. Connecticut* also somewhat modified the distinction that Waite and Field had made between beliefs and actions. Justice Owen Roberts, writing for the Court, first restated the distinction in tempered form: "[The First] Amendment embraces two concepts—freedom to believe and freedom to act. The first is absolute but, in the nature of things, the second cannot be. Conduct remains subject to regulation for the protection of society." . . . But the state's right to regulate conduct must be balanced in particular cases against the right of the individual or the church to free exercise: "In every case the power to regulate must be so exercised as not, in attempting a permissible end, unduly to infringe the protected freedom."

A few weeks after announcing the *Cantwell* decision, the Court swerved back toward the interest of the state in *Minersville School District v. Gobitis,* another case involving Jehovah's Witnesses, that at the time attracted far more public attention. The Gobitis children had been expelled from public school in Pennsylvania for refusing to salute the American flag in exercises prescribed by state law. According to the Jehovah's Witness faith of the Gobitis family, saluting the flag "of any earthly government" was idolatrous. The children's father, faced with the expense of providing them with a private education, brought suit.

Justice Felix Frankfurter (writing, it should be remembered, during the weeks when Hitler's armies were sweeping across the Low Countries and France, and the very survival of traditional Western civilization seemed threatened) delivered the opinion of the Court. While reaffirming application of the First Amendment to the states and not returning to the narrow distinction between belief and action proposed in the previous century by Chief Justice Waite, Frankfurter found an overwhelming state interest in instilling patriotic loyalty among the nation's youth. "We are dealing with an interest inferior to none in the hierarchy of legal values. National unity is the basis of national security." Frankfurter himself might question whether forced saluting of the flag was a truly effective means for instilling loyalty. "But this courtroom is not the arena for debating issues of educational policy. It is not our province to choose among competing considerations in the subtle process of securing effective loyalty to the traditional ideals of democracy, while respecting at the same time individual idiosyncrasies among a people so diversified in racial origins and religious allegiances."

Three years later, in *West Virginia State Board of Education v. Barnette,* the Court, perhaps influenced by instances of violence and discrimination against Jehovah's Witnesses, including children, that had followed *Gobitis,* reversed itself on the issue of compulsory flag-saluting by a vote of six to three. Justice Robert Jackson, writing for the majority, based the reversal on a First Amendment right to freedom of expression, which he maintained included nonparticipation in flag-saluting exercises, rather than on the right to free exercise of religion. "Those who begin coercive elimination of dissent," Jackson wrote, "soon find themselves exterminating dissenters. Compulsory unification of opinion achieves only the unanimity of the graveyard." . . .

By the time of the *Barnette* decision, the Court had further extended the right of free exercise by ruling that Jehovah's Witnesses selling religious tracts door-to-door must be exempted from a local ordinance requiring all itinerant solicitors to pay a small license fee. The case, *Murdock v. Pennsylvania,* went beyond the earlier *Cantwell* decision in that the government of Pennsylvania retained no discretion over whether the license should be issued. "Those who can tax the exercise of this religious practice can make its exercise so costly as to deprive it of the resources necessary for its maintenance." . . .

During the next three decades, the Court dealt with a large number of free exercise cases, gradually defining both the reach and the limits of the right. In 1961 the Court denied, to the anguish of many civil libertarians, the plea of an Orthodox Jewish merchant, Braunfeld, for exemption from a Pennsylvania law requiring that most retail stores be closed on Sunday. (The question of whether the Sunday-closing law itself violated the establishment clause of the First Amendment had already been decided.) Braunfeld's religion caused him to close his shop on Saturday, which he observed as the Sabbath. He therefore lost two days of business compared to his Gentile competitors' one. Nevertheless, wrote Chief Justice Earl Warren for the majority, "if the State regulates conduct by enacting a general law within its power, the purpose and effect of which is to advance the State's secular goals, the statute is valid despite its indirect burden on religious observance unless the State may accomplish its purpose by means which do not impose a burden."

Two years later, however, the Court, with a somewhat more liberal cast after the retirement of Frankfurter, in a similar case found a valid claim to free exercise. Sherbert, a Seventh Day Adventist, had been fired from her job in a South Carolina textile mill because she refused to work on Saturday, the Adventist's Sabbath. When she applied for unemployment compensation, she was denied benefits under South Carolina law that made a claimant ineligible "if he had failed, without good cause, to accept suitable work when offered him." This requirement, the Court held, violated Sherbert's right to free exercise by forcing her to "choose between following the precepts of her religion and forfeiting benefits, on the one hand, and abandoning one of the precepts of her religion in order to accept work, on the other." . . .

An Inherent Tension.   The most definitive opinion so far involving free exercise issues came in *Wisconsin v. Yoder* in 1972. A community of Old Order Amish (a German pietist sect) in Green County, Wisconsin, including Yoder, had defied the state law requiring children to attend public or private school up to the age of sixteen. To send their children to school beyond the eighth grade, Yoder and his coreligionists maintained, would "endanger their own salvation and that of their children."

Through an opinion written by Chief Justice Warren Burger, the Court found religious belief . . . a necessary but not in itself a sufficient condition for approving exemption of the Amish children from the state attendance law. The Amish claim, Burger emphasized, would not be valid if it were based on a merely "philosophical and personal" choice, like that of Henry David Thoreau when he turned away from "the social values of his time" in nineteenth century New England. Even after the claim's religious foundation had been verified, it would still be rejected by the Court if it were found to conflict seriously with the "State's interest in universal education." The actual effects of Amish practice, therefore, must decide.

Examination of the record of the Green County Amish showed that they "had never been known to commit crimes, that none had been known to receive public assistance, and that none were unemployed." Looking beyond the immediate community to the exemplary history of the Amish people over "three centuries and more than 200 years in this country," Burger found that there would be "at best a speculative gain, in terms of meeting the duties of citizenship, from an additional two or three years of compulsory formal education." Exemption of the Amish children from formal schooling beyond the eighth grade, the Court concluded, was therefore justified.

The *Yoder* decision, though approved by all but one participating justice, evidently caused the Court a good deal of soul-searching. Justice Byron White in a concurring opinion worried that some Amish children "may wish to become nuclear physicists, ballet dancers, computer programmers, or historians, and for these occupations, formal training will be necessary." White decided, however, that in this case, "although the question is close," the state had not demonstrated "that Amish children who leave school in the eighth grade will be intellectually stultified or unable to acquire new academic skills later."

Justice William Douglas, the lone dissenter, complained that the majority had given more consideration to the views of the Amish parents than to the interests of their children, which should have been paramount. . . .

The deeper significance of the *Yoder* case was that it placed beyond question the principle that under some circumstances, otherwise illegal actions as well as beliefs are entitled to protection of the free exercise clause. The Amish were declared a special class, defined by religion, exempt from some laws applying to everybody else. The right to free exercise, then, as long as vital interests of the state are not affected, may endow a particular religious group with unique privileges—moving close, some commentators have argued, to a selective establishment of religion. . . .

The Establishment Clause

In 1940, Justice Owen Roberts extended the establishment clause to the states, without elaboration, in his opinion in *Cantwell v. Connecticut,* although establishment had little or nothing to do with the case's substance. . . .

Whatever Roberts's reason, extending the establishment clause to the states opened questions that were sure to be both difficult and troublesome. Did prohibition of "establishment" make traditional practices of prayer and Bible reading in the public schools unconstitutional? Had state aid to religious education been taken out of the hands of the states altogether and placed under the interdict of the federal Constitution? Did exemption of church property from taxation, provided for in all the states, represent a form of "establishment"? What of such ministerial relationships as the appointment of chaplains by state legislatures? Were laws prohibiting some kinds of commercial activities on Christian days of worship unconstitutional?

Education for Salvation.   The first of these questions actually to be dealt with by the Court after *Cantwell* was the long-disputed issue of state aid to religious education. The men who passed and ratified the First Amendment had no experience with public education of the size or scope that developed in the United States during the nineteenth century. But they seem to have identified education with religion almost as a matter of course, as is shown by their mention of "religion" as one of the values to be promulgated through the schools in the Northwest Territory. . . .

During the early years of the twentieth century, many Protestants, joined by some Catholics and Jews, became concerned that their children were not receiving adequate education in religion. The Sunday school movement launched by Protestant churches in the nineteenth century had been created to help fill this gap, but few believed that instruction given for an hour or two on Sunday mornings by volunteer teachers could match the quality of training in secular subjects being provided by professional educators in the public schools. A program to deal with this problem, under which students were released from the public schools for one or more periods each week to go to the church of their parents' choice for religious instruction, was introduced in Gary, Indiana, in 1914. The so-called released-time plan spread widely among the states. . . .

. . . [A] variation on released time [was] introduced in Champaign, Illinois, in 1940. Under the Champaign plan, religious instruction was provided within the public school itself at a common time by instructors hired and paid by the community's interfaith council, composed of representatives of Protestant, Catholic, and Jewish denominations. Protestant students, who were in the majority, received instruction in their regular classrooms, while Catholics and Jews moved to rooms elsewhere in the building. Students whose parents indicated a preference for nonparticipation in the program were sent to a designated area, theoretically for supervised study. The Jewish program was soon discontinued, and most Jewish parents thereafter enrolled their children in the Protestant classes. The Champaign plan was also widely copied. Fifteen percent of all American school districts were providing religious education in public school buildings during school hours by 1949. . . .

. . . The ax fell . . . on the Champaign plan, . . . in *McCollum v. Board of Education* in 1948. Mrs. McCollum, a resident of Champaign, had indicated preference for nonparticipation in religious education for her son, a student in the fifth grade. During the period set aside for religious education, the boy was sent to a desk in the hall outside his classroom, a place sometimes used for disciplinary purposes, where he was subjected to teasing by passing students. Mrs. McCollum brought suit challenging the constitutionality of the religious instruction program.

Justice Black, . . . writing for the majority, found that the Champaign plan violated the standard he had set forth . . . for separation of church and state and was therefore unconstitutional. . . .

The *McCollum* decision was almost universally condemned by the nation's churches. . . .

In *Zorach v. Clausen* in 1952 the Court seemed to draw back. Justice Douglas, who had joined Black in *McCollum,* switched sides along with two other justices and, writing for the majority, found that New York City's released-time program, which made no use of public school buildings, did not violate the First Amendment. Releasing students to attend religious instruction off school premises, Douglas concluded, was no more than an adjustment of school schedules to "accommodate the religious needs of the people." In words that now astonish (he became the Court's most uncompromising separationist) Douglas held that "we are a religious people whose institutions presuppose a Supreme Being. . . . When the state encourages religious instruction or cooperates with religious authorities by adjusting the schedule of events to sectarian needs, it follows the best of our traditions. . . . To hold that it may not would be to find in the Constitution a requirement that government show a callous indifference to religious groups. That would be preferring those who believe in no religion over those who do believe. . . ."

Prayer in Schools.   In 1962 the Court at last faced up to the inherent conflict between *Cantwell* and the traditions of prayer and Bible reading in the public schools. At the time, devotional exercises in the public schools, while widely practiced, were by no means universal. . . .

During the 1950s, feeling on both sides of the issue became more intense. Among liberals a consensus gradually developed that state-sponsored prayer and Bible reading in the schools were unconstitutional invasions of civil liberties and should be stopped. Groups particularly concerned with the challenge of international communism or the perceived decline of domestic morality, on the other hand, became more resolute in their support for religious observances in the schools. One important group switched sides: after more than a century of opposition to religious exercises with a Protestant orientation in the public schools, the Catholic church now favored almost any means that would prevent the schools from becoming completely secularized.

Trying to bridge these conflicting points of view, the New York Board of Regents in 1951 composed a prayer for use in the schools that could not be identified with any particular denomination: "Almighty God, we acknowledge our dependence upon thee, and we beg thy blessings upon us, our parents, our teachers, and our country." The Board made provision that children who did not wish to participate in the prayer should be permitted to remain silent or, upon presentation of a written request from parents, could leave the classroom. In 1962 a case brought by parents of five children in the schools of New Hyde Park, New York, who challenged the constitutionality of the Regents' prayer reached the Supreme Court. With *Engel v. Vitale* the Court dodged no longer.

Once more leading the majority, Justice Black found the establishment clause "must at least mean that in this country it is no part of the business of government to compose official prayers for any group of the American people to recite as a part of a religious program carried on by government." . . .

The wave of condemnation raised against *Engel* made the criticisms that had been directed at *McCollum* in 1948 seem like a summer squall. Catholic clergy took the lead. Cardinal Francis Spellman of New York was "shocked, and frightened, that the Supreme Court has declared unconstitutional a simple and voluntary declaration of belief in God by public school children." Cardinal Richard Cushing of Boston was sure that "the Communists are enjoying this day." . . . The fury of Catholic spokesmen was matched by many Protestant ministers, particularly, though not only, among evangelicals. Billy Graham, the best known of the new wave of evangelical revivalists attracting national audiences, found the decision "another step towards the secularization of the United States." Episcopal Bishop James Pike of San Francisco announced that "the Supreme Court has just deconsecrated the nation."

Conservative politicians of both parties, whose irritation with the Warren Court had in any case been growing, denounced the decision, sometimes in apocalyptic terms. . . . Some Southern politicians found a connection between the prayer decision and the Court's 1954 decision requiring racial desegregation of the public schools. "They put the Negroes in the schools," said Congressman George Andrews of Alabama, "and now they've driven God out." . . .

A factor appeared in the reaction to *Engel,* however, that had generally been absent after *McCollum* fourteen years before: numerous liberal voices were raised to defend the decision or at least to advise compliance. Most, though not all, of the Jewish clergy supported the decision. A substantial number of liberal Protestant ministers agreed with Harold Fey, editor of the *Christian Century:* "The Court's decision protects the integrity of the religious conscience and the proper function of religious and governmental institutions." President Kennedy, who had recently been through an election in which religion had been a significant factor, was cautious. "The Supreme Court has made its judgment. A good many people obviously will disagree with it; others will agree with it. But I think it is important for us, if we're going to maintain our constitutional principle, that we support Supreme Court decisions even when we may not agree with them. . . ."

Fundamentalism and Politics

NANCY AMMERMAN

As fundamentalism reemerged in the United States in the late twentieth century after a period of apparent hibernation, no two words better captured its public image and agenda than the late 1970s term "Moral Majority," and later, in the 1990s, the phrase "family values." In 1979 independent Baptist pastor Jerry Falwell declared that people concerned about the moral decline of the United States were a majority waiting to be mobilized. He set out to accomplish that task, and since then through the Moral Majority and its successor organizations, especially the Christian Coalition, conservative voters have been registered, rallies held, and legislators elected. Ronald Reagan recognized religious conservatives as an important constituency, speaking at their rallies and inviting their leaders to the White House. And in 1988, politically active conservative pastors again had the ear of the president, Republican George Bush. Currently the Republican Party is dependent on this vote to win office at all levels, from regional to national.

Pastoring churches and establishing schools were long the most likely strategies of people who called themselves fundamentalists. Not all saw politics and social change as their mission, and many had discounted such activities as useless, even counterproductive. At the same time that some fundamentalists were lobbying in the White House, others were waiting anxiously for the Rapture, the time when they would be transported to heaven. A book appeared that set 1988 as the date for this eschatological event, and many were convinced by its claims that the Jewish New Year, Rosh Hashanah, would be the appointed time. Like many dates before it, this appointment with the end times went unkept, but believers were reminded again of how important it was to be "Rapture ready" and to seek the salvation of others.

Fundamentalists in North America can be found in both camps—waiting for the Rapture and lobbying in the White House—although our own times have seen an unprecedented growth in fundamentalist Christian activism in the electoral sphere. In both cases, whether anticipating the Rapture or struggling to influence state and local politics, believers have drawn on a distinctive view of the world that emerged about a century earlier. They are willing to argue that certain beliefs are "fundamental," and they are willing to organize in a variety of ways to preserve and defend those beliefs.

In the last quarter of the nineteenth century, many leaders in U.S. Protestantism were actively seeking ways to adapt traditional beliefs to the realities of "modern" scholarship and sensibilities. They were met head-on, however, by people who saw the adaptations as heresy and who declared that they would defend traditional beliefs from such change. In the first two decades of the twentieth century, the latter group produced essays that furthered their defensive cause. Among the most important was a series of short scholarly essays issued over a five-year period (1910–1915) entitled "The Fundamentals"—a name widely used to designate the threatened beliefs. In 1920, Curtis Lee Laws, editor of the Northern Baptist newspaper *The*

Nancy Ammerman, "North American Protestant Fundamentalism," in *Media, Culture, and the Religious Right,* ed. Linda Kintz and Julia Lesage (Minneapolis: University of Minnesota Press, 1998), 21–50.

Watchman-Examiner, wrote that a "fundamentalist" is a person willing to "do battle royal" for the fundamentals of the faith. The term "fundamentalism" was both a description and a call to action, and the name stuck. During the 1920s fundamentalists actively fought against modernism in their churches and against the teaching of evolution in their schools. They lost those battles but retreated and reorganized into a network of institutions that has housed much of the conservative wing of U.S. Protestantism ever since.

However, "fundamentalist" is not synonymous with "conservative." It represents, rather, a subset of the larger whole. Fundamentalists share with other conservative Christians their support for "traditional" interpretations of such doctrines as Jesus' Virgin Birth, the reality of the miracles that Scripture reports (including Jesus' Resurrection from the dead), and Christ's eventual return to reign over this earth. Like other conservatives, they tend to support supernatural interpretations of events, whereas liberals tend to seek naturalistic explanations.

In U.S. society, conservatism in religion is widespread. In the U.S. population, 72 percent say that the Bible is the word of God, with over half of that number (39 percent) saying that the Bible should be taken literally. Almost two-thirds are certain that Jesus Christ rose from the dead. Nearly three-fourths say they believe in life after death. And almost half (44 percent) could be called "creationists," since they believe that God created the world in "pretty much its present form" sometime in the last ten thousand years.

Not all these people, however, are fundamentalists. Conservative Protestantism has a number of significant divisions. Among other things, not everyone agrees on that most central of doctrines: how people are saved, that is, how they make themselves acceptable to God. One branch of conservative Protestantism places primary emphasis on historic creeds of faith and membership in a church that confesses those beliefs. People are baptized, initiated, as infants into a community of faith. These "confessional" churches are often conservative but are not usually the home of fundamentalists.

Fundamentalists are more often found in the other, much larger branch of conservative Protestantism that identifies itself as "evangelical." For these people, only an individual decision to follow Jesus will suffice for salvation. They are concerned not only about their own eternal fate but about the destiny of those around them. They seek to "win souls for Christ" by their words and deeds, testifying to the necessity of a life-changing decision to become a Christian. They often speak of that experience as being "born again." This experience gives them a sense of personal and intimate communion with Jesus, and it often shapes their lives and conversations in noticeably pious ways. . . .

Pentecostal and charismatic Christians in North America also belong in the evangelical family but are a distinct group within it. Beginning with the Pentecostal revivals near the turn of the twentieth century, new denominations such as the Church of God, the Church of God in Christ, and the Assemblies of God were formed. These emphasized "gifts of the spirit" (such as speaking in tongues and healing) as evidence of the believer's spiritual power. By the 1960s a similar emphasis on the Holy Spirit's power had also found its way into many mainline denominations, with prayer and healing groups meeting around the country in the parish halls of Catholic, Episcopal, Presbyterian, Methodist, and many other local churches. . . .

African American churches, Pentecostals, and Mormons occupy the same general religious territory as fundamentalists. They are all conservative and evangelical, but they are still distinct from each other and from fundamentalists. Mormons have their own scripture; African Americans are defined more by race than by doctrine; and Pentecostals trust the revelatory power of experience more than do the more rationally oriented fundamentalists who seek to confine revelation to Scripture alone. . . .

. . . During most of the first half of the twentieth century, "fundamentalist" and "evangelical" meant roughly the same thing. People might use either name to describe those who preserved and practiced the revivalist heritage of soul-winning and maintained a traditional insistence on orthodoxy.

But as orthodox people began to organize for survival in a world dominated by the nonorthodox, two significantly different strategies emerged. Seeking a broad culture base for their gospel, one group saw benefits in learning to get along with outsiders. They did not wish to adopt the outsider's ways, but they wanted to be respected. They began, especially after World War II, to take the name "evangelical" for themselves. Billy Graham can be seen as their primary representative. The other group insisted that getting along was no virtue, and they advocated active opposition to liberalism, secularism, and communism. This group retained the name "fundamentalist." . . .

When fundamentalists describe how they are different from other people, they begin with the fact that they are saved. They clearly affirm their kinship with other evangelicals on this point. Much of their organized effort is aimed at seeking converts. . . .

Inerrancy

Fundamentalists also claim that the only sure path to salvation is through a faith in Jesus Christ that is grounded in unwavering faith in an inerrant Bible. As fundamentalists see the situation, if but one error of fact or principle is admitted in Scripture, nothing—not even the redemptive work of Christ—is certain. When asked what else makes them distinctive, fundamentalists will almost invariably claim that they are the people who "really believe the Bible." They insist that true Christians must believe the whole Bible, the parts they like along with the parts they dislike, the hard parts and the easy ones. The Bible can be trusted to provide an accurate description of science and history, as well as morality and religion. . . .

Some aspects of modern science, of course, are not questioned (the earth's roundness and orbit around the sun, for instance). The interpretive task that fundamentalists undertake, then, requires a careful balancing of facts about the world presumed by moderns to be true with the assumption that the Bible contains no factual errors. . . . Likewise, moral teaching in Scripture that seems to condone slavery or polygamy must be neutralized. . . .

Premillennialism

Fundamentalists do not simply read the Bible to learn history or moral principles. They also expect to find in Scripture clues to the destiny of this world, to what will happen in the end times. . . . [T]oday most fundamentalists are "pre-Tribulation dispensational premillennialists." The ideas that go with that label are almost as complicated as the label, but one of the most important is the idea of the Rapture. . . .

. . . Believers are not content to know that Jesus is coming for them; they want to know when and what will happen next. For these clues they turn to the apocalyptic books of Daniel (in Hebrew Scripture) and the Revelation (at the end of the New Testament). Here there are great images of destruction and horror preceding the ultimate triumph of God. Believers interested in prophecy dissect these images to create a systematic scheme (often pictured in elaborate charts) that chronicles the Tribulation of the earth following the believers' departure, the rise of a world ruler (the Antichrist), and the final battle (Armageddon) in which the forces of good and evil will meet. Only then will Christ establish a kingdom of peace and righteousness on this earth. That fundamentalists believe Christ will have to return before the millennium (thousand-year reign on earth) makes them "premillennialists" (in contrast to the more optimistic "postmillennialists," who thought human effort might usher in the reign of God). That they think the Rapture will happen before the upheavals of the Tribulation makes their position "pre-Tribulation." . . .

The ultimate characteristic that has distinguished fundamentalists from other evangelicals has been their insistence that there can be tests of faith. Fundamentalists insist on uniformity of belief within the ranks and on separation from others whose beliefs and lives are suspect. The fundamentalist, then, is very likely to belong to a church with strict rules for its own membership and for its cooperative relations with others. It is likely to be an "independent" church, since so many of the denominations are seen as infected with apostasy and compromise. . . .

At the same time that fundamentalists were battling modernism in their churches, they joined forces with others to battle Darwinism in society. Ever since evolutionary ideas had come to prominence in the previous century, they had been fought by conservatives who saw each biological species (especially humanity) as God's unique creation accomplished in a historical period recent enough to be recounted in the pages of Scripture. World War I, however, gave the ideological battle new urgency. George Marsden argues that fundamentalists saw in the war the ultimate manifestation of a "survival of the fittest" mentality. If one believes that the strong are destined to displace the weak, then war on one's neighbors seems only natural. The war became, then, a struggle between Christian civilization and German barbarism. Conservative minds linked the presumed German acceptance of evolution (and the role of German scholars in producing the historical-critical method of interpreting Scripture) to German aggression. Just as the United States was called on to defend Christian civilization against that aggression, so Christians were called to attack the ideas at the root of Germany's sin: evolution.

Fundamentalist concern about evolution might have remained a matter confined to religious circles had not William Jennings Bryan chosen in 1920 to take up the cause. For the next several years anti-evolutionism became a national fad. It drew together denominational conservatives and dispensational premillennialists, northerners and southerners, farmers and city dwellers. Fundamentalists organized rallies, at which Bryan spoke. People throughout the country became convinced that the future of civilization depended on banishing this atheistic and harmful dogma from the schools. And premillennialists who had thought political action useless in the face of an imminent Rapture found themselves obsessed with seeking social change.

In twenty states, as diverse as New York and Georgia, activists introduced bills in their legislatures seeking to prohibit the teaching of evolution. In the Northeast those efforts never got very far. Many southern states saw real fights, but in most cases newspapers and universities could rally support among the educated public for freedom of thought. In two border states, Kentucky and Texas, the fights were especially bitter, and in Kentucky it took religious intervention to work out a compromise. Yet in neither state did a law against evolution succeed. But in Oklahoma, then Florida, followed by Tennessee, Mississippi, Louisiana, and Arkansas, the outcome was the reverse: In these states anti-evolution forces got laws on the books with relatively little effort. For many in those regions, teaching evolution was simply inconceivable. Outlawing it was not difficult.

Nor would enforcement have been much of a problem in Tennessee had it not been for the intervention of outside forces. Whether John Scopes tested the law on his own or was induced to do so does not matter as much as what happened after he was charged with the crime of teaching evolution in Tennessee's public schools. The American Civil Liberties Union sent in a team of lawyers, headed by Clarence Darrow, to defend him, and the anti-evolutionists dispatched William Jennings Bryan. The result was a highly publicized clash between new and old, between science and religion, between city and country. Scopes was convicted as charged. But "in the trial by public opinion and the press, it was clear that the twentieth century, the cities, and the universities had won a resounding victory, and that the country, the South, and the fundamentalists were guilty as charged."

In the days following the debacle in Dayton, Tennessee, anti-evolutionists organized furiously, but their efforts were increasingly radical and marginal to the larger culture. . . . After 1925 fundamentalism lost its credibility and with it the ability to rally national or even denominational support for attacks against Christian civilization's enemies. . . .

For fifty years fundamentalism had been largely invisible on the U.S. political scene. A few fundamentalists had joined 1950s anticommunist crusades, but most had remained relatively inactive in politics, preferring instead to put energy into the churches and institutions that made their view of the world possible. Evangelism and missions far outweighed efforts toward social reform. However, a number of things happened in the 1960s and 1970s to mobilize fundamentalists again as a social movement. In some ways, the culture itself pulled fundamentalists into the public arena; in other ways, internal changes pushed them outward. . . .

[The] seeming disintegration of society [in those decades] lent the evangelistic task extra urgency. Such chaos could only mean the Rapture was near. Such rapid change is the stuff of which sermons are made. And it is the stuff of which converts are made. Individuals often experienced cultural change as an intolerable shaking of the foundations. From burned-out hippies to disillusioned liberals to ordinary seekers, they made their way into fundamentalist churches. . . . In fundamentalist churches, . . . former rebels found answers and order, love and stability. . . .

The 1960s revolution had . . . pulled the entire U.S. polity toward new partisan alignments. The Democratic Party's hold on the South disintegrated with that party's embrace of civil rights. And working-class whites outside the South also began to drop their Democratic allegiance. Both northern and southern Democrats became more interested in moral and lifestyle issues than in traditional party interests and loyalties—interested enough to vote for Republicans who caught their fancy. With political choices to be made, people searched for the grounds on which to make them. At least some people began to wonder if churches might help them in that process.

Meanwhile, the U.S. government itself was creating a certain alarm in fundamentalists' minds. The retreat from Vietnam raised fears that the nation might no longer enjoy its world supremacy. Fundamentalists cared deeply about that possibility, partly because they feared communism's growth but also because they saw U.S. military and economic might as guarantors of their ability to evangelize the world. For fundamentalists, the United States has always been the "city on a hill," ordained by God as the light to the nations. From the beginning, they had been committed to foreign missions. Now they wondered if the gospel's light might go out because it would have no great chosen nation to carry it.

Their fear for the country's future was intensified by the 1963 U.S. Supreme Court decision that outlawed prescribed prayers in public schools. It seemed impossible that in this Christian nation children should be told not to pray in school. Over the next decade, the evidence mounted in fundamentalists' minds that the nation was being run by people intentionally hostile to their beliefs and determined to stamp out all vestiges of traditional religion in coming generations. Attacks on home, school, and church seemed so systematic that they surely must have come from a single ideological source, identified in Tim LaHaye's popular 1980 book, *The Battle for the Mind,* as secular humanism. . . .

Courts, schools, and legislatures seemed to dare fundamentalists to come out of their separatist institutions to defend their right to exist.

Though fundamentalist churches were enjoying the revival brought their way by increasing numbers of seekers, they were also being pulled out of their institutional subculture by broader concerns. They had a growing sense that if "God's people" did not stand up against an aggressive government in this generation, there might not be another generation of believers. The sense of urgency coming from the culture was matched by the momentum of institutional strength coming from within. In the late nineteenth century, conservatives concerned about the culture's drift into modernism had created new institutions to support their cause. In the late twentieth century, those institutions were already in place. They were, in fact, thriving. . . .

Nowhere was this . . . organizational power more apparent than in the television ministries. Television offered an enormously powerful medium for raising money, and it constantly pushed evangelists along by the sheer power of its resources. They not only raised money to stay on the air and preach the gospel; they also raised money for whatever enterprises their imagination and charisma could create and sustain. . . .

The Movement Organized

Christian Academies.   Following World War II, a few conservative churches began to organize their own day schools, but the movement accelerated rapidly during the 1960s. Some outsiders saw the move toward private church-sponsored schools as merely a retreat from racial integration—and some of it was clearly that—but the motivations were much larger. Fundamentalists had concluded that the public schools were actively hostile to their children's faith. Now that they had the resources, they took matters into their own hands. Between 1965 and 1983, enrollment in evangelical schools increased sixfold, and the number of schools reached about 10,000. . . .

The Christian Right.   The other major effort of 1980s fundamentalists toward gaining control over their world was their active entry into politics. Ironically, U.S. news media first glimpsed conservative religion's political potential not in terms of fundamentalists themselves but in terms of Jimmy Carter, who better fits the label "evangelical." Far from making his religion his political agenda, Carter strictly adhered to the traditional Baptist belief in separation of church and state. And fundamentalists soon saw that Carter shared few of their foreign or domestic policy positions. . . .

. . . [I]n 1979, some pastors of huge "superchurches" decided the time had come to organize to promote morality in U.S. life. With the help of conservative political organizers Richard Viguerie and Ed McAteer, they put together a nonpartisan political organization, the Moral Majority. Its head was to be Jerry Falwell, with other board members James Kennedy (Presbyterian from Florida), Greg Dixon (independent Baptist from Indianapolis), Tim LaHaye (conservative ideologue from California), and Charles Stanley (Southern Baptist from Atlanta). Other conservative religious political groups were being organized as well—the Religious Roundtable, the American Coalition for Traditional Values, and Christian Voice—but the Moral Majority captured the public imagination (and the news media), symbolizing a revitalized, politically potent fundamentalist movement. The group built on two primary organizational bases: the independent church network in existence since the 1930s and the television fund-raising mechanisms developed to a fine art in the 1970s. With pastors as primary organizers, the movement spread quickly into their spheres of influence, often large suburban churches. And television preachers and their direct-mail fund-raising lists broadened the net further.

The Moral Majority's strategy involved the full range of political activities. They distributed information through newsletters, seminars, and broadcast ministries. They registered voters and lobbied Congress. And they trained and encouraged conservatives in the fine art of running for office. No public office or bureaucratic position was too low; as political organizers, they realized that their crusade must begin from the ground up. And like the network of independent churches on which they built, Moral Majority activities often happened out of public sight, varying in form and emphasis from one location to another. . . .

. . . Though their efforts were at first ill-timed and ineffective, as they gained experience they were able to defeat the Equal Rights Amendment (ERA) to the U.S. Constitution and to enable "equal access" legislation (for after-hours religious activities in public schools).

The issues around which fundamentalists have attempted to rally support have ranged from gun control and the Panama Canal to drugs and pornography. The fight against the teaching of evolution had already been revived in a new form in the effort to institute the teaching of "scientific creationism" alongside evolution. Other public school issues included efforts to reinstitute prayer in the classroom and initiatives against many forms of secular humanism. . . .

The central theme of the fundamentalist foray into politics was to protect the traditional family, the basic unit of society. This meant a legally married man and woman, with their children, preferably supported solely by the husband's labor. From this flowed the movement's opposition to gay rights, pornography, the Equal Rights Amendment, and laws designed to protect abused wives and children. For the nation to be strong, its families should be constituted according to God's rules, rules including man's heading the family and parents' physically disciplining children. Concern for the family became most acute, however, on the issue of abortion. Evoking holocaust images, pro-life speakers and writers decried the immorality that leads to unwanted pregnancy in the first place, greedy doctors who make a living destroying life, and morally bankrupt government agencies and courts that allow such a practice to flourish. Stopping the slaughter of innocent unborn babies became the rallying cry that has mobilized many previously inactive conservatives.

Abortion also became the issue that tested the limits of fundamentalist activism. In 1988 a group called Operation Rescue arose as a vehicle for the promotion of civil disobedience in opposition to abortion. The group not only picketed abortion clinics but sought to prevent women from entering. The protesters sat down, formed human blockades, and pleaded with those who came and went. When clinics obtained court orders against them, they were not deterred, and many went to jail. During that summer's Democratic National Convention, Operation Rescue demonstrators filled Atlanta's jails, many giving only Jane Doe or John Doe as identification. While leaders of the Christian Right sympathized with their cause, most drew the line at civil disobedience. Jerry Falwell, who declared himself their "cheerleader," was himself not yet ready to go to jail. Mainstream fundamentalists would stick to standard political means while this new group explored more radical measures.

The abortion issue not only divided fundamentalists into differing tactical camps, it also united fundamentalists and other religious conservatives who had otherwise shunned each other as doctrinal inferiors or heretics. Catholics, long seen as allies of the Antichrist by many fundamentalists, were embraced by those active in the pro-life movement. Other issues brought together other unlikely coalitions: Feminists joined the fight against pornography; Mormons opposed the ERA; and Jews wanted partners in supporting Israel. In the Moral Majority, Falwell adamantly insisted such partnerships were essential, boldly asserting his organization's commitment to "pluralism."

FURTHER READING

Alley, Robert S. *The Supreme Court on Church and State* (1988).
Allitt, Patrick. *Catholic Intellectuals and Conservative Politics in America: 1950–1985* (1993).
Ammerman, Nancy. *Bible Believers: Fundamentalists in the Modern World* (1987).
Anderson, Robert. *Vision of the Disinherited: The Making of American Pentecostalism* (1979).

Balmer, Randall. *Mine Eyes Have Seen the Glory: A Journey into the Evangelical Subculture in America* (1989).

Bendroth, Margaret. *Fundamentalism and Gender, 1875 to the Present* (1993).

Blumhofer, Edith. *Defending the Faith: The Assemblies of God, Pentecostalism, and American Culture* (1993).

Capps, Walter. *The New Religious Right: Piety, Patriotism and Politics* (1994).

Carpenter, Joel. *Revive Us Again: The Reawakening of American Fundamentalism* (1997).

Eve, Raymond, and Francis Harrold. *The Creationist Movement in Modern America* (1991).

Frankel, Marvin E. *Faith and Freedom: Religious Liberty in America* (1994).

Greeley, Andrew. *An Ugly Little Secret: Anti-Catholicism in North America* (1977).

Handy, Robert. *Undetermined Establishment: Church-State Relations in America, 1880–1920* (1991).

Harrell, David, Jr. *Oral Roberts: An American Life* (1985).

Hutcheson, Richard G., Jr. *God in the White House* (1988).

Larson, Edward. *Summer for the Gods: The Scopes Trial and America's Continuing Debate over Science and Religion* (1997).

Marsden, George. *Understanding Fundamentalism and Evangelicalism* (1991).

Martin, William. *A Prophet with Honor: The Billy Graham Story* (1991).

———. *With God on Our Side: The Rise of the Religious Right in America* (1997).

Menendez, Albert. *The December Wars: Religious Symbols and Ceremonies in the Public Square* (1993).

Neuhaus, Richard. *The Naked Public Square* (1984).

Numbers, Ronald. *The Creationists* (1992).

Silk, Mark. *Unsecular Media: Making News of Religion in America* (1995).

———. *Spiritual Politics: Religion and America Since World War II* (1988).

Wertheimer, Jack. *A People Divided: Judaism in Contemporary America* (1993).

Wuthnow, Robert. *The Restructuring of American Religion: Society and Faith Since World War II* (1988).

———. *The Struggle for America's Soul: Evangelicals, Liberals, and Secularism* (1989).